New Frontiers in Regional Science: Asian Perspectives

Volume 56

This series is a constellation of works by scholars in the field of regional science and in related disciplines specifically focusing on dynamism in Asia.

Asia is the most dynamic part of the world. Japan, Korea, Taiwan, and Singapore experienced rapid and miracle economic growth in the 1970s. Malaysia, Indonesia, and Thailand followed in the 1980s. China, India, and Vietnam are now rising countries in Asia and are even leading the world economy. Due to their rapid economic development and growth, Asian countries continue to face a variety of urgent issues including regional and institutional unbalanced growth, environmental problems, poverty amidst prosperity, an ageing society, the collapse of the bubble economy, and deflation, among others.

Asian countries are diversified as they have their own cultural, historical, and geographical as well as political conditions. Due to this fact, scholars specializing in regional science as an inter- and multi-discipline have taken leading roles in providing mitigating policy proposals based on robust interdisciplinary analysis of multifaceted regional issues and subjects in Asia. This series not only will present unique research results from Asia that are unfamiliar in other parts of the world because of language barriers, but also will publish advanced research results from those regions that have focused on regional and urban issues in Asia from different perspectives.

The series aims to expand the frontiers of regional science through diffusion of intrinsically developed and advanced modern regional science methodologies in Asia and other areas of the world. Readers will be inspired to realize that regional and urban issues in the world are so vast that their established methodologies still have space for development and refinement, and to understand the importance of the interdisciplinary and multidisciplinary approach that is inherent in regional science for analyzing and resolving urgent regional and urban issues in Asia.

Topics under consideration in this series include the theory of social cost and benefit analysis and criteria of public investments, socio-economic vulnerability against disasters, food security and policy, agro-food systems in China, industrial clustering in Asia, comprehensive management of water environment and resources in a river basin, the international trade bloc and food security, migration and labor market in Asia, land policy and local property tax, Information and Communication Technology planning, consumer "shop-around" movements, and regeneration of downtowns, among others.

Researchers who are interested in publishing their books in this Series should obtain a proposal form from Yoshiro Higano (Editor in Chief, higano@jsrsai.jp) and return the completed form to him.

Masamichi Kawano • Karima Kourtit •
Peter Nijkamp • Yoshiro Higano
Editors

Theory and History in Regional Perspective

Essays in Honor of Yasuhiro Sakai

Springer

Editors
Masamichi Kawano
Professor in Emeritus of Kwansei Gakuin University
Sanda, Hyogo, Japan

Karima Kourtit
Open University in the Netherlands
Utrecht, Utrecht, The Netherlands

Peter Nijkamp
VU University
Leiden, Zuid-Holland, The Netherlands

Yoshiro Higano
University of Tsukuba
Tsukuba, Ibaraki, Japan

ISSN 2199-5974 ISSN 2199-5982 (electronic)
New Frontiers in Regional Science: Asian Perspectives
ISBN 978-981-16-6694-0 ISBN 978-981-16-6695-7 (eBook)
https://doi.org/10.1007/978-981-16-6695-7

This Springer imprint is published by the registered company Springer Nature Singapore Pte Ltd.
The registered company address is: 152 Beach Road, #21-01/04 Gateway East, Singapore 189721, Singapore

Foreword: Professor Yasuhiro Sakai and His Personality

Professor Yasuhiro Sakai, after graduating from Kobe University, earned Ph.D. from the University of Rochester and then taught economics at the University of Pittsburgh in the USA, Hiroshima, Tsukuba, and Shiga Universities, and finally at Ryukoku University in Japan.

He had taught mainly microeconomics especially focused on the economics of risk and uncertainty. All the students liked his style of lectures and personality as his classes were full of academic atmosphere and humor. For instance, when he talked about "risk," he always wore two watches, each on his right and left wrist. He said, "I am always using two watches as a behavior towards risk."

He also advised graduate students as well as doctoral students eagerly and friendly. The students loved him because they enjoyed the fellowship with him after class at a coffee shop near his office. They also enjoyed listening to interesting stories about the academic life which he experienced in the USA and in which he explained the importance of academic life. He had encouraged the students when they failed a presentation at an academic conference, saying that "Don't worry. If you do the same one-hundred times, you will surely be an expert."

At Shiga University, he had promoted establishing students' journal of graduate school, *Biwako Journal of Economics*, in which he artistically wrote the title letter by calligraphy, which is still on the cover of the journal.

He is stirring and benevolent; we his students are very thankful.

Kwansei Gakuin University, Sanda,
Hyogo, Japan

Masamichi Kawano

Foreword: Yasuhiro Sakai and His Achievements

This book is a tribute by the students and colleagues of Yasuhiro Sakai in order to celebrate the life and works of the outstanding and distinctive scholar ranging in scope in the fields of risk and uncertainty with applications to regional science; information transmission and distribution channels; the role of merchants in the market economy; insurance and culture; microeconomics with applications; and history of risk and economic thought. As his distinguished achievements and activities cover a widespread area, contributors to this book include not only his former Ph.D. students but also scholars of multiple talents in international regional science communities such as Regional Science Association International (RSAI), Pacific-Regional Science Conference Organization of RSAI, and, of course, Japan Section of RSAI.

Having had graduated from Kobe University, Department of Economics, in 1963, he had gone on to Graduate School of Economics, Kobe University, and earned his M.A. degree in 1965. His first career in the academic field had started in the Department of Economics, Kobe University, as Instructor in 1965. To my limited knowledge, Kobe University was a Mecca of Modern Economics which had a unifying power equal to Osaka University in the western part of Japan during the several decades just after the last Second World War. He has chosen to study Modern Economics although most scholars specialized in Economics chose to study Marxian Economics, which had reflected academic freedom after experiencing the dark moment of history during and before the War. While he was affected by Marshallian economics, he participated in classes offered in the Department of Mathematics and had studied Galois (group) theory, Lebesgue integral, topology, etc.

He had left for the USA in 1968 when student movement activists raged on at universities in Japan. Having stayed at Economics Institute, University of Colorado, as Special Researcher, he enrolled in Graduate School of Economics, University of Rochester. The university was one of famous universities, in which famous mathematical economists served. Completing his M.A. and Ph.D. courses in Economics at the University of Rochester from 1968 to 1972, he had advanced his career by working in the Department of Economics at the University of Rochester as Research Assistant from 1968 to 1970 and at the University of Pittsburgh as Assistant Professor from 1971 to 1975, being recommended by his supervisor, Professor Lionel W. McKenzie, who was one of gurus in the field of Mathematical Economics, especially General Equilibrium Theory.

Yasuhiro Sakai's research interest in Rochester was put on fundamental theorems of microeconomics with axiomatic approach. The title of his Ph.D. thesis is "Axiomatic foundations of consumption and production theories," and he had completed his Ph.D. Degree in 1972. Academic achievements were represented by Sakai (1973, 1974, 1975, 1977a). Sakai (1974) was a gem in that it clarifies substantial meaning of "integrability (or continuity) condition of demand function" in the content of Samuelson's weak axiom vs. Houthakker's strong axiom of revealed preference. More specifically, he had successfully specified a brand-new and *weak* regularity condition under which it is proved that weak and strong axioms of revealed preference are equivalent.

He had experienced big turning point in his life in Pittsburgh. Before he left for USA in 1968, he became skeptical about utopian socialism or its variants. While he studied and completed his Ph.D. thesis by gurus in the fields of mathematical economics at the University of Rochester, he had sometimes felt weird about beauteousness that is the right essence of the equilibrium theory. He might have become skeptical about a kind of utopian capitalism found in the beauty. In reminiscence of life, Sakai (2015c), he later on mentioned about a prescience given by Kitaro Shimizu, a famous Japanese sociologist, "... economic thought tends to develop through clash and feud between two schools of thought. One can be splendent because of such clash and feud. Sooner or later, one is eclipsed by loss in the other's luster ...."

Yasuhiro Sakai's skepticism was strengthened by experience during his lecture in Pittsburgh. A student from Turkey gave a naïve question to him, which was a very pointed question whether and to what extent is the general equilibrium theory applicable to the betterment of developing countries such as Turkey. He was shocked as it was a thunder out of the blue. He barely replied to her and all students in the class. "...Now, I would like to say. Let us study together to carefully examine the applicability of pure theory to more complicated economies as they really are ...."

He had a chance to talk to Dr. Oskar Morgenstern, who had visited the university to give a special lecture and was given an advice to study economics of risk and uncertainty, an emerging new field of economics. Since then, he devoted all energies to research of economics of risk and uncertainty while he gave lectures on subjects in mathematical economics to undergraduate and graduate students in Pittsburgh.

He returned to Japan in 1975 and restarted his academic career in Japan in the Department of Economics at Hiroshima University as Associate Professor. His early works in the field of economics of risk and uncertainty are represented by Sakai (1977b, 1978, 1981, 1982a, b, 1985a). Sakai (1978) is an excellent work in that he has proved failure of the Rybczynski and Stolper-Samuelson theorems—

fundamental in trade theories—when firms in the uncertain sector exhibit decreasing absolute risk aversion behavior.

He had moved to the University of Tsukuba in 1977, working at the Institute of Social Sciences as Associate Professor till 1990, and worked at the same institute as Professor till 2002 when he has retired from the university. While he worked at the University of Tsukuba, he stayed at the Department of Economics, University of Pittsburgh, as Visiting Professor and served as Research Associate at New York University from 1990 to 1998. During Tsukuba, he has deepened his works in the field of economics of risk and uncertainty by dealing with the meaning of "information" in order to specify substantial risky and uncertain situations in the conventional analytical framework of modern economics, especially in imperfect competition models. In this content, his works are represented by Sakai (1985b, 1986a, 1988, 1989, 1990, 1991a, b, 1993, 2016b, c, d). Sakai (1985b) has shown the value of information about stochastic economic situation in which two firms have to face to optimize their behavior in a simple duopoly game framework. It has shown improved information with one firm may or may not be detrimental to the other firm and/or consumers depending on the variances of stochastically variable cost function parameter with both firms and the covariance between the parameters, which suggests the importance of information gathering about the rival's cost structure rather than its own. This shows substantial aspect of the information sharing, e.g., through trade associations, etc. Sakai (1986) developed the analysis using Cournot and Bertrand models and has shown possible invalidity of propositions by X. Vives.[1]

After Tsukuba, he worked at the Graduate School of Economics, Shiga University, as Professor from 2002 to 2006, and as Special Appointed Professor from 2006 to 2010. After retirement at Shiga University in 2006, he worked at the Graduate School of Economics, Ryukoku University, as Professor from 2006 to 2012. He currently serves as International Advisor, Center for Risk Research, Shiga University, since 2006.

Moving to Hikone, Shiga prefecture, he expanded his research interest to the role of the distribution sector as intermediaries in the market economy. It might be a coincidence that the old name of Shiga prefecture is Ohmi, and it is famous with "Ohmi merchants" who cleverly behave for interests of both producers and consumers as well as themselves by not only fulfilling the spatial gap between producers and consumers but also getting back customer needs to producer. Typical works in this content are represented by Sakai and Sasaki (1992, 1996), and Sakai (1994, 2011, 2014a, 2018, 2021). Sakai and Sasaki (1972) is an insightful work in that raison d'être of distribution sectors such as wholesale and retail, which is clarified using a la Stackelberg oligopoly model with uncertainty, in which the distribution sector functions as an information transmitter between consumers and producers.

He expanded his research frontier by incorporating historical and cultural as well as ethical views into his works since the 1980s. This was amplified by the fall of the

[1]Xavier Vives (1984) Duopoly information equilibrium: Cournot and Bertrand. Journal of Economic Theory 34(1):71–94.

Berlin Wall all of a sudden in 1989, followed by the total collapse of the mighty Soviet Union into so many independent countries in 1991. As he wrote in reminiscence of his life, Sakai (2015c) "... it reminded me of my young days when the issue of 'socialism versus capitalism' was a lively discussion topic among fellow students. At the same time, I wondered if the collapse of one social system would sooner or later lead to the decline and even breakdown of its rival. As the saying goes, power will collapse, and absolute power will collapse absolutely!" The author just guesses that he had a sense of crisis against Modern Economics by experiencing the Great Depression in 2008, the zero/minus economic growth with deflation in Japan, and Great East Japan earthquake in 2011 because "economics or economist" is unable to fix the issues at all and it looks as if it is overlooked that human dignity is lost cruelly.

Works in this content are represented by Sakai (1986b, 2010, 2012, 2014b, 2016a, e, 2019a, b, c, 2020a, b). A series of works of Sakai (2019a, b, c, 2020b) are unique and impactful in that he deals with the substance of probability or uncertainty by shedding new light on old controversy between Émile Borel and John Maynard Keynes, Knightian uncertainty, and other related classics, namely whether probability is measurable, whether uncertainty is quantifiable, whether probabilities are comparable, how and to what extent probability (in the mathematical definition) is related to non-measurability and (psychological) ambiguity, etc.

He has received many awards. Major awards are: Ministry Award for Outstanding Achievement, Japanese Ministry of Post and Telecommunication, in 1999; Society Award for Outstanding Achievement, Japan Society for Risk Research, in 2002; Association Prize for Outstanding Achievement, Japan Section of RSAI (JSRSAI), in 2005; President Award for Outstanding Service, Shiga University, in 2010, etc.

Yasuhiro Sakai has contributed a lot to the development of academic associations in the field of regional science, modern economics, etc. In regional science related fields, he served as Council Member of Japanese Economic Association, from 1980 to 1995. He served as President of the Society for Risk Analysis, Japan, from 2000 to 2002 while he served as Council Member from 1992 to 2010. He also served as President of the Japan Society for Household Economics (JSHE) from 2001 to 2002 while he served as Council Member from 1992 to 2010. He served as Council Member of the Japan Society for Evolutionary Economics from 2006 to 2010. Further, he served as a member of Science Council of Japan from 2006 to 2009, representing JSRSAI and JSHE.

Of course, we cannot end this Foreword with no mention of his contribution to the development of JSRSAI. In 1991, he had become a member of JSRSAI. The recommender was Professor Yasuhiko Oishi, a founder and the second President of JSRSAI.

Yasuhiro Sakai was already an established scholar both nationally and internationally in the 1980s. In the early 1980s, JSRSAI had started a kind of campaign called internationalization, which means active participation by JSRSAI members in international RSAI Meetings, increase in articles accepted in *Studies in Regional Science*, a journal of JSRSAI, which are written in English by Japanese as well as foreign contributors, regular organization of international meetings and workshops, in which foreign scholars actively participate, etc. Executives of JSRSAI all welcomed Yasuhiro Sakai to join JSRSAI because it could be highly expected that he would be able to contribute to the development of JSRSAI in two roles: providing foundations for the rigid theoretical analysis of regional science topics; and enhancing the campaign of internationalization. He had already the flexibility to well adapt to the philosophy of regional science although it was sometimes taken as a kind of "fabulous animal" and poked fun at by so-called and sometimes self-designated mathematical economists in Japan. He rather recognized and appreciated that an association of regional science (JSRSAI) is one possibility to remove a cooped-up feeling brought by gaps between realities observable here and there in the world and refined sciences. It was unusual that he has so quickly become a Council Member of JSRSAI in 1992.

He loves the atmosphere of JSRSAI—an open-minded and friendly competition to try to improve by learning from others. In the 1990s, a kind of early bird session started in the annual meeting of JSRSAI. He took the role of Chair (and sometimes a la supervisor for graduate students) with good grace and punctually made comments and suggestion related to the theme under study. It is not an exaggeration to say that many young prosperous regional science scholars have left the nest owing to him, and now actively participate in international RSAI Meetings.

He served as a Council Member of JSRSAI till 2010 while he has served as Vice-President of JSRSAI, 2001–2002, and President of JSRSAI, 2003–2004. He is a Honorary Member of JSRSAI since 2008. He is now serving as Chair of the Association Prize Committee since 2007, Honorary Advisor to Council of JSRSAI since 2011, and Member of Advisory Board of *Asia-Pacific Journal of Regional Science* since 2016.

As he has confessed in his memoir, Sakai (2015c), he was not necessarily happy at the University of Tsukuba because of the human environment of the Institute of Social Science to which he belonged. The institute was still managed by a group of economists who were competitive against modern economists. He was treated unreasonably with his promotion. Just when other institutes in the university expressed skepticism about the matter and a big mass media took it up, he finally became Professor at the age of 49. It was not too early considering his nationally as well as internationally well-recognized achievements.

He believes the oriental saying—hardship makes the man or adversity is the parent of virtue. Therefore, he was unflattering against his Ph.D. students. Of course, he was bitter reasonably and meaningfully. On the other hand, he has an outgoing personality as well. He has distinct esprit and humor. He always participates in reception and/or dinner party which is held during international meeting/workshop as a matter of convention in order to enhance internationalization and provide members of JSRSAI opportunities to directly communicate with invited distinguished scholars. A party is warmed up by his speech of wit and it is filled with amiable atmosphere. I believe he has also contributed to the development of JSRSAI by establishing unshaken friendship between JSRSAI and international regional science communities. This is why not only his former students and colleagues but also so many internationally distinguished scholars have contributed to the book.

It is a great honor for his former students as well as the members of JSRSAI and the broader regional science community when this book is accepted as a token of their appreciation of Yasuhiro Sakai's long friendship and outstanding contribution to the community and regional science generally.

List of Major Publications

Sakai Y (1973) An axiomatic approach to input demand theory. Int Econ Rev 14(3): 735–752

Sakai Y (1974) Equivalence of the weak and strong axioms of revealed preference without demand continuity assumptions: a "regularity condition" approach. J Econ Theory 8(3) 292–304

Sakai Y (1975) Substitution and expansion effects in production theory: the case of joint production. J Econ Theory 9(3):255–274

Sakai Y (1977a) Revealed favorability, indirect utility, and direct utility. J Econ Theory 14(1):113–129

Sakai Y (1977b) The theory of the firm under price uncertainty. Econ Stud Q 28(1): 31–39

Sakai Y (1978) A simple general equilibrium model of production: comparative statics with price uncertainty. J Econ Theory 9(2):287–306

Sakai Y (1981) Uncertainty and the multiproduct firm: a duality approach. Econ Stud Q 32(1):66–76

Sakai Y (1982a) The economics of uncertainty. Yuhikaku Publishing, Tokyo (in Japanese)

Sakai Y (1982b) On the economics of uncertainty: perspectives and prospects. Lectures on mathematical analysis 22. Institute of Mathematical Analysis, Kyoto University (in Japanese)

Sakai Y (1985a) International trade models with uncertainty. Lectures on mathematical analysis 25. Institute of Mathematical Analysis, Kyoto University (in Japanese)

Sakai Y (1985b) The value of information in a simple duopoly model. J Econ Theory 36(1):36–54

Sakai Y (1986a) Cournot and Bertrand equilibria under imperfect information. J Econ 46(3):213–232

Sakai Y (1986b) Saving theory under uncertainty: historical perspectives. In: Theory of savings: a survey. Japanese Ministry of Telecommunications, Tokyo (in Japanese)

Sakai Y (1988) The economics of uncertainty and information. J Behav Psychol Stat 16(1) (in Japanese)

Sakai Y, Yamato T (1989) Oligopoly, information and welfare. J Econ 49(1):3–24

Sakai Y, Yamato T (1990) On the exchange of cost information in a Bertrand-type duopoly model. Econ Stud Q 41(1):48–64

Sakai Y (1990) Theory of oligopoly and information. Toyo Keizai Publishing, Tokyo (in Japanese)
Sakai Y (1990) Information sharing in oligopoly: overview and evaluation: part I alternative models with a common risk. Keio Econ Stud 27(2):17–41
Sakai Y (1991a) Information sharing in oligopoly: overview and evaluation: part II private risks and oligopoly models. Keio Econ Stud 28(1):51–71
Sakai Y (1991b) Risk and information: toward new economics. Keiso Shobo, Tokyo (in Japanese)
Sakai Y, Yoshizumi A (1991a) The impact of risk aversion on information transmission between firms. J Econ 53(1):51–73
Sakai Y, Yoshizumi A (1991b) Risk aversion and duopoly: is information exchange always beneficial to firms? Pure Math Appl 2(1)
Sakai Y (1991c) Risk and cost-benefit analysis: overview and evaluation. J Soc Risk Anal Jpn 3(1)
Sakai Y, Sasaki K (1992) Demand uncertainty and distribution systems: the role of intermediaries in the market economy. Stud Reg Sci 23(1):131–142
Sakai Y (1993) The role of information in profit-maximizing and labor-managed duopoly models. Manage Decis Econ 14(5)
Sakai Y (1993) Safety and risk in economics. J Int Traffic Safety 19(4) (in Japanese)
Sakai Y (1994) On moral hazard and society. J Secur 72(1) (in Japanese)
Sakai Y (1994) The market economy versus planned economy: the role of information and distribution. J Int Coop 2(2) (in Japanese)
Mizushima K, Sakai Y et al (1995) Insurance and culture: risk and Japan. Chikura Publishers (in Japanese)
Sakai Y (1995) Repeated contract negotiations with private information: comment. Jpn World Econ 7(4):475–479
Sakai Y, Sasaki K (1996) Demand uncertainty and distribution systems: information acquisition and transmission. In: Sato R, Ramachandran R, Hori H (eds) Organization, performance and equity. Research monographs in Japan-U.S. Business & Economics, vol 1. Springer, Boston, pp 59–91.
Sakai Y (1996) The economics of risk: information and culture. Yuhikaku Publishing, Tokyo (in Japanese)
Sakai Y (1997) Economic analysis of risk and insurance. J Soc Risk Anal Jpn 8(1)
Hara S, Sakai Y (1997) Introduction to the economics of household. Toyo Keizai Publishing Co., Tokyo (in Japanese)
Sakai Y (1998) Thought of risk supports decision-making. Energy Rev 205 (in Japanese)
Sakai Y (1998) Comments on "Sample selection in credit scoring models" by W. Greene. Jpn World Econ 10(3):317–320
Sakai Y (1999) Risk and insurance problems. J Soc Risk Anal 10(1)
Sakai S, Ikeda S, Tawada M (2004) Risk, environment and economy. Keiso Shobo (in Japanese)
Sakai Y (2006) Views of risk society. Iwanami Shoten, Publishers, Tokyo (in Japanese)

Sakai Y (2007) Risk in economics. In: Tachibanaki T et al (eds) What is risk?, vol I: Risk science: an introduction. Iwanami Shoten, Publishers, Tokyo (in Japanese)
Maeda Y and Sakai Y (2007) Risk financing through captive insurer: economic influences of captives on corporations and the first domicile in Japan. J Risk Res 10(6):793–803
Sakai Y, Sakai T (2007) A risk analysis of the liquid crystal display industry. J Risk Res 10(6):871–882
Sakai Y (2008) On the working of the market mechanism under asymmetric information: a study in the economic thought of risk. Hikone Ronso 374:53–86 (in Japanese)
Sakai Y, Maeda Y (2009) Japanese risk management as a product of social culture: with special reference to insurance companies. CRR working paper, series A-13, Center for Risk Research, Shiga University
Kubo H, Sakai Y (2009) On long-term credit risk assessment and rating: towards a new set of models. CRR Working Paper, Series B-10, Center for Risk Research, Shiga University
Sakai Y (2010) Economic history of risk and uncertainty. Minerva Shobo Publishers, Tokyo (in Japanese)
Sakai Y (2010) Comparative theories of economic systems: Werner Sombart versus John R. Hicks. Hikone Ronso 386:94–117
Sakai Y (2011) Current topics in insurance science and related fields: with a focus on risk, insurance, economy, and the Ohmi Merchant. J Insurance Sci 612:1–20
Kubo H, Sakai Y (2011) On long-term credit risk assessment and rating: towards a new set of models. J Risk Res 14(9):1127–1141
Sakai Y (2011) A risk-economic analysis of nuclear power generation: from "The Myth of Absolute Safety" to "The Occurrence of Unthinkable Events". CRR discussion paper, series J-15, Center for Risk Research, Shiga University
Sakai Y (2012) The economic thought of Frank Knight: with special reference to risk and uncertainty. CRR discussion paper, series J-19, Center for Risk Research, Shiga University
Sakai Y (2014a) Information and distribution: the role of merchants in the market economy with demand risk. Hikone Ronso 399:66–81
Sakai Y (2014b) J. M. Keynes and current economic theory. In: Toshiaki Hirai (ed) Why "now" we necessitate Keynes? The modern sense from the global perspectives. Sakuhin Publishers, Tokyo (in Japanese)
Sakai Y (2015a) Risk aversion and expected utility: the constant-absolute-risk aversion function and its application to oligopoly. Hikone Ronso 403:172–187
Sakai Y (2015b) On environmental risk management: the interactions of economic and on-economic factors. CRR discussion paper, series A-14, Center for Risk Research, Shiga University
Sakai Y (2015c) From the era of the cold war to the age of uncertainty: the evolution of economic science and my academic life for seven decades after the Second World War. Hikone Ronso 406:38–59

Sakai Y (2016a) J. M. Keynes and F. H. Knight: how to deal with risk, probability and uncertainty. CRR discussion paper, series A-15, Center for Risk Research, Shiga University

Sakai Y (2016b) Information exchanges among firms and their welfare implications (part I): the dual relations between the Cournot and Bertrand models. CRR discussion paper, series A-16, Center for Risk Research, Shiga University

Sakai Y (2016c) Information exchanges among firms and their welfare implications (part II): alternative duopoly models with different types of risks. CRR discussion paper, series A-17, Center for Risk Research, Shiga University

Sakai Y (2016d) Information exchanges among firms and their welfare implications (part III): private risks and oligopoly models. CRR discussion paper, series A-18, Center for Risk Research, Shiga University

Sakai Y (2016e) J. M. Keynes on probability versus F. H. Knight on uncertainty: reflections on the miracle year of 1921. Evol Inst Econ Rev 13(1):1–21

Sakai Y (2017) On environmental risk management: the interactions of economic and noneconomic factors. In: Shibusawa H, Sakurai K, Mizunoya T, Uchida S (eds) Socioeconomic environmental policies and evaluations in regional science. New frontiers in regional science: Asian perspectives, 24. Springer, Singapore

Sakai Y (2018) Liverpool merchants versus Ohmi merchants: how and why they dealt with risk and insurance differently. Asia-Pac J Reg Sci 2(1):15–33

Sakai Y (2019a) J.M. Keynes versus F.H. Knight. Evolutionary economics and social complexity science 18. Springer, Singapore

Sakai Y (2019b) Daniel Ellsberg on J.M. Keynes and F.H. Knight: risk ambiguity and uncertainty. Evol Inst Econ Rev 16(1):1–18

Sakai Y (2019c) Economics of pessimism and optimism: theory of Knightian uncertainty and its applications, Kiyohiko G. Nishimura and Hiroyuki Ozaki. Springer, Japan (2017). ISBN:978-4-431-55901-6. J Econ Psychol 72:51–53

Sakai Y (2020a) The Hicks-Morishima approach reconsidered: another look at the interdependence of several markets. Hikone Ronso 424:72–88

Sakai Y (2020b) Émile Borel, John Maynard Keynes, interval-valued probability, ambiguity. Discussion paper, series E-1, The Institute for Economic and Business Research, Faculty of Economics, Shiga University

Sakai Y, Sasaki K (2021) Information and distribution: the role of merchants in the market economy under uncertainty. New frontiers in regional science: Asian perspectives 49. Springer, Singapore

University of Tsukuba, Tsukuba, Japan

Yoshiro Higano

Preface

A visit to any annual conference of the Japan Section of the Regional Science Association International (JSRSAI) is always an unforgettable experience, for two reasons. In the first place, the academic level and the intellectual contributions of Japanese scholars are always a great delight for any regional scientist. And secondly, the scholarly impacts and the humoristic contributions by Yasuhiro Sakai at these meetings form another source of great pleasure, both scientifically and socially. Over the past decades, he has functioned as a major gravity attractor in a neo-Newtonian force field in Japan. His presence was always a glue in the Japanese regional science community, by his collegial talks with senior scientists, by his friendly talks with young Japanese researchers, and by his accessible and open attitude to many foreign colleagues. He provided always warm home feelings for those who came from far to attend the JSRSAI conferences.

Yasuhiro Sakai is not only a great human being and an eminent scholar, he has also been very instrumental in shaping a strong sense of internationalization for the Japanese regional science community. Together with Hirotada Kohno and Yoshiro Higano, he has laid a solid foundation for the impressive achievements of Japanese regional science, by producing high-quality research, by acting as a role model for Japanese students and young scholars, by stimulating many researchers to join regional science meetings, and by mobilizing many foreign scientists—from Europe, Australia, and the Americas—so as to join the Japanese regional science community. He is one of the cornerstones of Japanese regional science. Surprisingly enough, Yasuhiro Sakai is a very modest person; he is a great gentleman, in the right sense of the word.

This "liber amicorum"—containing a variety of scholarly contributions prepared for him by colleagues and friends—is a gesture to a "man of dignity" who deserves to be put in the spotlight. It is a sign of gratitude to a man who has played a pivotal role in the history and development of regional science.

The present volume contains three major parts that provide a Kaleidoscopic view of contemporary advances in regional science. These parts address the following themes, respectively: history and theory of space, applied spatial studies, and spatial data analytics. These fields of regional science research capture the main interest of professor Sakai.

The first part comprises eight contributions. The list of studies is opened by *Peter Batey* who interprets geodemographics and urban planning from the perspective of its rich history dating back to the second half of the last century (Chap. 1). Next, an original theoretical contribution to creative class research is provided by *Amit Batabyal* and *Seung Jick Yoo*, who focus in particular on inter-urban competition in this domain of research (Chap. 2). An informative study on Marshallian versus Walrasion stability in an experimental market is subsequently offered by *Junyi Shen*, *Ken-Ichi Shimomura*, *Takehiko Yamato*, *Takinao Ohtaka*, and *Kiyotaka Takahashi* (Chap. 3), followed by an interesting contribution written by *Daisuke Nakamura* on the relationship between spatial economics and transportation policy, against the background of regional welfare improvement (Chap. 4). *Sen Eguchi* then pays attention to difficult NIMBY conflict resolutions, from the perspective of game theory (Chap. 5), while *Hidekazu Sone* describes the existence and sustainability conditions for long-standing firms (Chap. 6) and *Atsuro Shibata* reexamines the logic behind the formation process of Japanese type of spin-offs (Chap. 7). After an examination of urbanization processes in developing countries, by *Masamichi Kawano* (Chap. 8), the first part of the volume is concluded with an insightful study on optimal openness, written by *Tomaz Ponce Dentinhoi* (Chap. 9).

The second part of the volume seeks to confront theory with practice. This part sets the tone with a well-crafted study on settlement and migration patterns of immigrants subdivided according to visa classes in Australia: the authors are *Dagmara Laukova, Aude Bernard*, and *Thomas Sigler* (Chap. 10). Next, *Karima Kourtit, Peter Nijkamp*, and *Soushi Suzuki* present a new stepwise application of Data Envelopment Analysis (DEA) to cultural performance of large cities in the world (Chap. 11). *Eujume Kim, Ayoung Kim*, and *Inseok Moon* then provide a study on the Seoul housing market, seen through the lenses of tax reforms in the real estate market (Chap. 12). A quantitative study on university impacts on regional economies in Australia is next pursued by *Robert Waschik, Jonathan Chew, John Madden, Joshua Sidgwick*, and *Glen Wittwer*; they use an integrated data model to map out the effect of universities on regional development (Chap. 13). *Cheng Tang* then takes an interesting practical case, viz. financial literacy and household borrowing behavior in China (Chap. 14). Important issues related to climate change and impacts of adaptation technologies of fruit production on Japanese regional economy are subsequently investigated by *Suminori Tokunaga, Mitsuru Okiyama*, and *Maria Ikegawa* (Chap. 15), while environmental consciousness of Palauan people is analyzed by *Yoko Fujita, Kaoruko Miyakuni*, and *Lincy Lee Marino,* revealing Palauan people's valuation of coral reefs in the Rock Island Southern Lagoon (Chap. 16). A final study in the applied part of the book, *Masakazu Maezuru* has analyzed impacts of activated lobbying with subsidization to environmental goods sectors on the world environment using two countries model of international trade in environmental goods (Chap. 17).

The third and final part of the book is more methodologically oriented and zooms in on spatial data analytics. This part takes off with an interesting methodological study of *Gordan Mulligan* on features of the well-known Herfindahl index (Chap. 18). Next, *Yuji Maeda* addresses an interesting phenomenon, viz. risk cultures, based on a comparative analysis of risk management between cultures (Chap. 19), while another interesting study focuses on risk assessment and communication in a science context by *Kami Seo* (Chap. 20). Importance of proficiency of insurance sales in individually providing information to customers to earn their trust is analyzed by Nobuko Aoba using human capital model (Chap. 21). The impacts of state level differences of COVID-19 policies are next statistically analyzed by *Kingsley Haynes, Rajendra Kulkarni, Meng-Hao Li,* and *Abu Bakkor Siddique* (Chap. 22). The emerging complexity of metropolitan economies in relation to their internal and external structure is next studied by *Lei Wang* and *Geoffrey Hewings* (Chap. 23). And finally, *Yoshiro Higano*, providing an alternative to Alonso-Muth urban spatial model in a dynamic content, has shown that dynamic land price is a negative exponential function in the distance to the city center, and analyzed impacts of sales tax and deemed tax on urban sprawl (Chap. 24).

The present volume encapsulates and illustrates the scientific wealth and policy relevance of contemporary regional science. There is no question that regional science has gained a powerful position in the analysis of the space economy, ranging from small-scale to macro-scale developments. In the development of this strong profile of regional science, Yasuhiro Sakai has played a pivotal role in Japan, and elsewhere. And therefore, this book may be seen as a tribute of colleagues and friends to his great dedication to regional science.

Sanda, Hyogo, Japan — Masamichi Kawano
Utrecht, The Netherlands — Karima Kourtit
Leiden, Zuid-Holland, The Netherlands — Peter Nijkamp
Tsuchiura, Ibaraki, Japan — Yoshiro Higano

Contents

Part I
History and Theory of Space

Chapter 1
Geodemographics and Urban Planning Analysis: An Historical Review

Peter Batey

Abstract The focus in this chapter is on geodemographics—essentially the analysis of people by where they live—from the perspective of those involved in planning and policy-making. Like other analysts, they seek to distil the main sources of social and economic variation in cities. However, what distinguishes them is usually some practical purpose directly related to policy formulation, analysis, and evaluation. The chapter takes the form of an historical review in which four main themes are examined: (1) early efforts to apply rudimentary geodemographic classifications, in order to inform and influence policy; (2) harnessing advances in computing and multivariate statistics that make it possible to handle the large datasets needed to explore urban spatial structure; (3) pioneering applications of geodemographics to enable local authorities to identify multi-dimensional needs and to indicate priorities for spatial targeting of resources, and (4) geodemographics in action as an evaluation tool to measure the success of spatial targeting of area-based policy initiatives and identify potential improvements. In a final section, some aspects of the present status of geodemographics are considered and related to the findings of the historical review.

Keywords Geodemographics · History of planning methods · Spatial targeting · Surveys of London life and labour · Charles Booth

1.1 Introduction

Geodemographics is concerned with the classification of neighbourhoods into categories or clusters based on their socio-economic characteristics. In lay-person's terms, it can be said to be 'the analysis of people by where they live' (Harris et al. 2005, pp. 16–17). It uses a qualitative description—a 'pen portrait'—to summarise

---

P. Batey (✉)
University of Liverpool, Liverpool, UK
e-mail: pwjbatey@liverpool.ac.uk

M. Kawano et al. (eds.), *Theory and History in Regional Perspective*, New Frontiers in Regional Science: Asian Perspectives 56,
https://doi.org/10.1007/978-981-16-6695-7_1

the distinctive attributes of each category or cluster. It works on the principle that 'birds of a feather flock together': people who live close by (i.e. in the same neighbourhood) are assumed to have more in common than a random group of people. This is a well-established notion in human geography, commonly known as Tobler's first law of geography: 'everything is related to everything else, but near things are more related than distant things' (Tobler 1970, p. 236; Harris et al.[1] 2005, pp. 16–17). Furthermore, geodemographics works on the principle that people tend to align themselves with the behaviour and aspirations of the local communities in which they live (Alexiou et al. 2016, p. 382).

Urban planners and policy-makers have long had a practical interest in geodemographics, usually directly related to policy formulation, analysis, and evaluation. Typically, the aim is to develop a consistent and systematic approach to spatial resource allocation, involving the definition of priority areas to receive favoured treatment. Such areas may be defined in relation to particular policy sectors, such as education, housing, crime or health or, in a more general sense, as in the case of designating 'inner city areas'. The geodemographic classification here serves as a composite measure of need and is usually constructed using census data, where feasible supplemented by other sources of small area data. It generally takes the form of a map displaying the spatial distribution of neighbourhood types, together with a set of pen portraits.

Without doubt, geodemographic classifications have made a major contribution to the regional scientist's toolkit since their introduction more than 50 years ago. This applies especially to those whose background training is in the quantitative branches of geography, planning, and sociology but not, it must be said, economics. Over the years, geodemographics has retained its strong empirical focus and has largely operated as a separate sub-field of applied regional science. Unlike many of their regional scientist colleagues, the proponents of geodemographics seem not to have chosen to engage with recent and current theoretical debates in regional economics and the burgeoning field of the New Economic Geography, preferring to concentrate on more technical matters at a fine level of spatial detail. However, as will be demonstrated later in this chapter, there are encouraging signs of new developments in *integrated* analysis, bringing together geodemographics with other forms of regional analysis, such as spatial interaction modelling.

In what follows, the emphasis will be on the public sector: how can and does geodemographics support the development of public policy in general and urban planning in particular? The chapter will take the form of an historical review, examining key developments in geodemographics through the medium of a series of themes, beginning with Charles Booth's pioneering street-by-street surveys and poverty maps of the late nineteenth century. As Singleton and Spielman (2013)

[1]Harris et al. (2005, p. 17) suggest that Tobler's Law should be modified when viewed in a geodemographic context: not only are nearby populations related but so too are populations living in the same type of neighbourhood. In other words, near and far things are related—by neighbourhood type.

observe, in the US most applications of geodemographics take place in a commercial environment and involve proprietary geodemographic classifications. The situation in the UK is different, largely thanks to a long tradition of making classifications accessible to public sector and academic users at very little cost.

Private sector applications, including retail planning, locational analysis and market segmentation, are a vast topic in themselves, and to cover them adequately would be well beyond the scope of the present chapter. They are, however, documented in the key geodemographics texts: see, for example, Webber and Burrows (2018); Harris et al. (2005); and Leventhal (2016). These texts also provide accounts of applications elsewhere in the world.

The chapter is organised into four main themes:

- *Precursors of geodemographics*: early efforts to apply rudimentary geodemographic classifications, in order to inform and influence policy.
- *Exploring urban spatial structure*: harnessing advances in computing and multivariate statistics that make it possible to handle the large datasets needed to explore urban spatial structure.
- *Pioneering geodemographic classifications* enabling local authorities to identify multi-dimensional needs and to indicate priorities for spatial targeting of resources
- *Geodemographics and the evaluation of spatial targeting:* geodemographics in action as an evaluation tool to measure the success of spatial targeting of area-based policy initiatives.

Interspersed in the text is a series of discussions that draw together some of the main points that emerge from the review, while in the final section there is an attempt to relate the historical advances covered in the chapter to a number of recent and current developments in geodemographics.

1.2 Precursors of Geodemographics

1.2.1 Charles Booth's Descriptive Map of London Poverty 1889

Charles Booth's *Descriptive Map of London 1889*, first published in 1891, is generally regarded as the earliest antecedent of geodemographic classifications. Booth,[2] a wealthy ship-owner and businessman from Liverpool, was also an energetic social reformer deeply committed to finding out the full extent of poverty in

[2] See Pfautz (1967, pp. 43–46) for a detailed account of Booth's life, character, and the motivation that lay behind his prodigious efforts to understand and campaign on poverty among London's population; see also Morgan (2019, pp. 40–41).

London. This was just one part of his broader lifetime mission to foster a deeper understanding of the origins of poverty in urban Britain.

His privately funded city-wide enquiry aimed to discover how many of London's residents were living in poverty, what kept them in that state and what might be done to alleviate it (Vaughan 2018, p. 69). In addition to his study of poverty, Booth made a series of detailed studies on the working conditions in the principal London industries. This ended with an inquiry into religious influences, including interviews with clergy to ascertain church attendance (Vaughan 2018, p. 70). The results of his research, including his poverty map, were published in a series of 17 volumes under the general heading of the *Life and Labour of the People of London* over the period 1886–1903.[3]

Booth was an empiricist who believed in collecting evidence to gain political support for a more systematic approach to the elimination of poverty than was being provided by the 'sporadic and untargeted efforts of the charitable classes' (Webber and Burrows 2018, p. 32). He was a member of the official committee in charge of the 1891 Census which suggests that he clearly understood the value of systematic data collection, even though he had no formal education in statistics (Webber and Burrows 2018, p. 32).

Booth began his study of poverty at Tower Hamlets in London's East End, in 1887, extending the inquiry a year later to include the people of East London and Hackney. Reaction from the press and the public was favourable and this gave Booth the confidence to turn his attention to gathering data on the rest of the city. His plans for the London-wide survey were ambitious. The outline of each street in London was carefully shaded on a 6″ to the mile base map to indicate the general socio-economic condition of the residents. The basis of the classification was the reports of the school board visitors (SBVs) to households in each street. These reports contained detailed records compiled from continuous home visits, of every family with children of school age, (Vaughan 2018, p. 70). The SBVs had been established as a result of the Compulsory Education Act of 1877 as a means of tracking the children of the poor in order to ensure they were receiving an adequate education. Each SBV kept a 'detailed record of every poor family in his district, noting such details as the occupation, his income, the number, ages, and sexes of the children, the parents' habits of sobriety, the cleanliness of the household, and so on' (Selvin and Bernert 1985, p. 73).

Booth preferred to interview SBVs rather than household members on the grounds that a direct interview would have been considered an 'invasion of privacy'. Each SBV was interviewed for 20–30 h based upon the contents of their notes and record books (Bales 1991). After carefully checking their returns, Booth personally inspected each neighbourhood covered by the SBV, and checked his findings with data from the census whose collection he also oversaw. It is significant that people

[3]The work is divided into three parts: the Poverty series (four volumes); the Industry series (five volumes); and the Religion series (seven volumes). The final volume is a conclusion to the whole work.

Table 1.1 Booth's classification of streets in London by general condition of inhabitants

Colour code	Description (or 'pen portrait')	Class	Description (or 'pen portrait')
Black	The lowest grade (corresponding to Class A), inhabited principally by occasional labourers, loafers and semi-criminals—the elements of disorder	A	The lowest class—occasional labourers, loafers and semi-criminals
Dark blue	Very poor (corresponding to Class B), inhabited principally by casual labourers and others living from hand to mouth	B	The very poor—casual labour, hand-to-mouth existence, chronic want
Light blue	Standard poverty (corresponding to Classes C and D) inhabited principally by those whose earnings are small (say 18 s (shillings—a unit a currency) to 21 s a week for moderate family), whether they are so because of irregularity of work (C) or because of a low rate of pay (D)	C and D	The poor—including alike those whose earnings are small, because of irregularity of employment, and those whose work, though regular, is ill-paid
Purple	Street mixed with poverty (usually C and D with E and F, but including Class B in many cases)	E and F	The regularly employed and fairly paid working class of all grades
Pink	Working class comfort (corresponding to Classes E and F, but containing also a large proportion of the lower middle class of small tradesman and Class G). These people usually keep no servant	G and H	Lower and upper middle class and all above this level
Red	Well-to-do; inhabited by middle-class families who keep one or two servants		
Yellow	Wealthy; hardly found in East London and little found in South London; inhabited by families who keep three or more servants and whose houses are rated at £100 or more		

Source: Harris et al. (2005)

living and working in an area were asked about the *neighbourhood* they lived in, not their own *personal* circumstances (Bales 1991).

These data were then used to place each household into one of eight mutually exclusive and exhaustive categories of 'class', rank ordered from A to H in ascending order of status. The eight were then grouped into five higher order categories (Webber and Burrows 2018, p. 32; Pfautz 1967, p. 91) again ordered by social status, as shown in Table 1.1.

Table 1.1 describes each of the classes by means of a pen portrait, a vivid description of the conditions experienced by London's residents. The idea of using pen portraits was novel at the time but proved very effective when used in conjunction with the maps emerging from the street survey. It has stood the test of time and still today forms an important component of a geodemographic classification.

The streets covered by the survey were mapped using the colour scheme described in Table 1.1. Booth recognised that the spatial distribution of these different classes of household was far from random. Although the pattern was not entirely uniform, for the most part households in similar classes tended to be 'clustered' in close spatial proximity to each other (Webber and Burrows 2018, p. 33). Booth was 'the first, and by no means the last, to use colour to indicate the locations where distinct categories of household lived' (Vaughan 2018, p. 71). Moreover, in mapping streets he permitted some streets to be assigned to more than one class, representing streets of a mixed socio-economic character, an idea which caught the attention of analysts much later when commercial geodemographic classifications[4] were being designed in the 1980s.

The map itself was published in 1891, in 12 sheets, as the *Descriptive Map of London Poverty 1889*. Figure 1.1 shows two extracts from the poverty map, the first centred on Bloomsbury, an affluent area of central London, and the other focusing on Lincolns Inn Fields not far away, a more mixed area. What is striking is that both areas contain such a variety of socio-economic conditions with many instances of the poorest living cheek by jowl with some of those most well off.

The map of poverty and the survey results was widely disseminated and proved very effective in drawing attention to the scale of poverty experienced by London's residents.

***Discussion 1*: The Wider Influence of Booth's London Survey and the Prospect for Follow-ups**

Charles Booth's work in compiling the *Life and Labour of the People of London* proved to be very influential and led to similar studies being carried out elsewhere, especially in the UK and the USA. Notable examples, referred to by Vaughan (2018, pp. 92–128), are Rowntree's studies of York; Hull-House in Chicago; and Du Bois' map of the seventh ward in Philadelphia. Of particular interest here is the *New Survey of London Life and Labour*, 1928–35, conducted under the leadership of Hubert Llewellyn Smith, one of Booth's former assistants. Like the earlier survey, the New Survey focused on poverty and was intended to make comparisons with the earlier *Life and Labour* survey, 40 years on. It aimed to replicate the methods used in Booth's survey.

The *New Survey* was well received, particularly in its examination of urban change. It showed a general rise in income, with a shorter working day and improved literacy and more money to spend in increased leisure time. However, there were still substantial numbers of people continuing to live in poverty (Alexander 2007).

Maps were just as important in the *New Survey* as they had been in the first survey. The study area was covered by six sheets at 4″ to the mile and Booth's colour

[4]Such classifications became known as fuzzy geodemographics, in view of the overlapping cluster boundaries. See Flowerdew and Leventhal (1998).

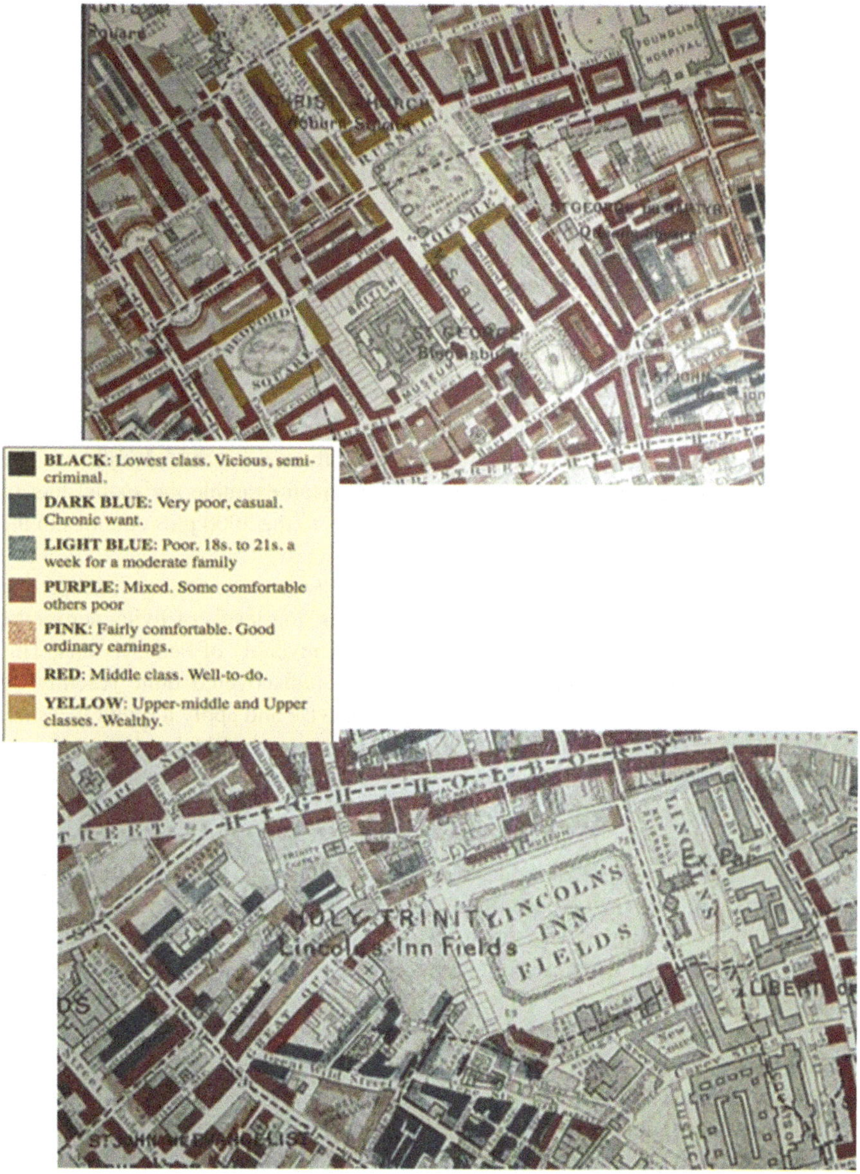

Fig. 1.1 Two extracts from Charles Booth's Descriptive Map of London Poverty 1889: Lincoln's Inn Fields and Bloomsbury

scheme was largely repeated. In the nine volumes that accompanied the maps, there is a huge amount of detailed analysis of the spatial structure of the city pinpointing areas of continuity and change. While poverty was now more dispersed, it remained entrenched in some areas (Vaughan 2018, pp. 115–125).

By the late 1950s there was a proposal to undertake a third survey. Emanating from the newly established Centre for Urban Studies based at University College London, the *Third Survey of London Life and Labour*, would again make a detailed analysis of residential areas, but this time making extensive use of small area data from the 1961 Census of Population. As will be seen later in this chapter, the Centre was in the forefront of developments in census analysis at that time, work that led on to a range of applications of geodemographics in the public sector, from the late 1960s onwards.

1.2.2 Carter Goodrich and the Plane of Living

The second example has been chosen partly because it illustrates geodemographic analysis at a different spatial scale. Whereas Booth was concerned with the fine detail of poverty in London's streets, in this American example the spatial unit of analysis is the county and the map in question refers to the 3000 plus counties in the whole country.

The subject of interest here is the so-called *Plane of Living*, a concept first developed during the 1930s as a means of characterising levels of living across the entire USA by Carter Goodrich et al. based at the University of Pennsylvania. This work, largely forgotten over the years, has been rediscovered quite recently by Carruthers and Mulligan (2008). The aim was to devise and apply a rough measure, by small geographical units, that would enable comparisons of the level of prosperity in various parts of the country immediately before the onset of the Great Depression. Which were the areas where the standard of living was low before 1929? Did people succeed in moving from the worse to the better areas? Did those who left the country for the city gain by moving? (Goodrich et al. 1935, p. 14). To be able to judge this, it was important to measure all parts of the country in a consistent manner, recognising the difficulties of finding indices that were equally applicable to both urban and rural areas. Hence the need for a careful comparison of possible measures before a final selection could be made.

The original *Plane of Living* map was prepared by Warren Thornthwaite[5] on behalf of Goodrich's team and is reproduced in Fig. 1.2. The map displays a composite index of three variables that reflects, as a percentage of the national average: (1) household income; (2) the proportion of homes having radios; and (3) the proportion of homes having telephones, equally weighted.

The *Plane of Living* data used here, expressed at county level, refer to the period 1928–1929, immediately before the Great Depression. Overlaid on the map are mining and manufacturing areas, a particular concern of Goodrich's research, as

[5] At this time, Thornthwaite was working as an urban geographer. Later in his career, he was to become a renowned climatologist, known for a climate classification still in use more than 70 years after it was first conceived.

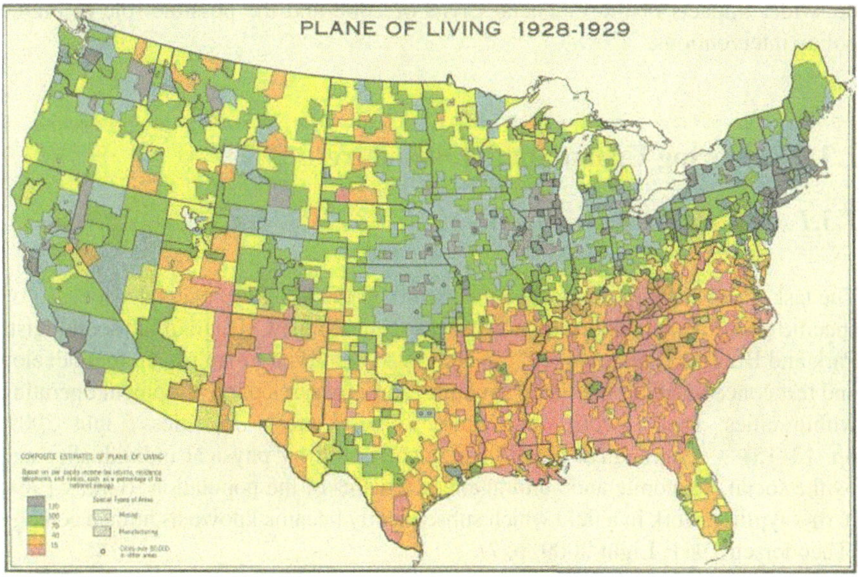

Fig. 1.2 Planes of Living in the United States 1928–1929 (Source: Goodrich et al. (1935))

well as towns with more than 50,000 population. A noteworthy feature is the concentration of low *Plane of Living* scores in the rural South, a reflection of the deficiency in 'those attributes of a modern standard of life' (Hoover 1948, p. 204). Only in a limited number of *urban areas* of the South are these attributes to be found. Here and elsewhere in the USA, the research team carried out a remarkably thorough analysis of the *Plane of Living* results and their implications for public policy.

At the time of Goodrich's research project, policy-makers wanted to understand how the distribution of the population had evolved in the period leading up to the Great Depression—and, going forward, how to influence migration flows in a way that enhanced economic opportunity and personal well-being (Goodrich 1936). It was vital that the analysis extended to the entire country rather than particular localities.

***Discussion 2:* Connecting Place-to-Place Variations in the Quality of Life to the Greater Economic Landscape**

Carruthers and Mulligan viewed the *Plane of Living* map as one of the earliest examples of what would now be regarded as geodemographics. They could see that it had a valuable role in explicitly connecting place-to-place variation in the quality of life to the greater economic landscape (Greenwood and Hunt 2003). Considered by Carruthers and Mulligan as exceptionally innovative for its time, the work of Goodrich and his team 'helped establish an enduring framework wherein living conditions are viewed as fundamental to a wide array of socio-economic processes and outcomes' (Carruthers and Mulligan 2008, p. 2). Carruthers and Mulligan proceeded to apply the *Plane of Living* concept in their own research examining the wider impacts of the Financial Crisis of 2008 and the possible role of public policy interventions.

1.3 Exploring Urban Spatial Structure[6]

1.3.1 United States

The task of identifying urban spatial structure in the USA has generally focused on specific cities. Among the best-known work is that of the Chicago urban sociologists Park and Burgess (Park et al. 1925). They used empirical urban research to develop and test concepts about the form, structure, and processes of development operating within cities. Park's work on defining 'natural areas' in cities (Light 2009, pp. 12–15)—'geographical units distinguished both by physical individuality and by the social, economic and cultural characteristics of the population' (Gittus 1964, p. 6)—typified work in a field which subsequently became known as human ecology (Theodorsen 1961; Light 2009, p. 7).

Early attempts at 'within city' classification, particularly those which involved the definition of natural areas, generally lacked methodological rigour. It is not clear how the various classification criteria (social, housing, ethnicity, etc.) were combined, nor was it evident as to which classification method was used. Despite these shortcomings, natural areas, once defined, remained in use as a summary device for reporting census and local statistics. Rees (1972) quotes the example of the *Local Community Factbook* for the Chicago Metropolitan Area which in 1960 was still using a city-wide application of the natural area concept in which 75 community areas defined 30 years earlier were employed as basic statistical units. Such areas had been classified according to a vaguely specified combination of historical, social, physical, commercial, and transportation criteria (Kitagawa and Taeuber 1963).

An undoubted stimulus to research in human ecology was the availability, for an increasing number of cities in the USA, of tabulations of data for census tracts, each with a population of about 4000. Census tracts had been introduced in 1910 when the US Bureau of the Census agreed to prepare tabulations of such areas as New York, Baltimore, Boston, Chicago, Cleveland, Philadelphia, Pittsburgh, and St Louis. Over the years, the number of tracted areas grew rapidly so that by the time of the 1960 Census, there were as many as 180 tracted areas, of which 136 were entire Standard Metropolitan Statistical Areas (Robson 1969, p. 42). Local advisory committees helped in the definition of tracts and where possible boundaries were drawn to follow permanent recognisable lines and to contain people of similar racial and economic status and areas of similar housing.

Notable among the studies that made extensive use of census tract data were those of Shevky and Williams (1949) and Shevky and Bell (1955) for Los Angeles and

[6]This section is a revised and expanded version of a section in Batey and Brown (1995).

San Francisco. They classified the census tracts of those cities into a number of classes that, because of their geographical proximity, were called social areas. The form of analysis was referred to as 'social area analysis'[7] and centred around three theoretical constructs: economic status, family status, and ethnic status. Shevky and his co-workers proposed three indices, one per construct, made up from one to three census variables, to measure the status of census tract population on scales of economic, family, and ethnic status, and to enable tracts to be classified on the basis of their scores on the indices (Berry and Horton 1970, p. 314). Social area analysis thus used classification criteria unique to each particular case study, which meant that the original analysis was incapable of being replicated by research workers in other cities. Rees (1972) includes a comprehensive bibliography of studies carried out in the USA and elsewhere following the principles set out by Shevky, Williams, and Bell.

Social area analysis was used to perform a variety of functions: to delineate socially homogeneous sub-areas within the city; to compare the distribution of such areas at two or more points in time; and compare the social areas in two or more places; and to provide a sampling framework; to enable other types of research to be undertaken, particularly for the design and execution of behavioural field studies (Rees 1972, p. 275).

In its original form social area analysis was severely criticised on two counts: first in terms of its theoretical basis (the theory underlying the constructs); and secondly for empirical reasons (the method of measuring the constructs).

Efforts were made subsequently to test the correctness of the census variables used to measure the constructs by employing factor analysis (Bell 1955). This work had some initial success, but extension to a wider range of cities revealed the shortcomings of the original choice of census variables (van Arsdol et al. 1958). It led to the inclusion of a wider range of socio-economic census variables and to the adoption of factor analysis (or the related technique of principal component analysis) as a standard method for identifying the underlying dimensions of urban social and spatial structure. This development of social area analysis became known as factorial ecology and was widely used by quantitative geographers in the 1960s and 1970s, not only in the USA but also in a range of cities throughout the world (Rees 1972; Berry and Horton 1970). Factorial ecology generally led to the production of maps and cross-sections using factor scores for each of the main factors. In this way it was possible to summarise the main features of spatial variation in socio-economic and demographic characteristics.

In some instances, the scores from the two factors were used to cross-classify census tracts. Rees's study of Chicago (Berry and Horton 1970), for example, employs a simple graphical technique to categorise areas according to the economic status of their residents. It was uncommon at this time to proceed one step further and

[7] Over time the term 'social area analysis' has been used in a number of different ways. For example, later in this chapter, the term will be used again to refer to work carried out in Liverpool in the late 1960s and 1970s.

use cluster analysis to create a multivariate classification of social areas. One exception, Tryon's (1955) study of the San Francisco Bay Area, was of limited value because of the imprecise way in which cluster analysis was used. Other researchers found it difficult to reproduce the results that Tryon had obtained (Robson 1969, p. 51).

1.3.2 United Kingdom

In Britain, early studies of urban spatial structure were hampered by the almost complete absence of small area census data. For many years the smallest units for which census data was published were the ward and civil parish and even here the range of information was small. Gittus (1964) describes attempts made in 1951 to define zones within the major conurbations that were relatively uniform with respect to the siting of industry and commerce, the rate of population change, and the age and type of housing. Within zones, distinctive areas, both natural and planned, were recognised and their boundaries determined on the basis of 'purely local considerations' (Gittus 1964, p. 9). These divisions and sub-divisions were intended to provide a more rational basis for presenting social data than that offered by administrative boundaries. However, it proved difficult to achieve consistency from one conurbation to another and in practice little use was made of the zones in comparative studies.

A more promising initiative was the establishment of the Inter-University Census Tract Committee. This committee, formed in Oxford in 1955, was originally intended to consider the definition of census tracts similar to those used in the USA. The city of Oxford served as the prototype for British census tracts and some 48 tracts were delineated with an average population of 2645 (Robson 1969, p. 44). Although these census tracts were similar to their American equivalents, they were nevertheless fairly large aggregates, likely to exhibit a high degree of internal heterogeneity. One possible advantage compared with other geographical units was that they were more certain of retaining their boundaries over time, allowing comparisons to be made.

However, the British Registrar General's Department had a different idea. Instead of adopting census tracts, it would make data available by enumeration district.[8] Such units were considerably smaller, containing on average less than 1000 people. Data on this scale were purchased for most of the conurbations included in the 1951 scheme and for a smaller number of smaller administrative areas. Members of the Inter-University Committee continued to meet and began to develop a series of

[8]An enumeration district was the area covered by a single census enumerator, distributing and collecting census forms.

comparative studies of urban structure. Gittus (1964) used 1951 Census data for sub-divisions[9] of the Merseyside and South East Lancashire conurbations in an experimental project, applying correlation analysis and principal component analysis to a set of 27 census variables. This preliminary work paved the way for further studies using 1961 Census enumeration district data, including Gittus's study of South Hampshire and Merseyside (Gittus 1963–1964) and Robson's study of Sunderland (Robson 1969; Robson 1984, pp. 110–112).

The work of the Centre for Urban Studies at University College London, under the direction of urban sociologist Ruth Glass, was probably the most important in terms of the development of method, scale of study and influence upon other research. Founded in 1958, one of its early projects was a pioneering inter-urban study of British towns. This study, carried out by two researchers at the Centre, Claus Moser and Wolf Scott, drew upon 60 variables for 157 towns in England and Wales with a population of more than 50,000 and classified them into 14 groups, using principal component analysis and a graphical plot of scores from the first two components (Moser and Scott 1961). The study was based on a combination of 1951 Census data and other sources of social and health data, while other variables were intended to measure change over time. Undoubtedly, the British Towns study was a remarkable achievement given the size of the data set and the limits of computing power available at the time. It provided the stimulus for much of the work in the UK on what was to become known as 'geodemographics'.

The Centre's original research programme included plans to undertake a *Third Survey of London Life and Labour*, intended to carry on some aspects of Charles Booth's *Life and Labour of the People in London* (1886–1903) and its follow-up the *New Survey of London Life and Labour* (1930–35), both of which were referred to earlier. The *Third London Survey* was seen as an opportunity to study how London had changed over time. And, rather than focus largely on poverty, as the earlier surveys had done, the scope would be wider, including London's economy, society, and culture. Like its two predecessors, the *Third Survey* would not be a purely academic exercise but where possible would use the survey results to influence social policy (Glass 1963, p. 181).

The Centre's research plan envisaged that four volumes would be published, covering: (1) Thirty Years of Change (essays on the main features and trends of change); (2) The Socio-Geographical Pattern (mainly the report on the analysis of special census tabulations; (3) The Diverse London (studies of particular areas, groups, problems, and aspects); (4) Maps and Sources (Descriptive material, as well as detailed tables relevant to the other three volumes). The second of the proposed volumes is of particular relevance here and reflected the Centre's:

[9] Sub-divisions consisted of a mix of smaller local authority areas and sub-divided larger local authority areas. They were used extensively by local planning authorities at that time to analyse population and employment change.

> . . . interest in developing large scale comparative analyses of urban patterns, both of intra-urban and inter-urban classifications—which make it necessary to identify types of towns and of urban components (Glass 1963 p. 182).

Here the intention was to make extensive use of the 1961 Census in the expectation that enumeration district data would become available early on in the Survey. Some 7000 enumeration districts were covered, 5000 of which referred to the County of London and the remainder in an out-county ring. A classification of enumeration districts in terms of their socio-economic characteristics would be produced.

The Centre research team experimented with 1961 Census data at both the ward and enumeration district levels. For Inner London[10] they produced a six-fold classification of enumeration districts using principal component analysis and a least-squares cluster analysis (Norman 1969). Several features of this work stand out, as may be seen in Table 1.2 which presents the results of the Inner London classification. First, and no doubt influenced by Charles Booth's poverty mapping, the naming of clusters ('Upper Class', 'Bed Sitter', 'Poor', 'Stable Working Class', 'Almost Suburban', 'Local Authority Housing'); secondly, the use of location quotients[11] to produce a statistical profile of each cluster); thirdly, the use of these statistical profiles to produce a verbal description of the main census characteristics of each cluster; and fourthly, the considerable variation that was found in the size of clusters: in this example, the Stable Working Class cluster accounted for almost a third of all enumeration districts, a fair reflection of the spatial structure of Inner London at that time. From that point onwards, these four features would become standard elements of geodemographic classifications.

The *Third Survey* was initiated in 1961 at a time when proposals were being considered for a comprehensive re-structuring of London's administration: by 1965, the Greater London Council (GLC) had been created. On the one hand, this new structure was bound to generate considerable interest in the results of the *Third Survey* and what it said about London's changing characteristics; while on the other hand some of the *Survey*'s findings would, by this time, be looking rather dated based as they were on the 1961 Census. Added to this, the newly established GLC would have its own technical capability in its Research and Intelligence Unit to carry out the same kind of census analyses.

---

[10] Inner London represented the area covered by the old (pre-1965) London County Council. There is no evidence that the Centre for Urban Studies team produced an enumeration district classification for the entire *Third Survey* study area.

[11] Table 1.2 shows location quotients that compare the cluster mean value of a variable with the Inner London value of the same variable. A quotient of less than 100 indicates the variable is under-represented in a cluster while a value of more than 100 indicates over-representation. See Batey and Brown (1995, pp. 95–102).

Table 1.2 Selected characteristics of six types of enumeration district in Inner London, 1961 Census

Number and Name of Variable		Enumeration District Type						All Inner London	
		Type 1 Upper Class	Type 2 Bed Sitter	Type 3 Poor	Type 4 Stable Working Class	Type 5 Local Authority Housing	Type 6 Almost Suburban	Mean	Coefficient of Variation
1.	% Population under 5	57	60	140	111	99	86	7.0	37
2.	% Population under 15	58	52	110	105	133	92	19.2	31
3.	% Population 65 and over	120	94	83	103	77	123	11.8	34
6.	Female/male ratio, all ages	130	105	92	96	94	102	1.123	21
7.	Female/male ratio, 25-44	126	91	115	95	106	105	1.005	22
8.	% women 20-24 never married	45	51	119	125	85	104	50.9	40
9.	% adults single	139	167	101	88	113	87	28.7	30
11.	% one-person households	149	205	112	94	58	77	22.5	51
12.	% one- and two-person households	125	144	105	99	141	97	52.6	25
13.	% households of five or more persons	68	44	97	94	159	92	12.4	50
15.	% all households overcrowded	49	159	228	91	86	32	6.9	83
16.	No. of persons per room	83	104	118	99	114	81	0.78	18
18.	% households sharing dwelling	38	66	218	122	18	62	29.1	105
19.	% households sharing dwelling stove sink	48	206	239	104	28	48	6.9	119
20.	% households sharing WC	57	159	195	120	390	63	30.4	78
21.	% households sharing dwelling stove sink WC	45	206	235	97	26	43	6.5	18
22.	% owner-occupiers	92	56	128	79	25	244	15.3	112
23.	% council tenants	23	16	31	63	352	42	21.2	146
24.	% private tenants, furnished accom.	138	355	182	68	13	68	13.0	110
25.	% private tenants, unfurnished accom.	118	83	120	135	35	94	46.0	56
28.	% born in India, Pakistan and Ceylon	190	350	120	50	30	80	1.0	150
30.	% born in British Caribbean	19	76	324	105	14	48	2.1	171
32.	% born outside British Isles and New Commonwealth	281	290	129	58	33	51	6.9	112
36.	% born in Ireland (both parts)	92	59	200	90	57	59	4.9	82
37.	% moved within year into local authority area	206	242	120	68	59	80	8.3	102
38.	% early school leavers	46	55	116	114	118	95	73.5	29
40.	% males in prof./ manag. occupations	304	191	200	55	39	128	13.2	111
41.	% males in manual occupations	44	63	119	115	118	85	65.3	32
	%of ed's of each type	9.1	7.3	14.9	31.1	18.2	19.4	100	

Source: modified from Norman (1969)

This is largely what happened in practice. The recent availability of the 1966 10% Sample Census[12] opened the way for a classification of the 32 newly created London Boroughs (Kelly 1971); a report, also by Kelly, on the methodology used to construct this classification, including helpful advice on the choice of input variables and clustering methods (Kelly 1969); and a classification of wards in Greater London by Daly (1971) that comes closest to what had been intended in the *Third Survey*. The notion of a classification based on 1966 Census enumeration districts was postponed because of concerns about sampling and enumeration errors (Kelly 1969, p. 18). In due course the 1971 Census, containing a substantial amount of 100% data, would prove more suitable for this kind of analysis.

The GLC's classification work as described here was strongly influenced by that of the Centre for Urban Studies and fully acknowledged the methodological contribution of Ruth Glass. Its practical value lay in enabling systematic comparisons to be made at different spatial scales across the whole of Greater London. It is certainly the case that its didactic reports did much to encourage other local authorities in the UK to carry out their own census classification.[13]

In the meantime, some of the research findings from the *Third Survey* were published but never the full range that had been promised when the idea was first contemplated.[14]

1.4 Pioneering Geodemographic Classifications

1.4.1 The City of Los Angeles and its Urban Information System

A pertinent example of an early application of the public sector use of geodemographics in the USA concerns the city of Los Angeles. In the late 1960s and 1970s, the city's administration began to develop a comprehensive urban information system that integrated a wide range of spatial data relevant to the

[12]The 1966 10% Sample Census was intended to plug the gap left between decennial censuses which was felt to be too long. However, sample censuses have never been repeated, largely because of difficulties in measuring change at a local level caused by incompatible enumeration district boundaries, confidentiality problems, and sampling error.

[13]For example, in 1972 the present author carried out a multivariate analysis, at ward level, of the 1966 Census for the Greater Manchester area. The approach taken was strongly influenced by the Greater London studies.

[14]The Third Survey reports were announced as 'forthcoming' as late as 1973 (Glass 1973). A Fourth Survey, *Working Capital: Life and Labour in Contemporary London* (Buck et al. 2002) was carried in the late 1990s and published to coincide with the centenary of Charles Booth's survey in 2002. Based on an extensive programme of interviews across London and on detailed analysis of socio-economic data, the book's main message was that despite London's outstanding economic success as a global city, the city's prosperity was unequally distributed and was increasingly marred by social exclusion and deprivation.

activities of the city council, particularly in housing and planning. A recent retrospective review by Mark Vallianatos considered this ambitious venture into computer-assisted data and policy analysis to be well ahead of its time, comparing favourably with current initiatives to create 'smart cities' (Vallianatos 2015).

In establishing its Community Analysis Bureau (CAB), Los Angeles sought new tools to address the old challenges of deteriorating housing by providing detailed local data to identify neighbourhoods showing early signs of obsolescence. The bureau's data would, it was felt, help identify blighted areas across the city and inform measures aimed at alleviating the poverty that led to blight in the first place.

The US Census Bureau had gathered and reported statistics on housing quality between 1940 and 1960 but had abandoned this approach when it became clear that it was seriously over-estimating the amount of dilapidated housing. After 1960, the Census Bureau recommended looking at other characteristics such as building age, lack of plumbing, and overcrowding to infer housing quality. The CAB adapted and developed a range of analytic approaches to assess housing (and related social) conditions to fill this void left by the Census Bureau, and provide detailed local data to identify neighbourhoods showing early signs of obsolescence. First, however, the bureau had to digitise and centralise relevant information from the US Census, the Los Angeles Police Department, the LA County Assessor, and other private and public sources. In an effort to create a comprehensive Los Angeles Urban Information System, the bureau assembled a database containing 550 categories available to analyse individual census tracts. As Vallianatos (2015) points out, given the computing power then available, this would certainly have been regarded as 'big data'.

The CAB used cluster analysis in order to allow "the data to suggest its own 'natural' grouping." Clustering could identify parts of the city that might be geographically far apart but shared important social and physical characteristics. Sixty-six key items were chosen from the database, including population, ethnicity, education, housing, and crime data, and an environmental quality rating and LA's 750 census tracts were sorted into 30 clusters. It emerged that nowhere near 66 data variables were needed to identify which parts of the city had the worst blight and poverty. Three sets of data considered together—birth weight of infants, sixth-grade reading scores, and age of housing—were found to be an accurate indicator of housing decline and socio-economic deprivation. The bureau's data and analyses were intended to spur interventions in the city. They helped the city to move away from the traditional approach to urban renewal, with its focus on the treatment only of physical problems, to a more broadly-based approach that dealt with the social, economic, and physical nature of urban decay. Ultimately, however, the CAB was a victim of its own success. The data it collected proved so useful in securing federal grants that the city focused the CAB's activities on grant development and administration, with continued data analysis to justify these funds. Instead of using research to guide the city's actions, the bureau found itself reacting to the city's predetermined goals as set out in funding applications. By 1980, it had stopped producing research reports and had been absorbed into the city's community development department (Fig. 1.3).[15]

1.4.2 Liverpool and its Social Area Analyses

In the late 1960s, the city of Liverpool in North West England was in serious social and economic decline. The City Council was engaged in a massive programme of slum clearance and new house building as part of efforts to regenerate the city. To help achieve these goals, the planning function in the City Council was being strengthened by creating a strong social research orientation. Planning was now seen as much broader in scope than physical planning. The City Council's role in social and community development was under active discussion in the aftermath of the UK Government's Seebohm Committee report (1968) which recommended fundamental changes in how social services were to be organised and delivered.

In 1967, the City Council hosted a conference to discuss community development in Liverpool. Attending the conference were city councillors, council officials, and representatives of community organisations in the city. The conference agreed that the city planning department should undertake a study to identify areas with large numbers of social problems, to help guide the allocation of social services resources and the establishment of a community development programme.

The so-called *Social Malaise Study,*[16] commenced in 1968, would concentrate on three elements: (1) an examination of 'social malfunction' throughout the city, to guide the allocation of extra physical and social resources; (2) an exploration of the degree of association between malaise and census indices, and of the important of better coordination of services to those in need; (3) a consideration of the impact of slum clearance and housing redevelopment, as well as various economic factors on the distribution of problem areas within the city. The information collected would guide policy but would also serve as an as educational exercise for city officials, helping to improve their understanding of the complex processes at work in the city. Unusually for a British local authority, the study team was advised in its early stages by an expert in community development, Professor Arthur Dunham, from the University of Michigan (Batey and Brown 1995, pp. 83–84). The City Council clearly wanted to be seen as a leading local authority in this field and the appointment of an international adviser would, no doubt, add to the prestige of the study.

Like the Los Angeles study described earlier, the *Social Malaise Study* assembled data from a range of sources:

- 1966 Census data, at enumeration district level (58 variables).
- Operational data assembled for 36 social malaise indicators from six City Council departments and from a wide range of other agencies on, e.g. job instability,

[15]For a full account of the Los Angeles Community Analysis Bureau, see Light (2003, pp. 78–83).
[16]See Flynn et al. (1972) for a comprehensive account of the Social Malaise Study.

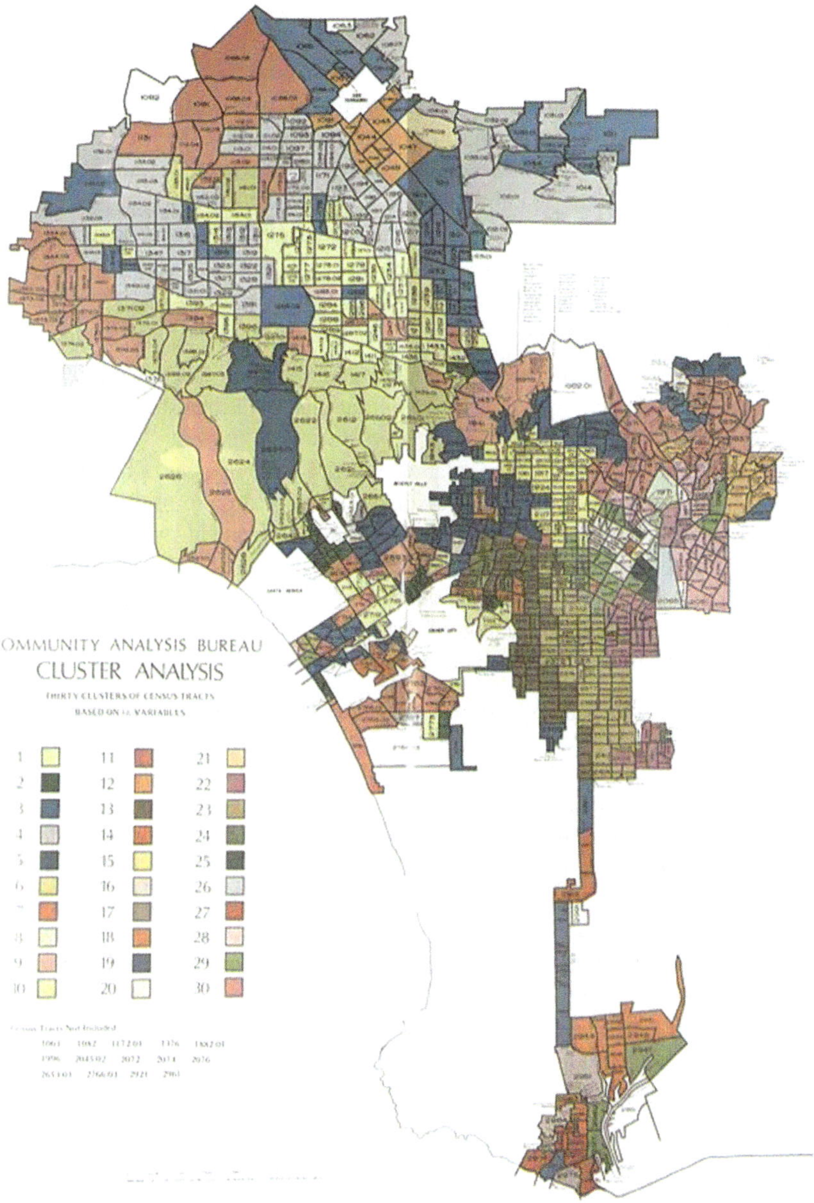

Fig. 1.3 The state of the city: a cluster analysis of Los Angeles, 1974 (Source: Vallianatos (2015))

crime, debtors, and possession orders, together with six housing variables (Amos 1969).

The task of collecting data was formidable and met with widespread resistance from those unconvinced as to the value of the study, as well as technical problems in coding operational data to the census enumeration districts. A correlation exercise was carried out for census and social malaise data at ward level, leading to a principal component analysis. The loadings on the first principal component were used as weights in creating a single index of social malaise which could then be used to define priority areas in the city.

The City Council was prepared to learn from the experience of this first *Social Malaise Study*. Four practical lessons were identified[17]:

- By concentrating on a single aggregate measure (score on principal component 1), the study failed to recognise the different kinds of urban stress experienced in cities.
- The proportion of the city's population shown to live in areas of severe need was out of all proportion to the funds available for allocation to priority areas.
- The analysis was carried out in the Planning Department, with other agencies playing little part in the project design and so not having much 'buy in' to the study, despite its high profile nationally.
- The technical capability was not retained with the result that further analysis that could have been done never materialised.

As the first of its kind, the *Social Malaise Study* proved controversial[18] attracting a lot of attention both locally and nationally: it was widely emulated by other local authorities in the early 1970s. This led to the holding of a conference in 1970 at which representatives from a range of disciplines were encouraged to criticise the study and suggest how it might be improved. The critics, who were largely academics, unsurprisingly pointed out the lack of underlying theory, limitations of the statistical analysis and the fact that, in the 3 years since the initial 1967 conference, the institutional and policy context had changed, as the Central Government implemented the Seebohm Committee's recommendations on the management and delivery of social services. In fairness, however, the scope of these changes could not have been fully anticipated by those commissioning the study.

The story of Liverpool's engagement with social area analysis does not end there. By 1974, there were calls for a new study. These came from a variety of sources: Liverpool City Council which was keen to extend its initial *Social Malaise Study* with the benefit of 1971 Census data; consultants Hugh Wilson and Lewis

[17] Webber (1975, p. 12).

[18] Some of the controversy arose because of the sensitive nature of the data being collected and the probability that some areas would be stigmatised as a result of high social malaise scores. The social malaise report was duly marked as 'highly confidential'.

Womersley who wanted an objective basis for defining boundaries of the Government-commissioned Liverpool Inner Area Study[19]; the newly established Merseyside (Metropolitan County Council), embarking on a strategic spatial plan and interested in developing cross-county information systems; the Centre for Environmental Studies and its Planning Research Applications Group (PRAG) which was seeking a test-bed for its area classifications and their application; and the Office of Population Censuses and Surveys (OPCS) which was interested in partnering PRAG in their census classification work.

This led to PRAG being commissioned to carry out a *Liverpool Social Area Study*. This was to be a well-resourced four-year study demonstrating advanced practice in assembling data sets, using computer-based analytical techniques and a range of actual and potential applications of the methodology. At the heart of the Study was a two-level geodemographic classification with 25 clusters and 5 so-called families (groupings of clusters).

The results of the study were widely disseminated in a number of reports each with a different target audience. The City Council produced a report combining the Social Area Analysis with more traditional methods for studying urban structure and long-term change in Liverpool and in comparator cities (Evans 1977); PRAG's report, written by leading census analyst Richard Webber as a demonstration project aimed at a wider audience of practitioners and academics (Webber 1975); PRAG's report on behalf of the Inner Area Study consultants making extensive use of visual and graphical techniques to illustrate clusters to show how they differed (Wilson and Womersley 1977); and a report showing how the classification had been extended to the wider area of Merseyside County and focusing on a range of applications (Webber 1978; Webber and Burrows (2018, pp. 54–61).

The collaboration with the OPCS proved to be very fruitful, leading to PRAG creating a series of classifications of parliamentary constituencies, the system of post-1974[20] local authorities in Britain and a number of individual local authorities. It culminated in the creation of two 1971 Census-based classifications, of wards and parishes and of enumeration districts, for Great Britain as a whole. These national classifications were to prove an important stepping stone for Webber as they started to generate serious interest from the private sector. Market analysts were quick to see the potential of area classifications. CACI, a leading US marketing company, made the first move and recruited Webber in order to help them launch ACORN[21] the first UK commercial product of its kind. ACORN was essentially a re-branding of the national classification that Webber had developed while working for PRAG (Batey and Brown 1995; Webber and Burrows 2018, pp. 62–63). For Webber, who had

[19]Inner Area Studies were commissioned by the UK Government in the early 1970s and were concerned with developing policy responses to a growing problem of multiple deprivation in the inner cities of England. Three studies were carried out: Liverpool, Birmingham, and Lambeth (London).

[20]In 1974 the system of local government was re-organised and a new, two-tier system of counties and districts was introduced. Local authority boundaries were comprehensively revised, hence the need to understand the socio-economic spatial structure of the new authorities.

[21]The term ACORN was an acronym for 'A Classification Of Residential Neighbourhoods'.

been the leading figure in developing public sector census classifications, this now opened up a highly successful career spent largely working in a commercial marketing environment.

From 1980 onwards there was a rapid growth in the development of proprietary area classifications, with several companies competing in the market place with products based on the 1981 Census. These products benefited greatly from increases in computing power and from new clustering methods that enabled much larger datasets to be handled. Although there were some variants, generally the statistical methodology adopted was very similar. Henceforth the field was to be known as 'geodemographics'.

***Discussion 3*: Los Angeles and Liverpool Experience Compared**
It is interesting to note the parallels between the experience in Liverpool and that in Los Angeles. Both cities were engaged in a major programme of urban renewal/slum clearance and had started to question the wisdom of pursuing an entirely physical approach. There was general agreement on the need to consider the social dimension of housing renewal and to collect data that would enable this to be done. Data collection would involve a multi-agency approach and considerable effort would be needed to ensure consistency in this data. Careful planning was essential if all participant organisations were to be persuaded to 'buy in' to the project and, importantly, stay with it beyond the early stages. Both cities were conscious of the fact that what they were attempting to do was new and untried and at the limits of technical and computing capability of that time. The two cities were also in the throes of reorganising their community development provision making it difficult to maintain the information function that had been built up during the project.

Whereas Liverpool was fortunate in very soon after being part of a multi-faceted project leading to some important developments nationally in geodemographic analysis, in Los Angeles the City Council re-structuring meant an end to the urban information system by the late 1970s. However, this was not the end of the story in Los Angeles. An executive order from the city mayor in December 2013 instructed each city department to gather all the data it collects and share it on a publicly accessible website. By later the following year, Los Angeles had appointed its first Chief Innovation Officer and launched DataLA, the city's online data portal. Forty years on, the era of 'big data' and Smart City had finally arrived (Vallianatos 2015).

1.5 Geodemographics in Action as an Evaluation Tool

1.5.1 Area-Based Urban Policy Initiatives (ABIs)

Much of the discussion so far has viewed geodemographic classifications as a tool to guide the spatial targeting of resources.[22] In this section, the process is reversed and

[22] For a comprehensive guide to the uses and limitations of geodemographic classifications in a public policy context, see Lupton et al. 2011).

geodemographics is used to evaluate targeting that has already been done by other means, which may or may not be rational. The focus is on urban policy operating at a neighbourhood scale in the UK.

For at least 40 years, area-based initiatives (ABIs) have been an important feature of urban policy in the UK and have been seen as an effective means of targeting the poor. Successive governments have pursued a spatial targeting approach and introduced a range of policies and programmes identified through the use of area deprivation indices (for example, the Index of Deprivation (1980s); the Index of Local Conditions (1990s); and the Index of Multiple Deprivation (2000s) (Harris et al. 2005, pp. 42–45)). This prompts the question: how effective is spatial targeting in reaching the people for whom an urban policy initiative is intended and where areas are targeted as a proxy for individuals? With this question in mind a geodemographic evaluation tool will now be introduced and tested.[23]

What is the purpose of targeting associated with ABIs? Potentially, there is a wide range of possibilities. At one extreme, there could be a situation where the sole purpose of targeting is to identify a group of individuals who share a common set of characteristics that are relevant to the initiative (individual-, or people-oriented targeting). In this case, the attraction of an area-based approach is that it gives ready access to a concentration of such individuals and may help in the delivery of the initiative. At the other extreme, there could be an initiative that is entirely geographically-based, to the extent that the characteristics of the local population are completely irrelevant (area- or place-oriented targeting).

In practice, ABIs invariably lie somewhere between these two extremes. Even initiatives that appear at first sight to be either place-oriented or people-oriented turn out to be a combination of the two. What distinguishes them is the relative importance attached to targeting the individual and the area.

Following a study of government urban policy initiatives, Tunstall and Lupton (2003) put forward two simple concepts that help in considering the effectiveness of targeting: the notions of *efficiency* and *completeness*. Because the population of any given area is never perfectly differentiated by income, every area is, to some extent, mixed. This means that a degree of inefficiency is built into targeting by area, because people who are not the intended beneficiaries will be included. At the same time, the targeting will be incomplete, because deserving cases living outside the targeted area will be excluded.

The Tunstall and Lupton concepts can be put into practice by developing a method to measure the degree to which spatial targeting is successful. The proposed method draws upon a geodemographic classification system. The utility of the method is demonstrated by employing the P^2 People and Places geodemographic system[24] to assess the targeting of the Sure Start initiative in eight large provincial cities in England.

---

[23] A fuller account of the geodemographic evaluation tool and its application is provided in Batey and Brown (2007).

[24] P^2 People and Places was a proprietary geodemographic classification based on the 2001 Census. It was developed jointly by Beacon Dodsworth Ltd. and researchers at the University of Liverpool.

1.5.2 Characterising ABIs

Geodemographic classification systems may be used to establish the main types of residential neighbourhood associated with particular area-based initiatives. Moreover, they provide a means of judging how well the boundaries of regeneration initiatives reflect the spatial distribution of socio-economic need.

Any targeted area may be described in terms of a series of census Output Areas.[25] Local examples of the areas defined for ABIs are generally larger than a single Output Area and, although the match will not be perfect, it should be relatively easy to list the relevant Output Areas that constitute a targeted area. Describing targeted areas in this way enables them to be linked to the geodemographic classification which itself is based on Output Area level data. In the geodemographic system, each Output Area is assigned to a specific residential neighbourhood type (cluster), along with other Output Areas sharing similar characteristics.

The neighbourhood types conveniently summarise the main features of the population that is being targeted by an initiative. In practice several different neighbourhood types will be needed, rather than a single dominant type. Two closely related technical issues are important here: the mechanism by which these neighbourhood types are identified; and the task of measuring the closeness of fit between these neighbourhood types and the population targeted by the initiative. The objective here is to obtain the best possible approximation.

Two complementary approaches have been adopted in identifying the list of relevant neighbourhood types. The first of these is referred to as a 'penetration ranking' or concentration approach and identifies the neighbourhood types that have the greatest over-representation of the ABI population. The second approach employs a method of ranking based on the overall similarity between particular neighbourhood types and the general socio-economic profile of the ABI. This is described as a programme profile distance approach. In drawing up a final list of neighbourhood types, elements of the two approaches are combined.

By studying the composition of neighbourhood types that make up local instances of targeted areas across the complete set of local authorities, it is possible to establish whether there are particular types that occur more frequently than others. Taken together, such neighbourhood types are likely to account for the bulk of the total population resident in the targeted areas. These may be regarded as *Category 1 Neighbourhoods*. These neighbourhoods are likely to play an important part in characterising the areas targeted by a particular initiative.

The latest (2011) version of P^2 People and Places is described on the Beacon Dodsworth website: https://beacon-dodsworth.co.uk

[25] In the 2001 UK Census, Output Areas replaced enumeration districts as the smallest spatial units used to publish census data. They were designed to align with postcode geography and were created by aggregating unit postcodes. This made it possible to link post-coded data with small area census data much more accurately than had been possible previously, with obvious benefits for spatial targeting. By the time of the 2011 Census there were approximately 190,000 Output Areas in the UK, containing an average of 125 households.

However, it is also important to recognise that certain types of neighbourhood are concentrated in particular parts of the country, and may not emerge near the top of a national ranking of prevalent neighbourhoods. The method used here must be sufficiently flexible to reflect local and regional distinctiveness of this kind. To do this, it is necessary to define a second group of neighbourhood types, namely *Category 2 Neighbourhoods*. Such neighbourhoods have to satisfy the criterion that they are locally important (local here could mean a particular local authority area) in that they are over-represented in that area.

Inevitably, some neighbourhood types will lie outside Categories 1 and 2. These are defined as Category 3. Successful spatial targeting implies that most of the targeted areas are either Category 1 or 2 Neighbourhoods (reflecting the *efficient* targeting of the initiative), and that the incidence of Category 1 and 2 neighbourhoods outside the targeted areas is kept to a minimum (reflecting more *complete* targeting of those whose needs are greatest).

1.5.3 Measures of Targeting Performance

A number of simple measures can be calculated to describe how successful targeting has been, based on the cell values contained in a 2 × 2 table. To illustrate these, an example has been selected for the city of Nottingham. Here the characterisation of an unspecified area-based initiative has been done using the P^2 People and Places geodemographic system referred to earlier. The different categories of residential neighbourhood were identified using the Branch (40 cluster) level in P^2 People and Places by adopting the procedure outlined earlier (see Batey and Brown (2007) for a more detailed account). The generalised socio-economic profile of the initiative is based on the combined evidence of targeting across the entire set of eight cities.

In Table 1.3 the two rows represent the combination of Category 1 and Category 2 neighbourhoods (i.e. those whose needs are greatest) and Category 3 neighbourhoods (i.e. those whose needs are least), and the two columns represent, respectively, output Areas within, and outside, the areas on which the ABI programme is targeted.

In this table, the two main diagonal entries represent *correct targeting*—comprising, respectively, the *deserving* Categories (1 and 2) that fall within the defined initiative area boundaries and the *undeserving* Category (3) that fall outside the defined area. This "correctness" can be translated into a rate by adding the two figures together and dividing by the total population of the city and expressing the result as a percentage.

In this table, the two main diagonal entries represent *correct targeting*—comprising, respectively, the *deserving* Categories (1 and 2) that fall within the defined initiative area boundaries and the *undeserving* Category (3) that fall outside the defined area. This "correctness" can be translated into a rate by adding the two figures together and dividing by the total population of the city and expressing the result as a percentage.

Table 1.3 The match between targeted areas and neighbourhood categories: a population analysis for Nottingham

	Targeted areas	Non-targeted areas	Total
Category 1 or 2	42,648	40,294	82,942
Category 3	31,090	141,956	173,046
Total	73,738	182,250	255,988

Source: Batey and Brown (2007)

The two off-diagonal entries each represent different types of error, as follows:

Type 1 Error refers to *inefficiency*, or the capturing, within the initiative area, of people who are in the less deserving Category 3, and *Type 2 Error* refers to *incompleteness*, or the omission, from the defined area, of people who are in the more deserving Categories 1 and 2.

Table 1.3 shows the relevant counts relating to Nottingham for the selected area-based initiative. These counts are then used to derive the corresponding measures of inefficiency and incompleteness, as follows:

1. *Correct Targeting*: (42,648 + 141,956) × 100/255988 = 72.1%
2. *Targeting Error*: 100−Correct Targeting = 27.9%
3. *Type 1 Error (Inefficiency)*: 31090 × 100/255988 = 12.1%, or 43.6% of total error
4. *Type 2 Error (Incompleteness)*: 74719 × 100/255988 = 15.7%, or 56.4% of total error

In this example, approximately three-quarters of Nottingham's population is found to be correctly targeted, implying that the remaining quarter is not. For this quarter, it is possible to apportion the error between Types 1 and 2. Here, Type 2 (incompleteness) turns out to be appreciably more important than Type 1 (inefficiency). The implication is that in Nottingham, the boundary of the area-based initiative needs to be drawn more extensively, to include a greater number of people living in Category 1 and 2 neighbourhood types.

1.5.4 Application to a Specific ABI

The Sure Start programme is used here to demonstrate the practical application of the geodemographic assessment tool. By concentrating on a comparison between eight large provincial cities, the application also provides an opportunity to demonstrate how the assessment tool can be used to identify variations in targeting performance between areas with markedly different social and economic conditions.

Sure Start was a £3bn. 10-year national programme, launched in 1998, in which the intention was to work with parents, parents-to-be, and children to promote the physical, intellectual, and social development of babies and young children, particularly those that are disadvantaged. The programme was focussed on combating

Table 1.4 Comparison of inefficiency and incompleteness in the definition of Sure Start areas by city

	Sure start rate	Correct targeting (%)	Targeting error (%)	Type 1 error (inefficiency) (%)	Type 2 error (incompleteness) (%)
Bristol	138	86.6	13.4	61.7	38.3
Sheffield	194	82.2	17.8	58.7	41.3
Birmingham	119	79.5	20.5	43.3	56.7
Leeds	146	77.7	22.3	50.1	49.9
Newcastle	335	73.8	26.2	70.3	29.7
Liverpool	285	73.4	26.6	35.2	64.8
Nottingham	288	72.1	27.9	43.6	56.4
Manchester	312	67.1	32.9	41.8	58.2
All 8 Cities	199	77.2	22.8	51.5	48.5

Source: Batey and Brown (2007)

child poverty in neighbourhoods with concentrations of children aged 0–4 by reshaping existing support services (see Sure Start 2005).

Districts in receipt of Sure Start funding were selected according to levels of deprivation, but detailed decisions about the definition of individual Sure Start programme area boundaries were made locally. The starting point in each case was the national list of the 20% most deprived wards, as measured by the IMD (Index of Multiple Deprivation) 2000 (Noble et al. 2000). Draft Sure Start area boundaries were then modified using local knowledge (Frost 2005).

Table 1.4 presents the results for the eight cities. The first column shows the Sure Start rate: the number of local residents targeted by Sure Start per 1000 total population in each city. It indicates that there is substantial variation among the cities in the penetration of the Sure Start initiative. The next four columns show the measures of correct targeting and targeting error introduced in the Nottingham example. The resulting values provide a basis for ranking the eight cities. This ranking places Bristol at the top, with a correct targeting measure of 86.6 or 12% above the average for the eight cities as a group. The complement, targeting error, ranges from 13.4% for Bristol to 32.9% for Manchester, the latter 44% higher than the eight-city average of 22.8%.

The same table also records the two components of targeting error: Type 1 (Inefficiency) and Type 2 (Incompleteness). The table reveals that, in those cities with a higher rate of correct targeting, there is a tendency for Inefficiency to exceed Incompleteness, i.e. for a larger number of less deserving people to be included in Sure Start areas than should be. Similarly, towards the bottom of the table, notably in Liverpool (with the highest value of 64.8%), Nottingham and Manchester, incompleteness is more marked, implying that, in these cities, the Sure Start area boundary has been drawn too tightly, causing a greater proportion of potentially deserving recipients to be excluded.

A clear indication of the success of spatial targeting can be obtained by mapping the Category 1 and 2 neighbourhoods and the boundaries of the ABI. Figure 1.4

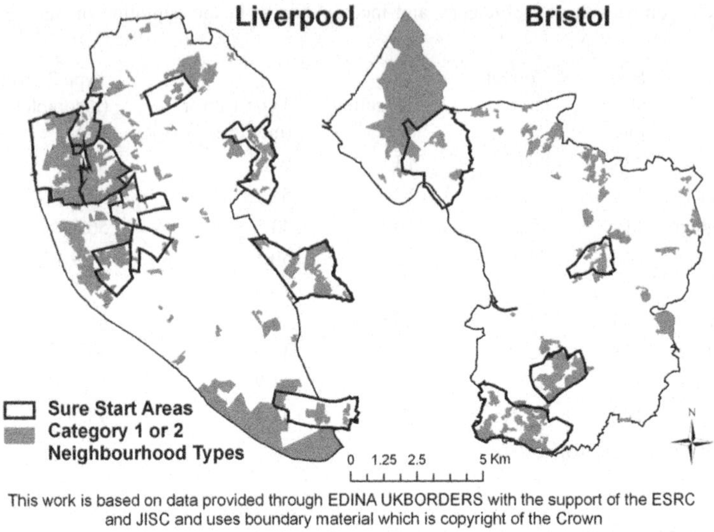

Fig. 1.4 The relationship between Sure Start areas and Category 1 and 2 neighbourhood types in Bristol and Liverpool (Source: Batey and Brown (2007))

presents maps of Bristol (where the targeting is relatively successful) and Liverpool (where it is less successful). The maps reveal that in both cities there are substantial areas that could equally well have been targeted and that there are some neighbourhoods where the targeting is hard to justify.

***Discussion 4*: Benefits of a Geodemographic Evaluation Tool**

This case study has shown how a geodemographic approach can be employed to measure the success of spatial targeting of area-based urban policy initiatives. Even though the original basis for targeting may be obscure, and reflect political as much as technical factors, the approach presented here allows targeted areas to be analysed consistently and systematically. The geodemographic approach works by characterising the main types of residential neighbourhood that account for the bulk of the population in targeted areas. Some neighbourhood types are widely represented while others are distinctive to particular localities. Neighbourhoods that have been wrongly targeted can be easily identified, as can those that have been missed in targeting.

The geodemographic approach is flexible. The Sure Start case study used here has shown that it is possible to compare targeting performance in one city with that in other cities and thus to draw conclusions about the consistency with which particular nationally initiated area-based initiatives are implemented. In some instances, poor targeting is found to be a product of incomplete targeting, where the definition of targeted areas has stopped short of including the full complement of deserving areas. In other cases, the poor targeting outcome reflects an inefficient definition in which areas are targeted wrongly, resulting in a targeted population that includes a mixture of neighbourhood types, only some of which are closely related to the socio-economic profile for Sure Start.

Some degree of spatial mis-targeting is inevitable and, indeed, it may be argued that this is no bad thing since it implies that, in any given targeted area, there will be some less deprived households that can serve as positive role models for those households intended to benefit from the policy initiative. However, the empirical results presented here in relation to Sure Start indicate that the quality of targeting is highly variable among cities and reveal that, even in the best cases, there is a substantial amount of mis-targeting. Taken as a whole, these results do give cause for concern and suggest that there is a plenty of scope for achieving better spatial targeting of urban policy initiatives. The geodemographic assessment tool described here provides clear guidance about where the emphasis should be placed in making these improvements.

1.6 Geodemographics Now

In this final section attention is drawn to two important developments of the last 10 years: *open geodemographics* in which data and computer software is made available free of charge to potential users in the public sector and in academia; and *geodemographics and spatial interaction data combined*, making it possible to join together residential and workplace classifications.

1.6.1 Open Geodemographics

Open geodemographics is intended to be highly flexible, in terms of geography, spatial scale, and choice of classification variables. The UK Office of National Statistics (ONS) first collaborated with Leeds University on constructing an Output Area Classification (OAC) based on the 2001 Census, and later worked in conjunction with University College London on a new classification based on the 2011 Census. The end product in each case was an Output Area Classification (OAC), with a hierarchical structure containing three levels, 8 Supergroups, 26 Groups, and 76 Subgroups in the 2011 version. The classification was based entirely on census data and the use of Output Areas—more than 190,000 covering the UK—meant that it was possible to tap the full spatial detail of the Census. There were 60 census variables in all, covering five domains: demographic; household composition; housing; socio-economic; and employment, broadly similar in scope to the variables used by the Centre for Urban Studies in the Third Survey enumeration district classification (Norman 1969).

The 2011 OAC went much further in terms of flexibility, allowing users to create their own classification based on a different geography and a different set of classification variables if desired.[26] A good case in point was London. In earlier, national classifications, in the 1990s and 2000s, London had proved problematical because, in many respects, it differed markedly from the UK as a whole and with each successive census these differences were becoming more pronounced. For the many users requiring a London classification, it was felt preferable to create a separate classification—L(ondon) OAC—to be made of the Greater London area with a set of more appropriate classification variables.[27] The successful creation of the LOAC led on to local authorities throughout the country being offered geo-data packs containing data specific to their area and access to software that enabled them to produce a tailor-made classification, without the need for specialised expertise and without cost, a major attraction to the many local authorities running tight budgets.

Alongside the 2011 OAC, the ONS created further classifications for different geographies and spatial scales. Like the OAC, these were hierarchical classifications with three levels, in this case 8 Supergroups, 16 Groups, and 24 Subgroups. Notable among these was a classification of UK local authorities, reminiscent of Moser and Scott's British Towns Study of the early 1960s. As shown in Fig. 1.5, there is a clear spatial structure to the classification, particularly in south east England where a series of concentric rings of area types radiate from the centre of London.

The second example of open geodemographics, *Patchwork Nation*, is quite different from the classifications described so far. Begun at the time of the 2008 US elections, the project was intended to create a usable, easily understandable tool for the media that would help combat simplistic views about America's socio-economic and political divides. It brought together academic social scientists and journalists working for a range of news media outlets, including the *Christian Science Monitor*, *PBS*, *Politico*, and the *Wall Street Journal*. Funding was provided by the Knight Foundation, a not-for-profit philanthropic organization that supports innovative projects in journalism, communities, and the arts, and the project hosted by the Jefferson Institute in Washington DC.

Like the *Planes of Living* example described earlier, *Patchwork Nation* used the 3144 counties as the building blocks for its area classification. However, unlike *Planes of Living*, which relied on just three classification criteria the *Patchwork Nation* project assembled a huge database, consisting of 150 variables, the vast majority drawn from the US Census. Chosen by the researchers for their relevance to present-day American politics, the scope of the variables was very wide indeed. It included data on population, local economic activity, and occupational mix, categories of consumer expenditure, racial and ethnic composition, religious adherence,

[26]The design of the 2011 OAC benefited from feedback gathered from users of the earlier OAC. See Gale et al. (2016).

[27]The London Datastore (https://data.london.gov.uk) is a free and open data sharing portal where anyone can access data relating to London. The LOAC may be accessed at https://data.london.gov.uk

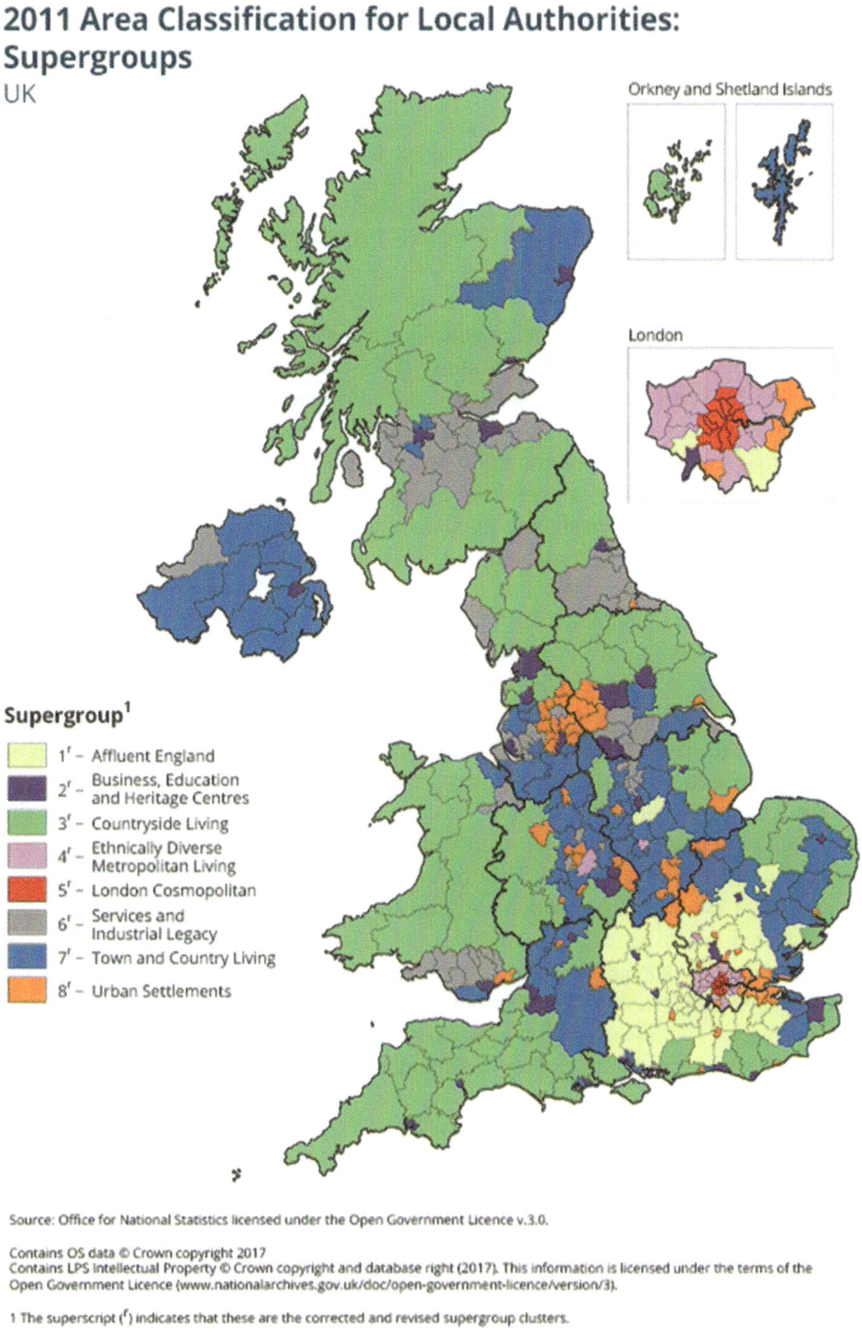

Fig. 1.5 2011 Area classification for UK local authorities: Groups (Source: https://www.ons.gov.uk/methodology/geography/geographicalproducts/areaclassifications/2011areaclassifications/maps,website accessed 17 Feb 2021)

immigration, education level, population density, housing stock, as well as several measures of income. There were also a number of variables measuring change, primarily relating to population. Where appropriate variable counts were converted into rates or percentages.

At the heart of *Patchwork Nation* was a geodemographic classification of the USA into different types of community. The methodology used to construct the classification was relatively simple and relied upon a standard principal component analysis in which all variables were included. Unlike many of the classifications described earlier in this chapter, there was no cluster analysis. Instead, the study focused on the leading principal components, in terms of overall variance explained, and the component score for each county on each of the principal components was used to decide to which of 12 community types a county should be assigned. The choice of 12 types was fairly arbitrary and reflected perceived ease of use by potential users as much as any particular statistical consideration.

Having created the 12 community types, considerable effort went into creating a profile of each type, along with specific examples of particular types. Journalists had an important role here, producing popular articles and features for both local and national media. Dante Chinni and James Gimpel, whose idea the project was, published a book that provided a more systematic account of each of the community types (Chinni and Gimpel 2010).

Table 1.5 shows the 12 community types, their labels and brief pen portraits in much the same manner as Charles Booth's poverty maps,[28] albeit with far less granularity. Figure 1.6, reminiscent of Carter Goodrich's *Plane of Living*, presents the community typology in interactive map form, enabling the reader to see how individual counties relate to the whole scheme of things.

As well as making *Patchwork Nation* comprehensible and accessible to the educated lay-person, the project team went out of its way to encourage readers to carry out their own analyses. This could involve producing maps for different geographies (state, region, nation), re-classifying counties according to different criteria, and maps for single variables. For this purpose the *Patchwork Nation* website supplies spreadsheets containing both the database as a whole and the database relating specifically to the 12 community types. Indeed the whole purpose of *Patchwork Nation* can be seen to be educational, aimed at achieving a better informed electorate able to see beyond traditional stereotypes.

1.6.2 Geodemographics and Spatial Interaction Data

Thus far in this chapter, geodemographics has been presented as a separate research tradition without any suggestion as to how it might link to other research fields of regional science. There are signs, however, that the picture is changing, with more

[28] See Fig. 1.1

Table 1.5 *Patchwork Nation* community types

Cluster name		Pen portrait
	Boom towns	Fast growing communities with rapidly diversifying population
	Immigration nation	Communities with large Latino populations and lower-than-average incomes, typically clustered in the south and south west
	Monied 'burbs	Wealthier, highly educated communities with a median income of $15,000 above the national country average
	Campus and careers	Cities and towns with young, educated populations; more secular and Democratic than other American communities
	Industrial metropolis	Densely populated, highly diverse; incomes trend higher than the national average and voters lean Democratic
	Mormon outposts	Homes to a large share of members of the Mormon Church and slightly higher median household incomes
	Emptying nests	Home to many retirees and aging baby boomer populations: less diverse than the nation at large
	Military bastions	Areas with high employment or related to the presence of the military and large veteran populations
	Service worker centers	Midsize and small towns with economies fuelled by hotels, stores and restaurants and lower than average median household income by country
	Evangelical epicenters	Communities with a high proportion of Evangelical Christians found mostly in small towns and suburbs; slightly older than the US average; loyal Republican voters
	Minority central	Home to large pockets of black residents but a below average percentage of Hispanics and Asians

(continued)

Table 1.5 (continued)

Cluster name		Pen portrait
	Tractor country	Mostly rural and remote smaller towns with older populations and large agricultural sectors

Source: https://patchworknation.org/regions-page, website accessed 15 Feb 2021

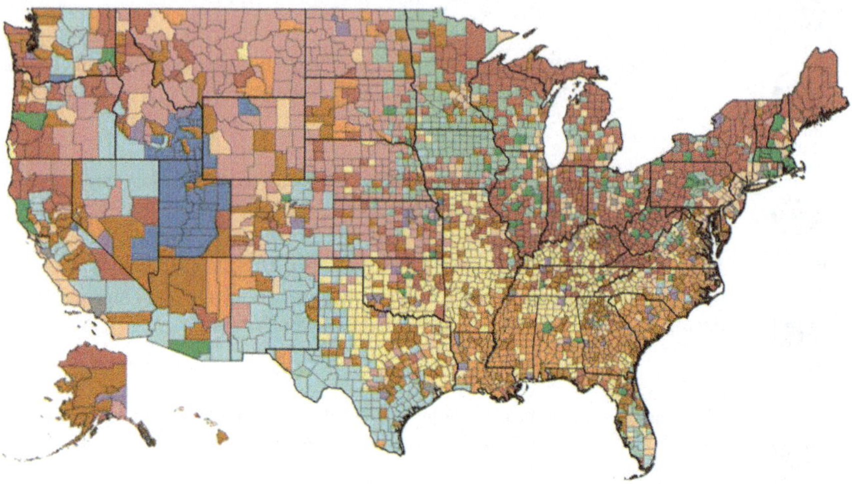

Fig. 1.6 Map of *Patchwork Nation* community types (Source: https://patchworknation.org/regions-page, website accessed 15 Feb 2021)

attention being paid to various forms of integrated analysis that includes geodemographics.

A good opportunity is the link between geodemographics and spatial interaction data. In a study examining the effectiveness of area-based urban regeneration policy, Buck and Batey (2021) showed how, by combining small area census data on migration with a geodemographic classification of residential neighbourhoods, much could be learnt about the structure of migration patterns. Using 13 geodemographic area types, they were able to show the key elements of these patterns: an underlying pattern of migration to more affluent area types; three migration sub-systems showing strong interaction within groupings of affluent area types, deprived area types, and metropolitan area types; and an outlier representing new starters in the housing market. Moreover, the study was able to draw firm conclusions about the impact of spatially targeted urban policy initiatives upon migration between these geodemographic area types.

Without exception, the geodemographic classifications examined up till this point have been residential classifications. Thanks to a number of refinements in the 2011 Census, it became possible for the first time to construct a workplace geodemographic classification, COWZ-EW. The refinements consisted of a wider spread of workplace variables and a system of purpose-designed Workplace Zones that replaced the Output Areas that up till then had had to suffice in representing workplace data.

In an important and ambitious paper, Martin et al. (2018) not only built a workplace classification, to stand alongside the 2011 OAC residential classification, but went a step further in constructing a classification of travel-to-work flows.[29] In doing so, they were able to analyse the 26 million travel-to-work flows in England and Wales, and to understand more clearly the different types of flow. This is likely to prove an important innovation that would find applications in a number of policy fields that had so far remained largely untouched by geodemographics, such as transport planning, labour market analysis, economic development, population mobility, gender studies, and energy consumption and pricing.

References

Alexander S (2007) A new civilisation? London surveyed 1928-1940s. Hist Workshop J 64:296–320

Alexiou A, Singleton AD, Longley P (2016) A classification of multi-dimensional open data for urban morphology. Built Environ 42:382–395

Amos FJC (1969) Social malaise in Liverpool: report on social problems and their distribution. Liverpool City Council, Liverpool

Bales K (1991) Charles Booth's survey of Life and Labour of the People in London. In: Bulmer M, Bales K, Sklar KK (eds) The social survey in historical perspective. Cambridge University Press, Cambridge, pp 1880–1940

Batey PWJ, Brown PJB (1995) From human ecology to customer targeting. In: Longley P, Clarke G (eds) GIS for business and service planning. GeoInformation International, Cambridge, pp 77–103

Batey PWJ, Brown PJB (2007) The spatial targeting of urban policy initiatives: a geodemographic assessment tool. Environ Plan A 39:2774–2793

Bell W (1955) Economic, family and ethnic status: an empirical test. Am Sociol Rev 20:45–52

Berry BJL, Horton FE (1970) Geographic perspectives on urban systems. Prentice-Hall, Englewood Cliffs

Buck M, Batey PWJ (2021) Migration, neighbourhood chance and the impact of area-based urban policy initiatives. In: Cochrane W et al (eds) Labor markets, migration and mobility. Singapore, Springer Nature

Buck N, Gordon I, Hall P, Harloe M, Kleinman M (2002) Working capital: life and labour in contemporary. Routledge, London

Carruthers J, Mulligan GF (2008) The plane of living and the pre-crisis evolution of housing values in the US. J Econ Geogr 12(1):739–773

Chinni D, Gimpel J (2010) Our patchwork nation: the surprising truth about the 'real' America. Gotham Books, New York

Daly M (1971) Greater London research: characteristics of 12 clusters of wards in Greater London, Research Report 13. GLC Department of Planning and Transportation, London

Evans ESP (1977) City in transition. Liverpool City Council, Liverpool

Flowerdew R, Leventhal B (1998) Under the microscope. New Perspect 18:36–38

[29] See also Hincks et al. (2018) for a similar geodemographic classification of commuting flows.

Flynn M, Flynn P, Mellor N (1972) Social malaise research: a study in Liverpool. Social Trends 2: 42–52

Frost M (2005) Principles of GIS: a review of applications. http://bbk.ac.uk/geog/study/courses/pgis.pdf

Gale CG, Singleton AD, Bates AG, Longley PA (2016) Creating the 2011 area classification for output areas (2011 OAC). J Spat Inf Sci 12:1–27

Gittus E (1964) The structure of urban areas: a new approach. Town Plan Rev 35:5–20

Glass R (1963) The Centre for Urban Studies: extracts from the Quinquennial Report. Town Plan Rev 34:169–184

Glass R (1973) The mood of London. In: Donnison D, Eversley D (eds) London, urban patterns, problems and policies. Heinemann, London

Goodrich CB (1936) Migration and economic opportunity: the report of the study of population redistribution. University of Pennsylvania Press, Philadelphia

Goodrich CB, Allin W, Hayes M (1935) Migration and planes of living: 1920–34. University of Pennsylvania Press, Philadelphia

Greenwood MJ, Hunt GL (2003) The early history of migration research. Int Reg Sci Rev 26:3–37

Harris R, Sleight P, Webber R (eds) (2005) GIS, geodemographics, and neighbourhood targeting. Wiley, Chichester

Hincks S, Kingston R, Webb B, Wong C (2018) A new geodemographic classification of commuter flows. Int J Geogr Inf Sci:663–684

Hoover EM (1948) The location of economic activity. McGraw Hill, New York

Jefferson Institute. https://patchworknation.org/regions-page, website accessed 15 Feb 2021

Kelly F (1969) Classification of urban areas, Quarterly Bulletin of the Research and Intelligence Unit, 9. Greater London Council, London, pp 13–19

Kelly F (1971) Classification of the London Boroughs, Greater London Research and Intelligence Unit, Research Report 9. Greater London Council, London

Kitagawa EM, Taeuber KE (1963) Local community fact book Chicago metropolitan area 1960. Chicago Community Inventory, University of Chicago, Chicago

Leventhal B (2016) Geodemographics for marketers: using location analysis for research and marketing. Kogan Page, London

Light JS (2003) From warfare to welfare; Defense intellectuals and urban problems in Cold War America. The Johns Hopkins University Press, Baltimore

Light JS (2009) The nature of cities. Johns Hopkins University Press, Baltimore

Lupton R, Fenton A, Tunstall R, Harris R (2011) Place typologies and their policy applications, CASE Report 65. Centre for the Analysis of Social Exclusion, London School of Economics, London

Martin D, Gale C, Cockings S, Harfoot A (2018) Origin-destination geodemographics for analysis of travel to work flows. Comput Environ Urban Syst 67:68–79

Morgan MS (2019) Charles Booth's poverty maps. Thames & Hudson, London

Moser CA, Scott W (1961) British towns: a statistical study of their social and economic differences. Oliver and Boyd, Edinburgh

Noble M, Smith G, Penhale B, Dibben C, Owen T, Lloyd M (2000) Measuring multiple deprivation at the local level: indices of deprivation 2000. Department of Environment, Transport and the Regions, London

Norman P (1969) Third survey of London life and labour: a new typology of London districts. In: Dogan M, Rokkan S (eds) Quantitative ecological analysis in the social sciences. MIT, Cambridge, pp 371–396

Park RE, Burgess EW, Mackenzie RD (eds) (1925) The city. University of Chicago Press, Chicago

Pfautz HW (1967) The times, the man and the inquiry. In: Pfautz HW (ed) Charles Booth on the city: physical pattern and social structure. University of Chicago Press, Chicago, pp 3–46

Rees PH (1972) Problems of classifying sub-areas within cities. In: Berry BJL, Smith KB (eds) City classification handbook: methods and applications. Wiley, London, pp 265–330

Robson BT (1969) Urban analysis: a study of city structure. Cambridge University Press, Cambridge

Robson BT (1984) A pleasant pain. In: Billinge M, Gregory D, Martin R (eds) Recollections of a revolution: geography as spatial science, vol 104-16. Macmillan, London

Selvin H, Bernert C (1985) Durkheim, Booth and Yule: the non-diffusion of an intellectual innovation. In: Bulmer M (ed) Essays on the history of British sociological research. Cambridge University Press, Cambridge, pp 70–82

Shevky E, Bell W (1955) Social area analysis: theory, illustrative application and computational procedures. Stanford University Press, Stanford

Shevky E, Williams M (1949) The social areas of Los Angeles: analysis and typology. University of California Press, Berkeley

Singleton AD, Spielman SE (2013) The past, present and future of geodemographic research in the United States and the United Kingdom. Prof Geogr 66:558–567

Theodorsen GA (ed) (1961) Studies in human ecology. Harper & Row, New York

Tobler W (1970) A computer movie. Econ Geogr 46:234–240

Tryon RC (1955) Identification of social areas by cluster analysis. University of California Press, Berkeley

Tunstall R, Lupton R (2003) Is targeting deprived areas an effective means to reach poor people? An assessment of the rationale, CASE Paper 70. Centre for Analysis of Social Exclusion, London School of Economics, London

Vallianatos M (2015) Uncovering the early history of ‘big data’ and ‘smart cities’: a critical appreciation http://www.boomcalifornia.com/2015/06/uncovering-the-early-history-of-big-data-and-the-smart-city-in-la/ Accessed on 15 Jan 2021

Van Arsdol MD, Camilleri SC, Schmid CF (1958) The generality of urban social area indexes. Am Sociol Rev 23:277–284

Vaughan L (2018) Mapping society. UCL Press, London

Webber R (1975) Liverpool social area study, 1971 data, PRAG Technical Paper 14. Centre for Environmental Studies, London

Webber R (1978) The social characteristics of residential neighbourhoods: Merseyside, PRAG Technical Paper 24. Centre for Environmental Studies, London

Webber R, Burrows R (2018) The predictive postcode: the geodemographic classification of British society. Sage, London

Wilson H, Womersley L (1977) Inner area study Liverpool social area analysis. Department of the Environment, London

Chapter 2
When Is Competition Between Cities for Members of the Creative Class Efficient?

Amitrajeet A. Batabyal and Seung Jick Yoo

Abstract We use microeconomic theory and calculus to study two geographically contiguous cities A and B that compete for N members of the creative class by providing a local public good (LPG) that is of interest to these members. The members can costlessly move between cities A and B. We demonstrate that as a result of this mobility, the equilibrium number of members residing in each city must be such that the utility levels obtained by consuming the LPG on offer are equalized across the two cities. Next, we suppose that the LPG can be provided at unit cost and that the two cities share this cost equally among the resident members. In this setting, we show when a policy that aims to attract and retain members in a city by maximizing the utility of a representative resident member is efficient.

Keywords Creative class · Efficiency · Inefficiency · Local public good · Mobility

JEL Codes H40 · R11

2.1 Introduction

A basic point that arises out of a lot of Richard Florida's recent research—see Florida (2002, 2003, 2005, 2008, 2014)—is that cities and more generally regions that want to thrive in this era of globalization need to do all they can to attract and retain members of the so-called *creative class*. The creative class "consists of people who add economic value through their creativity" (Florida 2002, p. 68). In particular, this

A. A. Batabyal
Department of Economics, Rochester Institute of Technology, Rochester, NY, USA
e-mail: aabgsh@rit.edu

S. J. Yoo (✉)
Graduate School of International Service, Sookmyung Women's University, Seoul, Republic of Korea
e-mail: sjyoo@sookmyung.ac.kr

M. Kawano et al. (eds.), *Theory and History in Regional Perspective*, New Frontiers in Regional Science: Asian Perspectives 56,
https://doi.org/10.1007/978-981-16-6695-7_2

class is made up of professionals such as doctors, engineers, lawyers, scientists, university professors, and, notably, bohemians such as artists, musicians, and sculptors.

We focus on cities in this chapter and we accept Florida's (2002) key point that cities seeking to blossom economically need to attract and hold on to members of the creative class. Once this is done, a question that follows naturally is: "How are cities to do this?" Buettner and Janeba (2016), Batabyal et al. (2019), Batabyal and Yoo (2020), and Batabyal and Beladi (2021) have answered this question by pointing out that local public goods (LPGs) such as cultural amenities, quality schools, and public transit can be used by cities to carry out the dual "attract" and "retain" functions.[1]

Batabyal et al. (2019) examine a model in which the creative class members can migrate between the two cities being studied. Next, they characterize the equilibrium distribution of the creative class in the two cities and ascertain whether the provision of a LPG is efficient. Batabyal and Beladi (2021) build on this work and examine a model of competition between two cities that use a LPG to attract members of the creative class. They follow Batabyal and Beladi (2018) and divide the total creative class population into two groups known as *artists* and *engineers*. They then conduct the remainder of their analysis with a representative artist and a representative engineer. Finally, Batabyal and Yoo (2020) use a theoretical model and demonstrate that the use of a "representative artist and engineer" modeling strategy can lead one to concentrate on an inefficient equilibrium in an aggregate economy of two cities.

We continue this discussion of efficiency/inefficiency when two cities use a LPG to compete for members of the creative class. However, our specific focus is twofold. First, we explain when a policy that aims to attract and retain creative class members in a city by maximizing the utility of a representative resident member, is efficient. Second, we describe the circumstances in which such a policy is inefficient.

The remainder of this chapter is organized as follows. Section 2.1 delineates our stylized model of an aggregate economy of two geographically proximate cities that are denoted by A and B. These two cities compete for N members of the creative class by providing a LPG that is of interest to these members. Because cities A and B are geographically contiguous, we suppose that creative class members are able to costlessly move between cities A and B. Because of this mobility, Sect. 2.2 shows that the equilibrium number of members residing in either A or B must be such that the utility levels obtained by consuming the LPG on offer are equalized across these two cities. Section 2.3 ascertains the conditions under which a policy that aims to attract and retain members in a city by maximizing the utility of a representative resident member[2] is or is not efficient. Finally, Sect. 2.3 concludes and then suggests two ways in which the research delineated in this chapter might be extended.

[1] See Hansen and Niedomysl (2009), Richardson (2009), and Audretsch and Belitski (2013) for a discussion of related issues.

[2] It is important to point out that the use of "representative agent" models is common in the public finance and in the regional science literatures. For a more detailed corroboration of this point, see Nechyba (1994), Riaz et al. (1995), Conley et al. (2019), Batabyal and Yoo (2020), and Batabyal

2.2 The Model

2.2.1 *Preliminaries*

Consider an aggregate economy that is made up of two geographically contiguous cities denoted by the subscript $i = A, B$. Real world examples from the USA of the kind of cities we have in mind are (1) San Francisco and San Jose in the state of California, (2) Minneapolis and Saint Paul in the state of Minnesota, and (3) Buffalo and Rochester in the state of New York. The cities A and B compete for members of the creative class by providing a LPG that is of interest to these members. This LPG, which we denote by $L_i \geq 0$, $i = A, B$, can be provided at unit cost and the two cities share this cost equally among the resident members.

The reader should understand that the creative class, in general, consists of a variety of professionals such as engineers, lawyers, sculptors, and university professors and is therefore made up of a heterogeneous set of individuals. That said, observe that cities looking to attract members of the creative class are typically *not* looking to attract every conceivable member in this set. Therefore, to be concrete, cities such as San Francisco and San Jose are probably more interested in attracting engineers than sculptors. Similarly, a city like New York is probably more interested in attracting bankers and less interested in drawing in painters. In addition, it is unreasonable to think that engineers, lawyers, sculptors, and university professors can all be attracted to a particular city by offering them a *single* LPG.

Hence, to focus the subsequent discussion, we suppose that cities A and B are looking to attract and retain a particular *subset* of members of the creative class such as lawyers or bankers. There are $N \in \mathbb{N}$ members in this subset and because these members are either all doctors or all lawyers and so and so forth, we can think of this subset of members as *homogeneous*. This does *not* mean that the subset of individuals being studied is literally homogeneous but that the members of the subset are *sufficiently similar* that, from a modeling standpoint, we lose little by thinking of them as being homogeneous. That said, these N homogeneous creative class members can freely or costlessly migrate between cities A and B. As such, our next task is to demonstrate an implication of this free mobility.

2.2.2 *Equalization of Utility Levels*

Let n_A and n_B denote the number of creative class members—in the subset of interest—who choose to reside in city A and B, respectively. Because the total population of this subset or N is fixed, it follows that $n_B = N - n_A$. Let $I \geq 0$ denote the income of the representative member of the subset of the creative class that we

---

and Beladi (2021). As such, we are certainly *not* setting a precedent by employing a "representative resident member" construct in our analysis in this chapter.

are studying and let $x \geq 0$ denote this member's consumption of some private good. Because cities A and B share the cost of providing L_i equally among the resident members, the cost to the representative member if he chooses to reside in city i is L_i/n_i, $i = A, B$. Therefore, we can represent his budget or income constraint as

$$I = x + \frac{L_i}{n_i}, i = A, B. \tag{2.1}$$

This representative member obtains utility from consuming the private good x and the local public good L_i. Using Eq. (2.1), the private good $x = I - L_i/n_i$. Using this last result, the representative member's utility function is given by $U[\{I - (L_i/n_i)\}, L_i]$. Now, recall that the representative member is able to move freely or costlessly between cities A and B. This free mobility of all the N members between the two cities means that the equilibrium number of members residing in each city must be such that the utility levels obtained by consuming the LPG on offer are *equalized* across the two cities. Mathematically, this means that the condition

$$U\left(I - \frac{L_A}{n_A}, L_A\right) = U\left(I - \frac{L_B}{N - n_A}, L_B\right) \tag{2.2}$$

must hold.[3]

Observe that Eq. (2.2) implicitly gives us an equation for the number of members who choose to reside in city A or n_A as a *function* of the two LPG levels that are provided or L_A and L_B. If we denote this function by $f(\cdot, \cdot)$, then we can write

$$n_A = f(L_A, L_B). \tag{2.3}$$

Additional details about this function $f(\cdot, \cdot)$ can be obtained by totally differentiating the right- and left-hand sides of Eq. (2.3).

Suppose, for concreteness, that we replace the *general* utility function in Eq. (2.2) with a constant returns to scale Cobb–Douglas utility function given by $\{I - (L_i/n_i)\}^{1/2} L_i^{1/2}, i = A, B$. Then, for this particular functional form, the equivalent of Eq. (2.2) is

[3]Our rationale for equalizing the utilities across the two cities stems from the fact that in an equilibrium, there cannot be any reason for wanting to move from either city A to B or vice versa because an individual member is unhappy with the LPG provision in either city A or B. In addition, our goal here is *not* to use "the marginal utility of public goods" to determine the optimal allocation of a public good.

$$\left(I-\frac{L_A}{n_A}\right)^{1/2} L_A^{1/2}=\left(I-\frac{L_B}{N-n_A}\right)^{1/2} L_B^{1/2} \Rightarrow \left(I-\frac{L_A}{n_A}\right) L_A$$
$$=\left(I-\frac{L_B}{N-n_A}\right) L_B, \tag{2.4}$$

and Eq. (2.4) now implicitly gives us n_A as a function of the two LPG amounts L_A and L_B. Our final task in this chapter is to determine when a policy that aims to attract and retain members in a city by maximizing the utility of a representative resident member, is efficient.

2.2.3 Policy Efficiency

The objective of an apposite authority in city A, for instance, is to maximize the utility of the representative resident creative class member. Therefore, this authority solves

$$\max_{\{L_A\}} U\left(I-\frac{L_A}{n_A}, L_A\right) \tag{2.5}$$

subject to the constraint given by Eq. (2.3). It is straightforward to confirm that we can incorporate this constraint into the objective function given by Eq. (2.5). Doing this gives us the following unconstrained maximization problem for the city authority:

$$\max_{\{L_A\}} U\left(I-\frac{L_A}{f(L_A, L_B)}, L_A\right). \tag{2.6}$$

Differentiating this objective function with respect to the choice variable L_A gives us the first-order necessary condition (FONC) for an optimum. We get

$$-\frac{\partial U}{\partial x}\left[\frac{1}{n_A}-\frac{L_A}{n_A^2}\frac{\partial n_A}{\partial L_A}\right]+\frac{\partial U}{\partial L_A}=0 \tag{2.7}$$

where $x = I - (L_A/n_A)$.

The salient point to note now is that because, in general, we expect the partial derivative $\partial n_A/\partial L_A \neq 0$, the condition described by Eq. (2.7) is *not* an efficiency condition. In fact, for the choice of L_A delineated by Eq. (2.7) to be efficient, we need the condition

$$\frac{\partial U/\partial L_A}{\partial U/\partial x} = \frac{1}{n_A} \tag{2.8}$$

to be satisfied. This last condition is one way to represent the well-known "Samuelson rule" and it delineates the level of the LPG that city A ought to optimally provide.[4] Observe that this condition is satisfied if and only if the partial derivative $\partial n_A/\partial L_A = 0$.

Specializing the discussion to the case of the constant returns to scale Cobb–Douglas utility function introduced in Sect. 2.2, the maximization problem that is equivalent to the one specified in Eq. (2.6) is

$$\max_{\{L_A\}} \left(I - \frac{L_A}{n_A}\right)^{1/2} L_A^{1/2} \tag{2.9}$$

subject, once again, to the constraint in Eq. (2.3). The first-order necessary condition or FONC for a maximum is

$$\left(I - \frac{L_A}{n_A}\right)^{1/2} L_A^{-1/2} + \left(I - \frac{L_A}{n_A}\right)^{-1/2} L_A \left\{-\frac{1}{n_A} + \frac{L_A(\partial n_A/\partial L_A)}{n_A^2}\right\} = 0. \tag{2.10}$$

As before, we do not in general expect the partial derivative $\partial n_A/\partial L_A = 0$ and therefore the condition delineated by Eq. (2.10) is *not* an efficiency condition in this specialized Cobb–Douglas utility case that we are studying.

The reason why the choice of L_A, for instance, is inefficient in this chapter is that we have modeled the two cities in a way that allows the number of creative class members who choose to reside in a particular city to *adjust* in response to the *amount* of the LPG that is provided. This is the essence of the competition between cities A and B for members of the creative class that we are analyzing. If, instead, we permitted the two cities to choose not only the level of the LPG they provide but *also* the number of members they attract then we would have *two* decision variables which would generate two first-order necessary conditions (FONCs) and these two conditions would jointly give rise to efficient LPG provision levels.

It is reasonable to think that once an appropriate city A or B authority has attracted a sufficient number of, say, bankers, to its city, attracting additional bankers is not helpful and may even be counterproductive. In other words, there may be diminishing returns to attracting bankers in the sense that too many bankers impose a congestion like cost on each other. But what if there are no diminishing returns and hence no congestion like cost? In this case, theoretically speaking, it would make sense for the city authority to attract an infinite number of bankers! Why? This is because each new banker attracted to the city will benefit from the LPG on offer by exactly the same amount as the first banker attracted and this banker will *not*

[4] See Hindriks and Myles (2013, Chapter 6) for a textbook exposition of the "Samuelson rule."

diminish the benefit to bankers already resident in the city under consideration. Also, an additional banker will also *reduce* the average cost of LPG provision for all resident bankers. Therefore, the net benefit of resident bankers will *rise* as new bankers are attracted to the city and, in principle, this process has no limit. This concludes our discussion of when competition between two cities for members of the creative class is efficient.

2.3 Conclusions

In this chapter, we studied two geographically contiguous cities A and B that competed for N members of the creative class by providing a LPG that was desired by these members. The members could costlessly move between cities A and B. Because of this mobility, the equilibrium number of members residing in each city had to be such that the utility levels obtained by consuming the LPG on offer were equalized across the two cities. The LPG was provided at unit cost and the two cities split this cost equally among the resident members. In this setting, we analyzed whether a policy that aimed to attract and retain creative class members in a city by maximizing the utility of a representative resident member, was efficient.

The analysis conducted in this chapter can be extended in a number of different directions. Here are two possible extensions. First, it would be useful to study the efficiency/inefficiency properties of the LPG provision decision when creative class members and city authorities interact with each other over time, in, for example, a repeated game. Second, it would also be instructive to analyze the efficiency/inefficiency of an equilibrium in which cities attempt to attract and retain members of the creative class with policies in addition to LPGs. Studies that analyze these aspects of the underlying problem will provide additional insights into the efficiency and the inefficiency of equilibria in models of interactions between creative class members and cities.

Acknowledgments We thank an anonymous reviewer and Karima Kourtit for their helpful comments on a previous version of this chapter. This research was supported by the Ministry of Education of the Republic of Korea and by the National Research Foundation of Korea (NRF-2016S1A3A2925230). Batabyal acknowledges financial support from the Gosnell endowment at RIT. The usual disclaimer applies.

References

Audretsch DB, Belitski M (2013) The missing pillar: the creativity theory of knowledge spillover entrepreneurship. Small Bus Econ 41:819–836

Batabyal AA, Beladi H (2018) Artists, engineers, and aspects of economic growth in a creative region. Econ Model 71:214–219

Batabyal AA, Beladi H (2021) On the existence of an equilibrium in models of local public good use by cities to attract the creative class. In: Suzuki S, Patuelli R (eds) A broad view of regional science. Springer Nature, Singapore, pp 25–35
Batabyal AA, Yoo SJ (2020) Using a local public good to attract representative creative class members: the inefficient equilibrium case. Theor Econ Lett 10:40–46
Batabyal AA, Kourtit K, Nijkamp P (2019) Using local public goods to attract and retain the creative class: a tale of two cities. Reg Sci Policy Pract 11:571–581
Buettner T, Janeba E (2016) City competition for the creative class. J Cult Econ 40:413–451
Conley JP, Driskill R, Wang P (2019) Capitalization, decentralization, and interregional spillovers in a Tiebout economy with a durable public good. Econ Theory 67:1–27
Florida R (2002) The rise of the creative class. Basic Books, New York
Florida R (2003) Cities and the creative class. City Community 2:3–19
Florida R (2005) The flight of the creative class. Harper Business, New York
Florida R (2008) Who's your city? Basic Books, New York
Florida R (2014) The creative class and economic development. Econ Dev Q 28:196–205
Hansen HK, Niedomysl T (2009) Migration of the creative class: evidence from Sweden. J Econ Geogr 9:191–206
Hindriks J, Myles GD (2013) Intermediate public economics, 2nd edn. MIT, Cambridge
Nechyba TJ (1994) Fiscal federalism and local public finance: a general equilibrium approach with voting. In: Proceedings of the Annual Conference on Taxation Held Under the Auspices of the National Tax Association—Tax Institute of America, vol 87. BiblioLife, Arkose Press, London, pp 136–141
Riaz K, Shogren JF, Johnson SR (1995) A general model of rent seeking for public goods. Public Choice 82:243–259
Richardson KE (2009) What lures and retains the international creative-class family? A case study of the family unit found in Vancouver's biotechnology sector. Comp Technol Transf Soc 7:323–345

Chapter 3
Revisiting Marshallian Versus Walrasian Stability in an Experimental Market

Junyi Shen, Ken-Ichi Shimomura, Takehiko Yamato, Tokinao Ohtaka, and Kiyotaka Takahashi

Abstract We study dynamics in pit market trading by a laboratory experiment. Our exchange economy model contains two types of consumers and two kinds of commodities, and three competitive equilibria exist. The two equilibria with the lowest and the highest relative prices are beneficial for one type of the consumers, and the intermediate price gives an equitable allocation. The theory of Walrasian tatonnement dynamics predicts that relative prices diverge from the intermediate equilibrium towards the lowest equilibrium or the highest equilibrium depending on initial prices. On the other hand, Marshallian quantity adjustment process leads the total supplied volume to the intermediate equilibrium only regardless of initial states. In order to examine how robust the equilibrium selection is, we conducted a manual experiment of pit market trading with different combinations of ethnicities of subjects in Kenya. Our result shows strong support for the convergence to the intermediate equilibrium, which is unstable in Walrasian tatonnement dynamics and is stable in Marshallian quantity adjustment process.

Keywords Marshallian stability · Walrasian stability · Experiments · Pit market · Kenya

---

J. Shen
Research Institute for Economics and Business Administration, Kobe University, Kobe, Japan

School of Economics, Shanghai University, Shanghai, China
e-mail: shen@rieb.kobe-u.ac.jp

K.-I. Shimomura
Research Institute for Economics and Business Administration, Kobe University, Kobe, Japan
e-mail: ken-ichi@rieb.kobe-u.ac.jp

T. Yamato (✉)
Department of Industrial Engineering and Economics, School of Engineering, Tokyo Institute of Technology, Tokyo, Japan
e-mail: yamato.t.aa@m.titech.ac.jp

T. Ohtaka · K. Takahashi
Department of Social Engineering, Graduate School of Decision Science and Technology, Tokyo Institute of Technology, Tokyo, Japan

M. Kawano et al. (eds.), *Theory and History in Regional Perspective*, New Frontiers in Regional Science: Asian Perspectives 56,
https://doi.org/10.1007/978-981-16-6695-7_3

JEL Codes C92 · D51

3.1 Introduction

We investigate dynamics adjustment processes in pit market trading by a laboratory experiment. We explore two issues in this paper. The first is the fact finding of natures of disequilibrium and equilibration processes in trading on the floor or "pit" markets. Historically, such markets have been widely used in actual trading places. In spite of that, studies on dynamic adjustment process in pit markets have been limited, while most scholars have investigated this issue in double auction markets. The key difference between a pit market and a double auction market is whether or not bids and asks as well as prices are public information.[1]

In the experimental economics literature, it has been known that pit market experiment was first conducted by Chamberlin (1948), who wanted to present that the model of perfect competition does not predict well. Smith (1962) used the double auction to show that repeated trades with public information about bids, asks, and trading prices tend to lead markets to perfectly competitive prices. In our experiment of pit markets (not *double auction* as in Smith 1962) with repeated trades, different from Chamberlin (1948), bids and asks were known to the buyer and the seller only in each trade, and what were publicly revealed to markets are quantities agreed to exchange. We conducted the experiment repeatedly by setting the initial holdings to be constant in each period of a sequence of experiment to observe tendencies of market prices. We had a conjecture that the sequence of market prices would converge to a competitive equilibrium because buyers and sellers can freely trade as many times as they want then information about exchange rates will become public gradually.

The second issue is the extent to which theoretical models based on adjustment help with understanding this trading pit process. Almost all dynamic models of perfect competition are formulated with the Walrasian tatonnement, which is the only system that manipulates a market price by raising a price when the commodity is excessively demanded and lowering a price when the commodity is excessively supplied. The dynamic stability of an experimental market is usually analyzed as if the process of equilibrium price discovery is the Walrasian tatonnement even when it is obviously not. Existing experiments have examined whether or not data of market prices in continuous double auctions are consistent with the predictions by Walrasian tatonnement (e.g., Smith 1962; Anderson et al. 2004; Crockett et al. 2010).

To the best of our knowledge, there is no such evidence with experimental results from trading pit which support any theory of dynamics in markets. We expected that the Walrasian adjustment process would work because a market price goes up whenever the commodity is excessively demanded and the price falls whenever the commodity is excessively supplied regardless of styles of trading. We thus

[1]We would like to give special thanks to Charles Plott for pointing out this issue.

actually conducted an experiment of trading pit to investigate what kind of dynamics of market prices appears.

The model to experiment is an exchange economy with two types of consumers and two kinds of commodities in which three competitive equilibria exist. One type of consumers initially owns the more of the first good, and the less of the second good, than the other type of consumers have. Consumers of the same type are all given identical commodity bundles of the endowment. We choose the second good as the numeraire, the price of which is always fixed to be one, and focus on the behavior of the relative price of the first good. In our model, the supply and demand curves intersect at three points, namely, there are three equilibrium prices. The lowest relative price is beneficial for the type of consumers having more of the second good, and the highest relative price is advantageous to the type of consumers having more of the first good. The intermediate price gives an "equitable" allocation.

According to the Walrasian dynamics, relative prices diverge from the intermediate equilibrium towards the lowest equilibrium or the highest equilibrium depending on initial prices. It means that the market mechanism causes an income inequality and the "invisible hand" leads the economy to an efficient but inequitable state. We thus have strong interest in conducting an experiment of our exchange model with multiple equilibria. We simply conjectured that trading outcomes would converge to one of the extreme equilibria because they are stable in Walras' sense. However, our results obtained in Kenya show strong support for the convergence to the intermediate equilibrium on average. Thus, our observations tell that pit market trading does not cause large inequalities of income or welfare. This is the opposite result that the theory of Walrasian stability predicts.

We therefore investigate our model with another dynamic stability concept of a market mechanism called the Marshallian adjustment process,[2] in which sellers increase supplies when the supply price is higher than the demand price and decrease them when the supply price is lower than the demand price. It then turned out that, in our model, the stability of each equilibrium is different in Walras' and Marshall's sense. It means that the lowest and highest equilibria are stable in Walras' sense but unstable in Marshall's sense, and the intermediate equilibrium is unstable in Walras' sense but stable in Marshall's sense.[3] Our experimental results of trading pit show that the market prices converged to the intermediate equilibrium, which is unstable in Walras' sense and stable in Marshall's sense.

Here we refer to the previous experimental studies related to our paper, for which double auction markets are adopted: Smith (1962) invented the method of continuous double auction by using an upward-sloping supply curve and a downward-sloping demand curve intersecting at the unique competitive equilibrium, which is

---

[2] We would like to thank Shyam Sunder, who suggested us to check Marshallian stability of equilibria for our model.

[3] Shapley and Shubik (1977) is a pioneering work that presents a simple exchange economy model with multiple competitive equilibria. Different from the current study, they investigated the Walrasian stability of the three equiribria, but did not discuss the Marshallian stability. See also Sakai (2020) for the Walrasian stability of multiple equilibria in two-good economies.

globally stable in Walras' sense. Plott and George (1992), Plott and Smith (1999), and Plott (2000) investigated multiple competitive equilibria for each of which the Walrasian and Marshallian models make the opposite predictions on the stability. In order to examine which model is appropriate, they conducted continuous double auction experiments in which the stability of each equilibrium was reversed in the middle of their experiments by changes in the demand or supply function. Plott and George (1992) changed demand functions while keeping the same downward-sloping supply curve attributed to "forward-falling" individual supplies due to external economies of scale. Plott and Smith (1999) switched supply curves in the middle of their experiment with the same demand curve which is upward-sloping because of the existence of a consumption externality. In both experiments, stability was supported by the Marshallian model of dynamics. Plott (2000) reported the convergence of prices, the stability of which is predicted by the Walrasian model, in the case of the downward-sloping supply curve derived from "backward-bending" individual supplies due to negative income effects. These experiments are concerned with partial equilibrium models of economies with externalities.

On the other hand, Anderson et al. (2004) considered a general equilibrium model of an exchange economy without externalities which Scarf (1960) constructed to show the possibility of limit cycles of price fluctuation. They presented the occurrence of the limit cycles from their double auction experiment. Crockett et al. (2010) also examined a simple exchange model with two commodities which Gale (1963) originated to prove the possibility of divergence of market prices. They reported strong support to the instability of price dynamics in their double auction experiment. The predictions by Scarf (1960) and Gale (1963) are both based on the Walrasian model. According to these studies, as Plott (2000) pointed out, which theory of dynamics, Walrasian or Marshallian one is appropriate for a double auction market is observed to depend on the underlying reasons for demand and supply shapes. This view has been already well accepted.

The paper is organized as follows. In Sect. 3.2, we present the model of an exchange economy with three competitive equilibria which we used to conduct our experiment. We also discuss the Walrasian stability and the Marshallian stability of each equilibrium. In Sect. 3.3, we explain the design and procedures of our experiment. Namely, we describe how we transformed the theoretical model into the experiments. In Sect. 3.4, we analyze the results of the experiment to find tendencies of the data and effects of our scientific controls. Discussions are provided in Sect. 3.5. Finally, Sect. 3.6 is for concluding remarks.

3.2 An Exchange Economy with Multiple Equilibria

We consider the following exchange economy model with two kinds of commodities called X and Y and two types of consumers named 1 and 2. The utility functions of consumers 1 and 2 are of "Leontief-nested" types in the following forms:

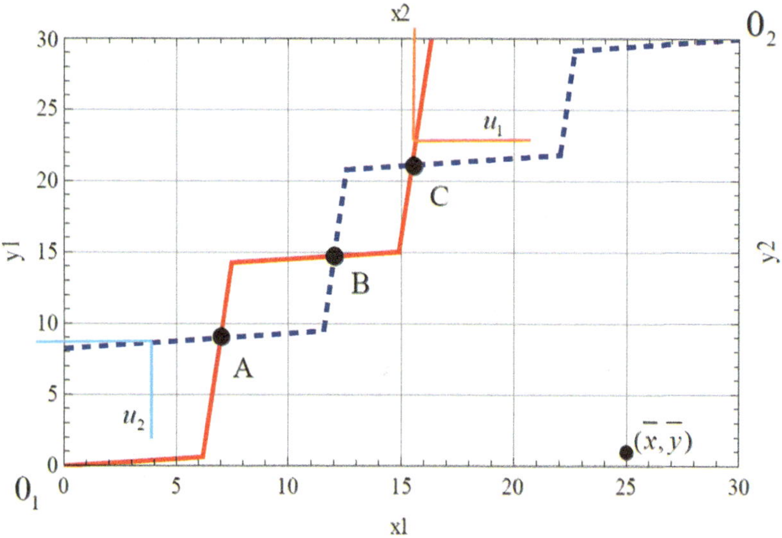

Fig. 3.1 Exchange economy with three competitive equilibria

$$\begin{aligned} U_1(x_1, y_1) &= a_1 \min\left[g_1(x_1), y_1\right] + b_1 \quad \text{and} \\ U_2(x_2, y_2) &= a_2 \min\left[g_2(x_2), y_2\right] + b_2 \end{aligned} \tag{3.1}$$

In the experiment, we set $a_1 = 52.58$, $b_1 = 669.96$, $a_2 = 50$, $b_2 = 695.07$,

$$\begin{aligned} g_1(x_1) &= x_1/9.8 && \text{if } x_1 \in [0, 6.2] \\ &= 10x_1 - 6.2(10 - 1/9.8) && \text{if } x_1 \in [6.2, 7.5] \\ &= x_1/9.8 + 1.3(10 - 1/9.8) && \text{if } x_1 \in [7.5, 14.9] \\ &= 10x_1 - 13.6(10 - 1/9.8) && \text{otherwise} \end{aligned}$$

and

$$\begin{aligned} g_2(x_2) &= x_2/9.1 && \text{if } x_2 \in [0, 7.35] \\ &= 11.3x_2 - 7.35(11.3 - 1/9.1) && \text{if } x_2 \in [7.35, 8] \\ &= x_2/9.1 + 0.65(11.3 - 1/9.1) && \text{if } x_2 \in [8, 17.45] \\ &= 11.3x_2 - 16.8(11.3 - 1/9.1) && \text{if } x_2 \in [17.45, 18.45] \\ &= x_2/9.1 + 1.65(11.3 - 1/9.1) && \text{otherwise} \end{aligned}$$

The individual endowment of consumer 1 is given by $(\bar{x}_1, \bar{y}_1) = (25, 1)$ and the individual endowment of consumer 2 is $(\bar{x}_2, \bar{y}_2) = (5, 29)$.

Figure 3.1 displays this economy in an Edgeworth box. The solid (resp. dashed) piecewise linear line denotes consumer 1's (resp. consumer 2's) "offer curve," derived by varying prices and asking the consumer how much she would like to

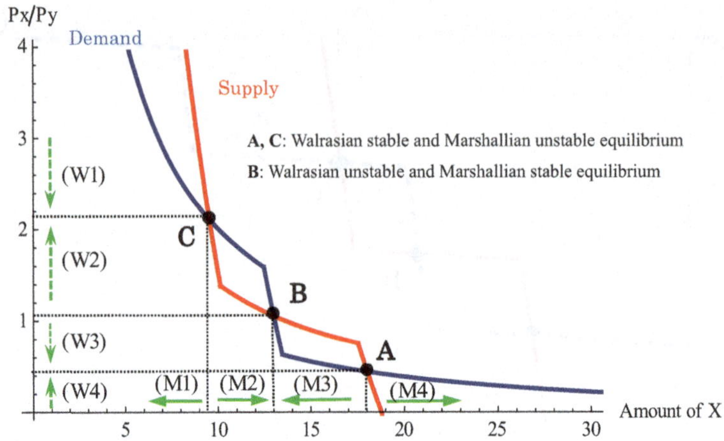

Fig. 3.2 Local Walrasian and Marshallian Stability of Three Competitive Equilibria in a Demand-Supply Diagram. (**a**, **c**) Walrasian stable and Marshallian unstable equilibrium. (**b**) Walrasian unstable and Marshallian stable equilibrium

trade to maximize her utility at each price. Notice that the offer curves are given by $y_1 = g_1(x_1)$ and $y_2 = g_2(x_2)$, because the utility maximization points are the loci of the vertices of the L-shaped indifference curves. There are three competitive equilibrium allocations denoted by the points of intersection of the two offer curves: $A = (7.00, 9.01)$, $B = (12.01, 14.74)$, and $C = (15.48, 21.13)$ in terms of agent 1's consumption bundle. Figure 3.1 can be also regarded as demonstrating symmetric equilibrium outcomes in a market with n traders on each side when all traders of the same type take the same action.

Figure 3.2 represents a diagram of the demand and supply curves for good X which are derived from our two-good economy model.[4] Notice that the supply curve is downward-sloping. The intuitive reason is as follows. Suppose that the price for X relative to good Y, Px/Py, decreases. Then the income of consumer 1 who initially has a large amount of X becomes smaller. Because consumer 1's utility function is of a Leontief type, there is no substitution effect and a large income effect. Therefore, consumer 1's demand for X decreases, implying that the supply (endowment minus demand) of X by consumer 1 increases. Since consumer 1 is the only supplier of X, the supply for X increases when the relative price for X decreases.

Figure 3.2 shows three equilibria at which the demand and supply curves intersect: $A = (x_A, p_A) = (18.00, 0.44)$, $B = (x_B, p_B) = (12.99, 1.06)$, and C = $(x_C, p_C) = (9.52, 2.11)$. There are two well-known concepts of local stability of a competitive equilibrium: Walrasian and Marshallian stability. These concepts give opposite answers to the question of whether each of the three equilibria is locally

[4]We only need to focus on trades of good X because, based on the Walras' law, the market of good X is clear when that of good Y is clear. Notice that Walras' law holds in our model since the utility functions of all consumers satisfy local nonsatiation.

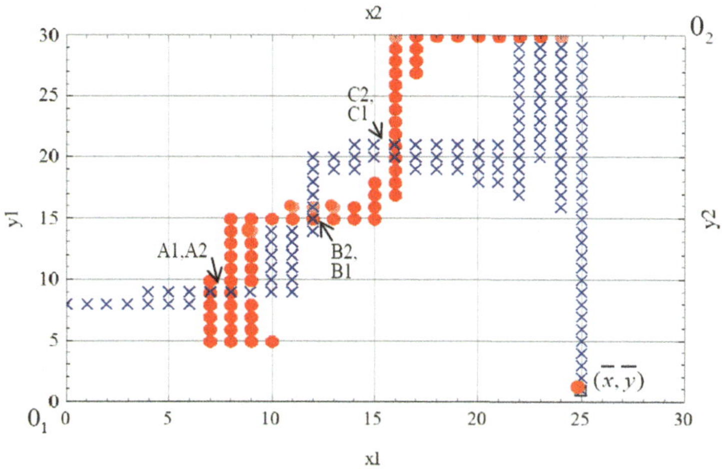

Fig. 3.3 Discrete version of the exchange economy

stable or unstable. First of all, let us consider Walrasian dynamics of price adjustment process, which works off equilibrium in the market. According to this dynamics, if the relative price of X, $p = Px/Py$, is lower than p_A (higher than p_C), the demand for X is larger (smaller) than the supply for X, so that p increases (decreases). If p lies between p_A and p_B (between p_B and p_C), the demand for X is smaller (larger) than the supply for X, so that p decreases (increases). Therefore, the equilibrium B is locally unstable in Walras' sense, whereas the other two equilibria A and C are both locally stable in Walras' sense.

Next let us examine Marshallian dynamics of quantity adjustment process. According to this dynamics, if the quantity of X, x, is larger than x_A (smaller than x_C), the demand price at x is higher (lower) than the supply price at x, so that x increases (decreases). If x lies between x_A and x_B (between x_B and x_C), the demand price at x is lower (higher) than the supply price at x, so that x decreases (increases). Therefore, the equilibrium B is locally stable in Marshall's sense, whereas the other two equilibria A and C are both locally unstable in Marshalls' sense.[5]

In our experiment, subjects chose integers as trading units, not real numbers as in usual theory. Therefore, it is important to consider a discrete version of the exchange economy corresponding to the experimental setting to make a rigorous theoretical prediction. Figure 3.3 shows this discrete exchange economy in an Edgeworth box. The locus of circles (●) (resp. multiplication signs (×)) denotes consumer 1's (resp. consumer 2's) offer curve, which is thick, in the discrete economy. The two offer curves intersect at seven points indicating competitive equilibria. In terms of consumer 1's consumption bundles, these equilibria are given by $A1 = (7, 8)$,

[5] See Appendix 1 for the formal definitions of local stability and instability of equilibrium according to Walrasian price adjustment process and those according to Marshallian quantity adjustment process.

Table 3.1 Theoretical predictions about discrete equilibria

	Allocation					Payoff	
	Type 1 ($x1$, $y1$)	Type 2 ($x2$, $y2$)	Price	Walrasian stability	Mashallian stability	Type 1 $U1$	Type 2 $U2$
$A1$	(7, 8)	(23, 22)	0.39	Stable	Unstable	1091	1745
$A2$	(7, 9)	(23, 21)	0.44	Stable	Unstable	1143	1745
$A3$	(8, 9)	(22, 21)	0.47	Stable	Unstable	1143	1739
$B1$	(12, 15)	(18, 15)	1.08	Unstable	Stable	1445	1445
$B2$	(12, 16)	(18, 14)	1.15	Unstable	Stable	1445	1395
$C1$	(16, 20)	(14, 10)	2.11	Stable	Unstable	1722	1136
$C2$	(16, 21)	(14, 9)	2.22	Stable	Unstable	1669	1136

$A2 = (7, 9)$, $A3 = (8, 9)$, $B1 = (12, 15)$, $B2 = (12, 16)$, $C1 = (16, 20)$, and $C2 = (16, 21)$ together with the corresponding equilibrium price ratios $P_X/P_Y = 0.39, 0.44, 047, 1.08, 1.15, 2.11$, and 2.22, respectively.

Table 3.1 summarizes the equilibrium predictions. The equilibria $A1$, $A2$, and $A3$ with low relative prices of commodity X, P_X/P_Y are beneficial for type 1 consumer having more of commodity Y, while the equilibria $C1$ and $C2$ with high relative prices of commodity X is advantageous to type 2 consumer having more of commodity X. In this sense, these four equilibria are not equitable. From the viewpoint of stability, these four equilibria are locally stable in Walras' sense, but locally unstable in Marshall's sense.

On the other hand, the equilibria $B1$ and $B2$ with intermediate prices give allocations that generate the minimal difference between the payoffs to the two types of consumers. We say that the equilibrium and allocation are fair. In particular, each type receives the same equilibrium payoff at $B1$. They are locally unstable in Walras' sense, but locally stable in Marshall's sense. There are trade-off between local Walrasian stability and "equity" of the competitive equilibria, whereas local Marshallian stability and allocation equity are compatible.

3.3 The Experimental Design and Procedures

The experiment was conducted at the University of Nairobi in Kenya during August 10–12 of 2010. We recruited subjects from three ethnic groups (i.e., Luo, Kikuyu, and Kalenjin) to attend the experiment.[6] The subjects were students at major Kenya universities such as the University of Nairobi, Kenyatta University, Moi University, Egerton University, Mount Kenya University, Kimathi University College of Technology, and Jomo Kenyatta University of Agriculture and Technology. No subject

[6]We investigated whether ethnicity affects subjects' trading behavior in another study (see Shimomura and Yamato (2012)). However, there are several differences in both the experimental design and procedures between that study and the current one (see detailed discussions in Sect. 3.5).

Table 3.2 Time schedule of the experiment

	8/10/2010	8/11/2010	8/12/2010
AM	L1–L2: 20 subjects	Ka1–Ka2: 20 subjects	Ka1*–Ka2*: 20 subjects
	Ki1–Ki2: 20 subjects	Ki1*–Ki2*: 20 subjects	L1*–L2*: 20 subjects
PM	L1–Ki2: 20 subjects	Ka1–Ki2*: 20 subjects	Ka1*–L2*: 20 subjects
	Ki1–L2: 20 subjects	Ki1*–Ka2: 20 subjects	L1*–Ka2*: 20 subjects

Notes: The roles of type 1 and type 2 that subjects played are indicated by the numbers 1 and 2, respectively. *L*, *Ki*, and *Ka* refer to Luo, Kikuyu, and Kalenjin subjects, respectively

had prior experience in market experiments. The number of subjects from each of the three ethnic communities was 40 for a total of 120 distinct subjects. For each ethnic group, 20 subjects played the role of type 1 consumer and another 20 subjects did the role of type 2 consumer. Their roles were fixed throughout the experiment.

Each subject participated in two sessions. In the first session they played with subjects from the same ethnic group and in the second session they played with those from a different ethnic group. In each session, there were 10 subjects who played the role of type 1 and 10 subjects who played the role of type 2. The subjects who played the same role in each session were always from the same ethnic group. As a result, a total of 12 sessions was conducted. Table 3.2 presents the details of these sessions. In the table, the roles of type 1 and type 2 that subjects played are indicated by the numbers 1 and 2, respectively, and *L*, *Ki*, and *Ka* refer to Luo, Kikuyu, and Kalenjin subjects, respectively. For example, L1–L2 and L1*–L2* refer to the sessions in which Luo subjects of type 1 played with Luo subjects of type 2, refer to the session in which Luo subjects of type 1 played with Kikuyu subjects of type 2, etc. In addition, it should be noted that the subjects participated in the experiment changed every day. For example, the Luo subjects in L1–l2 session on the first day differed from those in L1*–L2* session on the third day, and the Kikuyu subjects in Ki1–Ki2 session on the first day differed from those in Ki1*–Ki2* session on the second day, etc.

The procedure in each session was exactly the same. At the beginning of a session, each subject received one experimental instruction, one record sheet, one payoff table, and one name tag.[7] The name tag of each subject indicated her team name (A, B, C, . . ., or T) and her identification number (1 or 2). Ten subjects (A–J) played the role of type 1, and ten subjects (K–T) played the role of type 2. Each subject was given pink cards and/or white cards in an envelope. One pink card was one unit of commodity *X* and one white card was one unit of commodity *Y*. We explicitly noticed to every subject that she was not allowed to reveal any information regarding her payoff table or endowed color cards to any other subject.

Then, the subjects walked around a relatively large laboratory room and found a subject to trade. We prohibited any subject from trading any amount of commodity *X* or *Y* more than what they held. In addition, the trading ratio of *Y* to *X* should be

[7] The experimental instruction and payoff tables are provided in Appendices 2 and 3, respectively..

greater than or equal to 1/4 = 0.25 to avoid extremely low price ratio trading.[8] We told the subjects to trade commodity *X* for *Y* or *Y* for *X* when two subjects reached an agreement. After writing the trading results in their record sheets, the subjects reported them to the experimenter. The following information on the results was entered into the computer and displayed publicly through a projector: the team name giving commodity *X*, the amount of the traded *X*, the team name giving *Y*, the amount of the traded *Y*, and the trading ratio of the commodities (=*Y*/*X*). This was the end of one trade. The subjects had 10 min for each period and they were allowed to trade as many times as they wanted within the time limit. For the next trading partner, the subjects could choose any subject as they wanted. That is to say that the next partner might be the same as or different from one of the subjects they had already traded. After each period, the subjects went back to their seats and the experimenter collected all commodity cards. This was the end of one period.

At the beginning of the next period, the subjects received the same materials as those of the previous period. In particular, holdings of commodities were reset at the end of the previous period and each subject held the same endowment as that at the beginning of the previous period. After a 2-min break, the next period started. One session had five periods, which means that the above steps were repeated five times.

Earnings of each subject or team depended on the final payoff that she or her team earned in one randomly selected period from the experiment. This period was chosen by a random device after the experiment. The two sessions in which each subject participated required approximately 3 hours and half to complete in total. The mean payoff per subject was 3026 Ksh (One US dollar approximately exchanged for 80 Ksh in August of 2010). The maximum payoff among the 120 subjects was 3865 Ksh and the minimum payoff was 2068 Ksh.

3.4 Experimental Results

In this section, we are going to exhibit whether our experimental results support the Walrasian adjustment process or the Marshallian adjustment process based on the discussions on the ratio of the three equilibria, the average distances to the fair equilibrium, price movement, and final holdings of commodity *X*.

Table 3.3 provides the ratios of the three equilibria (i.e., *A*2, *B*1, and *C*1) bundles and the ratios of bundles near these three equilibria in the end-of-period holdings of *X* and *Y*. These ratios are also presented in Fig. 3.4 to help understanding visually.[9] The bundles near *A*2, *B*1, and *C*1 are defined as being within 1 unit of *A*2, *B*1, *C*1 for

[8] We set this floor price only, but it is more desirable to set a ceiling price such as 4 to avoid extremely high price ratio trading. Fortunately, these extremely high ratio trades were not observed in our experimental data.

[9] In Fig. 3.4, Panel I is for the ratios of the three equilibria bundles and Panel II is for the ratios of bundles near these three equilibria.

Table 3.3 Ratios of three equilibria bundles to all final holdings

	Type 1	Type 2	Both types
*A*2	0.17% (=1/600)	0.33% (=2/600)	0.25% (=3/1200)
Near *A*2 (±1)	0.50% (=3/600)	1.00% (=6/600)	0.75% (=9/1200)
*B*1	7.83% (=47/600)	6.33% (=38/600)	7.08% (=85/1200)
Near *B*1 (±1)	27.83% (=167/600)	27.33% (=164/600)	27.58% (=331/1200)
*C*1	1.00% (=6/600)	0.17% (=1/600)	0.58% (=7/1200)
Near *C*1 (±1)	2.67% (=16/600)	0.67% (=4/600)	1.67% (=20/1200)

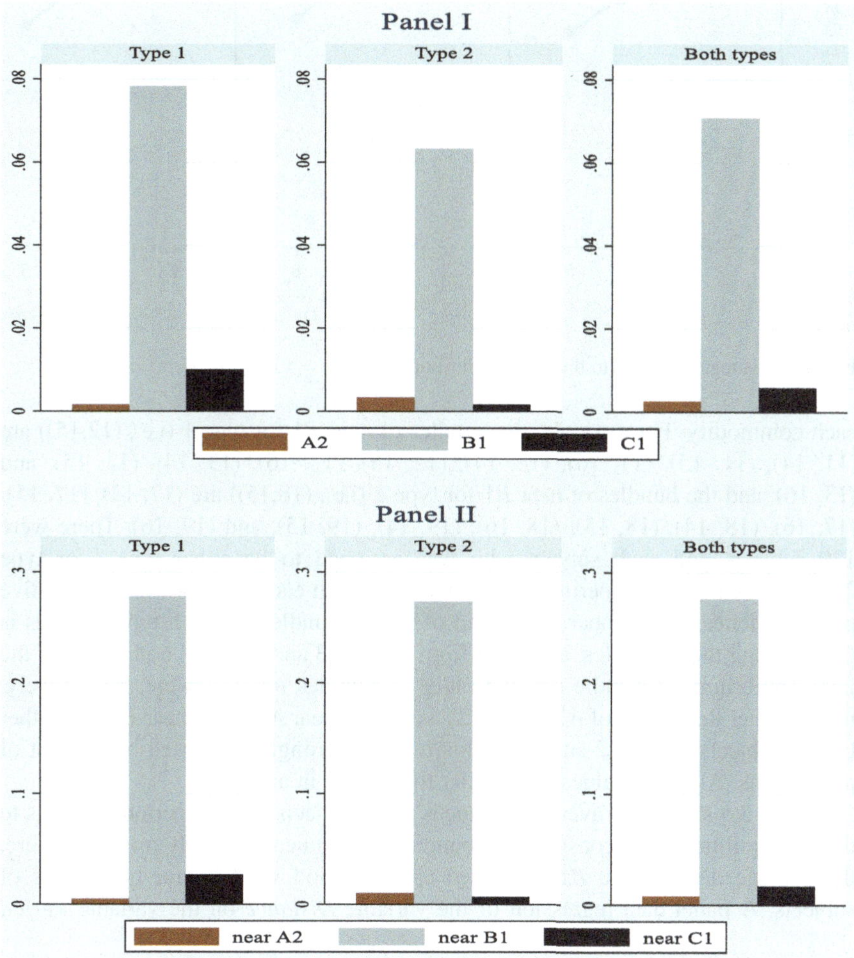

Fig. 3.4 Ratios of three equilibria bundles to all final holdings

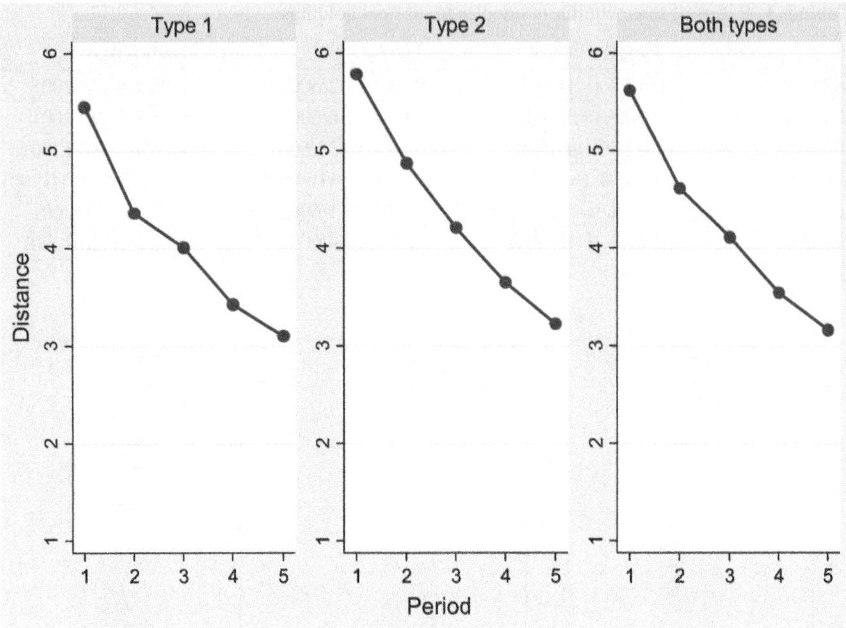

Fig. 3.5 Average distances to the fair equilibrium $B1$

each commodity. For example, the bundles of near $B1$ for type 1 (i.e., (12,15)) are (11, 14), (11, 15), (11, 16), (12, 14), (12, 15), (12, 16), (13, 14), (13, 15), and (13, 16), and the bundles of near $B1$ for type 2 (i.e., (18,15)) are (17, 14), (17, 15), (17, 16), (18, 14), (18, 15), (18, 16), (19, 14), (19, 15), and (19, 16). There were 120 subjects and each subject who was assigned to be either type 1 or type 2 participated in two experimental sessions in which each session consisted of five periods. Hence, the number of the end-of-period bundles for each type subjects is 600. Among these bundles, as shown from Table 3.3 and Fig. 3.4, both ratios of the fair equilibrium $B1$ bundle and the ratios of bundles near $B1$ were, respectively, much higher than those of $A2$ (resp. $C1$) and those near $A2$ (resp. near $C1$) for either type 1 subjects or type 2 subjects. This result is strongly supported by the test of proportions. All the p values are smaller than 0.001 in any cases.

Figure 3.5 shows the average distances from subjects' end-of-period holdings to the fair equilibrium $B1$ consumption bundle.[10] As indicated clearly from the figure, the average distances to $B1$ decreased as the period went by for both types of subjects. A panel data regression of the variable *Distance* on the variable *Period*

[10]Here the distance of each subject at each period is defined as the Euclidean distance, which can be written as $\sqrt{(X_{it}-12)^2+(Y_{it}-15)^2}$ for type 1 subjects and $\sqrt{(X_{it}-18)^2+(Y_{it}-15)^2}$for type 2 subjects, where i and t refer to subject and period indices, and X and Y stand for a subject's end-of-period holdings of commodities X and Y, respectively.

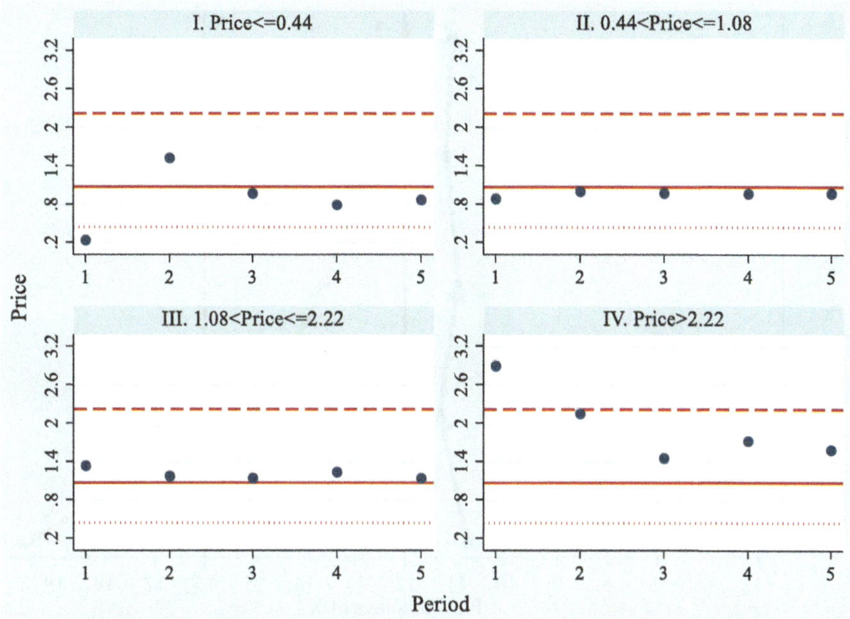

Fig. 3.6 Price movement by periods

was run to test whether this decrease is statistically significant. We found that the coefficient of *Period* was negatively significant at 0.1% level in either type-separated case or type-pooled case, which confirms that the decreasing tendency in Fig. 3.5 is significant.

Figure 3.6 shows the price movements of P_X/P_Y by periods. The three equilibria (i.e., the low, middle, and high equilibria) are also presented by the dot, solid, and dash lines, respectively. To draw these price movements, we first divided the subjects into four groups according to their prices in Period 1 and then trace their movements of the prices in Periods 2–5. The prices were calculated by subjects' end-of-period holdings of commodities X and Y, and the four groups were based on four price intervals: (1) price $\leq$ 0.44 (2.93% of subjects); (2) 0.44 $<$ price $\leq$ 1.08 (50.13% of subjects); (3) 1.08 $<$ price $\leq$ 2.22 (41.17% of subjects); and (4) price $>$ 2.22 (5.77% of subjects). As shown in the figure, a certain level of fluctuation in the price can be observed among the subjects whose prices in Period 1 were either not larger than the price at $A2$ (see Fig. 3.6—I) or larger than the price at $C1$ (see Fig. 3.6—IV). For the majority of subjects (91.3% of subjects), when their prices in Period 1 were between the prices at $A2$ and $B1$ (resp. between the prices at $B1$ and $C1$), an upward (resp. a downward) tendency towards the middle equilibrium can be observed. Although the panel data regression of the variable *Price* on the variable *Period* confirmed the significance of these two tendencies ($p < 0.05$ in both

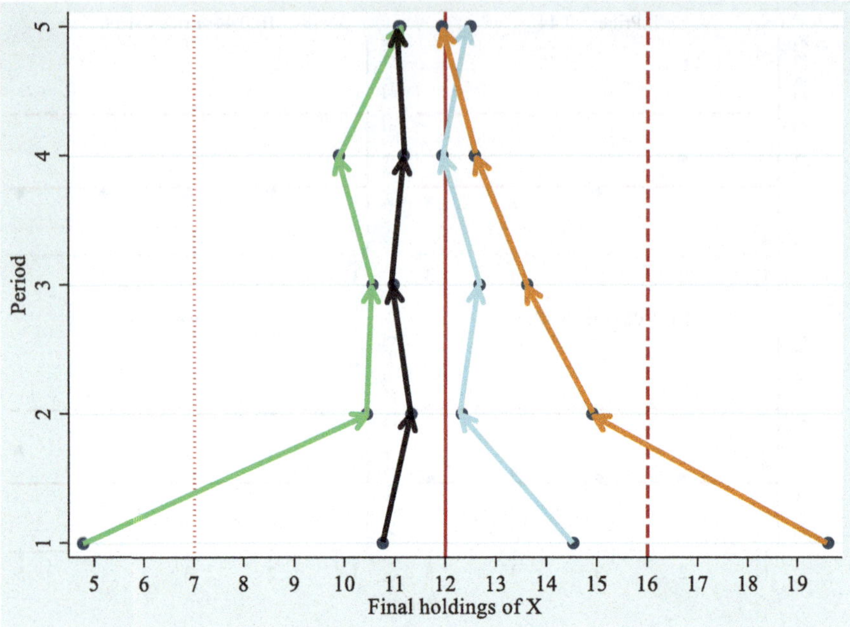

Fig. 3.7 Final holdings of *X*

cases), the results obtained from a Wilcoxon signed-rank test indicates that it is only in the case of the initial price being between 1.08 and 2.22 that the price in Period 5 is equal to the middle equilibrium price ($p = 0.3842$).[11]

Figure 3.7 presents the movements of the type 1 subjects' final holdings of commodity *X* by periods.[12] The three equilibria (i.e., the low, middle, and high equilibria) are again presented by the dot, solid, and dash lines, respectively. Similar to the case of the price movements, to draw the movements of final holdings of *X*, we first divided the type 1 subjects into four groups according to their final holdings of *X* in Period 1 and then trace their movements of the amount of *X* in Periods 2–5. The final holdings of *X* in Period 1 were based on four intervals: (1) $X \leq 7$; (2) $7 < X \leq 12$; (3) $12 < X \leq 16$; and (4) $X > 16$. As indicated from the figure, it seems that no matter where they started the final holdings of commodity *X* converged to the middle equilibrium with the passing of periods. By combining the results from the panel data regression and the Wilcoxon signed-rank test

[11] For other two initial price intervals, the prices in Period 5 are also significantly not equal to the middle equilibrium price.

[12] By Walras' law, we only need to focus on market of commodity *X*. In addition, by feasibility it is sufficient to consider the movements in final holdings of subjects of type 1 only.

together, we confirmed that the end-of-period holdings of X converged to the middle equilibrium in Period 5 in three of four intervals that mentioned above.[13] The only exceptional interval was that the final holdings of X in Period 1 were between the low equilibrium and the middle equilibrium (i.e., $7 < X \leq 12$). In this interval, we found that the variable *Period* did not have significant effect on the final holdings of X, and the amount of X was statistically equal to 11 in all the 5 periods (see the black line in Fig. 3.7).

Summing up the above descriptions, our results exhibit that Marshallian dynamics is supported in a pit market.

3.5 Discussions

Shimomura and Yamato (2012) studied how different compositions of ethnicities (i.e. Kikuyu, Luo, and Kalenjin) in Kenya trade in the similar market environment as in the current study. They found that ethnic diversity plays an important role in the evolution of markets. In sessions with Luo and/or Kikuyu subjects only, there was no convergence of allocations. However, in the sessions with Kalenjin subjects, allocations converged to the intermediate allocation, especially in later periods. Moreover, convergence to the intermediate equilibrium occurs considerably faster with Kalenjin subjects and the frequency of transactions with Kalenjin subjects is significantly lower than that with Luo and/or Kikuyu subjects only. They concluded that less frequent transactions resulted in the more efficient outcomes of the experimental market. In the current study, we also perform a robustness check to investigate whether our findings of Marshallian path in a pit market are similarly driven by the Kalenjin subjects. The comparison results for the data with and without Kalenjin subjects show that Marshallian dynamics is supported in both the sessions with and without Kalenjin subjects, and it is more obvious in the sessions where Kalenjin subjects participated than those with Luo and/or Kikuyu subjects only.[14]

In our view, the evidence that there is no convergence to the intermediate equilibrium in sessions with Luo and/or Kikuyu subjects only in Shimomura and Yamato (2012) might be due to the differences in experimental design between their study and ours. These differences are threefold. First, the parameterization of subjects' utility functions is different. In Shimomura and Yamato (2012), the parameterization led the payoff of the intermediate equilibrium for both types of subjects to be 2000 tokens, while in the current study we avoid this happening because the number of 2000 might be too conspicuous to attract subjects' notice. Second, different from that each trader in the current study is individual, each trading

[13]The panel data regression was run by regressing the variable *Final holdings of X* on the variable *Period*, and the Wilcoxon signed-rank test was conducted to test whether the end-of-period holdings of X was equal to 12. These results are available upon request.

[14]These results are not reported here, but are available upon request.

group in Shimomura and Yamato (2012) contained two subjects from the same ethnicity, which allows them being able to discuss with each other within each group. Third, each subject in Shimomura and Yamato (2012) participated in three experimental sessions, while that number in the current study is two. Given that the above-mentioned differences might lead to different experimental behavior, more research in future is needed to verify our findings.

3.6 Concluding Remarks

Our laboratory experiment is designed to study dynamics in pit market trading. In our exchange economy model, three competitive equilibria exist. The two equilibria with the lowest and the highest relative prices are beneficial for one type of the consumers, and the intermediate price gives an equitable allocation. Our result shows strong support for the convergence to the intermediate equilibrium, which is unstable in Walrasian tatonnement dynamics and is stable in Marshallian quantity adjustment process. In our experiments, Marshallian path predicts that consumers in the market finally reach at an "equitable" allocation where payoffs for both types of consumers are identically the same.[15] This naturally raises the question of whether our experimental results were due to subjects' fairness preferences on payoffs. However, our experimental design rules out this possibility, because each type of subjects can only know their own payoffs.

Plott (2000) reported that *in a double auction market* the Marshallian model works well when supply curves are forward-falling, in contrast, in the backward-bending case stability is captured by the Walrasian model and the Marshallian model of dynamics is rejected. Given this result, under what conditions Marshallian dynamics work *in a pit market* remains still unknown to us. In a recent study on investigating the change in the price in call market experiments, Plott and Pogorelskiy (2015) demonstrated that the Newton-Jaws model based on the Newton method provides a better description of how the markets operate than the Walrasian model. The Newton method (see details in Bossaerts and Plott (2008)) might be a useful tool for examining this question. We leave this issue open and welcome any efforts to explore it.

Acknowledgments We thank an anonymous referee, Jean Ensminger, Emiko Fukuda, Hiroyuki Hino, Anjan Mukherji, Charles Plott, Shyam Sunder, and Motoki Takahashi for their comments and suggestions. We appreciate special supports to conduct this experiment in Kenya by Mohamud Jama, Michiharu Masui, Joseph Onjala, and Kohei Yoshida. Financial supports from Japan International Cooperation Agency, the Murata Science Foundation, and the Japanese Ministry of

[15] In our data, both two-tailed *t*-test and Wilcoxon rank sum test cannot reject that mean and median payoffs are the same in Period 5, respectively (t test: $p = 0.6294$; Wilcoxon rank sum test: $p = 0.7022$).

Education, Culture, Sports, Science and Technology through Grant-in-aid for Scientific Research (C)19K01541 and (C)19K01558 are gratefully acknowledged.

Appendix 1: Local Stability Conditions of Price and Quantity Adjustment Processes in Two-Consumer Two-Good Exchange Economies

First of all, we give formal definitions of "two-good exchange economy" and "competitive equilibrium":

Definition 3.1 A *two-good exchange economy* is a list (I, U, ω) such that I is a nonempty finite set, $U = (U_i)_{i \in I}$ is a profile of real-valued functions from R^2_+, and $\omega = (\omega_i)_{i \in I}$, where $\omega_i = (\overline{x_i}, \overline{y}_i)$, is a profile of points of R^2_+. Then an element of I is called a *consumer*. For each $i \in I$, U_i and ω_i are called the *utility function, and the individual endowment, of consumer i*, respectively. The profile of non-negative vectors $(x_i, y_i)_{i \in I}$ is called an *allocation of* (I, U, ω) if $\sum_{i \in I} x_i = \sum_{i \in I} \overline{x_i}$ and $\sum_{i \in I} y_i = \sum_{i \in I} \overline{y_i}$.

Definition 3.2 Let (I, U, ω) be a two-good exchange economy. Then the vector $((x_i^*, y_i^*)_{i \in I}, (p_X^*, p_Y^*)) \in (R^2_+)^I \times R^2$ is a *competitive equilibrium*, or simply *equilibrium, for* (I, U, ω) if

1. for each $i \in I$, $p_X^* x_i^* + p_Y^* y_i^* \le p_X^* \bar{x}_i + p_Y^* \bar{y}_i$, and $U_i(x_i*, y_i*) \ge U_i(x_i, y_i)$ for each $(x_i, y_i) \in R^2_+$ such that $p_X^* x_i + p_Y^* y_i \le p_X^* \bar{x}_i + p_Y^* \bar{y}_i$;
2. $\sum_{i \in I} x_i^* = \sum_{i \in I} \bar{x}_i$ and $\sum_{i \in I} y_i^* = \sum_{i \in I} \bar{y}_i$.

The profile of non-negative vectors $(x_i*, y_i*)_{i \in I}$ and the vector (p_X*, p_Y*) are called an *equilibrium allocation* and an *equilibrium price vector, for* (I, U, ω), respectively.

We next investigate local dynamics of price adjustment process, which work in neighborhoods of equilibria. Simply speaking, the price adjustment process, or "Walrasian" adjustment process, means that the relative price of X goes up when X is excessively demanded, and the relative price of X goes down when X is excessively supplied. We first give the definitions of market excess demand function, and the local stability and instability of Walrasian adjustment process.

Definition 3.3 Let (I, U, ω) be a two-good exchange economy and d_i^X be the demand function for X of consumer $i \in I$. Define the set of the demanders ID(P) for X and the set of the suppliers IS(P) of X by

$$\mathrm{ID}(P) = \{i \in I | d_i^X(P, 1) - \bar{x}_i \geq 0\} \quad \text{and}$$
$$\mathrm{IS}(P) = \{i \in I | d_i^X(P, 1) - \bar{x}_i < 0\}$$

for each $P > 0$. Then the *market demand function,* simply *demand function for X* is defined by

$D^X(P) = \sum_{i \in \mathrm{ID}(P)} (d_i^X(P, 1) - \bar{x}_i)$the *market supply function,* simply *supply function of X* is defined by

$$S^X(P) = \sum\nolimits_{i \in \mathrm{IS}(P)} (\bar{x}_i - d_i^X(P, 1)),$$

and the *market excess demand function,* simply *excess demand function for X* is defined by

$$E^X(P) = D^X(P) - S^X(P) = \sum\nolimits_{i \in I} (d_i^X(P, 1) - \bar{x}_i)$$

for each $P > 0$.

Definition 3.4 Let (I, U, ω) be a two-good exchange economy. Suppose that $D^X(P^*) = S^X(P^*) = x^*$. Then *Walrasian adjustment process with the excess demand function* E^X is the ordinary differential equation: $\dot{P} = W(E^X(P))$, where W is a real-valued function from R such that $W(0) = 0$ and $W'(z) > 0$ for each $z \in$ R. We say that (x^*, P^*) is *locally Walras-stable* (resp. *locally Walras-unstable*) if $E^{X\prime}(P^*) < 0$ (resp. $E^{X\prime}(P^*) > 0$). The competitive equilibrium $((x_i*, y_i*)_{i \in I}, (p_X*, p_Y*))$ for (I, U, ω) is called a *locally Walras-stable equilibrium* (resp. *locally Walras-unstable equilibrium*) if $(D(p_X*/p_Y*), p_X*/p_Y*)$ is locally Walras-stable (resp. locally Walras-unstable).

The local Walrasian stability and instability of a competitive equilibrium for a two-consumer economy is characterized in an Edgeworth box in the following way: Let $((x_1*, y_1*), (x_2*, y_2*), (P^*, 1))$ be a competitive equilibrium, then $E^X(P^*) = 0$. Suppose that $((x_1*, y_1*), (x_2*, y_2*), (P^*, 1))$ is a locally Walras-stable equilibrium such that $\bar{x}_1 - x_1^* > 0$. Then $E^{X\prime}(P^*) < 0$. Draw the budget line passing through the competitive allocation and the initial allocation. Note that $(\bar{x}_1 - x_1^*)/(x_2^* - \bar{x}_2) = 1$ because $x_1^* + x_2^* - \bar{x}_1 - \bar{x}_2 = 0$. Consider a relative price slightly higher than P^*, draw the new budget line, and find the intersections with the offer curves of the consumers. Denote by (x_1, y_1), and (x_2, y_2) the intersections of the budget line with the offer curves of consumers 1 and 2, respectively. Recall $E^{X\prime}(P^*) < 0$, then the zero excess demand at P^* becomes negative when the relative price is marginally higher than P^*. Thus, $x_1 + x_2 - \bar{x}_1 - \bar{x}_2 < 0$, namely $(\overline{x_1} - x_1)/(x_2 - \overline{x_2}) > 1$. Then X is excessively supplied, so that the relative price decreases and converges to P^*. Similarly, by considering a relative price slightly lower than P^*, we can have $x_1 + x_2 - \bar{x}_1 - \bar{x}_2 > 0$, namely $(\overline{x_1} - x_1)/(x_2 - \overline{x_2}) < 1$. Then X is excessively demanded, and thereby the relative price increases and converges to P^*. The points A and C in Fig. 3.8, therefore, represent locally Walras-stable equilibria.

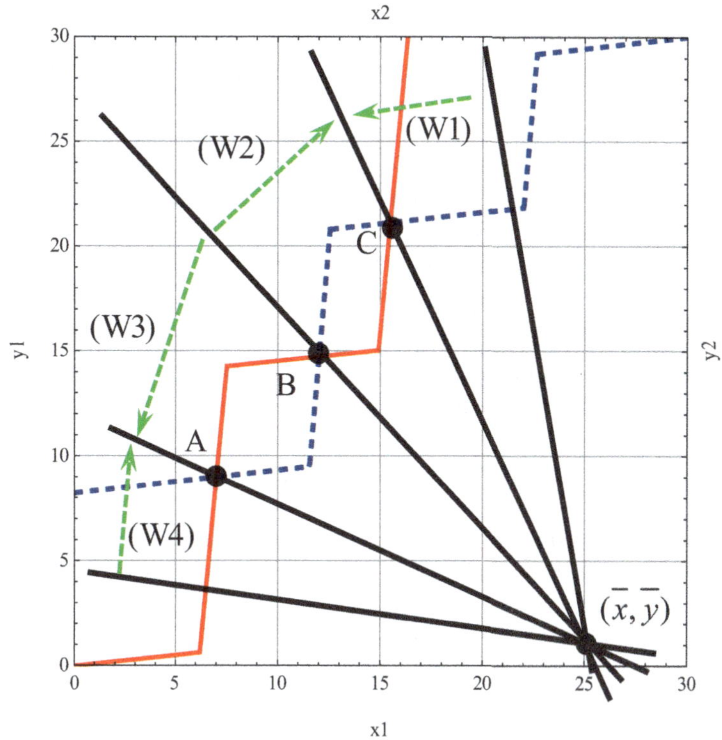

Fig. 3.8 Local Walrasian stability of three competitive equilibria

On the other hand, suppose that $((x_1*, y_1*), (x_2*, y_2*), (P^*, 1))$ is a locally Walras-unstable equilibrium such that $\bar{x_1} - x_1^* > 0$. Then $E^{X\prime}(P^*) > 0$, and $(\overline{x_1} - x_1)/(x_2 - \overline{x_2}) = 1$. Consider a relative price slightly higher than P^*, and choose (x_1', y_1'), and (x_2', y_2') in the same way as a locally Walras-stable equilibrium is considered. Then we can see that the zero excess demand at P^* becomes positive when the relative price marginally goes up. Thus, $x_1' + x_2' - \bar{x}_1 - \bar{x}_2 > 0$. Hence, $(\overline{x_1} - x_1')/(x_2' - \overline{x_2}) < 1$. Similarly, by considering a relative price slightly lower than P^*, we can have $x_1' + x_2' - \bar{x}_1 - \bar{x}_2 < 0$, namely $(\overline{x_1} - x_1')/(x_2' - \overline{x_2}) > 1$. The point B in Fig. 3.8, therefore, describes a locally Walras-unstable equilibrium.

We next discuss dynamics of quantity adjustment process. We give the definitions of local stability and instability of "Marshallian" adjustment process. To formulate them, we define the "demand price function" and the "supply price function" of an exchange economy, which are, respectively, "local inverse functions" of the demand and supply functions.

Let D^X and S^X be the demand function and the supply function, for$X$, respectively. Let $D^X(P^*) = S^X(P^*) = x^*$ and assume $D^{X\prime}(P^*) \neq 0$. Then, by the inverse function theorem, there exists an open interval V in R_{++} such that $x^* \in V$ and a function Δ^X from V to R_{++} such that $P^* = \Delta^X(x^*)$, $x = D^X(\Delta^X(x))$, and $\Delta^{X\prime}(x) = 1/D^{X\prime}(\Delta^X(x))$ for each $x \in V$. The function Δ^X is a local inverse function of D^X. Similarly, by assuming $S^{X\prime}(P^*) \neq 0$, we can show that there exists an open interval W in R_{++} such that $x^* \in W$ and a differentiable function Σ^X from W to R_{++} such that $P^* = \Sigma^X(x^*)$, $x = S^X(\Sigma^X(x))$ and $\Sigma^{X\prime}(x) = 1/S^{X\prime}(\Sigma^X(x))$ for each $x \in W$. The function Σ^X is a local inverse function of S^X. Notice that $G = V \cap W$ is an open interval in R_{++} such that $x^* \in G$. Hence, suppose that $G = V = W$. By considering the neighborhood[16] G of x^*, we may define the following concepts:

Definition 3.5 Suppose that $D^X(P^*) = S^X(P^*) = x^*$, $D^{X\prime}(P^*) \neq 0$, and $S^{X\prime}(P^*) \neq 0$. Let G be a neighborhood of x^*. The *demand price function for X on G* is defined by

$$\Delta^X(x) = \{P > 0 | x = D^X(P)\}$$

for each $x \in G$. The *supply price function of X on G* is defined by

$\Sigma^X(x) = \{P > 0 | x = S^X(P)\}$for each $x \in G$. The *excess demand price function for X on G* is defined by

$$\Phi^X(x) = \Delta^X(x) - \Sigma^X(x)$$

for each $x \in G$.

Notice that $\Phi^X(x^*) = \Delta^X(x^*) - \Sigma^X(x^*) = P^* - P^* = 0$.

Definition 3.6 Suppose that $D^X(P^*) = S^X(P^*) = x^*$, $D^{X\prime}(P^*) \neq 0$, and $S^{X\prime}(P^*) \neq 0$. Let G be a neighborhood of x^* and Φ^X be the excess demand price function for X on G. Then *Marshallian adjustment process with the excess demand price function Φ^X on G* is the ordinary differential equation: $\dot{x} = M\left(\Phi^X(x)\right)$, where M is a real-valued function from R such that $M(0) = 0$ and $M'(z) > 0$ for each $z \in R$. We say that (x^*, P^*) is *locally Marshall-stable* (resp. *locally Marshall-unstable*) if $\Phi^{X\prime}(x^*) < 0$ (resp. $\Phi^{X\prime}(x^*) > 0$). The competitive equilibrium $((x_i*, y_i*)_{i \in I}, (p_X*, p_Y*))$ for (I, U, ω) is called a *locally Marshall-stable equilibrium* (resp. *locally Marshall-unstable equilibrium*) if $(D^X(p_X* / p_Y*), p_X* / p_Y*)$ is locally Marshall-stable (resp. locally Marshall-unstable).

The local Marshallian stability and instability of a competitive equilibrium for a two-consumer economy is characterized in an Edgeworth box in the following way: Suppose that $((x_1*, y_1*), (x_2*, y_2*), (P^*, 1))$ is a locally Marshall-stable competitive equilibrium such that $\bar{x_1} - x_1^* > 0$. Then, $S^X(P^*) = \bar{x_1} - x_1^* = x_2^* - \bar{x_2} = D^X(P^*)$. This means that consumer 1 is the supplier, and consumer 2 is the demander, for X at the relative price P^*. Define $x^* = S^X(P^*) = \bar{x_1} - x_1^*$, then $\Phi^{X\prime}(x^*) < 0$. Draw the

[16]We call an open interval containing the real number x^* a *neighborhood of* x^*.

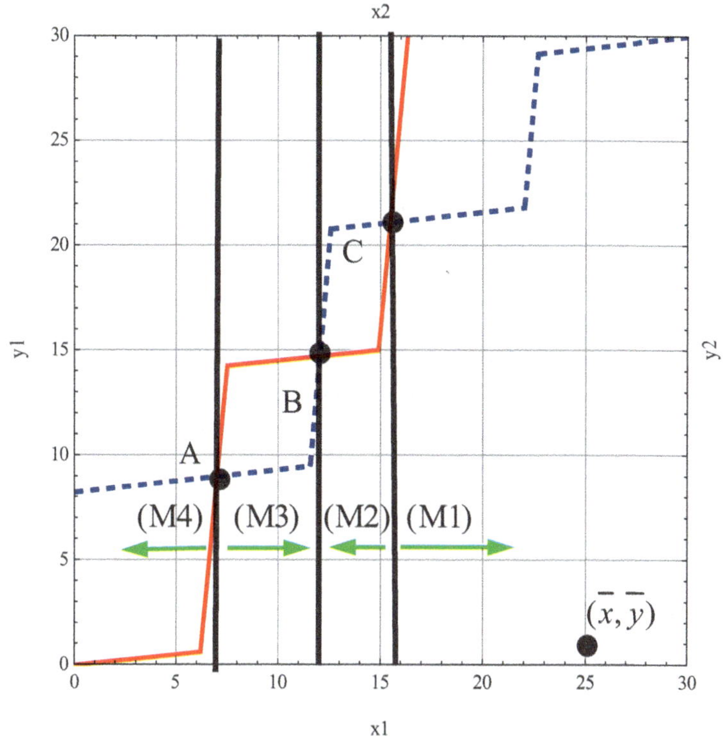

Fig. 3.9 Local Marshallian stability of three competitive equilibria

vertical line passing through the competitive allocation. Note that $(\bar{x_1} - x_1^*)/(x_2^* - \bar{x_2}) = (y_1^* - \bar{y_1})/(\bar{y_2} - y_2^*) = 1$ because $x_1^* + x_2^* - \bar{x_1} - \bar{x_2} = y_1^* + y_2^* - \bar{y_1} - \bar{y_2} = 0$. Consider a supply of X by consumer 1 slightly more than $\bar{x_1} - x_1^*$ under the feasibility constraint of X, $x_1^* + x_2^* - \bar{x_1} - \bar{x_2} = 0$. Draw the vertical line at the new supply level of X, and find the intersections with the offer curves of the consumers. Denote by (x_1, y_1) and (x_2, y_2) the intersections of the vertical line with the offer curves of consumers 1 and 2, respectively. In addition, let P_1 and P_2 be the associated supply price of consumer 1 and demand price of consumer 2, respectively. Recall $\Phi^{X\prime}(x^*) < 0$, then the zero excess demand price at x^* becomes negative when the supply of X is marginally greater than x^*. Thus, $P_2 - P_1 < 0$, namely $P_2 < P_1$. Then consumer 2, the demander, appreciates X less than consumer 1, the supplier, does at the level x^*, so that the supply of X decreases and converges to x^*. Similarly, by considering a supply level slightly less than $\bar{x_1} - x_1^*$, we can show $P_2 > P_1$. Then the demander 2 appreciates X more than the supplier 1 does, so that the supply of X increases and converges to x^*. The point B in Fig. 3.9, therefore, represents locally Marshall-stable equilibria.

On the other hand, suppose that $((x_1*, y_1*), (x_2*, y_2*), (P^*, 1))$ is a locally Marshall-unstable equilibrium such that $\bar{x_1} - x_1^* > 0$. Then, $S^X(P^*) = \bar{x_1} - x_1^* =$

$x_2^* - \bar{x_2} = D^X(P^*)$. Define $x^* = S^X(P^*) = \bar{x_1} - x_1^*$, then $\Phi^{X\prime}(x^*) > 0$. Draw the vertical line passing through the competitive allocation. Note that $(\bar{x_1} - x_1^*)/(x_2^* - \bar{x_2}) = (y_1^* - \bar{y_1})/(\bar{y_2} - y_2^*) = 1$ because $x_1^* + x_2^* - \bar{x_1} - \bar{x_2} = y_1^* + y_2^* - \bar{y_1} - \bar{y_2} = 0$. Consider a supply of X by consumer 1 slightly more than $\bar{x_1} - x_1^*$ under the feasibility constraint of X, $x_1^* + x_2^* - \bar{x_1} - \bar{x_2} = 0$. Draw the vertical line at the new supply level of X, and find the intersections with the offer curves of the consumers. Denote by (x_1, y_1) and (x_2, y_2) the intersections of the vertical line with the offer curves of consumers 1 and 2, respectively. In addition, let P_1 and P_2 be the associated supply price of consumer 1 and demand price of consumer 2, respectively. Recall $\Phi^{X\prime}(x^*) > 0$, then the zero excess demand price at x^* becomes positive when the supply of X is marginally greater than x^*. Thus, $P_2 - P_1 > 0$, namely $P_2 > P_1$. Then consumer 2, the demander, appreciates X more than consumer 1, the supplier, does at the level x^*, so that the supply of X increases and diverges from x^*. The points A and C in Fig. 3.9 therefore describe locally Marshall-unstable equilibria.

Appendix 2: Experimental Instruction

This is an experiment about decision making and economics. The instructions are simple. If you follow them carefully and make good decisions, you might earn a considerable amount of money that will be paid to you. In this experiment, you will make decisions to trade or hold two kinds of commodities, called X and Y in a sequence of trading periods.

2.1 Introduction

1. There are (20) traders in total. Please make sure that you have the following items:
   (a) "Payoff Table" (one)
   (b) "Record Sheet" (three)
   (c) Name tag (one).
2. Please check whether your trader name (A, B, C...) in your "Record Sheet" is the same as the *first* letter in your name tag.
3. Your "Payoff Table" is your own SECRET information. *You are NOT allowed to reveal the information regarding your "Payoff Table" to any other person.* We will show you how to read the "Payoff Table" later.
4. At the beginning of each period of the experiment, you will be given some *amounts of Commodity X and/or Y. These amounts are shown in the first row of your "Record Sheet." This endowment is also your own SECRET information,* so *you are NOT allowed to reveal the information regarding your endowment to any other person.*

2.2 Trading Rules

The trading rules are as follows:

1. First of all, please put on your name tag so that the other traders can see your trader name.
2. Each trader will be given pink cards and/or white cards in an envelope. One pink card is one unit of commodity *X* and one white card is one unit of commodity *Y*. The number of pink cards (resp., white cards) equals to the amount of Commodity *X* (resp., Commodity *Y*) in the first row of your "Record Sheet." You can take pink and white cards (Commodities *X* and *Y*) out of the envelope only when you check the number of cards or trade them.
3. Walk around this room and find a person to trade. *Be careful NOT to reveal to any other person your "Payoff Table" and "Record Sheet."* The same notice applies to the following steps 4, 5, and 6.
4. Start a negotiation when you find a person that wants to trade with you. *You CANNOT give Commodity X or Y more than you hold. Moreover, the trading ratio of Y to X (= (Amount of Y)/(Amount of X)) should be greater than or equal to (1/4 = 0.25). Remember that the trading ratio of Y to X cannot be less than (1/4 = 0.25).*
5. If you reach an agreement, then report the agreement to an experimenter. In front of the experimenter, trade Commodity *X* with Commodity *Y* according to the agreement. After that, write the trading result in your "Record Sheet." *This is the end of one trade.*
6. Repeat the above steps 3–5 after one trade is completed. *You have (12) minutes for each period.* You can trade as many times as you want within the time limit. For the next person to trade with, you can choose any person: she/he may be the same as or different from one of the persons you have already traded. We accept only agreements that have reached within the time limit.
7. Please go back to your seat after each period. Please make sure that all commodity cards you traded are in your envelope. This is the end of the first period.
8. At the beginning of the second period, you will receive the same materials as those of the first period. That is, the amounts of Commodities *X* and *Y* you initially have at Period 2 are the same as those at the *beginning* of Period 1. We will distribute pink cards and/or white cards in an envelope. Those amounts are shown in your "Record Sheet." We will also collect the commodity cards and the envelope used in Period 1. After a 2-min break, Period 2 starts. This experiment has (5) periods. The above steps are repeated (5) times.

2.3 An Example

We will give you an example to explain how to read the "Payoff Table" and how to fill out the "Record Sheet" by way of an example. In the following explanations, we

Table 3.4 Record Sheet Example 1

Record Sheet

Date (day/month/year): Time: ~

Trader Name: **A**

Your Name Tag ID: xxxxx Your Name xxxxx xxxxx

Period 1

Trade Number	Amount of Change in X	Amount of Change in Y	Person You Trade with	Amount of X	Amount of Y	Payoff
0				**9**	**8**	**4905**
1						

will use *the "Pilot Payoff Table" which has nothing to do with the "Payoff Table,"* but the "Pilot Payoff Table" should help you read the "Payoff Table" in the experiment.

1. Suppose that your trader name is "A."
2. Take a look at Table 3.4. Your endowment is shown in the second row of the "Record Sheet." In this example, you are given endowment of 9 units of Commodity *X* and 8 units of Commodity *Y*.

   Next see Table 3.5. This table represents a part of the "Pilot Payoff Table." In this table, the horizontally aligned numbers denote the amounts of Commodity *X* and the vertically aligned numbers denotes the amounts of Commodity *Y*. You are endowed with 9 units of Commodity *X* and 8 units of Commodity *Y*, so your initial payoff is the number in the cell of column 9—row 8, that is, 4905. This number is the value shown in the "Payoff" of "Trade Number 0" in the "Record Sheet."

   Let us begin the first trading.
3. Suppose that you negotiate with Trader B, and you and B reach the agreement that "4 units of Commodity *X* that you have are traded for 7 units of Commodity *Y* that Trader B has."
4. Report the agreement to the experimenter. The experimenter will fill out the following table on the blackboard for you.

   In this case, as shown in Table 3.6, the experimenter writes "A" in the blank of "Trader that gave *X*," "4" in "Amount of *X*," "B" in "Trader that gave *Y*," and "7" in "Amount of *Y*." *Remember that the trading ratio of Y to X (=Y/X) should be greater than or equal to (1/4 = 0.25).*

Table 3.5 Pilot Payoff Table

Pilot Payoff Table

Amount of Y

25	....	7209	7284	7359	7434	7509	7584	7659	7734	....
24	....	7145	7220	7295	7370	7445	7520	7595	7670	....
23	....	7073	7148	7223	7298	7373	7448	7523	7598	....
22	....	6994	7069	7144	7219	7294	7369	7444	7519	....
21	....	6907	6982	7057	7132	7207	7282	7357	7432	....
20	....	6810	6885	6960	7035	7110	7185	7260	7335	....
19	....	6703	6778	6853	6928	7003	7078	7153	7228	....
18	....	6585	6660	6735	6810	6885	6960	7035	7110	....
17	....	6455	6530	6605	6680	6755	6830	6905	6980	....
16	....	6311	6386	6461	6536	6611	6686	6761	6836	....
15	....	6152	6227	6302	6377	6452	6527	6602	6677	....
14	....	5976	6051	6126	6201	6276	6351	6426	6501	....
13	....	5781	5856	5931	6006	6081	6156	6231	6306	....
12	....	5566	5641	5716	5791	5866	5941	6016	6091	....
11	....	5328	5403	5478	5553	5628	5703	5778	5853	....
10	....	5066	5141	5216	5291	5366	5441	5516	5591	....
9	....	4776	4851	4926	5001	5076	5151	5226	5301	....
8	....	4455	4530	4605	4680	4755	4830	4905	4980	....
7	....	4101	4176	4251	4326	4401	4476	4551	4626	....
6	....	3709	3784	3859	3934	4009	4084	4159	4234	....
5	....	3276	3351	3426	3501	3576	3651	3726	3801	....
4	....	2798	2873	2948	3023	3098	3173	3248	3323	....
3	....	2269	2344	2419	2494	2569	2644	2719	2794	....
2	....	1685	1760	1835	1910	1985	2060	2135	2210	....
1	....	1039	1114	1189	1264	1339	1414	1489	1564	....
0	....	325	400	475	550	625	700	775	850	....
	....	3	4	5	6	7	8	9	10	....

Amount of X

5. Following the experimenter's guidance, trade Commodity *X* for *Y* according to the agreement. You give 4 pink cards (Commodity *X*) to Trader B and instead receives 7 white cards (Commodity *Y*) from Trader B.
6. Next please fill out your "Record Sheet." See Table 3.7. Write "−4" in the blank of "Amount of Change in *X*," "7" in "Amount of Change in *Y*," and "B" in "Person You Trade with" in the second row of "Trade Number 1" of the "Record Sheet."

Table 3.6 Agreement Example 1

Deal				
Trader that gave X	Amount of X	Trader that gave Y	Amount of Y	Ratio(=Y/X)
A	4	B	7	1.75

Table 3.7 Record Sheet Example 2

Record Sheet

Date (day/month/year): Time: ~

Trader Name: **A**

Your Name Tag ID: xxxxx Your Name xxxxx xxxxx

Period 1

Trade Number	Amount of Change in X	Amount of Change in Y	Person You Trade with	Amount of X	Amount of Y	Payoff
0				9	8	4905
1	-4	7	B	5	15	6302
2						

As a result of this trade, you now hold 5 units of Commodity *X* and 15 units of Commodity *Y*. According to the "Pilot Payoff Table" (Table 3.5), you will find that your payoff is "6302."

Write "5" in the blank of "Amount of *X*," "15" in "Amount of *Y*," and "6302" in "Payoff."

Then, the first trading is completed. Now, let us move on to the second trading.

7. Suppose that you negotiate with Trader K and agree "to trade your 2 units of commodity *Y* for Trader K's 3 units of commodity *X*."
8. Report the agreement to the experimenter. The experimenter will fill out the following table on the blackboard for you.

Table 3.8 Agreement Example 2

Deal				
Trader that gave X	Amount of X	Trader that gave Y	Amount of Y	Ratio(=Y/X)
A	4	B	7	1.75
G	5	H	4	0.8
L	12	F	14	1.17
K	3	A	2	0.67

Table 3.9 Record Sheet Example 3

Record Sheet

Date (day/month/year): Time: ~

Trader Name: **A**

Your Name Tag ID: xxxxx Your Name xxxxx xxxxx

Period 1

Trade Number	Amount of Change in X	Amount of Change in Y	Person You Trade with	Amount of X	Amount of Y	Payoff
0				9	8	4905
1	-4	7	B	5	15	6302
2	3	-2	K	8	13	6156

As shown in Table 3.8, the experimenter writes "K" in the blank of "Trader that gave *X*," "3" in "Amount of *X*," "A" in "Trader that gave *Y*," and "2" in "Amount of *Y*."

9. Following the experimenter's guidance, trade commodities according to the agreement. You will give 2 white cards (commodity *Y*) to Trader K, and in turn take 3 pink cards (commodity *X*).

10. Then, fill out your "Record Sheet" as follows. Look at the row of Trade 2 of Table 3.9. Write "3" in the blank of "Amount of Change in *X*," "−2" in "Amount of Change in *Y*," and "K" in "Person You Trade with."

As a result of this trading, you own 8 units of *X* and 13 units of *Y*. According to the "Pilot Payoff Table," your payoff is found to be 6156. So write "8" in the blank of "Amount of *X*," "13" in "Amount of *Y*," and "6156" in "Payoff."

Then, the second trading is completed.

Arrows in the "Pilot Payoff Table" indicate the changes in your payoff. In our experiment, you can make as many trades as you want within (12) minutes.

Now we will explain about your earnings. Your earnings depend on the *final payoff* that you earn in *one randomly selected period from the experiment.* This period is chosen by a random device after the experiment, so nobody can tell during the experiment. Your earnings are computed in the following way:

Your earnings = (your final payoff at one period randomly chosen) × (1.14) Ksh

For example, suppose that (1) Period 1 is randomly selected after the experiment, and (2) your final payoff at the end of Period 1 is (6156) as in Table 3.9. Then your earnings are (7018) Ksh because (6156) × (1.14) = (7018). We round off the decimal places.

That's all. If you have any questions, please raise your hand.

Now, let us start the experiment. First, look at your "Payoff Table." We will give you 5 min so that you can look over the table and understand it very well. During this period, please make sure that you completely understand all the rules.

If you have any questions, please let us know quietly. Our staff will come to help you. Please remember that *you are NOT allowed to communicate with any other person until the experiment starts.*

Meantime, our staff will distribute pink and/or white cards in an envelope. Notice that the trading period number is printed in each card. *You can only use cards with the same number as the numbers of the period going on.* For example, in Period 3, you can only use cards with "3."

Remember that you are NOT allowed to reveal the information regarding your "Payoff Table" or the information regarding your "Record Sheet" to any other person. If this happens, the experiment will be stopped at that point.

Appendix 3: Payoff Tables

Amount of Y \ Amount of X	0	1	2	3	4	5	6	7	8	9	10	11	12	13	14	15	16	17	18	19	20	21	22	23	24	25	26	27	28	29	30
30	670	675	681	686	691	697	702	1145	1424	1429	1434	1440	1445	1450	1456	1516	2068	2247	2247	2247	2247	2247	2247	2247	2247	2247	2247	2247	2247	2247	2247
29	670	675	681	686	691	697	702	1145	1424	1429	1434	1440	1445	1450	1456	1516	2068	2195	2195	2195	2195	2195	2195	2195	2195	2195	2195	2195	2195	2195	2195
28	670	675	681	686	691	697	702	1145	1424	1429	1434	1440	1445	1450	1456	1516	2068	2142	2142	2142	2142	2142	2142	2142	2142	2142	2142	2142	2142	2142	2142
27	670	675	681	686	691	697	702	1145	1424	1429	1434	1440	1445	1450	1456	1516	2068	2090	2090	2090	2090	2090	2090	2090	2090	2090	2090	2090	2090	2090	2090
26	670	675	681	686	691	697	702	1145	1424	1429	1434	1440	1445	1450	1456	1516	2037	2037	2037	2037	2037	2037	2037	2037	2037	2037	2037	2037	2037	2037	2037
25	670	675	681	686	691	697	702	1145	1424	1429	1434	1440	1445	1450	1456	1516	1984	1984	1984	1984	1984	1984	1984	1984	1984	1984	1984	1984	1984	1984	1984
24	670	675	681	686	691	697	702	1145	1424	1429	1434	1440	1445	1450	1456	1516	1932	1932	1932	1932	1932	1932	1932	1932	1932	1932	1932	1932	1932	1932	1932
23	670	675	681	686	691	697	702	1145	1424	1429	1434	1440	1445	1450	1456	1516	1879	1879	1879	1879	1879	1879	1879	1879	1879	1879	1879	1879	1879	1879	1879
22	670	675	681	686	691	697	702	1145	1424	1429	1434	1440	1445	1450	1456	1516	1827	1827	1827	1827	1827	1827	1827	1827	1827	1827	1827	1827	1827	1827	1827
21	670	675	681	686	691	697	702	1145	1424	1429	1434	1440	1445	1450	1456	1516	1774	1774	1774	1774	1774	1774	1774	1774	1774	1774	1774	1774	1774	1774	1774
20	670	675	681	686	691	697	702	1145	1424	1429	1434	1440	1445	1450	1456	1516	1722	1722	1722	1722	1722	1722	1722	1722	1722	1722	1722	1722	1722	1722	1722
19	670	675	681	686	691	697	702	1145	1424	1429	1434	1440	1445	1450	1456	1516	1669	1669	1669	1669	1669	1669	1669	1669	1669	1669	1669	1669	1669	1669	1669
18	670	675	681	686	691	697	702	1145	1424	1429	1434	1440	1445	1450	1456	1516	1616	1616	1616	1616	1616	1616	1616	1616	1616	1616	1616	1616	1616	1616	1616
17	670	675	681	686	691	697	702	1145	1424	1429	1434	1440	1445	1450	1456	1516	1564	1564	1564	1564	1564	1564	1564	1564	1564	1564	1564	1564	1564	1564	1564
16	670	675	681	686	691	697	702	1145	1424	1429	1434	1440	1445	1450	1456	1511	1511	1511	1511	1511	1511	1511	1511	1511	1511	1511	1511	1511	1511	1511	1511
15	670	675	681	686	691	697	702	1145	1424	1429	1434	1440	1445	1450	1456	1459	1459	1459	1459	1459	1459	1459	1459	1459	1459	1459	1459	1459	1459	1459	1459
14	670	675	681	686	691	697	702	1145	1406	1406	1406	1406	1406	1406	1406	1406	1406	1406	1406	1406	1406	1406	1406	1406	1406	1406	1406	1406	1406	1406	1406
13	670	675	681	686	691	697	702	1145	1354	1354	1354	1354	1354	1354	1354	1354	1354	1354	1354	1354	1354	1354	1354	1354	1354	1354	1354	1354	1354	1354	1354
12	670	675	681	686	691	697	702	1145	1301	1301	1301	1301	1301	1301	1301	1301	1301	1301	1301	1301	1301	1301	1301	1301	1301	1301	1301	1301	1301	1301	1301
11	670	675	681	686	691	697	702	1145	1248	1248	1248	1248	1248	1248	1248	1248	1248	1248	1248	1248	1248	1248	1248	1248	1248	1248	1248	1248	1248	1248	1248
10	670	675	681	686	691	697	702	1145	1196	1196	1196	1196	1196	1196	1196	1196	1196	1196	1196	1196	1196	1196	1196	1196	1196	1196	1196	1196	1196	1196	1196
9	670	675	681	686	691	697	702	1143	1143	1143	1143	1143	1143	1143	1143	1143	1143	1143	1143	1143	1143	1143	1143	1143	1143	1143	1143	1143	1143	1143	1143
8	670	675	681	686	691	697	702	1091	1091	1091	1091	1091	1091	1091	1091	1091	1091	1091	1091	1091	1091	1091	1091	1091	1091	1091	1091	1091	1091	1091	1091
7	670	675	681	686	691	697	702	1038	1038	1038	1038	1038	1038	1038	1038	1038	1038	1038	1038	1038	1038	1038	1038	1038	1038	1038	1038	1038	1038	1038	1038
6	670	675	681	686	691	697	702	985	985	985	985	985	985	985	985	985	985	985	985	985	985	985	985	985	985	985	985	985	985	985	985
5	670	675	681	686	691	697	702	933	933	933	933	933	933	933	933	933	933	933	933	933	933	933	933	933	933	933	933	933	933	933	933
4	670	675	681	686	691	697	702	880	880	880	880	880	880	880	880	880	880	880	880	880	880	880	880	880	880	880	880	880	880	880	880
3	670	675	681	686	691	697	702	828	828	828	828	828	828	828	828	828	828	828	828	828	828	828	828	828	828	828	828	828	828	828	828
2	670	675	681	686	691	697	702	775	775	775	775	775	775	775	775	775	775	775	775	775	775	775	775	775	775	775	775	775	775	775	775
1	670	675	681	686	691	697	702	723	723	723	723	723	723	723	723	723	723	723	723	723	723	723	723	723	723	723	723	723	723	723	723
0	670	670	670	670	670	670	670	670	670	670	670	670	670	670	670	670	670	670	670	670	670	670	670	670	670	670	670	670	670	670	670

A. Payoff table for the type 1 subjects

Amount of Y \ Amount of X	0	1	2	3	4	5	6	7	8	9	10	11	12	13	14	15	16	17	18	19	20	21	22	23	24	25	26	27	28	29	30
30	695	701	706	712	717	723	728	734	1103	1108	1114	1119	1125	1130	1136	1141	1147	1152	1465	1723	1728	1734	1739	1745	1750	1756	1761	1767	1772	1778	1783
29	695	701	706	712	717	723	728	734	1103	1108	1114	1119	1125	1130	1136	1141	1147	1152	1465	1723	1728	1734	1739	1745	1750	1756	1761	1767	1772	1778	1783
28	695	701	706	712	717	723	728	734	1103	1108	1114	1119	1125	1130	1136	1141	1147	1152	1465	1723	1728	1734	1739	1745	1750	1756	1761	1767	1772	1778	1783
27	695	701	706	712	717	723	728	734	1103	1108	1114	1119	1125	1130	1136	1141	1147	1152	1465	1723	1728	1734	1739	1745	1750	1756	1761	1767	1772	1778	1783
26	695	701	706	712	717	723	728	734	1103	1108	1114	1119	1125	1130	1136	1141	1147	1152	1465	1723	1728	1734	1739	1745	1750	1756	1761	1767	1772	1778	1783
25	695	701	706	712	717	723	728	734	1103	1108	1114	1119	1125	1130	1136	1141	1147	1152	1465	1723	1728	1734	1739	1745	1750	1756	1761	1767	1772	1778	1783
24	695	701	706	712	717	723	728	734	1103	1108	1114	1119	1125	1130	1136	1141	1147	1152	1465	1723	1728	1734	1739	1745	1750	1756	1761	1767	1772	1778	1783
23	695	701	706	712	717	723	728	734	1103	1108	1114	1119	1125	1130	1136	1141	1147	1152	1465	1723	1728	1734	1739	1745	1750	1756	1761	1767	1772	1778	1783
22	695	701	706	712	717	723	728	734	1103	1108	1114	1119	1125	1130	1136	1141	1147	1152	1465	1723	1728	1734	1739	1745	1750	1756	1761	1767	1772	1778	1783
21	695	701	706	712	717	723	728	734	1103	1108	1114	1119	1125	1130	1136	1141	1147	1152	1465	1723	1728	1734	1739	1745	1745	1745	1745	1745	1745	1745	1745
20	695	701	706	712	717	723	728	734	1103	1108	1114	1119	1125	1130	1136	1141	1147	1152	1465	1695	1695	1695	1695	1695	1695	1695	1695	1695	1695	1695	1695
19	695	701	706	712	717	723	728	734	1103	1108	1114	1119	1125	1130	1136	1141	1147	1152	1465	1645	1645	1645	1645	1645	1645	1645	1645	1645	1645	1645	1645
18	695	701	706	712	717	723	728	734	1103	1108	1114	1119	1125	1130	1136	1141	1147	1152	1465	1595	1595	1595	1595	1595	1595	1595	1595	1595	1595	1595	1595
17	695	701	706	712	717	723	728	734	1103	1108	1114	1119	1125	1130	1136	1141	1147	1152	1465	1545	1545	1545	1545	1545	1545	1545	1545	1545	1545	1545	1545
16	695	701	706	712	717	723	728	734	1103	1108	1114	1119	1125	1130	1136	1141	1147	1152	1465	1495	1495	1495	1495	1495	1495	1495	1495	1495	1495	1495	1495
15	695	701	706	712	717	723	728	734	1103	1108	1114	1119	1125	1130	1136	1141	1147	1152	1445	1445	1445	1445	1445	1445	1445	1445	1445	1445	1445	1445	1445
14	695	701	706	712	717	723	728	734	1103	1108	1114	1119	1125	1130	1136	1141	1147	1152	1395	1395	1395	1395	1395	1395	1395	1395	1395	1395	1395	1395	1395
13	695	701	706	712	717	723	728	734	1103	1108	1114	1119	1125	1130	1136	1141	1147	1152	1345	1345	1345	1345	1345	1345	1345	1345	1345	1345	1345	1345	1345
12	695	701	706	712	717	723	728	734	1103	1108	1114	1119	1125	1130	1136	1141	1147	1152	1295	1295	1295	1295	1295	1295	1295	1295	1295	1295	1295	1295	1295
11	695	701	706	712	717	723	728	734	1103	1108	1114	1119	1125	1130	1136	1141	1147	1152	1245	1245	1245	1245	1245	1245	1245	1245	1245	1245	1245	1245	1245
10	695	701	706	712	717	723	728	734	1103	1108	1114	1119	1125	1130	1136	1141	1147	1152	1195	1195	1195	1195	1195	1195	1195	1195	1195	1195	1195	1195	1195
9	695	701	706	712	717	723	728	734	1103	1108	1114	1119	1125	1130	1136	1141	1145	1145	1145	1145	1145	1145	1145	1145	1145	1145	1145	1145	1145	1145	1145
8	695	701	706	712	717	723	728	734	1095	1095	1095	1095	1095	1095	1095	1095	1095	1095	1095	1095	1095	1095	1095	1095	1095	1095	1095	1095	1095	1095	1095
7	695	701	706	712	717	723	728	734	1045	1045	1045	1045	1045	1045	1045	1045	1045	1045	1045	1045	1045	1045	1045	1045	1045	1045	1045	1045	1045	1045	1045
6	695	701	706	712	717	723	728	734	995	995	995	995	995	995	995	995	995	995	995	995	995	995	995	995	995	995	995	995	995	995	995
5	695	701	706	712	717	723	728	734	945	945	945	945	945	945	945	945	945	945	945	945	945	945	945	945	945	945	945	945	945	945	945
4	695	701	706	712	717	723	728	734	895	895	895	895	895	895	895	895	895	895	895	895	895	895	895	895	895	895	895	895	895	895	895
3	695	701	706	712	717	723	728	734	845	845	845	845	845	845	845	845	845	845	845	845	845	845	845	845	845	845	845	845	845	845	845
2	695	701	706	712	717	723	728	734	795	795	795	795	795	795	795	795	795	795	795	795	795	795	795	795	795	795	795	795	795	795	795
1	695	701	706	712	717	723	728	734	745	745	745	745	745	745	745	745	745	745	745	745	745	745	745	745	745	745	745	745	745	745	745
0	695	695	695	695	695	695	695	695	695	695	695	695	695	695	695	695	695	695	695	695	695	695	695	695	695	695	695	695	695	695	695

B. Payoff table for the type 2 subjects

References

Anderson CM, Plott CR, Shimomura K-I, Granat S (2004) Global instability in experimental general equilibrium: the scarf example. J Econ Theory 115:209–249

Bossaerts P, Plott CR (2008) From Market Jaws to the Newton method: the geometry of how a market can solve systems of equations. In: Plott CR, Smith VL (eds) Handbook of experimental economics results, vol 1. Elsevier B.V, Amsterdam

Chamberlin EH (1948) An experimental imperfect market. J Polit Econ 56:95–108

Crockett S, Oprea R, Plott CR (2010) Extreme Walrasian dynamics: the Gale example. Am Econ Rev 101:3196–3220

Gale D (1963) A note on global instability of competitive equilibrium. Nav Res Logist Q 10:81–87

Plott CR (2000) Market stability: backward-bending supply in a laboratory experimental market. Econ Inq 38:1–18

Plott CR, George G (1992) Marshallian vs. Walrasian stability in an experimental market. Econ J 102:437–460

Plott CR, Pogorelskiy K (2015) Call market experiments: efficiency and price discovery through multiple calls and emergent Newton adjustments. Social science working paper 1404. Division of the Humanities and Social Sciences, California Institute of Technology

Plott CR, Smith J (1999) Instability of equilibria in experimental markets: upward-sloping demands, externalities, and fad-like incentives. South Econ J 65:405–426

Sakai Y (2020) The Hicks-Morishima approach reconsidered: another look at the interdependence of several markets. The Hikone Ronso no. 424, pp 72–87

Scarf H (1960) Some examples of global instability of the competitive equilibrium. Int Econ Rev 1: 157–171

Shapley LS, Shubik M (1977) An example of a trading economy with three competitive equilibria. J Polit Econ 85:873–875

Shimomura K-I, Yamato T (2012) Impact of ethnicities on market outcome: results of market experiments in Kenya. In: Hino H, Lonsdale J, Ranis G, Stewart F (eds) Ethnic diversity and economic stability in Africa. Cambridge University Press, Cambridge, pp 286–313

Smith VL (1962) An experimental study of competitive market behavior. J Polit Econ 70:111–137

Chapter 4
Analysis of Spatial Economic System and Adaptive Transportation Policy for Regional Welfare Improvement

Daisuke Nakamura

Abstract There are potentially problematic regions in which the local population constantly decreases and the regional government must coordinate a sustainable local economy. These areas may be required to reorganise the spatial economic structure so that sufficient levels of economic environment and regional well-being are present. This paper introduces a location model that applies the established notion of agglomeration economies in rural areas. It shows that an adjustment of the spatial system of goods and services, by means of a rearrangement on the local transportation network, may keep the regional system above a minimum sufficient level to satisfy local demand and supply of goods and services. The change in the transportation network partly employs interregional cooperative coordination by utilising the spatial planning and policy.

Keywords Transportation policy · Regional welfare · Rural development · Spatial planning

JEL Classifications D62 · I31 · O18 · R12

4.1 Introduction

Many countries, particularly developed nations, have faced population declines and problems relating to population ageing. According to the methodological framework of the hierarchical central place system (Lösch 1944 [1954]), upper hierarchically ordered regions, such as the capital city, experience smaller declines in the local population and in the variety of economic activity compared with lower

The original version of the paper was presented at the 56th Annual Meeting of Japan Section of Regional Science Association International (JSRSAI) at Kurume in September 2019.

D. Nakamura (✉)
Faculty of Global Management, Chuo University, Tokyo, Japan
e-mail: dnakamura@tamacc.chuo-u.ac.jp

M. Kawano et al. (eds.), *Theory and History in Regional Perspective*, New Frontiers in Regional Science: Asian Perspectives 56,
https://doi.org/10.1007/978-981-16-6695-7_4

hierarchically ordered regions or rural areas. The worst-case scenario in lower hierarchically ordered regions or rural areas is that local market system—including publicly-operated services such as the local transportation system—does not work sufficiently because of a constant shortage in demand. A shrinking of the market structure may decrease a region's attractiveness, which can then cause further declines in the local population. To avoid such a negative sequence in the market system, sustainable regional economic management and policy may play important roles. These can be examined in location economic models because regional economic management and policy can partly include the optimisation of the spatial economic structure, which may improve the regional welfare level.

The welfare level might be measured or analysed by employing the conceptual framework introduced by Pigou (1932), who explicitly discussed the term 'social welfare' in economics, although its theoretical approach was not developed further following the introduction of Arrow's impossibility theorem (Arrow 1950; Arrow and Scitovsky 1969) and other critics of social welfare analysis. For instance, social welfare cannot be calculated by the sum of individual satisfaction or utility. Indeed, Pigou only focused on the measurable economic welfare by comparing different individuals. This approach of direct comparison was criticised by Robbins (1932).

Instead of using the cardinal utility function, the ordinal utility function was introduced later as the 'Pareto criterion' within the framework of 'efficiency'. Those are referred to as the 'compensation principle', 'compensation test', and 'welfare criterion'. In addition, Kaldor (1939) formulated a criterion by employing the utility possibility curve. However, Scitovsky (1941) found that this had a logical paradox, and Hicks (1939) stated an alternative criterion. Hicks' criterion itself contained another paradox, and both problems were solved by the Scitovsky criterion, although its methodological failure was found by Gorman (1955). Samuelson (1948) provided a different approach to avoid such issues, but a very limited condition was strictly given. The social welfare function was then formally introduced by Samuelson (1948) and Bergson (1938). However, this was not extended further by Arrow's (1950) impossibility theory. In addition, Little (1950) introduced a 'piecemeal approach' to conduct these evaluations. Later, further investigations were made by Sen (1970) and other successors.

The framework of welfare from the field of regional science was given by Isard (1975) in his discussion of 'conflict resolutions' based on location model analyses such as that by Isard (1956). While welfare studies have several barriers to further development, as indicated above, studies for measuring welfare level are important and some expansional attempts should be made using alternative scenarios. In this paper, we hypothesised that it is better to have an accessible market so that a greater variety of goods and services are available, which benefits both the individual and society. Capello (2015) noted that the development of a transportation network may not only bring about local economic growth but also increase economic competition because the barrier to protect is lower. The threat can be more serious if external regions have much greater economic strength. We concern interregional transportation. In this model, all regions have equally weak economic forces, which mean that none of them have any immediate problem regarding the threat of economic competition. Hence, reorganising the local transportation system may improve the regional welfare in lower hierarchically ordered regions or rural areas.

This paper initially introduces a simple location model that employs the notion of social welfare in a spatial term. In addition, regional agglomeration economies, which are 'external to the firm and the industry but internal to the region,' are considered (see Nakamura 2018a). These comprise an extensive framework of conventional agglomeration economies, which were classified by Parr (2002), and might share some similarities with the notion of 'regional externalities' in Parr (2015). The examination here analyses location forces such as the hierarchical central place system and the cost of transportation partly employing Weber's (1909 [1928]) location triangle model, which may work with above stated economic factors. We address an optimal regional system from the standpoint of location economics. Here, the optimal regional system implies that the local population is large enough and economic activity is sufficiently varied with cooperative behaviour with neighbouring regions ensuring an effective local public transportation policy.

4.2 Regional Economic Model

In this section, a regional economic model is examined regarding a representative household's utility maximisation under a given budget constraint, as indicated in Eqs. (4.1) and (4.2).

$$\max \quad U = U(x, A), \tag{4.1}$$

$$\text{s.t.} \quad M = p(t_x, d_x)x + \rho(t_A, d_A)A, \tag{4.2}$$

where this individual's utility level U is determined by the quantity demanded of composite good x ($x \geq 0$) with its price p, a unit transportation rate, t_x ($0 \leq t_x \leq 1$), and distance to access d_x ($d_x \geq 0$). In addition, this also includes an indicator of her living environment, denoted as A ($A \geq 0$) with a unit transportation rate, t_A ($0 \leq t_A \leq 1$), and distance to access d_A ($d_A \geq 0$). That is, A is related to non-market intangible elements such as access to clean air, unpolluted water, quiet spaces, and so on, and has the implicit price ($\rho \geq 0$). Here, we suppose that both composite good and non-market intangible elements are available from other regions and that every individual travels to other regions to receive composite good and non-market intangible elements, so the transportation rate can be denoted as a single framework. Hence,

$$t_x = t_A = \hat{t}. \tag{4.3}$$

Note that the more efficient transportation becomes, the closer the value to 1. In other words, the parameter $\hat{t}$ approaches 1 as the physical accessibility becomes increasingly well-coordinated.

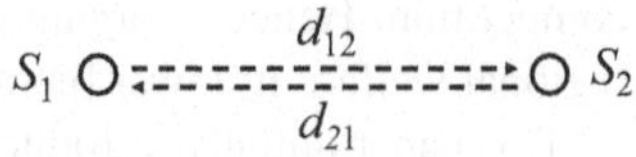

Fig. 4.1 Two-region model and its transportation network

From Eqs. (4.1) and (4.2), it is clear that less efficient transportation causes a much tighter budget constraint in Eq. (4.2), which lowers the utility level in Eq. (4.1). Here, we may assume that less efficient transportation reduces convenient access to the destination or objective of the economic activity. For instance, a lower operation frequency of public transportation is one example. The operation frequency of public transportation depends on the level of demand for public transportation. Demand relies on unit transportation cost, which includes not only monetary expenses (that is, the fare) but also time taken and the level of inconvenience to use public transportation.

Figure 4.1 illustrates a simple transportation network model and shows a transportation route between two regions, S_1 and S_2. Here, there are two separate regions, which have centres S_1 and S_2, respectively. The two regions are assumed to be similar in terms of population and variety of economic activity and the local transportation operator may earn insufficient profit because of a shortage of demand. The physical distance between each centre of two cities is $d_{12}(=d_{21})$.

If the local population decreases, each region has another problem. Because of the decrease in the quantity demanded of local goods and services, serving various goods and services can be difficult. This may cause a shrinking of the market structure, which would decrease a region's attractiveness and cause further declines in the local population because the market's 'love of variety' cannot be met (c.f., Dixit and Stiglitz 1977; Ethier 1982). Lower regional welfare would further accelerate decline of the local population, and such an event in one area may cause a negative sequence in the regional market system.

In this way, it can be difficult to organise a self-sufficient market system in regions S_1 and S_2. If these regions have no pre-coordinated cooperation to distribute goods and services, various goods and services may be limited to the local economic scale within S_1 or S_2. In other words, it is possible to apply the framework of comparative advantage (or interregional trade) by means of pre-coordinated coordination between the two regions. In that case, for households, fare and frequency of transportation are important factors in location theory. As long as the number of individuals travelling to other regions is limited because of high transportation costs, public transportation demand is kept at a minimum. If costs decrease, citizens can access other regions and the utility level recovers because of their 'love of variety'. In the following section, several hypothetical scenarios are examined to demonstrate regional spatial arrangements that may enhance the efficiency of the local transportation system.

4.3 Hypothetical Analysis

We have shown that the decision on the local transportation operation frequency may depend on a combination of fare, quantity demand, and operation costs. Hence, it is necessary to examine the representative transportation operator's economic behaviour. As already argued, the worst-case scenario in lower hierarchically ordered regions or rural areas is that the local transportation system does not work sufficiently because of a constant shortage in demand. Now, we examine how transportation operators may make more frequent services available in less populated areas. Here, physical transportation facilities such as road infrastructure have already been established for reasons of simplicity.

We have focused our firm analysis on the local transportation operator, which maximises profit π according to the following expressions.

$$\max \quad \pi = \tau(\hat{t})y_{ij}(d_{ij}) - cz_{ij} \tag{4.4}$$

$$\text{s.t.} y_{ij} = f(z_{ij}) \tag{4.5}$$

In Eq. (4.4), τ ($\tau \geq 0$) = the transportation fare to passengers, y_{ij} ($y_{ij} \geq 0$) = the number of passengers, travelling from region i to region j. This may be affected by a physical distance between two regions. In addition, c ($c \geq 0$) = the unit cost of operation under zero marginal cost condition for reasons of simplicity, and z_{ij} ($z_{ij} \geq 0$) = the quantity supplied of transportation service (i.e., frequency of operation) between two regions. In addition, the number of passengers y_i depends on the parameter z_{ij} as expressed in Eq. (4.5).

There is also a representative economic agent: private firms that produce goods and services. Their profit-maximising economic behaviour, particularly location decision-making, would affect welfare level of regions. Their location factors include location costs for rent, wages, capital, transportation on assembly, and distribution. Because the analysis of this paper mainly focuses on regional transportation, these factors are discussed in Sect. 4.4 as extensive notes.

It is apparent that an effective adjustment of the local transportation system plays an important role for a sustainable regional economy, while the system relies on economic behaviour of local households and transportation operators with several given physical constraints. This section now examines regional transportation policy within the framework of central place theory under a hierarchical spatial structure. There are three different types of hypothetical scenarios, Cases 1–3.

***Case 1*: Two Centres of Equivalent Lower Hierarchical Order**

In the first scenario, there are two separate regions (as shown in Fig. 4.2). As the regional population decreases, the hierarchical order of the urban system decreases

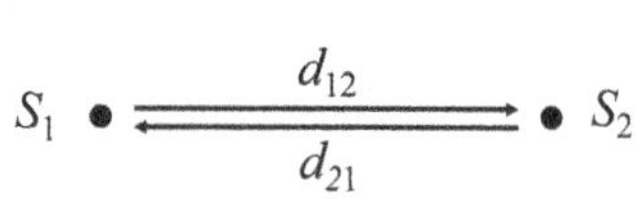

Fig. 4.2 Two-region scenario

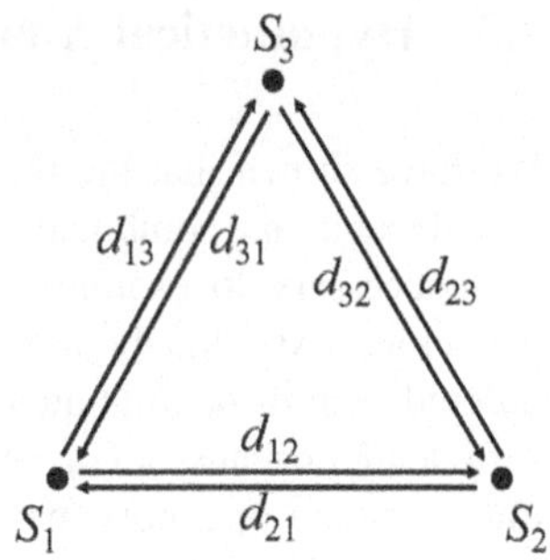

Fig. 4.3 Three-region scenario

from the original hierarchical level. Each region is then denoted in Fig. 4.2 as a small dot; the original spatial configuration in Fig. 4.1 was shown using circles (a higher hierarchical order than the small dot). Here, these two regions are assumed to be similar in terms of population and variety of economic activity, but some available goods and services and types of job may be different.

By using Eq. (4.4), the local transportation system between S_1 and S_2 can be expressed as Eq. (4.6).

$$\pi = 2\tau(y_{12} + y_{21}) - 2cz_{12} \tag{4.6}$$

The above expression shows a simplified form of the profit of the local transportation operator under a round-trip (denoted by the multiplication by 2 in the equation). Hence, the regional system and its transportation may be sustainable if

$$\tau \geq c\frac{z_{12}}{y_{12} + y_{21}}. \tag{4.7}$$

***Case 2*: Three-Region Scenario**

If the existing transportation system cannot sustain a sufficient operation frequency to satisfy local demand, an alternative transportation network must be coordinated. One alternative is illustrated in Fig. 4.3; this system involves an additional neighbouring region, S_3. Now, there are three regions and the demand for public transportation increases because of the emergence of this additional region.

The second case illustrates a situation in which all three centres are of an equivalent hierarchical order, can be established if

$$\pi = 4\tau(y_{12} + y_{23} + y_{31}) - 2c(z_{12} + z_{23} + z_{31}) \tag{4.8}$$

The above expression shows a simplified form of the local transportation operator's profit under a round-trip for two different directions (therefore, some parts are multiplied by 4 in the equation). Hence, the regional system and its transportation may be sustainable if

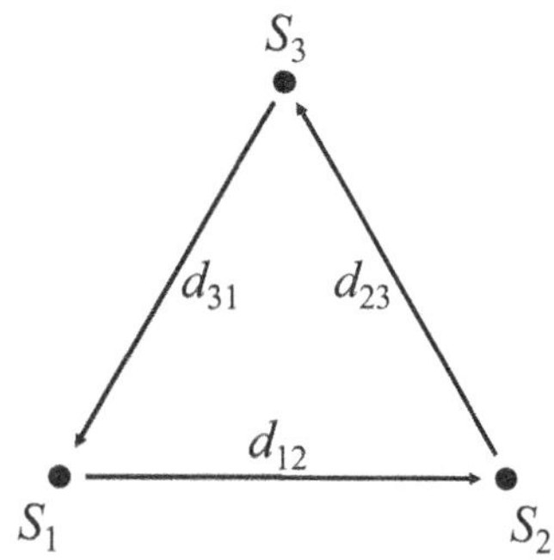

Fig. 4.4 Case with a one-way transportation network

$$\tau \geq \frac{1}{2}c\frac{z_{12}+z_{23}+z_{31}}{y_{12}+y_{23}+y_{31}}. \tag{4.9}$$

***Case 3*: Three-Region One-Way Network**

The final case illustrates a situation in which the transportation network can be integrated into a one-way structure, as depicted in Fig. 4.4 if

$$\begin{aligned}\pi &= \tau(y_{12}+y_{23}+y_{31}) + \tau(y_{23}+y_{12}+y_{31}) + \tau(y_{31}+y_{12}+y_{23}) \\ &\quad - c(z_{12}+z_{23}+z_{31}) \\ &= 3\tau(y_{12}+y_{23}+y_{31}) - c(z_{12}+z_{23}+z_{31}).\end{aligned} \tag{4.10}$$

Hence, the regional system and its transportation may be sustainable if

$$\tau \geq \frac{1}{3}c\frac{z_{12}+z_{23}+z_{31}}{y_{12}+y_{23}+y_{31}}. \tag{4.11}$$

Note that each of these listed scenarios is valid within neighbouring regions. In other words, it may not be applicable between non-neighbouring or remote areas because of the condition $y_{ij} = y_{ij}(d_{ij})$ and $\frac{\partial y_{ij}}{\partial d_{ij}} < 0$. Also, each scenario requires interregional coordination and negotiation among S_1, S_2, and S_3. A similar argument with more details can be found in Nakamura (2018b). The following section discusses the feasibility of interregional cooperative coordination in real-world cases.

4.4 Further Research

We have shown that interregional coordination and negotiation are essential for sustainable regional economic growth in rural areas with lower populations. However, straightforward interregional cooperative coordination may not be feasible because of the extra short-term cost burden to every economic agent. As described by Nakamura (2018b), additional incentives to motivate cooperation would be needed. This has also been argued by Isard (1975) in his comments on conflict resolution. Our analysis should now be expanded to solve the following socio-economic problem. When the regional population decreases, accessibility to goods and services diminishes as the transportation supply exceeds its demand level. In addition, an ageing society limits the availability of public finance, which means that subsidiary payments to local transportation could be further restricted. These restrictions would leave more people outside the region and local retailers and service providers would gradually exit the local market. Such vicious circles would diminish the social welfare level in those areas.

To avoid a negative sequence in the market system, restructuring the public transportation system may enable the construction of a well-coordinated interregional transportation network. An advanced system could feasibly enable economic agents to merge their locations into a single representative site such as a local retail store or service centre. As long as these locations are easily accessible, sustainable economic growth in rural areas is possible. Although the physical scale or area has not been precisely defined here, this concept is fundamental to regional agglomeration economies. These can be methodologically connected with the 'regional externalities' described by Parr (2015) by means of arguing for regional development in Parr (1970).

Although the interregional cooperative coordination increases the cost burden of each economic agent in the area in the short term, a proper spatial policy will improve the level of social welfare in the long term. For instance, first, a secured availability of goods and services maintains the region's attractiveness at a sufficient level. Second, less heavy dependence on private vehicles decreases excess income expenses and other costs including traffic congestion, accidents, and environmental damage. These decreases can improve the local community's safety and security. As a wider regional concept may be applicable, but the real-world situation would likely result in less cooperative behaviour, policy makers should clearly state the long-term advantages. It would be ideal if spatial social welfare function can describe these advantages under careful procedure of formalisations.

While this paper provides a theoretical demonstration of the regional transportation system, empirical analysis should be applied with relevant datasets to fit each hypothetical framework. This can be especially useful to examine rural regions. Another possibility to expand the framework of this paper is to employ the argument of 'overall Pareto optimality'. This may include a discussion of the judgement of whether public transportation should become a public service, for instance. Such an expansion can involve the taxation policy. These examinations are beyond the scope of this paper but will be necessary to investigate elsewhere.

4.5 Concluding Comments

This paper has studied regions in which the local population and the variety of economic activities decrease and demonstrated how a region can recover its attractiveness by focusing on a regional transportation policy. The argument partly involved regional externalities to determine the optimal level of economic activity associated with social welfare in spatial terms. The analysis showed that effective regional transportation management and reorganisation may enable households to attain much higher utility in an aggregate term, which would increase regional social welfare to a sufficient level to sustain the regional economic system. In addition, this paper has stressed the necessity and importance of interregional cooperative coordination and warned that such an arrangement may face difficulties without well-organised interregional negotiation and management.

References

Arrow KJ (1950) A difficulty in the concept of social welfare. J Polit Econ 58:328–346
Arrow KJ, Scitovsky T (1969) Readings in welfare economics. Richard D. Irwin, Northampton
Bergson A (1938) A reformulation of certain aspects of welfare economics. Q J Econ 52 (2):310–334
Capello R (2015) Regional economics, 2nd edn. Routledge, London
Dixit AK, Stiglitz JE (1977) Monopolistic competition and optimum product diversity. Am Econ Rev 67:297–308
Ethier WJ (1982) National and international returns to scale in the modern theory of international trade. Am Econ Rev 72:389–405
Gorman WM (1955) The intransitivity of certain criteria used in welfare economics. Oxford Economic Papers, New Series 7:25–35
Hicks JR (1939) Value and capital. Oxford University Press, Oxford
Isard W (1956) Location and space-economy. MIT, Cambridge
Isard W (1975) Introduction to regional science. Prentice-Hall, Englewood Cliffs
Kaldor N (1939) Welfare propositions of economics and interpersonal comparisons of utility. Econ J 49:549–552
Little IMD (1950) A critique of welfare economics. Oxford University Press, Oxford
Lösch A (1944 [1954]) Die Raümliche Ordnung der Wirtschaft, 2nd edn. Fischer, Jena. English translation by W. H. Woglom and W. F. Stolper, The Economics of Location, Yale University Press, New Haven
Nakamura D (2018a) Analysis on firm behavior and individual's utility maximization through regional agglomeration economies. In: Hosoe M, Kim ILT, Yabuta M, Lee W (eds) Applied analysis of growth, trade, and public policy. Singapore, Springer Nature
Nakamura D (2018b) Analysis of a sustainable rural economic system for wider-areal regional management. Conference Paper for the Special Academic Session of the Regional Science Academy (TRSA) at the 55th Annual Meeting of Japan Association of Regional Science Association International in October 2018 at Sapporo
Parr JB (1970) Regional development. In: Bacon P (ed) Focus on geography. National Council for the Social Studies, Washington, DC
Parr JB (2002) Missing elements in the analysis of agglomeration economies. Int Reg Sci Rev 25: 151–168

Parr JB (2015) The city and the region as contrasts in spatial organization. Ann Reg Sci 54:797–817
Pigou AC (1932) The economics of welfare, 4th edn. Palgrave Macmillan, Hampshire
Robbins L (1932) An essay on the nature and significance of economics science. Macmillan, Toronto
Samuelson PA (1948) Theory in terms of revealed preference. Economica 15:243–253
Scitovsky T (1941) A note on welfare propositions in economics. Rev Econ Stud 9:77–88
Weber A (1909 [1928]) Über den Standort der Industrien. Tübingen, Mohr. English version: Weber A (1928) Alfred Weber's Theory of the location of industries (trans: Friedrich CJ). University of Chicago Press, Chicago

Chapter 5
Effects of Nominating an Area as the Candidate Place of a New NIMBY Facility: A Consideration

Sen Eguchi

Abstract Generally, when a local government releases the construction plan for a "not in my backyard" (NIMBY) facility to the public, they nominate only one area as the candidate area of the proposed facility and fail to mention other areas that would benefit from it. This study theoretically explores the implications of releasing the NIMBY facility's construction plan to the public in this manner, especially whether the candidate area's nomination compels its residents to accept the facility. Our analysis shows that, if a candidate area's nomination induces the public to perceive that there is no alternative to building the facility in the nominated area, the nomination requires residents in the nominated area to approve the facility. On the other hand, residents in the nominated area would not be content to accept the facility if it came under such public perception, excluding the possibility of the facility being built in other areas. They would hope for such public perceptions to be corrected and the siting to be reconsidered without excluding other possibilities. Our analysis also investigates the conditions under which the abovementioned reactions occur, which do not necessarily oppose the proposed facility, but hope for a site to be selected without the exclusion of any possible sites. Our analysis suggests that residents in the candidate area know (or can specify) the residents in the non-nominated areas are crucially important for the emergence of such reactions.

Keywords NIMBY conflict · Prisoners' dilemma · Siting decision · Candidate area · Nomination

S. Eguchi (✉)
Faculty of Economics, Niigata Sangyo University, Niigata, Japan
e-mail: eguchi@econ.nsu.ac.jp

M. Kawano et al. (eds.), *Theory and History in Regional Perspective*, New Frontiers in Regional Science: Asian Perspectives 56,
https://doi.org/10.1007/978-981-16-6695-7_5

5.1 Introduction

A region or town usually consists of mutually distinctive, heterogeneous areas, such as "uptown" and "downtown" or "East" and "West" of a railroad station. In addition, it is common to produce local public goods/services for the residents of such a region in a facility constructed in one of these distinctive areas within the region. Although the region's residents consume local public goods/services produced at the facility equally, only the residents around the facility experience some production costs, especially environmental costs such as a noisy environment around the facility. Examples of such facilities include incinerators, public schools, and bus stops. Residents often agree on the necessity of a facility but oppose its construction in the area in which they reside, making siting the facility difficult. This study addresses such "not in my backyard" (NIMBY) responses and/or conflicts among residents.[1]

Looking closely at the real NIMBY conflicts, governments often release NIMBY facility construction plans by nominating one candidate area, but seldom mention the other areas, each of which would also benefit from the facilities.[2] Once nominated as the candidate area, residents in that area are required to express their opinions and/or decisions, either accepting or opposing and if they oppose, this is regarded as the emergence of a NIMBY conflict. The public, including researchers, often believe that there is no alternative than to build the facility in the nominated area, highlighting its focus on the residents in the candidate area.[3] Consequently, the latter are often criticized as "selfish" if they refuse the construction plan, making it difficult for residents to oppose it.

The purpose of this study is to theoretically investigate whether an area's nomination as the candidate area has the abovementioned effect of enforcing acceptance on its residents. In doing so, we consider a region's model comprising two potential candidate areas for a new NIMBY facility. In the model, when selecting the facility's site, residents (one in each area, Residents 1 and 2) express their opinions (welcoming or opposing the facility). The facility's site is determined only when the two residents agree (one resident "opposes" and the other "welcomes" the facility). Additionally, we suppose that there is a third party (player 3) residing outside the

[1] Facilities generating NIMBY conflicts are sometimes called "NIMBY facilities," and we use this term in this study.

[2] For example, as described in Shimizu (1999) and Siniawer (2018), in 1966, before the "war on garbage" in Tokyo in the 1970s, the Tokyo metropolitan government released a plan for constructing an incinerator to the residents in the Suginami ward in Takaido district in Suginami, but the government did not mention (the names of) other districts in Suginami that would also benefits from the incinerator in Takaido.

[3] The responses of the Takaido residents in Suginami ward in 1966 are reported in several case studies and/or articles (e.g., Shimizu (1999) and Siniawer (2018)), but the responses and/or attitudes of the residents in other districts in Suginami at that time are not reported. The same is true for many case studies on NIMBY analyzing other cases, including those referred in Eguchi (2020) (e.g., Flynn (2011), Guidotti and Abercrombie (2008), Sakurai (2010), Shimizu (1999, 2002), Zheng and Liu (2018)).

region who is not familiar with the region but would regard NIMBY as what solely generated by the residents' attitudes in the candidate area toward the facility and, hence, would criticize the resident in the candidate area when NIMBY conflicts arise.

In this environment, the government releases the NIMBY facility construction plan, nominating an area as the candidate area. We suppose that nomination provides the public (player 3), a wrong perception that the facility has no other possibility than to be built in the nominated area, and if the resident in the candidate area chooses "oppose," it is criticized by player 3, based on the wrong perception, to be "selfish." Our analysis shows that in such an environment, the nomination of either area as the candidate area of a NIMBY facility, followed by player 3's tendency to criticize the residents in the candidate area if the residents oppose, has effects of enforcing the resident in the nominated area to accept the facility, which may explain why governments often release construction plans by nominating candidate areas.

However, the residents in the nominated area will be dissatisfied if the facility is decided to be built in the nominated area, excluding the possibility it being built in any other area from site consideration. The residents in the nominated area would hope for such public perception to be corrected, and the siting to be reconsidered, with other possibilities also taken into account from the beginning. Although the residents in candidate areas in real NIMBY conflicts often insist angrily that the site should be reconsidered from the beginning,[4] in our view, such responses do not simply mean opposition/hatred toward the proposed facility, but hope for the abovementioned public perception to be corrected and the site to be reconsidered without excluding any possibilities. Our analysis shows that such responses would occur when the resident in the candidate area knows (or can search and specify) the particular resident in the non-nominated area. Such a result might explain why governments seldom mention the other areas that benefit from the facility when releasing construction plans while nominating the candidate area, although it is not an appropriate way of releasing the construction plan according to our view.

As referred to in Eguchi (2020), there are several studies on NIMBY from a theoretical viewpoint.[5] However, no research has investigated the possible influences/effects of nominating an area as the candidate area of a NIMBY facility on the choices and responses of the residents in the nominated area.

[4]The case of the Takaido residents in Suginami ward reported in Shimizu (1999) would be an example.

[5]For example, Burningham et al. (2006), and Suzuki (2011) provided useful surveys for discussions and research on NIMBY conflicts. Eguchi (2020) also refers to Fredriksson (2000), Feinerman et al. (2004), and Bellettini and Kempf (2013) investigating the NIMBY possibility to be efficiently resolved through appropriately designed processes or plausible political processes, Kunreuther and Kleindorfer (1986) and Mitchel and Carson (1986) seeking to find decentralized decision-mechanisms that would lead to the agreement, Frey et al. 1996, Frey and Oberholzer-Gee (1997), and Besfamille and Lozachmeur (2010) investing NIMBY from different viewpoints.

		Resident 2	
		oppose	welcome
Resident 1	oppose	(b_1 , b_2)	(FB_1 , sb_2)
	welcome	(sb_1 , FB_2)	(a_1 , a_2)

Fig. 5.1 Payoff matrix

Section 5.2 briefly introduces the analysis by Eguchi (2020), and Sect. 5.3 presents the main analyses. Finally, Sect. 5.4 concludes the study.

5.2 The Model and Analysis of Eguchi (2020)

Figure 5.1, a two-person normal form game, exhibits the model of a region consisting of two areas, outlined in Sect. 5.1 above: the players are residents 1 and 2, with either "welcome" or "oppose" strategies for both residents.[6] In Fig. 5.1, if one resident chooses "oppose" and the other "welcome," the facility is built in the latter's area, while the former obtains the payoff denoted FB_i $(i = 1, 2)$, the first-best utility attainable in area i, whereas the other resident obtains $sb_j \equiv SB_j - ENV_j$, where SB_j $(j = 1 \; or \; 2, j \neq i)$, $SB_j < FB_j$ is the second-best utility of living in area j with the NIMBY facility. ENV_j $(j = 1, 2)$ is the envy disutility and/or fear of risk.[7] The payoffs b_i $(i = 1, 2)$ are those under the battling situation when both residents "oppose" the facility, and a_i $(i = 1, 2)$ are those under the "peaceful competition" of both residents welcoming (accepting) the facility, although this is not expected to happen in the real world. This is the game into which the residents are supposed to be

[6] Figure 5.1 of this study is the same as that of Eguchi (2020), with the permission of the Japanese Section of Regional Science Association International, 2020.

[7] From the economics viewpoint of uncertainty, Sakai (2015) and Sakai (2019) provide explanations of how residents would feel and react when confronted with a nuclear power generation plant, one of the largest sources of risks, including possible unknown risks, which they would have to live with every day.

thrown into, when the government releases its intention to construct a NIMBY facility, in Eguchi (2020).

Figure 5.1 presents two notable points. First, Fig. 5.1 provides a perspective on the NIMBY conflicts. For the agreement of one resident "opposes" and the other "welcomes" the facility to be achieved voluntarily by the residents, the game must have at least one Nash equilibrium in the pure strategy of one agent "accept" and the other "oppose." Whether the games have such Nash equilibria depends on the relative positions of b_i and a_i concerning FB_i and sb_i, where $sb_i < FB_i$. Second, the facility brings the residents the payoff FB_i if it is built in the opposite area and sb_i if it is built in its area, where $sb_i < FB_i$. This means that either location/result is "favorable for one agent but less favorable for the other," the same feature as the battle of sexes and the war of attrition.

5.2.1 *Possible Causes and Results*

Eguchi (2020) argued that FB_i, sb_i, b_i, and a_i in Fig. 5.1 satisfy the relations $sb_i < FB_i$ and $b_i < a_i < FB_i$, but the relationship between $\{b_i, a_i\}$ and sb_i should be allowed to vary among the cases. Accordingly, each resident can plausibly be in either of the following two cases:

$$\text{Case A}: sb_i < b_i < a_i < FB_i,$$

$$\text{Case B}: b_i < sb_i < a_i < FB_i.$$

Thus, Fig. 5.1 can take only three possible cases: <A-A> (both residents in Case A) and <B-B> and <A-B> (one resident in Case A and the other in Case B). Eguchi (2020) analyzed these three cases and showed that the <A-A> case is the Prisoner's Dilemma, in which NIMBY conflicts of both residents choosing "oppose" will inevitably occur,[8] whereas the <B-B> case is the War of Attrition, in which different kinds of NIMBY conflict, the conflicts over the choice of the pure strategy Nash equilibrium in the War of Attrition, may occur.[9] Contrastingly, in the asymmetric <A-B> case, the game has a unique pure strategy Nash equilibrium of one agent "accept," and the other "oppose," and hence, NIMBY conflicts are unlikely to occur.

---

[8]For example, the facility whose site being decided later by coin tossing if both residents oppose, belong to <A-A>, where the value of b_i is, if the residents are risk-neutral, the average of FB_i and sb_i, which is greater than sb_i, and both residents would choose "oppose."

[9]The games belonging to <B-B> have a mixed strategy Nash equilibrium in which residents choose "oppose" with the probability $p_i = (-FB_j + a_j)/(a_j + b_j - FB_j - sb_j)$ $(i,j = 1 \text{ or } 2, j \neq i)$. When a NIMBY conflict, which is the conflict over the choice of a Nash equilibrium, occurs in a situation belonging to <B-B>, the residents might engage in this mixed strategy equilibrium, and the conflicting situation of both choosing "oppose" might follow with probability $p_1 p_2$.

5.3 When Announcing a Construction Plan with a Candidate Area for the Facility

In this section, we modify the model in Sect. 5.2 and consider a different situation. We suppose that there is another player in the game, player 3 resides outside the region. We suppose that the payoff of player 3 is unaffected by the facility itself or by the final facility site, but it is allowed (by the government) not only to pay attention to the facility's siting decision but also to affect the residents' payoff in the manner specified below.[10]

Under this setting, suppose that the government wanting to build a new NIMBY facility that brings the <A-A> case of the Prisoner's Dilemma of Fig. 5.1[11] releases the construction plan to both residents and player 3, with nominating area 2 as the facility's candidate area, encouraging the residents to choose the pure strategy profile of "oppose" for resident 1 and "welcome" for resident 2. We suppose that both residents 1 and 2 know that both areas 1 and 2 are potential candidate areas for the new NIMBY facility, but player 3 does not. Thus, residents 1 and 2 know that the true game that should be played to determine the facility's site is shown in Fig. 5.1. We suppose that the site for the facility is again determined only when the two players reach an agreement (one resident "opposes" and the other "welcomes" the facility).

5.3.1 *The Case of Common Knowledge*

First, we suppose that residents 1 and 2 are common knowledge, known by all players who they are, although player 3 is anonymous (i.e., two residents and the government do not know who it is). Here, once nominated as a candidate area, resident 2 is put in a position to be asked to answer either to "accept" or "oppose" the facility. However, resident 1 chooses "oppose" because it is not only the dominant strategy for him/her but also the strategy assigned to choose by the government in the construction plan. Thus, resident 1 did not need to negotiate the facility siting with resident 2. The situation is that resident 2 is forced to engage in the "one-player game" of the upper half of Fig. 5.1, where resident 1 is already choosing "oppose" in Fig. 5.1 without being noticed by player 3, although resident 2 knows it.

Perception of the Game by Player 3: We suppose that outside the region, player 3, who is not familiar with the region, perceives the situation incorrectly. As the

[10] Not only the media but also scholars in social science (for example, Feldman and Turner (2010) in the field of environmental philosophy), who are paying their attention to the NIMBY conflicts and often expressing their opinions about the conflicts, would correspond to player 3 in our model.

[11] In Sect. 5.2, we observed that in Eguchi (2020)'s framework, the typical NIMBY conflict of every resident opposes the facility is a phenomenon that occurs in the <A-A> case of the Prisoner's Dilemma. Thus, we focus on the <A-A> case in the rest of this study.

government nominated area 2 as the candidate place, player 3 perceives that whether the facility is built depends on resident 2, and in unison, does not notice resident 1 who chooses "oppose" from the strategy set {"welcome," "oppose"} secretly within the government's construction plan. Thus, the game perceived by player 3 is the "one-player game" of the upper half of Fig. 5.1 by resident 2, where player 3 can observe payoffs b_1, b_2, FB_1, and sb_2.

In addition, player 3, paying attention to how resident 2 responds, sometimes criticizes resident 2 based on the upper half of Fig. 5.1, its perception of the situation, affecting the payoffs of resident 2 as follows: if resident 2 choose "oppose," the government cannot build the facility in area 2, interpreted by player 3 as the emergence of a NIMBY arose by resident 2. In this case, player 3 criticizes resident 2, and resident 2 obtains the payoff $\{b_2 - \text{SELFISH}_2\}$ instead of b_2 in the case of Fig. 5.1, where SELFISH_2 is the fatigue of being criticized as "selfish" by player 3.[12] However, if resident 2 chooses "welcome," the facility is built without conflict. Here, player 3 would not criticize resident 2. However, the facility is built in area 2, and resident 2 obtains a payoff sb_2, like that obtained in Fig. 5.1.

To summarize the interaction described above, the true situation surrounding the facility is described in Fig. 5.1 of the Prisoner's Dilemma. Both residents 1 and 2 were aware of it. However, once the government nominates area 2 as the candidate area, resident 1 is allowed to choose "oppose" without notice from player 3. Resident 1 is not required to negotiate the site with resident 2 because, in its plan, the government considers area 2 as the candidate place. As resident 1 is already choosing "oppose," resident 2 is forced to engage in a "one-player game" in the upper half of Fig. 5.1. However, player 3 perceives the situation as the "one-player game" of the upper half of Fig. 5.1, where resident 1 can play no role as to the construction, and whether the facility is built or not depends solely on how resident 2 decides. Thus, the game that resident 2 is forced to engage in coincides with that perceived by player 3, although player 3 does not notice that player 1 is choosing "oppose." Player 3 may criticize resident 2 based on its perception of the situation, modifying the payoffs of Fig. 5.1 into those of Fig. 5.2. Resident 2 knows who resident 1 is. Resultantly, resident 2 is forced to engage in a "one-player" game of the upper half of Fig. 5.2.

The Equilibrium: In the "one-player game" of the upper half of Fig. 5.2, if $\{b_2 - \text{SELFISH}_2\} > sb_2$, resident 2 will choose "oppose," regarded as the NIMBY emergence. However, resident 2 will choose "welcome" if $\{b_2 - \text{SELFISH}_2\} < sb_2$. In the latter case, player 2 will choose "welcome" voluntarily in the game of the upper half of Fig. 5.2 because of the effect of SELFISH_2, possible criticisms from player 3 expressed based on the situation's perception. Thus, nominating area 2 as the candidate area of the facility has the effect of enforcing resident 2 in the nominated area to accept the facility, under the criticism based on the wrong

[12] In the real world, the residents under NIMBY conflict are criticized by the public, sometimes through the media. However, we do not specify the way player 3 criticize resident 2.

		Resident 2	
		oppose	welcome
Resident 1	oppose	$(b_1, b_2 - \text{SELFISH}_2)$	(FB_1, sb_2)
	welcome	(sb_1, FB_2)	(a_1, a_2)

Fig. 5.2 The modified payoff matrix

perception of the situation by player 3, explaining why governments often release construction plans by nominating a candidate area.

Remark: In the upper half of Fig. 5.2, resident 2 will choose "oppose" and the NIMBY would arise if $\{b_2 - \text{SELFISH}_2\} > sb_2$ and, hence, the whole two-by-two payoff matrix of Fig. 5.2 belongs to the <A-A> case of the Prisoner's Dilemma. However, if $\{b_2 - \text{SELFISH}_2\} < sb_2$ under increased values of SELFISH_2, and the whole matrix of Fig. 5.2 belongs to the <A-B> case, resident 2 will choose "welcome" and the NIMBY conflict will not occur. This implies that to criticize/bash residents engaging in NIMBY activity in the real world to be selfish is, even with or without the intention to do so, nothing more than an activity trying to change the whole payoff matrix of Fig. 5.2 from <A-A> to the <A-B> type.

Emergence of NIMBY: In Sect. 5.3.1, we concluded that by considering the equilibrium of the one-player game in the upper half of Fig. 5.2, if $\{b_2 - \text{SELFISH}_2\} > sb_2$, NIMBY would arise, whereas if $\{b_2 - \text{SELFISH}_2\} < sb_2$, it would not. This may seem to be a trivial result, saying that when there is a third party (player 3) who will criticize the residents in the candidate area if they oppose the facility to be built in their area selfishly, the residents may accept the facility and NIMBY may not arise.

However, such a conclusion does not necessarily apply to real NIMBY facilities. In the model in this section, we assume that residents 1 and 2 are common knowledge. In such a circumstance, even in the case of $\{b_2 - \text{SELFISH}_2\} < sb_2$, resident 2, who knows who resident 1 is, would try to explain to the government and player 3 with costs that resident 1 also has "welcome" in its strategy set and, hence, the true game which should be played is the whole two-by-two payoff matrix in Fig. 5.1, not the one-player game in the upper half of Fig. 5.2. Here, resident 2 has to prove that resident 1 not only has the strategy of "oppose" but also "welcome" and, thus, is a player in Fig. 5.1. In this case, resident 2 would refuse the construction plan in which the government would nominate area 2 from the beginning itself, and insisted that the plan including the siting should be reconsidered from the beginning, with the site for the facility to be redecided through the game in Fig. 5.1 with both residents 1 and 2 attendings.

5.3.2 The Case of Asymmetric Information

In this section, we suppose that residents 1 and 2 do not know who the other resident is, although the government knows who they are. This supposition would be justified if we look at our real life: in real life, often the residents in an area do not know "who is residing in other areas of the region." Also, although it is usual in real life that several areas of a region benefit from the building of a NIMBY facility, the residents in such beneficial areas often hide that they would also benefit from the facility, pretending that they have no relationship with the facility siting problem. Thus, it is not easy for the residents in the candidate area to specify the areas (and the residents) that should be concerned with the facility siting problem.

In this case, the situation is the same as that in Sect. 5.3.1, except that resident 2 does not know who resident 1 is. Therefore, through the same analysis as that in Sect. 5.3.1, we can conclude that if $\{b_2 - \text{SELFISH}_2\} > sb_2$, resident 2 will choose "oppose," the emergence of NIMBY, whereas resident 2 will choose "welcome" if $\{b_2 - \text{SELFISH}_2\} < sb_2$.

Non-Emergence of NIMBY: In Sect. 5.3.2, we assume that resident 2 does not know who resident 1 is. In the circumstance of Sect. 5.3.2, when $\{b_2 - \text{SELFISH}_2\} < sb_2$, resident 2 would again hope to explain to the government and player 3 that the true game that should be played is that in Fig. 5.1 between residents 1 and 2, not the one-player game in the upper half of Fig. 5.2. However, it would be difficult for resident 2 to do so in this case, contrary to the case in Sect. 5.3.1. To do so, resident 2 must first find and specify who resident 1 is, alone. Second, resident 2 would again have to prove that resident 1 has "welcome" in its strategy set and, hence, the actual game that should be played is that in Fig. 5.1 between residents 1 and 2.[13]

The difference from the case of Sect. 5.3.1 is thus the existence of the costs of searching and specifying resident 1. If these costs are not so large, resident 2 would search and find resident 1, and insist that the site should be reconsidered from the beginning, decided again through the game in Fig. 5.1 with both residents 1 and 2 joining. However, the costs of searching and specifying who resident 1 is would often be tremendously large, and resident 2 would have to abandon to engage in such activities.

[13] It would be difficult to prove that resident 1 has also the strategy "welcome," without specifying who resident 1 is.

5.4 Concluding Remarks

When a local government publicly releases a NIMBY facility construction plan, it nominates only one area as the candidate area of the facility to be built, often inducing the public's attention focusing on the residents' responses in the candidate area. We suppose that nomination provides the public the incorrect perception that there is no alternative than to build the facility in the nominated area, and whether the facility is constructed depends solely on the attitudes of the candidate area's residents toward the public's facility. Supposing that the public expresses criticism to the residents in the candidate area based on such a perception about the situation surrounding the facility, this study investigates whether a resident in the candidate area would accept the facility.

According to our findings, residents in the candidate area often choose to reject the construction plan, and even when it is better to agree than to face public opposition, they would try to prevent the facility from being built in their area, insisting that the site be reconsidered from the beginning. However, such activities would be abandoned when the residents in the candidate area cannot search and specify who the residents in the non-nominated areas are. In our view, such reactions are mostly merely hoping for the site to be reconsidered without removing any possibilities for the siting. The policy implication is that governments should not put residents in the "one-player game" but those of Fig. 5.1 when releasing construction plans.

Several assumptions in the models in Sect. 5.3 have been posed as plausible ones, concerning the situations of multiple, over [A16] two areas siting. Extending the analysis of Sect. 5.3 to such multiple settings explicitly, in which several areas comprise the region whose local government has to construct a NIMBY facility for the residents in one area would be a natural and meaningful extension. There would arise a room for the residents of non-nominated areas who want a "free-ride" to cooperate in the multiple-area scenario. Such interactions among the residents in the not-nominated areas would interest not only by themselves but also provide conclusions that would provide and enforce the plausibility of the several suppositions in Sect. 5.3.2, including that the residents do not know who the other residents, and that the resident in the candidate area cannot search and specify the residents in the other area. Also, under such multiple-player circumstances, the role of third parties outside the region who might be Benthamian would increase because the members of the region increase. We intend to address these issues in the future research.

Acknowledgment I am grateful to an anonymous referee for helpful comments. I am also thankful to the Japanese Section of Regional Science Association International 2020—one of the academic associations to which Professor Sakai has long contributed—for permitting me to use Figure 1 of Eguchi (2020) in this study.

References

Bellettini G, Kempf H (2013) Why not in my backyard? On the location and size of a public facility. Region Sci Urban Econ 43:22–30. https://doi.org/10.1016/j.regsciurbeco.2012.11.001

Besfamille M, Lozachmeur J-M (2010) NIMBY and mechanism design under different constitutional constraints. Int Tax Policy Finance 17:114–132

Burningham K, Barnett J, Thrush D (2006) The limitations of the NIMBY concept for understanding public engagement with renewable energy technologies: A literature review, Working Paper 1.3. The School of Environment and Development, University of Manchester, Manchester

Eguchi S (2020) NIMBY (not in my backyard) Conflicts: a simple game-theoretic analysis. Asia-Pacific J Reg Sci 4(3):821–833. https://doi.org/10.1007/s41685-020-00166-4

Feinerman E, Finkelshtain I, Kan I (2004) On a political solution to the NIMBY conflict. Am Econ Rev 94(1):369–381

Feldman S, Turner D (2010) Why not NIMBY? Ethics Place Environ 13(3):251–266. https://doi.org/10.1080/1366879X.2010.516493

Flynn G (2011) Court decisions, NIMBY claims, and the siting of unwanted facilities: Policy frames and the impact of judicialization in locating a landfill for Toronto's solid waste. Can Public Policy 37(3):381. https://doi.org/10.3138/cpp.37.3.381

Fredriksson PG (2000) The siting of hazardous waste facilities in federal systems: The political economy of NIMBY. Environ Resource Econ 15:75–87. https://doi.org/10.1023/A:1008313612369

Frey BS, Oberholzer-Gee F (1997) The cost of price incentives: An empirical analysis of motivation crowding-out. Am Econ Rev 87(4):746–755

Frey BS, Oberholzer-Gee F, Eichenberger R (1996) The old lady visits your backyard: A tale of morals and markets. J Polit Economy 104(6):1297–1313

Guidotti TL, Abercrombie S (2008) Aurum: A case study in the politics in NIMBY. Waste Manag Res 26(6):582–588. https://doi.org/10.1177/0734242X08092023

Kunreuther H, Kleindorfer PR (1986) A sealed-bid auction mechanism for siting noxious facilities. Am Econ Rev 76(2):295–299. Paper and Proceedings

Mitchel RC, Carson RT (1986) Property rights, protest, and the siting of hazardous waste facilities. Am Econ Rev 76(2):285–290. Paper and Proceedings

Sakai Y (2015) J.M Keynes versus Knight: Comparing the two economic giants in the age of uncertainty (in Japanese). Minerva, Kyoto

Sakai Y (2019) An application to nuclear power generation: From Daniel Bernoulli to Keynes, J.M. and Knight, F.H. In: J.M. Keynes versus F.H. Knight evolutionary, Economics and Social Complexity Science, 18. Springer, Singapore. https://doi.org/10.1007/978-981-13-8000-6_8

Sakurai H (2010) Nimbyism: Prospects under increased international resource recycling activities (in Japanese). Kikan Seisaku/keiei kenkyu 3:51–71, Mitsubishi UFJ Bank, 2010

Shimizu S (1999) NIMBY Syndrome Kou (Thinking about NIMBY syndrome, in Japanese). Tokyo Shimbun Shuppan-Kyoku, Tokyo

Shimizu S (2002) Haikibutsu shori shisetsu no ricchi to Juumin Goui keisei (Siting of unwanted facility and consensus building among residents, in Japanese). J Center Regional Aff Fukushima Univ 14(1):3–13

Siniawer EM (2018) A war against garbage in postwar Japan. Asia-Pacific J 16(22):5217. https://apjjf.org/2018/22/Maruko.html. Accessed 30 Nov 2019

Suzuki K (2011) NIMBY studies: Problems and prospects (in Japanese). Proceedings of JITA annual conference, December 2011, Japan Institute of Tourism, pp 17–20

Zheng G, Liu W (2018) Same projects, different endings: Comparative case studies on NIMBY facility construction in Beijing. Cities 73:63–70. https://doi.org/10.1016/j.cities.2017.10.010

Chapter 6
On the Existence and Sustainability of Long-Standing Japanese Shinise Firms

Hidekazu Sone

Abstract The purpose of this study is to explore the interdependent relationships between regional economies and long-standing firms in Japan. Research on family businesses is scarce, so this study analyses the actions of successive generations of family run businesses, interweaving their knowledge of management strategy, society, and history. In this study, we provide a field study on Suzuyo & Co., Ltd., a major logistics company rooted in Shizuoka City, Shizuoka Prefecture (Shimizu area) which has been operating for nine generations over the last 200 years. We discuss this case from the perspectives of innovation, business system, and socio-emotional wealth (SEW). Suzuyo's business style is based on sound region-customer relationships and is the biggest contributing factor to their long existence. This study offers a strong contribution to the literature due to its research methods, which included interviews and historical materials provided by the people at Suzuyo. In particular, we were able to interview President and Chairman Yohei Suzuki, the eighth generation of the family within the company. His effort ensured that our analysis was fact-based, allowing us to clarify the factors behind the firm's long-standing operation and the relationship of successive family generations with the local community.

Keywords Shinise (Long-standing firm) · Business system · Innovation · Socio-emotional wealth · Business succession

---

H. Sone (✉)
Faculty of Cultural Policy and Management, Shizuoka University of Art and Culture, Shizuoka, Japan
e-mail: h-sone@suac.ac.jp

M. Kawano et al. (eds.), *Theory and History in Regional Perspective*, New Frontiers in Regional Science: Asian Perspectives 56,
https://doi.org/10.1007/978-981-16-6695-7_6

6.1 Introduction

There has been a considerable regarding growth in management studies in Japan; however, little research has been conducted with the keyword of continuance. Additionally, there is insufficient research that examines the relationship between organizational culture and competitive strategy in Japanese companies. This study attempts to provide one answer to this question through an examination of how Suzuyo & Co., Ltd. (hereafter Suzuyo), a long-standing logistic firm in Japan, integrates social responsibility and innovation into its competitive strategy.

Suzuyo is currently headquartered at Shimizu Harbour in Shizuoka City (previously Shimizu City), Shizuoka Prefecture, Japan. The firm was established in 1801 as Harimaya Yohei and dates back to its first store at the center of Shimizu's wholesale port, where he took over the store of an oversea trading broker.[1]

The Suzuki family has inherited Suzuyo since its establishment. The current chairman and owner of the firm is Mr. Yohei Suzuki, the eighth generation of the family, while his son, Mr. Kenichiro Suzuki, is the current president.

The purpose of this study is, therefore, to explore how Suzuyo owners have created their competitive strategies and innovations. To do so, we have conducted interviews in addition to data collection from public sources such as books, academic papers, and periodicals. To create a meaningful case study, as suggested by Yin (1994), Gerring (2007), and Miles and Huberman (1994), we identified and analysed critical events during interviews and in public information.

The study is conducted by focusing on business systems, innovation, and socio-emotional wealth. Kagono and Inoue (2004) defined business systems as "systematic assembly of management resources in a determined structure that results from planning the progress from determination of either of two factors: first, what activities the company undertake, or second, what type of relationship the company establish with various external trading partners, with respect to specialization of work, establishment of an incentive system, information, product, and income."[2]

[1]Currently, in addition to distribution and logistics, the firm has seven business lines with over 140 branches, which include sales of food, construction, information system, and fuel trading, among others. The enterprise produces an annual revenue of around JPY 460 billion. Furthermore, the firm had to face hard times such as failure in speculative trading in the U.S. market, World War II, and the oil shock. The firm overcame these crises by restructuring its internal organization in response to the changing environment while also exploring new ventures. For example, Suzuyo had committed to developing Shimizu Harbour, selling coal, and exporting green tea and oranges overseas.

[2]Regarding business system studies in the field of business history, Cochran (1957), Cole (1964), and others used business systems as a dominant concept to scientifically discuss the major issues of economic developments based on case studies. Later, in business strategy theories, business management theories, etc., many researchers have been emphasizing business systems, particularly when discussing Japanese corporations. Kagono and Yamada (2019) defined a business systems as "a business framework being a cooperative systemized framework within a corporation and among corporations."

Theoretically, business systems are closely related to innovation as well as socio-emotional wealth (SEW).[3] The goal of SEW is to achieve good economic performance, but more importantly to prioritize how to pursue non-financial utility generated from other factors at the same time. Those factors include social image on the company's names, brand names, and family names that gain the ability to exercise identity and influence.[4] Therefore, one prime objective of SEW is to have the family business survive and succeeded into future generations (Miller and Le Breton-Miller 2014).

Upon investigating Japan's local production areas and long-established firms, one can identify many similarities between the business system theory and SEW theory. The business system theory has been widely used in Japanese management studies for approximately 20 years, and in recent years, the SEW theory is garnering attention as well.

6.2 Literature Review[5]

This paper rethinks the research into Shinise (long-standing firms) as it has been discussed relative to preservation, indicating its problematic points, and aims to approach the core of the subject by way of a new chronological analysis using case studies of various firms. Research on family businesses in Japan has been actively conducted in recent years as attention paid to long-established firms increases. However, many studies are limited to introducing the status of family businesses or the results obtained from the simple processing of questionnaire surveys as the field of expertise is still relatively new. Full-scale academic research began when The Family Business Review was launched in the USA in 1988. Further accumulation of theoretical and empirical research is required not only in Japan, but also in Europe and America.

---

[3] SEW has been actively discussed by many researchers in the USA and Europe since around 2010. SEW has also attracted attention from Japanese researchers in recent years, but the interpretation of SEW appears exaggerated. Thus, we use early research on SEW in the USA and Europe as a main reference for this study.

[4] Gomez-Mejia et al. (2007) investigated the attitudes of family business toward risks, that is, the facts that they are risk averse depending on their, nature which leads to the failure or reduction of SEW. Gomez-Mejia et al. (2011) distinguished family businesses from other types of businesses by emphasizing the role of uneconomic factors when referring to previous studies. In his 2011 research, he pointed out three distinct factors that the family business has inherited: a strong emotional overtone which the family has built up through its persistent memory and long existence as a social organization; the penetration of their family's idiosyncratic sense of value into the organization; and altruistic behaviour among owners of the family business.

[5] The literature review on business system and innovation is cited from the discussion in Ibrahim et al. (2011), Sone and Lam (2013), Lam and Sone (2018), and Sone et al. (2020) which is partly modified.

Keeping innovative culture in an organization is complex. For example, the transfer of a family business from one generation to another is a complex process that involves many factors (Ibrahim and Ellis 2004; Davis and Harveston 1998; Sone 2019). In industries that depend on craftmanship and skills, transfer of those skills from one generation to another is a must in maintaining sustainability and long-term success, especially for family businesses.

The family firms have a noticeable vision that has been passed across generations while non-family firms do not have an identifiable vision. This characteristic provides family firms with a competitive advantage over non-family firms (Habbershon and Williams 1999; Chua et al. 1999; Sone 2019).

Distinct differences in organizational culture have also been identified between family and non-family firms (Denison et al. 2004). Dyer (1986) argues that the values created by the founder have been transferred from one generation to another. Recent findings demonstrated that family firms are likely to be more innovative (Duran et al. 2016; Kammerlander and van Essen 2017; Padilla-Melendez et al. 2015; Astrachan 2010).

This fact articulates with the innovative culture created by a family and is embedded within its organization. The evidence that the family firm is likely to be more efficient in using innovative processes supports the hypothesis that a family firm creates more output with less R&D monetary inputs (Duran et al. 2016). Furthermore, family firms are more responsive to the changes in the market and customer demand. Newman et al. (2016), for example, found that there is a positive relationship between family firms and customer orientation on the use of exploratory innovation to scan the market for opportunities.

Kagono (1999) also demonstrated that an innovative culture in a family firm is used to empower employees and to leverage its trust with external networks. Family firms use the "family system" to build a clan culture that promotes teamwork while non-family firms rely on the "business system" to build their organizational culture (Sone et al. 2006; Yoshimura and Sone 2006; Sanchez-Marin et al. 2016; Kammerlander and van Essen 2017; Sone 2019). This concept is similar to the idea that the values created by the founder are associated with other stakeholders surrounding the family business (Poza et al. 1997). Firms' business cultures are heavily influenced by the regional social culture[6] (James 2005; Saxenian 1994; Lam and Sone 2018).[7]

We will discuss the case study of Suzuyo in the following chapter.

[6]Culture here means "a complex whole which includes knowledge, belief, art, morals, law, custom, capabilities and habits." Culture defines the members of a specific society (Tylor 1871). The culture of a regional society determines whether the society tolerates risk and changes, celebrates the success of others, collaborates and cooperates, and accepts failure as part of the normal process of doing business (Saxenian 1994; Stephan and Uhlaner 2010; Mason and Brown 2014; Spigel 2017). There are characteristics of a society that is conductive to a firm's innovation.

[7]The region's history of commerce, therefore, provides an insight as to why certain areas maintain a persistent level of entrepreneurial activities over a long period of time (Shane 1993; Aoyama 2009; Fritsch and Storey 2014; Sone et al. 2020).

6.3 Case Study: Competitive Strategy of Suzuyo[8]

This study uses Suzuyo as a case to explain the role of an innovative culture for the competitive strategy of a family firm. It also analyses the role of the firm's location in developing an innovative culture and associated behaviours with respect to the diversification and internationalization under four generations of the family firm.

6.3.1 Business Crisis in Edo Period and Foundation Establishment in Meiji Period

Shimizu Harbour has been the heart of Japan's marine ports since *Kamakura Period*. Together with *Ejirijuku of Tokaido*, this location in the eastern sea area is vitally important in terms of both marine and land transportation. *Tokugawa Ieyasu*, a leader of the *Tokugawa* clan, won a battle in the summer of 1615 at Osaka when special business rights were granted to the 42 local marine trade brokers, who then formed a monopoly in the marine trading business. The founder of Suzuyo took over the business of a marine trade broker called *Minatoya Heiemon* in 1801 and then established *Harimayayohei*.

We were unable to find information about the first two generations of the firm other than what was in their tombs and records. The first owner was born in 1752 and the second in 1774. The founder took over the capital when he was around 50 years old, which explains why his son, later the second generation's leader, had managed the business with the founder since the establishment.

Nevertheless, the monopolistic privilege disappeared when the special business right, the economic privilege of trade brokers in Shimizu Harbour, was suspended during the Tenpo Reforms in 1841. This change forced the traditional business environment to be a free competitive market. That change led to the closure of traders and the sales of the stocks, leaving only 38 marine trade brokers in operation, causing the marine transportation business at Shimizu Harbour to fall into economic depression.

When the third generation's leader took over the firm in 1812 and used his full strength to protect the business, he tried to make a good relationship with the *Fukatsu* and *Sawano* families. In 1856, he arranged to have his daughter married

[8]For this paper, primary materials were examined, while secondary materials and inhouse company documents were referred to. Interviews were conducted with Mr. Takafumi Mori, a former Suzuyo board member, and one other person on March 14, 2017, and with Mr. Daisuke Goto, an adviser to the company, and one other person on October 6, 2018. On July 1 and 28, 2020, Mr. Yohei Suzuki, the chairman and eighth-generation founder, was interviewed. At least ten rounds of investigation were conducted, including informal inquiries. We used a longitudinal case research method (Gerring 2007; Stake 1995) where we started with the company's founder and continued to the present leader of the ninth generation.

to the third son of *Sawano Niemon*. It was his son-in-law, *Gihei*, who took over the business. He then passed away in 1869, after he witnessed the business's well-being.

6.3.2 Suzuyo's Reform in the Transitions in Meiji Period

In *Gakuyo Meishiden* (notable persons in Gakuyo), published in 1891, the fourth Yohei Suzuki is described as a veteran chief merchant and scholar with a keen understanding of business opportunities.

The fourth generation's leader took over the business in the early Meiji Era, when it was in chaos. He diversified the business with new ventures and expanded. When the Japanese government decided to open a new railway (*Tokaido Line*) and *Shimizu Port* in 1889,[9] it was a turning point for the firm. The firm started trading salt, tea, and coal for expansion.[10] The firm changed its name to *Suzuki Yohei Shoten* during that time period. The fourth generation contributed tremendously to the family business, as well as to the regional community for where he was elected as the regional leader at the age of 25 and then became a *Shimizu Town* Mayor.

He was called "*Monarch of Meiji*" and had five major achievements. First, he created a strong foundation for *Suzuki Yohei Shouten*. Second, he contributed to the establishment of Japanese Tea-house in Yokohama by inviting *Mitsubishi* steamships to the harbour.[11] Third, as a response to the opening of the new railway, he used coal as a new resource for energy. Fourth, he renovated *Shimizu Harbour* to be a public wharf to support international trading business.[12] Firth, in 1899, he succeeded in obtaining government approval for the harbour to be used as an international trading port. His efforts helped the community in Shimizu develop tremendously.

An adopted son in 1865, *Keijiro Yamanashi* took taken over the name *Yohei* to become the fifth generation's leader. As a representative person of *Suzuki Yohei*, he

---

[9]It had been previously said that developing railways would have a negative effect on marine transportation, but it actually had a positive influence.

[10]Mr. Yohei Suzuki, the leader of the eighth generation, said, "Since Kushiro and Shimizu are not big harbour but rather medium-sized, no major companies came in. As a result, there were business opportunities for Suzuyo. Harbour of Shimizu, unlike Kushiro, had liners visit regularly, and therefore, they were able to export tea and tangerines from Meiji Period. Exports were usually operated by a large shipping company, but in the case of Shimizu, the business was entrusted to a local company. Running such a business required the workers to be able to speak English, and for this reason, they needed relatively high-calibre workers to do the job of the distributors. The quality of employees was quite high at Suzuyo because such personnel were combined with the work at the harbour."

[11]Opening teahouses at Yokohama was crucial for the community because exporting tea was mainly conducted at Yokohama port at that time.

[12]The fourth generation's leader played a leading role in the marine transportation industry at that time. He helped build up a wharf company, *Hakuunsha Co., Ltd.*, which accelerated the harbour development.

supported the expansion of *Shimizu Harbour*. For example, he was committed to exporting Japanese tea to the USA. Because of predecessors' orders, he continued the sales of salt while also expanding the business to include the delivery of wood, management of ships, and sale of marine insurance. He passed away at the age of 55 in 1917 after his adopted son-in-law succeeded the business as the sixth generation's leader.

There are very few documents on the first, second, and third Yohei Suzuki; thus, many things remain unclear. The fourth and fifth Yohei Suzuki managed the business without any major problems. Suzuyo expanded significantly under the sixth Yohei Suzuki.

6.3.3 Business Expansion and Management Philosophy

The sixth generation's leader made tremendous efforts in expansion and diversification of the business while he contributed to a large extent to the industrialization of *Shimizu Harbour*. He started trading coke, a fuel which is a by-product of coal, and obtained a license to sell reprocessed salt. Furthermore, he incorporated the business of warehouse management as a prospect for the future. He also founded *Shimizu Food* as a corporate social responsibility.

During this generation, the business was modernized. The proprietary organization was changed to a stock company in 1936, when the firm's name was changed from *Suzuyo Shoten* to *Suzuyo Shoten Co., Ltd*. The company also had to train employees and teach them the company's mission to support widely diversified business.

For example, the firm encouraged *"Tomoiki"* activities, in which employees support each other and live together. These activities were inspired by *Benkyo Shiio*, an influential monk from the *Jodoshu* Buddhist School, in 1922. The guiding philosophy of the "*Tomoiki Movement*" was the idea that "everything on earth are friends because grass and trees are all coexisting." The sixth generation's leader incorporated the concept of coexisting into the business philosophy, which became a fundamental support for employees.[13]

As a result, a voluntary group called *Suzuyo Shiseikai* was formed in 1927. Suzuyo night schooling started and encouraged employees of all ages and in all business units to attend.[14] The sixth generation's leader passed away at the age of 58 in 1940, leaving behind four mottos: serve with honesty, value harmony, work with persistence and self-respect, and mutual understanding. The sixth generation's

[13]Mr. Yohei Suzuki, eighth generation leader, wrote, "The business is all about its people" is a commonly known proverb, similarly our company history is also exactly "the history of the people of Suzuyo" (Suzuyo & Co., Ltd. 1987).

[14]Subjects taught were accounting, business administration, communications, classical Chinese, Japanese, and English.

leader has been recognized both internally and externally as a person who led to the modern Suzuyo.[15]

Mr. Yohei Suzuki, eighth generation leader, said, "I think the 6th generation, my grandfather, was an impressive person. He had a rough life. This may not be something I should say about a relative, but he went to Hitotsubashi University and was influenced by Professor Kanzo Uchimura to become a Christian. But he gradually drifted to Buddhism after returning to Shimizu and died early."

6.3.4 *The Chaotic Post-war Period, Rebirth, and the Rapid Economic Growth*

Upon the death of the sixth generation leader, his first son took over the seventh generation.[16] He had graduated from Kyoto University after majoring in economics, and was trained in marine trading at *Yamashita Kisen Steamship Co., Ltd.* After 2 years with *Yamashita*, he joined Suzuyo as a senior managing director and assisted the sixth generation's leader. His younger brother, Yoji, supported the seventh generation's leader along with a team of experienced and well-trained employees. Yoji had resigned from *Nosawa Gumi Trading* and joined Suzuyo after the sudden death of the sixth generation leader; Yoji later became a vice president and president. Yoji and the seventh generation's leader led the company and overcame the crisis caused by World War II, even though most of the company's assets were damaged during that period.

The seventh generation's leader recovered from the damage during the post-war period by progressively implementing automation, switching from coal to fossil fuel trading, in response to the rapid economic growth in Japan.[17] For example, he restructured the marine transportation business for expansion[18] by dividing it into

[15]The sixth Yohei Suzuki modeled the company like a terakoya school. He provided education, such as lessons on bookkeeping, reading and writing, and abacus, to his employees. The local community acknowledged this endeavor; thus, Suzuyo was able to recruit talented students from local higher elementary schools, because it was understood that employees would be able to study if they joined the company. These talented students contributed to Suzuyo's growth during the pre-war period. The management, led by the head clerk, laid the company's strong foundation.

[16]In addition to the position as the president of *Suzuyo Shoten*, he took over the position of president at partner companies and was a member on their boards. Mr. Yohei Suzuki, eighth generation leader, wrote, "The eighth generation describes his father, the seventh generation, as 'a quiet man'" (Suzuyo & Co., Ltd. 1996).

[17]Mr. Yohei Suzuki, eighth generation leader, wrote, "As the head of the company, my father must have been doing whatever he could to get through the turbulent times of the Pacific War, Japan's defeat in the war, and the post-war period. When I think of my father, a lump forms in my throat, as I think of a man who did not seem to have been blessed with talent as an entrepreneur but worked hard as he could" (Suzuyo & Co., Ltd. 1996).

[18]The annual sales value of the Transport Division increased from JPY 1.3 billion in 1961 to JPY 2.9 billion in 1965, then to JPY 2.9 billion in 1969.

three units; sales of marine transportation, woods, administration, and production to optimize the operation.

He also created a pier to use exclusively for coal trading to accelerate modernization in harbour operations and reform transportations. Within the organization, he adopted computers for efficient administrative operations in a designated electronic calculation office in 1968. Furthermore, in 1977, he opened a representative office in Antwerp and expanded the business internationally, to Los Angeles, New York, and Dusseldorf.

How he handled the business of SSK (*Shimizu Food*) illustrates that he was an excellent successor to the sixth generation leader. When SSK reported sluggish sales results in 1970s, most managers almost gave up on the business. It was, however, the seventh generation's leader who insisted that SSK should be continued. As the first son of the sixth generation, who founded SSK, he is said to have been strongly committed to SSK, believing that he had inherited the will of six generations.

The seventh generation's leader was always aware of his responsibility to contribute to the local community.[19] To carry out the will of his predecessor, who served as a chairman in *Shimizu City Council* for 16 years (over four periods), he donated JPY 150,000 to establish *Shimizu City Hospital*. He also served as a chairman of *Shimizu City Welfare Committee*, which formed in 1951 and provided opportunities for students who need special care by initiating a specialized class at *Shimizu City Elementary School*. Other elementary and junior high schools followed the trend.

He was willing to offer a place at Suzuyo headquarters for an institution for the mentally disabled to have their administrative office. He, along with other enterprises, raised a trust fund for the institution because they showed trust and respect to Suzuyo as the head of organization. This allowed *Anabara Gakuen School* to open. In 1975, *Anabaraso*, a lifelong support facility for those with mental disabilities, was also opened. He was a chairman of the organization and managed the team by himself. In 1978, he opened *Shimizu Harbour Museum* to introduce the local history and culture to other communities.[20]

---

[19]Mr. Yohei Suzuki, the leader of the seventh generation, wrote, "History (of Suzuyo) is directly linked to the development of Shimizu Port. Suzuyo, who has lived together with Shimizu Port, is grateful that it has grown with the prosperity of the port, and this is our basic spirit. ... Suzuyo's mission to be born in the hometown and live with the hometown is becoming more and more important, and we are keenly aware that we must have the responsibility and awareness to always return the benefits we have been given, both mentally and physically"(Company magazine, *Suzuyo*, Vol.1).

[20]Mr. Yohei Suzuki, the leader of the eighth generation, said, "My father (the seventh generation) was not really the one who took the lead, but rather was supported by my uncle (the younger brother of the seventh generation). I also think the support from university graduate shopkeepers who joined the company when my grandfather was the head was big. They really supported my father."

6.3.5 Reforms and Breakthrough by the Eighth Generation

The eighth generation's leader graduated from Tokyo University and majored in economics; he started his career with *Nippon Yusen* and later joined Suzuyo. He was promoted to the role of president at the age of 36 in 1977, after the sudden death of his uncle, Yoji.

He implemented policies for reform and breakthrough. The change was clear. Statements made on New Year's days included: "Pick up challenges and start a voyage while preserving traditions" in 1978; "We don't want those who are afraid of failure" in 1979; and "We will improve the skill of our employees to enhance the organization" in 1980.

This change was initiated because he discovered that the management failed to supervise the bottom of the organization during the seventh generation due to the rapid expansion. He then put a lot of effort in establishing the system of three business unit managers over administration, transportation, and sales so that the presidential policies were transparent and handled smoothly.

He updated the computer system installed by the previous generation and used the system for accounting and administration to increase the efficiency of operations. He also thoroughly reviewed and evaluated each project, and eventually terminated the projects burdened with deficits, such as *Shimizu Food*, *Fuji Plywood*, and *Shimizu Transports*. He admitted in later years, "It was indeed not easy to revitalize the company which had enjoyed a peaceful environment while I rushed into immediate restructuring to solve many problems."

Mr. Yohei Suzuki, the eighth generation, said, "When I became president, things were extremely tough. The union movement also flourished, and companies and unions that have never gone into the black since their founding were strong and it was as if we were on the verge of being knocked out. In my first year, I didn't know why the personnel department couldn't count the number of employees."

In addition to internal reforms, the eighth generation's leader, based on his international experience, had to expand into international trade in the logistic business by building both domestic and global relationships much earlier than competitors did. By collaborating with the largest broker in the USA and making it a place for international expansion, he incorporated a company, *Suzuyo Koku Kamotsu,* in 1987. Furthermore, companies for lease, insurance, security, distribution, pest control, building maintenance, and airline businesses had been established. He stated in interviews, "We were not expanding without plans. Every initiative started in response to the request from the local community. As a result, we added each company one by one into our group."

Recently, the firm accepted a request to manage *Shimizu S-Pulse*, a local professional soccer team in J-league. It opened "*S-Pulse Dream Plaza*" as an integrated commercial facility and as a hot spot for tourists to revitalize *Shimizu Harbour*. The eighth generation's leader also helped in the project of opening *Mt. Fuji Shizuoka Airport* and established *Fuji Dream Airlines (FDA).* Through this, the firm enhanced its ties with the local community. We found that the business strategy of Suzuyo is indeed consistent; it was based on the philosophy of coexistence with the customers, the local society, and the employees. The firm consistently attempted to build long-term and sustainable networks with time, costs, and efforts for coexistence rather than striving for short-term profits.

In 1990, Suzuyo donated JPY 1 billion to the opening of *Shizuoka Institute of Science and Technology* when the eighth generation leader became the first chairman of the board. He aimed to educate people through science and engineering so that they become researchers or engineers in the future who would contribute to development of the local society.

In fact, it was the eighth generation's leader who put together fundamental policies in the year of 1992. He argues that the reason why Suzuyo survived its difficulties was the consistent efforts and transformation made by ancestors after dramatic changes in the society and value perception.

He made sure that policies regarding business acts and employees' attitudes were clear. He had 12 principles that he shared for further development: conduct sincere business so that it endures judgements by history; be encouraged to hold and attain esteem; constantly seek reforms; proactively seek new investments; attempt to create a solid system by reserving retained earnings; establish good relationships with external stakeholders; attempt to unify the directions for effective management; communicate with formal written documents for every activity in the organization; have representatives and management be the driving force of the organization; ensure that every employee is always treated fairly; comply with the rules as fundamentals for all organizational activities; educate people.

Those 12 principles have become the present fundamentals for all Suzuyo employees. In August 2015, the eighth generation's leader was promoted to be the chairman of the board and his first son, *Kenichiro*, has become the new president. The smooth transition is expected to motivate people to further develop the firm.

Actions taken by successive generations illustrated that the factors for survival and the roles of long-established firms should have their roots deep in the region. The eighth generation indicated in an interview that the company had created solid roots in the region but was also willing to change.[21] This is critical. According to him, the most important role of a founder, when change is necessary, is to be able to have control at that time. The successive generations of the family have played a major role in the development of Shimizu port and the urban areas, and they also took responsibility as a coordinator within the industry.

The eighth generation mentioned the importance of attending the local schools until high school as an example of how he was deeply involved in the local community. He indicated that someone who is going to be a leader of area should live with the people of the community. The fourth and the sixth until the ninth

[21]The eighth Yohei Suzuki moved the company away from its local orientation (Sone and Yoshimura 2019).

generations had worked for other companies for this reason.[22] They recognized the importance of close relationships with the local community for the education of human resources as well as gaining knowledge and technology.[23]

6.3.6 *Carrying on Reforms in line with the Environment*

Mr. Kenichiro Suzuki is the eldest son of Mr. Yohei Suzuki. He joined NYK Line in 2000 after graduating from Waseda University, and became a Suzuyo director in 2009. In 2011, as managing director, he oversaw the group's food business and served as the manager of the logistics division. After serving as senior managing director, he was appointed president and representative director at the age of 40 in 2015.

In addition to the existing logistics business, he is focusing on the areas of open innovation and platform business for the future while simultaneously pursuing operational reforms. Mr. Kenichiro Suzuki, the leader of the ninth generation said, "Suzuyo has been self-reforming in accordance with its business environment. I will steadfastly follow this path as the ninth-generation founder.[24]" He is expected to lead the company as it expands further and contribute to the local community.

[22] Mr. Yohei Suzuki, the leader of the eighth generation, said, "This is how salaried workers live, this is how they work, the bosses are like this, they learn their work this way, and this is the kind of lifestyle they go through. Every single realization should teach us something. Even at my company we tell our workers to cherish their co-workers. Workers of shipping companies are nice to each other, and they're good friends. I want that kind of culture to be present in our company as well."

[23] Mr.Takafumi Mori said, "I am immensely grateful that you are so enthusiastic about Suzuyo. Though it has been 10 years since I retired, I still feel glad that I worked for this company."

[24] https://globis.jp/article/5259

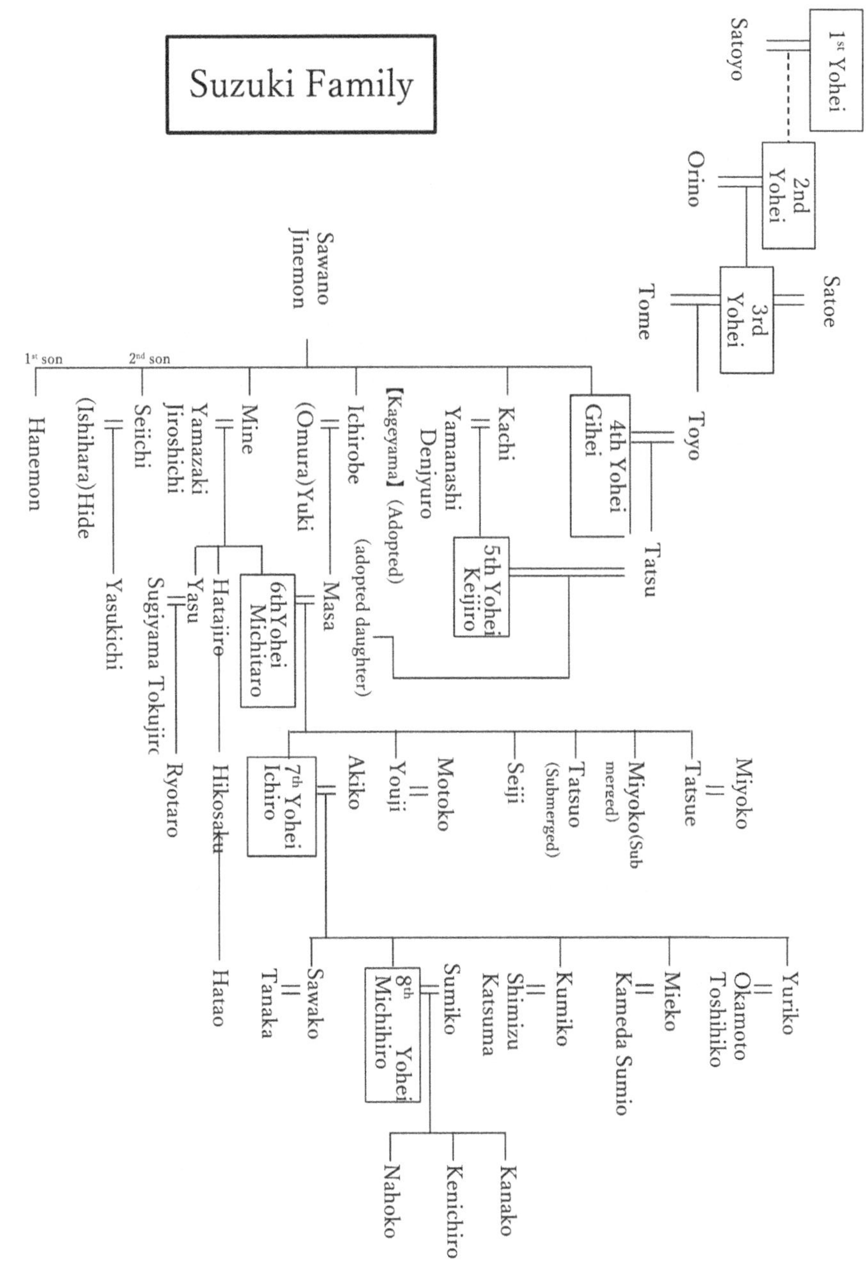

Source: Written by the author based on Suzuyo company history, internal magazines

6.4 Conclusions

The conclusions in this paper offer diverse theories and examples but can be summarized as below. This study identifies the fact that the firm has been developing through various innovations, but at the same time it has contributed tremendously to the development of the local community.

This study has the following contributions to the academic literature: First, the study focused on innovation, business system, and socio-emotional wealth of a family business, which had remained unexplored. Second, it analysed the enterprise, Suzuyo, from various aspects and from its positioning in the local community. The studies on socio-emotional wealth have become pervasive recently, and thus this paper leads to future studies. Third, we conducted many interviews with the owners and members of management team to check facts, which method we believe valuable for the study.

The study repeatedly mentioned that the firm has deep roots in the local community since their foundation. We understood that the firm has made the local community a high priority and thus coordinated with the local people to work because the firm stood for a long time in that local community and worked together with them. While keeping its tradition is important, the firm strived for innovations and breakthroughs to keep the business sustainable. Furthermore, we conclude that when an organization is willing to expand, internal training and education are indeed necessary.

To sum up, we found that the three theoretical viewpoints identified in this paper, which are innovation, business system, and socio-emotional wealth, are indeed important and affected each other as prime reasons for the long-standing operation of Suzuyo.

Finally, future issues are described. Although this paper is a single case study, it is believed that the importance of this case can be further enhanced by conducting a comparative study with other companies in the same industry.

Acknowledgments This work was supported by JSPS KAKENHI Grant Number 18K01760, 18H00886 and 16H03656. This paper has been corrected and revised from the paper by Sone, Lam, Kagono and Maeda (2020).

I would like to express my gratitude to Suzuyo for providing information over the years as I prepared this paper. In particular, Mr. Yohei Suzuki (eighth generation) gave me a number of interviews lasting several hours and answered my questions in letters; his humorous and thoughtful replies were fascinating. I also learned what it means to be a researcher, as well as about life in general, by interacting with him. In addition, Mr. Takafumi Mori told me about the eighth-generation founder's appeal, providing the impetus to begin this study.

References

Aoyama Y (2009) Entrepreneurship and regional culture: the case of Hamamatsu and Kyoto, Japan. Reg Stud 43(3):495–512

Astrachan J (2010) Strategy in family business: toward a multidimensional research agenda. J Fam Bus Strat 1(1):6–14
Chua JH, Chrisman JJ, Sharma P (1999) Defining the family business by behaviour. Entrepr Theory Pract 23(4):19–39
Cochran TC (1957) The American business system: a historical perspective 1900–1955. Harper & Row, New York
Cole AH (1964) The business system and economic advance. An attempt at historical generalization, Private printed, Mass
Davis PS, Harveston PD (1998) The influence of family on the family business succession process: a multi-generational perspective. Entrepr Theory Pract 22(3):31–49
Denison D, Leif C, Ward J (2004) Culture in family-owned enterprises: recognizing and leveraging unique strengths. Fam Bus Rev 17:61–71
Duran P, Kammerlander N, van Essen M, Zellweger T (2016) Doing more with less: innovation input and output in family firms. Acad Manage J 59(4):1224–1264
Dyer WG Jr (1986) Cultural change in family firms: anticipating and managing business and family transitions. Jossey-Bass, San Francisco
Fritsch M, Storey DJ (2014) Entrepreneurship in a regional context: historical roots, recent developments and future challenges. Reg Stud 48(6):939–954
Gerring J (2007) Case study research: principles and practices. Cambridge University Press, Cambridge
Gomez-Mejia LR, Haynes KT, Nunes-Nickel M, Jacobson K, Moyano-Fuentes J (2007) Socioemotional wealth and business risks in family-controlled firms: evidence from Spanish olive oil mills. Adm Sci Q 52(1):106–137
Gomez-Mejia LR, Cruz C, Berrone P, De-Castro J (2011) The bind that ties: socioemotional wealth preservation in family firms. Acad Manage Ann 5(1):653–707
Habbershon TG, Williams M (1999) A resource-based framework for assessing the strategic advantage of family firms. Fam Bus Rev 12(1):1–25
Ibrahim AB, Ellis WH (2004) Family business management: concepts and practice, 2nd edn. Kendall/Hunt, Dubuque
Ibrahim AB, Sone H, Lam J, Kagono T (2011) A longitudinal study of longevity in two family firms. In: Proceedings of the 11th International Conference on Family Enterprise Research Academy, 178–179
James A (2005) Demystifying the role of culture in innovation regional economies. Reg Stud 39(9): 1197–1216
Kagono T (1999) Kyousouyuuino system: Jigyousenryaku no shizukanakakumei. PHP Institute, Kyoto
Kagono T, Inoue T (2004) Jigyou system senryaku. Yuhikaku, Tokyo
Kagono T, Yamada K (2019) Nihon no business system. Yuhikaku, Tokyo
Kammerlander N, van Essen M (2017) Research: family firms are more innovative than other firms. Harv Bus Rev. Retrieved from https://hbr.org/2017/01/research-familyfirms-are-more-innovative-than-other-companies
Lam J, Sone H (2018) Innovation culture in a family business, business 2025: driving growth through strategic innovation. Entrepr Digit:178–181
Mason C, Brown R (2014) Entrepreneurial ecosystems and growth-oriented entrepreneurship. Background paper prepared for the workshop organized by the OECD LEED Programme and the Dutch Ministry of Economic Affairs on entrepreneurial ecosystems and growth-oriented entrepreneurship. Retrieved from: http://www.oecd.org/cfe/leed/entrepreneurialecosystems.pdf (Accessed on 23 May 2019)
Miles M, Huberman AM (1994) Qualitative data analysis, 2nd edn. Sage, Beverly Hills
Miller D, Le Breton- Miller, I. (2014) Deconstructing socioemotional wealth, managing for the long run. Entrepr Theory Pract 19(1):713–720
Newman A, Prajogo D, Atherton A (2016) The influence of market orientation on innovation strategies. J Serv Theory Pract 26(1):72–90

Padilla-Melendez A, Dieguez-Soto J, GarridoMoreno A (2015) Empirical research on innovation in family business: literature review and proposal of an integrative approach. Rev Bus Manage 17(56):1064–1089
Poza E, Alfred T, Maheswari A (1997) Stakeholders perception of culture and management practices in family firms. Fam Bus Rev 10(2):135–155
Sanchez-Marin G, Carrasco-Hernandez AJ, Danvila del Valle I, Sastre-Castillo MA (2016) Organizational culture and family business: a configurational approach. Eur J Fam Bus 6(2):99–107
Saxenian A (1994) Regional advantage: culture and competition in Silicon Valley and Route 128. Harvard University Press, Cambridge
Shane S (1993) Cultural influences on national rates of innovation. J Bus Ventur 8(1):59–73
Sone H (2019) Shinisekigyou no sonzoku mechanism. Chuo Keizaisha, Tokyo
Sone H, Lam J (2013) Business systems of long-established family firm: a study of Marinelli, Italy's oldest firm. Fam Bus Rev 3:33–45
Sone H, Yoshimura N (2019) Suzuyo kabusikigaisha no chiiki ni nezashita sonzoku senryaku, Working Paper Series. Faculty of Economics, Wakayama University, Wakayama, 19-05
Sone H, Sarac V, Nonaka M, Yoshimura N (2006) Preliminary research on the corporate creed observed in the living company, Kongo Gumi in Japan, Working Paper Series. Faculty of Economics, Wakayama University, Wakayama, 06-02
Sone H, Lam J, Kagono T, Maeda Y (2020) Competitive strategy of Suzuyo in Japan: a long standing logistic firm from a viewpoint of innovation business system and socioemotional wealth. Fam Bus Rev 8-9:13–31
Spigel B (2017) The relational organization of entrepreneurial ecosystems. Entrepr Theory Pract 41(1):49–72
Stake RE (1995) The art of case study research. Sage, Thousand Oaks
Stephan U, Uhlaner L (2010) Performance-based vs socially supportive culture: a cross-national study of descriptive norms and entrepreneurship. J Int Bus Stud 41(8):134–136
Suzuyo & Co., Ltd. (1987) Shinobugusa. Suzuyo & Co., Ltd., Shizuoka
Suzuyo & Co., Ltd. (1996) Shichidai Suzuki Yoheiden. Suzuyo & Co., Ltd., Shizuoka
Tylor EB (1871) Primitive culture, vol 2. Brentano's, New York
Yin RK (1994) Case study research: design and methods, 2nd edn. Sage, Beverly Hills
Yoshimura N, Sone H (2006) Observations of Kongo Gumi's corporate creed. Ann Econ Soc Wakayama Univ 10:143–152

Chapter 7
The Formation Process and Logic of the Spin-off Governance Mode: A Case Analysis of the Morimura Zaibatsu

Atsuro Shibata

Abstract The purpose of this article is to reexamine the logic behind the Japanese spin-off governance mode by revealing the formation process of Japanese spin-offs. In order to achieve that purpose, this paper will conduct a case analysis centered on companies belonging to the Morimura Zaibatsu, while paying special attention to the formation process of the parent-subsidiary relationship between Morimura-gumi and Nippon Touki Gomei Kaisha.

In conclusion, this paper clarifies that there may be limits to previous explorations of the Japanese spin-off governance mode focusing on the process of forming Japanese spin-offs, and points out that the nature of Japanese companies may play an important role in the logic behind Japanese firms adopting the spin-off governance mode.

Keywords Japanese spin-offs · Corporate governance · Management dispute · Personal association

7.1 Previous Explanations of the Logic Behind Japanese Spin-Offs

The academic concept of Japanese spin-offs was developed by Ito (1995) and refers to a type of strategic behavior which is particular to Japanese firms.

First, this paper begins by examining previous research on what Japanese spin-offs are, and why Japanese firms tend to adopt this type of strategic behavior.

This paper is an English translation of a paper published in the *Journal of Business Management*, Vol. 22 in 2008.

A. Shibata (✉)
Faculty of Economics, Shiga University, Hikone, Shiga, Japan
e-mail: a-shibata@biwako.shiga-u.ac.jp

M. Kawano et al. (eds.), *Theory and History in Regional Perspective*, New Frontiers in Regional Science: Asian Perspectives 56,
https://doi.org/10.1007/978-981-16-6695-7_7

7.1.1 What Are Japanese Spin-Offs?

Why do Japanese firms spin-off new businesses with future growth potential? Ito (1995) launches his explanation, which hinges on the transaction cost theory,[1] with the following three points and suggests there are three alternative methods of managing new businesses: (1) through the market, (2) through a hierarchy, and (3) through a spin-off.

Generally, where the degree of parent firm ownership of a new business is α, in the case of the market, $\alpha = 0$, or in other words, complete divestment. In the case of a hierarchy, $\alpha = 100$, complete integration in which the parent firm retains complete ownership of its new business. With a spin-off, the equation becomes $0 < \alpha < 100$ or a quasi-market relationship between the parent firm and its new business. Basically, spin-offs are defined as firms which adopt an intermediate ownership structure that is neither a market nor a hierarchy. Ito (1995) argues that the parent firm will select one of these modes of governance with a view to greater economic efficiency of its transactions with the new business.

7.1.2 Why Do Japanese Firms Tend to Adopt the Spin-off as a Type of Governance Mode?

Why do Japanese firms tend to choose the spin-off as the mode of governance? First, Ito (1995) ascribes this tendency to the social environment of Japanese firms, in which parent firms have little need to retain all residual rights of control over the spin-off and integrate it within the parent firm. The risk of acquiring a new business in a heterogeneous social environment seems to prompt US firms to either completely integrate the new business or sell it off entirely, primarily for the purpose of profit. Japan, on the other hand, is a homogeneous society, with a social environment that enables parent firms to constrain the opportunistic behavior of its subsidiaries through sanctions imposed by social networks. As a result, Ito notes that parent firms do not necessarily have to ensure the complete possession of residual rights of control through full ownership.

Ito (1995), therefore, concludes that Japanese firms use the spin-off mode of governance because in Japan, sanctions imposed by social networks serve to complement ownership-based control, making the spin-off mode an economically rational choice.

Ito (1995) also focuses on the aspect of separation of core competencies with dominant logic as well as aspects of Japan's labor market conditions and practices as two other reasons for adopting the spin-off governance mode.

[1] For this point, see Williamson (1975), Grossman and Hart (1986).

Ito (1995) points out that when a Japanese firm sets up a new business spin-off, it tends to create a business possessing more advanced technology independent of the existing business, and thus the parent firm adopts the spin-off governance mode. Technically, if the parent firm's old management systems and core competencies with dominant logic are unfit for the new business, the better option is to separate the new business from the parent firm, because this unfitness is likely to become the biggest impediment to growing the new business based on its own dominant logic. This is especially true if the new business generates few synergistic effects with the existing business.

Why Japanese firms adopt the spin-off governance mode can also be found in aspects of labor market conditions and practices of Japanese firms. It is well known that Japanese firms have a well-developed internal labor market based on the premise of lifetime employment. In other words, Japanese companies need to secure new upper management posts for senior employees and respond to pressure of the internal labor market by spinning off new businesses.

In summary, there are three reasons why Japanese firms spin-off new businesses with future growth potential. The main reason lies in the aspect of "economies of transaction cost" with Japanese firms operating in Japan's homogeneous social environment where the monitoring and sanction of subsidiaries based on social networks can complement ownership-based control. As a result, a parent firm can constrain the opportunistic behavior of its subsidiary without having to own the subsidiary completely, giving an economic rationality to the spin-off that allows it to balance the cost associated with hierarchy and market transactions. The second reason concerns the aspects of "economies of separation of the core competencies with dominant logic." Separating a new business from a parent firm means separating the new business from the parent firm's older management systems and core competencies with dominant logic. As a result, the new business once separated from the parent will be able to develop its own core competencies that match the business environment. The spin-off governance mode not only generates growth of the subsidiary based on multiple uses (namely economies of scope) of the parent firm's managerial resources, but also has the economies of fostering the development of core competencies with dominant logic unique to the subsidiary. The third reason is the aspect of "efficiency of the internal labor market." This is to say that the spin-off governance mode also plays a role in making the internal labor market of Japanese firms work better by creating new senior managerial posts.

In this paper, we focus on the process of forming Japanese-style spin-offs by analyzing the Morimura conglomerate, especially the initial spin-off, or Nippon Touki Gomei Kaisha (hereafter referred to as Nitto), clarify why these Japanese companies adopted the spin-off governance mode, and critically examine the previous research through case analysis.

7.2 A Case Analysis of the Morimura Zaibatsu

The Morimura Zaibatsu is the oldest corporate group in Japan and one of the largest corporate groups, along with KYOCERA Corporation, in the ceramics industry. The starting point of the corporate group called the Morimura Zaibatsu goes back to the establishment of a trading company named Morimura-gumi, which was founded by Ichizaemon Morimura, together with his younger brother Toyo Morimura, in 1876.

Morimura-gumi's business initially involved the export of Japanese antiques to the USA through Morimura Brothers, which was a retail store in New York City in the USA (Sunagawa 1998). As the popularity of Japanese-made pottery became clear, Morimura-gumi's business gradually evolved from the export of Japanese antiques to the production and export of porcelain, especially Western-style dinnerware sets, to meet the growing demand in the USA.

However, the development of Western-style dinnerware sets proved extremely difficult, because technology in Japan at that time could not produce the pure white porcelain clay required for making Western-style dinnerware sets. The research and development of the pure white clay was carried out mainly by Magobei Okura, the head clerk of Morimura-gumi, his son Kazuchika Okura, and Kotaro Asukai, the chief engineer. After studying abroad in Germany, a company named "Nippon Touki Gomei Kaisha" was established at the same time as the successful development of a pure white porcelain clay called Nitto 3.3.

7.2.1 Dispute Resolution and Corporate Control Not Based on Capital Principles

Nitto was established in 1904 in Noritake, Nagoya City, Aichi Prefecture, and the enterprise form of Nitto was a general partnership. According to the articles of incorporation, Nitto had five investors comprised of Ichizaemon Morimura, Magobei Okura, Morikata Murai, Kazuchika Okura, and Kotaro Asukai. The breakdown of capital was 30,000 yen for Ichizaemon Morimura, 25,000 yen each for Magobei Okura and Morikata Murai, 15,000 yen for Kazuchika Okura, and 5000 yen for Kotaro Asukai, for a total of 100,000 yen. All investors were members of the trading company Morimura-gumi.

The firm intended to produce export porcelain using automated manufacturing processes, but a major problem soon emerged. The firm was unable to manufacture the largest dinner plates of about 23 cm in diameter that formed part of the standard 93-piece Western-style dinnerware set because of issues with the pure white porcelain clay known as Nitto 3.3. As a result, Nitto recorded substantial deficits in its first several years of operation. Against this backdrop, a dispute emerged among Nitto's management personnel in around 1908 (Sunagawa 2000).

The clash was between Morimura-gumi, where founder Morimura Ichizaemon was calling for a return to business principles, and the Nitto camp comprising Nitto's head clerk, Magobei Okura, and his son Kazuchika who wanted the company to focus on manufacturing. The Nitto view was that mercantilism did not produce good factories, and that the firm needed to adopt a stronger emphasis on manufacturing. At the time, employees entered the gates at Noritake with the Nitto plant to the right and the Morimura-gumi office to the left. Every day, according to which way they turned through the gates, staff would be abused as "those *Morimura-gumi* chumps" or "those Nitto dummies." The internal clash between Ichizaemon and Morimura-gumi on the one hand and Magobei, Kazuchika, and the Nitto camp on the other escalated beyond a personal dispute among company executives into a companywide division.

In response to this dispute, Magobei and the Nitto camp developed a hard line, agreeing to continue handling American orders as a service to Morimura-gumi as long as Nitto was given discretion with regard to all other work. They argued that Nitto did not need Morimura Brothers for ceramicware sold on a yen basis in Nagoya (Ise 1957). This division between Morimura-gumi and Nitto became increasingly pronounced, and the situation deteriorated to the point that Ichizaemon finally decided to split the company.

Attempting to mediate the situation was Morikata Murai, who later became Morimura-gumi's general manager. Ichizaemon met with Murai, noting that various circumstances had prompted a request from Okura to split the company, and that he had no choice but to concede. Murai was asked to handle the aftermath accordingly.

After arriving in Nagoya, Murai visited the Nitto factory and found such a state of turmoil that it was difficult to know where to start. He first built a home in Shumoku-cho, invited Ise, a Morimura-gumi head office accountant, to Nagoya to serve as his secretary, and set about resolving the dispute.

Murai quickly recognized the cause of the dispute: the employees' dedicated approach to their work made them determined to have their own way, which in turn had them at odds with each other. As for the relationship between Morimura-gumi and Nitto, he believed the two should separate, but becoming two entirely separate entities, as per Nitto's request, also meant that the newly completed factory would be of no business use. Accordingly, even in the event of a split, the situation would have to be arranged calmly rather than in a spirit of anger in order to maintain psychological ties going forward (Oonishi 1943; Ise 1957).

Murai's first task for his newly appointed secretary was to draw up an agreement, the key issue of which was that while Morimura-gumi and Nitto would be separate entities, they would have to maintain psychological ties. The question was how to divide the controlling rights between Morimura-gumi and Nitto.

After much thought, Murai made Ichizaemon the company president and gave the controlling rights to the president, to be passed down to successive generations of the Morimura family. Magobei pushed for himself to become vice-president of Morimura-gumi, but to avoid creating a "two-headed snake," Murai made him an advisor to the company president. In addition, where Murai had previously managed Morimura Brothers, Morimura-gumi's US branch, his official designation was now as Morimura-gumi's general manager. In terms of handling Nitto, which had been the greatest point of dispute, the administration of Nitto was given to Kazuchika, who had been elected as a representative partner, and the administration of Morimura-gumi was limited in the director of the materials division.

This agreement was determined with the participation and consent of Ichizaemon and Magobei, the two parties to the dispute. Unlike the articles of ordinary companies, the agreement was not announced formally, but was an internal document intended to unify the various parties' mindsets (Oonishi 1943; Ise 1957).

Thanks to the determined efforts of Murai and Ise, the clash between Morimura-gumi executives Ichizaemon and Magobei began to cool. This was achieved through the use of an internal agreement formed on the basis of discussions with old and new executives, the main parties to the dispute included. In the end, the control of Morimura-gumi went to Ichizaemon with Murai as manager, while head clerk Magobei was made advisor to the president. Nitto itself became Morimura-gumi's materials division, supplying materials to Morimura-gumi on a monopoly basis. At first glance, it appears that the negotiations went entirely in the favor of Morimura-gumi.

However, interestingly enough, in 1908, Nitto itself became completely independent of Morimura-gumi in terms of capital, with Magobei and his son Kazuchika taking over company ownership. Ichizaemon, who was the biggest investor when Nitto was established, and Murai, who stood as the second biggest investor with the same capital amount as Magobei, resigned as Nitto partners (Nippontouki70nensihensyuuiinkai 1974).

Wanting to integrate Nitto with Morimura-gumi, the latter laid out its internal regulations, defined its philosophy, and restructured its organization. If Morimura-gumi and Nitto became separate firms, Morimura-gumi would not be able to export porcelain dinnerware sets to the US market created from the pure white porcelain clay that the company needed in order to grow. Given this situation, the rational solution would have been to bring Nitto completely under the Morimura-gumi umbrella even in terms of capital. However, Ichizaemon and Murai, key Morimura-gumi figures, withdrew their capital entirely from Nitto, which was then turned over to the ownership and control of Magobei and Kazuchika and made independent of Morimura-gumi capital. As a result, while capital relations between the two firms were dissolved, the danger of a complete corporate split was avoided.

7.2.2 Monitoring and Influence Not Based on Capital Principles

Around this time, Nitto partner and chief engineer Asukai was spearheading concerted efforts to develop dinner plates. Dinner plates were the largest plates in a 93-piece dinnerware set, measuring 23 cm in diameter. The technical problem in manufacturing these big plates was the weight of the materials causing the center to sag when the plates were fired. Extensive use of gairome clay to strengthen the mix muddied the color, but limiting the use of this clay to the point where the color was not affected resulted in misshapen plates (Nippontouki70nensihensyuuiinkai 1974).

In 1909, around the time when Asukai's plate development efforts seemed to have stalled, Magoemon Ezoe graduated from the Tokyo Higher Technical School and joined Nitto as an engineer. Ezoe first worked at the saggar factory, but Ise brought him over on an "urgent mission," and he found himself tackling the development of dinner plate clay. This situation caused another clash, this time between Asukai and the newcomer Ezoe. Ezoe undertook a comparative analysis of the constituents of the Nitto 3.3 clay mix and the clay used in Limoges porcelain to work out what was wrong with the Nitto 3.3 mix. He found that Nitto 3.3 clay contained a lot of silicic acid and little aluminum oxide, clearly identifying a higher ratio of aluminum oxide as the key issue.

Asukai felt threatened by Ezoe's actions and began to dislike the new engineer. Given that Asukai had graduated ahead of Ezoe from the same university, and had far more seniority status within Morimura-gumi and Nitto than Ezoe, this emotionally charged friction was probably inevitable. Ise notes that he received a secret report about a plot to give Ezoe a beating under the cover of darkness. Ise begged Ezoe to persevere, but in the end, Ezoe decided that he had no choice but to resign. The confrontation between Asukai and Ezoe related directly to differences over the direction of dinner plate clay development, but evolved into an attempt to isolate Ezoe at the organizational level, with Ezoe eventually deciding to leave the company.

The clash ultimately evolved into a major management headache of whether to retain Asukai or promote Ezoe. In 1910, Murai and Ise discussed the pros and cons of firing Asukai. Morimura-gumi executives were for terminating him immediately, but Murai was hesitant to take such a course because of potential implications. However, he ultimately decided that Asukai would have to go.

Murai's decision was communicated to Kazuchika, the Nitto representative partner. Kazuchika noted that while he regretted the move, the circumstances permitted no other choice. He asked to be allowed to inform Asukai himself as part of his job responsibilities. In the end, Asukai was handed his notice at Kazuchika's home on 29 October 1910, and Ezoe was informed of his appointment as managing head of the technical division. In this case, Morimura-gumi managed to influence Nitto's management even in the absence of capital relations between the two.

7.2.3 From Capital Split to the Japanese Spin-off Governance Mode

After Asukai left the company, Nitto's technical team led by Ezoe continued its desperate efforts to develop Western-style dinnerware sets for export to the USA. Then in 1913, 3 years after Asukai leaving, Ezoe and his team finally succeeded in

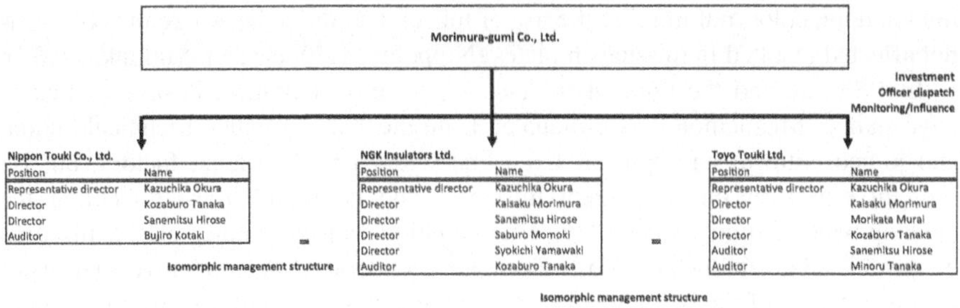

Fig. 7.1 Similarities in the management structures of the Nippon Touki Gomei Kaisha affiliates (Source: Shibata (2008))

making a 23-centimeter plate, and in 1914, mass production at the factory became possible. Roughly 10 years of research and development were spent on the development of Western-style dinnerware sets.

What status was given to Ise, who was dispatched to Nitto to mediate a dispute and then handed the role of monitoring Nitto's management? Ise became a Nitto partner in 1912, and in the same year, Momoki Saburo also became a partner, followed by Tsunekichi Takeuchi and Kozaburo Tanaka in 1913. Ise and Tanaka both had ties with Morimura-gumi. At that stage, the clash between Morimura-gumi and Nitto had been completely resolved, and while the two firms no longer had capital relations, their cooperative relationship seems to have stabilized.

Nitto subsequently became Nippon Touki Co., Ltd. When the firm changed from a general partnership to a joint stockholding company, both the Morimura family and the Okura family bought company stock, but Kazuchika was appointed as representative director, with Tanaka Kozaburo and Hirose Sanemitsu as directors. Tanaka and Hirose were core members of the Morimura-gumi Trading Company. The system whereby Kazuchika of the Okura family controlled Nitto's management while Morimura-gumi's people monitored and, where necessary, influenced the management seems to have been maintained here too.

In 1913, having been selected as a Nitto partner, Ise was appointed as auditor to NGK Insulators Ltd.,[2] a spin-off from Nitto's insulator division that had been capitalized as a joint stockholding company. This established what could be described as a federation-style governance mode called a spin-off, and was the origin of the Japanese spin-off governance mode, or a type of strategic behavior whereby cooperative arrangements are maintained even as the corporate body is segmented. An overview of this management structure is shown below (Fig. 7.1).

It should be noted that Kazuchika was appointed as representative director of NGK and Toyo Touki Ltd.,[3] both of which were spun off from Nitto, and that Kaisaku Morimura, who was Ichizaemon's successor, along with Tanaka and Hirose as core members, were appointed as directors and auditors. When the two companies

[2]Below, NGK.

[3]Below, TOTO (current title) and for this company, see Sasaki and Ikeda (1988).

became joint stockholding companies, the Morimura family and Morimura-gumi's people put up the capital, but management was controlled entirely by the Okura family. In other words, while the Morimura-gumi side invested in the spin-offs, they sought to do no more than monitor and influence the management by dispatching officers to these firms. This illustrates that corporate control, in which human ties are more influential than capital principles, had a great influence on the formation process of the Japanese spin-off governance mode. The invention of this governance mode made it possible to accumulate capital within a corporate group while avoiding a capital split of the company. As a result, this corporate group grew to become known as the Morimura Zaibatsu.

7.3 Findings

In the previous sections, we looked closely at the formation process of the governance mode known as the spin-off. Here we outline the findings of the case study and consider in greater detail the logic behind the formation of the Japanese spin-off governance mode.

1. The main factor prompting the 1908 spin-off, or in other words, the capital split, was the clash of management. This clash was mediated by Murai, who at the time was in charge of Morimura-gumi's US branch. To avoid a complete separation, Murai defined the corporate philosophy and established a particular mindset for Morimura-gumi and Nitto personnel. He gave control over Morimura-gumi affairs to the Morimura family, and control over Nitto affairs to the Okura family, withdrawing from Nitto those funds invested by Ichizaemon, a powerful Morimura-gumi member, and then his own investment in light of his subsequent position as manager of Morimura-gumi. Murai created an organizational structure and appointed Magobei as an advisor to Morimura-gumi as a way to constrain Magobei's influence within Morimura-gumi, while also dispatching to Nitto his own confidant, Ise. The dispatch of Ise gave Morimura-gumi an effective means of monitoring and, where necessary, influencing Nitto's management, but disputes were resolved through discussion and not on the basis of capital logic (Fig. 7.2).
2. These arrangements were relatively successful, but a new dispute between Asukai and Ezoe emerged within Nitto with regard to the direction of product development. Ise intervened in this process and sought to mediate, but ultimately Asukai left the company. This result represented the successful exercise of influence by Morimura-gumi executives, who had been unhappy with Asukai's policy. It is worth noting there was no capital relations between Nitto and Morimura-gumi at the time, and Asukai's dismissal was not based on capital principles.
3. Subsequently, Ise, who had been dispatched from Morimura-gumi as an ordinary worker, became a Nitto partner, while Tanaka, a key Morimura-gumi member, also became a Nitto partner. It was at this point that the pattern whereby

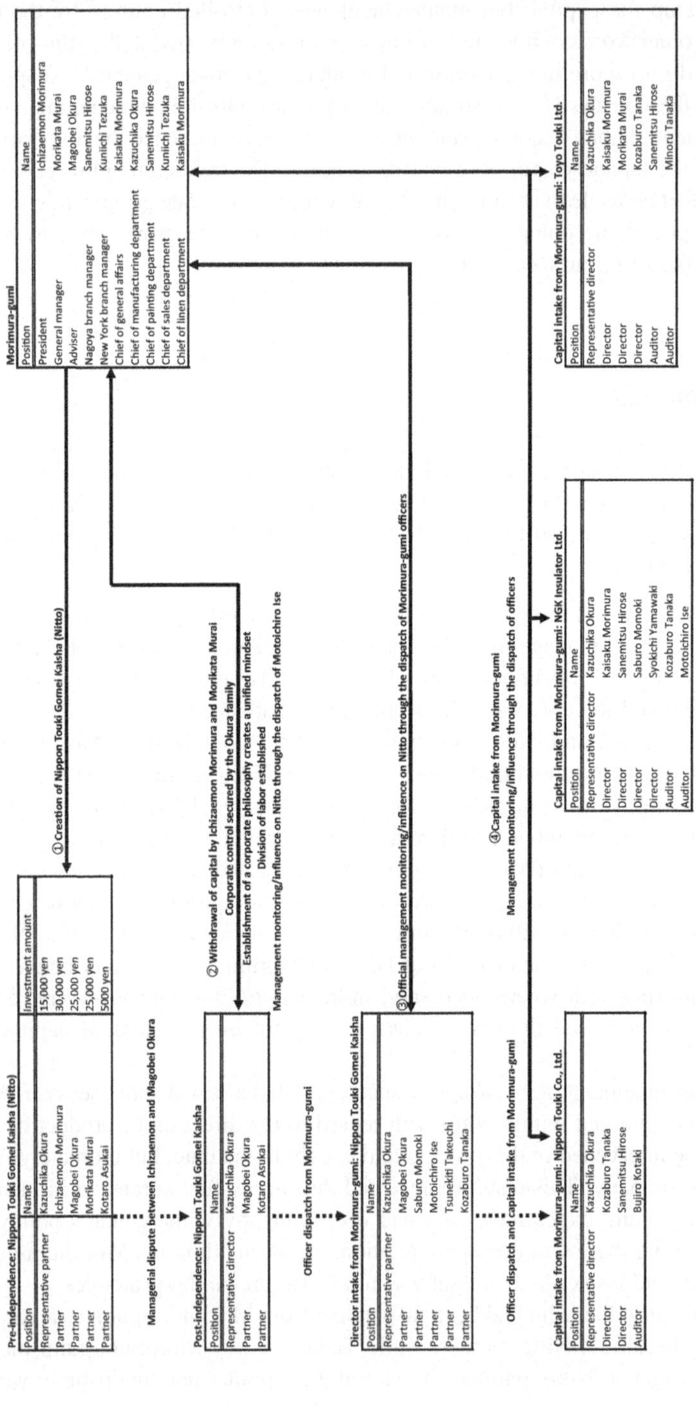

Fig. 7.2 Dispute resolution process and the Japanese spin-off governance mode formation process (Source: Shibata (2008))

Morimura-gumi would dispatch officers to Nitto as a means of monitoring and, where necessary, influencing Nitto management stabilized as a formal mechanism.

4. In addition, the year 1917 saw Nitto become a joint stockholding company. Nitto's head, Kazuchika, also invested in Nitto, but the bulk of the capital came from the Morimura family, which was a party to the 1908 dispute. Kazuchika became the representative director, while the directors and auditors were all Morimura-gumi people. The same governance modes were evident in TOTO, a spin-off from Nitto's hygiene ceramics division, and NGK, a spin-off from Nitto's insulator division.

7.4 Discussion

In the previous section, we undertook a detailed examination of the corporate spin-off process with a focus on the Nitto case, noting the findings that we regard as important in terms of the essence of the Japanese spin-off governance mode as a form of strategic behavior. What do the above facts signify in terms of understanding the form of strategic behavior known as the Japanese spin-off?

Ito (1995) suggests that the key to the Japanese spin-off governance mode as a form of strategic behavior by Japanese firms is the reduction of transaction costs. He notes three alternative methods of managing new businesses: (1) through the market; (2) through a hierarchy; and (3) through a spin-off. Transaction costs, he states, determine which trading relationship between the parent firm and the subsidiary will be selected. In particular, Ito argues that the homogeneity of Japanese society compared to the USA means that opportunistic behavior of subsidiaries can be constrained through monitoring and sanctions imposed by tight social networks in Japan, with the result that parent firms can control their subsidiaries' behavior through partial ownership of their stock without having to seek complete control of the businesses by means of ownership. How valid is this interpretation in terms of understanding the phenomenon of the Japanese spin-off governance mode?

What we first observe is the fact that companies at the time were not operated on the basis of capital principles, as seen in the dispute resolution process within Nitto. The development of the Western dinner plate, which was part of the standard 93-piece dinnerware set, had become a bottleneck in developing Western dinnerware sets for the US market. Because dinner plate development required a substantial injection of capital, a dispute emerged between Ichizaemon on the one hand, who focused on the business aspects and consequently felt that dinner plates did not have to be developed in-house, and Magobei on the other, who insisted on in-house development. This dispute, however, was not resolved by majority investment.

In addition, the dispute between Morimura-gumi leaders Ichizaemon and Magobei was not the only one to arise in the process of dinnerware set development. A clash also arose between Asukai, a Morimura-gumi engineer and Nitto partner, and Ezoe, a new Nitto engineer. As noted earlier, this clash resulted in Asukai leaving the company and his departure marked the successful exercise of influence by Morimura-gumi executives, unhappy over the slow progress of dinner plate development. This influence was also not based on capital principles. The two firms certainly enjoyed cooperative relations, with the division of labor between Morimura-gumi and Nitto at the time having the former handling the export business side and the latter supplying the materials for export ceramicware. In capital terms, however, the firms were entirely separate entities.

Corporate control was not conducted on the basis of the capital principles of majority investment and ownership, nor was Asukai's opportunistic behavior checked on the basis of these principles.

Summarizing the above, the explanation given by Ito (1995) for the phenomenon of Japanese spin-offs appears to be limited in that companies at the time, at least as far as the Nitto case suggests, did not attempt corporate control on the basis of capital principles such as ownership rights embodied in majority investment. In the dispute resolution process, capital principles were not used at all as a means of resolution; corporate behavior was instead influenced by other means. Nitto's spin-offs were created not on the economically rational grounds of reducing transaction costs, but because of differences between management personnel in regard to the company's future direction—in other words, differences in their strategies. This would suggest the need to revisit the very framework put forward by Ito, which only categorizes firms according to the degree of ownership and views them as being controlled only on the basis of ownership. In other words, in the case of Japan, the foundation of corporate activities may be human ties rather than capital ties.

Looking at the cases of influence not based on capital principles, there appears to be some evidence of the constraining effect that Ito (1995) argues to be exercised over potential opportunistic behavior of subsidiaries through sanctions based on social networks. However, if sanctions from social networks were in fact entirely effective, there would be no spin-offs. Moreover, from the Nitto case it could even be argued that spin-offs are created because of sanctions from social networks. In that sense, the influence of sanctions from social networks as indicated by Ito could well be positioned as a central factor in understanding the Japanese spin-off governance mode. At the same time, the Nitto case obviates the consideration of the function of social networks in the sense indicated by Ito as a key factor in the formation of the Japanese spin-off governance mode.

There is a more fundamental problem when it comes to using the transaction cost theory to understand the Japanese spin-off governance mode as a form of strategic behavior by Japanese firms. The transaction cost theory is premised on a product and service vertical trading relationship between the parent firm and the subsidiary. A vertical trading relationship was needed between Morimura-gumi as an exporter and Nitto as a dinnerware set manufacturer in that Nitto's dinnerware sets were exported to the USA by Morimura-gumi. This trading relationship clearly had to be established between the two firms even after the corporate split, and the importance invested in sustaining that relationship is borne out by the great lengths to which Murai as mediator went in resolving the Ichizaemon-Magobei dispute to ensure that the companies did not become entirely separate entities. NGK, by contrast, made high-pressure insulators in the construction materials sector that were used in domestic power stations, electric lights, and telegraphic communications, while TOTO focused on manufacturing hygiene ceramics to meet Western-style construction demand, which was growing in response to Japan's Europeanization policy. In other words, while Morimura-gumi and Nitto had a vertically continuous trading relationship, NGK and TOTO had no need to build such a relationship with Morimura-gumi or Nitto to further their businesses. From the standpoint of trading products and services, there are evidently some limits to understanding the phenomenon of Japanese spin-offs from the perspective of the transaction cost theory.

Ito (1995) also puts forward the explanation that the significance of the Japanese spin-off governance mode is in separating the subsidiaries from the parent firm's core competencies with dominant logic. If this were true, how would we explain the appointment of Kazuchika as representative director of Nitto, NGK, and TOTO, or the inclusion of many personnel from Morimura-gumi and the parent firm Nitto in the management ranks of the spin-offs? If the significance of Japanese spin-offs lies in the separation of core competencies, the same result could be achieved through rigorous decentralization. Even where the further step of creating a spin-off is taken to the extent that management ranks are filled with personnel from the parent firm, separating subsidiaries from the parent firm's core competencies becomes a logical impossibility. In the case of Nitto, as Ito suggests, it may be possible to understand that sharing human resources between the parent firm and the subsidiary is more suitable for transaction costs because of the high relevance in the business of spin-offs. However, it may be understood as an example of corporate control based on human principles (i.e. human ties) rather than capital principles.

Finally, another explanation given alongside the separation of core competencies relates to Japan's labor market conditions and practices, namely the need for Japanese firms to create new upper management posts for senior employees as part of the Japanese practice of lifelong employment. Ito (1995) suggests that the creation of spin-offs is a response to pressure from internal labor markets. If firms need to create new upper management posts for senior employees as part of lifelong employment, they can do so by simply increasing the number of upper management posts within the parent firm. Moreover, it is unclear whether the practice of lifelong employment actually existed back then.[4] In fact, NGK fired 120 employees in order to ride out the recession at the time of the Russo-Japanese War.[5] In other words, Nitto was creating spin-offs back in a time when the practice of lifelong employment had not yet emerged in Japanese firms. Japanese labor market conditions and practices appear to be an extremely narrow explanation of Japanese spin-offs.

---

[4] Fujimura (2006) notes the difficulty in to proving whether or not prewar Japanese firms followed the practice of lifelong employment.

[5] Shibagaki et al. (1995) state that NGK fired 120 factory hands because of the temporary recession caused by the Russo-Japanese War.

What key factors can be identified in terms of understanding Japanese spin-offs as a form of strategic behavior among Japanese firms? The dispute resolution process at Nitto offers some hints. First is the nature of the company. The direct cause of the Nitto split was the dispute between Morimura-gumi's founder, Ichizaemon, and the head clerk, Magobei. Nitto was engaged in the production of export ceramicware for the US market using automated manufacturing processes, but not only did Nitto fail to show a profit, the company could not even make the products. Dissatisfied with this situation, Ichizaemon wanted to re-focus on the business aspects, while Magobei was working actively to produce export ceramicware using an automated manufacturing setup, and wanted the emphasis to remain on the factory. These differences in direction between Morimura-gumi and Nitto—in other words, differences in strategy—were the fundamental cause of the dispute. The dispute was not resolved through a capital majority, but rather by appointing Ichizaemon head of Morimura-gumi and pulling the capital of Ichizaemon and Murai out of Nitto in order to pass control of Nitto to Magobei and Kazuchika.

What does all this mean? It indicates that corporate control at the time was not based on majority investment embodying ownership rights. As an expedient means of dispute resolution, ownership rights, or the majority capital embodying these rights, did not have any meaning for firms at the time. In other words, companies at the time used the nature of "personal association" that prioritized human ties rather than capital ties.

At one point, Morimura-gumi and Nitto appeared to have split entirely, at least in terms of capital, yet they subsequently succeeded in building a cooperative relationship. When Nitto became a joint stockholding company, it was the Morimura family and other Morimura-gumi personnel who put up most of the capital. This investment was not linked to corporate control. If it had been tied to corporate control in the conventional sense, the company might well have split again as the result of further disputes. To avoid a situation detrimental to the survival and growth of the firm, a form of investment was created which entailed providing funds without seeking control.

Naturally, this form of investment was not without a quid pro quo. Many of Nitto's investors were top Morimura-gumi personnel who dispatched officers to Nitto to monitor the firm's management and also exercise a certain amount of influence over the controlling Okura family's management policies through constraining actions. The emergence of this form of investment was the primary reason why Morimura-gumi and Nitto were able to develop a cooperative arrangement, creating as a result the mode of governance known as the Japanese spin-off governance mode.

7.5 Conclusion

This paper offers a detailed examination of the formation process of the Japanese spin-off governance mode, a form of strategic behavior pronounced among Japanese firms. The major factor behind the Nitto spin-off was a management dispute. For companies back then, the majority capital that usually embodies ownership rights was not an effective means of resolving this kind of management-level dispute. Company spin-offs occurred because of the nature of firms as personal associations.

However, the nature of firms as personal associations was not the direct factor in the formation of the Japanese spin-off governance mode. Rather, it was the premise upon which external capital was gathered or rallied to form the particular governance mode known as the Japanese spin-off. This investment did not take the conventional form whereby majority capital is linked directly to corporate control. Investors were not aspiring to corporate control; they aimed purely to monitor and, where necessary, influence management through the dispatch of officers.

The Japanese spin-off governance mode did not emerge from the intention to control subsidiaries on the basis of capital principles, nor were spin-offs planned as a means of fostering the subsidiaries' core competencies. And spin-offs were certainly not designed with a view to increasing management posts in line with the practice of lifelong employment.

The prototype for the governance mode known as Japanese spin-offs was developed as a last resort in response to what could be described as an unplanned outcome with the aim of overall optimization of the Morimura-gumi and Nitto businesses in the face of the crisis situation of a possible complete corporate split. The Japanese spin-off governance mode can therefore be characterized as a radical management innovation enabling the creation of interfirm cooperative arrangements premised on the basic nature of Japanese firms in past days as personal associations.[6]

Acknowledgment This work was supported by JSPS KAKENHI Grant Number JP20K01914.

References

Fujimura S (2006) Teinentaishoku no kigen. Liaison Newslett 43(6)
Grossman SJ, Hart OD (1986) The costs and benefits of ownership: a theory of vertical and lateral integration. J Polit Econ:691–719
Ise I (1950) Kindainippontougyohattenhishi. Gihoudou
Ise I (1957) Tougyoushinkou no kakushin. Gihoudou
Ito K (1995) Japanese spin-offs: unexplored survival strategies. Strateg Manage J 16:431–446
Nippontouki70nensihensyuuiinkai (1974) Nippontouki70nenshi. Nippontouki Co., Ltd.
Oonishi R (1943) Murai-Morikataden. Murai-Morikataaikyoukai
Sasaki T, Ikeda M (1988) Toutoukiki70nenshi. Totokikikabushikikaisya

[6]For other cases, see Shibata (2006).

Shibagaki K, Ito M, Hasegawa S, Kikkawa T (1995) Nippongaishi75nenshi. Nippongaishikabushikikaisya

Shibata A (2006) Tougikisangyou niokeru kaishaseido nikansuru kenkyuu. Doctoral Dissertation. Kobe University Graduate School of Business Administration, Kobe

Shibata A (2008) Japanese-style spin-off strategy: formation process and logic, A case study of Nippon Touki Gomei Kaisha. J Bus Manage 22:41–52

Sunagawa Y (1998) Morimura-Ichizaemonmuyoku no shougai. Soushisha

Sunagawa Y (2000) Seitououkoku wo kizuitatiti to ko: Okura-Magobeito Okura-Kazuchika. Shobunsha

Williamson OE (1975) Markets and hierarchies: analysis and antitrust implications. Free Press, New York

Chapter 8
Dynamic Model of Urbanization with Public Goods

Masamichi Kawano

Abstract We try to examine the optimal number of the regions or the optimal number of the population would be? The Henry George theorem is about the optimal supply of local public goods. The theorem asserts that the optimal population of a region is attained when the total expenditure on the public goods equals the total revenue of the land rents. This theorem had been discussed in static frameworks. We examine this theorem in a dynamic framework. We used an overlapping-generations model and derived the optimal dynamic path of the economy, and we try to examine the theorem. As the result, it is shown that the theorem holds in a steady state, but does not hold on the optimal path which is converging to the steady state.

Keywords Henry George theorem · Public goods · Urbanization · Optimal population

JEL Classification O21, R13

8.1 Introduction

In this paper, we try to examine how many regions[1] are necessary or how the size of each region should be?[2] The Henry George theorem relates to this kind of question. This theorem relates to the optimal supply of local public goods. The theorem asserts

---

This paper is a revised version of Kawano (2014).

---

[1]The term *region* in this paper implies the area where people live together and jointly consume the service of the same public goods.

[2]In China, people in agricultural sector are moving to urban sector. About 51% of the total population live in urban area now. However, there are 16% of the non-registered residents in

---

M. Kawano (✉)
Kwansei Gakuin University, Nishinomiya, Japan

M. Kawano et al. (eds.), *Theory and History in Regional Perspective*, New Frontiers in Regional Science: Asian Perspectives 56,
https://doi.org/10.1007/978-981-16-6695-7_8

that the optimal population of a region is attained when the total expenditure on the public goods equals the total revenue of the land rents. That is, the revenue of the land rent should be all taxed and the revenue of the government should be all spent only on the public goods. Then the optimal number of the population in each region is attained, or in other words, optimal number of the regions in a country is attained, since the total population is given and all regions are assumed homogeneous.

The theorem was named after the Single Tax theory of Henry George (1942). Flatters et al. (1974) first introduced this theorem into regional economics. They called this theorem "Golden Rule." The term Henry George theorem was first used by Arnott and Stiglitz (1979). The theorem is related to the efficiency of the production side of the economy, and it guarantees the maximum per-capita consumption for any given level of the public good. It does not guarantee the optimal supply of the public goods. Together with the optimal supply condition of the public good shown by Samuelson (1954), the total optimality is attained.

The theorem had been mainly discussed in the framework of statics. See Arnott (2004); Hartwick (1980); Kanemoto et al. (1996). When we consider the optimal strategy of urbanization in developing economies, we desire to check whether the theorem still holds in dynamic framework. Thus, we extend the theorem to a dynamic context. Fu (2005),[3] based on the same purpose, tried to extend the Henry George theorem, and derived that the theorem holds in the sense that the present value of the total land rents over all time periods equals the present value of the public goods expenditure over all time periods. But in each period, the theorem does not hold and the land rents and the optimal public goods expenditure are not equal.

The main purpose of this paper is to examine the Henry George theorem in the transient state in our model. We use the overlapping-generations model, where we assume that the land is succeeded over generations, and the method of saving is only to possess the land. The interest income for the saving is the capital gain of the land plus the land rent net of the tax payment.

Total population is fixed for the sake of simplicity. There are no population growth in sum, but for each region the population changes since the number of the regions is determined by the government. The government divides the population to regions equally at every period. Public good is also distributed for each regions equally. Total amount of the public goods evolves according to the total investment and depreciation. Under these assumptions, we derive the optimal path of the economy. On the optimal path, the population of each region moves monotonically and converges to the steady state. That is, if the population of each region is smaller than the optimal steady state level at the starting point of the plan, the optimal

urban regions, and they cannot receive enough public services from the governments. This is an important urbanization problem in China. See Ehara (2013), Kaniwa (2013). However, we cannot discuss this kind of problem and we limit our discussion in purely economic field in this paper.

[3]Especially, Chapter 1 of his dissertation, "Dynamic Henry George Theorem and Optimal City Sizes."

population level should increase. (or, the number of the regions should decrease.) We derive that, also in this model, the Henry George theorem holds in the steady state but, in the transient state, it does not hold also in this model.

In the next section, we will present the basic model, which discusses the optimal consumption of private goods. In Sect. 8.3, welfare maximization is discussed. The governmental optimal policy is to give the optimal number of the population per region, and that is equivalent to determine the optimal number of the public goods in each region. Also we discuss on the Henry George theorem both in steady state and transient state. Section 8.4 concludes the discussions.

8.2 The Basic Model

We assume that the population of a country is distributed equally over homogeneous regions. The number of the total population is fixed and there is no population growth in a country. Each individual lives for two periods. He works at the first period in the agricultural sector, and earns the wage income. He consumes a part of the wage income and saves the rest. In the next period, he does not work, but he becomes the owner of the land, buying the land with the saving of the young age. The generations overlap, and there are young workers and the same number of old land owners.

Let us assume, for the sake of simplicity, that the square of the land available for a region is equally limited.[4] All regions are physically homogeneous. The production factor of each region is labor, and the production function is given by

$$Y_t = F(N_t), \quad F' > 0, \;\; F'' < 0, \tag{8.1}$$

where N_t is the amount of labor, that is, the younger generation at period t, Y_t is the amount of the product at period t. We assume that the land is another production factor, however, we ignore it from consideration since the size of the land in each region is assumed fixed at the same level.

The worker of the period t, i.e., the generation t, earns the wage income w_t, and he faces the interest rate r_{t+1}, which will be explained later. Then, the budget constraint is given by

$$w_t = C_t^1 + \frac{C_{t+1}^2}{1 + r_{t+1}}, \tag{8.2}$$

where C_t^1 is the per-capita consumption of the young age at period t, and C_{t+1}^2 that of the old age at period $t + 1$. He maximizes the utility function,

[4]Fujita (1989) and others derived the physical size of the city endogenously. We assume the physical size is fixed for the sake of simplicity. This assumption does not affect the result crucially.

$$u_t = u^1\left(C_t^1, C_{t+1}^2\right) \tag{8.3}$$

subject to the budget constraint (8.2). The individual of the generation t determines the consumption of the periods t and $t + 1$ so as to maximize the utility function (8.3), then we have the consumption functions

$$C_t^{1*} = C^1(w_t, r_{t+1}) \tag{8.4}$$

and

$$C_{t+1}^{2*} = C^2(w_t, r_{t+1}). \tag{8.5}$$

Thus, the saving is given by

$$S_t = w_t - C^1(w_t, r_{t+1}). \tag{8.6}$$

Since the public goods are supplied by the government, the individuals take them as given. Here we assume that the public good G has no external effect on the consumption functions (8.4) and (8.5). Let us assume that there is only one way of storing wealth that is to possess the land. The saving S_t is all spent to buy the land. We assume that the older generation of any regions can buy the land of any other regions. Since we assume that the government can determine the number of the regions at each period, there should be some regions which happen to be unpopulated suddenly. Then some land owners suffer loss in the reality. In order to avoid this kind of asymmetry among landowners, we assume that all landowners are homogeneous, and people can buy any land of any other regions and the expected profit rate is common to all lands. Let V_t denote the total land value of one region, then the total land value of a country is given by $V_t n_t$, where n_t stands for the number of the regions at period t. Since the total population of each generation is fixed at p, we have $n_t = p/N_t$. At each period, the number of the regions changes since it is a policy variable of the government. The younger generation as well as the older generation together move across the border of the regions.[5] Thus, since the saving of the total population of this country is all invested into the land, we have

$$\frac{V_t}{N_t} = S_t \tag{8.7}$$

g_t is the country's total investment for the public good, but if it is seen from the individual's side, the total tax, and $\frac{g_t}{p}$ is the tax-per capita. Then $\frac{g_t N_t}{p}$ is the total tax per region.

[5] At each period, two generations co-exist, so the total population is $2p$.

The total income of the old generation, *i.e.*, the generation t at the period $t + 1$ is given by

$$\left(V_{t+1} + F(N_{t+1}) - N_{t+1}F'(N_{t+1}) - \frac{g_{t+1}N_{t+1}}{p}\right)n_{t+1} \tag{8.8}$$

that is the revenue from selling the land to the next generation $V_{t+1}n_{t+1}$, plus the total land rent $\left(F_{t+1} - N_{t+1}F'_{t+1}\right)n_{t+1}$ net of tax payment $g_{t+1}N_{t+1}n_{t+1}/p$. Since the total revenue of the older generation is all spent for the consumption for the old age of the period $t + 1$, we have

$$\left(V_{t+1} + F(N_{t+1}) - N_{t+1}F'(N_{t+1}) - \frac{g_{t+1}N_{t+1}}{p}\right)\frac{n_{t+1}}{p} = C^2_{t+1}. \tag{8.9}$$

Then the interest rate for the saving for the generation t is given by

$$\begin{aligned} r_{t+1} &= \frac{\frac{V_{t+1}}{N_{t+1}}p + \left(F(N_{t+1}) - N_{t+1}F'(N_{t+1}) - \frac{g_{t+1}N_{t+1}}{p}\right)n_{t+1}}{\frac{V_t}{N_t}p} - 1 \\ &= \frac{w_{t+1} - C^{1*}_{t+1} + \frac{F(N_{t+1}) - N_{t+1}F'(N_{t+1})}{N_{t+1}} - \frac{g_{t+1}}{p}}{w_t - C^{1*}_t} - 1 \end{aligned} \tag{8.10}$$

from (8.6), (8.7) and $n_t = p/N_t$. Since the wage rate is given by the marginal productivity of labor, we have $w_t = F'(N_t)$, then we denote the wage rate as the function of N,

$$w_t = w(N_t). \tag{8.11}$$

Hence the wage rate is determined by the number of the workers in each region.

8.3 Welfare Analysis

We discuss the government's behavior to maximize the social welfare. We assume that the welfare of this society is composed of the sum of each generation's utility. The utility of each generation is given by

$$u^{\mathrm{C}}\left(C^{1*}_t, C^{2*}_{t+1}\right) + u^{\mathrm{G}}(N_tG_t/p), \tag{8.12}$$

where G_t is the stock of the public good all over the country in sum. The first term is the utility from the private goods, and the second, the public good. G_t/p is the per-capita public good, and N_tG_t/p denotes the total amount of the public good available in one region, which determines the utility of the public goods for each individual.

G_t is the public good at the beginning of the period t, and it depreciates at the rate of δ. Hence, the dynamic equation of the total public good is given by

$$G_{t+1} = g_t + (1 - \delta)G_t. \tag{8.13}$$

The government of the country tries to maximize the sum of the utility (8.12) over the generations to an infinity subject to the dynamic equation of the total public good (8.13),

$$\begin{aligned} &\text{maximize} \sum_{t=0}^{\infty} \left[u^{C}(C_t^{1*}, C_{t+1}^{2*}) + u^{G}(N_tG_t/p) - B\right] \\ &\text{subject to } \; G_{t+1} = g_t + (1 - \delta)G_t, \end{aligned} \tag{8.14}$$

where B is the bliss, *i.e.*, the maximum utility attainable among possible steady states.[6] Here the strategic variables for the government are the time path of $\{g_t\}$ and $\{N_t\}$.[7] The movement of the public good can be shown by (8.13) and which implies that the total public goods in this model are effectively used and never discarded. This implies that the public goods can move across the border of the regions with individuals.

In order to solve this government problem and derive a clear-cut result, we have to introduce the simplifying assumptions on the production and utility functions.

8.3.1 *Specialization of the Model*

For the sake of simplicity, we assume that the production function is given by

$$F(N_t) = \sqrt{N_t}. \tag{8.15}$$

Then the wage rate is given by $w_t = \frac{1}{2\sqrt{N_t}}$, and the utility function is specified as

[6]The bliss is introduced for a mathematical purpose, that is, for the objective function not to expand to an infinity, and it does not have essentially important meaning economically. See Ramsey (1928).
[7]This can be said as $\{G_t\}$ and $\{n_t\}$.

$$u^{\mathrm{C}} = \frac{1}{2}\ln C_t^1 + \frac{1}{2}\ln C_{t+1}^2. \tag{8.16}$$

Then from (8.2), (8.10), and (8.16), we obtain

$$C_t^{1*} = \frac{1}{4\sqrt{N_t}} \tag{8.17}$$

and

$$C_t^{2*} = \frac{3}{4\sqrt{N_{t+1}}} - \frac{g_{t+1}}{p}. \tag{8.18}$$

Thus, we obtain that $u^{\mathrm{C}}\left(C_t^{1*}, C_{t+1}^{2*}\right)$ as a function of N and g_{t+1}.

Next, we introduce public goods. Government supplies the public goods, that is, for the individuals it is exogenous variables and they cannot control them. We showed that the utility of the public goods is given by $u^{\mathrm{G}}\left(\frac{G_tN_t}{p}\right)$. However, the specified utility function of the public good is given by $\frac{AG_tN_t}{p}$, where A is the co-efficient parameter of the public good.

The utility function of the consumptions of the generation t is log-linear additive separable as follows:[8]

$$U_t = \frac{1}{2}\ln C_t^1 + \frac{1}{2}\ln C_{t+1}^2 + \frac{AG_tN_t}{p}. \tag{8.19}$$

Hence we derive that the utility is given by (8.17)–(8.19) as

$$U_t = \frac{1}{2}\ln\left(\frac{1}{4\sqrt{N_t}}\right) + \frac{1}{2}\ln\left(\frac{3}{4\sqrt{N_{t+1}}} - \frac{g_{t+1}}{p}\right) + \frac{AG_tN_t}{p}, \tag{8.20}$$

The government problem is to maximize the sum of the utility U_t subject to the dynamic equation of the public good, given by (8.13). But here for the sake of simplification we assume that $\delta = 1/2$. Then the Lagrangean for the maximization is given by

[8]If we assume symmetric utility function, $U_t = \beta_1 \ln C_t^1 + \beta_2 \ln C_{t+1}^2 + \beta_3 \ln\left(\frac{G_tN_t}{p}\right)$, then we cannot derive steady state equilibrium.

$$L = \sum_{t=0}^{\infty} \left[\begin{array}{l} \frac{1}{2} \ln\left(\frac{1}{4\sqrt{N_t}}\right) + \frac{1}{2} \ln\left(\frac{3}{4\sqrt{N_{t+1}}} - \frac{g_{t+1}}{p}\right) + \frac{AG_{t+1}N_{t+1}}{p} \\ +\mu_{t+1}\left\{g_t + \frac{G_t}{2} - G_{t+1}\right\} - B \end{array} \right]. \quad (8.21)$$

Differentiating (8.21) w.r.t N_t, G_t. g_t and μ_t, we obtain the following first order conditions:

$$\frac{\partial L}{\partial N_t} = \frac{1}{2} \frac{-2g_t\sqrt{N_t} + 3p}{N_t(4g_t\sqrt{N_t} - 3p)} + \frac{AG_t}{p} = 0, \quad (8.22)$$

$$\frac{\partial L}{\partial G_t} = \frac{AN_t}{p} + \frac{\mu_{t+1}}{2} - \mu_t = 0, \quad (8.23)$$

$$\frac{\partial L}{\partial g_t} = \frac{-\frac{1}{2}N_t}{p\left(\frac{3}{4}\sqrt{N_t} - \frac{g_tN_t}{p}\right)} + \mu_{t+1} = 0, \quad (8.24)$$

$$\frac{\partial L}{\partial \mu_t} = g_t + \frac{G_t}{2} - G_{t+1} = 0. \quad (8.25)$$

From these first-order conditions, the optimal dynamic equations can be derived. This dynamic system is essentially second order difference equation system in μ_t and G_t and other variables N_t and g_t are connected to them. First, let us derive the difference equations in G_t andμ_t, eliminating N_t andg_t. From (8.24) we obtain

$$g_t = \frac{1}{4}\left(\frac{3p}{\sqrt{N_t}} - \frac{2}{\mu_{t+1}}\right). \quad (8.26)$$

From (8.23), we have

$$N_t = \frac{p}{A}\left(-\frac{1}{2}\mu_{t+1} + \mu_t\right). \quad (8.27)$$

From (8.22), (8.26) and (8.27), we obtain a difference equation to give μ_{t+1} by μ_t and G_t, as

$$G_t - p\left(\frac{3\sqrt{2}p\mu_{t+1} + 2\sqrt{\frac{(-\mu_{t+1}+2\mu_t)p}{A}}}{4A\left(\frac{-\mu_{t+1}+2\mu_t}{A}\right)^{3/2}}\right) = 0. \quad (8.28)$$

Next, we derive a difference equations for μ and G, from (8.25) by (8.26) and (8.27),

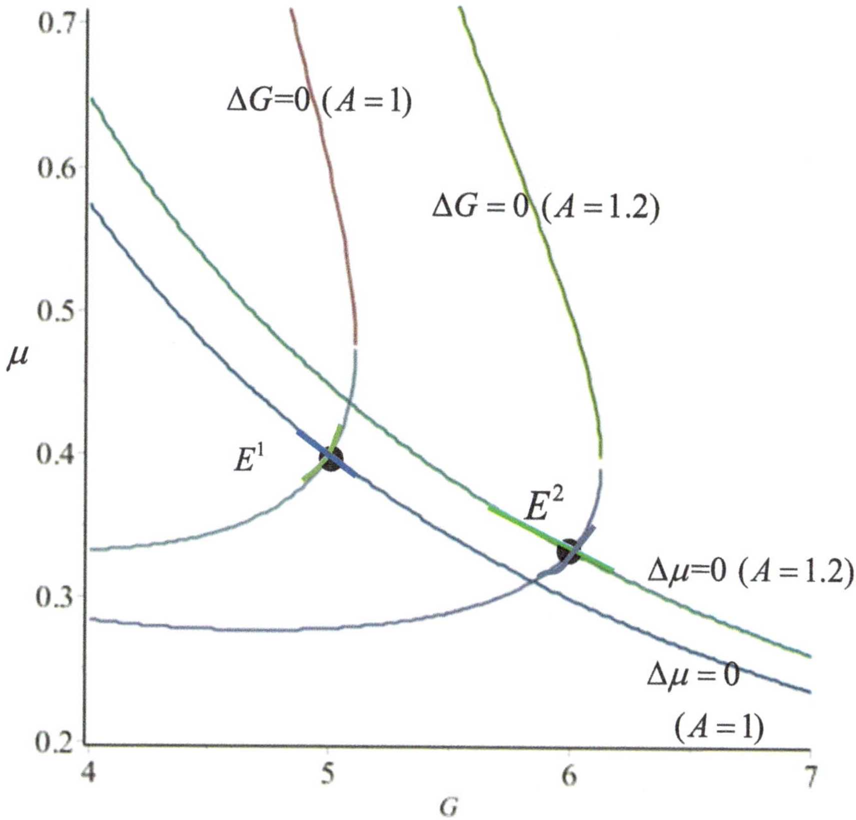

Fig. 8.1 Steady state equilibrium

$$G_{t+1} - \frac{3\sqrt{2}p}{4\sqrt{\frac{(-u_{t+1}+2u_t)p}{A}}} + \frac{1}{2u_{t+1}} - \frac{G_t}{2} = 0 \tag{8.29}$$

This is an implicit function of $(\mu_{t+1}, \mu_t, G_{t+1}, G_t)$, In order to derive the dynamic path of the system, we have to obtain the following type two difference equations $\mu_{t+1} = \varphi(\mu_t, G_t)$ and $G_{t+1} = \psi(\mu_t, G_t)$. The former is already obtained as (8.28), but the latter is not yet derived. In order to obtain the latter difference equation, we have to solve nonlinear simultaneous equations given by (8.28) and (8.29). That is essentially solving cubic simultaneous non-linear equations. But, we could solve them by *Maple*, but the solutions are too complicated that we do not show them here. But, we can show here the graphs of $\Delta\mu_t = 0$ and $\Delta G_t = 0$. Figure 8.1 shows the graph of $\Delta\mu_t = 0$ and $\Delta G = 0$, assuming two cases of parameters, i.e., $(A, p) = (1, 5)$ and $(1.2, 5)$. We showed a comparative statics result graphically. E^1 is the steady state equilibrium when $(A, p) = (1, 5)$, and E^2 when $(A, p) = (1.2, 5)$. It shows that if the efficiency parameter of the utility of the public good A increases (decreases), then μ decreases (increases) and G increases (decreases).

We have derived the graphs of $\Delta\mu = 0$ and $\Delta G = 0$, but in order to derive the movement of the variables, we need the phase diagram. For this purpose, we want to obtain the linear approximation of the system around the steady state. Hence, at first, we have to derive the steady state equilibrium.

8.3.2 Steady State Equilibrium Analysis

From (8.28), (8.29) and $\mu_{t+1} = \mu_t$ and $G_{t+1} = G_t$, we derive the steady state values,

$$(\mu^*, G^*) = \left(\frac{2}{Ap}, Ap\right).$$

For the steady states values of N and g, we take (8.26), (8.27) into (8.28), (8.29), we obtain the steady state levels for all the variables,

$$(\mu^*, G^*, g^*, N^*) = \left(\frac{2}{Ap}, Ap, \frac{Ap}{2}, \frac{1}{A^2}\right) \tag{8.30}$$

We summarize these results as the following lemma:

Lemma 8.1: Steady State Equilibrium *On the steady state equilibrium, the product of the parameters, Ap, (the productivity of the utility of public good times the total population) determines* μ^*, G^*, g^*, *but* N^* *since* $(\mu^*, G^*, g^*, N^*) = \left(\frac{2}{Ap}, Ap, \frac{Ap}{2}, \frac{1}{A^2}\right)$. *The steady state population of a region is determined independently from p.*

8.3.3 Optimal Path of the Transient State

Let us back to the transient state analysis. Assuming $(A, p) = (1, 5)$, we analyze the movement around the steady state, $(\mu^*, G^*) = \left(\frac{2}{5}, 5\right)$, by linear approximation.

Firstly, we linearize our fundamental difference equation system (8.28) and (8.29) around the steady state. We derived

$$\mathrm{d}\mu_{t+1} = \frac{22}{17}\mathrm{d}\mu_t + \frac{16}{425}\mathrm{d}G_t, \tag{8.31}$$

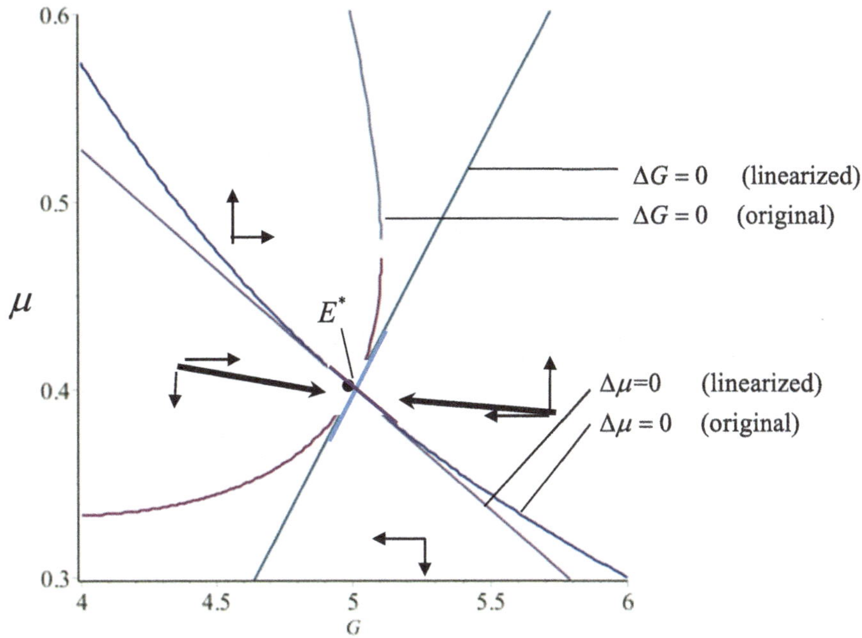

Fig. 8.2 Linear approximation of the optimal path. (These graphs are made by *Maple*)

$$dG_{t+1} = \frac{25}{34} d\mu_t + \frac{27}{34} dG_t. \tag{8.32}$$

These two equations show the movement of μ_t and G_t near the steady state. Arranging these equations, we have

$$d(u_{t+1} - \mu_t) = \frac{5}{17} d\mu_t + \frac{16}{425} dG_t, \tag{8.33}$$

$$d(G_{t+1} - G_t) = \frac{25}{34} d\mu_t - \frac{7}{34} dG_t. \tag{8.34}$$

The movement of μ_t and $G_t$is as shown by the arrows in Fig. 8.2. From (8.33), we have $\frac{\partial(u_{t+1} - \mu_t)}{\partial \mu_t} = \frac{5}{17}$, which shows that if μ_t moves to upward (downward) from the $\Delta\mu_t = 0$ curve, then it moves to still more upward (downwards) and never come back. Similarly, from (8.34), we have $\frac{\partial(G_{t+1} - G_t)}{\partial G_t} = -\frac{7}{34}$, which shows that if G_t moves to leftward (rightward) from the $\Delta G_t = 0$ curve, then it moves to leftward and return to the curve. Our dynamic equation system is difference equation system, not a differential equation system, so the movement of the variables is slightly different, such as the overshooting exists in difference equation system. For the sake of simplicity of discussion, assuming that the system is as if a differential system, we show the optimal behavior of the variables.

Then as shown by the arrows in Fig. 8.2, there exists one pair of the stable paths of μ_t and G_t which converge to the steady state equilibrium $E^* = (\mu^*, G^*)$, monotonically. Global movement can be drawn by using the graphs of the original $\Delta\mu_t = 0$ and $\Delta G_t = 0$. The linearized ones only helped us to know the signs of $\Delta\mu_t$ or ΔG_t near the steady state.

Transient optimal path of the economy is one pair of the stable path shown by the bold arrows which converge to the steady state equilibrium in $G - \mu$ plane shown in Fig. 8.2. One path starts from a smaller public good than G_t, then μ_t decreases and G_t increases on the optimal path. Another path starts from the excess public capital, and it decreases and μ_t increases on the optimal path.

Then the problem is to show the other important variables such as N_t and g_t's behaviors. These can be derived from (8.26) and (8.27), which gives g_t and N_t. Totally differentiating the system (8.26)–(8.29), we linearize the system and derive

$$\mathrm{d}N_t = \frac{30}{17}\mathrm{d}\mu_t - \frac{8}{85}\mathrm{d}G_t, \tag{8.35}$$

$$\mathrm{d}g_t = \frac{25}{34}\mathrm{d}\mu_t + \frac{5}{17}\mathrm{d}G_t. \tag{8.36}$$

From (8.35), on the optimal path, we have

$$\frac{\mathrm{d}N_t}{\mathrm{d}G_t} = \frac{30}{17}\frac{\mathrm{d}\mu_t}{\mathrm{d}G_t} - \frac{8}{85} < 0 \tag{8.37}$$

because, it is evident that $\frac{\mathrm{d}\mu_t}{\mathrm{d}G_t} < 0$ holds on the optimal path. Equation (8.37) shows that N_t and G_t move to the opposite directions on the optimal path.

Next, we derive the behavior of g_t. From (8.36), we have

$$\frac{\mathrm{d}g_t}{\mathrm{d}G_t} = \frac{25}{34}\frac{\mathrm{d}\mu_t}{\mathrm{d}G_t} + \frac{5}{17}. \tag{8.38}$$

Because $\frac{\mathrm{d}\mu_t}{\mathrm{d}G_t} < 0$ holds on the optimal path, the sign of $\frac{\mathrm{d}g_t}{\mathrm{d}G_t}$ is not clear. But from Fig. 8.2, $\frac{\mathrm{d}\mu_t}{\mathrm{d}G_t}$ on the optimal path is greater than the gradient of the curve $\Delta\mu_t = 0$, which is $\left.\frac{\mathrm{d}\mu_t}{\mathrm{d}G_t}\right|_{\Delta\mu=0} = -\frac{16}{425} / \frac{5}{17}$ from (8.33), and which is smaller than the gradient of the optimal path as shown in Fig. 8.2. Hence, from (8.39), we have

$$\frac{\mathrm{d}g_t}{\mathrm{d}G_t} = \left.\frac{25}{34}\frac{\mathrm{d}\mu_t}{\mathrm{d}G_t}\right|_{\substack{\text{optimal}\\ \text{path}}} + \frac{5}{17} > \left.\frac{25}{34}\frac{\mathrm{d}\mu_t}{\mathrm{d}G_t}\right|_{\Delta\mu=0} + \frac{5}{17} = \frac{1}{5} > 0, \tag{8.39}$$

from (8.33) and (8.36). This shows that g_t and G_t move to the same direction.

We summarize the above results as the following theorem:

Theorem 8.1: Optimal Transient State *On the optimal path, G_t and μ_t move to the opposite directions monotonically, and converge to the steady state. G_t and g_t move to the same direction, and also μ_t and N_t also move to the same directions and converge to the steady state.*

8.3.4 The Henry George Theorem

Our purpose is to examine the Henry George Theorem in the transient state. Firstly, however, let us examine the theorem in the steady state.

From (8.30), the total revenue of the land rent of each region at the steady state is given by

$$F(N^*) - F'(N^*)N^* = \frac{1}{2}\sqrt{\frac{1}{A^2p^2}} = \frac{1}{2Ap} \tag{8.40}$$

where asterisk denotes steady state equilibrium. The total investment expenditure for the public good of a region is

$$\frac{g^*N^*}{p} = \left(\frac{Ap^2}{2}\right)\left(\frac{1}{A^2p^2}\right)\frac{1}{p} = \frac{1}{2Ap}. \tag{8.41}$$

In our specified model, the Henry George theorem holds in the steady state.

Lemma 8.2: The Henry George Theorem in the Steady State *The Henry George Theorem holds in the steady state.*

Next we examine the Henry George theorem in a linearized system, and derive that the theorem does not hold even in the neighborhood of the steady state.

In the previous section, we derived the optimal path of the system graphically. Here we derive the path analytically, because it is required in examining the Henry George theorem in the transient state.

Equations (8.31) and (8.32) show the optimal dynamic path of the linearized economy. We make the co-efficient matrix of the difference equation system as follows:

$$M = \begin{pmatrix} \frac{22}{18} & \frac{16}{425} \\ \frac{25}{34} & \frac{27}{34} \end{pmatrix}. \tag{8.42}$$

The behavior of the linearized dynamic model is given by

$$\begin{pmatrix} d\mu_{t+1} \\ dG_{t+1} \end{pmatrix} = M \begin{pmatrix} d\mu_t \\ dG_t \end{pmatrix}. \tag{8.43}$$

Let the characteristic roots of the matrix Mbe λ_1 and λ_2, then we have

$$\lambda_1 = \frac{71 - \sqrt{417}}{68}, \quad \lambda_2 = \frac{71 + \sqrt{417}}{68}. \tag{8.44}$$

And also let their characteristic vectors be v_1 and v_2, respectively. Then, we make matrix $P = (v_1, v_2)$ and we have

$$P^{-1}MP = \begin{pmatrix} \lambda_1 & 0 \\ 0 & \lambda_2 \end{pmatrix}. \tag{8.45}$$

Then we obtain

$$\begin{pmatrix} d\mu_t \\ dG_t \end{pmatrix} = M^t \begin{pmatrix} d\mu_0 \\ dG_0 \end{pmatrix}, \tag{8.46}$$

where

$$M^t = P\underbrace{(P^{-1}MP) \cdot (P^{-1}MP) \cdot (P^{-1} \ldots MP)}_{t} \cdot P^{-1} = P\begin{pmatrix} {\lambda_1}^t & 0 \\ 0 & {\lambda_2}^t \end{pmatrix}P^{-1}. \tag{8.47}$$

Let $P$and P^{-1} be[9]

$$P = \begin{pmatrix} \alpha_1 & \beta_1 \\ \gamma_1 & \delta_1 \end{pmatrix}, \quad P^{-1} = \begin{pmatrix} \alpha_2 & \beta_2 \\ \gamma_2 & \delta_2 \end{pmatrix}, \tag{8.48}$$

respectively. Then (8.49) can be derived

[9] P and P^{-1} can be derived as $P = \begin{pmatrix} 1 & 1 \\ \frac{-25\sqrt{417} - 425}{64} & \frac{25\sqrt{417} - 425}{64} \end{pmatrix}$, and $P^{-1} = \begin{pmatrix} \frac{417 - 17\sqrt{417}}{837} & \frac{-32}{25\sqrt{417}} \\ \frac{417 + 17\sqrt{417}}{837} & \frac{32}{25\sqrt{417}} \end{pmatrix}$, respectively.

$$\begin{pmatrix} \mathrm{d}\mu_t \\ \mathrm{d}G_t \end{pmatrix} = M^t \begin{pmatrix} \mathrm{d}\mu_0 \\ \mathrm{d}G_0 \end{pmatrix}$$
$$= \begin{pmatrix} {\lambda_1}^t \alpha_1(\alpha_2 \mathrm{d}\mu_0 + \beta_2 \mathrm{d}G_0) + {\lambda_2}^t \beta_1(\gamma_2 \mathrm{d}\mu_0 + \delta_2 \mathrm{d}G_0) \\ {\lambda_1}^t \gamma_1(\alpha_2 \mathrm{d}\mu_0 + \beta_2 \mathrm{d}G_0) + {\lambda_2}^t \delta_1(\gamma_2 \mathrm{d}\mu_0 + \delta_2 \mathrm{d}G_0) \end{pmatrix}. \tag{8.49}$$

From (8.44), since we have $|\lambda_1| < 1$, $|\lambda_2| > 1$, the co-efficient for ${\lambda_2}^t$of (8.49) must be zero, if not, (8.49) expands. Hence, in order for the optimal path to converge to the steady state,

$$\gamma_2 \mathrm{d}\mu_0 + \delta_2 \mathrm{d}G_0 = 0 \tag{8.50}$$

must hold. Since we have

$$\gamma_2 = \frac{17\sqrt{417} + 417}{835}, \quad \delta_2 = \frac{32}{25\sqrt{417}} \tag{8.51}$$

as shown in footnote 9. We derive that

$$\left.\frac{\mathrm{d}\mu_0}{\mathrm{d}G_0}\right|_{\substack{\text{optimal} \\ \text{path}}} = -\frac{\delta_2}{\gamma_2} = -\frac{64}{25\left(\sqrt{417} + 17\right)} \approx -0.068. \tag{8.52}$$

This must hold at any point on the optimal path, hence, this is the gradient of the linearized optimal path in Fig. 8.2.

Next, we examine the condition for the Henry George theorem to hold.
The term HG in (8.53) shows the gap between the land rent and public investment per region.

$$\mathrm{HG} = -\frac{\sqrt{N}}{2} + \frac{gN}{p}. \tag{8.53}$$

The land rent is $\frac{\sqrt{N}}{2}$ and the investment in the public good is given by $\frac{gN}{p}$, and those are equal when HG = 0. We already checked that HG = 0 holds at the steady state. What we have to check is that, whether it holds on the optimal transient path, holds. Our system is essentially composed of the two variablesμ and G as shown in Fig. 8.2, we try to explain HG by μ and G. We are discussing the linear approximation model on the assumption of $(A, p) = (1, 5)$. Totally differentiating (8.53), and using the steady state value (8.30), and (8.35) and (8.36) we have

$$\mathrm{dHG} = -\frac{10}{17}\mathrm{d}\mu - \frac{3}{85}\mathrm{d}G. \tag{8.54}$$

Arranging (8.54) we obtain

$$\frac{\mathrm{dHG}}{\mathrm{d}G} = -\frac{10}{17}\frac{\mathrm{d}\mu}{\mathrm{d}G} - \frac{3}{85}. \tag{8.55}$$

If the economy is on the optimal path, $\frac{\mathrm{d}\mu}{\mathrm{d}G}$ is given by (8.52), we obtain

$$\begin{aligned}\frac{\mathrm{dHG}}{\mathrm{d}G} &= -\frac{10}{17}\frac{\mathrm{d}\mu_0}{\mathrm{d}G_0}\bigg|_{\substack{\text{optimal}\\ \text{path}}} - \frac{3}{85} = \frac{640}{17(25\sqrt{417}+425)} - \frac{3}{85}\\ &\approx 0.004947.\end{aligned} \tag{8.56}$$

Thus, since (8.56) does not equal zero, we can say that the Henry George theorem does not hold in the transient state.[10]

Theorem 8.2 *Henry George theorem does not hold in the transient state.*

8.4 Concluding Remarks

We analyzed the optimal dynamics of urbanization process. We examined the dynamic movement of the population or the stock of the public goods, etc., in an overlapping-generations model. Public goods play an important role in urbanization. In one region, all residents can utilize all of the public good of the region. In this respect, the region is bigger the better. However, the marginal productivity of labor is decreasing, there exists optimal population in a region.

In this model, we called region, not city, because we had implicitly assumed that the production technology is like that of agriculture, since there is no capital stock is assumed and labor is only input for production. But even though the same production function is assumed, we can call this region as city, because this economy is well described for urban dynamic economy.

The main purpose of this paper is to examine whether the Henry George theorem holds in a transient state, though in the steady state it is easy to derive that it holds. In order to discuss the theorem in the transient state, we need to know the optimal path that economy is on. By linearizing the system near the steady state, we derived the optimal path of the economy analytically, and derived that the theorem does not hold on the optimal path. The model which we used in this analysis is very simple and very specified. We have to generalize the model in the future.

[10]In order for the Henry George theorem to hold, $\mathrm{HG} = 0$ must be satisfied, hence, from (8.54), we have $\frac{\mathrm{d}\mu}{\mathrm{d}G} = \frac{-3}{50} = -0.06$. On the other hand, however, on the optimal path $\frac{\mathrm{d}\mu}{\mathrm{d}G} \approx -0.068$ holds. There exists a gap.

References

Arnott RJ (2004) Does the Henry George Theorem provide a practical guide to optimal city size? Am J Econ Sociol 63:1057–1090

Arnott RJ, Stiglitz JE (1979) Aggregate land rents, expenditures on public goods, and optimal city size. Q J Econ 93:471

Ehara N (2013) Urbanization of China. Int Trade Invest 91:49–64

Flatters F, Henderson V, Mieszkowski P (1974) Public goods, efficiency and regional fiscal equalization. J Public Econ 3:99–112

Fu S (2005) Essays on urban agglomeration economies. Ph.D dissertation, Boston College

Fujita M (1989) Urban economic theory. Cambridge University Press, Cambridge

George H (1942) Progress and poverty. Water J. Black, Inc., New York

Hartwick JM (1980) The Henry George Rule, optimal population, and interregional equity. Can J Econ 13(4):695–700

Kanemoto Y, Ohkawara T, Suzuki T (1996) Agglomeration economies and a test for optimal city sizes in Japan. J Jpn Int Econ 10:379–398

Kaniwa Y (2013) Possibility of the growth of Chinese economy by urbanization (in Japanese). Monthly Report, Sumitomo Mitsui Trust Bank

Kawano M (2014) Optimal process of urbanization in a developing country-dynamic Henry George Theorem. Lett Spat Resour Sci 7(3):196–204

Ramsey F (1928) A mathematical theory of saving. Econ J 38(152):543–559

Samuelson PA (1954) The pure theory of public expenditure. Rev Econ Stat 36(4):387–389

Chapter 9
Optimal Openness

Tomaz Ponce Dentinho

Abstract The chapter addresses the question of how open should a city region be? The approach is rooted in the literature on Spatial Interaction Models enlarged to integrate a productive space conceptualized as interconnected channels in which size can change instead of a space if inert links. The argument begins with the formulation of an open spatial interaction model with two channels: *Cardo* for the internal interaction and *Decumanus* for the external connection; both constrained by energy, environmental, technological, and economic restrictions. Results indicate that the optimal openness depends on relative structural centrality of the city region, or the length of *Cardo* and *Decumanus*, on the environmental capacity of the channels and on the multiplier effect of external connections.

Keywords Spatial interaction · Urban size · Optimization

9.1 Introduction

Regional Science looks into human creative interaction within space (Kourtit et al. 2015). The organic interaction within space evolve naturally to congested channels; this is what happens in some urban areas when it is difficult to manage flows in the city and into the city or to have means and viability to adjust channel capacity to the flows they carry. Alternatively, rational interaction leads to the calibration of channels that maximize interaction flows.

The maximization of creative human interaction within space is an interesting conceptual objective for humans that acknowledge love as a shared objective. Like Mother Teresa says, "Some call Him Ishwar, some call Him Allah, some simply God, but we all have to acknowledge that it is He who made us for greater things, to love and to be loved" (Fig. 9.1). From this perspective, love for the self and love for

T. P. Dentinho (✉)
University of Azores, Azores, Portugal
e-mail: tomas.lc.dentinho@uac.pt

M. Kawano et al. (eds.), *Theory and History in Regional Perspective*, New Frontiers in Regional Science: Asian Perspectives 56,
https://doi.org/10.1007/978-981-16-6695-7_9

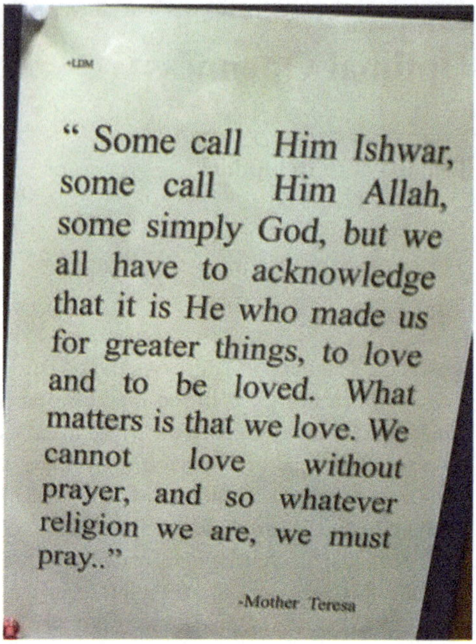

Fig. 9.1 Photo of a say of Mother Teresa near her thumb in Kolkata

the other, assessed by the creative spatial interaction between people, organizations, places, regions, and countries, can be the objective function of conceptual and operational economic models. The great advantage is to overcome and still include the subjective selfishness of individual satisfaction proposed by Adam Smith (1776).

Closed systems die and very open systems disintegrate (von Bertalanffy 1969; Chadwick 1978). The question is about the optimal openness regarding the defined aim and unavoidable constraints. Optimal openness is implicit in the studies of the dimension of firms (Williamson 1985), based on transaction costs and benefits. Cities also receive considerable attention by various authors that return to the topic cyclically (Von Thünen 1826; Alonso 1971; Richardson 1972; Henderson 1974; Fujita and Krugman 1995; Camagni et al. 2013) associating the optimal dimension to the marginal costs and benefits of city size.

There is a large literature on international economics rooted in the seminal and textbooks' work of David Ricardo (1817) that relate the optimal openness to the endogenous features such as the elasticity of substitution between domestic and imported goods and services or the price effects of border controls (Romer 1993; Epifani and Gancia 2009).

The novelty of this chapter is that, whereas previous studies assume that the aim is to maximize net benefits, measured as product or utility, the present analysis adopts the maximization of internal and external human interactions as the objective function enlarging the scope of the analysis to the optimal openness. In other words, optimal proximity between people, households, neighbourhoods, cities, regions or countries. Furthermore, in line with regional economists, space that

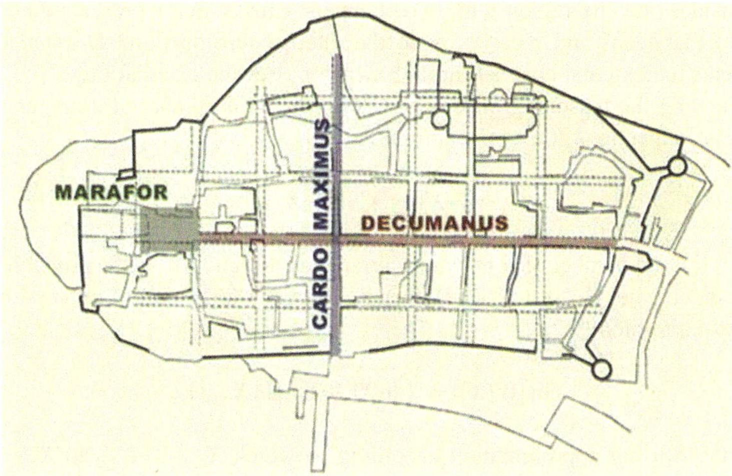

Fig. 9.2 Cardo and Decumanus, which relation defines the optimal openness

structures proximities appears clearly in the analysis, mainly because space becomes tractable in the analysis of human interactions within space.

The chapter addresses the question of how open should be a household, a neighbourhood, a city, a region or a country? The approach is rooted in the literature on Spatial Interaction Models (Wilson 2010) and Economic Base Models (Fujita et al. 2001). The analysis begins with the formulation of an open spatial interaction model with two channels: *Cardo* for the internal interaction and *Decumanus* for the external interactions (Muntaha 2005) (Fig. 9.2).

The chapter develops as follows. Section 9.2 presents a model of human and organic interaction within a Cardo–Decumanus spatial framework. Section 9.3 explains the optimized equilibrium of this model constrained by energy, environmental, technological, and economic constraints. Section 9.4 discusses the results by doing some simulation experiments to perceive the effect of the various constraints on the outcome of the city region. Finally, Sect. 9.5 suggests conclusions, recommendations, and future work.

9.2 Model of Human Interaction

The analysis of human interactions within space is under scrutiny for a long time in the studies of Von Thünen (1826), Christaller (1933), Losch (1954). More recently the works of Wilson (1970), Paelinck and Nijkamp (1976), Nijkamp and Reggiani (1988), Sen and Smith (1995), Echenique et al. (2013), and Andersson and Andersson contributed strongly to the understanding of the interaction of people and places.

Consider one city region with two channels: *Cardo*, that represents the internal channel that feeds and receives from the internal territory; and *Decumanus* that represents the external channel through which passes the external flows.

Following the reasoning of Wilson (1970) the total number of arrangements of channels connections comes in expression (9.1)

$$W(X) = X!/\Pi_{c;\,d}X_{c;\,d}! \tag{9.1}$$

where X = total number of connections arrangements; and $X_{c;d}$ = the probability that the given channel ($X_{c;d}$), (c) or (d) occurs. Thus, the logarithm of expression (9.1) leads to expression (9.2).

$$\ln\left[W(X)\right] = \{\ln X! - \Sigma_{c;\,d}\ln X_{c;\,d}!\}, \tag{9.2}$$

using the Stirling approximation according to which $X_{c;d}! = X_{c;d}\ \ln\ X_{c;d} - X_{c;d}$ expression (9.2) becomes Eq. (9.3).

$$\ln\left[W(X)\right] = \{\ln X! - \Sigma_{c;\,d}X_{c;\,d}(\ln X_{c;\,d} - 1)\} \tag{9.3}$$

Since (ln X!) is constant, expression (9.3) of the total number of channel arrangements results in an entropy function (9.4) very similar to the Shannon's (1948) expression where flows are a function of the channel. Adding ($W_{c;d}$) as an *ex-ante* aimed levels of network provision that maximizes interaction, total interaction (F) result from the flows in (c) and (d) generated by the channels (X_{cd}) having in mind the aimed levels of channel provision ($W_{c;d}$).

$$F = -\sum_{c;\,d}\left[X_{c;\,d}\left(\ln\ \frac{X_{c;\,d}}{W_{c;\,d}} - 1\right)\right] \tag{9.4}$$

There is a maximum of interactions when [$X_d = W_d$ and $X_c = W_c$], shown in Fig. 9.3, that also presents the graphic of expression (9.4) reporting the interaction as a function of *Cardo* and *Decumanus* channels ($X_{c;d}$), with two aimed levels of channel provision ($W_{c;d}$). Notice that the maximum interaction corresponds to the aimed dimension for the channels ($W_c = 1$; $W_d = 1$).

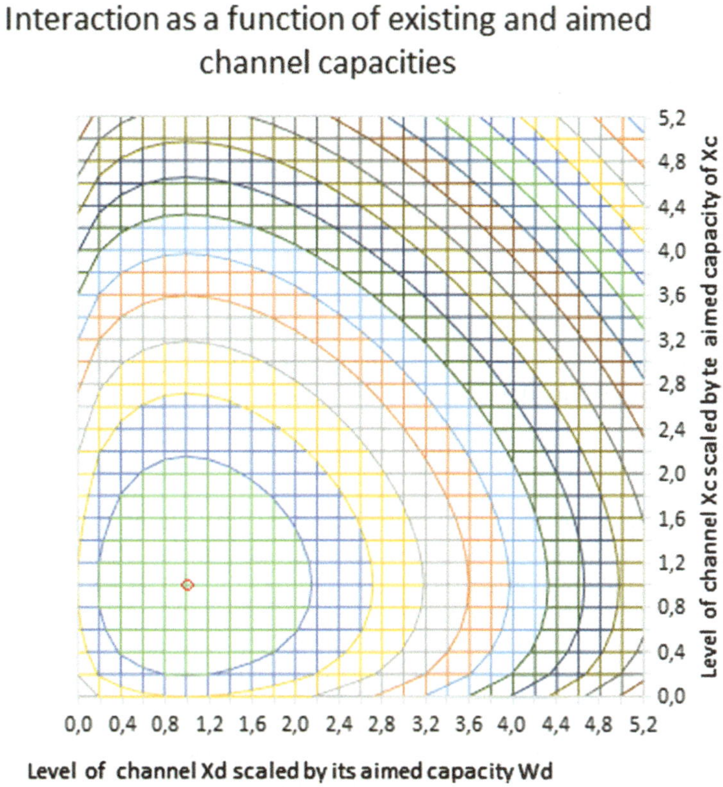

Fig. 9.3 Interaction and channels as a function of existing and aimed channels

9.3 Human Interaction Constrained by Energy, Environmental, Technological, and Economic Restrictions

Human interaction maximizes interactions by managing the size of channels ($X_{c;d}$) taking into account ex-ante aimed sizes of these channels ($W_{c;d}$) as presented in expression (9.4) but considering also three types of constraints: (a) technological and economic; (b) environmental; and (c) related to energy costs.

9.3.1 *Technological and Economic Constraints*

The technological and economic constraints state that there is a relation between the Cardo and Decumanus defined by the multiplier effect of the base model [$m = 1/$

$(1 - rs)]$ where the employment multipier of the basic employment (m) is the inverse of one minus the activity rate (r) minus the service rate (s).

The service rate (s) equals the quotient between Cardo and the sum of Cardo and Decumanus multiplied by the inverse of the activity rate ($s = X_c/r\sum_{c;\,d}X_{c;\,d}$).

Being so, there is a technological and economic relation between Cardo and Decumanus through the multiplier effect (m) expressed in Eq. (9.5) that says that the dimension of Cardo, associated to internal connections, derives from the dimension of Decumanus, linked with external connections:

$$X_c = X_d(m - 1) \tag{9.5}$$

Similarly the target level for these interactions $[W_c;\, W_d]$ should be related, as presented in expression (9.6):

$$W_c = W_d(m - 1) \tag{9.6}$$

The substitution of Eqs. (9.5) and (9.6) in Eq. (9.4) leads to a very simple expression of the interaction as a function of the Decumanus channel, actual and aimed, and the multiplier effect (m).

$$F = -m\left[X_d\left(\ln\frac{X_d}{W_d} - 1\right)\right], \tag{9.7}$$

which maximization on (X_d) leads to the simple result that ($X_d = W_d$).

The multiplier effect (m) also has an important role. When ($m \leq 1$), there is no interaction. When ($m > 1$), interaction occurs. Nevertheless, since the aimed value for Cardo relates with the aimed value for the Decumanus in expression (9.6), the best interaction is achieved when ($m = 2$) as simulated in Fig. 9.4. The simulation is done because the partial derivative of expression (9.7) is undetermined.

9.3.2 *Energy Constraint*

The energy constraint defines that there are energy costs ($g_{c;d}$) associated with each channel ($X_{c;d}$) should be lower than a threshold on energy expenditures (G). If we assume that the energy cost associated with Cardo, for the internal interactions, is zero ($g_c = 0$), we can get the following constraint.

$$g_d X_d = G \tag{9.8}$$

With this new element, expression (9.8) becomes expression (9.9).

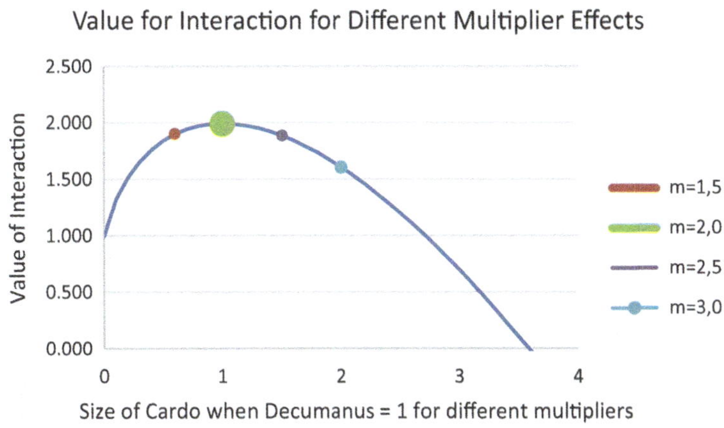

Fig. 9.4 Simulation of the Optimal Multiplier Effect when the ex-ante aimed Decumanus equals 1

$$F = m\left[-X_{\mathrm{d}}\left(\ln \frac{X_{\mathrm{d}}}{W_{\mathrm{d}}} - 1\right)\right] + \beta(G - g_{\mathrm{d}}X_{\mathrm{d}}), \tag{9.9}$$

where (β) is the bid rent of the energy costs assuming a maximum energy cost (G) and the energy costs of the Decumanus (g_{d}), (m) is the technological and economic multiplier effect, and (W_{d}) is the ex-ante aimed capacity of the Decumanus.

Expression (9.10) optimizes the Decumanus (X_{d}) to maximize interactions (F), dependent on energy constraints ($\beta(g_{\mathrm{d}})$), technological and economic coefficients (m), and ex-ante aimed levels of the Decumanus (W_{d}). It is clear that with the inclusion of energy costs the optimal dimension of the Decumanus ($X_{\mathrm{d}} = W_{\mathrm{d}}$), defined for the model with no contraints (Eq. 9.4) and with technological constraints (Eq. 9.8) does not hold for the model with the energy constrains where the aimed ex-ante capacity (W_{d}) is limited by the energy costs ($\exp\left(-\frac{\beta g_{\mathrm{d}}}{m}\right)$) and the multiplier ($m$).

$$X_{\mathrm{d}} = W_{\mathrm{d}} \exp\left(-\frac{\beta g_{\mathrm{d}}}{m}\right) \tag{9.10}$$

Actually, as can be seen in Fig. 9.5, the inclusion of the energy costs associated to Decumanus shifts the optimum to the left of the ex-ante capacity (W_{d}).

The multiplier (m) continues to have an important role. Once more when ($m \leq 1$) there is no interaction. Although the partial derivative of expression (9.9) on (m) is undetermined, it is interesting to perceive that the optimal dimension of Cardo is not when ($X_{\mathrm{c}} = X_{\mathrm{d}}(m - 1)$) but, instead, when ($X_{\mathrm{c}} = mX_{\mathrm{d}}$).

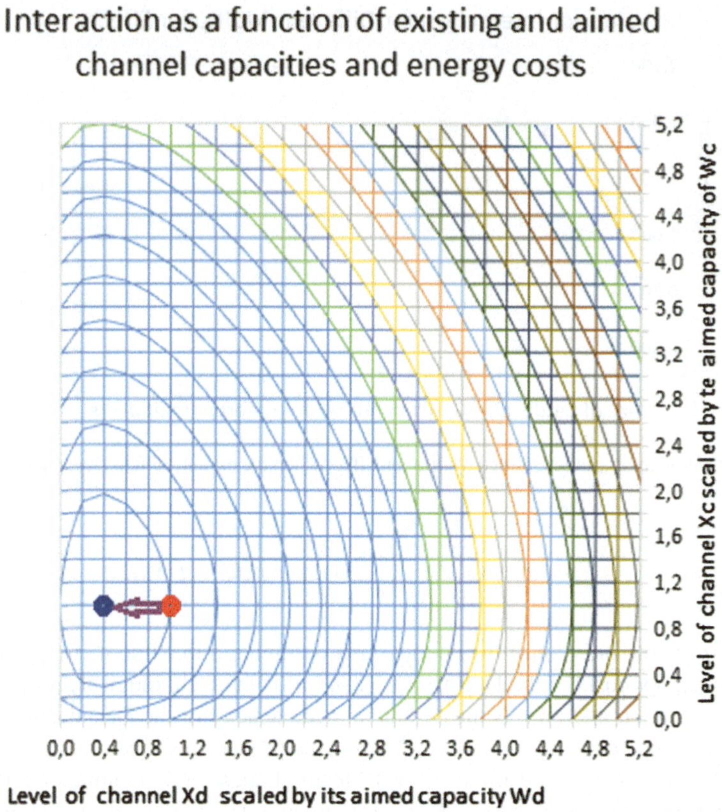

Fig. 9.5 Interaction as a function of existing and aimed channel capacities and energy costs

9.3.3 Environmental Constraints

The environmental constraint D_d can be associated with the aimed level of Decumanus ($W_d = D_d$). Actually, the Decumanus pushes the regional economy from the outside being limited by the capacities of the region (D_d) whereas the Cardo is the result of the local demand stimulated by the Decumanus through the multiplier effect (m). Therefore, the final model is similar to expression (9.9) with the only difference that the aimed level of Decumanus is in fact the capacity of the region to export ($W_d = D_d$).

$$F = m\left[-X_d\left(\ln\frac{X_d}{D_d} - 1\right)\right] + \beta(G - g_d X_d), \qquad (9.11)$$

Being the optimal level defined by expression (9.10).

$$X_{\mathrm{d}} = D_{\mathrm{d}} \exp\left(-\frac{\beta g_{\mathrm{d}}}{m}\right) \tag{9.12}$$

9.4 Discussion of the Optimal Openness

According to expression (9.12) the optimal openness defined for the Decumanus Channel (X_{d}), depends on the environmental capacity of the region (D_{d}), on the attrition costs along the Decumanus (X_{d}) and on the technological and economic conditions of the multiplier effect (m).

Through numerical analysis it is possible to define best value for Cardo ($X_{\mathrm{c}} = mX_{\mathrm{d}}$), which can be accepted if there is not an environmental limitation on Cardo ($D_{\mathrm{c}} > mD_{\mathrm{d}}$). This liberates the reasoning from the very limiting condition of model (Eq. 9.8) that requested an optimal multiplier equal to 2, allowing also the possibility of larger multiplier effects that come with economic growth (Pred 1966).

The entropy-constrained model proposed to discuss the issue of optimal openness goes in line with the seminal texts of Adam Smith (1776) on the advantages of openness for the wealth of people and places, follows the enduring work of David Ricardo (1817) that highlight the role of exogenous and endogenous capacities, and confirms the idea that close systems die (von Bertalanffy 1969; Chadwick 1978). Moreover, attrition costs and exports capacity related to the border of entities defended for companies by Williamson (1985). The bid-rents of the entropy-constrained model related to the discussion of the optimal size of cities by regional economists established when marginal costs of the city size equals the marginal benefits (Alonso 1971; Richardson 1972; Henderson 1974; Fujita et al. 1999; Camagni et al. 2013). Finally, the unifying perspective of this simple model also encompasses the price effects of border controls associated to the cost of energy (Romer 1993; Epifani and Gancia; 2009).

9.5 Conclusions

The chapter addresses the question of how open should and economy be? The approach is rooted in the literature on Economic Base Theory and on Spatial Interaction Modelling. The argument begins by assuming entropy as the objective function for human interaction, which is then constrained by technological, economic, energy, and environmental constraints. Results show the importance of space. Not only as productive system revealed by the environmental capacity to export represented by the dimension of the export channel (Decumanus), but also as a distance that show up as a critical element to liberate the formal limitation of the multiplier effect.

Future work is due on the application of the model that assumes the idea of a productive or creative space constrained by the physical space. Furthermore, it make sense to explore different levels of the model linking them to different levels of aggregation.

References

Alonso W (1971) The economics of urban size. In: Papers and Proceedings of the Regional Science Association, vol 26, pp 67–83

Camagni R, Capello R, Caragliu A (2013) One or infinite optimal city sizes? In search of an equilibrium size for cities. Ann Reg Sci 51:309–341. https://doi.org/10.1007/s00168-012-0548-7

Chadwick G (1978) A systems view of planning. Towards a theory of the urban and regional planning process, 2nd edn. Pergamon. ISBN: 9781483139388

Christaller W (1933) Central places in southern Germany (trans: Baskin CW). Prentice-Hall, Englewood Cliffs, NJ

Echenique MH, Grinevich V, Hargreaves AJ, Zachariadis V (2013) LUISA: a land-use interaction with social accounting model; presentation and enhanced calibration method. Environ Plann B Plann Des 40(6):1003–1026. https://doi.org/10.1068/b38202

Epifani P, Gancia G (2009) Openness, government size and terms of trade. Review of Economic Studies Limited, Oxford, pp 629–668. https://doi.org/10.1111/j.1467-937X.2009.00546.x

Fujita M, Krugman P (1995) When is the economy monocentric? von Thünen and Chamberlin unified. Reg Sci Urban Econ 25(4):505–528

Fujita M, Krugman P, Mori T (1999) On the evolution of hierarchical urban systems. Eur Econ Rev 43(2):209–251

Fujita M, Krugman P, Venables A (2001) The spatial economy. In: Cities, regions and international trade. The MIT Press, London

Henderson J (1974) The sizes and types of cities. Am Econ Rev 64:640–656

Kourtit K, Royuela V, Dentinho T, Nijkamp P (2015) Envisioning experiments on regional science frontiers. Investig Reg 36(36):35–61

Losch A (1954) The economics of location. Yale University Press, New Haven, CT. ISBN 978-0-300-00727-5. OCLC 876506870

Muntaha S (2005) Urban planning in a seaport city, Beirut from Hellenistic to Byzantine period. In: Morhange C, Saghieh-Beydoun M, Ala'eddine A (eds) La Mobilité des Paysages Portuaires Antiques du Liban. Bulletin d'Archéologie et d'Architecture Libanaises, Hors-série II, pp 147–184

Nijkamp P, Reggiani A (1988) Entropy, spatial interaction models and discrete choice analysis: static and dynamic analogies. Eur J Oper Res 36(2):186–196

Paelinck J, Nijkamp P (1976) Operational theory and method in regional economics. Saxon House, Lexington

Pred AR (1966) The spatial dynamics of U.S. urban industrial growth. MIT Press, Cambridge

Ricardo D (1817) Princípios de Economia Política e Tributação. Fundação Calouste Gulbenkian, Lisbon. 2015

Richardson H (1972) Optimality in city size, systems of cities and urban policy: a sceptic's view. Urban Stud 9(1):29–47

Romer D (1993) Openness and inflation: theory and evidence. Q J Econ 108(4):869–903. https://doi.org/10.2307/2118453

Sen A, Smith TE (1995) Gravity models of spatial interaction behavior. Springer, Berlin

Shannon CE (1948) The mathematical theory of communication. Bell Syst Tech J 27:379–423. 623–656, July, October 1948

Smith A (1776) Riqueza das Nações. Fundação Calouste Gulbenkian, Lisbon. 1981 e 1983. 2 vols
Von Bertalanffy L (1969) General system theory: foundations, development, applications. George Braziller, Inc., New York, NY
Von Thünen JH (1826) Derisolierte Statt in Belziehung auf Landwirtschaft und National ökonomie. Part I. Pethers, Hamburg
Williamson O (1985) The economic institutions of capitalism. Free Press, New York, NY
Wilson AG (1970) Entropy in urban and regional modelling. Pion, London
Wilson A (2010) Entropy in urban and regional modelling: retrospect and prospect. In: Geographical analysis, vol 42. The Ohio State University, Columbus, OH, pp 364–394

Part II
Applied Spatial Studies

Chapter 10
Settlement and Migration Patterns of Immigrants by Visa Class in Australia

Dagmara Laukova, Aude Bernard, and Thomas Sigler

Abstract Migration is a key theme in regional science, as it concerns the movement and distribution of human populations and the impacts thereof. The twenty-first century has witnessed increasingly diverse forms of migration, in particular the bifurcation of migrants into permanent migrants and temporary migrants, among others. In this chapter, we focus on the specific case of Australia to uncover how the stratification of migrants by visa class helps to explain the mobility of migrants after arrival. It draws on two new powerful datasets that link visa status with census data to examine the settlement and migration patterns of immigrants by visa class. Our analysis reveals important variations by visa class that are missed when migrants are lumped together. The results confirm that early years post-arrival constitute an important period of adjustment as immigrants seek to establish themselves in the labour and housing markets, but they show that this process is particularly pronounced for skilled migrants who exhibit heightened levels of mobility. While the visa types used in this analysis are specific to Australia, they are underpinned by distinct reasons for immigrating, namely employment, family reunification, and humanitarian motives, which remain the primary drivers of international migration in most countries.

Keywords International migration · Internal migration · Immigrants · Age-standardisation · Skilled migrants · Humanitarian migrants · Permanent and temporary migrants

D. Laukova (✉) · A. Bernard · T. Sigler
Queensland Centre for Population Research, School of Earth and Environmental Sciences, The University of Queensland, Brisbane, QLD, Australia
e-mail: d.laukova@uq.edu.au; a.bernard@uq.edu.au; t.sigler@uq.edu.au

M. Kawano et al. (eds.), *Theory and History in Regional Perspective*, New Frontiers in Regional Science: Asian Perspectives 56,
https://doi.org/10.1007/978-981-16-6695-7_10

10.1 Introduction

The analysis of migration is an increasingly important theme in regional science, given its diverse forms. Migration in the twenty-first century has transitioned from the large waves of migration that preceded it toward more nuanced, and arguably more complex forms. One example of this is the increasing intensity of South-South migration to complement South-North and North-North flows. A complementary process is the stratification of migrant groups by skill level, and accordingly by visa category. This has implications for where and how migrants settle in new countries, but also for their mobility after arrival.

The focus of this chapter is on the mobility of migrants post-arrival with particular regard to the impacts of visa class. This is particularly relevant to regional science, as migration is a key mechanism for addressing uneven development both between and within countries. This chapter adds a unique dimension to understandings of migration that most focus on either international *or* internal migration (King and Skeldon 2010), but rarely on the internal mobility of international migrants.

As the majority of developed countries around the world have transitioned to Stage Four and beyond of the demographic transition, with low or even below replacement levels of fertility, migration has become the leading driver of population change. While internal migration is free and unrestricted in most countries, international migration is limited and controlled by system of visa grants with the exception of European Union where cross-border migration is unrestricted for all member states. Commonly, the different visa systems share the same basic immigration categories based on motives to move—work, family, and humanitarian/refugee visas. The distinction of various visa types combined with novel datasets offers a new perspective in studying settlement patterns of immigrants in host countries. Australia is one of the ideal candidates for this type of research.

With 28% of its population born overseas (ABS 2017), Australia is a major immigration country. It has long recognised the twin roles of international migration in promoting national and regional economic growth by addressing skill shortages and more recently in moderating the pace and extent of population ageing (McDonald 2018). Over the last 25 years, increased emphasis has been placed on skilled migrants, who now account for 70% of total permanent migrants intake, compared with less than 50% in the mid-1990s (MCA 2015). As a result, family migration, which represented up to 80% of the permanent migration intake in the 1990s, declined to below 50% by the early 2000s and has now stabilised at 30% (Larsen 2013). At the same time, the share of temporary migrants has risen dramatically in an effort to improve skills matching through the introduction in the mid-1990s of temporary skilled visas that provide more flexible arrangements to employers (Khoo et al. 2009). Combined with the growth in working holiday makers (Hugo 2004), international students, and the introduction of graduate visa schemes that provide post-graduation working rights (Faggian et al. 2016), these changes have led to a rapid rise in the share of temporary migrants in the overall annual intake from 64% in 2004 up to 77% in 2017 (ABS 2018a). Collectively, these changes have contributed to a substantial growth in Australia's annual net migration intake, reaching 240,000 in 2017, which is nearly double the 1981 net intake (ABS 2018b). While the proportion of skilled migrants has increased, Australia's humanitarian migration intake has progressively decreased, and now contributes to less than 10% of Australia's annual permanent migrant intake (Karlsen 2016).

Traditionally, the Australian immigration policy has been concerned with shaping the level and composition of the immigration intake (Hugo 2011). However, there have been increased attempts by successive governments to influence the place where migrants settle upon arrival. Since the inception of State-Specific Regional Migration programmes in the mid-1990s, a series of new visa categories have been introduced to encourage migrants to settle in regional areas in an effort to redirect population growth away from metropolitan areas and mitigate any regional skill shortages. While the efficacy of such schemes remains unclear given the very limited research on the migration trajectories of the overseas-born in regional areas (Hugo 2008), recent synthetic estimates suggest that there is low retention of immigrants in regional Australia (Baffour and Raymer 2019).

Both the initial settlement patterns and subsequent moves of overseas-born migrants exert a significant effect on the growth, composition, and geographic distribution of Australia's population (Bell and Hugo 2000). Subsequent moves are an important component of immigrants' settlement process in destination countries (Reher and Silvestre 2009). Immigrants are known to display a preference to live in major cities and to be especially mobile upon arrival as they adjust their housing and locational needs and preferences (Bell and Hugo 2000; Hugo 2011; Maher and McKay 1986; Reher and Silvestre 2009; Rowland 1979). Variations exist, however, by country of birth (Raymer and Baffour 2018), with some groups more likely to live in non-metropolitan areas (Wilson and Charles-Edwards 2017), including in communities with little prior experience in receiving migrants (McAreavey and Argent 2018). Long-term permanent visa holders through the skilled and family streams have a much greater bearing on the growth, composition, and geographic distribution of Australia's population than temporary visa holders (Parr 2018), yet temporary migrants play an important role by providing a ready and growing pool from which the majority of permanent migrants are selected (McDonald 2018). It is therefore important to establish the impact of visa type on immigrants' locational preference and movement within Australia.

In this chapter, we explore variations in settlement and migration patterns by visa type, something that has long been an implicit focus of migration studies (Faggian et al. 2016; Hugo 2014), but not explicitly studied in the Australian context. In particular, we examine the extent to which permanent and temporary migrants exhibit similar levels of spatial mobility and whether they follow the same spatial patterns of settlement. Recent improvements in data availability, in particular the linked visa status and census datasets, represent an unprecedented opportunity to establish the mobility level of immigrants in Australia in order to create a comprehensive evidence base to inform policy development. Drawing on these new datasets, the analysis considers the way age and period of residence affect mobility and explores differences by type of move (i.e. change of residence, inter-regional, and inter-state migration). Section 10.2 summarises prior work on the spatial mobility of the overseas-born population in Australia and in other advanced economies. In Sect. 10.3, we introduce census data and specify the spatial framework used in the analysis. Sections 10.4–10.7 present the results of our empirical analysis focusing on the spatial patterns of settlement of the overseas-born (Sect. 10.4), their level of spatial mobility (Sect. 10.5), its impact on population redistribution (Sect. 10.6) and the spatial pathway they follow (Sect. 10.7). Each segment of the analysis provides a unique perspective and together they offer a comprehensive understanding of the migration behaviour of immigrant populations in Australia. In Sect. 10.8, we summarise key findings and discuss avenues for future research.

10.2 Prior Studies

A small but growing literature has emerged on the post-settlement migration of overseas-born populations, particularly in high immigration countries in North America, Australasia, and Europe, particularly in the United Kingdom. This body of work has shown that the overseas-born are more mobile that the native-born (Belanger and Rogers 1992; Darlington-Pollock et al. 2018; Fielding 1992; Hatton and Tani 2005; Kritz and Nogle 1994; Newbold 1996, 1999; Rogers 1999), particularly in the early years post-arrival. As a result, the movement of overseas-born populations can exert an important impact on the overall redistribution of the population within a country (Nogle 1997) and contributes to net population gains and losses in particular regions. This is the case in Australia, where early studies have revealed distinct internal migration patterns of overseas-born characterised by high levels of mobility (Bell and Cooper 1995; Bell and Hugo 2000). Subsequent studies have demonstrated a strong preference for city living (Hugo 2011, 2014), which is the result of initial settlement in metropolitan areas, particularly Sydney (Hugo 2008), combined with a low retention of immigrants in regional and remote areas (Baffour and Raymer 2019). At the same time, important variations in settlement and migration patterns distinguish migrants from different birth countries, as they often tend to follow their compatriots and concentrate in established settlements (Kritz and Nogle 1994). As a result, internal migration can reinforce the concentration of some birthplace groups, while dispersing others (Raymer and Baffour 2018). In Australia, Asian migrants tend to move toward major centres of Asian settlement in Sydney and to a lesser extent Melbourne (Bell and Hugo 2000) and this preference has persisted over the last 30 years (Raymer et al. 2018). As a result, Sydney and Melbourne together are home to three-quarters of Australia's China-born and about two-thirds of its India-born (Wilson and Charles-Edwards 2017). Despite important variations in the settlement and migration patterns of different overseas-born groups, little consideration has been given to date to variations by visa class. While a couple of studies examined the employment and settlement patterns of international students (Faggian et al. 2016), and humanitarian migrants (Hugo 2014), no systematic comparison of visa classes has been undertaken because of the absence, until recently, of adequate datasets. Because the entry visa class is directly linked to the purpose of the stay, one might expect that there are different migration patterns based on migrants' visa classes.

10.3 Migration Data

As in most countries around the world, migrants can enter Australia on a permanent or temporary basis depending on the length of their stay and the purpose of their visit. Permanent residency can be granted through three main pathways—family reunification, skills, and humanitarian grounds—and allows migrants to reside in Australia indefinitely and apply for citizenship after a minimum of 4 years. Temporary visa holders, on the other hand, can reside in Australia only for a defined period of time, the length of which varies by visa class. The main visa classes, other than tourism, include temporary skilled migrants, students, working holiday makers, New Zealand citizens, and bridging visa holders as listed in Appendix 1.

In an effort to expand the range of data available for research and policy purposes, the Australian Bureau of Statistics (ABS) released the Australian Census and Migrants Integrated Dataset (ACMID) for the first time in 2014. The ACMID probabilistically matches individual-level records from the 2011 census to the visa status of permanent migrants—skilled, family, and humanitarian—who were granted permanent residency any time after the 1st of January 2000 based on the records from the Department of Home Affairs. In 2018, the ABS updated ACMID for the 2016 census to create a database of over two million migrants who were granted permanent residency anytime between the 1st of January 2000 and the 9th of August 2016. Many of them would have first entered Australia on a temporary basis and transitioned to permanent residency later, but visa transitions are not made available in this dataset. A total of 31% of permanent migrants arrived in Australia before 2005, 46% between 2006 and 2011, and 23% between 2012 and 2016. About a half of them have become Australian citizens by the 2016 census. The majority (58.5%) were granted permanent residency through the skilled stream. Breakdown by visa sub-classes indicates that 78% were on independent or employer-sponsored visas, while regional visas which require residing in a regional area for a defined period of time are less common, accounting for only 14% of permanent skilled migrants. Family migrants account for 31.6% of total permanent migrant intake, while humanitarian migrants represent only 9.9% of migrants who were granted permanent residency since 2000.

To complement ACMID, in 2019 the ABS released for the first time a census-based dataset for temporary migrants, the Australian Census and Temporary Entrants Integrated Dataset (ACTEID). This dataset does not include temporary entrants whose visa is for tourism, short stay business or visiting relatives, but comprises all other types of temporary visa holders. In this chapter we consider only temporary skilled migrants. This is because students are tied to their place of study and working holiday makers reside in Australia for short periods of time.

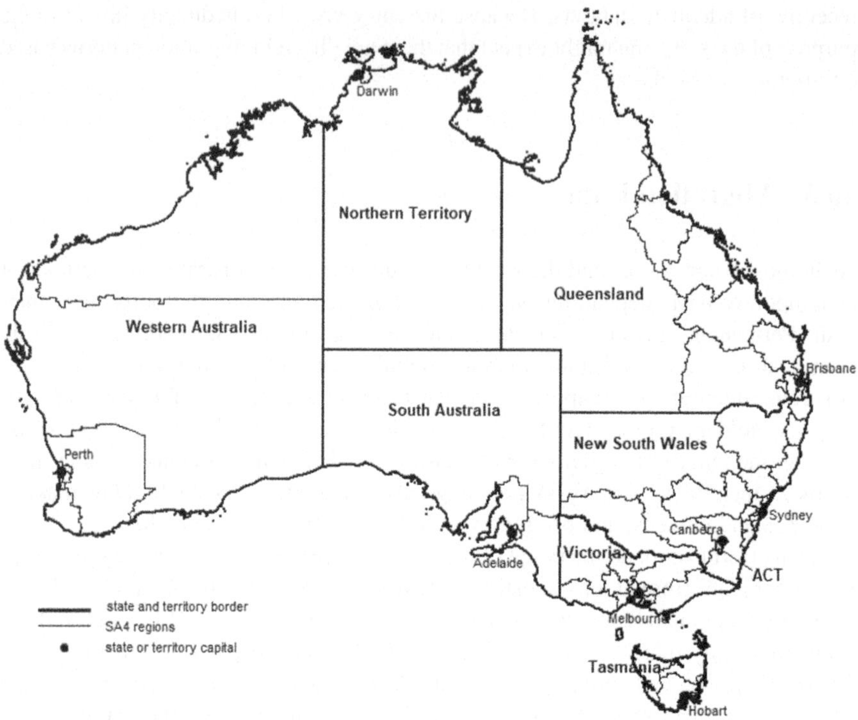

Fig. 10.1 States and territories and SA4 regions in Australia in 2016

Bridging visa holders represent a heterogeneous category of migrants changing visa status with little intrinsic meaning and New Zealand citizens are allowed to reside in Australia indefinitely despite their classification as temporary migrants.

The two datasets are conceptually different in that ACTEID provides a stock count of all temporary migrants in Australia at the 2016 census, while ACMID includes any migrants who were granted permanent residence in the last 16 years. To ensure comparability, we therefore compare temporary and permanent skilled migrants who arrived between 2012 and 2016. For confidentiality purposes, both datasets have been released only at an aggregate level.

The Australian census measures internal migration as a transition by comparing current place of usual residence to that 1 and 5 years prior to the census (Bell et al. 2002). One-year data is more sensitive to short-term variations and, for that reason, 5-year is often preferred. However, in order to capture recently arrived migrants and temporary migrants who typically reside in Australia less than 5 years, we chose to use 1-year migration data instead. The migration data used in this chapter is based on Statistical Area Level 4 or SA4s as represented on Fig. 10.1 along with states and territories and their capital cities. These 88 regions are the largest sub-state regions in the Main Structure of the Australian Statistical Geography Standards and broadly correspond to labour markets. For example, Greater Sydney is divided into fourteen

SA4 regions, while Greater Brisbane is made up of five, and the Northern Territory of only two. This spatial framework enables the analysis of migration flows between states and territories and between metropolitan and non-metropolitan areas. Within states and territories, the ABS divides Australia into 5 classes of remoteness status based on the relative access to services—major cities, inner regional, outer regional, remote and very remote areas—which allows the examination of migration flows up and down the urban hierarchy. While the changes of addresses are reported by the ABS in binary manner (yes/no), migration between SA4s and states has to be extracted from origin-destination matrices in TableBuilder, an online interface for disseminating aggregate census data. To mitigate the risk of re-identification potentially caused by data sparsity, the ABS does not make such data available for a subset of visas, which means that inter-regional migration can be obtained only for the most common visa classes. Despite these limitations, the data reported here allows the most spatially detailed examination of migration and settlement of different visa holders in Australia to date. Most results are compared to the Australian population, which comprises all individuals residing in Australia at the 2016 census whether they were born in Australia or not.

10.4 Spatial Patterns of Immigrant Settlement

In this section we first examine the distribution of immigrants between states and territories, and across the urban hierarchy before turning our attention to changes in distribution across SA4s by duration of residence. The population of Australia is well known to follow a particular geographic distribution characterised by a high proportion living in urban areas, particularly in state capital cities and a strong concentration in the south-eastern seaboard of the country. Consistent with the 2006 and 2011 censuses, Table 10.1 shows that about a third of the Australian population lives in New South Wales, followed by a quarter in Victoria and about 20% in Queensland. Immigrants follow broadly similar settlement patterns, with the majority settled in New South Wales and Victoria. Looking at each permanent migration programme separately, humanitarian migrants are more likely to settle in Victoria and South Australia, but less so in Queensland. While permanent skilled migrants are also less likely to settle in Queensland than the Australian population, they are overrepresented in Western Australia where demand for skilled labour was strong during the most recent resources boom, which ended just a few years before the 2016 census. The remote nature of work in the resources industry explains why Western Australia is the second biggest receiver of skilled migrants on regional visas after Victoria, despite its relatively small regional population. South Australia and the Northern Territory are also overrepresented by regional migrants, whereas Queensland has attracted proportionally fewer regional visa holders despite nearly 40% of its population living outside major cities. Finally, the concentration of family migrants in New South Wales (38.3%) is the result of migrants joining family members who are already established, primarily in the state's cosmopolitan capital

Table 10.1 Percentage distribution of the population across states and territories by visa status

		New South Wales	Victoria	Queensland	South Australia	Western Australia	Tasmania	Northern Territory	Australian Capital Territory	Total
Australian population		32.0	25.3	20.1	7.2	10.6	2.2	1.0	1.7	100
Permanent migrants	Skilled	29.8	27.1	15.6	6.5	17.4	0.5	1.0	1.9	100
	Skilled (Regional)	10.9	25.9	17.5	17.6	19.3	1.4	3.8	3.5	100
	Family	38.3	27.6	14.8	4.8	11.1	0.8	0.9	1.7	100
	Humanitarian	32.6	32.2	12.1	9.7	10	1.7	0.6	1.2	100
	Recently arrived[a] skilled	28.3	27.8	12.4	8.0	19.4	0.4	1.5	2.1	100
Temporary migrants	Recently arrived Skilled	40.9	23.1	13.5	3.2	15.4	0.6	1.9	1.4	100

Source: 2016 ACMID and ACTEID, authors' calculations
[a]Recently arrived migrants settled in Australia between 2012 and 2016, while other migrants settled between 2000 and 2016

Table 10.2 Percentage distribution of the population across the urban hierarchy by visa status

Remoteness area/visa type		Major cities	Inner regional	Outer regional	Remote	Very remote	Total
Australian population		71.2	18.2	8.5	1.2	0.8	100
Permanent migrants	Skilled	89.7	5.9	3.5	0.6	0.3	100
	Skilled (regional)	42.0	25.3	13.8	2.1	16.7	100
	Family	88.4	6.8	3.9	0.6	0.3	100
	Humanitarian	91.1	6.2	2.5	0.1	0.1	100
	Recently arrived skilled[a]	89.6	5.6	3.7	0.8	0.3	100
Temporary migrants	Recently arrived skilled[a]	86.9	6.3	4.9	1.1	0.8	100

Source: 2016 ACMID and ACTEID, authors' calculations
[a]Recently arrived migrants settled in Australia between 2012 and 2016, while other migrants settled between 2000 and 2016

of Sydney. Among the recently arrived migrants, temporary skilled migrants are significantly more likely to settle in New South Wales than permanent skilled migrants, with a staggering 40.9% of all temporary skilled workers concentrated in the country's most populous state.

In addition to variation by state, a look at remoteness classification allows us to better understand the distribution of urban, regional, and rural migrant populations in Australia. Given the country's settlement history, rural and remote parts of Australia tend to be less provisioned with basic services than similar places elsewhere. Overall, migrants display a strong preference for living in the largest cities and tend to be underrepresented in settlements down the urban hierarchy.

Table 10.2 shows a wide variation in remoteness by visa status. Concentration in major cities is particularly pronounced for humanitarian migrants (91.1%). The social process of chain migration by which new humanitarian migrants are located close to family members already established in Australia is a possible explanation for their strong preference for urban living. The settlement location of humanitarian migrants with no family links in Australia is decided by the federal Department of Social Services, who prioritise regional locations with adequate services and employment opportunities over urban areas. Our results suggest, however, that less than 10% of humanitarian migrants who arrived in the last 15 years fall into this category, which suggests that for this group, migration is a network-driven process that guides new arrivals toward pre-existing family ties. Furthermore, migrants are often able to leverage co-ethnic networks in larger cities, which can provide sources of employment, social life, and support for the transition to life in a new country. Our analysis of the Building a New Life in Australia (BNLA), a nationally-representative longitudinal study of humanitarian migrants who settled in Australia in 2013,[1] shows that of all migrating units interviewed, as many as

[1]For more information about the BNLA please refer to Edwards et al. (2018).

53.0% already had family members in Australia and 21.7% had friends from their country of origin. This explains why seven out of the top ten SA4 destinations for humanitarian migrants who arrived between 2012 and 2016, were also the SA4 regions with the largest established humanitarian migrant communities (i.e. settled prior to 2012). These are Sydney (Parramatta, South West, Inner South West, and Blacktown) in New South Wales, Melbourne (South East, West, North East, and North West) in Victoria, Logan-Beaudesert—an outer suburb of Greater Brisbane—in Queensland, and Perth (North West) in Western Australia. Combined, seven of these SA4s, all of which are in middle and outer suburbs of major cities, received over 50% of all humanitarian migrants who settled in Australia in the 5 years to 2016.

Regional skilled migrants are the only migrant group that is more likely to reside outside major cities compared with the Australia population. They are disproportionately located in smaller cities and towns, particularly in very remote areas (16.7%). Note, however, still over 40% of regional visa holders are residing in major cities, which suggest that a large proportion of them eventually move out of regional areas to settle in cities. Among the recently arrived skilled workers, the settlement patterns of temporary and permanent migrants are very similar.

We now turn our attention to the distribution of migrant population across the settlement system and to systematically establish patterns of concentration across Australia's 88 S4 regions we are using the Index of Dissimilarity (ID), which can be expressed as:

$$I_D = 0.5 \sum_{i=1}^{n} | x_i - y_i | \tag{10.1}$$

where n is the number of spatial units, 88 regions in this analysis, x_i is the proportion of a particular migrant group living in region i and y_i is the proportion of the reference group (the Australian population here) in region i. It can be interpreted as the percentage of a particular migrant group, which would have to change region of residence for its distribution to be the same as the Australian population. This index varies between 0 and 100, 0 indicating complete integration—the two populations have the same spatial distribution—while 100 indicates complete segregation with no one from the migration group in the same region as the reference population. Values of below 20 are often interpreted as an indication of little spatial separation, while values above 30 indicate significant segregation and values above 50 extreme segregation. We calculate this index separately for each visa type distinguishing between recently arrived migrants (2012–2016), settled migrants (2006–2011), and long-established migrants (2000–2005).

All migrant groups, regardless of their visa status, are more spatially concentrated than the Australian population. As evident from Table 10.3, the degree of spatial concentration of permanent migrants diminishes as the length of residence increases. This process of spatial integration (often referred to as 'spatial assimilation') is

Table 10.3 Index of Dissimilarity by visa status and year of arrival

Permanent migrants	Year of arrival	Index of dissimilarity
Skilled	2012–2016	35.0
	2006–2011	28.6
	2000–2005	25.6
Skilled (regional)	2012–2016	40.3
	2006–2011	34.8
	2000–2005	29.5
Family	2012–2016	29.2
	2006–2011	24.2
	2000–2005	24.2
Humanitarian	2012–2016	50.3
	2006–2011	47.9
	2000–2005	44.9
Temporary Skilled	2012–2016	38.9

Source: 2016 ACMID and ACTEID, authors' calculations

particularly apparent for skilled migrants. Within a decade of arrival, the Index of Dissimilarity decreases from 35.0 to 25.6.

As Hugo (2014) notes, this group is more likely to select areas to live according to socio-economic rather than ethnic factors, although temporary skilled migrants show a slightly higher degree of concentration. Decreasing, yet consistently high, dissimilarity for humanitarian migrants can thus be explained as a function of (lack of) relative economic opportunity and this group remains significantly separated in its spatial distribution more than 10 years after arrival (ID = 44.9). It is important to recognise that the data used here is not longitudinal and thus represents the experience of different arrival cohorts rather than single cohort tracked over time. Despite this limitation, there is clear evidence that the spatial patterns of settlement of immigrants change over time, as they become more spatially integrated. This suggests that immigrants are more spatially mobile in Australia in the early years after arrival. The next two sections examine this process, starting with their overall mobility level.

10.5 Level of Internal Migration

It is clear from our results that settlement patterns vary considerably by visa class and that migrants are rather more concentrated than the Australian population at large. The geographic distribution of the overseas-born is the result of their initial settlement patterns and subsequent relocation within Australia. This section focuses on the latter by examining internal migration levels by visa class. Drawing on 1-year transition data, we compute crude migration intensities (CMI) by dividing the number of individuals who changed place of residence in the last 12 months by

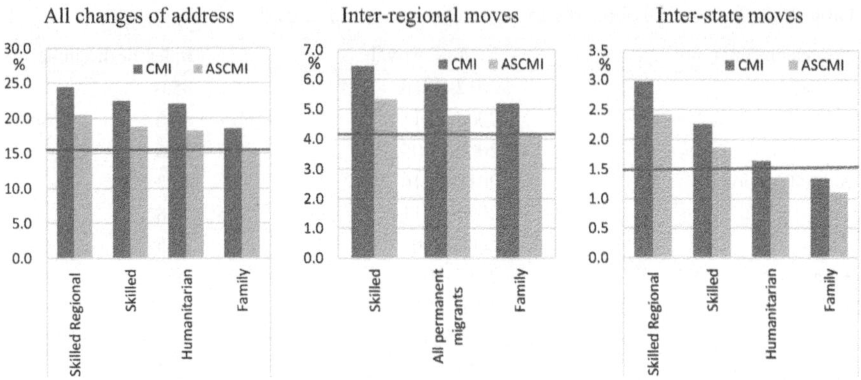

Fig. 10.2 Crude and age-standardised migration intensity by visa class, all changes of address, inter-regional migration within a state and inter-state migration. Note that the x-axis intersects the y-axis at the migration intensity of the Australian population thus representing a benchmark against which to interpret immigrants' mobility levels. Inter-regional migration cannot be obtained for all visa classes because of data scarcity. (Source: 2016 ACMID and ACTEID, authors' calculations)

the population at risk of moving measured at the time of the census and expressed it as a percentage. Populations with younger age structures exhibit higher overall migration levels, simply because young adults are more mobile (Bernard et al. 2014a, b; Rogers and Castro 1981). While all migrant groups are relatively young, median ages at the 2016 census ranged from 24.2 years for students to 30.7 years for humanitarian migrants and 34.4 years for permanent skilled migrants, compared with 38.1 years for the total population (Appendix 2). To robustly compare migration levels between different types of visa holders, we therefore age-standardise crude migration intensities (ASCMI), which has rarely been considered in previous studies. Because of small sample sizes, we use indirect age-standardisation method.[2] We compute CMIs and ASCMIs at three spatial scales: all changes of address, inter-regional and inter-state migration.

Figure 10.2 reports crude and age-standardised migration intensities by visa class compared with the Australian population. Even once differences in age structure are controlled for, all immigrant groups remain more mobile than the general population, with the exception of family visa holders. This suggests that immigrants' high levels of mobility are not only the product of different age structures, but reflect genuine variations in their underlying propensity to move. Drilling down to variation by visa class, the level of mobility (all changes of address) varies significantly from

[2]We compute age-specific migration intensities in five-year age groups for the Australian population. We then multiply them by the population in the corresponding age group for each visa class. The sum of these gives the total number of excepted internal migrants if these visa holders had the same internal migration behaviour as the Australian population. We then divide the number of observed migrations by the number of expected migrations to obtain a standardised migration ratio (SMR). Finally, we multiple the SMR by the observed CMI and obtain age-standardised migration intensities (ASMIs) that are directly comparable to the total population among visa holders.

20.4% for regional skilled migrants down to 18.2% of humanitarian migrants to 15.5% for family migrants—on par with the total population—as they presumably join family members who are already established in Australia. A similar gradient is observed for inter-regional migration. Note there was no statistically significant difference in mobility levels between permanent migrants who applied onshore and those who applied offshore (not shown here), which suggests that the lower levels of mobility of permanent migrants is not the product of differences in migration pathways to Australia.

Results from inter-state migration in confirm that skilled migrants are more likely to move interstate than the general population, particularly regional visa holders with 2.4% changing state of residence every year. This is possibly linked to visa requirements permitting departure from regional areas after an initial period of residence, although the absence of data on place of origin tabulated by place of destination precludes understanding motivations behind regional visa holders' movement up and down the urban hierarchy. Finally, family and humanitarian migrants show lower levels of inter-state migration than the general population, which probably reflects the strength of cultural ties and social networks among this groups who show a high degree of concentration in certain metropolitan areas as discussed earlier.

Some of the variation in mobility between immigrants and the general population has been explained by the length of residence (Bell and Hugo 2000). Early years in Australia represent a period of adjustment where immigrants seek to establish themselves in the labour and housing markets. Figure 10.3 examines this settlement process by reporting the proportion of migrants changing address by year of arrival and visa type. Note that migration intensities have been age-standardised and that the x-axis intersects the y-axis at the migration intensity of the total Australian population (15.1%), thus representing a benchmark against which to interpret immigrants' mobility levels. Figure 10.3 confirms that immigrants display above-average migration intensities in the early post-arrival years. However, mobility levels decline over time as length of residence in Australia increases and within about a decade, permanent migrants display mobility levels on par with the Australian population. Note that when differences in age structure are not controlled for, it takes 3–4 years longer for migrants to reach a mobility level similar to the Australian population. Looking at each permanent migration programme separately shows categorically lower levels of mobility among family migrants, whose mobility levels converge the fastest to that of the Australian population. As for temporary skilled migrants we were only able to trace their moves to 5 years ago, because of the low numbers of migrants staying on temporary visas over a longer period of time. Their initial mobility is higher than majority of permanent visa holders, but it is still noticeably lower than the levels of permanent skilled workers. This is most likely due to the fact that temporary skilled migrants are typically tied to an employer or a sponsor upon arrival as opposed to the majority (67%) of permanent skilled migrants who are not restricted to a particular employer.

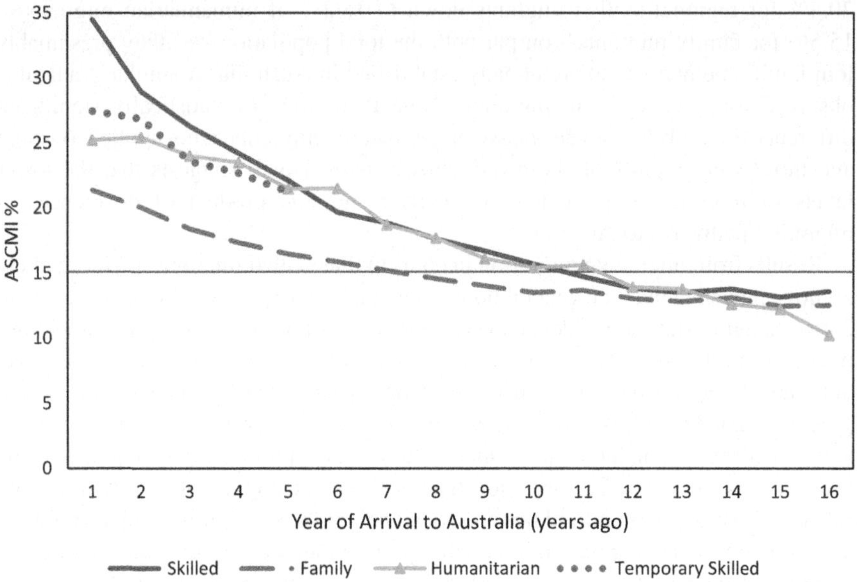

Fig. 10.3 Age-standardised crude migration intensities by visa class and single year of arrival. Note that the *x*-axis intersects the *y*-axis at the migration intensity of the Australian population (15.1%), thus representing a benchmark against which to interpret immigrants' mobility levels. (Source: 2016 ACMID and ACTEID, authors' calculations)

10.6 Redistribution of Population Through Migration

Migration does not necessarily bring about significant changes in the distribution of the population because some flows are offset by counter-flows in the reverse direction. This section examines the extent to which immigrants' movement contributes to the redistribution of the population. The net redistribution of population is the product of two parallel processes: (1) the intensity of movement measured by the crude migration intensity (CMI) discussed in the preceding section and (2) the degree of asymmetry between flows and counter-flows as measured by the migration effectiveness index (MEI), which can be mathematically expressed as follows:

$$\mathrm{MEI} = 100 * N/M \tag{10.2}$$

where N represent the net population redistribution between states and M the total number of migrants between states. The MEI measures the spatial imbalance of flows, but does not indicate the overall effect of migration on the settlement pattern. This is most effectively captured by the aggregate net migration rate (ANMR), which is the product of CMI and MEI divided by 100 (Bell et al. 2002).

Table 10.4 Inter-state migration indicators

		Crude migration intensity (CMI)	Migration effectiveness index (MEI)	Aggregate net migration rate (ANMR)
Australian population		1.45	9.42	0.14
Permanent migrants	Skilled	2.25	20.05	0.45
	Skilled (regional)	2.97	20.54	0.61
	Family	1.34	16.44	0.22
	Humanitarian	1.63	22.56	0.37
	Recently arrived[a] skilled	3.77	28.37	1.07
Temporary migrants	Recently arrived[a] Skilled	2.98	14.95	0.45

Source: 2016 ACMID and ACTEID, authors' calculations
[a]Recently arrived migrants settled in Australia between 2012 and 2016, while other migrants settled between 2000 and 2016

$$\text{ANMR} = 100 * \frac{N}{P} = \text{CMI} * \text{MEI}/100 \tag{10.3}$$

Thus, the ANMR quantifies the net shift of population between states per hundred persons residing in the country. It follows from Eq. (10.3) that the same impact of migration on population redistribution as measured by the ANMR may be achieved either through high MEI combined with low CMI or vice versa. Table 10.4 shows that overall redistributive effect is much higher for all migrant groups than the Australian population, except family migrants. Recently arrived permanent skilled migrants recorded the highest migration impact driven by equally high MEI and CMI, followed by regional skilled visa holders. For other visa classes, the impact of migration is lower, but the sources are quite different. For humanitarian migrants, low intensity is compensated by high migration effectiveness (i.e. spatially imbalanced flows), whereas for recently arrived temporary skilled workers high migration intensity is absorbed in reciprocal exchanges, resulting in low migration effectiveness, which limits the extent of population redistribution.

10.7 Spatial Patterns of Migration

The measures discussed in the preceding section provide summary indicators of the impact of migration on overall population redistribution, but they provide no information as to its spatial manifestation. We now turn our attention to the spatial outcomes of population movement, using net migration flows and rates (in-migration minus out-migration) as simple measures of the redistributive effect of migration between states in Table 10.5. Considering the entire population of Australia between 2015 and 2016, Victoria (14,371) and Queensland (10,568) recorded the largest net migration gains followed by Tasmania (1769), and Australian Capital Territory (1577), while all the other states recorded net losses, with New South Wales registering the highest net loss (10,849). Figure 10.4 shows the size and direction of net migration flows of internal migrants between states and territories. Victoria gained migrants from all the states, while Queensland gained from all the states but Victoria and Tasmania. Patterns of gains and losses for other states are more complex, but there is a clear movement from Western Australia to Victoria, Queensland and New South Wales.

Drilling down to visa class (Table 10.5), family migrants display migration patterns almost identical to the Australian population. Permanent skilled migrants follow broadly the same pattern, with net gains for Victoria and Queensland and net losses for almost all the other states (except ACT), although movement away from South Australia, Western Australia, Tasmania, and the Northern Territory is proportionally larger. Similar patterns characterise regional skilled migrants, with net gains for Victoria and Queensland and losses for all the other states, particularly Tasmania and the Northern Territory whose populations are predominantly located in non-metropolitan regions. This suggests that a significant proportion of regional visa holders eventually leave regional and remote areas, presumably in favour of metropolitan areas in Victoria and Queensland. While Victoria records a high net gain of humanitarian migrants, this group is also moving disproportionally away from Tasmania and the Northern Territory, ultimately reinforcing humanitarian migrants' settlement in major cities. New South Wales records net population gains only among recently arrived skilled migrants, both temporary and permanent, which confirms the persistence of Sydney as a gateway for skilled migrants who later move out. Recent temporary skilled migrants also stand out with a large proportion moving to Tasmania and to a lesser extent to the Northern Territory, and being the only group keeping a positive net inter-state rate in Northern Territory.

10.8 Discussion and Conclusion

As the level of international migration increases and the share of temporary migrants rises, new forms of analysis are required to better understand the nuanced processes of internal migration of overseas-born populations. This book chapter focuses on the settlement and migration patterns of Australian migrants by visa class. In doing so, we provide a novel approach to understanding how international migrants are distributed within Australia post-settlement and how they compare against the population at large.

Based on visa class, migrants within Australia can be broken down into two major categories: permanent and temporary. Permanent migrants are further classified as skilled, family or humanitarian. Likewise, temporary migrants are classified as either

Table 10.5 Net inter-state migration rates by visa class

		NSW	Vic	Qld	SA	WA	Tas	NT	ACT
Australian population		−0.16	0.27	0.25	−0.35	−0.47	0.39	−1.02	0.5
Permanent migrants	Skilled	−0.14	1.24	0.72	−2.72	−1.01	−1.88	−4.07	0.4
	Skilled (regional)	−0.35	2.02	0.58	−0.15	−0.89	−3.96	−5.15	−2.2
	Family	−0.26	0.5	0.42	−1.07	−0.52	1.55	−1.51	0.6
	Humanitarian	−0.49	1.12	0.01	−0.54	−0.8	−3.78	−1.65	0.6
	Recently arrived[a] skilled	0.82	2.16	2.14	−5.88	−1.96	−3.42	−5.13	−3.96
Temporary migrants	Recently arrived[a] skilled	0.44	0.79	−1.11	−2.06	−1.3	6.32	3.48	−0.3

Source: 2016 ACMID and ACTEID, authors' calculations

[a]Recently arrived migrants settled in Australia between 2012 and 2016, while other migrants settled between 2000 and 2016

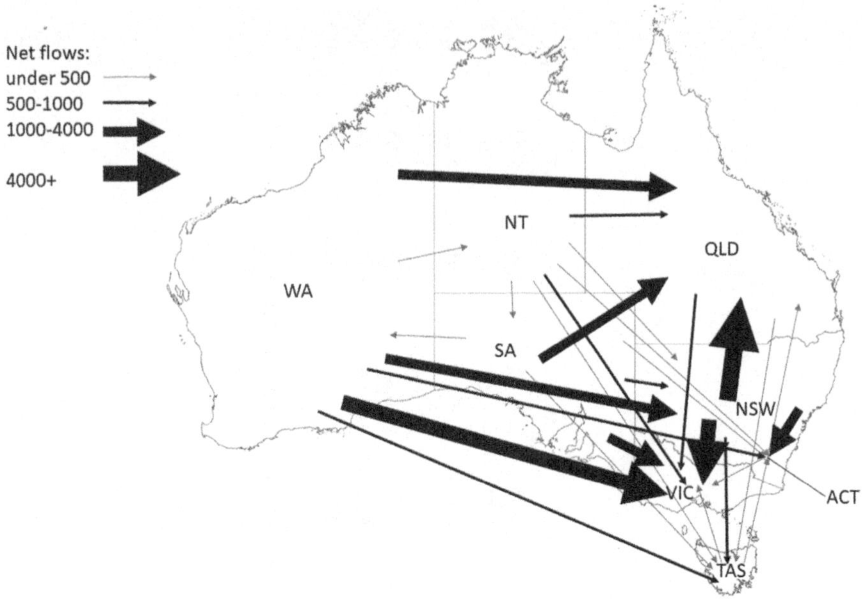

Fig. 10.4 Net inter-state migration flows, Australian population, 2015–2016. (Source: Census 2016, authors' calculations)

skilled, working holiday makers, students, or New Zealand citizens. There are several dozen sub-classifications, but these are beyond the scope of this analysis.

The overall settlement patterns of international migrants broadly mirror the population at large. Australia's population is heavily concentrated on the south-eastern seaboard, with large numbers in the major cities of Sydney and Melbourne. International migrants are even more concentrated in major cities, with particular visa classes such as the humanitarian more so than others. Over time, the dissimilarity index indicates that there is spatial de-concentration as the settlement patterns of the migrant population begin to resemble the non-migrant. This is because the level and pattern of internal migration of the overseas-born, which differ from the Australian population in early years, tend to converge towards those of the Australian-born as duration of residence increases. Interpreted through the lens of the assimilation theory, which posits that migrants become more similar to the native-born with increasing length of residence (Glick and Park 2016), these findings suggest that economic motives may take over social motives as migrants become more established, with the exception of humanitarian migrants who remain spatially segregated.

Our analysis has revealed important variations by visa classes that are missed when migrants are studied together as one group. First, recently arrived migrants are more mobile than established migrants, even after controlling for differences in age structures, and they display unique migration patterns characterised by a net gain for New South Wales, whereas the long-established migrants and the native-born move in the opposite direction with net losses for New South Wales (Sydney) and net gains for Victoria (Melbourne) and Queensland (Brisbane and surrounding regions). Permanent skilled migrants show migration patterns more broadly aligned with the Australian population, suggesting that there are similar forces shaping the internal migration of both groups. Second, family migrants exhibit a level and direction of internal migration that closely mirrors those of the Australian-born, even in the early post-arrival years. Because they join family members who are already established and have close family ties and connections to the Australian population, this group appears not to follow the same adjustment process as other migrant groups. While the visa types used in this analysis are specific to Australia, they are underpinned by distinct reasons for immigrating namely employment, family reunification and humanitarian motives, which remain the primary drivers of international migration in most countries.

Overall, a very small proportion of international migrants live outside major centres, with the notable exception of the skilled regional stream. Past and present efforts to locate migrants away from cities, including those on humanitarian visas, have largely been thwarted by a tendency to migrate to major cities as shown by movement away from Tasmania and the Northern Territory, towards established centres of humanitarian migrants' settlement in Melbourne. The movement of regional visa holders away from Tasmania and the Northern Territory towards Victoria suggests a low retention of these migrants in non-metropolitan areas. While successive policy measures have attempted to redress the imbalanced distribution of immigrants in Australia, further investigation is needed into the effects of these migrations over time to understand the long-term retention of regional visa holders and the effect of population churn on receiving regions.

Our results confirm that early years post-arrival constitute an important period of adjustment as immigrants seek to establish themselves in the labour and housing markets, having shown that this process is particularly pronounced for skilled migrants who exhibit heightened levels of mobility. As frequent residential relocation and migrations can be detrimental to mental health outcomes and integration into receiving communities (Stokols and Shumaker 1982), there is a need to better understand early years in Australia and the impact of high mobility on a series of life outcomes. Immigrants' movement in Australia is closely linked to the transition from one visa class to another as temporary workers gain the status of permanent residents and students acquire working rights upon graduation. These processes remain poorly understood and there is a need for a longitudinal dataset tracking migrants upon arrival. Building a New Life in Australia is an example of such dataset for humanitarian migrants. Such a survey could be extended to other visa holders as there is a need to better understand how migrants transition from one visa to another as they progress from temporary to permanent residency. While such datasets are currently not available in Australia, the forthcoming release of a longitudinal census dataset, which tracks individuals over three censuses, should permit better understanding how migrants circulate between places in Australia and offer a longitudinal perspective that would reveal how migration choices interface across space and time over the life-course of immigrants who settled in Australia before 2006. Further insights into the spatial integration of the overseas-born could also be gained by considering variation by key socio-demographic characteristics, such as sex, country of birth, and level of educational attainment. Finally, ACMID and ACTEID provide an opportunity to analyse the local factors attracting immigrants to particular regions by drawing on contextual social and economic variables in order to get a more fine-grained understanding of variations by visa types. These new datasets should stimulate further regional science research on migration in coming years.

Appendix 1: Visa Types, Classes and Sub-Classes

Visa type		Visa class	Visa Sub-class
Permanent	Permanent Skilled	Skilled Independent	Independent Entrant (126)
			Skilled—Independent (136)
			Skilled—Independent (175)
			Skilled—Independent Regional (Provisional) (495)
			Skilled—Independent Overseas Student (880)
			Skilled—Independent (885)
			Skilled—Independent (189)
			Skilled—Nominated (Permanent) (190)
			Skilled—Onshore Independent New Zealand Citizen (861)
		Skilled Entrepreneur	Business Innovation & Investment (Provisional) (188)
			Business Innovation & Investment (Residence) (888)
		Skilled Family or Government Sponsored	Concessional Family—Skilled—Australian Linked (105)
			Regional Family Sub-Class—Regional Linked (106)
			Skill Matching (134)
			State/Territory Nominated Independent (135)
			Skilled—State/Territory Nominated Independent (137)
			Skilled—Australian Sponsored (138)
			Skilled—Designated Area Sponsored (139)
			Skilled—Sponsored (176)
			Skilled—Regional Sponsored (475)
			Skilled—Regional Sponsored (487)

(continued)

Visa type		Visa class	Visa Sub-class
			Skilled—Designated Area Sponsored (Provisional) (496)
			Skilled—Designated Area Sponsored—Overseas Student (882)
			Skilled—Regional (887)
			Skilled—Other Family or Government Sponsored (993)
		Skilled Employer Sponsored	Regional Sponsored Migration Scheme (119)
			Labour Agreement (120)
			Employer Nomination Scheme (121)
			Skilled—Regional Sponsored (Provisional) (489)
			Labour Agreement (855)
			Employer Nomination (856)
			Regional Sponsored Migration Scheme (857)
			Skilled—Onshore Designated Area—Sponsored New Zealand Citizen (863)
			Skilled—Employer Nomination (186)
			Skilled—Regional Employer Nomination (187)
		Skilled Other	Business—General (123)
			Distinguished Talent (Australian Support) (124)
			Distinguished Talent and Special Service (Independent) (125)
			Business Owner—Business Skills (127)
			Business Skills (Senior Executive) (128)
			State/Territory Sponsored (Business Owner—Business Skills) (129)
			State/Territory Sponsored (Business Skills—Senior Executive) (130)
			Migrants—Investment Linked (131)
			Business Talent (132)
			Business Owner (160)
			Senior Executive (161)
			Investor (162)
			State/Territory Sponsored Business Owner (163)
			State/Territory Sponsored Senior Executive (164)
			State/Territory Sponsored Investor (165)

(continued)

Visa type		Visa class	Visa Sub-class
			Skilled (805)
			1 November Special (816)
			1 November Highly Qualified EP (818)
			Business Owner (840)
			Senior Executive (841)
			State/Territory Sponsored Business Owner (842)
			State/Territory Sponsored Executive (843)
			Investment—Linked (844)
			Established Business in Australia (845)
			State/Territory Sponsored (846)
			Distinguished Talent (858)
			Skilled—Onshore Australian-Sponsored New Zealand Citizen (862)
			Business Owner (890)
			Investor (Residence) (891)
			State/Territory Sponsored Business Owner (892)
			State/Territory Sponsored Investor (Residence) (893)
	Family	Family Partner	Spouse (100)
			Interdependency (110)
			Prospective Marriage (300)
			Spouse (Provisional) (309)
			Interdependency (Provisional) (310)
			Spouse (After Entry) (801)
			Interdependency (Permanent) (814)
			Spouse (Extended Eligibility) (820)
			Interdependency (826)
			Prospective Marriage Spouse (831)
		Family Other	Child (101)
			Child for Adoption (102)
			Parent (103)
			Preferential Family (104)
			Aged Dependent Relative (114)
			Remaining Relative (115)
			Carer (116)
			Orphan Relative (117)
			Designated Parent (118)
			Contributory Parent (143)
			Contributory Parent (Temporary) (173)

(continued)

Visa type		Visa class	Visa Sub-class
			Dependent Child (445)
			Child (After Entry) (802)
			Aged Parent (After Entry) (804)
			Compassionate Grounds (Family & Other Close Ties) (806)
			Confirmatory (Residence) (808)
			December 1989 (Permanent) (812)
			Close Ties (832)
			Remaining Relative (835)
			Carer (836)
			Orphan Relative (837)
			Aged Dependent Relative (838)
			Designated Parent (859)
			Contributory Aged Parent (Residence) (864)
			Contributory Aged Parent (Temporary) (884)
	Humanitarian	Humanitarian Refugee	Refugee (200)
			In-Country Special Humanitarian (201)
			Emergency Rescue (203)
			Woman at Risk (204)
		Humanitarian Special Humanitarian Programme	Humanitarian—Other Special Humanitarian (994)
			Global Special Humanitarian (202)
			Resolution of Status (Permanent) (851)
		Humanitarian Other	Refugee (After Entry) (803)
			Camp Clearance (205)
			East Timorese in Portugal (208)
			Citizens of Former Yugoslavia (Displaced Persons) (209)
			Minorities of Former USSR (Special Assistance) (210)
			Burmese in Burma (211)
			Sudanese (Special Assistance) (212)
			Burmese in Thailand (Special Assistance) (213)
			Cambodian SAC (214)
			Sri Lankan (Special Assistance) (215)
			Ahmadi SAC (216)
			Vietnamese SAC (217)
			PRC Citizen (Permanent) (809)
			1 November PRC (815)

(continued)

Visa type	Visa class	Visa Sub-class
	Permanent Other	Authority to Return/Return Endorsement (111)
		Former Citizen (150)
		Former Resident (151)
		Family Reunion (New Zealand Citizens) (152)
		Return Class A (154)
		Emergency (Seeking Permanent Residence) (302)
		Certain Unlawful Non-Citizens (833)
Temporary Visa	Bridging	Bridging Visa Class A (010)
		Bridging Visa Class B (020)
		Bridging Visa Class C (030)
		Bridging Visa Class D (040)
		Bridging Visa Class E (050)
		Bridging Visa Class F (060)
		Bridging Visa Class R (070)
	Special Category (New Zealand)	Special Category (444)
	Temporary Work (Skilled)	Temporary Work (Skilled) (457)
	Working Holiday Maker	Working Holiday (417)
		Work and Holiday (462)
	Student	Student (Temporary) (500)
		Independent ELICOS Sector (570)
		Schools Sector (571)
		Vocational Education and Training Sector (572)
		Higher Education Sector (573)
		Postgraduate Research Sector (574)
		Non-Award Foundation/Other Sector (575)
		AUSAID/Defence Sponsored Sector (576)
	Temporary Other	Temporary Work (Short Stay Activity) (400)
		Temporary Work (Long Stay Activity) (401)
		Training and Research (402)
		Temporary Work (International Relations) (403)
		Investor Retirement (405)
		Government Agreement (406)
		Retirement (410)
		Foreign Government Agency Staff (415)
		Special Programme (416)

(continued)

Visa type	Visa class	Visa Sub-class
		Entertainment (420)
		Media and Film Staff (423)
		Supported Dependent of Aust or NZ Citizen Temp in Australia (430)
		New Zealand Citizen (Family Relationship) (461)
		Skilled—Graduate (476)
		Temporary Graduate (485)
		Diplomatic (995)

Regional visa
Skilled—Independent Regional (Provisional) (495)
Regional Family Sub-Class—Regional Linked (106)
Skill Matching (134)
State/Territory Nominated Independent (135)
Skilled—State/Territory Nominated Independent (137)
Skilled—Designated Area Sponsored (139)
Skilled—Regional Sponsored (475)
Skilled—Regional Sponsored (487)
Skilled—Designated Area Sponsored (Provisional) (496)
Skilled—Designated Area Sponsored—Overseas Student (882)
Regional Sponsored Migration Scheme (119)
Skilled—Regional Sponsored (Provisional) (489)
Regional Sponsored Migration Scheme (857)
Skilled—Regional Employer Nomination (187)

Appendix 2: Median Age by Visa Type

	Median age
1 Total Population	38.08
4 Permanent Migrants	34.69
4.1 Skilled	34.35
4.1.1 Skilled Independent	34.27
2.1.2 Skilled Entrepreneur	23.32
2.1.3 Skilled Family or Government Sponsored	35.41
2.1.4 Skilled Employer Sponsored	34.08
2.1.5 Skilled Other	33.14
2.1.6 Skilled Regional	33.41
4.2 Family	36.15
4.3 Humanitarian	30.67

(continued)

	Median age
5 Temporary Migrants	28.1
5.1 Temporary Bridging Visa	30.51
5.2 NZ Citizen	38.06
5.3 Temporary Work Skilled	30.63
5.4 Working Holiday Maker	
5.5 Student	24.15
5.6 Other Temporary	28.16

Source: 2016 ACMID and ACTEID, authors' calculations

References

ABS, Australian Bureau of Statistics (2017) 2016 Census data. ABS, Canberra, ACT. extracted via Table Builder

ABS, Australian Bureau of Statistics (2018a) Migration, Australia, 2016–2017. ABS, Canberra, ACT. in catalogue no 3412.0

ABS, Australian Bureau of Statistics (2018b) Australian demographic statistics (3101.0). ABS, Canberra, ACT

Baffour B, Raymer J (2019) Estimating multiregional survivorship probabilities for sparse data: an application to immigrant populations in Australia, 1981–2011. J Demogr Res 40:463–502

Belanger A, Rogers A (1992) The internal migration and spatial redistribution of the foreign-born population in the United States: 1965-70 and 1975-80. Int Migr Rev 26(4):1–69

Bell M, Cooper J (1995) Internal migration in Australia 1986-1991: the overseas-born. Multicultural Australia. Bureau of Immigration and Research Population, Canberra, ACT

Bell M, Hugo G (2000) Internal migration in Australia: 1991-1996 overview and the overseas-born. Department of Immigration and Multicultural Affairs, Canberra, ACT

Bell M et al (2002) Cross-national comparison of internal migration: issues and measures. J R Stat Soc Ser A Stat Soc 165(3):435–464

Bernard A, Bell M, Charles-Edwards E (2014a) Improved measures for the cross-national comparison of age profiles of internal migration. Popul Stud 68(2):179–195

Bernard A, Bell M, Charles-Edwards E (2014b) Life-course transitions and the age profile of internal migration. Popul Dev Rev 40(2):231–239

Darlington-Pollock F, Lomax N, Norman P (2018) Ethnic internal migration: the importance of age and migrant status. Geogr J 185:68

Edwards B et al (2018) Cohort profile: building a new life in Australia (BNLA): the longitudinal study of humanitarian migrants. Int J Epidemiol 47(1):20–20h

Faggian A et al (2016) Evaluating the effects of Australian policy changes on human capital: the role of a graduate visa scheme. Environ Plan C Govern Pol 34(1):151–170

Fielding AJ (1992) Migration and social mobility: South East England as an escalator region. Reg Stud 26(1):1–15

Glick J, Park J (2016) Migration, assimilation and social welfare. International handbook of migration and population distribution (Springer), pp 505–524

Hatton TJ, Tani M (2005) Immigration and inter-regional mobility in the UK, 1982–2000*. Econ J 115(507):F342–FF58

Hugo G (2008) Australia's state-specific and regional migration scheme: an assessment of its impacts in South Australia. J Int Migr Integr 9(2):125–145

Hugo G (2004) A new paradigm of international migration: implications for migration policy and planning in Australia

Hugo G (2011) Changing spatial patterns of immigrant settlement. In: Multiculturalism and integration: a harmonious relationship. ANUE Press, Canberra, ACT, pp 1–40

Hugo G (2014) Change and continuity in Australian International Migration Policy. Int Migr Rev 48(3):868–890

Hugo G (2014) Immigrant settlement in regional Australia: patterns and processes. Rural change in Australia: population, economy, environment, pp 57–82

Karlsen E (2016) Refugee resettlement to Australia: what are the facts?

Khoo S-E, McDonald P, Hugo G (2009) Skilled temporary migration from Asia-Pacific countries to Australia. Asian Pac Migr J 18(2):255–281

King R, Skeldon R (2010) 'Mind the gap!' Integrating approaches to internal and international migration. J Ethn Migr Stud 36(10):1619–1646

Kritz M, Nogle J (1994) Nativity concentration and internal migration among the foreign-born. Demography 31(3):509–524

Larsen G (2013) Family migration to Australia. Parliamentary Library Australia, Canberra, ACT

Maher CA, McKay J (1986) Internal migration in Australia. Department of Immigration and Ethnic Affairs for Commonwealth, Canberra, ACT

MCA, Migration Council Australia (2015) Migration in focus: an analysis of recent permanent migration census data. Occasional paper. Australian National University. Centre of Oriental Studies, Canberra, ACT

McAreavey R, Argent N (2018) New Immigration Destinations (NID) unravelling the challenges and opportunities for migrants and for host communities. Elsevier, Amsterdam

McDonald P (2018) Australia should continue its current comprehensive population policy–at least for the next decade. Aust Pop Stud 2(2):3–11

Newbold KB (1996) Internal migration of the foreign-born in Canada. Int Migr Rev 30(3):728–747

Newbold KB (1999) Internal migration of the foreign-born: population concentration or dispersion? J Interdiscipl Stud 20(3):259–276

Nogle JM (1997) Internal migration patterns for US foreign-born, 1985–1990. Int J Popul Geogr 3 (1):1–13

Parr N (2018) What sort of population policy should Australia adopt? suggestions for migration, fertility and population research policy. Australian Popul Stud 2(2):12–21

Raymer J, Baffour B (2018) Subsequent migration of immigrants within Australia, 1981–2016. Popul Res Policy Rev 37(6):1053–1077

Raymer J et al (2018) The sources and diversity of immigrant population change in Australia, 1981–2011. Demography 55(5):1777–1802

Reher DS, Silvestre J (2009) Internal migration patterns of foreign-born immigrants in a country of recent mass immigration: evidence from new micro data for Spain 1. Int Migr Rev 43(4): 815–849

Rogers A (1999) The internal migration patterns of the foreign-born and native-born populations in the United States 1975–80 and 1985–90. Int Migr Rev 33(2):403–429

Rogers A, Castro LJ (1981) Model migration schedules. Research report RR-81-30. International Institute for Applied Systems Analysis, Luxemburg

Rowland DT (1979) Internal migration in Australia. Australian Bureau of Statistics, Canberra, ACT

Stokols D, Shumaker SA (1982) The psychological context of residential mobility and well-being. J Soc Issues 38(3):149–171

Wilson T, Charles-Edwards E (2017) The regional pattern of Australia's largest overseas-born populations. Reg Stud Reg Sci 4(1):227–231

Chapter 11
Culture and the City: An Application of Data Envelopment Analysis to Cultural Performance

Karima Kourtit, Peter Nijkamp, and Soushi Suzuki

Abstract This paper seeks to analyse the significance of cultural amenities in a city for its socio-economic performance. In particular, our study aims to provide an evidence-based answer to the question which cities are the most efficient in terms of their multidimensional economy-culture ratio, and why. This analysis is pursued by using a large database on 40 global cities extracted from the Global Power City Index (GPCI) data system. The methodology adopted here originates from Data Envelopment Analysis (DEA) complemented with a so-called Super-Efficiency Module (SEM) so as to arrive at unambiguous rankings of the cities at hand on a global cultural ladder. The DEA results are complemented with a multivariate analysis and regression models. By analysing the cultural productivity of these cities, it appears that our empirical results differ often from the usual urban ranking methods where cities such as London, New York, Paris, or Tokyo rank the highest. Large Asian cities appear to be able to obtain a good efficiency performance in terms of the ratio of (multidimensional) economic outcomes versus (multidimensional) cultural input resources.

Keywords Global cities · Data envelopment analysis (DEA) · Super-efficiency · Culture · Cultural efficiency · Cultural capability

---

K. Kourtit (✉) · P. Nijkamp
Open University of the Netherlands, Heerlen, The Netherlands

Alexandru Ioan Cuza University of Iasi, Iasi, Romania

University of Technology (UM6P), Benguérir, Morocco

S. Suzuki
Hokkai-Gakuen University, Sapporo, Japan
e-mail: soushi-s@lst.hokkai-s-u.ac.jp

M. Kawano et al. (eds.), *Theory and History in Regional Perspective*, New Frontiers in Regional Science: Asian Perspectives 56,
https://doi.org/10.1007/978-981-16-6695-7_11

11.1 Introduction

In the urban world history, cities are usually regarded as the cradles of culture and civilisation. Such historically shaped, contextual conditions act as magnets for urban development and power, as is not only witnessed by ancient cities but also by medieval and contemporary cities (see Glaeser et al. 2020). Modern cities such as New York, San Francisco, Paris, Tokyo, Rome or Amsterdam derive their attractiveness not only from a solid economic structure reflected in agglomeration benefits, but also from a multi-faceted portfolio of cultural and entertainment services that attract millions of people. So the cultural base of a city may—under certain conditions—be an escalator for urban progress and development. In a recent study (Kourtit and Nijkamp 2019) an extensive modelling study has been undertaken on the important magnet function of urban cultural amenities for the attraction of the creative class and subsequent urban development. In the above study also an extensive description and operational definition of cultural amenities in the city has been provided.

In the present paper, we will examine whether the presence of *cultural capital* (interpreted in a broad sense as 'the historical-social and cognitive assets linked to history, arts and culture', which embodies many public provisions for arts and culture, such as museums, art galleries, theatres, cinemas, or sports events; Kourtit and Nijkamp 2013a, b) has a positive influence on the city's socio-economic performance. We aim to assess the urban cultural gravity function from the perspective of measurable cultural capital in a city. We will apply this question to 40 global cities. The database on these global cities used in this study will be described in Sect. 11.3.

We posit in our study that culture is an enabling public amenity in a city. Its presence does not automatically—as a '*deus ex machina*'—generate economic growth of a city. It may be a desirable but not sufficient condition for urban economic development. This enabling role of culture will be called here *cultural capability*. This concept will be further articulated in Sect. 11.2.

In examining the role of culture in urban development we should recognise that in general big cities provide more opportunities to create and enjoy cultural amenities. Although in the developing world such big cities show often more problematic features, they are generally also enjoying relatively higher welfare levels compared to smaller places. In any case, it is a fact that larger cities all over the world score relatively high on the cultural performance ladder. Clearly, size matters. However, for an economist it is relevant to look at the scarce resources needed to generate a desired urban outcome, and to examine whether the translation of urban inputs into outputs takes place in an efficient way. In other way, for a meaningful comparison of the urban cultural impact it is pertinent to use an efficiency indicator that relates urban output to urban input. From this perspective, the notion of cultural capability receives also an appropriate meaning, as the question is: which cities are able to produce a maximum level of urban output with a given level of cultural input resources (or cultural capital)?

This latter efficiency question is the core of our research. In the present paper we will use an established method, data envelopment analysis (DEA), to relate multiple inputs to multiple outputs, and to infer conclusions on the relative efficiency of 40 global cities. For technical details on this DEA approach we refer to a book publication by Suzuki and Nijkamp (2017). This technique allows to derive an efficiency ranking of cities, especially if a so-called super-efficiency model is applied, which leads to an unambiguous ranking of all cities under consideration. Our study presents thus an application of DEA to the cultural efficiency performance of large cities. It also attempts to examine the quantitative effects of urban cultural provisions on general urban development and welfare indicators through the use of multivariate statistics and regression analysis.

This paper is organised as follows. Section 11.2 presents the storyline of the paper in which the role of urban culture and cultural capability is described. Then Sect. 11.3 presents the database and the methodological framing of our study. Next, Sects. 11.4 and 11.5 provide the empirical outcomes of our DEA model and of the econometric regression analysis, respectively. Finally, Sect. 11.6 concludes this paper.

11.2 Recent Interest in Culture in the City: A Capability Approach

In recent years we witness a rising interest in culture—as a broad concept referring to tangible and immaterial expressions of the human mind that create a sense of history, identity, or recognition—as an integral part of a balanced urban policy, as will be illustrated by a few examples. The 2030 Agenda for Sustainable Development, published by the United Nations (2015a) under the title '*Transforming our World*', presents a plan of action addressing five major concerns in the contemporaneous global policy arena, viz. *people*, *planet*, *prosperity*, *peace*, and *partnership*. It turns out that human settlements—including, in particular, cities—are directly and indirectly a focal point of this action agenda, witness the emphasis on poverty, human health, inclusive education, social empowerment, water management, sanitation, labour markets, infrastructure, urban safety, resilient cities, environmental quality, land degradation, and so forth. This UN declaration addresses explicitly also culture, and states: '*We acknowledge the natural and cultural diversity of the world and recognize that all cultures and civilizations can contribute to, and are crucial enablers of, sustainable development*' (item 36).

Over the past years, a series of policy documents focussing on tangible and intangible forms of culture (often related to cultural heritage in cities) has been published as part of a broader international policy agenda on sustainable development.[1] These documents were often produced against the background of rapid and usually uncontrolled world-wide urbanisation with inevitable—often adverse—consequences for culture and historical-cultural heritage. The common policy vision is that cultural amenities are to be harnessed to the benefit of communities, cities, and regions. In this context, historic towns and areas, cultural amenities (e.g., art galleries, museums, churches, theatres, festivals), lively historic districts or streets, or an authentic urban 'ambiance' may act as an attraction force for both residents and visitors, while they may also enable social cohesion and inclusion, especially if there is sufficient attractive public space for sharing identity, cultural values and jointly inspiring urban activities. Culture is then an enabler of mixed urban land use and of urban social buzz externalities favouring livability, inclusiveness, and sustainability in the modern urban fabric. In conclusion, culture is not a luxury, but an urgent necessity in any vital and creative city through its inherent value articulating the sense of place, history, and identity for inhabitants and visitors.

Studies on the importance of culture for modern life can be distinguished into two strands, viz. *micro-based* and *macro-based* research. In recent years, the micro-based perspective on culture—defined in a broad sense—has found many applications in individual perception and preference studies, in particular, in discrete choice models, contingency valuation models, and conjoint analysis (see e.g., Comim et al. 2008; Tellier 2009; Glaeser 2011; Taylor 2013; Archer and Bezdecny 2016; Acs 2016; Stanley et al. 2017; Kourtit and Nijkamp 2018a, b; Nijkamp 2016; Kourtit et al. 2015; Throsby 2001; Östh et al. 2021). A macro-based view looks more into '*cultural complexes*' in the city from a broader and collective policy perspective, and has found many applications in assessment studies based on cost–benefit analysis, multi-criteria analysis or urban imagineering studies (see e.g. Fusco Girard and Nijkamp 2009; Gravagnuolo et al. 2021; Mommaas 2004). A merger of a micro-based and a macro-based approach to a culture-based urban perspective can be found in Kourtit and Nijkamp (2013a, b), where individual facebook data were used in an assessment of alternative meso-development plans for a historico-cultural district in Amsterdam.

It is noteworthy that culture—as an organised social constellation and product of the human mind (see Bourdieu 1973)—helps enhance quality of human life, while in turn it is also shaped by the cognitive and creative ability of humankind (e.g., Sen 1999, 2008). In recent scientific and policy oriented debates on sustainable and inclusive development two important economic concepts have often come to the fore, viz. *needs* (or demand) and *capabilities*.

[1]Examples are: The Paris Declaration on Heritage as a Driver of Development (2011) (UNESCO, Paris); The UNESCO World.

Report: Investing in Cultural Diversity and Intercultural Dialogue (2009) (UNESCO, Paris); The Bali Promise (2011) (World Culture Forum, Bali); The Future We Want for All (2015b) (United Nations, New York); Cultural Heritage, the UN Sustainable Development Goals and the New Urban Agenda (2015) (ICOMOS, Paris); Cities of Tomorrow (2011) (European Union, Regional Policy, Brussels).

The notion of '*needs*' has already a long history, in both psychology and economics. The hierarchical needs ladder advocated by Maslow (1943) forms one of the cornerstones of behavioural psychology, while needs satisfaction under scarcity constraints is a core element in traditional economic utility and welfare theory. The concept of needs is not only relevant in conventional consumer theory (including marketing) in relation to the appreciation and choice for goods and services under a regime of scarcity, but has also a clear relevance in an urban context from the perspective of clients or consumers (residents and visitors); see also a study by Glaeser et al. (2001).

In a policy document by UN Habitat (2013) on '*The City We Need*', a new urban paradigm is launched, based on the premise that '*the battle for a more sustainable future will be won or lost in cities*'. It is argued that well-planned cities provide all citizens with the opportunity to lead a safe, healthy, and productive life, while they do also favour social inclusion, resilience, and prosperity. This UN document mentions several '*don'ts*' in urban planning and management in the form of policy lessons on things to avoid, such as: lack of uncoordinated urban policies, poor planning, and 'short-termism', disregard of urban-rural linkages, poorly regulated real estate markets, mismanagement by all actors and tiers of government, loss of urban identity, lack of effective participation, and absence of effective implementation and financing mechanisms. It is noteworthy that this report refers explicitly to the loss of urban identity caused by the regretful destruction of *cultural heritage*, local bio-diversity, and public space.

Generally speaking, cities have many opportunities—as a result of their indigenous resources and their agglomeration advantages—to grow and to become economic spearheads. Culture is one of the components of city capital and provides many development options for the city. It is an enabling factor, hence the term cultural capability.

Cultural capability is a key concept in our study and is formally defined as the potential of the city—measured in terms of a portfolio of direct and indirect (contextual) cultural amenities (cultural interaction capital, livability/environmental capital, and infrastructural capital)—to deliver a broad package of cultural services that may not only serve the own citizens, but also to attract in particular external or foreign visitors. Cultural capability—as a desirable condition for sustaining or creating culture—can lead to a better (i.e. more efficient) socio-economic outcome of a city; it is necessary but not sufficient condition: its presence does not necessarily or automatically lead to better outcomes; the latter depends on the context and on the use or customer conditions. It may thus be conceived of as an integrated set of productive input services that may be used as opportunities to generate or favour the cultural attractiveness of a city, in particular for visitors from elsewhere. Critical moderator variables are agglomeration advantages from urban size and prosperity effects from high-welfare urban areas.

In the context of the present study, the focus will be on culture (cultural amenities, historico-cultural or socio-political attitudes, authentic atmosphere or ambiance in a city, etc.) as one of the meso-based intermediate enabling constituents of urban performance (at the aggregate level of a city) and urban well-being or quality life (at a meso or micro level of consumers). In this context, the strength of a city is not formed by a closed 'island' character, but by its multi-tasking role in choosing smart options in a broad urban opportunity space. Open and accessible public spaces in cities, enabled and enriched by culture, arts, and community interaction, may be an effective therapy against such urban 'diseases' as congestion, crowdedness, social exclusion or stress, or—in general—urban degeneration. Culture—as an intermediate social constellation between emancipated citizens ('urban minds' or 'urban souls') and beautiful cityscapes ('urban bodies')—may be a promising vehicle on the way to urban regeneration and creative urban environments (Törnqvist 1983; Santagata 2009; Wahlström 2017; Kourtit et al. 2020). Against this background, cultural clusters and historic urban landscapes may be seen as prominent capability resources that favour sustainable and inclusive local development (see e.g., Allmendinger and Haughton 2009; Amin and Roberts 2008; Cooke and Lazzaretti 2008). Smart sectoral specialisation in a given domain (e.g., culture) may then be a meaningful developmental strategy of an intelligent or smart city, especially in a modern digital age (see Kopczewska et al. 2017).

In the same vein as the currently popular Tourism-Led Growth (TLG) concept (see Castro-Nuno et al. 2013; Inchausti-Sintes 2015; Bride et al. 2016; Liu et al. 2017; Li et al. 2020), we witness nowadays an increasing popularity of Culture-Led or Culture-Driven Growth (see e.g., Miles and Paddison 2005; Sacco et al. 2004; Throsby 2001; Wåhlin et al. 2016). In various recent studies the notion of cultural capital or cultural resources is employed as a conceptual framing of the idea that culture is a productive asset contributing to urban prosperity or performance (see Snowball 2008). The notion of cultural capital has already a long history. It plays a major role in the seminal work of Bourdieu (1986) who interprets cultural capital as a set of accumulated resources that empower individuals and groups to enhance their cultural competence and socio-economic position, e.g., through upward social mobility and rise in status of various kinds. Bourdieu's description of cultural capital differs from earlier views of Weber (1921) who conceives of local culture as an institutionalised set of local and historically shaped characteristics that determine the urban spirit from a structuralist perspective. Finally, the economic concept of creative and cultural capital and the notion of sustainable development in shaping urban well-being and quality of life have also quite a long history. They highlight the added value of urban cultural-oriented amenities which comprise locality-specific tangible and intangible assets (e.g. historical-cultural heritage, historical atmosphere in a city, historically determined social and political institutions or attitudes). Clearly, they also influence the different stakeholders' thinking and co-determine their preferences and values, choices, and behaviours. Studies on the latter issues can again be either micro-based or macro-based (see e.g., Russo and van der Borg 2010; Arribas-Bel et al. 2016; Romão et al. 2017; Kourtit and Nijkamp 2019).

As mentioned before, in our study we will investigate whether a favourable cultural profile of a city enables the city to attract cultural consumers (clients) in the form of visitors and foreign tourists, as might be reflected in its high socio-economic performance, based on the urban *cultural capability* approach. This may clearly lead to a high cultural appreciation, while then the subsequent question is whether city size and economic prosperity act as moderator variables for explaining this cultural performance of the city at hand. This intriguing question bears a clear resemblance to the so-called Kuznets discussion on the (positive or negative) relationship between economic growth and income disparity in a country. This issue has gained quite some prosperity in recent debates on 'environmental Kuznets curves' (see e.g., Wang et al. 2013; Kourtit et al. 2019). In the specific context of our study we address the question whether a higher level of prosperity and/or a larger city size is negatively or positively correlated with the cultural performance indicator of the city concerned. Hence, we refer here to the notion of a 'quasi-Kuznets' curve for a city's cultural quality with respect to economic welfare and urban size (see also Kourtit et al. 2019). Clearly, evidence-based empirical research is needed to test the validity of these concepts. This will be taken up in the subsequent sections.

11.3 Database and Analysis Framework

In our study on urban cultural efficiency performance, we will use the Global Power City Index (GPCI) system produced by the Institute of Urban Strategies (2019) (Mori Memorial Foundation). This is a very extensive multi-annual database (starting off from the year 2009) that captures in a systematic and annually updated manner a wide range of relevant urban indicators. This GPCI data set comprises 40 global cities from all continents and is, therefore, very appropriate as a database for comparative research on the cultural significance of cities. We use this data system as a statistical source for our DEA analysis. If we take the cultural performance indicators—conceived of as the ratio between input and output factors in the urban cultural system—from this GPCI database, we can depict the ranking of the 40 cities according to their aggregate cultural resources (i.e. the input resources in our DEA approach). This result for all cities can be found in Fig. 11.1, which depicts the comparative cultural input indicators (C-Index Scores) for all 40 cities under consideration. These are directly extracted from the GPCI database. These rankings more or less confirm our prior perceptions.

It should be noted that the comparative results on the cultural achievements of cities may be somewhat biased due to a statistical level correlation: rich and big cities may be expected to have a higher cultural performance outcome. To cope with this bias, it is appropriate to apply a Data Envelopment Analysis (DEA), so that the output performance is related to the input resources or supply conditions of the city concerned. Therefore, the next step of our analysis seeks to identify the efficiency in delivering cultural capabilities and services of the cities concerned.

The high degree of heterogeneity and level-collinearity among these 40 cities necessitates a subdivision into smaller subsets of cities that are more homogeneous and thus more similar in terms of size and prosperity level. Therefore, we have subdivided the 40 cities in a dichotomic classification of big (B) and medium-sized (M) cities, where the 20 largest cities are denoted as B-cities and the 20 relatively smaller as M-cities. A similar dichotomic segmentation of our sample is made for

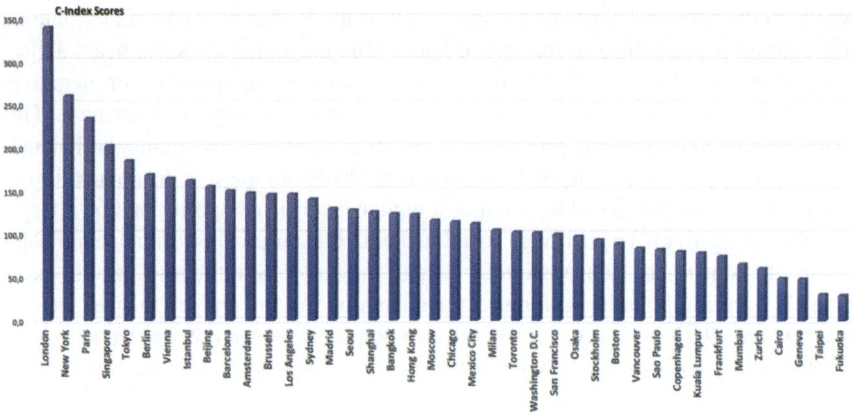

Fig. 11.1 The comparative cultural input indicators (C-Index Scores) for all 40 cities under consideration

relatively prosperous cities (H-cities) and relatively poor cities (L-cities). By combining both classifications, we may create a double (dichotomic) classification matrix, in which each quadrant contains ten cities (see Fig. 11.2). The underlying data on the two cross-classified indicators for the 40 cities are given in Annex 1, for each of the four quadrants for Fig. 11.2 (viz., the B-, M-, H-, and L-cities). As indicated above, this double dichotomic segmentation of the 40 cities at hand shows in each segment more homogeneity in cultural characteristics, according to size and in prosperity level, so that statistically more satisfactory results may be expected.

In several recent studies, the efficiency ranking of the 40 GPCI cities and their performance determinants have been subjected to a careful scrutiny, *inter alia* by employing various versions of Data Envelopment Analysis (DEA). DEA is essentially a method to judge the efficiency of the production of goods or services, by relating the outcomes (often multiple outputs) to the input resources (often multiple inputs). It is essentially based on a generalised fractional programming algorithm (see for details Cooper et al. 2006; Suzuki and Nijkamp 2017, 2020). Application of a comparative DEA to global cities will lead to a more fine-grained and strategic re-interpretation of the GPCI findings depicted in Fig. 11.1. We will in our study use a suitable DEA method to address the cultural sector (and its achievements) in the cities at hand. The specific DEA method employed in our analysis is based on the *Super-Efficiency* (SE) principle (SE-DEA) (see for details Anderson and Petersen 1993). The reason to adopt an SE-DEA approach is that in a standard DEA model, which serves to identify the most efficient actors (or Decision Making Units—DMUs) among their peers, we may end up with multiple equally-ranked efficient actors (i.e., several DMUs may have a DEA score equal to 1.0), so that then an unambiguous and conclusive ranking of DMUs is not possible. To avoid ambiguous final results, the SE-DEA algorithms aims to cope with this shortcoming by introducing auxiliary criteria to identify those DMUs which perform best in terms of their

City Size

Prosperity Level (GDP per capita)

	B			M		
	City	Population 2016 (1000 persons)	Ranking of Nominal GDP per capita (U.S. dollars per capita) 2016	City	Population 2016 (1000 persons)	Ranking of Nominal GDP per capita (U.S. dollars per capita) 2016
H	New York	8,550	8	Zurich	412	2
H	Los Angeles	3,972	8	Geneva	201	2
H	Chicago	2,721	8	San Francisco	865	8
H	Singapore	5,535	10	Washington D.C.	672	8
H	Sydney	4,921	11	Boston	667	8
H	Hong Kong	7,324	18	Copenhagen	591	9
H	Berlin	3,490	22	Stockholm	924	12
H	London	8,539	24	Amsterdam	822	15
H	Tokyo	9,297	25	Vienna	1,797	16
H	Seoul	10,297	33	Toronto	2,615	21
L	Madrid	3,142	34	Vancouver	649	21
L	Istanbul	14,657	70	Frankfurt	716	22
L	Moscow	12,330	77	Brussels	1,175	23
L	Sao Paulo	11,968	79	Osaka	2,695	25
L	Mexico City	8,872	80	Fukuoka	1,543	25
L	Shanghai	24,257	83	Paris	2,219	28
L	Beijing	21,516	83	Milan	1,360	31
L	Bangkok	8,305	102	Barcelona	1,605	34
L	Cairo	9,508	136	Taipei	2,704	42
L	Mumbai	12,478	169	Kuala Lumpur	1,733	75

Fig. 11.2 A cross-classified matrix of the 40 cities. (Source: Population datasets collected from GPCI-2016. GDP per capita datasets collected from The International Monetary Fund (IMF), http://www.imf.org/external/datamapper/NGDPDPC@WEO/OEMDC/ADVEC/WEOWORLD)

relative input endowments and output factors (Suzuki and Nijkamp 2017). This adjusted method will also be employed in our empirical analysis.

Next, to cope with multicollinearity and to reduce the dimensionality of the selected indicators for the direct and indirect (contextual) cultural amenities among the 49 relevant sub-indicators, we use first a principal component analysis (PCA) of each indicator category from the GPCI dataset, in order to reconstruct a smaller subset of uncorrelated explanatory factors. The PCA appears to allow the identification of a reduced number of three main factors, each containing an uncorrelated set of explanatory sub-variables that are appropriate for empirical measurement in our study.[2]

In our subsequent SE-DEA analysis, we have used the following classes of input and output indicators, followed by a brief interpretation. The input indicators extracted from the data set are:

- Input indicators of Factor 1: *Cultural Interaction*

  This main component refers in particular to supply elements, such as *Cultural Ambiance* and *Amenities for Foreign Visitors*, and can be further subdivided into distinct sub-categories of explanatory supply variables, which are primarily responsible for sustainable socio-economic development and competitive advantage.

Cultural Ambiance	• Number of Theatres and Concert Halls
	• Environment of Creative Activities
	• Attractiveness of Shopping Options
	• Number of Large World Class Cultural Events held
	• Number of Museums
Amenities for Foreign Visitors	• Opportunities for Cultural, Historical, and Traditional Interaction
	• Attractiveness of Dining Options
	• Number of Luxury Hotel Guest Rooms
	• Number of Hotels
	• Number of Stadiums
	• Number of Foreign Resident
	• Trade Value of Audiovisual and Related Services

- Input indicators of Factor 2: *Livability & Environment*

  This second important factor includes valuable environmental resources, in particular Safe Environment Quality and Local Attractiveness, and their decomposition is based on various sub-variables that create an added value regarding creative, resilient, and sustainable urban development.

Safe Environment Quality	• Water Quality of Rivers
	• Number of Medical Doctors per Population
	• Disaster Vulnerability
	• Openness and Fairness of Society
	• Level of Green Coverage
	• Comfort Level of Temperature
Local Attractiveness	• Variety of Retail Shops
	• Variety of Restaurants
	• Number of Companies with ISO 14001 Certification

[2]Results are available from the corresponding author on request.

- Input indicators of Factor 3: *Accessibility*

  This indicator comprises two main sub-categories, namely *Quality of Transport System* and *Transport Connectivity*. These are composed of interdependent aspects that may have a positive effect on the production and consumption side of the socio-economic performance of a city or region.

Quality of Transport System	• Commuting Convenience
	• Travel Time between Inner-city Areas and International
	• Taxi Fare
	• Transportation Fatalities per Population
	• Punctuality and Coverage of Public Transportation
Transport Connectivity	• Number of Arriving/Departing Passengers on International
	• Number of Cities with Direct International Flights
	• Number of Runways
	• Density of Railway Stations

  For the output indicators, we have only selected one key variable for urban cultural achievement, viz. visitors.

- Output Indicator: *Visitors*

  This indicator illustrates the total number of *Visitors from Abroad* in the cities concerned.

Magnet Indicator	• Number of Visitors from Abroad

Thus, the various types of city assets and resources (inputs) are here decomposed on the basis of three appropriate categories of direct and indirect (contextual) cultural amenities and resources and are used to deliver a broad package of cultural services that may attract (foreign) visitors as an output variable. Consequently, what matters is the ratio between output and inputs. For this reason, the SE-DEA approach is adopted (see Sect. 11.4).

11.4 Results of the DEA Approach

The key question is here how to use the above data for a cultural performance assessment of cities. As mentioned, the SE-DEA approach serves to assess the efficiency in the production of urban cultural performance, as it relates urban cultural output to the input needs. The application of the SE-DEA method—as a first step in our analysis—leads to the following overall ranking of the 40 cities (see Fig. 11.3).

The results from Fig. 11.3 show that an input–output based presentation of cultural efficiency outcomes leads to significant differences for most cities as compared to Fig. 11.1. It turns out that several big Asian cities—with a relatively low supply of input resources for culture—manage to attract quite a lot of visitors, e.g., Tokyo, Osaka, Bangkok, Hong Kong or Singapore, while also Istanbul scores

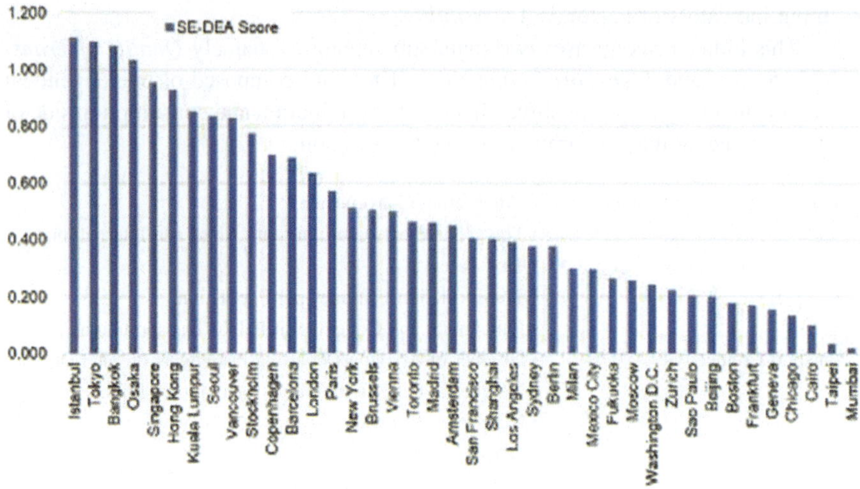

Fig. 11.3 Ranking of SE-DEA efficiency scores for cultural efficiency of 40 global cities

rather high. From an efficiency perspective, New York, London, Paris, Amsterdam, or Vienna score now much lower. There is apparently a big difference between absolute cultural performance scores and relative efficiency scores for cultural achievement. This is further clarified in Annex 1 where the findings for each segment from Fig. 11.2 are reported. Also, the results from Figs. 11.15 and 11.16 show a high degree of heterogeneity among cities, both in terms of urban size (viz., B- and M-cities) and urban prosperity (viz., H- and L-cities). It is noteworthy that even within the distinct B-, M-, H-, and L-categories the statistical variations are still significant. Apparently, urban cultural performance is a heterogeneous and multidimensional concept that may not be explained simply in terms of scale and prosperity of cities. However, the SE-DEA scores provide interesting results different from the C-Index scores.

The SE-DEA results offer thus intriguing results. It turns out that the absolute cultural indicators—as derived from the GPCI data base—leads to different findings compared to those derived from the SE-DEA approach. The latter rankings are efficiency-oriented and may—from an economic perspective—be seen as more meaningful outcomes on the (relative) cultural performance than the overall absolute cultural indicators; cultural rankings are in general not very suitable for evaluating cultural performance.

11.5 Regression Results of Urban Cultural Performance and Efficiency in Terms of Size and Prosperity

In Sect. 11.2 a reference was made to a 'quasi-Kuznets' phenomenon, in the sense that urban cultural quality or performance may depend on city size (through agglomeration advantages, e.g.) and/or prosperity level (through income-dependent cultural priorities, e.g.). It may, therefore, be interesting to examine whether the composite cultural capability indicators (derived from the GPCI data base) and/or the cultural efficiency scores from the SE-DEA experiments are correlated with either city size or general welfare level in urban areas.

Since both size and prosperity play essentially a discriminating role, it is pertinent to examine their distinct roles more explicitly. This calls for application of a partial OLS regression analysis—for the successive classes of sub-samples of 20 cities—so as to explore and trace an empirical correlation between performance/efficiency on the one hand and size/prosperity on the other hand.

We will start our exploratory analysis by mapping out the correlation between the overall GPCI scores for the 40 cities concerned (C-Index Score) and their SE-DEA Scores (i.e., the cultural efficiency indicators) (see Fig. 11.4). The correlation appears to show a positive relationship, while the statistical significance is high. Clearly, cultural performance indicators are to a large extent also related to cultural efficiency, but are not a precise linear predictor.

Our next step bears some resemblance to the previous steps in the analysis of cultural performance scores in Sect. 11.4 and Annex 1. It uses again the classification of Fig. 11.2 (based on both city size and prosperity) to explain the indicators for composite cultural performance (the C-Index) and the efficiency in the delivery of urban cultural amenities (the SE-DEA Score) for B-cities, M-cities, H-cities, and L-cities separately (see Figs. 11.5, 11.6, 11.7, and 11.8).

Figure 11.5 maps out the regression results for all 40 cities in terms of their cultural performance scores (C-Index) in relation to their size. The results show a slightly positive and significant correlation, despite the variety in city size. A more

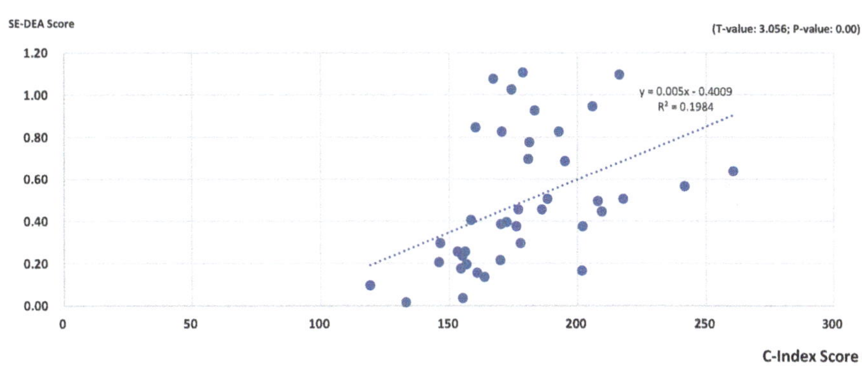

Fig. 11.4 Correlation between super-efficiency scores and the total GPCI scores for all 40 cities

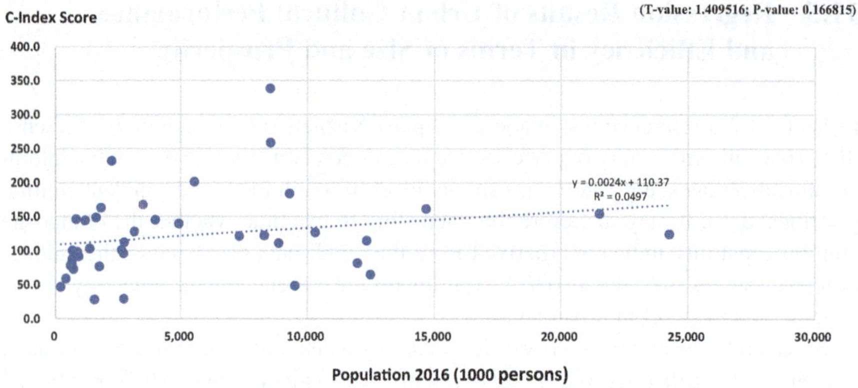

Fig. 11.5 Regression results for cultural performance scores and city size for all 40 cities

fine-grained regression analysis according to B- and M-classes (see Fig. 11.6) shows similar results; a positive and significant relation for the M-cities, and a positive, highly significant outcome for the B-cities. We find again that size matters!

We will next carry out a similar analysis on cultural performance for the prosperity levels of the 40 cities concerned (see Figs. 11.7 and 11.8).

The results from Fig. 11.7 are somewhat ambiguous. The influence of prosperity on urban cultural performance is small, and the overall result is insignificant. If we divide the cities according to H- and L-classes (see Fig. 11.8), it turns out that wealthy cities show a negative significant correlation with cultural performance, and less wealthy cities a significantly positive correlation.

From Figs. 11.5, 11.6, 11.7, and 11.8, we may infer that generally city size is positively correlated with cultural performance scores, for both the B- and M-cities. The results for prosperity are less unambiguous and differ according to the prosperity class concerned.

The next step will be a similar analysis, but now for the cultural efficiency (SE-DEA) scores from the SE-DEA model for the cities concerned (see Figs. 11.9, 11.10, 11.11, and 11.12).

The findings from Figs. 11.9 and 11.10 indicate that there is a negligible and insignificant generic effect of city size on cultural efficiency; urban size has a weak and insignificant effect on cultural efficiency—and hence cultural capability—for B-cities, and a slightly positive and weakly significant effect for M-cities.

We will, finally, pursue a similar analysis for the prosperity levels of the cities concerned (see Figs. 11.11 and 11.12).

The statistical results from Figs. 11.11 and 11.12 are less unambiguous. The overall correlation displays much heterogeneity and is less convincing. The partial results according to H- and L-classes are significant and confirm a negative

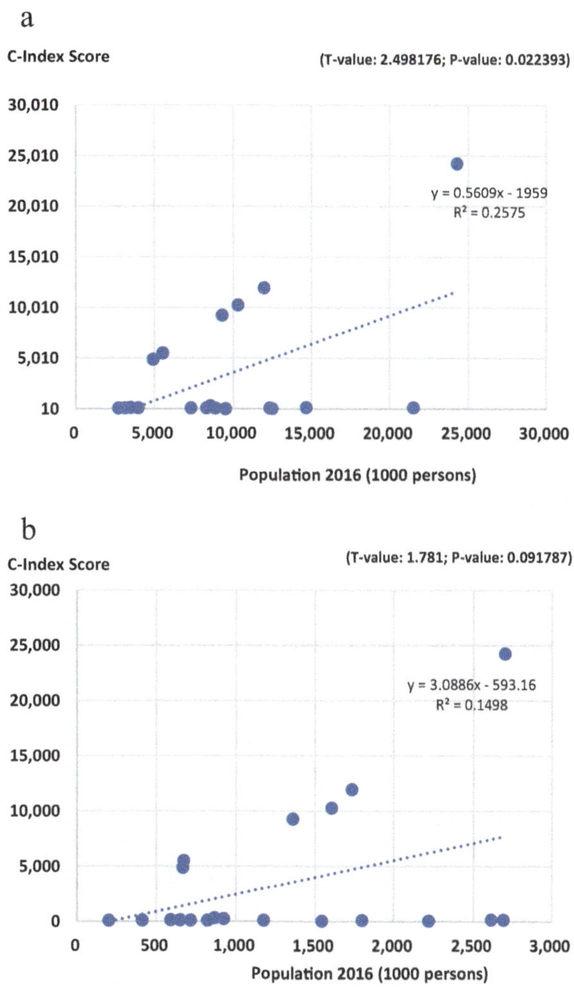

Fig. 11.6 Regression results for cultural performance scores depending on city size (two classes). (**a**) B-cities. (**b**) M-cities

correlation for H-cities and a positive correlation for L-cities. This implies essentially that cities in lower developed nations may—in a relative sense—still perform rather well in terms of their efficiency in the provision of cultural services.

The general results for cultural efficiency appear to be straightforward for city size, despite the complex input–output ratio in the SE-DEA calculation of these efficiency scores. The overall findings for prosperity as a determinant of cultural efficiency are rather convincing for specific classes of cities, despite the heterogeneous nature of the cities in the GPCI sample.

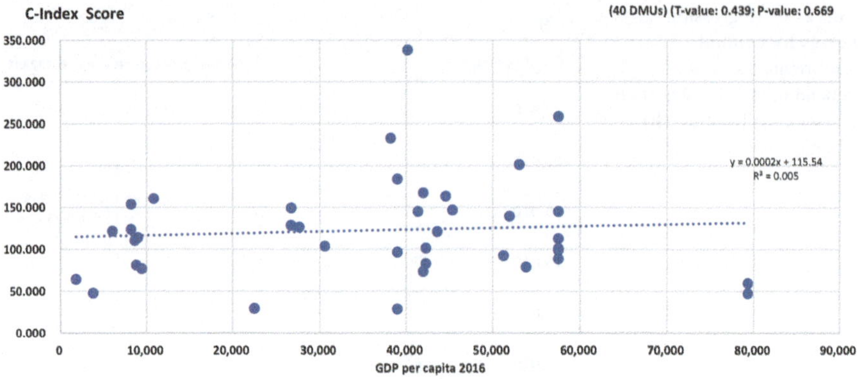

Fig. 11.7 Regression results for cultural performance scores and the level of prosperity for all 40 cities

11.6 Conclusion

Our study aimed to assess whether the variation in cultural attractiveness of global cities is related to its size, to its level of welfare or to other moderator variables. The analysis—based on a '*cultural capability*' perspective, inspired by Amartya Sen, combined with a '*quasi-Kuznets*' approach—was undertaken in two steps, viz. the aggregate GPCI scores for cultural achievement for 40 global cities and the urban cultural efficiency scores calculated through a SE-DEA model. The results show interesting outcomes, in particular:

- the structural urbanisation of our world prompts a strong inter-urban competition, not only in general, but also in particular regarding the cultural magnet function of global cities which may strengthen their socio-economic power.
- the systemic effects of size and prosperity of global cities as cultural magnets are weakly confirmed in our empirical analysis; this holds for both the cultural capability approach and the 'quasi-Kuznets' approach (in particular, in regard to prosperity).
- the capability theory framework offers a useful and operational contribution to a better understanding of the drivers of cultural performance and efficiency.
- the overall finding of our study is that cultural performance—as a magnet influence of large agglomerations—is an important spinoff of urban size and economic welfare in urban areas.

These results have also a clear policy relevance. Culture is in many cases associated with size and prosperity of cities, but is by no means a sufficient condition. Our results have shown that in the case of so many heterogenous cities

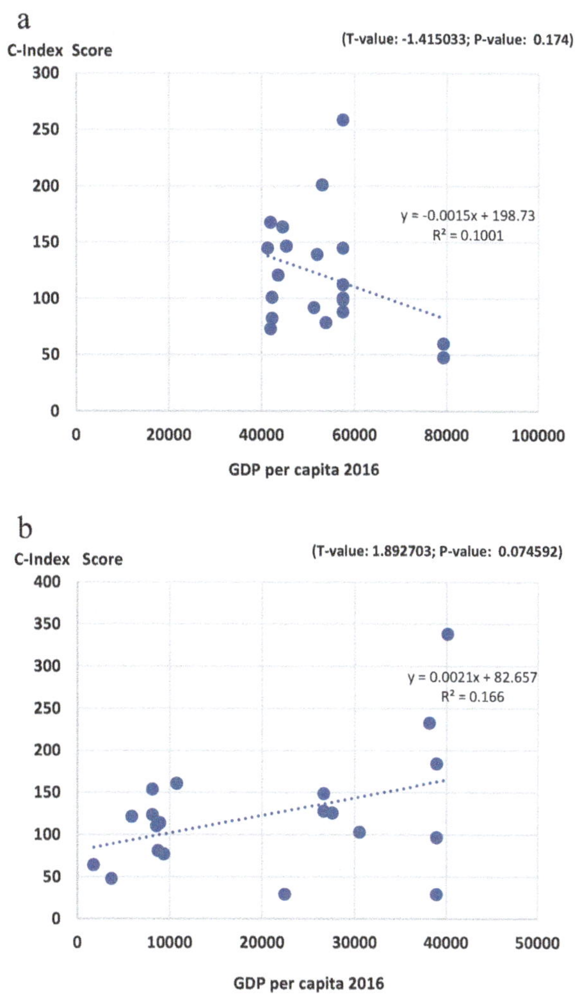

Fig. 11.8 Regression results for cultural performance scores depending on prosperity (two classes). (**a**) H-cities. (**b**) L-cities

in our world, there is a multiplicity of moderator variables which altogether create promising conditions for a successful urban ambiance.

Acknowledgments Karima Kourtit and Peter Nijkamp acknowledge the grant from the Axel och Margaret Ax:son Johnsons Stiftelse, Sweden. Karima Kourtit and Peter Nijkamp also acknowledge the grant from the Romanian Ministry of Research and Innovation, CNCS—UEFISCDI, project number PN-III-P4-ID-PCCF-2016-0166, within the PNCDI III project ReGrowEU—Advancing ground-breaking research in regional growth and development theories, through a resilience approach: towards a convergent, balanced and sustainable European Union (Iasi, Romania).

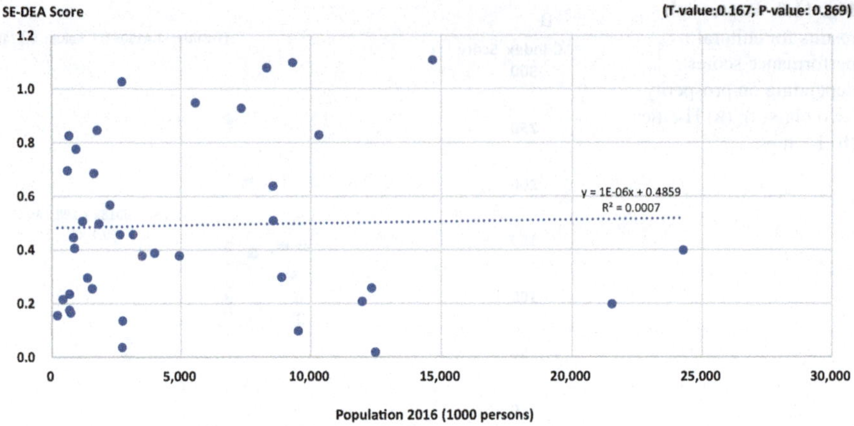

Fig. 11.9 Regression results for SE-DEA efficiency scores depending on city size for all 40 cities

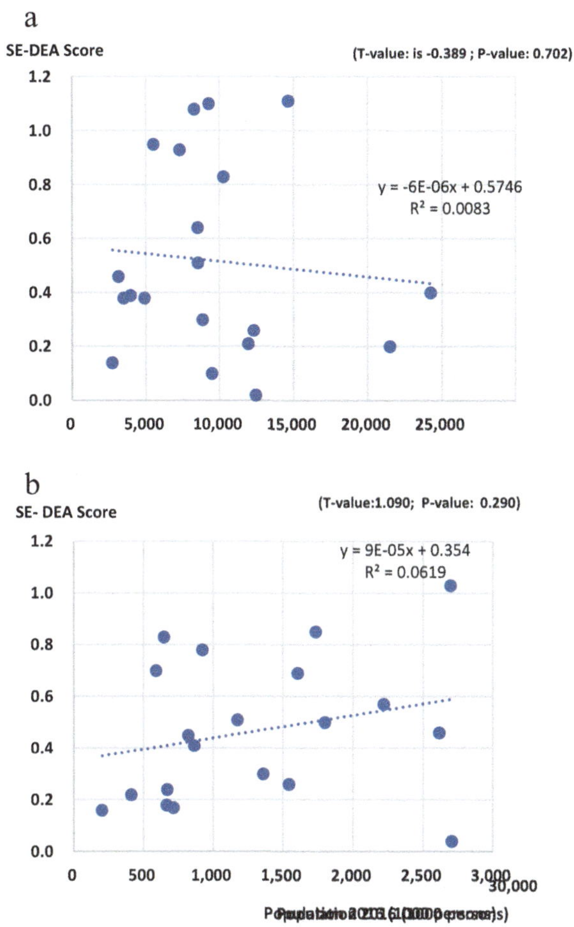

Fig. 11.10 Regression results for cultural efficiency scores depending on city size (two classes). (**a**) B-cities. (**b**) M-cities

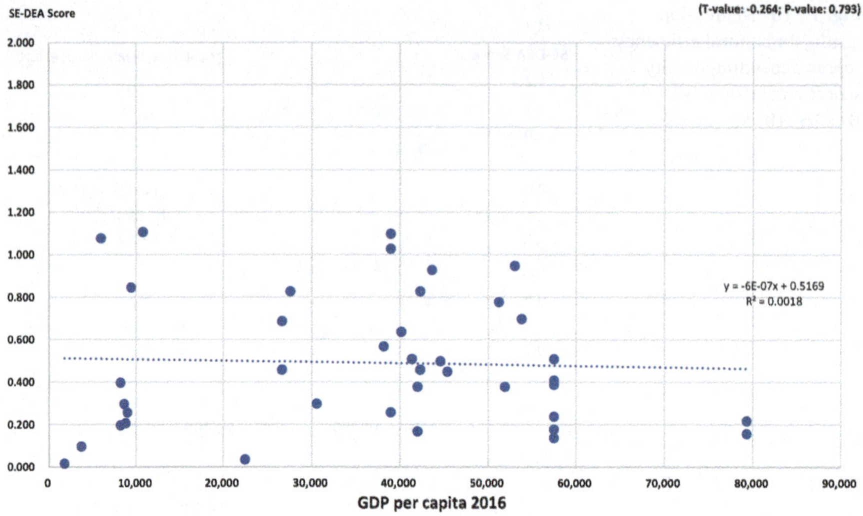

Fig. 11.11 Regression analysis for super-efficiency scores and the level of prosperity for all 40 cities

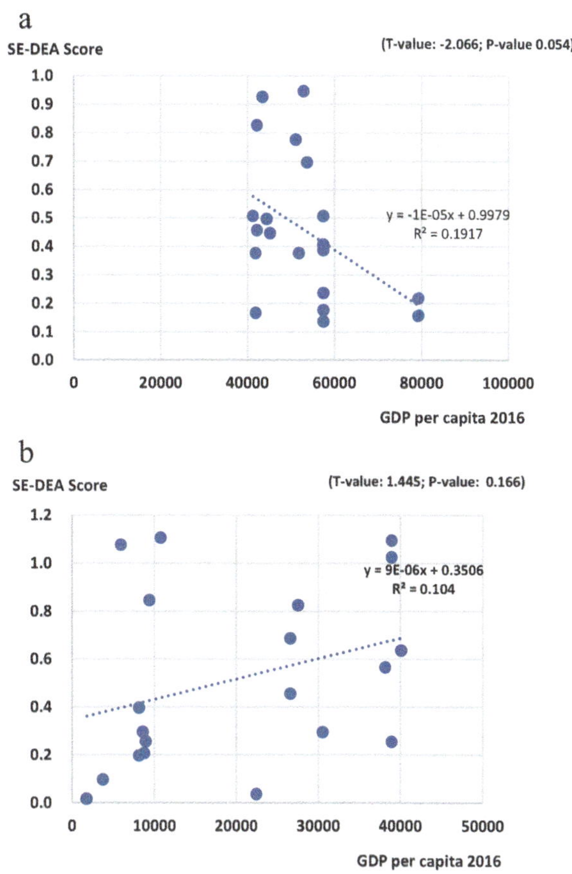

Fig. 11.12 Regression results for cultural efficiency scores depending on prosperity (two classes). (**a**) H-cities. (**b**) L-cities

Annex 1: Cultural Performance Results for Four Classes of Cities

We will present here the ranking results of the 40 global cities for each major segment of the double dichotomic classification, viz. for the B-cities and M-cities, and for the H-cities and L-cities, respectively. These results are given in Figs. 11.13 and 11.14, respectively.

Figure 11.13 shows for the big (B) global cities the expected results, with London on top and Moscow/Cairo in the lower ranks. For the class of relatively medium-sized/smaller cities, Barcelona, Milan, and Amsterdam appear to possess the top positions, while Fukuoka has—in a relative sense—the lowest cultural position.

The ranking results of cities according prosperity outcomes (see Fig. 11.14) show high scores for New York, Amsterdam, Vienna, and Singapore, and a relatively low

a

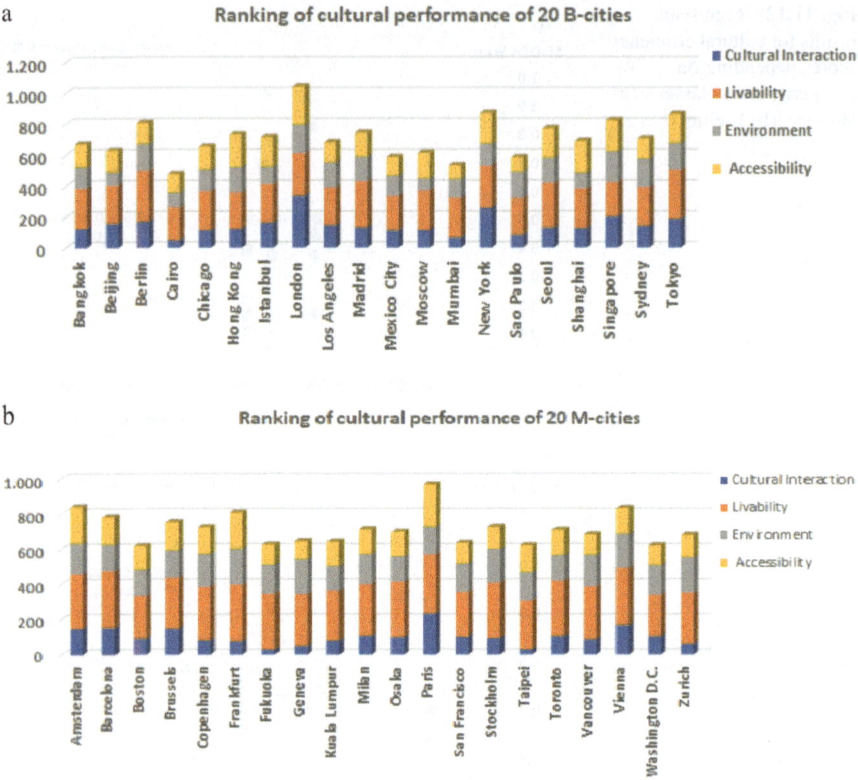

Fig. 11.13 Ranking results for cities based on two size classes. (**a**) B-cities. (**b**) M-cities

performance for Boston. Regarding the ranking results for less prosperous places, it turns out that London and Paris are at the top, whereas Moscow and Cairo have the lowest positions in the set of cities considered.

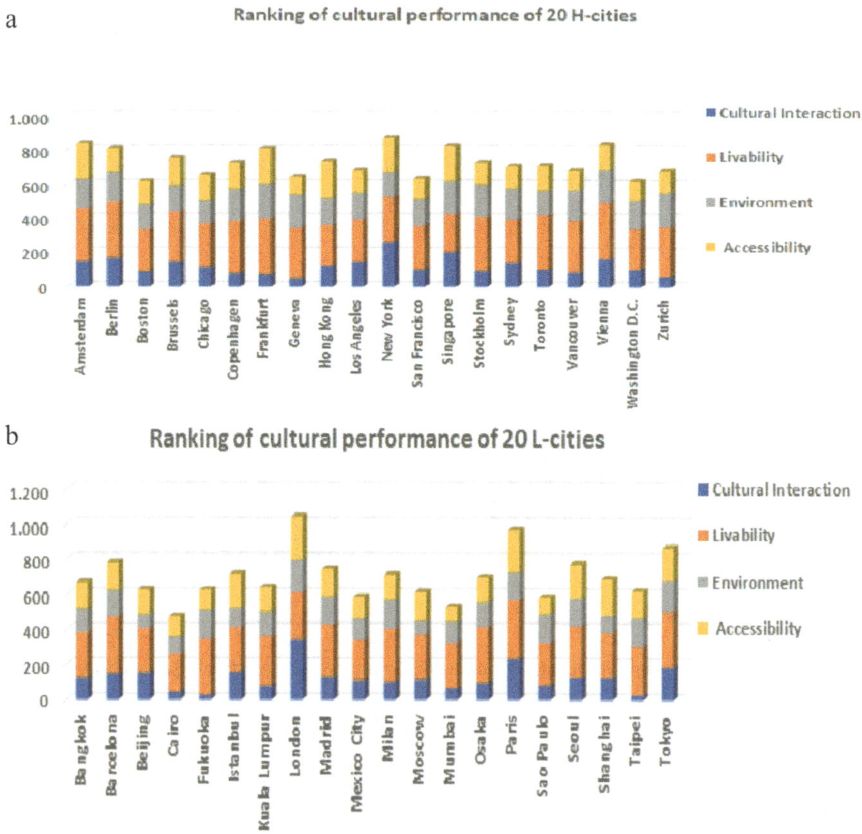

Fig. 11.14 Ranking results for cities based on two prosperity classes. (**a**) H-cities. (**b**) L-cities

Annex 2: SE-DEA Cultural Efficiency Results for Four Classes of Cities

Given the great heterogeneity among these cities, we may rank the efficiency of the cultural capability of these cities for each subcategory in the matrix in Fig. 11.2, viz. H-cities, L-cities, B-cities, and M-cities. These results can be found in Figs. 11.15 and 11.16.

Figure 11.15 shows much variation among the class of B-cities, with Tokyo, Bangkok, and Istanbul on top, while Mumbai and Cairo have the lowest positions. The ranking of M-cities leads to high positions for Osaka, Kuala Lumpur, and Vancouver, and to low ranks for Taipei or Boston. It is clear that the size class matters for the cultural performance assessment of cities.

Next, Fig. 11.16 provides the findings on the impact of urban prosperity on the cultural performance efficiency scores. From the wealthy cities, Singapore,

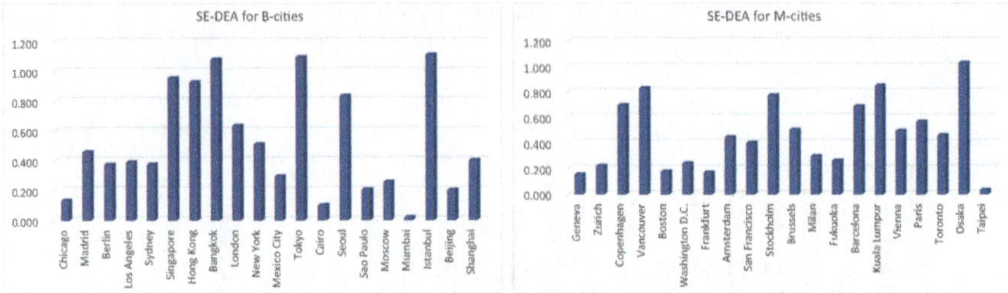

Fig. 11.15 Efficiency ranking results for cities based on two size classes. (**a**) B-cities. (**b**) M-cities

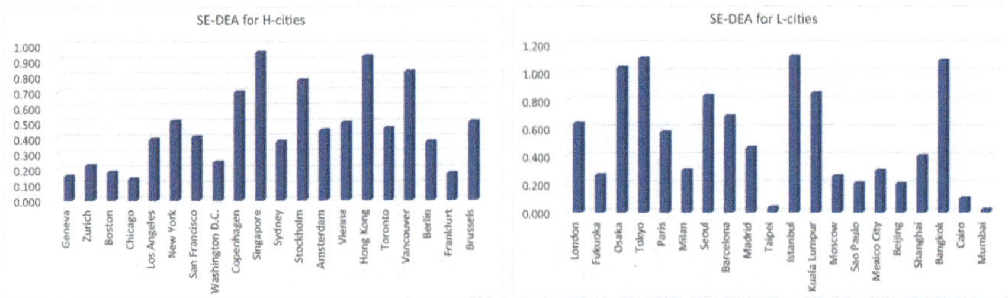

Fig. 11.16 Efficiency ranking results for cities based on two prosperity classes. (**a**) H-cities. (**b**) L-cities

Stockholm, Vancouver, and Hong Kong occupy high positions on the cultural performance efficiency ladder, with low positions for Frankfurt, Chicago, and Geneva. From the classes of relatively lower prosperous cities, Tokyo, Osaka, Istanbul, and Bangkok assume high ranks in terms of cultural efficiency, while Taipei, Beijing, and Mumbai are the lowest among their peers.

References

Acs Z (ed) (2016) The growth of cities. Edward Elgar, Cheltenham

Allmendinger P, Haughton G (2009) Soft spaces, fuzzy boundaries, and meta-governance. Environ Plan A 41:627–633

Amin A, Roberts J (eds) (2008) Community, economic creativity and organization. Oxford University Press, Oxford

Anderson P, Petersen NC (1993) A procedure for ranking efficient units in data envelopment analysis. Manag Sci 39(10):1261–1264

Archer K, Bezdecny K (eds) (2016) Handbook of cities and the environment. Edward Elgar, Cheltenham

Arribas-Bel D, Kourtit K, Nijkamp P (2016) The sociocultural sources of urban buzz. Environ Plan C 34(1):188–204

Bourdieu P (1973) Culture reproduction and social reproduction. In: Brown R (ed) Knowledge, education and social change. Tavistock, London, pp 71–112

Bourdieu P (1986) The forms of capital. In: Richardson JG (ed) Handbook of theory and research for the sociology of education. Greenwood, New York, NY, pp 241–258
Bride JG, Cortes-Jimenez I, Pulina M (2016) Has the tourism-led growth hypothesis been validated? A literature review. Curr Issue Tour 19(5):394–430
Castro-Nuno M, Molina-Toucedo JA, Pablo-Romero MP (2013) Tourism and GDP: a meta-analysis of panel data studies. J Travel Res 20(10):1–14
Comim F, Qizilbash M, Alkire S (2008) The capability approach. Cambridge University Press, Cambridge
Cooke P, Lazzaretti L (eds) (2008) Creative cities, cultural clusters and local economic development. Edward Elgar, Cheltenham
Cooper WW, Seiford LM, Tone K (2006) Introduction to data envelopment analysis and its uses. Springer, Berlin
European Union (2011) Cities of tomorrow. DG Regional Policy, Brussels
Fusco Girard L, Nijkamp P (eds) (2009) Cultural tourism and sustainable local development. Ashgate, Aldershot
Glaeser E (2011) Triumph of the city. Penguin Press, New York, NY
Glaeser E, Kolko J, Saiz A (2001) Consumer city. J Econ Geogr 1:27–50
Glaeser E, Kourtit K, Nijkamp P (eds) (2020) Urban empires. Routledge, London
Gravagnuolo A, Fusco Girard L, Kourtit K, Nijkamp P (2021) Adaptive re-use of urban cultural resources. City Cult Soc 26:100416. https://doi.org/10.1016/j.ccs.2021.100416
ICOMOS (2015) Cultural heritage. The UN Sustainable Development Goals and the New Urban Agenda, Paris
Inchausti-Sintes F (2015) Tourism: economic growth, employment and Dutch disease. Ann Tour Res 54:172–189
Institute for Urban Strategies (2019) Global power city index. The Mori Memorial Foundation, Tokyo. http://www.mori-mfoundation.or.jp/english/research/project/6/pdf/GPCI2019_English.pdf
Kopczewska K, Churski P, Ochojski A, Polko A (2017) Measuring regional specialisation. Springer, Berlin
Kourtit K, Nijkamp P (2013a) The use of visual decision tools in an interactive stakeholder analysis. Sustainability 5:4379–4405
Kourtit K, Nijkamp P (2013b) In search of creative champions in high-tech spaces. J Reg Sci 53 (5):749–777
Kourtit K, Nijkamp P (2018a) Impact of cultural ambiance on the spatial distribution of creative professions – a modelling study in The Netherlands. Int Reg Sci Rev 41(1):103–128
Kourtit K, Nijkamp P (2018b) Big data dashboards as smart decision support tools for I-cities – an experiment on Stockholm. Land Use Policy 71:24–35
Kourtit K, Nijkamp P (2019) Creative actors and historical-cultural assets in urban regions. Reg Stud 53:977. https://doi.org/10.1080/00343404/2018:1541077
Kourtit K, Nijkamp P, Stough R (eds) (2015) The rise of the city: spatial dynamics in the urban century. Edward Elgar, Cheltenham
Kourtit K, Nijkamp P, Suzuki S (2019) Are global cities sustainability champions? A double delinking analysis of environmental performance of urban agglomerations. Sci Total Environ 709(20):134963. https://doi.org/10.1016/j.scitotenv.2019.134963
Kourtit K, Nijkamp P, Wahlström M (2020) How to make cities the home of people – a 'soul and body' analysis of urban attractiveness. Land Use Policy. https://doi.org/10.1016/j.landusepol.2020.104734
Li H, Nijkamp P, Xie X, Liu J (2020) A new livelihood sustainability index for rural revitalization assessment—a modelling study on smart tourism specialization in China. Sustainability 12: 3148
Liu J, Nijkamp P, Lin D (2017) Urban-rural imbalance and tourism-led growth in China. Ann Tour Res 64:24–36
Maslow AH (1943) A theory of human motivation. Psychol Rev 50(4):370–396

Miles S, Paddison R (2005) Introduction: the rise of culture-led urban regeneration. Urban Stud 42 (5/6):833–839
Mommaas H (2004) Cultural clusters and the post-industrial city. Urban Stud 41(3):507–532
Nijkamp P (2016) The 'resourceful region'. J Reg Res 36:191–214
Östh J, Kourtit K, Nijkamp P (2021) My home is my castle - assessment of city love in Sweden. Int J Inf Manag 58:102213
Romão J, Kourtit K, Neuts B, Nijkamp P (2017) The smart city as a common place for tourists and residents: a structural analysis of the determinants of urban attractiveness. Cities 78:67. https://doi.org/10.1016/j.cities.2017.11.007
Russo AP, van der Borg A (2010) An urban policy framework for culture-oriented economic development: lessons from The Netherlands. Urban Geogr 31(5):668–690
Sacco P, Ferilli G, Tavano Blessi G, Nuccio M (2004) Understanding culture-led local development. Urban Stud 51(13):2806–2821
Santagata W (2009) White paper on creativity. Towards an Italian model of development. EBLA CENTER - International Center for Research on the Economics of Culture, Institutions and Creativity, Torino. http://www.eblacenter.unito.it/BOOKS/White%20paper%20Creativity%20JUNE%202009.pdf
Sen A (1999) Development as freedom. Knopf, New York, NY
Sen A (2008) The economics of happiness and capability. In: Bruni L, Comim F, Pugno M (eds) Capability and happiness. Oxford University Press, New York, NY
Snowball JD (2008) Measuring the value of culture. Springer, Berlin
Stanley J, Stanley J, Hansen R (2017) How great cities happen: integrating people, land use and transport. Edward Elgar, Cheltenham
Suzuki S, Nijkamp P (2017) Regional performance measurement and improvement: new developments and applications of data envelopment analysis. In: New frontiers in regional science: Asian perspectives 9. Springer, Singapore
Suzuki S, Nijkamp P (2020) High urban population density as a facilitator of energy–environment–economy performance–development of an autoconfiguration target model in data envelopment analysis. Asia Pac J Reg Sci 5:261. https://link.springer.com/article/10.1007/s41685-020-00161-9
Taylor PJ (2013) Extraordinary cities: millennia of moral syndromes. In: World-systems and city/state relations. Edward Elgar, Cheltenham
Tellier L-N (2009) Urban world history. Presse de l'Université du Québec, Québec, QC
Throsby D (2001) Economics and culture. Cambridge University Press, New York, NY
Törnqvist G (1983) Creativity and the renewal of regional life. In: Buttimer A (ed) Creativity and context: a seminar report. Lund studies in geography. B. Human geography, No. 50. Gleerup, Lund, pp 91–112
UN Habitat (2013) The city we need. UN Habitat, Nairobi. http://mirror.unhabitat.org/downloads/docs/The%20City%20We%20Need.pdf
UNESCO (2009) UNESCO world report: investing in cultural diversity and intercultural dialogue. UNESCO, Paris
UNESCO (2011) The Paris declaration on heritage as a driver of development. UNESCO, Paris
United Nations (2015a) Transforming our world: the 2030 agenda for sustainable development A/RES/70/1. United Nations, Division for Sustainable Development, Department of Economic and Social Affairs, New York, NY
United Nations (2015b) The future we want for all. UN, New York, NY. https://www.un.org/millenniumgoals/pdf/Post_2015_UNTTreport.pdf
Wang Y, Kang L, Wu X, Xiao Y (2013) Estimating the environmental Kuznets curve for ecological footprint at the global level: a spatial econometric approach. Ecol Indic 34:15–21

Wåhlin N, Kapsali M, Näsholm MH, Blomquist T (2016) Urban strategies for culture-driven growth. Co creating a European capital of culture. Edward Elgar, Cheltenham
Wahlström M (2017) What about the soul of the city? Applying a resident perspective in four Swedish cities. Roman J Reg Sci 11(1):36–36
Weber M (1921/1958) The city. Free Press, New York, NY
World Cultural Forum (2011) The Bali promise. UNESCO, Paris. http://www.cicop.net/joomla/images/cicop/docs/the.PDF

Chapter 12
Government Intervention in Real Estate Market: Is Tax Reform Effective in Seoul Housing Market?

Euijune Kim, Ayoung Kim, and Inseok Moon

Abstract This paper develops a dynamic economic analysis of fiscal housing policy effects on the housing market in Korea. The analytical framework integrates a standard Computable General Equilibrium (CGE) model with a housing market model. The housing model accounts for housing demand, investment, user costs, and multiregional migration. The market is disaggregated into four major regions; three regions (Seoul, Inchon, and Gyeonggi) in the Seoul Metropolitan Area and the rest of Korea to incorporate the regional heterogeneity in housing stocks. The policy simulations using the CGE model show that it would be more effective to increase the property tax rate than the acquisition tax to stabilize housing prices with a moderate increase in housing demand.

Keywords Housing market · Housing policy · Property tax · Acquisition tax · Dynamic CGE model

JEL D58 · H21 · O18 · R31

E. Kim (✉)
Department of Agricultural Economics and Rural Development, Integrated Program in Regional Studies and Spatial Analytics, and Research Institute of Agricultural and Life Sciences, Seoul National University, Seoul, South Korea
e-mail: euijune@snu.ac.kr

A. Kim
Department of Agricultural Economics, Mississippi State University, Starkville, MS, USA
e-mail: a.kim@msstate.edu

I. Moon
Department of Project Management, Savills Korea, Seoul, South Korea

M. Kawano et al. (eds.), *Theory and History in Regional Perspective*, New Frontiers in Regional Science: Asian Perspectives 56,
https://doi.org/10.1007/978-981-16-6695-7_12

12.1 Introduction

Government intervenes in the housing market to achieve socio-economic goals that include stabilization of housing markets and supplying affordable housing. The U.S. government has implemented various tax-based policies for the housing market, such as mortgage interest deduction, a first-time homebuyer tax credit, or tax rate changes for capital gains. Fannie Mae and Freddie Mac, which are U.S. government-sponsored organizations, also play an essential role in stabilizing the mortgage finance system. The main goals of those policies are to encourage homeownership and stimulate (or stabilize) the housing market. In China, the government has carried out active and direct housing market policies to control soaring housing prices. The housing purchase restriction rule in most Chinese cities prohibits resident households from buying more than two homes (Wu and Li 2018). Recently, a property tax pilot program was launched in Shanghai and Chongqing (Cao and Hu 2016). This was a critical change because the Chinese government has not imposed a property tax since the Communist takeover.

In Korea, government intervention in the housing market is more pervasive and more significant than in any other country through application of supply and demand regulations and fiscal and financial tools. Housing policy is one of the most important political agendas in presidential campaigns, and the real estate market is the major subject of interest. This is a result of the fact that the net worth of Korean households depends highly on real estate assets,[1] which have been considered to be the safest and most profitable investment vehicle since the 1970s. This has led to spatial sorting of wealth based on where people buy their homes. According to Korea Appraisal Board data, the average housing price increased by 56% between 2003 and 2020,[2] and the government has come under pressure to correct this housing market failure. The Korean governments have frequently implemented new sets of such measures. In particular, the Korean government has announced 22 sets of measures to invigorate or stabilize housing markets over the last 4 years that focus on Seoul metropolitan areas.

The socio-economic impact of housing policy has been highly controversial, along with the appropriateness of government intervention in the housing market. Researchers and policymakers are still debating whether the government can achieve its goals and whether their interventions result in better outcomes in the housing market. However, it cannot be doubted that housing policies using fiscal and financial tools enormously influence housing and financial markets as well as the national economy. Many studies shed light on the effect of the government's intervention in the housing market and report results in terms of partial equilibrium

[1] In 2018, 77.8% of total net worth in the Korean household was non-financial assets of which real estate makes up the vast majority of such assets (http://kostat.go.kr/portal/eng/pressReleases/1/index.board?bmode=read&aSeq=376338, accessed on February 19, 2021).

[2] http://www.r-one.co.kr/rone/resis/statistics/statisticsViewer.do?menuId=HOUSE_21111 (accessed on February 192,021).

prices, stocks, or ownership. Some researchers emphasize that disregarding equilibrium effects can lead to misleading results because house prices, renters, supply, demand, and household welfare are simultaneously determined in response to government housing policies. Most recently, Floetotto et al. (2016) and Sommer and Sullivan (2018) analyze the effects of homebuyer tax policies in an equilibrium framework that allows adjusting house prices, user costs, and quantities according to the U.S. tax code.

In the same framework, this paper not only suggests the equilibrium effect but also expands the general equilibrium model to include the dynamic computable general equilibrium (CGE) model which incorporates heterogeneous regional housing markets and multiregional migration. The frequent announcements of housing policy reflect that the Korean housing market is challenging to analyze with static or partial equilibrium models. Housing demand as a transaction of a consumption good is directly affected by policy. When the government performs actions to stabilize the housing market, housing prices stop rising rapidly, but this is mostly temporary. In practice, the Korean housing market cools down immediately when the government announces new measures, but the housing price rebounds shortly thereafter. Our dynamic CGE model includes both the short- and long-term impacts in the Korean housing market on prices, demand, tax revenue, and social welfare when simulating different types of fiscal instruments. It allows us to understand the mechanism of the policy application for the housing market in regional and national economic frames.

This paper analyzes policy impact on four regional housing markets, which work with localized demand and supply and allow interregional mobility of households as housing consumers. This is an essential component that reflects the substantial housing price gap between Seoul, the capital of Korea, and other regions. For instance, 16% of the total housing units in Seoul are worth over KRW 600 million (US $537,780 in 2018), on which the comprehensive real estate tax is imposed, while 2% of the total housing units in Korea are valued at exceeding the price. The government mainly focuses on stabilizing housing prices in Seoul by imposing a high tax rate or financial burden on holding houses and supplying houses in its neighboring regions to push the excessive housing demand out of Seoul. Therefore, our model classifies regions of interest into (1) Seoul, (2) Incheon, (3) the rest of the Seoul Metropolitan Area (ROS), Gyeonggi (the present region of highest housing prices and its neighboring regions), and (4) the rest of Korea (ROK) to find differential policy impacts on different markets.

This paper addresses how policy tools can contribute to a reduction in the price of housing in Seoul and affect other regional housing markets over ten periods and is structured as follows: (1) positive and negative effects of government fiscal tools on the housing market which are discussed in terms of methods and policy implications, and (2) the economic effects of housing acquisition and property tax rates on the Seoul housing market as a measure for the housing market stabilization issue that are calibrated by developing a CGE housing market model for Korea. Then, a summary of this approach as well as suggestions for future research are provided. This analysis from the CGE model provides policymakers and economic agents with practical insights regarding the costs and benefits of housing tax tools. The remainder of this paper is organized as follows: after the introduction, the next section provides some background on Korean policy in the housing market and reviews previous literature on the impact of housing policy. This is followed by the empirical section, which includes the dynamic CGE model structure, policy simulations, and results. The chapter ends with a summary and conclusion.

12.2 Background Information and Literature Review

The Korean government commonly uses tax policy to intervene in the housing market, leading to a complicated tax system. There are three types of taxes that are imposed on homeowners: an acquisition tax when buying a house, a capital gains tax when selling a house, and a property tax when owning a house. The acquisition and property taxes are local taxes and apply progressive rates levied on house value. The capital gains tax is a national tax imposed on profit margins realized through house sales. The tax rate is basically progressive but depends on whether the owner holds the property in the short term and has multiple houses and whether the house is located in a speculation restriction zone. Also, there is a group-targeted tax, called the Comprehensive Real Estate Tax (CRET), which was introduced in 2003. It is a national estate tax levied on residential houses that exceed a specific exemption level, i.e., KRW 600 million (roughly 0.6 million U.S. dollars) as the taxable value.[3]

The capital gains tax is known to have a lock-in effect that leads homeowners/investors to hold their assets for a longer time until realization to avoid taxation (Holt and Shelton 1962). The government has expected to reduce the speculative housing demand by imposing a heavier capital gains tax and CRET on excessive demands. Along with adjusting tax rates, regulating mortgage rules is also preferred to reduce speculative investments in real estate by increasing the cost of loans and tightening borrowing requirements. These fiscal and financial tools have been mostly applied to stabilize the housing market. On the other hand, these were also implemented to revitalize the housing market by lowering tax rates and easing mortgage regulations.

In 2011–13, the government cut the acquisition and capital gains tax rates and released financial constraints to shore up the housing market, which was depressed due to a high volume of unsold residential inventory during the global economic recession. To support the sluggish housing market, the government kept a low-interest rate and the easing of Loan to Value (LTV) and Debt to Income (DTI) ratio requirements. This was quite effective in inducing a large amount of demand and supply by reducing house purchase costs and expanding capital gains. The revitalization policy dramatically pushed up housing demand and kept prices high in the short run. However, this instant remedy could cause to fall into a housing price bubble without taking long-term adverse effects on the financial market into

[3]The CRET originally was designed with an exemption level at KRW 600 million, but the Korean government lowered the level to KRW 300 million in 2018.

Table 12.1 Korean housing tax rates by the latest set of housing policies

	Current rates	Revised rates
Real estate acquisition tax (Local tax)	– 1–3% of the actual market price for 1–3 homes owner – 4% for multiple-home owners above 4 units	– 1 to 3% of the actual market price for single homeowners – 8% for 2-home owners – 12% for multiple-home owners above 3 units
Comprehensive real estate tax (National tax)	0.5% to 3.2% for a high-value property above KRW 300 (taxable value), higher tax rates for multiple-property owners in speculation restriction zones	0.6% to 6% for a high-value property above KRW 300 (taxable value), higher tax rates for multiple-property owners in speculation restriction zones
Property tax (Local tax)	0.1–0.4% according to the tax base bracket	0.1–0.4% according to the tax base bracket
Capital gains tax (National tax)	– 50% for holding property less than a year – 40% for holding property for 1–2 years – 6–42% for holding property for 2 years +	– 70% for holding property less than a year – 60% for holding property for 1–2 years – 6–42% for holding property for 2 years +

Source: http://www.molit.go.kr/policy/stable/sta_b_01.jsp (accessed on February 20, 2021)

account. The new administration, which began in 2017, has been announcing sets of measures to stabilize the heated housing market but faced the same criticisms that the previous administration had.

Recently, the Korean government has proposed a set of new real estate regulations that are focused on raising tax rates targeting multiple-home owners in order to stabilize the housing market. This policy attempts to increase the burden of economic cost that speculators or multiple-property owners should pay through the periods of purchasing, holding, and selling properties. As shown in Table 12.1, the multiple-home owner is subject to a heavier acquisition tax rate from the current 1 to 4% to a further 12% when they buy an additional property. The property tax rate is 0.15–0.50% of the property values depending on the location of the property and the type of building. However, property tax rates are imposed up to an additional 0.20–2.80% on multiple-home owners. In particular, the homeowner who has a high-value property over roughly 0.3 million U.S. dollars as a taxable value, has to pay the comprehensive real estate holding tax as a kind of wealth tax. Its tax amount is between 0.6% and 6% of the housing value, depending on the land use type and the lot size. The capital gains tax is progressive, but the tax deduction is also given to long-term holdings.

The heavy sales tax is expected to generate a positive effect on reducing speculative investments to earn capital gains from short-term transactions, and the high property tax allows multiple-home owners to put their housing stocks on the market. However, the latest housing tax reform raised the tax rates for both transaction and possession of housing. Opponents argued that either the acquisition tax rate or the property tax rate should be relatively reduced to inch down the housing price by increasing the trading volume of housing units offered for sale in Seoul. Higher tax rates on acquisition and possession are capitalized and discourage homebuyers from entering the market.

Government intervention in the housing market has been debated with respect to its effectiveness because its evaluation is challenging. First, housing as a durable good has a complicated market linked with many other economic sectors, such as construction and financial markets. Second, even though governments have the same policy goals, for instance, promoting homeownership or cooling down inflated housing prices, they utilize different instruments or combinations to achieve their goals and to target various groups—i.e., the county as a whole, specific regions, income groups, homeowners, renters, primary homeowners, or second homeowners. The policy tools to modify housing markets vary from conventional tools—taxes, finances, or subsidies—to an aggressive intervention, such as housing purchase restrictions (Wu and Li 2018). Housing tax reform, however, is still one of the favorable policy tools that many countries have adopted to moderate housing price inflation and increase government revenue. As a consequence, a large number of studies have widely investigated the policy effectiveness of government intervention through tax policies from various perspectives using theoretical and empirical approaches. These are also the main research questions underlying this paper. How do governmental tax instruments affect the housing market and macroeconomic indicators? We evaluate the possible scenarios that the Korean government has considered with respect to the housing market to moderate housing price inflation through tax reform.

Housing tax policies are effective for the housing market through tax capitalization into user cost rather than a direct intervention like controlling demand or supply. Considerable studies across countries have been done on housing taxes, such as property taxes, transaction taxes, or capital gains tax as shown in Table 12.2. By and large, lower housing prices and the volume of transactions increase due to a tax burden increase, although the magnitudes of these effects vary across studies and countries. Those studies empirically analyze the impact of housing tax programs using various approaches such as hedonic models (Benjamin et al. 1993), difference-in-difference (Besley et al. 2014; Dachis et al. 2011; Guillaume and Trannoy 2017), an instrumental variable (Davidoff and Leigh 2013), a panel regression (Fritzsche and Vandrei 2019; Petkova and Weichenrieder 2017), and other innovative approaches (Bai et al. 2014; Cao and Hu 2016; Liberati and Loberto 2019). As a recent work example, Liberati and Loberto (2019) evaluated Italia's housing market taxation reforms in 2012 and found that property tax on owner-occupied homes has a negative effect on property and rental prices, whereas taxes on secondary homes have qualitatively opposite effects. The extent of property tax capitalization, however, is partial but significant as 60% on house prices which confirms Palmon and Smith (1998). Another body of studies focuses on the effect of tax rate reduction, removal of mortgage interest, or property tax deductibility (Anderson and Roy 2001; Bruce and Holtz-Eakin 1999; Cho and Francis 2011).

Empirical findings from the existing literature, including those mentioned above, are mostly based on the partial equilibrium perspective, and only focus on the

Table 12.2 Studies on the impact of housing tax policies

Tax policies	Studies	Methods
Real estate transfer tax Stamp duty	Benjamin et al. (1993) Besley et al. (2014) Bérard and Trannoy (2017) Dachis et al. (2011) Davidoff and Leigh (2013) Guillaume and Trannoy (2017) Hilber and Lyytikäinen (2013) Petkova and Weichenrieder (2017) Fritzsche and Vandrei (2019)	Hedonic model Bargaining model Difference-in-difference (DID) Discontinuity DID Instrumental variables DID Regression analysis Regression analysis Fixed effects panel regression
Property taxes	Bai et al. (2014) Cao and Hu (2016) Liberati and Loberto (2019) Poterba (1984)	Modified DID Microsimulation model Searching and matching model Dynamic asset market model
Tax deductibility Tax credit	Anderson and Roy (2001) Bruce and Holtz-Eakin (1999) Cho and Francis (2011) Floetotto et al. (2016) Gervais (2002) Sommer and Sullivan (2018)	Distributional analysis Dynamic numerical simulation DID General equilibrium Dynamic general equilibrium Dynamic general equilibrium
Others	Berkovec and Fullerton (1992) Chambers et al. (2009) Peng and Wang (2009)	General equilibrium Overlapping generational model General equilibrium

differential effects of the housing market. They clearly show that tax policy is effective in cooling down the housing market. The studies, however, are limited in that price is endogenously determined and other macroeconomic variables, which are directly or indirectly affected by the housing policies and prices, are excluded. For instance, Glaeser and Gyourko (2005) found that an upturn in house prices provides support to output in the construction sector, as firms find it more profitable to build new houses that lead to increasing supply and a move to a new price equilibrium. Several empirical studies demonstrated that housing prices are closely interrelated with macroeconomic variables (Rosenberg 2019).

Few studies have contributed to equilibrium models in order to analyze housing market policies. Berkovec and Fullerton (1992) apply a static disaggregated general equilibrium model that includes owner-occupied and rental housing demand as risky assets and endogenous consumption and investment decisions. Their simulation results show that taxes on owner-occupied housing would raise welfare, the overall rate of homeownership, and the removal of the property tax or mortgage interest deduction would reduce the amount of homeownership and the stock of housing. Peng and Wang (2009) develop a general equilibrium model with endogenous housing quality and prices and examine the effects of the reduction in housing-related tax policies on housing quality/prices, land rent, and urban structure. They numerically find housing quality and housing values rise as the urban fringe expands.

More recent studies using a general equilibrium model for the housing market focus on the impact of mortgage interest tax deduction in the U.S. Sommer and Sullivan (2018) extended their model based on Chambers et al. (2009), who analyze the relationship between the asymmetric tax treatment of owner- and tenant-occupied housing and the progressivity of income taxation. They find that eliminating the mortgage interest deduction causes house prices to decline, decreasing housing consumption by the wealthy, increasing homeownership by low-wealth and rent-occupied households, and reducing mortgage debt and improving welfare. Their findings stand in contrast to previous studies that show the removal of mortgage interest deductions could depress homeownership and reduce welfare. For instance, Gervais (2002) argued that repealing the mortgage interest deduction leads to a decline in homeownership because it increases the cost of ownership but does not reduce down payment requirements. These results are limited because house prices are kept fixed, and not endogenously determined.

Floetotto et al. (2016) examine the effects of homebuyer tax credits using a heterogeneous-agent overlapping-generations general equilibrium model. Their results suggest that homebuyer tax credits temporarily raise house prices and transaction volumes but have negative effects on welfare. We contribute to the evolving literature by using a dynamic computable general equilibrium model, which allows us to consider the direct goal of housing market policy and its macroeconomic effects. Our study quantifies the effect of government housing tax policy on the macroeconomic system, including housing prices and demand, tax revenue, and social welfare.

12.3 Analysis

12.3.1 Housing CGE Model

The Computable General Equilibrium (CGE) model is widely used to evaluate the growth and distribution effects of policies such as those focused on economic development, public finance, infrastructure, and regional and environmental economies as implemented in the late 1970s (Kim et al. 2014). The model framework has also been applied to housing policy studies. Kim and Ju (2003) used a CGE model to assess the economic effects of the housing supply on urban growth and income distribution in Seoul. Their results indicated that housing development on industrial land or green areas increased the Gross Regional Product by approximately 1% under the deterioration of income inequality. Bye and Åvitsland (2003) analyzed the welfare effects of a neutral housing taxation system in Norway, and developed an inter-temporal CGE model. They found that housing tax reform increased intra-temporal efficiency gains but decreased the real wage rate owing to high housing price inflation. Kim (2008) used the CGE model to evaluate government policies in terms of housing demand. It analyzed the impact of a comprehensive real estate tax and the Loan-To-Value ratio on income quintile groups. Their results showed that housing tax policy and financial regulations are effective in controlling housing demand for owner-occupied households.

Keast (2010) developed the bi-regional CGE model to analyze the regional impacts of housing policies in the South West housing market in the UK. That study's results showed that demographic factors stemming from increased space demands by households put greater pressure on the housing market, leading to a rise in the price of both new housing and housing services. Park et al. (2014) used the CGE model to classify households by real estate asset levels in order to analyze the influence of the economic ripple effect from changes in the real estate holding tax. They found that changes in the real estate holding tax decreased total disposable income and the social welfare of consumers by 0.1% to 0.3%. Feltenstein et al. (2016) examined the effects of tax reforms that reduce by half the taxes on homesteaded properties and increase the base and rate of the state sales tax in Georgia, U.S. Their results indicated that the proposed policy has no effect on the distribution of consumption across income classes but increased the percentage of owner-occupied housing units. In summary, these previous studies of the housing market using the CGE model analyzed the effects of housing policies on social utility in terms of the demand side. Our model, by contrast, addresses housing policies using a consolidated CGE model to integrate the commodity and service markets, including housing supplies, demands, and prices. The housing market is divided into four regional areas to take into account spatial interaction and linkages with respect to population migration and spillover effects of housing prices and demand.

In principle, the CGE model is an analytic tool based on general equilibrium theory to quantify impacts of external shocks on the behavior of economic agents. It achieves Walrasian equilibrium and determines the market price through an adjustment and interaction process with quantity. Namely, the model simultaneously captures optimal levels of prices and quantities, allowing a variety of functional linkages between economic agents in a supply–demand structure. The quantity is derived from maximization of each economic agent's goal subject to institutional constraint, and any imbalance between the supply and the demand can be made clear through price changes. The structure of the CGE model of the housing market in this paper is based on Kim (2008): a standard neoclassical-oriented CGE model and the housing market module. The former is composed of the supply, the demand, and the price equilibrium in industrial sectors. The latter includes housing demand, housing investment (supply), housing price, user costs, and multiregional migration. The housing markets are disaggregated into four major regions; three regions (Seoul, Inchon, and ROS) in the Seoul Metropolitan Area (SMA) and the rest of Korea (ROK). The economic agents consisted of 13 industrial sectors (housing construction and housing services by each region, agriculture and mining, manufacturing, construction, real estate services, and other services), four regional household groups (in Seoul, Inchon, ROS, and ROK), one central government, and the rest of the world (ROW).

Figure 12.1 shows our model structure.

The sectoral output is determined by a two-level structure of Leontief production function with intermediate inputs and value-added in the production sector. The

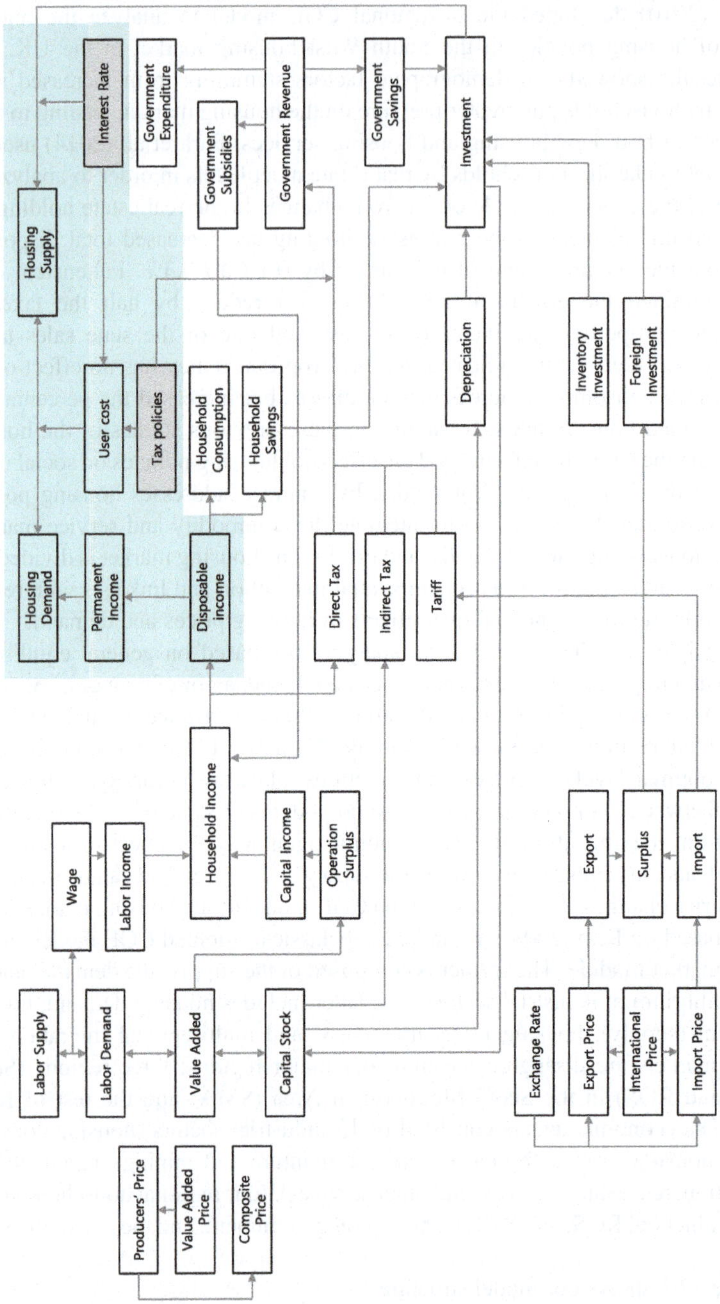

Fig. 12.1 Model structure

intermediate input is equal to the input–output coefficients multiplied by the output (Eq. 12.1). The value-added is generated by the Cobb–Douglas production function of traditional factor inputs, i.e., labor and capital (Eq. 12.2). The producer is assumed to select an optimal set of two factor inputs for profit maximization. The Keynesian employment condition is applied to the labor market as a macroeconomic closure rule such that an average wage and total labor demand are exogenous and endogenous variables, respectively (Eq. 12.3).

$$\mathrm{XD}_i = \min\left(\frac{\mathrm{VA}_i}{a_i}, \frac{\mathrm{IND}_{1i}}{io_{1i}}, \cdots, \frac{\mathrm{IND}_{ji}}{io_{ji}}\right) \tag{12.1}$$

$$\mathrm{VA}_i = A_i \cdot L_i^{\alpha_i} \cdot K_i^{1-\alpha_i} \tag{12.2}$$

$$L_i \cdot \mathrm{WA} \cdot w\mathrm{dist}_i = \alpha_i \cdot \mathrm{PVA}_i \cdot \mathrm{VA}_i \tag{12.3}$$

XD_i: Gross output of industry sector i
IND_{ji}: Intermediate input of industry sector j from i
VA_i: Value-added
K_i: Capital stock
$w\mathrm{dist}_i$: Wage distribution parameter
L_i: Labor input
WA: Average wage
PVA_i: Value-added price.

The sectoral demand is satisfied with supplies of domestic and imported commodities under Armington structure. With the relative price between two commodities and their imperfect substitution, the demander determines their consumption amounts through cost minimization. On the other hand, the Constant Elasticity of Transformation (CET) function is applied to specify the interaction between the domestic and exporting commodities with a fixed output: the profit maximization of the producer results in an optimal bundle of domestic demand and exporting commodities (Eqs. 12.4–12.9).

$$\min\ \mathrm{PM}_i \cdot M_i + \mathrm{PD}_i \cdot \mathrm{XXD}_i \tag{12.4}$$

$$\text{s.t}\ X_i = AC_i \cdot \left(\delta_i \cdot M_i^{-\rho c_i} + (1-\delta_i) \cdot \mathrm{XXD}_i^{-\rho c_i}\right)^{-\frac{1}{\rho c_i}} \tag{12.5}$$

$$\frac{M_i}{\mathrm{XXD}_i} = \left(\frac{\delta_i}{1-\delta_i} \cdot \frac{\mathrm{PD}_i}{\mathrm{PM}_i}\right)^{\frac{1}{1+\rho c_i}} \tag{12.6}$$

$$\max\ \mathrm{PE}_i \cdot E_i + \mathrm{PD}_i \cdot \mathrm{XXD}_i \tag{12.7}$$

$$\text{s.t}\ \mathrm{XD}_i = AT_i \cdot \left(\gamma_i \cdot E_i^{\rho t_i} + (1-\gamma_i) \cdot \mathrm{XXD}_i^{\rho t_i}\right)^{\frac{1}{\rho t_i}} \tag{12.8}$$

$$\frac{E_i}{\mathrm{XXD}_i} = \left(\frac{1-\gamma_i}{\gamma_i} \cdot \frac{\mathrm{PE}_i}{\mathrm{PD}_i}\right)^{\frac{1}{\rho t_i - 1}} \tag{12.9}$$

XXD_i: Domestically produced and consumed commodities
PM_i: Price of import commodity
PD_i: Price of domestic commodity
M_i: Import
PE_i: Price of export commodity
X_i: Composite commodity
E_i: Export.

The total income of each regional household is composed of labor and capital incomes from supplying production factors, government subsidies, and capital gains from the ROW. By budget constraint, consumers allocate the consumption amount based on maximization of the utility function, which is expressed by the Cobb–Douglas function.

$$\mathrm{YH}_m = \mathrm{YLC}_m + \mathrm{YKC}_m + \mathrm{YSUB}_m + \mathrm{YFC}_m \tag{12.10}$$

$$\mathrm{YD}_m = \mathrm{YH}_m - \mathrm{YTAX}_m \tag{12.11}$$

$$\mathrm{YSAV}_m = \mathrm{YD}_m \cdot \mathrm{YSAVP}_m \tag{12.12}$$

$$\mathrm{P}_i \cdot \mathrm{PC}_i = \sum_m (\mathrm{YD}_m - \mathrm{YSAV}_m) \cdot \mathrm{PCES}_{m\,i} \tag{12.13}$$

YH_m: Household income
YD_m: Disposable income
YLC_m: Labor income
YKC_m: Capital income
YSAV_m: Household savings
YSAVP_m: Marginal propensity to save
YSUB_m: Government subsidy
YTAX_m: Direct tax
YFC_m: Capital gains by the ROW
P_i: Price of commodity
PC_i: Private consumption
$\mathrm{PCES}_{m\,i}$: Marginal propensity of consumption from industry i in the region m.

There is one consolidated government, which is composed of the national and regional governments. Government revenue is constructed of an indirect tax from producers and a direct tax from households. Government expenditure includes government consumption expenditure, subsidies to households, and government savings. Total savings is equal to the total amount of investment, consisting of depreciation, household saving, government saving, and foreign saving.

$$\mathrm{GREV} = \sum_i \mathrm{INDTAX}_i + \sum_m \mathrm{YTAX}_m + \mathrm{TARIFF} \tag{12.14}$$

$$\mathrm{GUSE} = \sum_i \mathrm{GC}_i + \sum_r \mathrm{YSUB}_r + \mathrm{GSAV} \tag{12.15}$$

$$\mathrm{SAVINGS} = \sum_i \mathrm{DEPR}_i + \sum_m \mathrm{YSAV}_m + \mathrm{GSAV} - \mathrm{FSAV} \cdot \mathrm{ER} \tag{12.16}$$

GREV: Government revenue.
GUSE: Government expenditure.
INDTAX_i: Indirect tax
SAVINGS: Savings (=Investment).
DEPR_i: Depreciation
TARIFF: Tariff
GC_i: Government consumption
GSAV: Government savings
FSAV: ROW savings
ER: Exchange rate.

The housing model estimates the housing demand, the housing investment (supply), the user costs of owner and renter, and multiregional migration by region. The specification of the housing demand function follows Kim (2008) and Mankiw and Weil David (1989) in which the independent variables for the demand are housing price, household income, and demographic attributes such as the number of household members and ages, and the dependent variable is the area of the house (m^2). Table 12.3 shows the results of the housing demand function, which is estimated based on user cost, permanent income, and the number of household members categorized by age cohort. We utilize Korea Housing Survey data in 2010 and 2014 provided by the Ministry of Land, Transport, and Maritime Affairs. Since age-specific housing demands vary with the number of members and family structure in each household, this paper estimates the age-adjusted regression coefficient with a 10-year age cohort (0–14, 15–24, 25–34, 35–44, 45–54, 55–64, over 65) to reflect a life-cycle pattern. The values of income elasticity and price (user cost) elasticity are ranges of 0.363 (ROK) to 0.532 (Seoul) and −0.110 (ROS) to −0.071 (Seoul), respectively.

$$\ln(\mathrm{HD}_m) = \beta_0 + \beta_1 \ln(\mathrm{UC}_m) + \beta_2 \ln(\mathrm{PI}_m) + \sum\nolimits_j \alpha_n X_{mn} + \mathrm{dm}_{2010} + \epsilon_m \tag{12.17}$$

HD_m: Housing demand (Housing area)
UC_m: User cost of housing service
PI_m: Permanent income
X_{mn}: Number of household members m in age cohort n
dm_{2010}: Dummy for the year 2010
m: Household.

Table 12.3 Estimation of the housing demand function

$\ln(\text{HD}_m) = \beta_0 + \beta_1 \ln(\text{UC}_m) + \beta_2 \ln(\text{PI}_m) + \sum_n \alpha_n X_{mn} + \text{dm}_{2010} + \epsilon_m$								
	Parameter							
Variable	Seoul		Incheon		ROS		ROK	
β_0	0.040		1.257	***	1.123	***	1.491	***
$\ln(\text{UC}_m)$	−0.071	***	−0.092	***	−0.110	***	−0.102	***
$\ln(\text{PI}_m)$	0.532	***	0.379	***	0.414	***	0.368	***
X_{m1}	0.086	***	0.084	***	0.066	***	0.056	***
X_{m2}	0.046	***	0.041	***	0.053	***	0.013	***
X_{m3}	−0.002		0.006		0.011		−0.009	***
X_{m4}	0.010		0.011		0.028	***	0.011	***
X_{m5}	0.060	***	0.066	***	0.060	***	0.052	***
X_{m6}	0.167	***	0.167	***	0.148	***	0.134	***
X_{m7}	0.268	***	0.245	***	0.254	***	0.205	***
dm_{2010}	−0.058	***	−0.041	***	−0.115	***	−0.065	***
Number of samples	9300		3090		8742		27,792	
Adjusted R^2	0.433		0.323		0.360		0.355	

Note: *, **, and *** mean statistically significant at 10%, 5%, and 1%, respectively

The user cost is defined as the cost of occupying the housing service for a certain period rather than the housing (sale) price that is determined by an equilibrium between the housing supply and demand in the market. The user cost relies on an occupancy type such as owner-occupied or renter-occupied. That is, the cost is built on utilization not relevant to ownership (possession). The housing user cost is affected by macroeconomic indicators and the tax burden, taking into consideration government intervention in the market through regulations. Equations (12.18) and (12.19) are the formula for the user cost for the owner and the renter, respectively; these are revised from Kim (2008). Equation (12.20) shows the weighted interest rate, which is defined as the weighted housing finance loan and general mortgage (Sohn and Park 2005). The actual tax rate is derived for each household using the Korean Housing Survey data. The interest income tax rate is applied at 15.4%, which is the rate currently applied in Korea, and the depreciation rate for housing is 2.5%, based on Lee and Chung (2010). In addition, the growth rate in the housing price is 3.78%.[4]

$$\text{UC}_{\text{own}} = \{(1 - t_{\text{r}})\, r^* + t_{\text{a}} + t_{\text{p}} + m - (1 - t_{\text{g}})g\} V_{\text{h}} \tag{12.18}$$

$$\text{UC}_{\text{rent}} = (1 - t_{\text{r}})\, r^* V_{\text{h}} + R \times 12 \tag{12.19}$$

$$r^* = rq + r'(1 - q) \tag{12.20}$$

[4]This is derived from the housing sales price index by KB bank (2003.06–2013.06), and the average duration of homeownership is 10 years.

$$t_a = t'_a(1 + r')^l / l \tag{12.21}$$

UC_{own}: User cost for owner-occupied household
UC_{rent}: User cost for rented household
t_r: Interest income tax
r^*: Weighted interest rate
q: Ratio of loan to housing price
r: Housing mortgage interest rate
r': Market interest rate
t_a: Actual acquisition tax
t_a': Nominal acquisition tax
t_p: Actual property (ownership) tax
m: Depreciation rate of housing
t_g: Actual capital gains tax
g: Inflation rate of housing price
V_h: Housing price
R: Monthly rental price.

As discussed earlier, housing demand is determined by permanent income rather than annual income, taking into account the physical durability of the housing unit. The permanent income is estimated by annual income, assets, consumption, and age of the household head which is based on Kim (2008). The effects of income and assets on permanent income, as expected, are positive; the elasticity of current income with respect to user cost is estimated as 0.617 (Seoul) to 0.705 (ROK) (Table 12.4).

$$\ln(\text{PI}_m) = \beta_0 + \beta_1 \ln(\text{prop}_m) + \beta_2 \ln(\text{inc}_m) + \beta_3 \text{age}_m + \beta_4 \text{age}_m^2 \tag{12.22}$$

PI_m: Permanent income (consumption)
prop_m: Properties (real estate + finance + others)

Table 12.4 Estimation of the permanent income function

$\ln(\text{PI}_m) = \beta_0 + \beta_1 \ln(\text{prop}_m) + \beta_2 \ln(\text{inc}_m) + \beta_3 \text{age}_m + \beta_4 \text{age}_m^2 + \epsilon_m$								
	Parameter							
Variable	Seoul		Incheon		ROS		ROK	
β_0	1.124	***	0.969	***	0.879	***	1.008	***
$\ln(\text{prop}_m)$	0.077	***	0.044	***	0.072	***	0.045	***
$\ln(\text{inc}_m)$	0.617	***	0.687	***	0.662	***	0.705	***
age_m	0.0301	***	0.026	***	0.028	***	0.021	***
age_m^2	−0.0003	***	−0.0003	***	−0.0003	***	−0.0002	***
Number of samples	9300		3090		8742		27,792	
Adjusted R^2	0.694		0.698		0.687		0.760	

Note: *, **, and *** mean statistically significant at 10%, 5%, and 1%, respectively

Table 12.5 Estimation of the Housing Investment (Supply) Function

$\ln(\mathrm{HI}_{mt}) = \beta_0 + \beta_1 \ln(\mathrm{grdp}_{mt}) + \beta_2 \ln(\mathrm{defl}_t) + \beta_3 \ln(\mathrm{rate}_t) + \beta_4 \ln(\mathrm{supp}_{mt-1}) + \beta_5 \mathrm{dummy}_{01} + \beta_6 \mathrm{dummy}_{02} + \beta_7 \mathrm{dummy}_{03} + \beta_8 \ln(\mathrm{grdp}_{mt}) * \mathrm{dummy}_{01} + \beta_9 \ln(\mathrm{grdp}_{mt}) * \mathrm{dummy}_{02} + \beta_{10} \ln(\mathrm{grdp}_{mt}) * \mathrm{dummy}_{03} + \beta_{11} \ln(\mathrm{rate}_t) * \mathrm{dummy}_{01} + \beta_{12} \ln(\mathrm{rate}_t) * \mathrm{dummy}_{02} + \beta_{13} \ln(\mathrm{rate}_t) * \mathrm{dummy}_{03} + \epsilon_m$

Variable	Parameter	Variable	Parameter
β_0	5.904***	dummy_{03}	−17.705*
$\ln(\mathrm{grdp}_{mt})$	0.457***	$\ln(\mathrm{grdp}_{mt}) * \mathrm{dummy}_{01}$	1.088**
$\ln(\mathrm{defl}_t)$	−0.416***	$\ln(\mathrm{grdp}_{mt}) * \mathrm{dummy}_{02}$	1.282**
$\ln(\mathrm{rate}_t)$	−1.041***	$\ln(\mathrm{grdp}_{mt}) * \mathrm{dummy}_{03}$	0.824*
$\ln(\mathrm{supp}_{mt-1})$	0.504***	$\ln(\mathrm{rate}_t) * \mathrm{dummy}_{01}$	1.371**
dummy_{01}	−22.890**	$\ln(\mathrm{rate}_t) * \mathrm{dummy}_{02}$	1.348**
dummy_{02}	−24.650**	$\ln(\mathrm{rate}_t) * \mathrm{dummy}_{03}$	1.481**
Number of samples	377	Adjusted R^2	0.742

Note: *, **, and *** mean statistically significant at 10%, 5%, and 1%, respectively

inc_m: Income (= labor + business + properties + transfer)
age_m: Age of householder

The housing investment as the housing supply for the current period is estimated using the Gross Regional Product (GRP), construction material costs, real interest rate, and the previous year's supply amount. To reflect regional effects, a regional dummy and its interaction variables with the GRP and the interest rate are included in the model, too. If the GRP increases by 1%, the housing investment will increase by 0.457%, but this could be reduced by 1.041% by raising the interest rate by 1% (Table 12.5).

$$\begin{aligned}\ln(\mathrm{HI}_{mt}) = {} & \beta_0 + \beta_1 \ln(\mathrm{grdp}_{mt}) + \beta_2 \ln(\mathrm{defl}_t) + \beta_3 \ln(\mathrm{rate}_t) \\ & + \beta_4 \ln(\mathrm{supp}_{mt-1}) + \beta_5 \mathrm{dummy}_{01} + \beta_6 \mathrm{dummy}_{02} \\ & + \beta_7 \mathrm{dummy}_{03} + \beta_8 \ln(\mathrm{grdp}_{mt}) * \mathrm{dummy}_{01} + \beta_9 \ln(\mathrm{grdp}_{mt}) \\ & * \mathrm{dummy}_{02} + \beta_{10} \ln(\mathrm{grdp}_{mt}) * \mathrm{dummy}_{03} + \beta_{11} \ln(\mathrm{rate}_t) \\ & * \mathrm{dummy}_{01} + \beta_{12} \ln(\mathrm{rate}_t) * \mathrm{dummy}_{02} + \beta_{13} \ln(\mathrm{rate}_t) \\ & * \mathrm{dummy}_{03} + \epsilon_m \end{aligned} \tag{12.23}$$

HI_{mt}: Total value of order
grdp_{mt}: Gross regional domestic product
defl_t: Construction material costs
rate_t: Interest rate
supp_{mt-1}: Housing supply for the previous year
dummy_{01}: Seoul dummy
dummy_{02}: Incheon dummy
dummy_{03}: ROS dummy
m: Region (Seoul, Incheon, ROS, and the ROK),
t: Year (1991–2014)

In the model, the population of the current period is a sum of the natural growth of the lagged population size and net migration. The out-migration between regions is assumed to proceed in response to interregional differences in expected incomes, the population, and the housing prices of the origin and destination regions, which is revised from Todaro and Smith (2015). The expected income is defined as the GRP multiplied by the employment rate of the destination region, while Todaro and Smith (2015) argue that migrants tend to select residential locations based not on actual income or direct benefit but the income expectation and utility factors after migration. If the housing price in Seoul goes up by 1%, the number of migrants to Seoul would decrease by 0.309%. In addition, 1% growth of the share of expected income in Seoul to other regions induces an increase in the in-migration volume by 0.303% (Table 12.6).

Table 12.6 Estimation of the Migration Function

$$\ln(\mathrm{MOV}_{mn}) = \beta_0 + \beta_1 \ln(\mathrm{HP}_m) + \beta_2 \ln(\mathrm{HP}_n) + \beta_3 \ln(\mathrm{EI}_n/\mathrm{EI}_m) + \beta_4 \ln(\mathrm{pop}_n/\mathrm{pop}_m) + \beta_5 \mathrm{dummy}_{02} + \beta_6 \mathrm{dummy}_{03} + \beta_7 \ln(\mathrm{HP}_n) * \mathrm{dummy}_{02} + \beta_8 \ln(\mathrm{HP}_n) * \mathrm{dummy}_{03} + \beta_9 \ln(\mathrm{EI}_n/\mathrm{EI}_m) * \mathrm{dummy}_{02} + \beta_{10} \ln(\mathrm{EI}_n/\mathrm{EI}_m) * \mathrm{dummy}_{03} + \epsilon_m$$

	Parameter			
Variable	Seoul Destination	Incheon Destination	ROS Destination	ROK Destination
β_0	30.639***	25.909***	17.004***	19.522***
$\ln(\mathrm{HP}_m)$	−0.890***	0.286***	0.855***	−0.946***
$\ln(\mathrm{HP}_n)$	−0.309***	−1.379***	−1.270***	0.360***
$\ln\left(\frac{\mathrm{EI}_n}{\mathrm{EI}_m}\right)$	0.303***	0.140**	0.161**	0.063
$\ln\left(\frac{\mathrm{pop}_n}{\mathrm{pop}_m}\right)$	−0.689***	−0.698***	−0.629***	0.422***
dummy_{01}		−18.025***	−1.806 (5.525)	2.005
dummy_{02}	−11.028***		−13.326***	3.427*
dummy_{03}	−10.860***	−14.993***		
$\ln(\mathrm{HP}_n) * \mathrm{dummy}_{01}$		1.290***	0.310	−0.137
$\ln(\mathrm{HP}_n) * \mathrm{dummy}_{02}$	0.700***		0.888***	−0.337***
$\ln(\mathrm{HP}_n) * \mathrm{dummy}_{03}$	0.761***	1.070***		
$\ln\left(\frac{\mathrm{EI}_n}{\mathrm{EI}_m}\right) * \mathrm{dummy}_{01}$		0.623	−1.310*	−0.421***
$\ln\left(\frac{\mathrm{EI}_n}{\mathrm{EI}_m}\right) * \mathrm{dummy}_{02}$	−0.862*		1.371	−0.062
$\ln\left(\frac{\mathrm{EI}_n}{\mathrm{EI}_n}\right) * \mathrm{dummy}_{03}$	−0.796	0.749		
Number of samples	352	352	352	900
Adjusted R^2	0.897	0.909	0.884	0.784

Note: *, **, and *** mean statistically significant at 10%, 5%, and 1%, respectively

$$\ln(\mathrm{MOV}_{mn}) = \beta_0 + \beta_1 \ln(\mathrm{HP}_m) + \beta_2 \ln(\mathrm{HP}_n) + \beta_3 \ln(\mathrm{EI}_n/\mathrm{EI}_m) + \beta_4 \ln(\mathrm{pop}_n/\mathrm{pop}_m) + \beta_5 \mathrm{dummy}_{02} + \beta_6 \mathrm{dummy}_{03} + \beta_7 \ln(\mathrm{HP}_n) * \mathrm{dummy}_{02} + \beta_8 \ln(\mathrm{HP}_n) * \mathrm{dummy}_{03} + \beta_9 \ln(\mathrm{EI}_n/\mathrm{EI}_m) * \mathrm{dummy}_{02} + \beta_{10} \ln(\mathrm{EI}_n/\mathrm{EI}_m) * \mathrm{dummy}_{03} + \epsilon_m \quad (12.24)$$

MOV_{mn}: Number of migrants from m to n
HP_m: Housing price
EI_m: Expected income (GRP per capita * employment rate)
pop_m: Population
dummy_{01}: Seoul dummy
dummy_{02}: Incheon dummy
dummy_{03}: ROS dummy
m, n: Origin and destination regions.

The housing CGE model is a recursive or backward-looking dynamic model in which the value of every exogenous variable, such as government expenditures, is assumed to following a historical path from one period to another. For example, a difference between the current capital stock and its previous period's depreciated value is equal to new investment demand in a stock-flow model. The model is a square system of equations with 378 equations and 539 variables, including 161 exogenous variables. The numeraire variable of the model is the foreign exchange rate for which the prices of all the commodities and services are calculated on that basis. The Social Accounting Matrix (SAM) is used as benchmark data for this CGE model of the housing market. The SAM is calibrated using the regional input–output table in 2013 and the national accounts data from the Bank of Korea. It consists of six accounts of the production factor, the regional household, the production, the government, the capital, and the ROW, while the government account includes economic activities of the national and regional governments.

Traditionally there are three ways to resolve the parameters in the CGE model. The parameters in the first category are derived from a balancing system between incomes and expenditures or inputs and outputs in the SAM: those include the tax and savings rates, and the shift and the share parameters of production, export, and import functions. Those in the second type are employed to be used in similar works or model structures such as the elasticity values of the CET and the Armington functions in international trade. The last category is estimated with econometric models: all the equations in the housing model and the household consumptions in this paper are estimated utilizing actual panel or historical data. We examine model reliability and robustness using an iteration of sensitivity analysis on key parameter values as argued in Belgodere and Vellutini (2011). In this paper, the sensitivity analysis is applied to cases of elasticities of substitution for the Armington function and elasticities of the user cost with respect to the housing demand. Total household incomes and government revenues could increase by 0.06–0.15% and 0.16–0.17%, respectively, if two elasticity values go up by 10%.[5] This reveals that the housing CGE model seems to be stable for counterfactual analysis.

12.3.2 Policy Simulation

This section examines what measure leads to mitigation of housing prices in Seoul and the increase in housing demands. The Housing CGE model is applied to business-as-usual (BAU) and two alternative scenarios as follows:

BAU: business-as-usual.

Acquisition Option: increase of the acquisition tax rate by 1% point (from 1.46% to 2.46% at the base year).

Property Option: increase of the property tax rate by 1% point (from 0.34% to 1.34% at the base year).

The model finds dynamic equilibria path for ten periods by recursively updating the values of exogenous variables from the adaptive expectation methods proposed by Devarajan and Robinson (2013). The BAU scenario is a reference case without changes in the housing tax rates under the existing framework. If an external change in the housing tax is applied to the Housing CGE model, a new set of equilibria for the endogenous variables—prices and quantities in the market—could be calibrated. The simulation results for alternative scenarios are compared with those of the BAU case.[6] There is no computational difficulty in finding a set of unique solutions for multiple periods under the backward-looking approach.

Table 12.7 summarizes the effects of increases in housing acquisition and property tax rates on the markets. In principle, imposing higher tax rates has negative effects on housing transactions, housing demand, the user cost of housing, and household consumption, but has positive effects on the government revenue and thereby the government consumption. A 1% point increase in the acquisition tax rate would augment tax revenue and the housing demand in Seoul by 0.49% and 0.08% over a 10-period average, respectively. However, as expected, it would reduce the welfare of Seoul residents by 0.54% despite the drop in housing price by 0.83% compared with the BAU scenario. In this paper, the welfare index is measured by compensating variation. Over the ten periods, the positive effect on the revenue and the negative effect on welfare would be consistent and stable. The effect on tax revenue ranges from 0.43% to 0.56% over the simulation period. The marginal

[5]The range is appropriate because the upper and lower limits of the parameter are 10% of the average value in Belgodere and Vellutini (2011).

[6]The model cannot deal with housing consumption behavior by household by income class or property size since the housing CGE model is not classified in terms of property value, the number of privately owned housing units, the holding period, and the geographical location within regions due to limitations on data availability for these housing statistics.

Table 12.7 Dynamic impacts of 1% point increases in housing acquisition and property tax rates on tax revenue and housing markets (Unit: %)

(1) Housing acquisition tax

Period	1	2	3	4	5	6	7	8	9	10	Average
Tax revenue	0.56	0.54	0.52	0.51	0.49	0.48	0.46	0.45	0.44	0.43	0.49
Housing price	−0.73	−0.75	−0.78	−0.80	−0.83	−0.85	−0.87	−0.89	−0.91	−0.93	−0.83
Housing demand	−0.09	−0.05	−0.01	0.02	0.06	0.09	0.12	0.15	0.18	0.21	0.08
Welfare	−0.48	−0.49	−0.50	−0.52	−0.53	−0.54	−0.55	−0.57	−0.58	−0.60	−0.54

(2) Housing property tax

Period	1	2	3	4	5	6	7	8	9	10	Average
Tax revenue	1.81	1.75	1.69	1.64	1.58	1.54	1.50	1.46	1.43	1.40	1.58
Housing price	−10.00	−10.40	−10.78	−11.13	−11.47	−11.79	−12.09	−12.38	−12.66	−12.91	−11.56
Housing demand	−1.27	−0.66	−0.09	0.46	0.98	1.48	1.96	2.42	2.85	3.27	1.29
Welfare	−1.85	−1.90	−1.93	−1.96	−1.98	−1.99	−2.01	−2.02	−2.03	−2.05	−1.97

(negative) effect on the housing price would be larger than other variables. Increasing the acquisition tax rate has adverse effects on housing demand in the short run but turns into positive effects after the first three periods.

The magnitudes of the property tax effects on four variables are more considerable than for the acquisition case. Housing prices could fall off by 11.56%, along with improving housing demand by 1.29%. Welfare would be worsened but be unlikely to change substantially. The different sizes of scenario effects result not only from the lower rate of the property tax (0.34% on average) than that of the acquisition tax (1.23%) but also an intrinsic contribution to the property tax on price stabilization in the real estate market as argued by Park and Lee (2018). They showed that countries with a low property tax rate had reduced housing prices, while countries with already high rates could fail to mitigate housing prices due to transferring tax burdens to renters. Also, lowering the transaction tax rate would decrease housing prices. In summary, the government needs to raise the property tax rate but lower the transaction tax rates, such as acquisition and capital gains, on residential units if the policy goals are focused on decreasing housing prices and increasing housing demand. It is worthwhile to note that the trading amount of the housing sale cannot rise under a high transaction tax rate.

12.4 Summary and Further Research Issues

This paper develops a dynamic economic analysis of housing policy effects on the housing market in Korea. The framework is composed of the standard CGE model that integrates the housing market model, which accounts for housing demand, investment, user cost, and multiregional migration for three sub-regions in the Seoul Metropolitan Area and the rest of Korea. The policy simulations using the CGE model show that it would be more effective to increase property tax rate than acquisition tax to stabilize housing prices with a moderate increase in housing demand.

To address further research issues, the model needs to be extended into a multiregional CGE model to estimate spillover effects of housing demand and housing production on regional economies. In this paper, housing demands and households are classified into four regions, but producers excluding housing construction and the housing service sectors are regarded as representative of national economic activity. In addition, it is important to disaggregate the housing market at least into owned housing, deposit rent housing, deposit and monthly pay-rent housing, and monthly pay-rent housing according to tenure choice and payment system, while our model measures user costs only by housing tenure choice. The last issue is to integrate the CGE model of the housing market with a financial mechanism for housing loans. We define the house as a commodity to consume rather than as an asset or property in our analysis. However, housing represents 30% of world wealth, larger than bonds (27%) or equities (19%) (Kim and Bae 2015; Kim et al. 2017). If we can incorporate the expected return on housing investment into our model, we can deeply understand consumer behavioral responses to government policy. This paper shows a positive effect of interest rate on the housing market, but if we make a linkage between the current model and the loanable market, then the result might be inconclusive. The impacts of financial tools on the market may depend on financial portfolio choice for financial instruments (assets) and their costs. In addition, it would be of interest to examine how housing prices are affected by housing redevelopment projects to be financed by property tax revenues similar to a tax increment financing.

References

Anderson JE, Roy AG (2001) Eliminating housing tax preferences: a distributional analysis. J Hous Econ 10(1):41–58

Bai C, Li Q, Ouyang M (2014) Property taxes and home prices: a tale of two cities. J Econ 180(1):1–15

Belgodere A, Vellutini C (2011) Identifying key elasticities in a CGE model: a Monte Carlo approach. Appl Econ Lett 18(17):1619–1622

Benjamin JD, Edward Coulson N, Yang SX (1993) Real estate transfer taxes and property values: the Philadelphia story. J Real Estate Finance Econ 7(2):151–157

Bérard G, Trannoy A (2017) The impact of a rise in the real estate transfer taxes on the French Housing Market. In: AMSE Working Paper 1732. AixMarseille School of Economics

Berkovec J, Fullerton D (1992) A general equilibrium model of housing, taxes, and portfolio choice. J Polit Econ 100(2):390–429

Besley T, Meads N, Surico P (2014) The incidence of transaction taxes: evidence from a stamp duties holiday. J Public Econ 119:61–70

Bruce D, Holtz-Eakin D (1999) Fundamental tax reform and residential housing. J Hous Econ 8: 249–271

Bye B, Åvitsland T (2003) The welfare effects of housing taxation in a distorted economy: a general equilibrium analysis. Econ Model 20(5):895–921

Cao J, Hu W (2016) A microsimulation of property tax policy in China. J Hous Econ 33:128–142

Chambers M, Garriga C, Schlagenhauf DE (2009) Housing policy and the progressivity of income taxation. J Monet Econ 56(8):1116–1134

Cho S-w, Francis JL (2011) Tax treatment of owner occupied housing and wealth inequality. J Macroecon 33(1):42–60

Dachis B, Gilles D, Turner MA (2011) The effects of land transfer taxes on real estate markets: evidence from a natural experiment in Toronto. J Econ Geogr 12:327–354

Davidoff I, Leigh A (2013) How do stamp duties affect the housing market? Econ Rec 89(286):396–410

Devarajan S, Robinson S (2013) Contribution of computable general equilibrium modeling to policy formulation in developing countries. In: Dixon PB, Jorgenson DW (eds) Handbook of computable general equilibrium modeling. North-Holland, Oxford

Feltenstein A, Rider M, Sjoquist DL, Winters JV (2016) Reducing property taxes on homeowners an analysis using computable general equilibrium and microsimulation models. Public Finance Rev:1–27

Floetotto M, Kirker M, Stroebel J (2016) Government intervention in the housing market: who wins, who loses? J Monet Econ 80:106–123

Fritzsche C, Vandrei L (2019) The German real estate transfer tax: evidence for single-family home transactions. Reg Sci Urban Econ 74:131–143

Gervais M (2002) Housing taxation and capital accumulation. J Monet Econ 49(7):1461–1489

Glaeser EL, Gyourko J (2005) Urban decline and durable housing. J Polit Econ 113(2):345–375
Guillaume B, Trannoy A (2017) The impact of a rise in the real estate transfer taxes on the French housing market. In: AMSE working papers 1732. Aix-Marseille School of Economics, Marseille
Hilber CAL, Lyytikäinen T (2013) Housing transfer taxes and household mobility: distortion on the housing or labour market? In: Government Institute for Economic Research VATT Working Papers 47/2013
Holt CC, Shelton JP (1962) The lock-in effect of the capital gains tax rate. Natl Tax J 15:337–352
Keast S-J (2010) A bi-regional CGE model of the south west housing market. Unpublished Ph.D. Dissertation, Plymouth University
Kim A (2008) Impact of housing tax policies on housing demand and income distribution using CGE model. Unpublished Master Thesis, Seoul National University
Kim E, Ju J (2003) Economic analysis of urban land use and housing supply: an application of urban land use and a CGE model for Seoul. In: Computable general equilibrium approaches in urban and regional policy studies, vol 15, pp 167–186
Kim E, Hewings GJD, Nam K-M (2014) Optimal urban population size: national vs local economic efficiency. Urban Stud 51(2):428–445
Kim E, Bae Y (2015) Economic contribution of the private sector on financing and operation of a highway: financial computable general equilibrium. J Transp Econ Policy 49(3):397–414
Kim E, Hewings GJD, Amir H (2017) Economic evaluation of transportation projects: an application of financial computable general equilibrium model. Res Transp Econ 61:44–55
Lee S-Y, Chung E-C (2010) An analysis of impact of debt-to-income regulation on housing tenure decisions of urban households. Seoul Stud 11(1):83–101. (in Koran)
Liberati D, Loberto M (2019) Taxation and housing markets with search frictions. J Hous Econ 46: 101632
Mankiw NG, Weil David N (1989) The baby boom, the baby bust, and the housing market. Reg Sci Urban Econ 19(2):235–258
Palmon O, Smith BA (1998) New evidence on property tax capitalization. J Polit Econ 106(5):1099–1111
Park JB, Lee Y (2018) The real estate tax policy and the housing market stabilization—focused on the property possession tax and the transaction tax. J Real Estate Anal 4(1):1–19. (in Korean)
Park J, Lee T, Bae Y, Jeong H, Choi S (2014) An analysis on economic impacts of changes in property tax. Korea Research Institute for Human Settlements, 2014-29. (in Korean)
Peng S-k, Wang P (2009) A normative analysis of housing-related tax policy in a general equilibrium model of housing quality. J Publ Econ Theor 11(5):667–696
Petkova K, Weichenrieder AJ (2017) Price and quantity effects of the german real estate transfer tax. In: CESifo Working Paper Series, 6538
Poterba JM (1984) Tax subsidies to owner-occupied housing: an asset-market approach. Q J Econ 99(4):729–752
Rosenberg S (2019) The effects of conventional and unconventional monetary policy on house prices in the Scandinavian countries. J Hous Econ 46
Sohn K-H, Park C-G (2005) An empirical analysis on the consumer behavior for housing lending. J Korean Real Estate Soc 23:9–24. (in Korean)
Sommer K, Sullivan P (2018) Implications of US tax policy for house prices, rents, and homeownership. Am Econ Rev 108(2):241–274
Todaro MP, Smith SC (2015) Economic development, 12th edn. Pearson Addison Wesley Pearson, Boston
Wu Y, Li Y (2018) Impact of government intervention in the housing market: evidence from the housing purchase restriction policy in China. Appl Econ 50(6):691–705

Chapter 13
The Economic Effects on Regional Australia of RUN-Member Universities

Robert Waschik, Jonathan Chew, John Madden, Joshua Sidgwick, and Glyn Wittwer

Abstract The study analyses the impacts of selected regional universities on regional economies within Australia using a multi-regional CGE model, VU-TERM. Universities enhance a community's knowledge base through teaching and research, raising productivity within the region. To depict the regional economic contribution of universities, we simulate a hypothetical removal of regional campuses. This includes closing campus activities, plus demand-side shocks to remove student expenditures, and supply-side shocks to capture the campuses' productivity effects on their local economies. We estimate demand-side shocks using expenditure patterns of university enrollees. The major supply-side shocks use inputs from econometric studies estimating rates of return to levels of educational attainment. Simulation results show a wide variation in the effects of the campuses on host regions' gross regional product, varying from around half a per cent for regions with small campuses through to around 13% for the local economy of Armidale, which has a strong university presence.

JEL Classification Codes C68 · O18

Keywords CGE modelling · Regional universities · Economic contribution

---

R. Waschik (✉) · J. Madden · G. Wittwer
Centre of Policy Studies, Victoria University, Melbourne, VIC, Australia
e-mail: robert.waschik@vu.edu.au; john.madden@vu.edu.au; glyn.wittwer@vu.edu.au

J. Chew
Navitas Pty Ltd, Brisbane, QLD, Australia
e-mail: jon.chew@navitas.com

J. Sidgwick
Australian Bureau of Statistics, Canberra, ACT, Australia
e-mail: joshua.sidgwick@abs.gov.au

M. Kawano et al. (eds.), *Theory and History in Regional Perspective*, New Frontiers in Regional Science: Asian Perspectives 56,
https://doi.org/10.1007/978-981-16-6695-7_13

Table 13.1 Estimated funding cuts to RUN universities, 2018–2021

RUN-member university	Funding decrease %	Funding decrease $m
Southern Cross University (SCU)	5.7	33
The University of New England (UNE)	3.2	25
Federation University Australia (FED)	5.9	29
Central Queensland University (CQU)	15	147
University of the Sunshine Coast (USC)	8.7	66
University of Southern Queensland (USQ)	3.1	29

Source: ABC News (2018)

13.1 Introduction

Regional universities can provide substantial positive contributions to regional economies. The presence of a university provides more career development opportunities within a region. Tertiary students from elsewhere, either within Australia or overseas, increase regional demands for local goods, services, and housing. The presence of a local university may open up the possibility of local synergies between industries or essential services and the university (Uyarra 2010).

However, in recent years, cuts in the federal funding to Australian universities have impacted disproportionally on universities located in regional Australia. Nationally, a 2017 report by Universities Australia showed that "... students and universities have contributed around $3.9 billion in net savings between 2011–12 and 2016–17".[1] Details of the Commonwealth Government's December 2017 freeze to university funding, made available in June 2018, confirmed a further $2.3 billion of cuts to university funding over the period 2018–2021, equivalent to a 4.5% decrease in funding. Furthermore, as summarized in Table 13.1, a number of university members of the Regional Universities Network (RUN) face funding cuts over this period, which are considerably higher than the national average. The sensitivity of regional universities to these funding cuts is exacerbated by the fact that regional universities do not have the endowment and reputation of leading Australian universities, making them more vulnerable to downturns in public funding.

The objective of this study is to simulate the economic contribution that these regional universities make to their respective regional economies. To do so, we adopt the approach of Madden (2017) to economic contribution and conduct a simulation to answer the following question: "What would the regional economy where each RUN-member university has a campus look like if the campus had never existed?" We simulate the hypothetical removal of the regional campuses of universities that are members of the RUN using a Computable General Equilibrium (CGE)

[1]See "The Facts on University Funding" (April 2017), available from https://www.universitiesaustralia.edu.au/Media-and-Events/submissions-and-reports/The-facts-on-university-funding.

model of the Australian economy with sufficient regional detail to separately identify small regions (at the SA3 level under the Australian Statistical Geography Standard) which are home to a RUN-member university's regional campus. The losses that would result at the regional level from not having a local campus arise from several direct effects. First, regional universities are an important employer in regional communities. Absence of a campus would weaken the local job market. Adjustment at the local level is likely to result through a combination of lower real wages and interregional migration. Some university staff would have found jobs at other universities. Others would have remained in the community, in all probability with lower paid jobs. Others would have participated less in the labour force.

Absence of a university campus would mean lower demands for local services with a consequent drop in local income (approximated in the CGE model by total value added or GDP). This would mean lower demand for restaurants, health services, entertainment, community services, transport services, and other local services. Lower demand would also see lower local prices relative to otherwise, notably in the housing market.

In addition to lower local demands, skill acquisition arising from the presence of a local university would diminish in the community. This is evident in data from the Graduate Outcomes Survey showing that a substantial proportion of graduates from a regional university remain to take on employment within that region. For example, health services are an important employer in regional communities. Without a university, health-related professions would rely increasingly on training from outside of the region.

In addition to skill acquisition associated with university attendance, universities provide pervasive but small productivity improvements across all industries. For example, research in agricultural science disciplines contributes to productivity improvements that extend beyond the local region. We have not modelled the local productivity benefits that may arise from synergies between a regional university and, for example, a regional teaching hospital. Such synergies may be possible within both the teaching program and the provision of some health services.

Table 13.2 summarizes the economic structure of the regions in which individual campuses of RUN-member universities are located (see Fig. 13.1 at the end of the paper for a map showing the approximate location of each campus). Clearly, these vary widely. For example, Armidale has the largest university activity as a share of total regional economic activity. Consequently, Armidale's local economy is hit harder by a hypothetical removal of its university than other RUN regions. The final row of Table 13.2 reports regional gross domestic product, providing an indication of the relative size of the economies of these different regions.

The chapter proceeds as follows: In the next section, we describe the methodology used to determine the economic impact that RUN-member universities have on their regional economies. We describe the CGE model used for the study and detail the data and process used to determine the impact that these regional universities have on local demand and supply in their respective regional economies. In Sect. 13.3 we describe the assumptions made to close the model so that we simulate the long-run economic impacts of RUN-member universities. Results reported in Sect.

Table 13.2 Economic structure of each region (industry share of total regional value added, %)

	CQU								FED		
	Rockhmpton Qld	Mackay Qld	Gladstone Qld	Bundaberg Qld	CentHlnd Qld	TownsvillQld	CairnsSth Qld	Noosa Qld	Ballarat Vic	Latrobe VlVic	Grampians Vic
Primary	14.1	26.2	14.0	14.0	52.0	5.8	4.5	4.5	4.2	8.5	30.0
FoodProds	2.7	3.2	0.3	4.7	0.2	1.3	1.2	0.9	3.9	1.5	3.2
AlcoSmokes	0.0	0.0	0.0	0.3	0.0	0.0	0.0	0.0	0.2	0.1	0.5
HholdGoods	2.5	3.3	23.1	3.0	1.9	3.5	2.5	1.8	4.2	6.1	2.6
ClothingFtwr	0.0	0.0	0.0	0.0	0.0	0.0	0.0	0.0	0.1	0.0	0.0
CarCosts	1.1	1.2	0.8	2.0	0.9	1.1	1.5	1.1	2.3	1.3	1.2
Utilities	5.9	1.6	5.4	1.8	1.3	2.9	2.2	1.3	1.7	17.7	2.2
OthService	38.1	35.4	31.6	45.3	26.0	52.1	53.4	64.0	49.5	38.5	33.6
Transport	11.0	10.4	10.9	3.5	5.1	5.7	5.9	1.8	3.1	2.0	4.1
AirTransport	0.3	0.5	0.4	0.1	0.2	0.3	1.2	0.2	0.0	0.0	0.0
OwnerDwellng	8.4	7.9	7.1	9.3	6.9	8.6	9.9	11.0	9.5	7.6	7.8
OthEducation	4.5	3.1	2.5	5.3	2.2	5.1	5.1	4.6	5.9	4.8	4.1
TertiaryEdu	1.5	0.2	0.1	0.4	0.0	0.0	0.0	0.3	1.6	0.5	0.0
Health	5.3	3.8	2.1	6.4	1.7	6.9	6.7	5.3	8.1	5.6	6.2
ChildComCare	4.1	2.7	1.6	3.2	1.3	6.1	4.5	2.0	4.5	5.0	3.6
RecreatEnttn	0.3	0.2	0.2	0.4	0.2	0.5	1.0	1.0	1.2	0.5	0.7
ExpEdu	0.1	0.1	0.1	0.1	0.1	0.1	0.1	0.1	0.1	0.1	0.1
Total	100	100	100	100	100	100	100	100	100	100	100
GDP ($ bn)	8.1	9.1	6.1	4.0	2.9	14.2	5.9	2.1	5.6	4.9	3.5

	SCU			UNE	USQ		USC		
	RichValHnNSW	Coolangatta	CoffsHrbrNSW	ArmidaleNSW	Toowoomba Qld	IpsSprRdb Qld	Buderim Qld	GympiCool Qld	HerveyBay Qld
Primary	5.3	3.2	3.6	9.3	7.8	3.0	6.3	12.5	8.4
FoodProds	9.4	0.7	1.3	0.9	2.8	3.9	1.4	3.8	1.0
AlcoSmokes	0.1	0.3	0.0	0.3	0.0	0.1	0.0	0.1	0.0
HholdGoods	4.6	3.4	3.7	1.7	4.1	7.2	3.2	9.7	4.0
ClothingFtwr	0.0	0.1	0.0	0.0	0.0	0.0	0.0	0.1	0.0
CarCosts	2.2	1.0	1.8	1.3	1.6	1.8	1.5	2.0	1.8
Utilities	1.7	1.6	1.5	1.6	2.1	1.8	1.5	1.8	2.3
OthService	44.9	60.1	56.3	48.3	48.8	52.5	58.2	45.0	52.1
Transport	2.7	2.3	3.0	2.2	4.6	7.3	1.9	3.8	3.4
AirTransport	0.0	1.3	0.5	0.0	0.1	0.2	0.3	0.0	0.0
OwnerDwellng	10.6	10.2	11.0	11.7	9.2	9.1	10.4	9.6	10.5
OthEducation	5.6	4.8	6.0	5.1	5.4	3.9	4.0	4.3	5.2
TertiaryEdu	2.3	1.0	0.3	9.5	1.4	0.1	2.0	0.1	0.2
Health	6.4	6.0	6.5	4.6	6.5	4.9	6.2	4.0	7.1
ChildComCare	2.9	2.3	3.2	2.5	5.0	3.5	2.1	2.6	3.3
RecreatEnttn	1.1	1.4	1.1	0.7	0.4	0.4	0.8	0.4	0.5
ExpEdu	0.1	0.1	0.1	0.1	0.1	0.1	0.1	0.1	0.1
Total	100	100	100	100	100	100	100	100	100
GDP ($ bn)	3.3	3.1	4.4	1.9	9.6	11.8	3.2	2.2	2.1

Source: CoPS VU_TERM database

	CQU	postcode	SA3		SOUTHERN CROSS U	postcode	SA3
a	Rockhampton	4702	30803	l	Lismore	2480	11202
b	Mackay	4740	31202	m	Gold Coast	4225	30902
c	Gladstone	4680	30802	n	Coffs Harbour	2450	10402
d	Bundaberg	4670	31901		U NEW ENGLAND		
e	Emerald	4720	30801	o	Armidale	2351	11001
f	Townsville	4810	31802		U SOUTHERN QUEENSLAND		
g	Cairns	4870	30602	p	Toowoomba	4350	31701
h	Noosa	4566	31605	q	Springfield/Ipswich	4300	31003
	FEDERATION UNI				U SUNSHINE COAST		
i	Ballarat	3350	20101	r	Sippy Downs	4556	31601
j	Churchill	3842	20504	s	Gympie	4570	31903
k	Horsham	3400	21501	t	Fraser Coast	4655	31904

Fig. 13.1 Approximate location of RUN-member campuses

13.3 highlight the range of impacts that RUN-member universities have on their regional economies. In those regions where a RUN-member university has its dominant campus, the universities contribute from 3.5 to 12.9% to regional GDP and 1.9–9.6% to regional employment. Section 13.4 concludes.

13.2 Study Method

Universities have a range of effects on the regional economies in which they are located.[2] A university's operations increase demands for local goods, services, and housing. Potential impacts are greater than local demand increases.[3] Due to the nature of their output—primarily teaching and research—universities have an effect on the community's knowledge base and thus act to raise productivity, both in the university's own region and in other regions to which the new knowledge spills over.

There have been numerous regional economic impact studies of particular universities, mainly using input–output models, which capture the multiplier effects of university expenditure in the region—see Florax (1992) and Giesecke and Madden (2006). The literature on the knowledge effects of universities has been largely by way of econometric studies (see Florax (1992) and Henderson (2007)). The present study follows the general approach of Giesecke and Madden (2006) and Madden (2014, 2017) in modelling both local expenditure impacts and knowledge impacts in a CGE framework.

In the remainder of this section, we discuss our approach to modelling the contribution made by the regional campuses of the six universities that are members of the Regional Universities Network (RUN) to their local economy. The major innovations in the present study relate to the local area under examination. Giesecke and Madden (2006) analysed the economic effects of the University of Tasmania that is the only university within its state. Subsequent regional CGE studies of higher education by Hermannsson et al. (2014) and Madden (2014) model all universities in aggregate in regions (Scotland and Queensland, respectively) where cross-border commuting is limited, while Madden (2017) models local effects of a university located in a district of a large metropolis.[4] Here we examine the economic effects of RUN-member regional campuses, which are typically located at a distance from state capitals.

[2]There is an extensive literature on the benefits of universities to their local economies (see, for instance, Florax 1992, Feldman and Desrochers 2003, Drucker and Goldstein 2007, Fritsch and Slavtchev 2007, Dalziel et al. 2009, and Harris et al. 2011). We confine ourselves to only economic effects. Universities can also have non-market benefits, both of a private and public nature, but we do not deal with those in this study. See McMahon (2009) for a discussion of non-market benefits.

[3]Different industries can have varying regional economic impacts due to the composition and geographical sourcing of their inputs. A characteristic of the education industry is that, like certain other service industries (e.g. those operating tourist attractions and sports and other events), it attracts out-of-region visitors who increase local demand. This attribute is dealt with in items Sects. 13.2.2 and 13.2.3 below.

[4]Giesecke and Madden (2006), Madden (2014), and Hermannsson et al. (2014) all model changes in the sizes of universities, while Madden (2017) examines the local economic contribution of a university.

13.2.1 The Economic Model: VU-TERM

In the master database of VU-TERM, there are 192 industry sectors in 334 SA3 regions. In the version of VU-TERM used for the study, the model has been aggregated to 17 industry sectors (see Table 13.12 in Appendix) in 24 regions. The 24 regions correspond to the SA3 region in which each regional campus of the RUN-member Universities is located: CQU (8 campuses); Federation University (3 campuses); Southern Cross University (3 campuses); University of New England (1 campus); University of Southern Queensland (2 campuses); University of the Sunshine Coast (3 campuses); one rest-of-state region for each of New South Wales, Queensland, and Victoria, and an aggregate rest of Australia region. The RUN-member university regional campuses and the postcodes contained in each campus' SA3 region are detailed in the Appendix in Table 13.13.

In VU-TERM, each industry produces a single commodity. Investment is allocated across industries to maximize rates of returns to investors (households, firms). Capital creators assemble, in a cost-minimizing manner, units of industry-specific capital for each industry. Each region has a single representative household and a single government agency. Finally, there are foreigners, whose behaviour is summarized by export demand curves for the products of each region and by supply curves for international imports to each region.

As is standard in CGE models, VU-TERM determines the supply and demand for each regionally produced commodity as the outcome of optimizing behaviour of economic agents. Regional industries are assumed to choose labour, capital, and land so as to maximize their profits while operating in a competitive market. In each region a representative household purchases a particular bundle of goods in accordance with the household's preferences, relative prices and its amount of disposable income. Regions are linked via interregional trade, interregional migration, and capital movements. For a detailed description of the theoretical structure of the VU-TERM model, see Wittwer (2012) or Wittwer (2017).

13.2.2 Treatment of Foreign Students with VU-TERM

Of particular relevance to this study is VU-TERM's specific treatment of overseas students, captured by a separate exports-of-education ("ExpEdu") sector. This sector takes account of education export fees plus the living expenses of overseas students. Household demands in the original CGE database that reflect living expenses of students become intermediate inputs into "ExpEdu". There were 645,185 international enrolments in 2015 in Australia, equal to about 2.5% of the national population. Of these, 363,421 were enrolled in the tertiary sector, of which 8552 were accounted for by international students attending a RUN-member University regional campus. Expenditure shares for international students are lower than the population share for some commodities, but not air transport.

We identify two separate effects that universities have on their regional economies (Giesecke and Madden 2006). First, a "demand-side effect" reflects the impacts that a university's presence has on local expenditures. Second, universities contribute a "supply-side effect" through their teaching and research activities, raising the productivity of graduates who gain a tertiary qualification (a positive effect on labour productivity) and improving the productivity of industrial activities overall by producing research (a positive effect on all-factor productivity). The demand-side effects as they relate to RUN-member Universities are described in greater detail in Sect. 13.2.3, while the two supply-side effects, labour productivity and research productivity are described in Sect. 13.2.4.

13.2.3 Demand-Side Effects

To determine the effect of RUN-member University enrolments on demand in each region, we begin with the information about student expenditure patterns from Western et al. (2005), who report estimates of weekly spending for international higher education students in Australia. The expenditure data in Western et al. (2005) are used directly to determine an estimate of the expenditures of overseas students at RUN-member University regional campuses. We assume an international full-time student spends 40 weeks each year in the region in which they are enrolled and exclude all out-of-region expenditure. The data in Table 12 of Western et al. (2005) are for 2004. These data are converted to 2016 values using the ratio of consumer price indices of 2016 and 2004 for the state in which the campus is located (ABS cat. 6401.0, Table 5).

These updated data from Western et al. (2005) allow us to model the expenditure patterns of international students at RUN-member regional campuses. To determine the expenditure patterns of domestic students, however, we need to recognize that these will vary depending on the student's mode of study and the location of their home residence relative to the campus they attend. Students whose permanent residence is within commuting distance of their campus will spend only a fraction of their total expenditures on campus, and students who study via external mode typically attend lectures remotely and spend almost no time on campus.

To proceed, we use data on 2016 campus enrolments reported in Table 13.3[5] that decompose total enrolments into the following categories:

[5]The enrolment data in Table 13.3 include full-time and part-time commencing and continuing students by campus. These data are converted to equivalent full-time student load (EFTSL) figures using EFTSL-to-enrolment ratios for domestic and international students at each RUN-member university.

Table 13.3 Campus enrolment by origin of student

						Intra-region		Intra-state		Inter-state	
		Postcode	SA3	Overseas	Domest	Internal	Extern.	Internal	Extern.	Internal	Extern.
CQU	Rockhampton	4702	30803	160	12,416	1520	1110	667	6949	61	2109
	Mackay	4740; 4741	31202	6	633	541	18	61	1	11	1
	Gladstone	4680	30802	4	151	149	1	1	0	0	0
	Bundaberg	4670	31901	24	793	680	41	61	6	5	0
	Emerald	4720	30801	0	16	1	0	14	0	1	0
	Townsville	4810	31802	0	63	49	8	5	0	1	0
	Cairns	4870	30602	2	89	64	6	19	0	0	0
	Noosa	4566	31605	1	182	66	4	103	6	3	0
Federation University	Ballarat	3350	20101	599	5980	2347	77	2736	374	306	140
	Churchill	3842	20504	46	1552	725	3	802	9	12	1
	Horsham	3400	21501	0	21	20	1	0	0	0	0
Southern Cross	Lismore	2480	11202	174	8419	1081	472	1193	3180	236	2257
	Gold Coast	4225	30902	716	2996	462	45	1029	137	1173	150
	Coffs Harbour	2450	10402	25	1264	715	90	348	78	27	6
U New England	Armidale	2351	11001	1100	20,689	621	647	2204	11,116	372	5729
U Sth. Queenslnd	Toowoomba	4350	31701	3645	20,717	2499	1889	1587	10,700	205	3837
	Springfield/ Ipswich	4300; 4305	31003; 31004	168	2548	1261	0	1260	0	27	0
U Sunshine Coast	Sippy Downs	4556	31601	1568	11,284	2573	13	8445	78	163	12
	Gympie	4570	31903	0	238	222	0	16	0	0	0
	Fraser Coast	4655	31904	4	496	351	0	145	0	0	0

Source: Student enrolments across all RUN campuses from 2014 to 2016, mapped using ABS ASGS Correspondences

- Overseas: students whose reported home residence is overseas.
- Intra-region—internal: students whose reported home residence is in a postcode which is within the SA3 region in which the campus is located and whose mode of study is internal.
- Intra-region—external and multi-mode: students whose reported home residence is in a postcode which is within the SA3 region in which the campus is located and whose mode of study is external or multi-modal.
- Intra-state—internal: students whose reported home residence is in the state but not the SA3 region in which the campus is located and whose mode of study is internal.
- Intra-state—external and multi-mode: students whose reported home residence is in the state but not the SA3 region in which the campus is located and whose mode of study is external or multi-modal.
- Inter-state—internal: students whose reported home residence is in a state other than that in which the campus is located and whose mode of study is internal.
- Inter-state—external and multi-mode: students whose reported home residence is in a state other than that in which the campus is located and whose mode of study is external or multi-modal.

Following Giesecke and Madden (2006), we assume that the living costs of inter-state and intra-state students who study via internal mode are 80 and 60% of those for overseas students, respectively. This reflects the likelihood that a proportion of these students may have permanent residences within weekly or daily commuting distance of their campus.[6] Intra-state and inter-state students studying via external mode are assumed to behave like intra-region students, with expenditures that are 10% of those for overseas students. Intra-region students will live in their region whether or not they were studying on campus, so their expenditure multipliers are 0.1, except for those on housing, utilities, and entertainment/recreation expenditures, whose multipliers are 0. This methodology allows us to calculate estimates of expenditures for all students attending RUN-member University campuses in 2016.

13.2.4 Supply-Side Effects

The supply-side effects capture the two principal contributions that are made by universities on the supply-side of the economy: teaching and research. The former results in a labour force that is more skilled, evidenced by the tertiary qualifications held by RUN-member University graduates. These translate into improved labour productivity, the quantification of which is outlined in Sect. 13.2.5. Productivity

[6]Giesecke and Madden (2006) assumed that this intra-state student multiplier was 0.5, but their study looked at students in Tasmania. Since RUN-member campuses are located in much larger states, the proportion of students with permanent residences within a reasonable commute of campus will be smaller, so we use a multiplier of 0.6 instead of 0.5 for these students.

improvements derived from RUN-member University research activities are detailed in subsection Sect. 13.2.6.

13.2.5 Labour Productivity

The primary data source for labour productivity shocks is the file "DS_GOS_RUN2013–16.xlsx" (This file is the institute-specific outputs of the Graduate Outcome Survey from 2013 to 2016, supplied by RUN Strategic Information and Analysis Unit. The Graduate Outcomes Survey (GOS) is a national survey of recent higher education graduates being conducted for the Australian Government Department of Education and Training by the Social Research Centre, see https://www.srcentre.com.au/our-research/graduate-outcomes-survey) that reports the location of workplace by postcode of RUN-member University graduates over the period 2013–2016. For example, data reported in this file tell us that in 2016, 218 CQU Bachelor degree graduates were working in a postcode that is within the SA3 region of a CQU campus. A further 200 CQU Bachelor graduates were working in Queensland but in a postcode which is not within the SA3 region of a CQU campus. Table 13.4 reports the number of students working intra-region or intra-state for all RUN-member Universities by award category (Diploma, Bachelor, GradDip, MAPhD).[7] Clearly, there are large differences between RUN-member Universities in the share of graduates who work in a region in which the same RUN-member University has a campus. University of New England has only one campus, and far more UNE graduates work intra-state (i.e. in New South Wales but not in Armidale) than intra-region.

CQU graduates are the exception. For qualifications other than Masters and PhD degrees, more graduates from CQU are employed in CQU postcodes than elsewhere intra-state. A number of possible reasons may explain this. In Table 13.3, we see that less than 2% of enrollees at CQU are from overseas, whereas the proportion for all universities shown in Table 13.3 exceeds 9%. This alone might push up the proportion of graduates employed locally. It could be that differences in course offerings between CQU and elsewhere, perhaps based on the relative isolation of CQU campuses, influence the different proportions of graduates employed locally. An explanation of differences in graduate patterns is beyond the scope of the present study.

To translate these employment figures into labour productivity effects, we need to resolve the following issues:

[7]More specifically, "Diploma" includes the award categories Advanced Diploma (AQF), Associate Degree, Diploma (AQF), and Enabling; "Bachelor" includes Bachelor's Graduate Entry, Bachelor's Pass, Bachelor's Graduate Honours, Postgrad. Qual. Prelim and Non-award courses; "GradDip" includes Graduate certificate, Graduate (post) dip. (ext. area) and Graduate (post) dip. (new area); "MAPhD" includes Master's by coursework, Master's by research, PhD by coursework and PhD by research.

Table 13.4 RUN-member graduates employed by region and award

	Diploma	Bachelors	GradDip	MAPhD	Diploma	Bachelors	GradDip	MAPhD
	Central Queensland U—Intra-region				Central Queensland U—Intra-state			
2013	29	297	106	21	16	171	91	64
2014	28	327	94	25	27	174	98	49
2015	23	336	84	22	19	200	77	56
2016	21	218	55	16	17	200	35	21
	Federation U—Intra-region				Federation U—Intra-state			
2013	6	131	71	13	26	257	106	51
2014	1	185	29	21	1	336	57	86
2015		183	23	33	2	285	117	106
2016	1	18		18	3	45	4	27
	Southern Cross U—Intra-region				Southern Cross U—Intra-state			
2013	12	204	26	18	35	284	38	55
2014	8	175	25	16	21	270	41	47
2015	6	168	21	14	22	245	51	61
2016	7	107	16	24	16	171	24	34
	U of New England—Intra-region				U of New England—Intra-state			
2013	3	73	8	20	12	371	129	148
2014	1	72	14	35	28	458	185	167
2015	1	86	11	36	23	460	184	178
2016	1	69	7	20	31	437	121	179
	U of South Queensland—Intra-region				U of Southern Queensland—Intra-state			
2013	16	203	28	59	62	411	122	157
2014	12	243	41	59	71	354	141	181
2015	16	205	41	49	56	368	148	144

(continued)

Table 13.4 (continued)

	Diploma	Bachelors	GradDip	MAPhD	Diploma	Bachelors	GradDip	MAPhD
	Central Queensland U—Intra-region				Central Queensland U—Intra-state			
2016	15	203	33	68	73	359	166	166
	U of Sunshine Coast—Intra-region				U of Sunshine Coast—Intra-state			
2013	0	128	18	19	2	456	44	52
2014	0	133	13	19	2	508	54	64
2015	0	145	13	30	0	582	37	39
2016	0	77	10	13	6	444	55	64

Source: Graduate Outcome Survey from 2013 to 2016

1. Employment figures in Table 13.4 are based off the Graduate Student Survey, which only samples a fraction of total graduates, a smaller proportion of whom respond ($n = 6500$ surveyed, while $N = 20{,}000$ population of graduates from RUN)
2. Results from the Graduate Student Survey are at the University level—we need results at the campus level.
3. University graduates should be modelled as receiving a wage premium, the major component of which represents increased skills acquired through their university studies.

To deal with (1), we assume that the Graduate Student Survey is representative and apply a multiplier of 20/6.5 to the data in Table 13.4 to arrive on total graduates employed. To deal with (2), we allocate RUN-member graduates by University in Table 13.4 across RUN-member regional campuses using enrolment shares by award category calculated from the enrolment data in the file "RUN enrol data 2014–2016.xlsx" [This data contains information on student enrolments across all RUN campuses from 2014 to 2016, supplied by RUN Strategic Information and Analysis Unit and is consistent with Higher Education uCube data, see: http://highereducationstatistics.education.gov.au/. Mapping between postcode (POA) to SA3 used the ABS Australian Statistical Geography Standard (ASGS) Correspondences, see: http://www.abs.gov.au/websitedbs/D3310114.nsf/home/Correspondences]. To resolve item (3), we follow Madden (2017) and multiply the number of intra-region employees by a wage premium earned according to award type. We use the wage premia from the "log hourly wage" regressions that assume 10% upwards ability bias reported in Table 13.4 in Leigh (2008:244).[8] In particular, Diploma graduates are assumed to receive a wage premium of 13%, Bachelor graduates a premium of 32%, Graduate Diploma students a premium of 35%, and PhD graduates a premium of 41%.

These adjustments to the data in Table 13.4 allow us to estimate the number of graduates working in each region in which a RUN-member campus is located, reported in Table 13.5.

Of course, the actual number of RUN-member graduates working in each region is likely to be larger than the figure reported in Table 13.5, since we do not account for students who graduated before 2013. The number of omitted graduates may be small since pre-2013 graduates who were working in a RUN-member campus region may have moved to a different region. Ideally, we would adjust the data in Table 13.5 to account for the probability of relocation and use a longer time series to include students who graduated before 2013. Since these data are not available, we use the data in Table 13.5 on graduates working in each region and regard these data as conservative.

[8] We assume that the wage premia by award category are the same for each year over 2013–2016.

Table 13.5 RUN graduates employed in region

CQU	Rockhampton	1521	SCU	Lismore	535
	Mackay	53		Gold Coast	213
	Gladstone	9		Coffs Harbour	94
	Bundaberg	53	UNE	Armidale	481
	Emerald	0	USQ	Toowoomba	1215
	Townsville	9		Springfield/Ipswich	100
	Cairns	1	USC	Sippy Downs	608
	Noosa	25		Gympie	5
FED	Ballarat	680		Fraser Coast	23
	Churchill	64			
	Horsham	8			

Source: Graduate Outcome Survey from 2013 to 2016

13.2.6 Research Productivity

We measure the contribution of university research activity as the sum of the value of research income and the value of the time spent undertaking research activity by academics. Research income by RUN-member universities is available from Higher Education Research Data Collection (HERDC).[9] (HERDC data used is the HERDC time series maintained by Universities Australia, "HERDC time-series data dating back to 1992 (XLSX)", see: www.universitiesaustralia.edu.au/australias-universities/key-facts-and-data/Research-Intensity%2D%2D-Output, which is an accessible summary of the Higher Education Research Data Collection, see: https://www.education.gov.au/higher-education-research-data-collection.) To get an estimate of the value of time spent undertaking research activity, we follow the process outlined in Madden (2017:17). ABS (2014) biennial data for research income by state include the category "General university funds", which is an estimate of time spent at research activity by academics. If the share of "General university funds" out of total research income reported by the ABS is $x \in (0,1)$, then the remainder $(1-x)$ must be external research income as reported in HERDC. If we assume that the share of the value of research time for each RUN-member university is the same as the state average x, then the total value of research activity (i.e. the sum of research income plus the value of academics' time at research) will be given by $1/(1-x)$ times the value of RUN-member University external research income as reported in HERDC. Table 13.6 reports total HERDC research income (in $'000) as well as the share of the value of research time x for each RUN-member university, for each two-year period since 1992 (data in ABS (2014) are biennial).[10] These data are used to determine the total value of research activity for each RUN-member university.

[9] See https://www.education.gov.au/search/site/data

[10] Note how the general decrease in the shares made up by "General university funds" in Table 13.6 reflect the trend that Universities are now relying more on external research funds.

Table 13.6 Total HERDC research income ($'000) and ABS share of General University Funds

	1992–93	1994–95	1996–97	1998–99	2000–01	2002–03	2004–05	2006–07	2008–09	2010–11	2012–13	2014–15	2016
CQUniversity	$1996	$3104	$4639	$5107	$6573	$8966	$10,412	$12,071	$12,223	$13,135	$17,072	$16,247	$7604
	0.668	0.668	0.627	0.631	0.635	0.645	0.65	0.566	0.51	0.548	0.543	0.542	0.542
FederationUn	$777	$1022	$1933	$2606	$4630	$7340	$10,173	$10,124	$10,587	$7026	$7159	$10,639	$4847
	0.574	0.574	0.608	0.586	0.583	0.592	0.591	0.503	0.495	0.567	0.593	0.561	0.561
SouthCrossU	$844	$1530	$6131	$7552	$9218	$11,633	$17,480	$19,758	$18,209	$23,802	$26,555	$23,514	$11,508
	0.667	0.667	0.67	0.625	0.648	0.637	0.629	0.504	0.566	0.524	0.533	0.509	0.509
UNewEngland	$17,676	$19,281	$18,172	$17,802	$20,126	$26,875	$31,471	$34,648	$33,491	$38,791	$58,202	$63,499	$31,268
	0.667	0.667	0.67	0.625	0.648	0.637	0.629	0.504	0.566	0.524	0.533	0.509	0.509
USouthernQld	$1527	$2696	$3407	$4728	$6392	$11,085	$8077	$9513	$11,161	$15,040	$17,455	$26,106	$14,754
	0.668	0.668	0.627	0.631	0.635	0.645	0.65	0.566	0.51	0.548	0.543	0.542	0.542
USunshCoast	$0	$0	$0	$283	$735	$1277	$1489	$3073	$5440	$6879	$14,052	$23,420	$14,683
	0.668	0.668	0.627	0.631	0.635	0.645	0.65	0.566	0.51	0.548	0.543	0.542	0.542

Source: Calculated using HERDC time series maintained by universities Australia, "HERDC time-series data dating back to 1992"

For example, in 2016, the total value of research activity for UNE would be \$31,268.1·[1/(1−0.509)] = \$63,682.5 thousand.

The next step is to determine each RUN-member University's contribution to the total stock of research knowledge. This will be given by the summation of the value of research activity over the entire period 1992–2016, presuming that the stock of research knowledge depreciates. Following Madden (2017), we suppose that the stock of research knowledge depreciates at a rate of 10% per year. Finally, we use the most conservative estimate of the rate of return on the stock of research knowledge reported in Madden (2017) and adopt a value for this rate of return of 25%. For more detail, see the discussion in Section 3.2.2 of Madden (2017:16–19).

As in Section 13.2.5 for the labour productivity shocks, the data in Table 13.6 reflect the return on each RUN-member University's stock of research knowledge. These data need to be disaggregated across RUN-member regional campuses. To do so, we disburse each RUN-member University's return to its stock of research knowledge across regional campuses using each campus' share of Master's and PhD students. Ideally, we would use data on the share of research-active academic staff by campus, but these data are not available. Nonetheless, Master's and PhD students shares are likely to be quite similar to those on research-active staff by campus, since more staff engaged in research will work at larger campuses with larger enrolments of postgraduate students. We assume that none of the returns to the stock of research knowledge accrues specifically to the region in which the RUN-member University campus is located. Rather, the returns to the stock of research knowledge are shared equally across all regions in Australia. This implies that we have not considered the possible gains that may arise from synergies between a local university and local businesses or essential services. This was due to a lack of data.

13.3 Simulation Assumptions and Results

In order to assess the economic contribution of each RUN-member University's regional campus, we need to devise a simulation that projects what each regional economy as well as the economies of the other Australian regions would look like if the RUN-member regional campuses did not operate in their respective SA3 regions (i.e. the hypothetical or counterfactual scenario). When each campus is removed we assume that a share of university activities are relocated elsewhere in Australia. We conduct a counterfactual simulation that provides the long-run effects of such a hypothetical removal and partial relocation.

The implied assumption underlying this simulation is that it incorporates full adjustment to this hypothetical removal and partial relocation, thus mimicking the counterfactual of each RUN-member University having had no regional campuses for many years.[11] Hence, we assume that the aggregate level of Australian employment is unaffected by the presence of any RUN-member University's regional campus. Instead, the aggregate level of Australian employment is dependent in the long run on demographic and industrial relations factors. At the national level the real wage adjusts to accommodate this. At the regional level, labour is imperfectly mobile. This means that as a region's labour market weakens relative to other regions, regional adjustment occurs through a combination of migration to other regions, higher regional unemployment and lower real wages than other regions in the long run.

The rate of return on capital for each regional industry is assumed not to be affected by the location of RUN-member University regional campuses in the long run. Rather, rates of return are modelled as being dependent on the world interest rate level. Investment in individual regional industries is assumed to move approximately in line with changes in their long-run capital stocks.

To simulate the removal of RUN-member regional campuses, we introduce shocks to the model that reflect the effects that a campus' presence has on regional demand and supply as described in Sect. 13.2, as well as the effects on the Rest of Australia when a portion of university activities are relocated. We reduce demand in each region by the aggregate of expenditures by all domestic and overseas students studying via internal and external mode, by introducing the shocks to VU-TERM detailed in Table 13.7. For example, in simulating removal of CQU's Rockhampton campus, we reduce demand for processed food products by 1.08%, the share of total spending in Rockhampton on processed food products accounted for by domestic students. Shocks to reflect the absence of overseas students are reflected in the final "ExpEdu" column. Notice how the shocks in Table 13.7 reflect the characteristics of enrolments in Table 13.3: Shocks are larger in the region's dominant campus (i.e. Rockhampton for CQU or Sippy Downs for USC) and much smaller for the regional campuses with small enrolments. While Sippy Downs at USC and Rockhampton at CQU have a comparable number of intra- and inter-state students, a larger share at Sippy Downs study via internal mode while most at Rockhampton study via external mode. As a result, the negative demand shocks are larger at Sippy Downs than Rockhampton. Finally, we assume that when a RUN-member regional campus is removed, ¼ of the students study elsewhere in Australia, and introduce shocks that increase demand in the Rest of Australia by ¼ of the aggregate of expenditures by all domestic and overseas students at the campus that closes.

To simulate the changes in labour productivity due to a removal of the RUN-member regional campuses, we construct negative productivity shocks by dividing the product of the wage premium and our estimates of graduates working in each region in Table 13.5 by the value of regional employment. As with the demand shocks, we assume that ¼ of RUN-member graduates represented in

[11] Recall that the research productivity effect was calculated using discounted research income back to 1992, a sufficient period to justify the counterfactual of each RUN-member University having had no regional campus for many years.

Table 13.7 Demand shocks due to RUN-member campus removal

		Primary	Food Prods	Alco Smokes	Hhold Goods	Clothing Ftwr	Car Costs	Transport	Air Transport	Owner Dwellng	Oth Education	Tertiary Edu	Health	Child ComCare	Recreat Enttn	Exp Edu
CQU	Rockhampton	0.00	−1.08	−0.86	−0.02	−0.35	−0.20	−0.11	−0.40	−0.25	−0.53	−0.27	−0.19	0.00	−0.18	−35.41
	Mackay	0.00	−0.04	−0.05	0.00	−0.02	−0.01	−0.01	−0.02	−0.02	−0.04	−0.02	−0.02	0.00	−0.02	−13.51
	Gladstone	0.00	−0.01	−0.01	0.00	−0.01	0.00	0.00	−0.01	0.00	−0.01	−0.01	−0.01	0.00	0.00	0.00
	Bundaberg	0.00	−0.10	−0.10	0.00	−0.05	−0.02	−0.02	−0.05	−0.04	−0.10	−0.05	−0.03	0.00	−0.03	−52.28
	Emerald	0.00	−0.02	−0.02	0.00	−0.01	0.00	0.00	−0.01	−0.02	−0.02	−0.01	−0.01	0.00	−0.01	0.00
	Townsville	0.00	0.00	0.00	0.00	0.00	0.00	0.00	0.00	0.00	0.00	0.00	0.00	0.00	0.00	0.00
	Cairns	0.00	−0.01	−0.01	0.00	0.00	0.00	0.00	0.00	−0.01	−0.01	0.00	0.00	0.00	0.00	0.00
	Noosa	0.00	−0.12	−0.08	0.00	−0.02	−0.03	−0.03	−0.03	−0.11	−0.18	−0.08	−0.06	0.00	−0.06	−7.08
FED	Ballarat	0.00	−2.65	−1.79	−0.08	−1.00	−0.46	−0.52	−1.01	−1.57	−1.29	−0.62	−0.39	0.00	−1.72	−32.90
	Churchill	0.00	−1.17	−0.73	−0.02	−0.43	−0.19	−0.16	−0.41	−0.62	−0.39	−0.20	−0.11	0.00	−0.65	−8.89
	Horsham	0.00	0.00	0.00	0.00	0.00	0.00	0.00	0.00	0.00	0.00	0.00	0.00	0.00	0.00	0.00
SCU	Lismore	0.00	−1.96	−1.80	−0.07	−0.79	−0.35	−0.76	−0.78	−1.03	−1.65	−0.88	−0.67	0.00	−1.17	−26.17
	Gold Coast	0.00	−2.46	−1.69	−0.05	−0.74	−0.54	−0.43	−0.70	−1.91	−2.32	−0.88	−0.86	0.00	−1.44	−32.69
	Coffs Harbour	0.00	−0.41	−0.23	−0.01	−0.08	−0.05	−0.10	−0.09	−0.20	−0.21	−0.13	−0.08	0.00	−0.18	−19.06
UNE	Armidale	0.00	−9.31	−5.30	−0.23	−2.18	−1.26	−2.76	−2.10	−2.61	−5.30	−1.74	−2.44	0.00	−2.92	−35.99
USQ	Toowoomba	0.00	−1.36	−1.14	−0.03	−0.61	−0.26	−0.18	−0.54	−0.41	−0.59	−0.23	−0.22	0.00	−0.32	−19.45
	Springfield/ Ipswich	0.00	−0.33	−0.28	−0.01	−0.16	−0.06	−0.04	−0.13	−0.23	−0.22	−0.11	−0.08	0.00	−0.21	−22.17
USC	Sippy Downs	0.00	−9.15	−6.90	−0.20	−3.20	−1.92	−1.76	−3.24	−6.85	−8.65	−2.58	−3.31	0.00	−6.14	−31.79
	Gympie	0.00	−0.07	−0.06	0.00	−0.03	−0.01	−0.01	−0.03	−0.02	−0.07	−0.03	−0.02	0.00	−0.02	0.00
	Fraser Coast	0.00	−0.30	−0.21	−0.01	−0.09	−0.06	−0.05	−0.11	−0.17	−0.29	−0.14	−0.10	0.00	−0.14	−10.94

Source: Author calculations

Table 13.8 Supply shocks due to RUN-member campus removal (%)

		Labour product	Research product			Labour product	Research product
CQU	Rockhampton	3.33	0.0018	SCU	Lismore	2.07	0.0025
	Mackay	0.11	0.0018		Gold Coast	0.94	0.0025
	Gladstone	0.04	0.0018		Coffs Harbour	0.29	0.0025
	Bundaberg	0.18	0.0018	UNE	Armidale	3.28	0.0056
	Emerald	0.00	0.0018	USQ	Toowoomba	1.96	0.0021
	Townsville	0.01	0.0018		Springfield/ Ipswich	0.13	0.0021
	Cairns	0.00	0.0018	USC	Sippy Downs	2.62	0.0015
	Noosa	0.16	0.0018		Gympie	0.03	0.0015
FED	Ballarat	1.57	0.0011		Fraser Coast	0.13	0.0015
	Churchill	0.23	0.0011				
	Horsham	0.03	0.0011				

Source: Author calculations

Table 13.5 would work in the Rest of Australia upon closure of the RUN-member regional campus and apply a positive labour productivity shock to the Rest of Australia region.

Finally, the counterfactual assumes that when the RUN-member University campus is relocated, only ¼ of the returns to the stock of research knowledge are retained. Since we assume that the returns to the stock of research knowledge are shared equally across all regions in Australia, removal of any of the RUN-member universities implies the same negative shock to research productivity in all regions in Australia (Table 13.8).

13.3.1 Simulation Results

The values of the economic effects that the presence of the regional campuses of RUN-member Universities have on their region are detailed in this section (real consumption and GDP results are reported graphically in Fig. 13.2 near the end of the chapter). All tables report results where only ¼ of the labour and research productivity effects is retained in some other region(s) in the counterfactual simulation.[12] Table 13.9 reports results for the simulation of removing the Central

[12] As a less conservative counterfactual simulation, we also run simulations in which ¾ of the students in RUN campuses would study elsewhere in Australia. Consequently, ¾ of the labour productivity effects accrue to other regions in Australia, and ¾ of the returns to the stock of research knowledge are retained. For directly affected campus regions, the two assumptions generate almost identical impacts. This is so because we effectively assume that of the ¼ or ¾ of the residents who

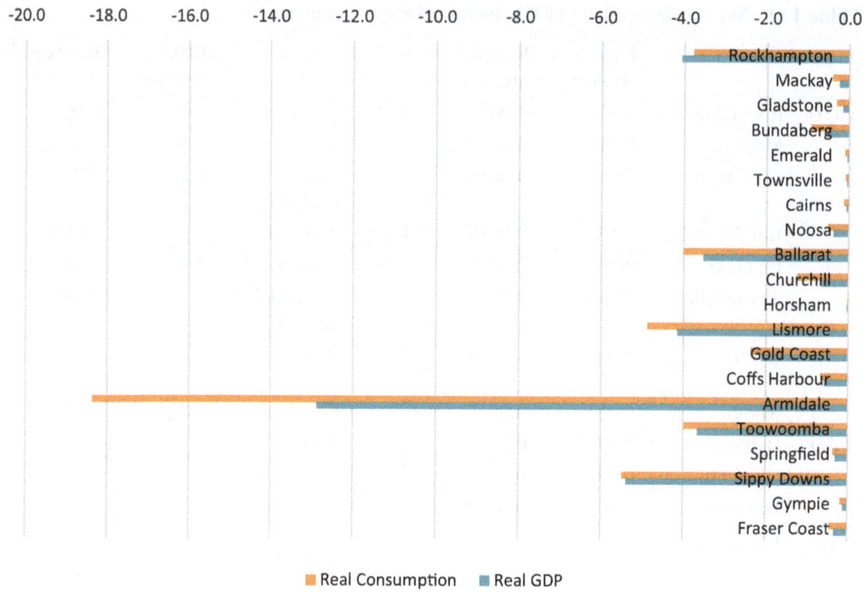

Fig. 13.2 Real GDP and consumption by campus (%Δ from base)

Queensland University's campus. Tables 13.10 and 13.11 report results for the other five RUN-member University campuses. All variables are reported in percentage changes, except real GDP results are also reported in $ million and employment in full-time equivalent workers.

The employment loss in the long run in Rockhampton relative to retaining the campus is similar to direct campus job losses. 2016 ABS census data indicate that 2% of Rockhampton's workforce is employed in the tertiary education sector. Input–output analysis, which assumes quantity adjustments without price or wage adjustments, would result in local employment multipliers and hence larger local job losses. But in VU-TERM, the long run adjustment to regional labour market weakening due to campus removal entails a combination of migration out of the region and a decline in regional real wages relative to national real wages. That is, we do not assume that the regional labour market adjustment is perfectly elastic, in

study elsewhere, none returns to their region of origin. That is, when CQU's Rockhampton campus closes, ¼ of those who studied there go on to study elsewhere in Australia, but none returns to Rockhampton after completing their studies. This is likely to be not too far from observed patterns of youth migration. For example, Hillman and Rothman (2007) note that over the period 1997–2004, "... just under three-quarters (74%) of non-metropolitan young people in 1997 were still in non-metropolitan areas". If we accounted for the small share of the 26% of those who were not in non-metropolitan areas and returned to Rockhampton (for example), this would slightly mitigate the losses reported for CQU-Rockhampton in Table 13.9, more so if the share of graduates who studied elsewhere was assumed to be ¾. In the rest of Australia, the two assumptions provide proportionally different impacts but they are both small in percentage terms.

Table 13.9 Effects of CQU campus removal on regional macroeconomic variables (% change from base)

Central Queensland University	Rockhampton	Mackay	Gladstone	Bundaberg	Emerald	Townsville	Cairns	Noosa
Real private consumption	−3.8	−0.4	−0.3	−0.9	−0.1	−0.1	−0.1	−0.5
Real private investment	−3.2	−0.2	−0.1	−0.6	0.0	−0.1	−0.1	−0.5
Average real wage	−1.9	−0.2	−0.2	−0.5	−0.1	0.0	−0.1	−0.3
Aggregate employment	−1.9	−0.2	−0.2	−0.5	0.0	0.0	−0.1	−0.2
Agg. Employment (units)	−870	−97	−38	−133	−5	−29	−22	−39
Capital stocks	−2.9	−0.2	−0.1	−0.4	−0.1	−0.1	−0.1	−0.3
Real GDP	−4.1	−0.2	−0.2	−0.5	0.0	−0.1	−0.1	−0.4
Real GDP ($ million)	−328	−22	−9	−22	−1	−7	−4	−8
GDP price index	0.5	−0.1	−0.1	−0.4	0.0	0.0	−0.1	−0.2
GNE price index	0.2	−0.1	0.0	−0.2	0.0	0.0	0.0	−0.1
Real disposable income	−3.8	−0.3	−0.2	−0.7	−0.1	−0.1	−0.1	−0.4

Source: Model simulations

Table 13.10 Effects of campus removal on regional macro variables: FED and SCU

	Federation U.			Southern Cross U.		
	Ballarat	Churchill	Horsham	Lismore	Gold Coast	Coffs Harbour
Real private consumption	−4.0	−1.2	0.0	−4.9	−2.4	−0.7
Real private investment	−4.5	−0.6	0.0	−5.3	−3.3	−0.8
Average real wage	−2.0	−0.6	0.0	−2.5	−1.2	−0.3
Agg. Employment	−2.0	−0.6	0.0	−2.5	−1.2	−0.3
Agg. Employment (units)	−875	−172	−3	−639	−271	−108
Capital stocks	−3.2	−0.5	0.0	−3.4	−2.1	−0.5
Real GDP	−3.5	−0.7	0.0	−4.2	−2.1	−0.6
Real GDP ($ million)	−198	−32	−1	−137	−65	−25
GDP price index	−1.3	−0.5	0.0	−1.3	−1.1	−0.2
GNE price index	−0.8	−0.3	0.0	−0.8	−0.7	−0.1
Real disposable income	−4.1	−0.9	0.0	−4.7	−2.5	−0.7

Table 13.11 Effects of campus closures on regional macro variables: UNE, USQ, USC

	U. New England	U. Southern Queensland		U. Sunshine Coast		
	Armidale	Toowoomba	Springfield	Sippy Downs	Gympie	Fraser Coast
Real private consumption	−18.4	−4.0	−0.4	−5.5	−0.2	−0.4
Real private investment	−17.7	−3.9	−0.4	−7.7	−0.1	−0.4
Average real wage	−9.6	−2.0	−0.2	−2.8	−0.1	−0.2
Agg. Employment	−9.6	−2.0	−0.2	−2.8	−0.1	−0.2
Agg. Employment (units)	−1412	−1243	−133	−646	−15	−38
Capital stocks	−11.2	−3.1	−0.3	−5.7	−0.1	−0.3
Real GDP	−12.9	−3.7	−0.3	−5.4	−0.1	−0.3
Real GDP ($ million)	−244	−352	−36	−170	−3	−7
GDP price index	−7.7	−1.0	−0.2	−2.3	−0.1	−0.2
GNE price index	−4.7	−0.6	−0.1	−1.6	0.0	−0.1
Real disposable income	−15.9	−4.0	−0.4	−6.1	−0.1	−0.4

Source: Model simulations

which case real wages would adjust by the same percentage across all regions. The lower real wage in Rockhampton (−1.9%, Table 13.9) relative to the national wage (−0.1%, not shown) in the long run alleviates to some extent regional job losses.

We can explain regional real GDP using a back of the envelope equation: GDP = f(K,L,1/A), where K is capital stocks, L aggregate regional employment, and 1/A productivity. In Rockhampton, L accounts for 53% of GDP on the income side and K 28%. The remaining 19% of income side GDP arises from land (unchanged) and indirect taxes (which change with economic activity). The contribution of primary factor losses to the overall GDP loss is only 1.8% [=0.53 · −1.9% + 0.28 · −2.9%] out of a total real GDP loss of 4.1%. In addition, there is a labour productivity decline in the region of 3.3%, which contributes an additional loss of 1.7% [=0.53 · −3.3%]. Most of the remaining loss arises from falling productivity associated specifically with the campus. Our assumption is that there is sharp fall in productivity of tertiary-education-specific labour and residual capital following campus removals. In Rockhampton, these industry-specific productivity losses account for most of the residual GDP losses (0.5%).

We also observe adjustment in the local housing market in the long run due to campus removals. These adjustments occur through a combination of falling prices and falling investment, which in turn leads to a reduction in the housing stock. House prices in Rockhampton fall by 3.4%, while the housing stock falls in quantity by 4.8% relative to base.

Results from Tables 13.10 and 13.11 show a similar pattern for other RUN-member campuses. For each RUN-member university's dominant campus, real GDP falls by 3.5–5.4%, and aggregate employment falls by 2.0–2.8%. For the smaller satellite campuses, real GDP and employment changes are typically much smaller than 1.0%. As expected, the University of New England's campus at Armidale is an outlier, contributing almost 13.0% to Armidale's regional GDP and 9.6% to regional employment.

13.4 Conclusion

While the majority of Australia's 40 universities have their major campuses located in large cities, typically state capitals, university campuses can be found now in many smaller Australian cities in what is often referred to as "regional" Australia. Six universities, which have their major campus outside the state capitals, and which generally have a number of other campuses located in cities and towns in rural areas, established the Regional Universities Network in 2011. RUN considers its member universities as important contributors to the economy of the region in which they are located. In this chapter we have undertaken CGE simulations to estimate the degree to which this is so.

Our approach to estimating a university's contribution to a regional economy is to simulate the situation where the university had not been established in the region. The difference between this counterfactual and the actual regional economy is taken as the university's regional economic contribution.

The shocks required to undertake the counterfactual cover the effects of the university on both the demand-side and the supply-side of the regional economy. The demand-side shocks relate to the demands generated by the university's operation, expenditure by out-of-region and retained students, and other associated demands. The demand-side effects are thus similar to other industries that involve induced tourism. Demand-side effects essentially act to pull resources into a region from other areas of the nation. Thus, while they may be important to the economy of the region itself, they have little impact at the national level.

The other set of shocks relates to the supply-side of the economy and relate to the effects of university study on human capital and in turn on labour productivity and to university research on all-factor productivity. To the degree that regional universities add to national skill acquisition and the stock of research knowledge, these supply-side effects do affect the economy at the national level. At the regional level, they affect both the university's own region and the regions to which these "knowledge" effects spill out, via inter-state migration of graduates and the typically public-good nature of research knowledge.

Simulations are conducted with the VU-TERM model, which for the current study is decomposed into 24 regions, of which 20 correspond to the SA3 regions in which RUN campuses are located. In estimating the shocks, we use data related to the RUN universities' cost structures, student numbers by home region and student living expenses information, numbers graduating and their post-graduation destinations, wage premia after allowing for returns to signalling, and HERDC and ABS information on externally funded research by RUN campuses and total (including general academic research) research expenditure, respectively.

The simulations show that RUN universities make a substantial contribution to those regions in which each university's major campus is located. Typical contributions are around 3–4% of these regions' value added and about 2–3% of regional employment. Satellite campuses tend to be smaller relative to the regional economies in which they are located. The effects of these campuses on the gross regional output of their local economies vary between 0.1 and 2.4% and are typically around half a per cent or less.

The one clear exception to these results is for Armidale, a university-town in which the University of New England (UNE) forms a major component of the city's total economic activity. UNE is shown to contribute almost 13% to gross regional output and almost 10% to regional employment. Nonetheless, while the contribution of RUN campuses varies across different campus locations, we can conclude that the cuts in the federal funding to Australian universities that were reviewed in the introduction could have important negative impacts on regions that host a RUN-member university campus.

Appendix

Table 13.12 Aggregated industries/commodities in VU-TERM

Name	Description of major activity
1. Primary	Primary products: Agriculture, mining, forestry, fishing
2. FoodProds	Processed food products
3. AlcoSmokes	Alcohol and tobacco
4. HholdGoods	Manufactured goods
5. ClothingFtwr	Clothing and footwear
6. CarCosts	Motor vehicles, petrol, car repairs
7. Utilities	Electricity, gas water
8. OthService	Other services
9. Transport	Transport services other than air transport services
10. AirTransport	Air transportation services
11. OwnerDwellng	Ownership of dwellings
12. OthEducation	Education other than tertiary education
13. TertiaryEdu	Tertiary education
14. Health	Health care services
15. ChildComCare	Child, aged and disabled care services
16. RecreatEnttn	Libraries, museums, art, sports, gambling
17. ExpEdu	Exports-of-education

Table 13.13 RUN-member university campuses, SA3 region, and postcodes (local postcode in bold)

University	Campus	SA3	Intra-region postcodes
CQU	Rockhampton	30,803	4699; 4700; 4701; **4702**; 4703; 4704; 4706; 4710; 4711; 4714
	Mackay	31,202	4737; 4738; **4740; 4741**; 4750; 4751; 4753; 4754; 4756; 4757; 4798; 4799
	Gladstone	30,802	4420; 4674; 4676; 4677; 4678; **4680**; 4694; 4695; 4697; 4715; 4716; 4718; 4719
	Bundaberg	31,901	4660; **4670**; 4673
	Emerald	30,801	4709; 4712; 4713; 4717; **4720**; 4722; 4723
	Townsville	31,802	**4810**; 4811; 4812; 4813; 4814; 4815; 4816; 4817; 4818; 4819
	Cairns	30,602	4865; 4868; 4869; **4870**
	Noosaville/ Noosa	31,605	4565; **4566**; 4567
Federation University	Ballarat	20,101	**3350**; 3351; 3352; 3355; 3356; 3357
	Churchill	20,504	3825; 3840; **3842**; 3844; 3854; 3856; 3869; 3870
	Horsham	21,501	3317; 3318; 3319; 3374; 3375; 3377; 3378; 3379; 3380; 3381; 3384; 3385; 3387;

(continued)

Table 13.13 (continued)

University	Campus	SA3	Intra-region postcodes
			3388; 3390; 3391; 3392; 3393; 3395; 3396; 3400; 3401; 3409; 3412; 3413; 3414;
			3415; 3418; 3419; 3420; 3423; 3424; 3477; 3478; 3485; 3487; 3488; 3489; 3491
Southern Cross	Lismore	11,202	2469; 2470; 2471; 2474; 2476; **2480**
	Gold Coast	30,902	4221; 4223; 4224; **4225**
	Coffs Harbour	10,402	**2450**; 2452; 2453; 2454; 2455; 2456
U New England	Armidale	11,001	2350; **2351**; 2354; 2358; 2365
U Sth. Queensland	Toowoomba	31,701	4343; 4344; 4345; 4347; **4350**; 4352; 4358; 4400
	Springfield/ Ipswich	31,003; 31,004	**4300**; 4301; 4303; 4304; 4305; 4306
U Sunshine Coast	Sippy Downs	31,601	**4556**; 4557
	Gympie/ Amamoor	31,903	**4570**; 4580; 4581; 4600; 4601
	Fraser Coast/ Wide Bay	31,904	**4655**

References

ABC News (2018) CGS estimates of base funding for Australian universities. Australian Broadcasting Corporation, https://assets.documentcloud.org/documents/4515140/CGS-estimates-of-base-funding-for-Australian.pdf

Dalziel P, Saunders C, Kaye-Blake W (2009) The role of universities in theories of regional development. In: Rowe JE (ed) Theories of local economic development: linking theory to practice. Ashgate, Farnham

Drucker J, Goldstein H (2007) Assessing the regional economic development impacts of universities: a review of current approaches. Int Reg Sci Rev 30:20–46

Feldman M, Desrochers P (2003) Research universities and local economic development: lessons from the history of the John Hopkins University. Ind Innov 10:5–24

Florax R (1992) The university: a regional booster? Economic impacts of academic knowledge infrastructure. Avebury, Aldershot

Fritsch M, Slavtchev V (2007) Universities and innovation in space. Ind Innov 14(2):201–218

Giesecke JA, Madden JR (2006) A CGE evaluation of a university's effects on a regional economy: an integrated assessment of expenditure and knowledge impacts. Rev Urban Reg Dev Stud 18: 229–251

Harris R, Li QC, Moffat J (2011) The impact of higher education institution-firm knowledge links on firm-level productivity in Britain. Appl Econ Lett 18:1243–1246

Henderson JV (2007) Understanding knowledge spillovers. Reg Sci Urban Econ 37:497–508

Hermannsson K, Lisenkova K, Lecca P, Swales JK, McGregor PG (2014) The regional economic impact of more graduates in the labour market: a 'micro-to-macro' analysis for Scotland. Environ Plan A 46:471–487

Hillman K, Rothman S (2007) Movement of non-metropolitan youth towards the cities, LSAY Research Reports, Longitudinal surveys of Australian youth research report n.50., https://research.acer.edu.au/lsay_research/54

Leigh A (2008) Returns to higher education in Australia. Econ Pap 27(3):233–249
Madden JR (2014) The economic effects of an expansion in the Queensland university sector. In: Report for the University of Queensland. Centre of Policy Studies, Victoria University, Melbourne
Madden JR (2017) University location and city development: the effects of Victoria University on the Western Melbourne economy. In: Centre of Policy Studies Working Paper G-272. Victoria University, Melbourne. http://www.copsmodels.com/elecpapr/g-272.htm
McMahon W (2009) Higher learning, greater good. The Private and Social Benefits of Higher Education, John Hopkins University Press, Baltimore
Uyarra E (2010) Conceptualising the regional roles of universities, implications and contradictions. Eur Plan Stud 18:1227–1246
Western M, Boreham P, Laffan W, Haynes M, Chesters J, Tighe M, Arts D (2005) Survey of international students' spending in Australia, UQSRC report to the Department of Education, Science & Training. Brisbane, University of Queensland Social Research Centre
Wittwer G (ed) (2012) Economic modeling of water: the Australian CGE experience. Springer, Dordrecht
Wittwer G (ed) (2017) Multi-regional dynamic general equilibrium modeling of the U.S. economy. Springer, Cham

Chapter 14
Financial Literacy and Consumer Debt: An Empirical Analysis Based on the CHFS Data

Cheng Tang

Abstract Against the backdrop of the rapidly expanding household debt in China, we have conducted this empirical analysis of the relationship between financial literacy and consumer debt. This paper focuses on the purpose of household borrowing, based on the data from Chinese Household Finance Survey (CHFS) data, and examines how exactly financial literacy affects actual household and consumer debt. This paper shows how financial literacy affects actual household debt accumulation and distribution. The main findings of the paper are as follows: (1) higher financial literacy is linked to household debt, but lower financial literacy correlates with excessive debt, which suggests that financial literacy helps households to rationally manage their assets, thereby effectively controlling household debt risk and reducing the risk of excessive debt. (2) Financial literacy has a strong positive impact on consumer debt, which has serious implications for the rapidly expanding household consumer finance market. Our study means that high level of financial literacy can push up consumer debt and in the process contribute to the expansion of the consumption market. Therefore, improving financial literacy can promote healthy borrowing behavior and reduce the risks associated with consumer finance and financial markets as a whole.

Keywords Financial literacy · Consumer finance · Consumer debt

14.1 Introduction

The borrowing behavior of a household, along with its asset allocation, is among the most important household financial activities. Based on the data from Chinese Household Finance Survey (CHFS), this paper demonstrates, through empirical analysis, how financial literacy influences household borrowing behavior, especially

C. Tang (✉)
Chuo University, Tokyo, Japan
e-mail: tang@tamacc.chuo-u.ac.jp

M. Kawano et al. (eds.), *Theory and History in Regional Perspective*, New Frontiers in Regional Science: Asian Perspectives 56,
https://doi.org/10.1007/978-981-16-6695-7_14

Table 14.1 Structural changes of household assets and liabilities

	2015	2017
Debt household ratio (%)	27.93	27.82
Debt balance (10,000 yuan)	3.5284	4.2325
Owning house (number of houses)	1.1169	1.1373
Net assets (10,000 yuan)	75.3543	93.845
(1) Business debt (10,000 yuan)	0.8862	0.9357
(2) Housing debt (10,000 yuan)	2.1873	2.7347
(3) Consumer debt (10,000 yuan)	0.1981	0.3800

Source: Estimated by the authors based on 24,679 identical households in CHFS 2015 and CHFS 2017

with regard to consumption debts, and explores factors that have contributed to the rapid expansion of household debts from the angle of financial literacy.

Some people have argued that household borrowing has the effect of balancing household consumption and contributing to economic growth, but excessive debts will function as a brake on household consumption and slow down economic growth by reducing demands (Note 1). It is still fresh in our memories that the Global Financial Crisis was triggered by the US subprime debts. Against this backdrop, there have been increasing concerns among economists and policymakers, both inside and outside China, over the rapid increase in the debt size of not only the corporate sector, but also the household sector in China in recent years (Tian et al. 2018; IMF 2018, etc.).

So, what is the current state of household debt in China? According to The People's Bank of China (PBC) and International Monetary Fund (IMF), China's total household debt expanded rapidly from 5.7 trillion yuan in 2007 to 46.8 trillion yuan in 2018, exceeding 41 trillion yuan in just 11 years, with the debt to GDP ratio also jumping from 19.1 to 52.4% during the same period. Not only macroeconomic data, but also microeconomic data from CHFS collected during the 2015 and 2017 period confirm the trend of household debt expansion.

Table 14.1 shows our estimate of the consequences that may result from changes in household debt pattern. In 2015, there were 27.93% families with debts. By 2017, the percentage dropped to 27.82%. Although the number fell by just 0.11 points, the amount of debt increased from an average of 32,716 yuan per household in 2015 to 40,504 yuan per household in 2017, which is a significant increase by 7788 yuan. If we further divide household debts according to their purposes, there are roughly three main categories: business debt, mortgage debt, and consumer debt. Of the 7788 yuan increase, 495 yuan goes to business debt, 5474 yuan to mortgage debt, and 1819 yuan for consumer debt. We have noted that the amount of debts related to business debt dropped from 27.08% in the total amount of debts in 2015 to 23.10% in 2017, falling by 3.98%, whereas housing and consumption related debts over the same period increased from 66.85% to 67.52%, a jump of 6.06% and 9.38%, respectively, during the two-year period.

An examination of the changes in the size of debt for the same household during the two-year period shows that although the number of households incurring debts decreased slightly, the debt size actually increased. As is illustrated by Table 14.1, housing debt contributes most to debt increase because both housing prices and homeownership per household have been on the rise, which pushes up housing debt. The same table also shows that consumption related debts doubled in the last two years. Although the percentage of consumption related debts is still relatively low in the overall household debts, the rate of its increase is next only to housing debts. The increase in consumption related debts has to do with two major developments since the 2010s: first, the growth in consumer credit market; and second, the rapid popularization of smartphones and related technologies, such as artificial intelligence and service platform based on big data.

It seems clear that consumption related debt is the major contributing factor to the increase in household debt size in recent years. However, borrowing behavior involves a complex decision-making process which is subject to influence from both the general economic climate and family financial constraints. For instance, a family may have to consider the size of the debt it can afford when purchasing a house, or the best way to use credit card, which is considered as consumption finance in China, to purchase durable goods (Wu et al. 2018). Apparently, to fully engage in this decision-making process requires financial literacy to calculate the affordable amount of debts, the interest rate, and the terms and conditions of the debts.

After the 2008 Global Financial Crisis, there has been a growing consensus among economists on the importance of financial literacy for consumers when it comes to borrowing, so much so that Lusardi and Tufano (2015) have even argued that inadequate financial literacy is responsible for the excessive household debt in the USA. The objective of this paper is to investigate if financial literacy influences household borrowing behavior, particularly in the area of consumption debt, and if so, in what ways. I hope to explore reasons for the rise in household debts in recent years by focusing on the role played by financial literacy.

To address these questions, I have carefully studied the CHFS data and found some characteristics in the debt structure that have emerged among the Chinese households in recent years. I will demonstrate, with empirical evidence, how household borrowing behavior, especially with regard to consumption related debts, is influenced by financial literacy.

This paper will consist of three parts: Part one reviews previous studies on the subject and provides a conceptual framework for the discussion about the relationship between financial literacy and household debts; part two proposes a hypothesis after surveying the statistics and conducting a descriptive data analysis; and part three proceeds with empirical case study, hypothesis testing, robustness test, and endogeneity test. Finally, at the end of the paper, I will provide a summary of the study, its intellectual contribution and the remaining issues in need of further research.

14.2 Literature Review

Although the term "financial literacy" has never been clearly defined, conventional wisdom tends to regard it as part of human capital, which entails not only the human ability to understand economic and financial information, but also the ability to process and make use of that information (Huang et al. 2009; Lusardi et al. 2017). In other words, financial literacy refers to common sense about finance, understanding of the basic financial concepts, and the ability to acquire, process, and apply knowledge about finance (Huston 2010)—all of which are necessary prerequisites to improve the quality of one's life.

Previous studies have established the connection between financial literacy and household needs for financing as well as its borrowing behavior by focusing on the following issues: First, household with improved financial literacy will have better understanding of the policies governing the consumer financial market and the borrowing processes, which leads to greater willingness to borrow and higher demand for debts. For example, households making efforts to collect information about the lenders will have higher success rate in securing loans (Akudugu et al., 2009).

Second, improved financial literacy will allow households to use financial means to create economic opportunities for themselves, especially when there are not enough innovation and investment opportunities. For example, households may want to use loans to invest in the financial markets (Van Rooij et al., 2011) or to start new businesses (Oseifuah 2010). When that happens, there will be greater demand for loans. It is safe to assume that financial literacy will help household to accumulate wealth, enhance its ability to pay off debts, and gives household better chance to secure a loan from well-established financial institutions (Lusardi and Mitchell 2007). Third, households with advanced financial literacy are better positioned to maintain good credit records, which in turn will make it easier for them to borrow more easily in the future (Kidwell and Turrisi 2004).

Although household borrowing behavior in China is not adequately studied, scholars have begun to pay attention to the issue in recent years (Song et al. 2017; Wu et al. 2018). There are two possible reasons for this increased scholarly attention to this area. First, the rapid expansion of household debt in recent years has attracted academic attention to this phenomenon. After the 2008 global financial crisis, some people have argued that households with insufficient financial literacy are more likely burdened by excessive debt. For example, Lusardi and Tufano have pinpointed the low financial literacy as an important contributing factor to the excessive debts among the US households (Lusardi and Tufano 2015). Their observation is supported by Disney and Gathergood with empirical research (Disney and Gathergood 2013) and confirmed by an analysis of Chinese data as well (Wu et al. 2018).

For the Chinese economy undergoing a transitional period, increasing household consumption through the mechanism of consumer financial market has serious policy implications. Some economists are of the view that financial literacy is a crucial factor in explaining households' borrowing behavior and increased consumption. For this reason, improving financial literacy is a necessity for a household's economic well-being (Song et al. 2017). Studies have shown that higher level of financial literacy not only improves the chances for households to take on loans, but also places households in better position to secure loans from reputable and well-established financial institutions and reduced the possibility of excessive debt (Wu et al. 2018). It should be noted that financial literacy seems irrelevant in decisions concerning short-term debt. In general, higher financial literacy is linked to an overall lower households' borrowing rate and higher percentage of the debts used for housing (Wu et al. 2019).

Since the 2010s, as the consumer finance business model has further developed and became more mature, services related to consumer finance are provided by four major players which compete with each other for business. They include state owned commercial banks, consumption oriented financial companies (Mashang Consumer Finance, Haiercash, Bank of Beijing Consumer Finance Company, and Bank of China Consumer Finance, internet based banks (aka. BATJ such as Baidu–Alibaba–Tencent–JD.com), and online financing platform (aka. P2P—peer-to-peer lending) (Note 2).

It is generally agreed that the development of the consumer finance market tends to promote the diversification of the market for household consumption. Modern families and individuals use loans for a variety of purposes. In addition to purchasing homes and cars, people also take loans to pay for durable goods such as home appliances and furniture, as well as for education, travel expenses, medical bills, and cosmetic services. In fact, studies based on empirical data have shown that financial literacy can increase a household's consumer credit worthiness (Song et al. 2019) and is considered a form of human capital which is closely related to consumer's borrowing behavior. Moreover, consumers with advanced financial literacy are more likely to utilize internet financial service (Yin and Qiu 2019). Their knowledge of the available financial services on the internet reduces the cost of borrowing for them and hence increases their willingness to borrow (Xiang and Guo 2019).

Although previous studies show that financial literacy is an important explanatory factor for Chinese households' borrowing behavior, most of them focus only on two types of lenders: legitimate and regulated financial institutions and non-regulated informal lending sources (Song et al. 2017; Peng, 2019; Wu et al. 2018), which may include relatives or other private lenders that charge high-interest rates. This latter type of lending practice is not subject to official oversight and supervision and usually predatory in nature, complex in practice, and opaque to outsiders.

Given the rapid development in the consumer finance market, the conventional focus on only two types of lenders is no longer helpful to our accurate understanding of the precise degree to which financial literacy influences household borrowing behavior. As consumer/borrower becomes increasingly diversified, so do the sources of financial service providers, as evidenced by the emergence of non-traditional lenders, such as BATJ and P2P. Therefore, we need to have a more accurate assessment of the degree to which financial literacy influences household debts.

To date, no previous studies have grasped the reality of the rapid increase in the size of household debt in recent years and the reasons behind this development.

For example, typical of this oversight in previous studies, the analysis of sample data of 6878 from 24 cities by Wu et al. (2018) are from the 2010–2011 period, which is outdated. A similar study by Wu et al. (2019) uses only 4503 valid samples from two surveys (aka. China Consumer Finance Survey and Investor Education Survey) conducted in 2011. Neither of them has offered explanation for the rapid growth in household debt and the statistics cited in both studies are not sufficient to be used as the basis to make generalization about overall state of financial market in China.

This paper can supplement previous studies by making the following contributions: first, the empirical data for this study are collected from the whole country, rather than from a few cities or regions; second, this paper approaches the impact of financial literacy on household consumption debt from a new angle, which focuses on how loans are used. This approach helps us understand what drives the rapidly expanding consumer financial market and, for the first time, illustrates beyond any doubt the important role played by financial literacy in household debt in the fiercely competitive consumer financial market.

It is our hope that this study, with its novel approach, will help us better assess the risk factors for both the borrowers and the lenders, contribute to the development of a stable financial system, and provide guidance for policymakers who want to promote sustainable economic growth through encouraging household consumption.

14.3 Summary of the Data and Descriptive Analysis of the Statistics

The empirical basis of this paper is the Chinese Household Finance Survey (CHFS) conducted by Xinan University of Finance and Economics in 2015 and 2017. With the notable exceptions of Xinjiang and the Tibetan regions, these surveys cover 29 provinces, cities, and regions that include 363 counties and 1439 villages, both urban and rural households. The effective sample sizes of 37,289 and 40,011 are produced by the three-tier PPS sampling method. This data includes information about the population (gender, age, household composition, and housing arrangement), household assets and liabilities, insurance, and safety net.

The primary objective of this paper is to explore how financial literacy affects borrowing behavior with regard to consumption debt which involves two most important variables: household consumer debt and financial literacy. A related issue concerns the relationship between household debt, excess debt, and financial literacy. The term "household consumer debt" means all debts other than mortgage and self-employed business debts, which include loans taken for cars, education, and other durable consumer goods. Financial literacy is measured by the rate of correct answer to the three questions prepared by CHFS. The following section describes the

Table 14.2 Responses to financial literacy question items (2015)

	Correct answer rate (%)	Wrong answer rate (%)	"Unknown" selection rate (%)
Interest calculation ability	28.4	22.8	48.8
Inflation understanding	16.1	37.7	46.2
Risk awareness level	51.7	4.6	43.7

Source: Estimated based on CHFS 2015

questions that were designed to gauge financial literacy and how well these questions were answered. In 2015 and 2017, the China Household Finance Survey designed three question items (Note 3) to measure the level of financial literacy of household heads. These questions focus on their ability to calculate interest rate, understanding of inflation, and awareness of risk.

This study adopted the principles used in the method of measuring household financial literacy in China developed by Yin et al. (2014) and applied the same method in its assessment of the level of financial literacy in China during the 2015 and 2017 period. Table 14.2 shows a summary of the answers to the questions on financial literacy in 2015. The rate of correct answers to questions about the ability to calculate interest stands at 28.4%, understanding of inflation 16.1% and awareness of risk 51.7%, respectively (Note 4). Moreover, it should be noted that among the answers collected, "I don't know" made up the majority of the responses to all question items. However, people who answered questions incorrectly and people who simply did not have answer are not at the same level of financial literacy (Note 5).

It should also be noted that this paper has incorporated many control variables that may affect household consumer borrowing behavior. More specifically, we have taken into consideration both the social attributes of the householder (gender, age, years of education, membership in the party, occupation, risk tolerance, marital status, etc.) and economic situation (family size, logarithm of household income, number of households, log of debt, etc.). As Barnes and Young (2003) have shown that demographic and sociological factors are among the major factors influencing the borrowing behavior of households in the USA. We expect to see similar pattern in China. Moreover, the fixed effect of the area is controlled by using the dummy variable of farmers and the provincial dummy variable. In the data processing, we selected the same households in 2015 and 2017 and excluded the sample with negative household income, more than 30 homeowners, and a householder age of 16 years or less. As a result, panel data of 24,689 actual samples were constructed.

Table 14.3 provides descriptive statistics for CHFS 2015 and CHFS 2017. According to this graph, although the number of households with debt has slightly decreased, the debt balance per household has increased from an average of 35,284 yuan per household in 2015 to an average of 42,325 yuan per household in 2017. The consumption debt has almost doubled from an average of 1981 yuan per household in 2015 to an average of 3800 yuan per household in 2017. In the

Table 14.3 Descriptive statistics

	2015			2017		
Variable name	Average value	Standard deviation	Number of responses	Average value	Standard deviation	Number of responses
Dependent variable						
Existence of household debt	0.2793	0.4487	24689	0.2782	0.4481	24689
Debt balance (10,000 yuan)	3.5284	17.8956	24689	4.2325	19.2859	24689
Excess debt (10,000 yuan)						
Consumer debt (10,000 yuan)	0.1981	1.4144	24689	0.3800	2.0573	24689
Variable of interest						
Financial literacy	39.5547	24.7060	24689	60.8501	29.2362	24689
Control variable						
Peasant dummy	0.3647	0.4814	24689	0.3628	0.4808	24689
Marriage dummy	0.8761	0.3295	24689	0.9526	0.2126	24689
Household income (10,000 yuan)	7.0648	22.2304	24689	8.0485	9.9889	24689
Household size	3.6849	1.7329	24689	3.2922	1.5794	24689
Risk appetite dummy	0.0817	0.2739	24689	0.0818	0.2740	24689
Male dummy	0.7826	0.4125	24689	0.8117	0.3910	24689
Household age (years)	54.6488	13.6138	24689	56.3919	13.4793	24689
Education age	8.9482	4.1104	24682	8.9818	4.0417	24682
Communist dummy	0.0826	0.2753	24689	0.0810	0.2729	24689
Household head high position dummy	0.0129	0.1129	24689	0.0001	0.0064	24689
Insurance dummy	0.8066	0.3950	24689	0.8477	0.3593	24689
Good health dummy	0.1061	0.3079	24689	0.1265	0.3325	24689
Bad health dummy	0.1777	0.3823	24689	0.1986	0.3989	24689
Number of homeowners	1.1169	0.5287	24689	1.1373	0.5619	24689
Net assets (10,000 yuan)	75.3543	127.3246	24689	93.8450	165.3371	24689

Source: Created by the author based on the same 24679 households in CHFS 2015 and CHFS 2017

meanwhile, the average household income has increased from 70,648 yuan in 2015 to 83,006 yuan in 2017 and the number of family members has decreased from 3.68 per household to 3.29 which suggests that nuclear family is becoming a norm. With regard to household heads, their average age is 54 and years of education about 9. About 8.5% of them are Communist Party members and 1.0% of them occupying a managerial position or above. 80.6% of the people surveyed purchased insurance policies and joined health insurance programs. That number increased to 80.6% per household in 2015 to 84.8% per household in 2017.

Furthermore, although the percentage of the household heads who reported as in good health was 10.6% in 2015 and 12.6% in 2017, the number of them reported as in "poor health" has also risen. It is worth noting that the number of homeowners has increased slightly from 2015 to 2017, with their net assets value increased by an average of 180,000 yuan over the past two years, an evidence of the conspicuous rise in housing price.

Based on previous studies and the descriptive statistical analysis of panel data, we believe that among all the factors affecting households' borrowing behavior, financial literacy is the most important one. We propose the following two hypotheses which will be elucidated in the subsequent discussion. The two hypotheses are: (1) the higher the financial literacy, the larger the size of debts and consumer debt and (2) the higher the income level and greater the number of homeownership, the more likely for a household to not only incur debt, but also at larger scale.

14.4 Model and Variables

14.4.1 The Model

In this paper, we examine various factors that may affect demand for household and consumption debt to determine the role of financial literacy in household borrowing behavior. In order to do so, we have relied on the same data from CHFS 2015 and CHFS 2017 to conduct regression analysis based on the panel data of the 24,679 households in the two surveys. The probit-type binary selection model of whether to hold debt and whether to fall into excess debt and the fixed effect of debt size and consumption debt.

This paper estimates the binary probit models of whether households hold debt and excessive debt and fixed effect regression analysis of debt size and consumption debt.

First, with respect to the probit model, those holding debts are assigned a value of one, while a value of 0 is assigned to those without debts (i.e.: with debts = 1; otherwise = 0; similarly, with excessive debts = 1; otherwise = 0), we have designed the following model to test probit model's validity.

$$\text{Dummy debt}_{it} = \beta_0 + \beta_1 \text{Financial Literacy}_{it} + \beta_2 X_{it} + v_i + \lambda_t + \epsilon_{it} \quad (14.1)$$

$$Y_{it} = \beta_0 + \beta_1 \text{ Financial Literacy}_{it} + \beta_2 X_{it} + v_i + \lambda_t + \epsilon_{it} \quad (14.2)$$

Next, since the dependent variables of the debt balance and consumption debt are continuous variables, we used fixed effect model to the text them. The basic model is as shown in Eq. (14.2).

Equation (14.1) examines whether financial literacy affects the presence or absence of household debt. (14.2) tests how financial literacy affects household debt, where, Y_{it} is the logarithmic value of each explained variable, the debt balance per household in household i in year t, business debt, housing debt, and consumer debt. $Financial\ Litercay_{it}$ is the control variable, an explanatory variable showing the characteristics of households, and it is also a regional control variable at the provincial level. β_i is a parameter vector, and ϵ_{it} is an error term, assuming that it follows the standard normal distribution.

The primary focus of this paper is to examine financial literacy as an explanatory variable. Based on the study by Wu et al. (2018), which shows a correlation between households' financial literacy and their ability to not only take on debts, but also do so from legitimate and regulated financial institutions, we approach the issue from a new angle, namely by focusing on the purpose of borrowing as a way to assess the role of financial literacy in a variety of household debts. We believe this approach is more appropriate in studying the rapidly developing consumer financial market in China.

In addition, as discussed earlier, this paper incorporates some controlled variables that may affect household borrowing behavior. Specifically, we have taken into consideration the attributes of household head (gender, age, years of education, membership in the party, occupation, risk aptitude, marital status, etc.) and households' economic standing (family size, household income, financial assets, homeownership, number of units, debt, etc.). Household income and homeownership are considered important control variables in borrowing behavior.

14.4.2 Estimated Results and Their Interpretation

Table 14.4 illustrates the estimated results of financial literacy as a variable on (1) with debt; (2) excessive debt; (3) debt scale; and (4) consumer debt. According to the results (1) financial literacy is positive, with 5% significance, which means that the higher the financial literacy, the easier the family to hold debt; in contrast, the results (2), the coefficient of financial literacy is significantly negative at the level of 10%, indicating that the lower the financial literacy, the more likely the family is to have excessive debt, which is consistent with the analysis result of Wu Zhiming (2018). In other words, families with high level of financial literacy can properly control their debt situation and reduce the adverse impact of excessive debt on families. The lack of financial literacy is directly linked to excessive debt, which validates the study by Wu et al. (2018);

In addition, the fixed effect model of debt scale and consumption debt Eq. (14.2) shows that the coefficient of financial literacy and debt scale (3) is significantly positive at the level of 10%. It can be said that high financial literacy plays a positive role in increasing debt scale. However, in (4) equation, financial literacy and consumer debt are positively correlated at the 5% significance level,

Table 14.4 Financial literacy and borrowing behavior estimation results

	With debt	Excess debt	Debt scale	Consumer debt
	(1)	(2)	(3)	(4)
	Probit	Probit	Fixed effect	Fixed effect
Financial literacy	0.0038*	−0.0251*	0.0429*	0.0354**
	(0.0021)	(0.0151)	(0.0230)	(0.0150)
Peasant dummy	0.0413	0.1707***	0.4051	0.1483
	(0.0276)	(0.0369)	(0.2836)	(0.1926)
Marriage dummy	0.0036	0.0016	0.0414	−0.0463
	(0.0100)	(0.0618)	(0.0987)	(0.0650)
Income logarithm	0.0106****	−0.1098***	0.1448***	0.0018
	(0.0022)	(0.0118)	(0.0240)	(0.0158)
Household size	0.0116***	−0.0019	0.1301***	0.0832***
	(0.0022)	(0.0100)	(0.0250)	(0.0166)
Risk dummy	0.0070	−0.0241	0.3126	−0.4378***
	(0.3478)	(0.0555)	(7.6191)	(0.0509)
Male dummy	−0.0214***	−0.0565	−0.2225**	−0.1188**
	(0.0083)	(0.0437)	(0.0893)	(0.0593)
Household age (years)	−0.0016***	0.0004	−0.0160***	−0.0121***
	(0.0004)	(0.0015)	(0.0044)	(0.0030)
Education age	0.0013	−0.0276***	0.0143	−0.0019
	(0.0012)	(0.0050)	(0.0136)	(0.0089)
Party member dummy	−0.0190	−0.0072	−0.2747	−0.0006
	(0.0217)	(0.0675)	(0.2362)	(0.1333)
Household head high position dummy	0.0325	−0.4692	0.2800	−0.0277
	(0.0278)	(0.3000)	(0.3044)	(0.1878)
Commercial insurance dummy	−0.0134*	−0.1680***	−0.1526*	−0.0321
	(0.0077)	(0.0382)	(0.0874)	(0.0584)
Good health dummy	−0.0158**	−0.1469**	−0.1584*	−0.1324***
	(0.0077)	(0.0576)	(0.0812)	(0.0543)
Poor health dummy	0.0238***	0.2152***	0.2091***	0.2104***
	(0.0071)	(0.0385)	(0.0751)	(0.0543)
Number of owned houses (cases)	−0.0358***	−0.4184***	1.1865***	−0.2322***
	(0.0011)	(0.0127)	(0.0675)	(0.0119)
Area dummy	Yes	Yes	Yes	Yes
Year dummy	Yes	Yes	Yes	Yes
*R*2	—	—	0.068	0.053
Sample	24679/ 49358	6880/13760	24679/ 49358	24679/49358

Note: (1) The excess debt dummy variable in (2) is calculated from households in (1) "with debt." 2) *,**,*** indicate significance of 10%, 5%, and 1%, respectively, and the non-uniform variance robust standard deviation is shown in parentheses indicating that the higher the financial literacy ability is, the larger the scale of household consumer debt is.

Our study has verified that financial literacy has an obvious impact on consumer debt. As discussed earlier, as the consumer credit market is developing rapidly and tend to be increasingly competitive, advanced financial literacy will place households in a more advantageous position by allowing them to have access to financial information, cutting the cost in time and expenses needed to secure a debt and enhancing their desire to take debts.

Among the control variables in Table 14.4, the logarithm of "household income" has a strong correlation with each of the explained variables. This suggests that the higher the household income, the lower the possibility of debt and excess debt, but the higher household income is also linked to larger housing debts. Conversely, the higher the income is, the smaller the consumption debt is. Age has a significantly negative correlation with each of the explained variables, except for excess debt in Eq. (14.2). Crook (2001) pointed out that the age of the household heads will have major influences on borrowing decisions, our study suggests that the older the age, the lower the probability of debt as well as the amount of debt. Conversely, the farmers dummy variable is significantly positively related to the non-explanatory variables: (1) the debt dummy and (2) the excess debt dummy, and because farmers have relatively less income and assets than the city residents, hence, the likelihood of excess debt for farmers increases.

In contrast, the "number of homeownership" is significant to all explained variables. This means the more houses one owns, the lower the probability one would take on debt and the less possibility of falling into excessive debt. Conversely, the results also show that the more housing ownership, the more debt scale, because as the housing price rises, house related debt dramatically expands the size of household debt. The continuously rising price for houses causes the expansion of household debt (Wu et al. 2013). Our findings also show that the higher income level tends to reduce the level of consumption debt. In other words, all evidence supports our hypotheses 1 and 2.

14.4.3 Robustness Check

In what follows, we conduct a robustness test to verify whether the estimation results indicated by the table are indeed constant and stable. We estimated the sample size by excluding the values below 1% and above 99% of each explained variable, that is, the debt balance and the "consumer debt" balance. The estimated results in Table 14.5 show that financial literacy had a significant positive correlation with "debt balance" of 10% and is significantly positively correlated with "consumer debt" by 5%. The robustness test also shows that the effect of financial literacy on household borrowing behavior is the same as Table 14.4. In other words, the higher popularization of financial literacy, the more objective householders' knowledge

Table 14.5 Robustness test

	(1) Winsorize processing method		(2) Endogenicity test (2SLS)		(3) Tobit model	
	Debt scale	Consumer debt	Debt scale	Consumer debt	Debt scale	Consumer debt
Financial Literacy	0.0429*	0.0354**	0.0165*	0.1604***	0.1773***	0.3091**
	(0.0230)	(0.0150)	(0.0890)	(0.0579)	(0.0654)	(0.1474)
Household head attribute variable	Yes	Yes	Yes	Yes	Yes	Yes
Year dummy	Yes	Yes	Yes	Yes	Yes	Yes
Other variables	Yes	Yes	Yes	Yes	Yes	Yes
R2	0.069	0.053	0.1117	0.0522	0.148	0.084
Sample	24679/49358	24679/49358	24679/49358	24679/49358	24679/49358	24679/49358

Note: *, **, *** indicate significance of 10%, 5%, and 1%, respectively, and the non-uniform variance robust standard deviation is shown in parentheses

about various consumer finance products, the more appropriate consumer debt a householder will gain based on his or her abilities.

It is widely agreed that there is a possibility of endogeneity exists in financial literacy, which is our variable of interest. This is because borrowing activities in households' daily lives will likely improve their financial literacy. Households' past experiences may also enhance their financial literacy. The existence of such an inverse correlation leads to an overestimation of the effect on the debt size or the consumer debt size for financial literacy. Although respondents answered questions related to financial literacy without using devices such as a calculator, the correct answer to a given question may be a coincidence.

In order to solve this problem, we use the level of financial literacy and income of other households living in the same community as an instrumental variable of the financial literacy index (Note 6).

It is considered that the explanatory variables by this method can satisfy the correlation of manipulated variables and the exogenous condition. The level of financial literacy of other households who live in the same community and have the same income level reflects the average level of financial literacy of households in this community, and households which have a higher level of financial literacy can teach other households in the surrounding community. Therefore, this instrumental variable and the financial literacy of households have a positive correlation and satisfy the relevance condition.

When considering the effect of the variable of interest, which is financial literacy in this case, on debt size, we have tried to use Tobit model to predict outcome. Because many of the explained variables are concentrated in 0, and the error term may not be normally distributed, this may cause a bias in the estimation parameter. However, as shown in Table 14.5 (3), the results are still robust, which is also consistent with the estimation results indicated in Table 14.4. Financial literacy does not affect housing debts, but the higher the level of financial literacy, the more positive the coefficient of household debt and consumable debt. The reason for this is that the Tobit model cannot estimate the panel estimation effect method, and many unobservable variables are missing, which may affect the estimation results significantly.

14.5 Conclusion

Against the backdrop of the rapidly expanding household debt in China, we have conducted this empirical analysis of the relationship between financial literacy, which is one of the important factors that determine the financial behavior of households, and the borrowing behavior of households, especially with regard to consumer debt. In contrast to other published studies, this paper focuses on the purpose of household borrowing, relying on national CHFS microdata, and examines how exactly financial literacy affects actual household and consumer debt.

The main findings of this paper are as follows:

1. The higher the financial literacy of the head of household, the more likely the household will take on debt. Conversely, the lower the financial literacy, the more likely a household will incur excess debt, a correlation observed by Wu et al. (2018) in their empirical study based on household data collected from urban areas. What this means is that financial literacy helps households manage their assets in a rational manner, effectively control their debt risk, and reduce the risk of excessive debt.
2. Financial literacy has a strong positive impact on consumer debt, which has serious implications for the rapidly expanding household consumer finance market. More specifically, this highlights the following changes in recent years: first, the expansion of financial services for consumers has largely changed the perception of privately operated financial services as unregulated and charging high-interest rates. In particular, the shift by commercial banks to "intelligent banking" and the emergence of the numerous mini-debt platformers such as Alibaba and Tencent have provided consumers more borrowing opportunities as well as the convenience and diversity of financial products.

Our study means that high level of financial literacy can push up consumer debt, and in the process contribute to the expansion of the consumption market. Conversely, households with low level of financial literacy are likely to be plagued by excess debt. Therefore, improving financial literacy can promote healthy borrowing behavior and reduce the risks associated with consumer finance and financial markets as a whole.

Although this study has confirmed the impact of financial literacy on household borrowing behavior by focusing on the purpose of debt, which has been absent in the published studies to date, further research is still needed to address the following issues: first, the purpose of households' debt requires more detailed and in-depth analysis and second, the exact degree to which financial literacy influences the borrowing behavior of households should be described more precisely, especially with regard to the difference between rural and urban areas.

Note 1: For example, recent research such as Mian et al. (2017), Lombardi et al. (2017) show that although the rapid increase of household debt can boosts economic growth in the short term. The economic growth rate will be reduced in the medium and long term.

Note 2: For details, please refer to iResearch "China Consumer Finance Business Report 2019." According to the report, by the end of 2018, the total amount of outstanding debts of China's household sector was 47.9 billion yuan, of which the outstanding balance of housing debts and car debts totaled 27.4 trillion yuan, and the outstanding balance of consumer finance reached 11.1 trillion yuan.

Note 3: In other words, (1) If the annual interest of a bank is 4% and 100 yuan is in a fixed deposit for one year, the principal and interest after one year ① is less than 104 yuan, ② is exactly 104 yuan, ③ is more than 104 yuan, ④ cannot be calculated, (2) If the annual interest rate of the bank is 5% and the annual inflation rate is 3%, and you deposit 100 yuan into the bank, one year later, your purchase amount is ① more than one year ago, ② the same as one year ago, ③ less than a year ago, ④ unable to calculate. (3) If you have two lottery tickets to choose from, one lottery ticket gives you a 100% chance to win 4000 yuan, the second chance is a 50% chance to win 10000 yuan, but the remaining 50% chance is 0%, which one do you choose?

Note 4: However, the average value of financial literacy in 2017 has greatly increased to 60.85. The reasons are as follows: first, in recent years, with China's increasing publicity and efforts on the concept of inclusive finance, the level of family financial literacy has improved to a certain extent. Second, the development of internet finance, especially the rapid development of new services such as internet mobile and mobile payment is considered to help households to gain knowledge of the financial market and improve the level of financial literacy. Similarly, according to the first National Financial Literacy Survey (18,600 samples) conducted by the people's Bank of China, the "Consumer Finance Assistance Survey Analysis Report 2017," 87.1% of the respondents recognize that "diffusion of financial knowledge is very important" or "relatively important," and the index of the average correct answer rate of consumer financial literacy is 63.7.

Note 5: According to Yin et al. (2014), in order to show the difference between the two, we established two dummy variables for the three questions of financial literacy: (1) whether they are correct and (2) whether the answer is direct. Then, a total of six dummy variables were created and exploratory factor analysis was performed to estimate factor 1 and factor 2. In addition, the values of the KMO (measure of sampling adequacy), factor analysis result of financial literacy, and the estimation result of the factor loadings are all above 0.6, which indicates that the sample size in this paper is suitable for factor analysis.

Note 6: In this paper, the meaning of "community" refers to the residential community in which in rural areas, villages are the unit, while in cities, certain areas are the unit. It is under the jurisdiction of "community neighborhood committee." For the method of operating variables, refer to Yin et al. (2014).

References

Akudugu MA, Egyir IS, Mensah-Bonsu A (2009) Women farmers' access to credit from rural banks in Ghana. Agric Fin Rev 69(3):284–299

Barnes, S. and Young, G. (2003), The rise in us household debt: assessing its causes and consequences, Bank of England Working Papers., No. 206.

Crook J (2001) The demand for household debt in the USA: evidence from the 1995 survey of consumer finance. Appl Fin Econ 11(1):83–91

Disney R, Gathergood J (2013) Financial literacy and consumer credit portfolios. J Bank Finan 37(7):2246–2254

Hung A, Parker A, Yoong J (2009) Defining and measuring financial literacy, Working Paper. Rand Corporation, Santa Monica

Huston SJ (2010) Measuring financial literacy. J Consum Aff 44(2):296–316

IMF (2018) A decade after the global financial crisis, are we safer? Global Financ Stab Rep, October

Kidwell B, Turrisi R (2004) An examination of college student money management tendencies. J Econ Psychol 25(5):601–616

Lombardi MJ, Mohanty M, Shim I (2017) The real effects of household debt in the short and long run. BIS Working Papers 607:1–42

Lusardi A, Mitchell OS (2007) Baby boomer retirement security: The roles of planning, financial literacy, and housing wealth. J Monet Econ 54(1):205–224

Lusardi A, Tufano P (2015) Debt literacy, financial experiences, and overindebtedness. J Pension Econ Fin 14(4):332–368

Lusardi A, Michaud PC, Mitchell OS (2017) Optimal financial knowledge and wealth inequality. J Polit Econ 125(2):431–477

Mian A, Sufi A, Verner E (2017) Household debt and business cycles worldwide. Q J Econ 132(4): 1755–1817

Oseifuah EK (2010) Financial literacy and youth entrepreneurship in South Africa. Afr J Econ Manag Stud 1(2):164–182

Peng JC (2019) Research on financial literacy and household loan behavior: evidence from financial surveys in Chinese urban household consumption. J Xiangtan Univ (Philos Soc Sci) 1:125–129. (in Chinese)

Song QY, Wu Y, Yin ZC (2017) Financial literacy and household borrowing behavior. J Financ Res 6:95–110. (in Chinese)

Song QY, Xiao JN, Yin ZC (2019) The effect of financial literacy on household consumption. Econ Rev 1:113–147. (in Chinese)

Tian G, Huang X, Ning L, Wang Y (2018) Safeguarding household debt crisis and associated systemic financial risks, Policy Research Report No. 58. Shanghai Univ Fin Econ. (in Chinese)

Van Rooij M, Lusardi A, Alessie R (2011) Financial literacy and stock market participation. J Financ Econ 101(2):449–472

Wu, W.X., Xu, Q. and Bai, X.H. (2013), A comparative study of group differences among debt decision-making of Chinese households. (in Chinese).

Wu WX, Wu K, Wang J (2018) Financial literacy and household debt: empirical studies using Chinese household survey data. Econ Res J 1:97–109. (in Chinese)

Wu WX, Zhang XY, Wu K (2019) The effect of financial literacy on household debt behavior. Res Financ Econ Iss 5:57–65. (in Chinese)

Xiang H, Guo ZZ (2019) An empirical study of financial literacy's impact on online lending consumption behavior: based on the mediating role of perceived risk. Consumption Econ 2: 62–70. (in Chinese)

Yin ZC, Qiu H (2019) Is financial knowledge important for internet financial participation? Finance Trade Econ 6:70–84. (in Chinese)

Yin ZC, Song QY, Wu Y (2014) Financial literacy, trading experience and household portfolio choice. Econ Res J 1:62–75. (in Chinese)

Chapter 15
A Computable General Equilibrium Analysis of the Impact of Climate Change on Regional Economies Through Japan's Fruit Tree Production Changes: Evidence from Panel Data and Spatial CGE Models

Suminori Tokunaga, Mitsuru Okiyama, and Maria Ikegawa

Abstract According to a report of Japan's Ministry of the Environment (2015), the severity and significance of climate change are "very high," and the urgency is "high" for paddy rice and fruit trees among crop cultivation. In this study, we focused on Japan's fruit tree production, assessing the impacts of climate change, particularly global warming, on regional economies through changes in Japan's fruit tree cultivation using a panel data model and a nine regional computable general equilibrium (9SCGE) model and the effects of adaptation technology and tariff reduction as recovery policies to mitigate the influence of climate change using this model. Our study revealed three findings: First, we estimated the panel data model of fruit tree production with climate change variables and demonstrated that the impact of high temperature became larger and production decreased when temperature exceeded a certain point, except in Hokkaido. Second, we constructed the 9SCGE model by combining the nine interregional social accounting matrix and the estimation results of the panel data model and conducted three simulated scenarios of global warming without adaptation technology, including the future temperature reaching the predicted maximum, mean, and minimum values. These simulation results revealed that global warming has different impacts on each region and results in regional economic disparities. For example, global warming has a positive impact on regional economies in Hokkaido, Tohoku, and Okinawa. Moreover, through the changes in producer prices for fruit trees and other agricultural products, farmers' sales will increase to differing degrees among regions. Third, we conducted simulated scenarios of global warming with adaptation technology under the assumption that the development of high-temperature-tolerant fruit trees results

---

S. Tokunaga (✉) · M. Ikegawa
Faculty of Economics and Business Administration, Reitaku University, Chiba, Japan
e-mail: tokunaga@reitaku-u.ac.jp

M. Okiyama
Reitaku Institute of Political Economics and Social Studies, Reitaku University, Chiba, Japan

M. Kawano et al. (eds.), *Theory and History in Regional Perspective*, New Frontiers in Regional Science: Asian Perspectives 56,
https://doi.org/10.1007/978-981-16-6695-7_15

in curbing global warming-induced productivity decline (with adaptation technology) as a recovery policy. This simulation revealed that the negative impact on fruit tree production to the west of Kanto will be lower than the range of decline and the equivalent variation gaps between Tohoku and Shikoku will decrease.

Keywords Climate change impacts · Spatial computable general equilibrium model · Panel data model · Japan's fruit tree production · Adaptation technology · Tariff reduction policy

15.1 Introduction

Amid the ongoing scholarly debate on the challenges of global warming since the 1980s, the "Intergovernmental Panel on Climate Change" (IPCC) was set up in 1988 as a forum to study global warming and review measures to reduce greenhouse gas (GHG) emissions. This review led to the emergence of a number of research papers on the effects of climate change on agricultural production. According to multiple papers, it is believed that agricultural production would be most affected by climate changes induced by global warming (Furuya et al. 2015; Okiyama and Tokunaga 2019; Kunimitsu et al. 2020). This will most strongly affect the food and beverage industries that depend on agriculture for inputs. As recently as 2017, the Japan Meteorological Agency (JMA) projected climate change in Japan based on a nonhydrostatic regional climate model using IPCC GHG emission scenario RCP8.5, revealing that the annual mean temperature could increase by about 4.5 °C in the national average by the late twenty-first century based on the averages from the late twentieth century. This scenario depicts the highest GHG emissions, and the rise in temperature is predicted based on the assumption that no policies will be implemented to curb GHG emissions that exceeds the present time.

The impact of climate changes on the rice production in Japan has been studied by many researchers since the early 2000s (Yokozawa et al. 2009; Kunimitsu et al. 2013). These studies identified the consequences of climate change on rice yield and its quality using regional panel data, including climate variables. For example, in their study based on crop models, Yokozawa et al. (2009) reported that the average national rice yield was expected to increase slightly until the temperature rose by approximately 3 °C during the warm season (May to October). If the temperature rise were to exceed 3 °C, it might reduce crop yield in various regions, except in Hokkaido and Tohoku. Furthermore, using macrodata, Fujimori et al. (2018) analyzed the macroeconomic impacts of future climate changes by examining projected changes in crop yields using both the crop model and the computable general equilibrium (CGE) model. Kunimitsu (2015) and Tokunaga et al. (2017, 2020b) analyzed the impacts of climate change on regional economies through changes in rice production using the regional CGE model, also determining that the impacts of climate change caused by global warming differed among regions.

In contrast to the previous studies on rice production, we focus on Japan's fruit trees. According to the Ministry of the Environment report (2015),[1] the severity and significance of climate change among crop cultivation for both paddy rice and fruit trees are "very high," and both urgency and confidence are "high." Using data based on the JMA's future temperature projections, a panel data model, and a nine regional computable general equilibrium (9SCGE) model with a social accounting matrix (SAM), we measured the impacts of global warming-induced climate change on nine regional economies through the changes in Japan's fruit tree production. We performed two simulations of adaptation technology and tariff reduction as recovery policies intended to mitigate the influence of climate change using the 9SCGE model with reference to our previous analysis method (Tokunaga et al. 2017, 2020a, b).

This chapter is organized into five sections: Section 15.2 measures the production function of fruit trees, including climate variables, using panel data for nine regions and studies the regional changes in fruit tree production based on the JMA's future temperature projections (2017). Section 15.3 provides an overview of nine regional SAMs and nine interregional CGE models. Section 15.4 explains the data, which include the simulation details, and analyzes the simulation results using the 9SCGE model. Finally, Sect. 15.5 presents the conclusions and the policy implications.

15.2 Estimation of Regional Fruit Tree Production and Future Temperatures

15.2.1 Changes in Fruit Tree Production for 1995–2017 and Temperatures for 1990–2017

In this section, we conduct a dynamic panel data analysis to examine the impact of climate change on fruit tree production in Japan. The panel data are compiled into nine regional divisions, including Hokkaido, Tohoku, Hokuriku, Kanto-Tosan, Tokai, Kinki, Chugoku, Shikoku, and Kyushu (excluding Okinawa). For this study, the agricultural product category selected to investigate the extent to which

[1] The Japanese Ministry of the Environment (2015) report projected the impact of climate change on fruit trees. (1) For satsuma mandarin oranges, the climate in the 2060s is projected to be more difficult than today for growing in many of today's prime production areas, and growing will become possible in areas that are currently not suited, including inland areas in the warm south-western region (relatively warmer areas such as southern Kyushu) and coastal areas along the Sea of Japan and southern Tohoku region. (2) For apples, by the 2060s, the climate is projected to be more difficult than today for growing in the central Tohoku plains, and many of today's prime production areas, such as the northern Tohoku plains, will reach temperatures similar to areas that produce warm-climate apple varieties today. (3) For grapes, peaches, and cherries, high temperature is expected to cause challenges for cultivation in major-producer prefectures.

climate change will affect agricultural products in Japan is fruit trees.[2] The data of fruit tree production, fixed capital of farmer's households, and cultivated land are compiled from 1995 to 2009 for five regions (Tokai, Kinki, Chugoku, Shikoku, and Kyusyu), and the data of production and cultivated land are compiled from 1980 to 2017 in Hokkaido, Tohoku, Hokuriku, and Kanto-Tosan. Figure 15.1a depicts the variation in total fruit tree production for 1995–2017. From this figure, we determine that fruit tree production trends downward yearly in each region, except Hokkaido and Hokuriku, where there is a small production volume and little change.

Figure 15.1b presents the variation in the annual average temperature by nine regions for 1990–2017. Meteorological data are provided by AMeDAS.[3] The data are cross-sectioned by municipality and monthly figures for temperature in fixed interval averages.[4] Even when examining variations in regional temperatures for less than 30 years, a slightly upward trend could be determined. However, the temperatures in 1994, 1998, 2004, 2007, 2010, and 2016 significantly exceeded normal values by roughly 1.0 °C, thus constituting abnormal weather. In addition, the current (1990–2009) annual mean temperature for each region is plotted in Fig. 15.1c.

15.2.2 Estimation of a Panel Data Model on Fruit Tree Production

First, we estimate the dynamic panel data model on fruit tree production with reference to Eq. (15.1) using the panel data of a sample period from 1996 to 2009

[2]Fruit tree production is calculated by multiplying five kinds of production (unit: tons) of mandarin orange (Citrus unshiu), apple, grape, persimmon, and Japanese pear using the 2005 annual wholesale price (amount per ton) for each fruit-producing region. In other words, the production in 2005 is the nominal amount of money, but fruit tree production in each other year is the amount of money fixed at the 2005 wholesale price. There are two reasons for constructing such data. One is that it was not possible to simply add up the production of the four kinds of fruits and it was necessary to multiply the weights in some way. Another is to make the same concept as the amount of fruit trees in 2005 SAM, which is a database of CGE models. The fruit trees are a nominal amount of money in 2005 SAM, but this amount of money is regarded as the production amount with the price set to 1. The monetary value is also displayed in the simulation result, but it is treated as the production amount.

[3]We used prefectural data processed by Dr. Nishimori, who belongs to the National Institute for Agro-Environment Sciences, according to specific observatory data of AMeDAS. We are grateful to him for his cooperation.

[4]Figures from 2010 to 2017 are provided by regional data on the difference between each annual mean temperature from 2010 to 2017 and the 1981–2010 average temperature calculated by regional data on the difference at 2009 using the meteorological observation database by JMA.

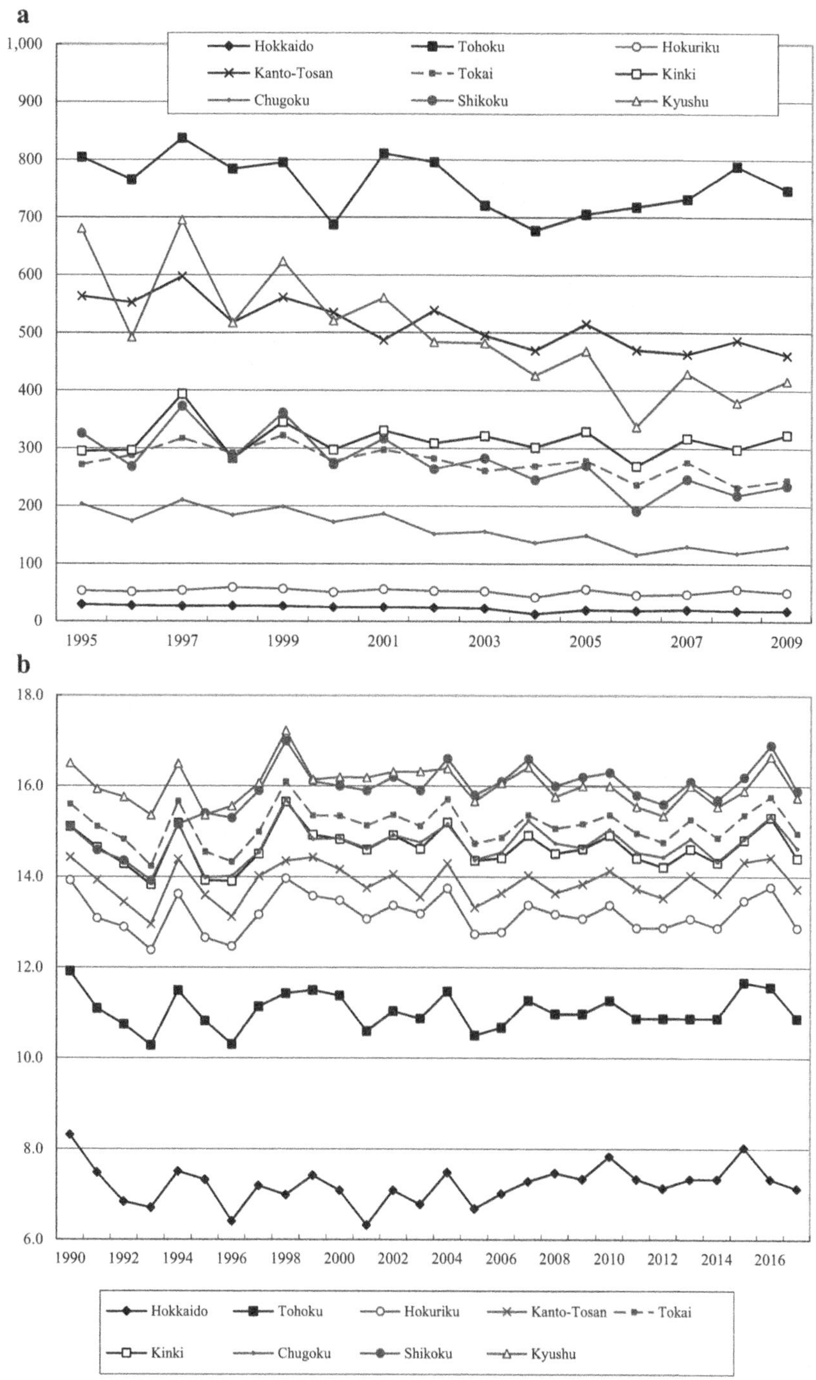

Fig. 15.1 (**a**) Trends in fruit tree production by region for nine regions (Source: The Ministry of Agriculture, Forestry and Fisheries, MAFF). Note: Unit in 1000 tons. Five kinds of fruit trees are examined, which include mandarin orange (unshiu mikan), apple, grape, persimmon, and Japanese pear. (**b**) Trends in annual average temperature by region (Source: AMeDAS). Note: Unit is °C. (**c**) Annual mean temperature change between present (1990–2009) and future (2076–2095) by region

c

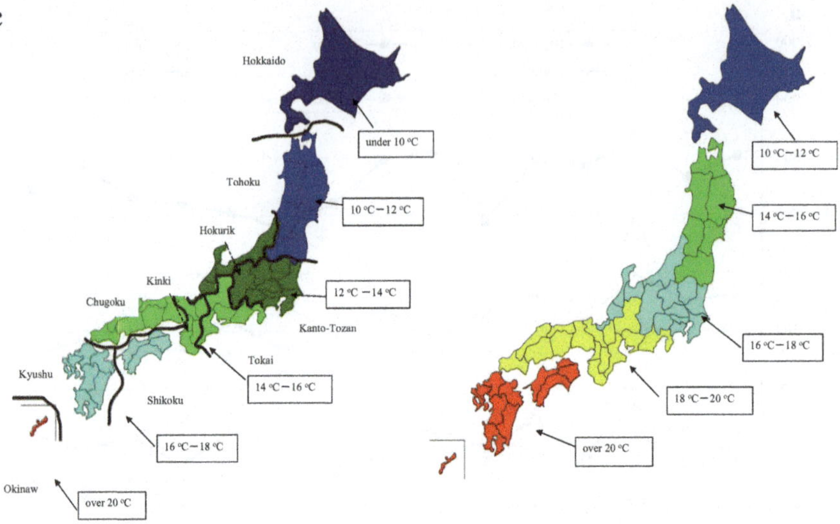

Fig. 15.1 (continued)

in nine regions (Hokkaido, Tohoku, Hokuriku, Kanto-Tosan, Tokai, Kinki, Chugoku, Shikoku, and Kyushu).[5]

$$\log\left(\frac{Y_{it}}{\text{Land}_{it}}\right) = \alpha + \beta_1 \log\left(\frac{Y_{it-1}}{\text{Land}_{it-1}}\right) + \beta_2 \log\left(\frac{K_{it}}{\text{Land}_{it}}\right) + \beta_3(\text{temp}it) + \beta_4\left(\text{temp}_{it}^2\right) + \varepsilon, it \tag{15.1}$$

where Y_{it} represents the fruit tree production of region i in year t (unit in tons), Land_{it} represents the cultivated area of region i in year t (unit in hectares), K_{it} represents the total real amount of fixed capital expended by all farming households of region i in year t (unit in million yens), temp_{it} represents the mean temperature for region i in year t, and temp_{it}^2 represents the square of the temperature variable. The estimation results are presented in Table 15.1. In the specification of Eq. (15.1), the coefficient estimates of capital stock per cultivated land and mean temperature are not statistically significant at the 0.05 level, and coefficient estimate of lagged fruit tree production per cultivated land is statistically significant at the 0.01 level but negative.

[5]For the panel data model, see Greene (2012), Tokunaga et al. (2015, 2016), and Tokunaga et al. (2017).

Next, we estimate in Eq. (15.2) using the same panel data of the sample period 1996–2009 in nine regions and the panel data of the sample period 1996–2009 in seven regions, excluding Hokkaido and Hokuriku. The estimation results are presented in Table 15.2. The results in the left-hand and middle sides of this table reveal that the coefficients of labor and two temperature variables are not statistically significant for both cases. Then, we estimate again in Eq. (15.2) using the panel data of the sample period 1996–2009 in five regions, excluding Hokkaido, Hokuriku, Tohoku, and Kanto-Tosan. The estimation results are presented in the right-hand side of Table 15.2. These results establish that the coefficients of the land and labor variables are statistically significant at the 0.1 level. In particular, the coefficient of the mean temperature variable is positive and statistically significant at the 0.1 level, and the coefficient of the square of the mean temperature variable is negative and statistically significant at the 0.1 level. These results show that the impact of high-temperature injury rises and yield decreases when temperature exceeds a certain point, as emphasized in previous studies for rice yields (Yokozawa et al. 2009; Tokunaga et al. 2017, 2020a, b).

$$Y_{it} = \alpha + \beta_1 \cdot \mathrm{Land}_{it} + \beta_2 \cdot L_{it} + \beta_3 \cdot \mathrm{temp} + it\beta_4 \cdot \mathrm{temp}_{it}^2 + \varepsilon_{it}, \tag{15.2}$$

where L_{it} represents the total labor time by the farming household of region i in year t that cultivates fruit trees (unit in thousand hours).

Therefore, for Hokkaido, Tohoku, Hokuriku, and Kanto-Tosan, where the above estimation results were not statistically significant, we estimated in Eq. (15.3) using the panel data and expanding the scope of the estimation period. The results are shown in Table 15.3. The first and second columns of this table show that the coefficients of two temperature variables are not statistically significant at the 0.1 level even when the estimation periods are 1995–2009 in the first column and 1995–2017 in the second column. However, during the estimation period 1980–2017, in the third column, we show that the two temperature variables are statistically significant at the 0.05 level and the sign conditions are satisfied.

$$Y_{it} = \alpha + \beta_1 \cdot \mathrm{Land}_{it} + \beta_3 \cdot \mathrm{temp} + it\beta_4 \cdot \mathrm{temp}_{it}^2 + \varepsilon_{it}. \tag{15.3}$$

We also predict the rate of change in fruit tree production with future temperatures in Hokkaido using the parameters in the third column of Table 15.3. The results are presented in Table 15.5. Because the forecasted values of annual mean temperature and fruit tree production in Hokkaido exceeded our expectations, we estimate the production function in Eq. (15.4) again using the time series data from 1980 to 2017 in Hokkaido. The results are presented in Table 15.4. The estimation results show that the coefficients of the land and temperature variables are positive and statistically significant at the 0.05 level.

Table 15.1 Estimation result of fruit tree production function using panel data in Eq. (15.1)

Independent variable	Fruit trees yield
Log (Y_{it}/Land$_{it}$)	Fixed-effect model
Dependent variables	Equation (15.1)
Log (Y_{it-1}/Land$_{it-1}$)	−0.3664 ***
	(−4.13)
Log (K_{it}/Land$_{it}$)	0.1042
	(1.46)
temp$_{it}$	0.1350
	(0.87)
(temp$_{it}$)^2	−0.0042
	(−0.79)
Constant term	0.6768
	(0.61)
F test Prob>*F*	19.74
Prob>*F*	0.00
Hausman test	14.55
Prob>χ^2	0.006
Current sample period	1996–2009
Number of regions	9
Number of observations	108

Note 1: *** <0.01, ** <0.05, * <0.1, *t*-statistics in parentheses
Note 2: Fixed effect model: *t*-statistics in parentheses
Note 3: 9 regions indicate Hokkaido, Tohoku, Hokuriku, Kanto Tosan, Tokai, Kinki, Chugoku, Shikoku, and Kyushu

$$Y_{it} = \alpha + \beta_1 \cdot \text{Land}_{it} + \beta_3 \cdot \text{temp} + it\varepsilon_{it}. \qquad (15.4)$$

Figure 15.2 presents the changes in fruit tree production using this elasticity for every 0.5 °C increase in the 2005 temperature. This figure also points out that production in Tohoku has decreased slowly and has declined to about 5% even if the temperature increases by 4 °C. In Tokai, Kinki, and Chugoku, growth does not turn negative when the temperature increases by approximately 1.0 °C–1.5 °C, but production decreases when the temperature increase exceeds 2 °C. In the other regions, except Hokkaido, production decreases when the temperature increases by 0.5 °C and exponentially decreases when the temperature increases even further. In particular, when the temperature rises beyond 3 °C, the impact of high-temperature injury becomes larger, and the rate of decrease in production tends to rise. For example, in the Tokai, Chugoku, and Kyushu regions, production declines to about 20%–30% with an increase in the temperature of 3 °C, and in Shikoku, it declines by nearly 60%. Conversely, the rate of change in production due to temperature increase in Hokkaido and Hokuriku is significantly different from the regions described above. When the temperature rises by more than 1.0 °C in Hokkaido, the production rise by about 1.5 times, but when the temperature exceeds 2.5 °C, the growth of production slows down. In Hokuriku, however, the production declines sharply as the temperature rises.

Table 15.2 Estimation results of fruit tree production function using panel data in Eq. (15.2)

Independent variable	Fruit trees amount of money		
Y_{it}	Fixed-effect model		
Dependent variables	Equation (15.2)		
Land_{it}	4.2677 ***	4.2742 ***	3.6731 ***
	(7.97)	(7.58)	(4.83)
L_{it}	0.0425	0.0426	0.3061 *
	(0.29)	(0.28)	(168)
temp_{it}	2616.59	5395.59	74,655.66 *
	(0.18)	(0.29)	(1.90)
$(\text{temp}_{it})^2$	−116.53	−203.16	−2435.16 *
	(−0.24)	(−0.32)	(−1.92)
Constant term	−8842.28	−29,877.01	−581,337.10 *
	(−0.08)	(−0.21)	(−1.90)
F test Prob>F	15.50	17.21	3.23
Prob>F	0.000	0.000	0.018
Hausman test	14.86	15.28	3.56
Prob>χ^2	0.000	0.000	0.313
Current sample period	1995–2009	1995–2009	1995–2009
Number of regions	9	7	5
Number of observations	117	105	75

Note 1: *** <0.01, ** <0.05, * <0.1, *t*-statistics in parentheses
Note 2: Fixed effect model: *t*-statistics in parentheses
Note 3: 7 regions indicate Tohoku, Kanto-Tosan, Tokai, Kinki, Chugoku, Shikoku, and Kyushu
Note 4: 5 regions indicate Tokai, Kinki, Chugoku, Shikoku, and Kyushu

15.2.3 Prediction of Temperature and the Regional Fruit Tree Production

Next, the maximum, mean, and minimum values of the annual temperature for the future climate in the nine regions (2076–2095 average) based on the present climate (1980–1999 average) are estimated. The future climate (2076–2095 average) predicted by the JMA (2017) and the regional changes in mean temperature and standard deviation are also estimated. The results are shown in column (b) in Table 15.5 and Fig. 15.1c. Future temperatures in Hokkaido rise up to 0.7 °C higher than Tohoku's 1990–2009 mean temperature, and future temperatures in Tohoku drop to 0.7 °C lower than Shikoku's 1990–2009 mean temperature. In the west of Tokai, the annual temperature will rise to 18 °C–19 °C, but it will not be equal to Okinawa's 1990–2009 mean temperature (23.8 °C for annual). Column (d) in Table 15.5 presents the results of the estimated impact on fruit tree production when the temperature rises from the 2005 levels to these future temperatures. However, Table 15.5 is based on the assumption that the factors of production, such as land, capital, and labor, remain constant. The following points were reviewed based on this table. The fruit tree production change in Hokkaido will increase greatly in the range of 300% even if the temperature increase is the minimum value in the future. The production in Tohoku and Kanto-Tosan will

Table 15.3 Estimation results of fruit tree production function using panel data in Eq. (15.3)

Independent variable Y_{it}	Fruit trees amount of money		
	Fixed-effect model		
Dependent variables	Equation (15.3)		
Land_{it}	4.0816 ***	5.4345 ***	5.1312 ***
	(5.55)	(11.33)	(15.51)
L_{it}	–	–	–
	–	–	–
temp_{it}	2896.41	9213.55	18,036.35 **
	(0.23)	(0.88)	(2.53)
$(\text{temp}_{it})^2$	−200.71	−426.39	−828.43 ***
	(−0.37)	(−0.94)	(−2.64)
Constant term	17,639.11	−49,282.99	−89,044.50 **
	(0.23)	(−0.79)	(−2.11)
F test Prob>F	3.23	0.66	8.37
Prob>F	0.030	0.578	0.000
Hausman test	9.91	1.63	26.73
Prob>χ^2	0.019	0.442	0.000
Current sample period	1995–2009	1995–2017	1980–2017
Number of regions	4	4	4
Number of observations	60	92	152

Note 1: *** <0.01, ** <0.05, * <0.1, *t*-statistics in parentheses
Note 2: Fixed effect model:t-statistics in parentheses
Note 3: 4 regions indicate Hokkaido, Tohoku, Hokuriku, and Kanto-Tosan

decrease by 10.2% and 25.7%, respectively, even if future temperatures increase to the maximum value. In each region of Tokai, Kinki, Chugoku, and Kyushu, fruit tree production will decrease greatly, in the range of 23% to 35%, even if the temperature increase is the minimum value in the future. Moreover, the degree of influence of the maximum values of the temperature is large in the west of Tokai. Shikoku and Hokuriku will be the most negatively affected regions. Shikoku will reduce by 89.4% in case of the mean value and by 69.6% in case of the minimum value, and Hokuriku will reduce by 200% in case of the minimum value in calculation.

15.3 Structure of the Nine Regional CGE Model

This section explains the framework of the nine regional CGE model used to simulate the effects of global warming on regional economies through fruit tree production.[6] First, the database used for the 9SCGE model is the nine interregional

[6]For the spatial CGE model, see Tokunaga et al. (2003), Ban (2007), Hosoe et al. (2010), EcoMod Modeling School (2012), Okiyama and Tokunaga (2016), and Tokunaga et al. (2017).

Table 15.4 Estimation result of fruit tree production function using time series data of Hokkaido in Eq. (15.4)

Independent variable	Fruit trees amont of money
Y_{it}	Time series model
Dependent variables	Equation (15.4)
Land_{it}	2.7486 ***
	(10.43)
L_{it}	–
	–
temp_{it}	683.57 **
	(2.63)
$(\text{temp}_{it})^2$	–
	–
Constant term	−6306.83
	(−2.81)
F test Prob>F	64.84
Prob>F	0.00
Adjusted R^2	0.775
Durbin-Watson statistic	1.996
Current sample period	1980–2017
Number of observations	38

Note 1: *** <0.01, ** <0.05, * <0.1, t-statistics in parentheses
Note 2: Fixed effect model: t-statistics in parentheses

SAM, including an interregional input–output table of competitive imports for the nine regions of Hokkaido, Tohoku, Kanto (the seven prefectures of the Kanto area in addition to the four prefectures of Niigata, Nagano, Yamanashi, and Shizuoka), Chubu (the five prefectures of Toyama, Ishikawa, Gifu, Aichi, and Mie), Kinki (the six prefectures of the Kinki area plus Fukui prefecture), Chugoku, Shikoku, Kyushu, and Okinawa. The data sources for the SAM include input–output tables of the 2005 Ministry of Internal Affairs and Communications report for Japan; the 2005 Ministry of Economy, Trade, and Industry's nine interregional input–output table and its nine intraregional input–output tables of competitive imports; and the Cabinet Office's fiscal 2005 Prefectural Accounts for 47 prefectures. The 9SCGE model is developed, comprising 20 agents (one household, 16 industries, one company, one regional government, and one investment bank) in the nine regions. Two agents, that is, the central government and overseas sector, are added. In addition, the market includes 16 commodity markets; three production factor markets of agricultural land, labor, and capital in the five agriculture sectors (rice, wheat and potatoes, vegetables, fruit trees, and livestock); and two factor markets of labor and capital in nonagricultural sectors.[7] Then, each endowment of agricultural land, labor, and capital is

[7] Agricultural land refers to the total amount of rent. We calculate land rent and owned land rent per cultivated land and owned land rent per farmer based on the "Statistics on Production Cost," the "Report of Statistics Survey on Farm Management and Economy," and the "Statistics on Crops" of the Ministry of Agriculture, Forestry, and Fisheries. The total amount of rent is determined by multiplying the rent per cultivated land of the farmer by the total cultivated land or total farmers.

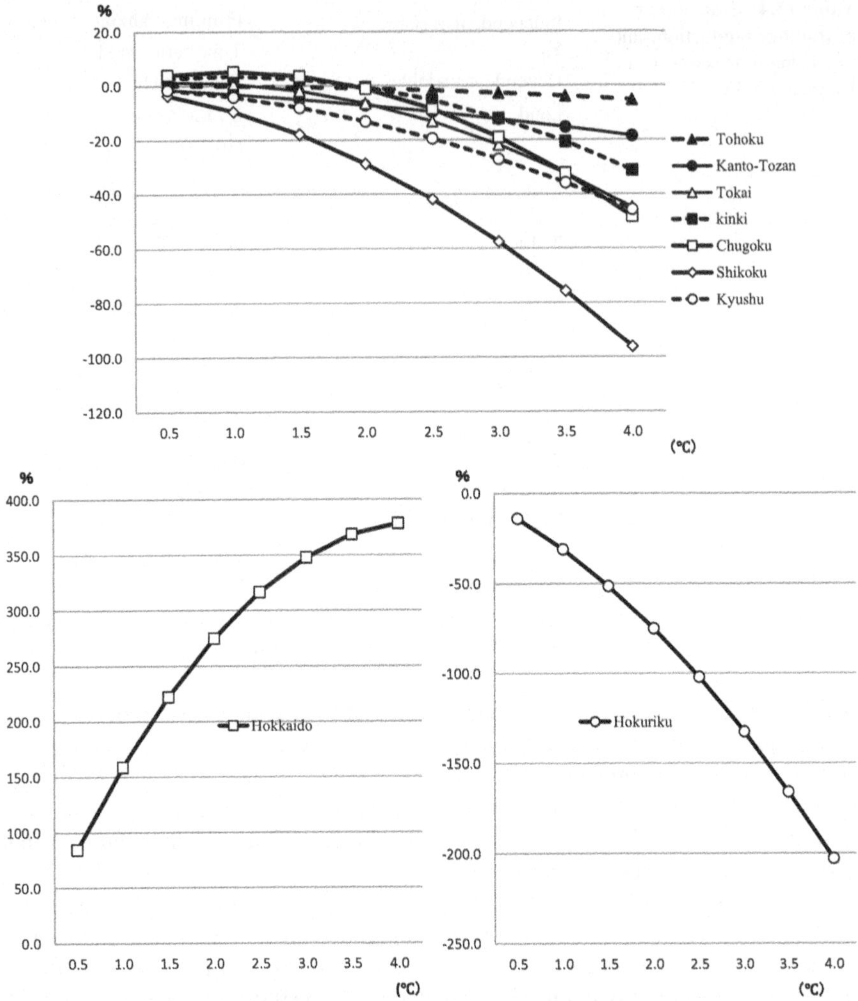

Fig. 15.2 Changes in regional fruit tree production by rise in temperature

exogenously fixed, and it is assumed that there are no transfers outside the region, although agricultural land can shift between agriculture sectors and both labor and capital can move between industries within the region. The structure of each block in the 9SCGE model, which focused on the flow of fruits tree products, illustrates in Fig. 15.3a: domestic production for fruit tree and non-fruit tree sectors, households, enterprise, regional and central government, savings and investment, and trade. Of these, the domestic production, household, government, and savings-investment blocks will be explained below.

Therefore, we can obtain the capital in agriculture sectors by deducting the total amount of rent from the sum of operation surplus and compensation of capital stock in the SAM. In addition, the households in the SAM can provide the total amount of rent as household income.

Table 15.5 Regional future temperature increase rate and regional prediction of fruit tree production growth rate

Region	(a) Current (1990–2009)	(b) Future(2076–2095)			(c) Changes in mean temperature from 2005 to 2076–2095			(d) Changes by a rise in temperature from 2005 to 2076–2095		
		Annual mean temperature (°C)			Annual mean temperature(%)			Fruit trees production (%)		
	Annual mean temperature (°C)	Max	Mean	Min	Max	Mean	Min	Max	Mean	Min
Hokkaido	7.1	12.4	11.7	11.0	85.4	74.9	64.4	332.0	366.1	379.2
Tohoku	11.0	15.9	15.3	14.6	51.5	45.3	39.2	−10.2	−7.7	−5.6
Hokuriku	13.2	17.9	17.3	16.7	48.7	41.2	34.3	−301.6	−248.5	−200.2
Kanto-Tozan	13.8	18.3	17.7	17.1	37.5	33.0	28.5	−25.7	−21.3	−17.2
Tokai	15.1	19.4	18.9	18.3	32.0	28.3	24.5	−66.4	−49.5	−35.0
kinki	14.6	19.1	18.5	18.0	32.7	28.9	25.0	−48.9	−34.6	−22.5
Chugoku	14.7	18.8	18.3	17.8	30.6	27.1	23.6	−63.2	−44.7	−29.2
Shikoku	16.0	20.1	19.6	19.1	27.5	24.3	21.1	−111.6	−89.4	−69.6
Kyushu	16.1	20.0	19.6	19.1	33.0	29.1	25.2	−54.1	−43.9	−34.7

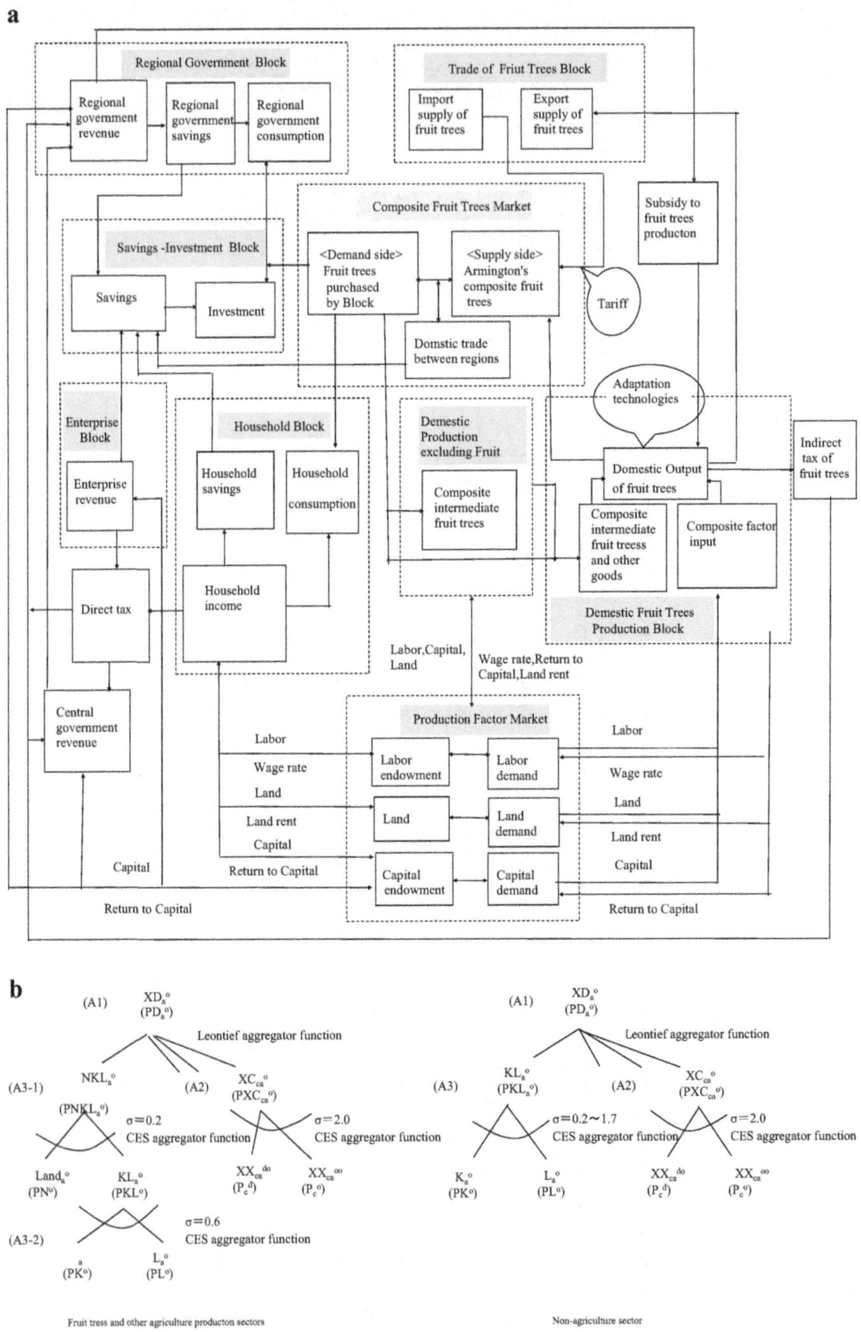

Fig. 15.3 (**a**) Structure of the 9SCGE model focused on the flow of fruit tree products. (**b**) Structure of the production sector. (**c**) Map of the nine regions of Japan in 9SCGE model

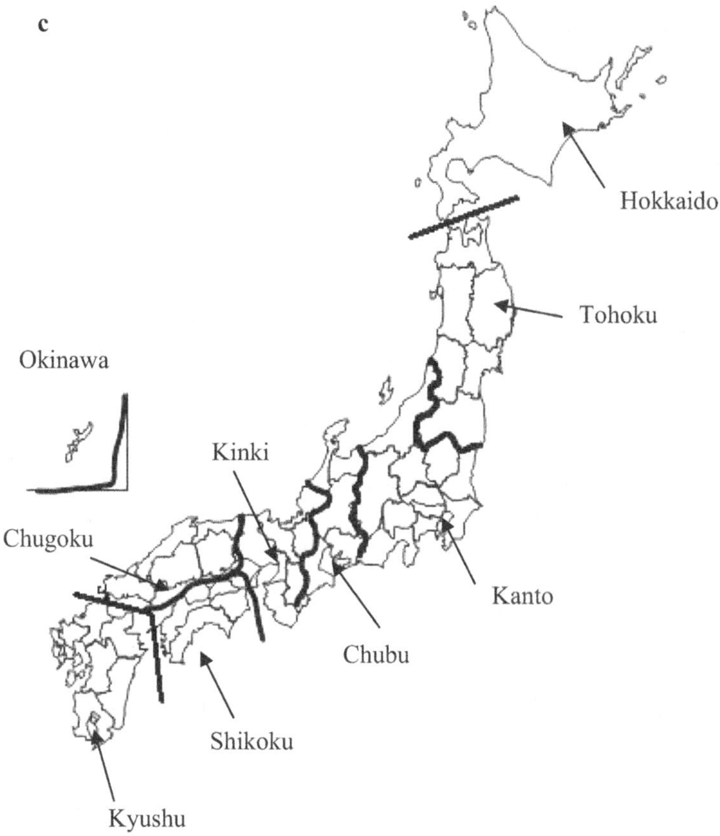

Fig. 15.3 (continued)

First, we will explain the main structure of the 9SCGE model. The domestic production sector employs a nested production structure (Fig. 15.3b). Each production sector $a(a \in A)$ in region $o(o \in S)$ is assumed to produce XD_a^o of one commodity $c(c \in C)$, maximize their profits, and face a multilevel production function. First, the structure of agricultural production on the left is explained. In Level 1 (A1), an industry in sector a constrained by Leontief technology takes the production function using each intermediate input good XC_{ca}^o aggregated from the 16 commodities and the added value NKL_a^o as a demand of an agricultural land–capital–labor bundle by firms. Because the producer price PD_a^o of sector a in region o holds true for the zero-profit condition, it follows that the income is equal to the production costs. In Level 2 (A2) on the right, we derive the intermediate goods aggregated for the 16 commodities from the composite commodity according to the Armington assumption XX_{ca}^{do} input from origin $d \in R$ in region d under the constraint of constant returns-to-scale CES technology and the o intraregional composite commodity according to the Armington assumption XX_{ca}^{oo}. In addition, we derive PXC_{ca}^o, the price of the intermediate goods aggregated from sector a of region o, by the income definition, considering the zero-profit condition for intermediate goods. By contrast, in Level 2 (A3), the added value portion consists of two levels. In Level 1 (A3–1), we derive NKL_a^o from agricultural land Land_a^o and the capital–labor bundle by the firms $\left(\mathrm{KL}_a^o\right)$ from sector a of the destination region o under the constraint of constant returns-to-scale CES technology. Next, in Level 2 (A3–2), we derive KL_a^o from capital K_a^o and the labor L_a^o under the constraint of constant returns-to-scale CES technology. Then, each price level of PNKL_a^o and PKL_a^o holds true for the zero-profit condition. Because there is a variation in the use of agricultural land, the rent PN^o is identical for agriculture sectors, and the return to capital PK^o and wage rate PL^o are identical for all industries in region o because they can shift between industries within region o. Next, the structure of nonagricultural production on the right is elaborated. In Level 1 (A1), an industry in sector a constrained by the Leontief technology takes the production function using each intermediate input good XC_{ca}^o aggregated from the 16 commodities and the added value KL_a^o. In Level 2 (A2) on the right, we derive the intermediate goods aggregated for the 16 commodities from the composite commodity in line with the Armington assumption XX_{ca}^{do} input from origin $d \in R$ in region d under the constraint of constant returns-to-scale CES technology and the o intraregional composite commodity based on the Armington assumption XX_{ca}^{oo}. In addition, even the added value portion (A3) is derived from capital K_a^o and labor L_a^o from sector a of destination region o under the constraint of constant returns-to-scale CES technology similarly as the intermediate goods sector. As the producer price PD_a^o of sector a in region o holds true for the zero-profit condition, it follows that the income is equal to the production costs. Finally, we arrive at PXC_a^o, the price of the intermediate goods aggregated from sector a in region o (by the income definition), considering the zero-profit condition for intermediate goods.

Next, for the household sector, we derive the behavior of maximizing the level of household utility UH^o. At Level B1, households in the destination region o maximize the linear-homogeneous Cobb–Douglas utility function for goods HC_c^o aggregated consumption budget CBUD^o. At Level B2, we obtain the aggregated goods from the composite commodity consistent with the Armington assumption XH_c^{do} imported from region d in origin region $d \in R$ under the constant returns-to-scale CES technology constraint and the intraregional o composite commodity based on the Armington assumption XH_c^{oo}. Household income comprises employment income, capital income, social security benefits, property income, and receipts from other current transfers. Household budget CBUD^o comprises payments of income tax from household income, household savings, social contributions, and payments from property income as well as other current transfers. Household savings is calculated from household income, assuming the fixed propensity to save.

The 9SCGE model is closed to prior savings, and in terms of investment, a bank agent allots savings S^o to investment demand IC_c^o from 16 goods in accordance with the linear-homogeneous Cobb–Douglas utility function. Here, the savings include the savings of household SH^o, company SN^o, regional government SLG^o, and central government SCG^o in addition to income transfers SDB^o and overseas savings SF^o to offset the interregional current account balances. Although the structure of the trade sector includes exports and imports between each region and the foreign sector, trade also occurs through imports and exports between regions. Finally, the relationship between regional and central governments, which coexist, is elucidated. The central government itself does not engage in spending; instead, its function is to distribute the taxes it collects to the nine regional governments and to create savings by taking a fixed proportion of the tax revenue and allocating it to the savings sector of the nine regions. Meanwhile, the governments in the nine regions have budgets that contain the differences between the revenues generated from tax receipts and regional allocation tax grants, among others, and the subsidies disbursed to each production sector. These budgets are then multiplied by a fixed ratio to create savings, and the expenditures comprise social security benefits to the household sector and transfers to other institutional sectors.

The function parameters for each sector were estimated with a calibration method that used the nine interregional SAM data and 2005 as the benchmark year.[8] However, in order to estimate these function parameters, one of the parameters must depend on an external database. Thus, to describe the setting of these parameters, we reference the values used in GTAP7.1 for the elasticity of substitution for labor and capital in the production sector and that for the CES-type (Armington) function of the trade sector. Then, in reference to previous studies by Ban (2007), Hayashiyama et al. (2011), and Tanaka and Hosoe (2009), we set the interregional elasticity of substitution for the production, household, and investment sectors; the elasticity of substitution of the CET-type function for the trade sector; and the elasticity of agricultural land and the capital–labor bundle in Table 15.6.[9]

15.4 Results of the Simulation Analysis

15.4.1 Setting Simulation Data

This section demonstrates the setting of the simulation data related to the changes in fruit tree production caused by climate change induced by global warming.

Before setting the simulation data for this section, we explain how the results obtained from fruit tree production function (estimated in Sect. 15.2) were reflected in the 9SCGE model. As shown in Fig. 15.3a, the function for the production block in the 9SCGE model cannot be used to directly indicate the impact of global warming-induced temperature rise on regional fruit tree production. Therefore, the

[8]For map of the nine regions of Japan in 9SCGE model, see Fig. 15.3c.

[9]Although the results of simulations with interregional elasticities changed from 2.0 to 0.5 were different, we adopted the elasticity values that have been commonly used in previous studies because we do not know which elasticity value will be optimal at a future point in time.

Table 15.6 List of the elasticity of substitution setup in this model

Production activities	Elasticity of substitution between land and capital-labor bundle in the CES function	Elasticity of substitution between capital-labor in the CES function	Elasticity of transformation in CET function	Elasticity of substitution of ARMINGTON function	Elasticity of substitution between intermediate goods of different origin in the CES function
Rice	0.2	0.6	2.0	5.0	2.0
Wheat and potatoes	0.2	0.6	2.0	3.0	2.0
Vegetables	0.2	0.6	2.0	2.0	2.0
Fruit trees	0.2	0.6	2.0	2.0	2.0
Livestock	0.2	0.6	2.0	2.0	2.0
Fisheries	0.2	0.6	2.0	1.2	2.0
Slaughtering and dairy products	–	1.2	2.0	4.0	2.0
Processed seafood	–	1.2	2.0	2.0	2.0
Grain milling and agricultural food stuffs	–	1.2	2.0	3.0	2.0
Other foods, beverage and tobacco	–	1.2	2.0	2.0	2.0
Mining and manufacturing products	–	1.3	2.0	3.2	2.0
Construction	–	1.4	2.0	1.9	2.0

Electricity, gas, and water supply	–	1.3	2.0	2.8	2.0
Commerce	–	1.3	2.0	1.9	2.0
Transport	–	1.7	2.0	1.9	2.0
Services	–	1.3	2.0	1.9	2.0

present study adopts a method to reflect the results of the growth rate of production obtained from the production function of fruit trees, which indicates the temperature variables shown in Sect. 15.2. The panel data in Sect. 15.2 (designed to estimate the production function and the nine regional SAM, a database for the 9SCGE model) differ extensively in terms of dataset timing and regional classification. In addition, the production functions in Sect. 15.2 and the 9SCGE model do not match in terms of the production function premises and explanatory variables (excluding temperature variables). Although these two models differ vastly, the present study interprets the production growth rate calculated by the rise of the temperature shown in Table 15.5 as the impact of global warming on regional fruit tree production. Moreover, each regional production growth rate matched is obtained from the rate of change of fruit tree production and agricultural land as the initial value of the impact of global warming on fruit trees (not affected by fruit trees in other regions) in regions corresponding to the 9SCGE model. Even if the initial value is obtained using the results obtained in Sect. 15.2, it is essential to develop methods to eliminate any doubts with regard to the credibility of the simulation results obtained by combining the results of one model with another model's simulation premises. The present study addresses this point using the JMA's future temperature prediction ranges (maximum and minimum values).

Next, specific steps to obtain the parameters for simulation conditions are elaborated. This study focuses on the efficiency parameter aF_a^o obtained from a calibration regarding the fruit tree production function, as shown in Eq. (15.5):

$$\mathrm{XD}_a^o = \frac{1}{b_a^o} \cdot \left(\alpha_a^o \cdot aF_a^o\right)\left(\gamma F_a^o \cdot \mathrm{Land}_a^{o\frac{-(1-\sigma F_a)}{\sigma F_a}} + \left(1-\gamma F_a^o\right)\mathrm{KL}_a^{o\frac{-(1-\sigma F_a)}{\sigma F_a}}\right)^{\frac{-\sigma F_a}{1-\sigma F_a}}, \quad (15.5)$$

where α_a^o represents the parameter that changes the productivity of fruit tree production in each region due to climate change[10] (hereafter, this parameter is called the global warming parameter). b_a^o represents the efficiency parameter for the agricultural land–capital–labor bundle in sector a's production function of region o, aF_a represents the elasticity of substitution between agricultural land and the capital–labor bundle in the CES function, and γF_a^o represents the CES distribution parameter for the capital–labor bundle in sector a's production function of region o.

However, an alternative approach is used to change this efficiency parameter because it cannot be directly altered using the information discussed in Sect. 15.2. This approach determines a global warming parameter, which changes the efficiency parameter (i.e., this parameter's default gives a value of 1.0 to the fruit tree

[10]This parameter represents the degree to which the output of fruit tree production is affected by global warming. In other words, if the output of fruit tree production calculated by the two efficiency parameters obtained from the calibration is not subjected to global warming, this parameter is set to 1. However, if the output of fruit tree production is reduced by 10% due to global warming, the productivity is reduced by 10% by multiplying the output of fruit tree production by 0.9 of this parameter. This parameter is obtained from the search frame shown in Fig. 15.4.

production activities in the nine regions) from the 9SCGE model simulations. Using this approach, simulations were run to determine a global warming parameter that can reproduce the fruit trees' growth rate amount obtained in Sect. 15.2 in the 9SCGE model for 24 cases (fruit trees in eight regions, except Okinawa, for the maximum, mean, and minimum values, respectively). Subsequently, it is revealed that the region where citrus fruits can be grown may be expanded to the north Kanto region and the Tohoku region in the future because of the influence of global warming. However, the present study does not incorporate this point. In order to reproduce the production growth rate in the 9SCGE model, in addition to fruit tree production in the regions that are to be changed, all endogenous variables in all regions will be changed. Consistent with the changes in fruit tree production, fruit tree production factors such as agricultural land and labor variables will also change. Therefore, the changed agricultural land and labor variables were included in the production functions in Eqs. (15.2), (15.3), and (15.4) to recalculate the fruit tree production growth rate and reproduce it in the 9SCGE model. By repeating these processes, a global warming parameter was obtained in which the results of Eqs. (15.2)–(15.4)'s production functions nearly matched those of the 9SCGE model, except Chubu and Shikoku, in terms of the maximum value.[11] Tables 15.7 and 15.8 present the results. The numerical values of the central part of Table 15.7 present the results of each simulation by region using the 9SCGE model, confirming that only some regions' fruit tree production is affected by global warming and other regions are not affected. The numerical values on the right-hand side of Table 15.7 are the results of fruit tree production, including the changes in land and labor obtained in an earlier simulation by the 9SCGE model using Eqs. (15.2)–(15.4).[12] The previously mentioned search framework is shown in Fig. 15.4.[13]

---

[11] Although these processes were repeated, the optimal global warming parameters could not be obtained in Chubu and Shikoku in case of the maximum value because we were unable to obtain an optimal solution in the 9SCGE model.

[12] Specifically, the rate of change in production in Hokkaido is calculated using the coefficients in Eq. (15.4). The rate of change in production in the Kanto region of the CGE model is calculated using the coefficients and the temperature in the future obtained by multiplying the coefficients in each production function and each temperature in the future in three regions of Hokuriku, Kanto-Tosan, and Tokai by the weight of the cultivated area of Niigata prefecture, Kanto-Tosan region, and Shizuoka prefecture, respectively. Similarly, the rate of change in production in the Chubu region is calculated based on the coefficients in each production function and each temperature in the future in the two regions of Hokuriku and Tokai, and the weight of the cultivation area of Ishikawa and Toyama prefectures and Tokai region, excluding Shizuoka prefecture, respectively. The rate of change in production in the Kinki region was obtained based on the coefficients in each production function and each temperature in the future in the two regions of Hokuriku and Kinki, and the weight of the cultivated area of Fukui Prefecture and Kinki regions, respectively. However, considering the result of Hokuriku in Table 15.5, the rate of change in Hokuriku's production was reduced by 100% for the maximum, mean, and minimum values.

[13] In the simulation analysis using the 9SCGE model, the capital stock changes with land and labor, but is not used in the search framework to replicate the output value, because the coefficient of the capital stock was not statistically significant in the estimation results of the production function using panel data.

Table 15.7 Comparison of the results of fruit tree production in Eq. (15.2) with the result of the 9SCGE model

Fruit trees changes in base value (2005)	Simulation results to obtain a global warming parameter through the repetition of these processes									The result of Eq. (15.2)–(15.4)		
	Changes in land (%)			Changes in Labor (%)			Changes in Production (%)			Changes in Production (%)		
	Max	Mean	Min	Max	Mean	Min	Max	Mean	Min	Max	Mean	Min
Hokkaido	−18.26	−15.48	−12.80	–	–	–	74.20	66.39	57.84	74.81	66.38	57.82
Tohoku	4.67	3.52	2.53	–	–		−5.70	−4.29	−3.09	−5.69	−4.32	−3.13
Kanto	6.71	6.31	5.43	7.06	6.63	5.71	−39.95	−31.13	−23.90	−39.94	−31.17	−23.86
Chubu	−17.59	−2.38	0.93	−19.00	−2.61	1.02	−80.08	−55.76	−40.11	−85.98	−55.74	−40.13
Kinki	5.37	5.11	3.89	6.03	5.74	4.36	−43.02	−29.30	−18.95	−43.10	−29.33	−18.92
Chugoku	13.05	10.70	7.52	14.68	12.01	8.41	−48.82	−32.99	−21.04	−48.85	−33.00	−20.95
Shikoku	9.15	15.04	13.09	11.75	19.59	16.98	−88.87	−69.80	−52.51	−99.69	−69.77	−52.56
Kyushu	12.68	10.70	8.71	15.40	12.95	10.50	−39.31	−31.44	−24.61	−39.35	−31.43	−24.59

Table 15.8 Setting of the nine regions' global warming parameters with/without adaptation technologies

	Adaptation technologies does not exist			Adaptation technologies exist
	A maximun rise in temperature	A mean rise in temperature	A minimun rise in temperature	A mean rise in temperature
Hokkaido	2.140	1.970	1.811	1.970
Tohoku	0.899	0.923	0.944	0.962
Kanto	0.561	0.646	0.720	0.823
Chubu	0.245	0.454	0.593	0.727
Kinki	0.537	0.669	0.777	0.835
Chugoku	0.447	0.599	0.729	0.800
Shikoku	0.100	0.254	0.408	0.627
Kyushu	0.528	0.609	0.684	0.805
Okinawa	1.000	1.000	1.000	1.000

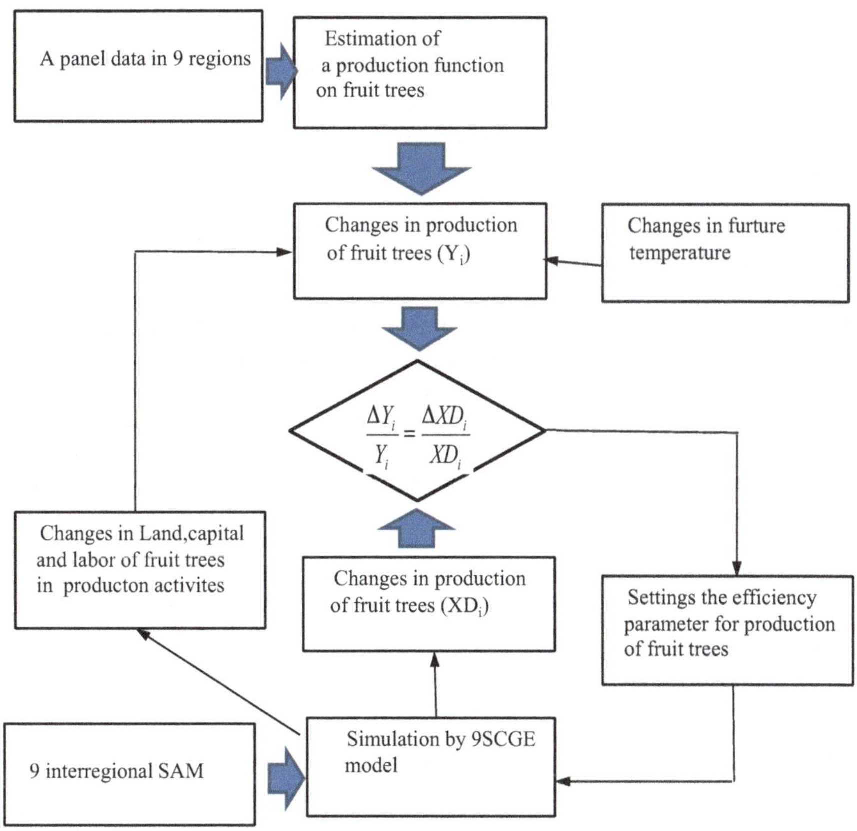

Fig. 15.4 Search framework for global warming parameters

By inserting the global warming parameters of the eight regions in Table 15.8 into the 9SCGE model, global warming simulations without adaptation technologies were performed using three scenarios: when the future temperature becomes (1) the maximum value, (2) the mean value, and (3) the minimum value. This was used to measure the impact of each scenario on regional economies and the economic welfare of each region as well as the economic spillover effects on agriculture, forestry, fishery, and food and beverage industries. Next, it was assumed that the development of high-temperature-tolerant fruit tree varieties has resulted in curbing global warming-induced productivity decline (with adaptation technologies, mean value) for regions in which global warming parameter when future temperature has a mean value of 1 or below. These global warming parameters were calculated on the basis of the assumption that productivity decline will improve by 50%.[14] This parameter was also used to run global warming simulations with adaptation technologies based on the 9SCGE model to measure the degree to which the negative economic impact can be mitigated by comparing the results of the former. In this simulation, two settings are made. One is a case wherein only the setting of the global warming parameter is changed. In this case, there are only adaptation technologies. In order to minimize the decrease in the supply of fruit trees to the market due to global warming, it is essential to increase the supply of imported fruit trees to the market using a method to abolish tariffs. In this case, there are adaptation technology and tariff reduction policies. In this simulation, the import tariff rate is set to 0% from plus 9.8% at 2005 (weighted average among regions) for fruit trees.[15]

15.4.2 Simulation Results

Table 15.9 reveals the following six points. First, in the simulations assuming alterations in regional fruit tree production owing to Japan's rise in temperature over the next 60–80 years (global warming simulations without adaptation technologies), the national equivalent variation (economic welfare) will decline by 142.69 billion yen when the impact of global warming is minimum and by 302.79 billion yen when the impact is maximum (compared to the 2005 standards). When this is

[14] The Yomiuri Shimbun on May 6, 2015, reported, "the Ministry of Agriculture, Forestry, and Fisheries will strengthen research to make agricultural products strong against heat and water shortage as a measure against global warming from 2015." Assuming that the annual average temperature rises by 2 °C in that, predicting to what extent crop yield and quality will decline for domestic major agricultural crops, with the aim of suppressing such damage to less than half.

[15] It has been pointed out that Japan's volume of imported goods has been small. The reason is not a result of a high import tariff rate but because there are nontariff barriers that prohibit importation unless quality standards are met. In response to these indications, the CGE model cannot simulate nontariff barriers per se, but it is possible to analyze by replacing the portion corresponding to the nontariff barrier with a higher import tariff rate than the present import tariff rate. Carrying out such a simulation will be for future study.

converted into per capita value, a decline will be in the range of 1123 to 2382 yen. Regionwise data reveal that eight regions, except Hokkaido, will be negatively affected, whereas Shikoku is affected the maximum by global warming, in which the decline will be up to 10,240 yen per person, creating a gap of 10,824 yen in comparison to Hokkaido, which will see a 584 yen increase. Similarly, considering the impact of global warming on regional economies, although the real GRP will decrease by 0.02%–0.05% from Tohoku to Kinki, the west of Chugoku will decline by more than 0.05%, and a decline in the real GRP will be the largest in Shikoku at −0.46%. Meanwhile, the real GRP in any region, except Hokkaido, whose real GRP will increase by 0.01%, will be negatively affected by global warming with regard to fruit trees.

Second, although global warming will increase fruit tree production in Hokkaido, Tohoku, and Okinawa, the production will decrease in the west of Kanto, except Okinawa, with a −17.36% to −31.87% national decline. Meanwhile, production in Hokkaido will witness an increase of 88.95% in case of the maximum value and 62.94% increase in case of the minimum value. In addition, production in Tohoku will increase by 0.08% to 1.51%. Comparing this rate of decrease with the simulation results (Table 15.7), assuming that only Tohoku will be negatively affected by global warming, the mean value will increase from −4.29% to 0.47%. In case of the maximum value, the rate of increase in production will grow +1.51% from −5.70%. This is because the outflow (exports) from Tohoku to other regions, which is negatively affected by global warming, will rise and the inflow (imports) to Tohoku from other regions will decrease because of the decline in the fruit tree production of other regions and the differences in the cost of fruit trees between Tohoku and other regions. A similar situation arises in Hokkaido and Okinawa.

Third, through changes in regional fruit tree production, we find that other agricultural products' production will be affected negatively in each region, except Hokkaido and a partial case of Chubu. This is because the three production factors of agricultural land, capital, and labor will shift from other agricultural products to fruit trees. As a result, other agricultural products will decrease in each region. It is to the west of Tohoku, as the productivity of fruit trees declines because of global warming, that the production factors are introduced to mitigate a possible decline in fruit tree production. As a result, the production factors of other agricultural products shift to fruit trees, and the production volume of other agricultural products decreases. Conversely, in Hokkaido, the productivity of fruit trees rises because of the positive effect of global warming, so there is no shift in the production factor for fruit trees due to global warming. However, as fruit tree production in the west of Kanto decreases, fruit tree exports from Hokkaido to the west of Kanto increase because of the differences in the price of fruit trees between regions as mentioned earlier. As a result, the production factor shifts from vegetables and livestock to fruit trees in order to increase the fruit tree production, and the production volume of these other products decreases even in this region. In case of the maximum value in Chubu, as fruit tree production drastically declines (77.15% decrease) as a result of global warming, the production volume of agricultural products will increase as production factors are shifted from fruit trees to rice and wheat/potatoes. The

Table 15.9 Simulation results using the 9SCGE model

Changes in output of base value (2005)			Economic welfare		Main index (unit: %)			Direct and indirect effect by global warming (unit: %)	
Region	With/Without adaptation technologies	Degree of a rise in temperture	Equivalent Variation unit: billion yen	E.V. per capita unit: yen	Real GRP	Total output	Farmer household's sales	Total crops	Rice
Whole country	Without adaptation technologies	Max	−302.79	−2382	−0.06%	−0.04%	−0.06%	−4.88%	−0.57%
		Mean	−206.56	−1625	−0.04%	−0.03%	0.22%	−3.69%	−0.48%
		Min	−142.69	−1123	−0.03%	−0.02%	0.23%	−2.70%	−0.36%
	With adaptation technologies (Mean value)	Only adapation technologies	−81.09	−638	−0.02%	−0.01%	0.13%	−1.66%	−0.22%
		With tariff reduction	−51.57	−406	−0.02%	−0.01%	−0.32%	−1.94%	−0.15%
Hokkaido	Without adaptation technologies	Max	3.15	584	0.01%	0.01%	0.54%	1.28%	0.60%
		Mean	3.80	706	0.01%	0.01%	0.49%	1.11%	0.58%
		Min	3.85	716	0.01%	0.01%	0.41%	0.93%	0.46%
	With adaptation technologies (mean value)	Only adapation technologies	5.21	968	0.01%	0.01%	0.35%	0.99%	0.31%
		With tariff reduction	6.91	1284	0.01%	0.02%	0.21%	0.83%	0.15%
Tohoku	Without adaptation technologies	Max	−7.02	−782	−0.05%	−0.04%	1.65%	−0.05%	−0.47%
		Mean	−5.08	−565	−0.03%	−0.03%	1.22%	−0.08%	−0.21%
		Min	−3.58	−398	−0.02%	−0.02%	0.86%	−0.07%	−0.10%
	With adaptation technologies (mean value)	Only adapation technologies	−2.20	−245	−0.01%	−0.01%	0.46%	−0.13%	−0.04%
		With tariff reduction	−1.47	−164	−0.01%	−0.01%	0.17%	−0.33%	−0.08%

Kanto	Without adaptation technologies	Max	−120.42	−2319	−0.04%	−0.03%	0.54%	−4.20%	−0.52%
		Mean	−88.67	−1707	−0.03%	−0.02%	0.38%	−3.26%	−0.27%
		Min	−64.90	−1250	−0.02%	−0.02%	0.25%	−2.51%	−0.17%
	With adaptation technologies (mean value)	Only adapation technologies	−37.28	−718	−0.01%	−0.01%	0.13%	−1.53%	−0.09%
		With tariff reduction	−25.97	−500	−0.01%	−0.01%	−0.44%	−1.94%	−0.03%
Chubu	Without adaptation technologies	Max	−37.97	−2802	−0.05%	−0.01%	−2.95%	−6.51%	0.83%
		Mean	−23.44	−1730	−0.03%	−0.01%	−1.17%	−4.74%	−0.18%
		Min	−15.88	−1172	−0.02%	−0.01%	−0.60%	−3.41%	−0.31%
	With adaptation technologies (mean value)	Only adapation technologies	−9.56	−705	−0.01%	−0.01%	−0.32%	−2.21%	−0.24%
		With tariff reduction	−4.28	−316	−0.01%	0.00%	−0.83%	−2.37%	0.03%
Kinki	Without adaptation technologies	Max	−44.57	−2072	−0.04%	−0.02%	−2.05%	−8.38%	−0.18%
		Mean	−30.54	−1420	−0.03%	−0.02%	−0.99%	−5.61%	−0.02%
		Min	−20.06	−933	−0.02%	−0.01%	−0.47%	−3.57%	0.02%
	With adaptation technologies (mean value)	Only adapation technologies	−13.52	−629	−0.01%	−0.01%	−0.38%	−2.63%	−0.01%
		With tariff reduction	−7.91	−368	−0.01%	0.00%	−1.19%	−3.18%	0.13%
Chugoku	Without adaptation technologies	Max	−25.21	−3389	−0.08%	−0.05%	−0.08%	−8.15%	−0.84%
		Mean	−16.48	−2216	−0.05%	−0.04%	0.58%	−5.16%	−0.27%
		Min	−10.39	−1397	−0.03%	−0.03%	0.68%	−3.08%	−0.05%
	With adaptation technologies (mean value)	Only adapation technologies	−6.92	−930	−0.02%	−0.02%	−0.11%	−2.67%	−0.02%
		With tariff reduction	−5.12	−688	−0.02%	−0.01%	−0.26%	−2.67%	0.01%

(continued)

Table 15.9 (continued)

Changes in output of base value (2005)			Economic welfare		Main index (unit: %)			Direct and indirect effect by global warming (unit: %)	
Region	With/Without adaptation technologies	Degree of a rise in temperture	Equivalent Variation unit: billion yen	E.V. per capita unit: yen	Real GRP	Total output	Farmer household's sales	Total crops	Rice
Shikoku	Without adaptation technologies	Max	−39.38	−10,240	−0.46%	−0.24%	−7.10%	−22.00%	−2.64%
		Mean	−22.19	−5770	−0.33%	−0.25%	−3.11%	−17.82%	−5.05%
		Min	−13.80	−3588	−0.23%	−0.20%	−1.60%	−13.30%	−4.59%
	With adaptation technologies (mean value)	Only adapation technologies	−6.83	−1775	−0.13%	−0.12%	−0.55%	−7.56%	−3.00%
		With tariff reduction	−6.12	−1591	−0.13%	−0.11%	−1.13%	−7.81%	−2.56%
Kyushu	Without adaptation technologies	Max	−30.46	−2340	−0.12%	−0.10%	1.15%	−6.07%	−2.24%
		Mean	−23.26	−1787	−0.09%	−0.08%	0.85%	−4.79%	−1.64%
		Min	−17.42	−1338	−0.07%	−0.06%	0.59%	−3.73%	−1.22%
	With adaptation technologies (mean value)	Only adapation technologies	−9.71	−746	−0.04%	−0.04%	0.38%	−2.13%	−0.71%
		With tariff reduction	−7.53	−579	−0.04%	−0.03%	−0.05%	−2.38%	−0.56%
Okinawa	Without adaptation technologies	Max	−0.93	−646	−0.01%	0.00%	4.76%	4.01%	−4.48%
		Mean	−0.70	−488	0.00%	0.00%	3.21%	2.72%	−2.66%
		Min	−0.51	−356	0.00%	0.00%	2.18%	1.85%	−1.68%
	With adaptation technologies (mean value)	Only adapation technologies	−0.29	−204	0.00%	0.00%	1.16%	0.99%	−0.84%
		With tariff reduction	−0.08	−53	0.00%	0.00%	0.51%	0.42%	−0.28%

			Spillover effect to non-agriculture output (unit: %)					
Wheat and potatoes	Vegetables	Fruit trees	Livestock	Slaughtering and dairy products	Grain milling and agricultural food stuffs	Other foods, beverage and Tobacco	Mining and manufacturing products	Services
−0.94%	−0.20%	−31.87%	−0.22%	−0.16%	−0.46%	−0.41%	0.05%	−0.02%
−0.85%	−0.18%	−23.80%	−0.17%	−0.13%	−0.39%	−0.29%	0.03%	−0.01%
−0.66%	−0.14%	−17.36%	−0.13%	−0.10%	−0.29%	−0.20%	0.02%	−0.01%
−0.40%	−0.08%	−10.66%	−0.07%	−0.06%	−0.18%	−0.11%	0.01%	−0.01%
−0.22%	−0.05%	−13.10%	−0.05%	−0.03%	−0.11%	0.54%	0.02%	−0.01%
0.02%	−0.06%	88.95%	−0.20%	−0.13%	−0.07%	−0.35%	−0.01%	0.01%
0.04%	−0.05%	74.67%	−0.14%	−0.10%	−0.06%	−0.20%	−0.01%	0.00%
0.04%	−0.04%	62.94%	−0.10%	−0.07%	−0.04%	−0.13%	−0.01%	0.00%
0.04%	−0.01%	69.37%	−0.06%	−0.05%	0.00%	−0.08%	−0.02%	0.00%
0.07%	0.01%	59.14%	−0.04%	−0.03%	0.04%	−0.05%	−0.01%	0.00%
−1.02%	−0.14%	1.51%	−0.11%	−0.10%	−0.43%	−0.16%	−0.01%	−0.02%
−0.76%	−0.10%	0.47%	−0.08%	−0.07%	−0.35%	−0.12%	0.00%	−0.02%
−0.54%	−0.07%	0.08%	−0.05%	−0.05%	−0.26%	−0.08%	0.00%	−0.01%
−0.32%	−0.04%	−0.52%	−0.03%	−0.03%	−0.15%	−0.05%	0.00%	−0.01%
−0.15%	−0.03%	−1.57%	−0.01%	−0.01%	−0.09%	−0.03%	0.02%	−0.01%
−1.31%	−0.18%	−30.24%	−0.09%	−0.09%	−0.39%	−0.44%	0.04%	−0.02%
−1.02%	−0.14%	−23.86%	−0.06%	−0.07%	−0.30%	−0.30%	0.03%	−0.01%
−0.76%	−0.10%	−18.54%	−0.05%	−0.05%	−0.22%	−0.21%	0.02%	−0.01%
−0.45%	−0.06%	−11.32%	−0.03%	−0.03%	−0.13%	−0.12%	0.01%	0.00%
−0.19%	−0.03%	−15.01%	−0.01%	0.00%	−0.07%	1.39%	0.03%	−0.01%
0.42%	−0.01%	−77.15%	−0.03%	−0.06%	−0.26%	−0.45%	0.06%	−0.02%
−1.25%	−0.12%	−50.90%	−0.06%	−0.08%	−0.33%	−0.30%	0.03%	−0.02%
−1.28%	−0.11%	−35.38%	−0.05%	−0.06%	−0.28%	−0.21%	0.02%	−0.01%
−0.88%	−0.07%	−22.65%	−0.03%	−0.04%	−0.18%	−0.12%	0.01%	−0.01%

(continued)

Table 15.9 (continued)

			Spillover effect to non-agriculture output (unit: %)					
Wheat and potatoes	Vegetables	Fruit trees	Livestock	Slaughtering and dairy products	Grain milling and agricultural food stuffs	Other foods, beverage and Tobacco	Mining and manufacturing products	Services
−0.20%	−0.02%	−26.49%	−0.01%	−0.01%	−0.08%	−0.08%	0.01%	−0.01%
−0.91%	−0.26%	−41.92%	−0.05%	−0.11%	−0.30%	−0.33%	0.03%	−0.01%
−0.93%	−0.23%	−28.08%	−0.06%	−0.09%	−0.25%	−0.24%	0.02%	−0.01%
−0.71%	−0.18%	−17.89%	−0.04%	−0.07%	−0.19%	−0.18%	0.01%	−0.01%
−0.50%	−0.12%	−13.11%	−0.03%	−0.04%	−0.12%	−0.10%	0.01%	0.00%
−0.03%	−0.02%	−16.53%	0.03%	−0.01%	−0.06%	−0.07%	0.03%	−0.01%
−3.65%	−0.42%	−43.60%	−0.33%	−0.27%	−0.89%	−0.63%	0.03%	−0.04%
−3.08%	−0.35%	−28.12%	−0.27%	−0.22%	−0.70%	−0.43%	0.01%	−0.02%
−2.24%	−0.25%	−16.96%	−0.19%	−0.16%	−0.50%	−0.29%	0.00%	−0.02%
−1.47%	−0.16%	−14.96%	−0.12%	−0.10%	−0.31%	−0.17%	0.00%	−0.01%
−0.97%	−0.11%	−15.25%	−0.08%	−0.06%	−0.23%	−0.13%	0.02%	−0.01%
−1.69%	−0.06%	−88.68%	−0.17%	−0.15%	−1.17%	−0.61%	0.39%	−0.11%
−3.52%	−0.23%	−68.32%	−0.27%	−0.20%	−1.46%	−0.47%	0.12%	−0.09%
−3.20%	−0.21%	−50.04%	−0.24%	−0.17%	−1.21%	−0.34%	0.04%	−0.07%
−2.10%	−0.14%	−27.97%	−0.15%	−0.11%	−0.76%	−0.19%	0.01%	−0.04%
−1.73%	−0.12%	−29.53%	−0.12%	−0.08%	−0.61%	−0.16%	0.02%	−0.04%
−2.45%	−0.43%	−32.39%	−0.50%	−0.44%	−1.07%	−0.43%	0.06%	−0.03%
−1.84%	−0.32%	−25.93%	−0.38%	−0.33%	−0.81%	−0.32%	0.03%	−0.02%
−1.37%	−0.23%	−20.38%	−0.28%	−0.25%	−0.61%	−0.23%	0.02%	−0.02%
−0.81%	−0.14%	−11.62%	−0.16%	−0.15%	−0.35%	−0.13%	0.01%	−0.01%
−0.59%	−0.10%	−13.75%	−0.12%	−0.10%	−0.26%	−0.10%	0.02%	−0.01%
−0.72%	−0.47%	14.41%	−0.05%	−0.07%	−0.58%	−0.09%	0.01%	−0.01%
−0.48%	−0.30%	9.67%	−0.03%	−0.05%	−0.45%	−0.07%	0.01%	−0.01%

−0.32%	−0.19%	6.56%	−0.02%	−0.03%	−0.33%	−0.06%	0.01%	−0.01%
−0.16%	−0.10%	3.49%	−0.01%	−0.02%	−0.19%	−0.03%	0.00%	0.00%
−0.08%	−0.05%	1.49%	0.00%	−0.01%	−0.12%	−0.02%	0.01%	−0.01%

regional production of agricultural products throughout the nation will decrease by 2.70%–4.88%. When the impact of global warming is the mean value and the minimum value, the farmers' sales will increase by 0.22% and 0.23%, respectively. However, in case of the maximum value, farmers' sales will decrease by 0.06%. Farmers' sales will change along with these changes in producer prices for fruit trees and other agricultural products, following four different outcomes among regions. The first outcome is farmers' sales will increase in Hokkaido as both the production volume of fruit trees will increase more than the rate of decline in producer price and the production volume of rice and wheat/potatoes will increase in addition to a rise in producer prices. The second outcome is that farmers' sales will increase in Tohoku and Okinawa as producer prices of agricultural products, including fruit trees, will rise more than the rate of decrease in production volume of agricultural products, excluding fruit trees. The third outcome is that farmers' sales will increase in Kanto, Kyushu, and Chugoku, except the maximum value, as producer prices of agricultural products, including fruit trees, will rise more than the rate of decrease in production volume of agricultural products, including fruit trees. The fourth outcome is that farmers' sales will decrease in Chubu, Kinki, Shikoku, and Chugoku in case of the maximum value as the decline in fruit tree production will be higher than the producer prices of fruit tree production. As shown earlier, the impact of global warming on fruit trees is demonstrated to widen the gap in the farmers' income among regions.

Fourth, we consider the spillover effects of global warming on other industries impacted by global warming on the production of agricultural products. Livestock production will be negatively affected in all regions. In the case of the agriculturally dependent food and beverage industries, these industries will experience a negative impact in all regions with a −0.20% to −0.46% national decline. Considering the production in the mining and manufacturing industries as well as in the service industry, the mining and manufacturing industries in all regions, except Hokkaido and Tohoku in case of the maximum value, will be positively affected with a 0.02%–0.05% national rise, but the service industry will be negatively affected with a −0.01% to −0.02% national decline in all regions, except Hokkaido. Meanwhile, in Hokkaido, service industries will remain nearly constant.

Fifth, assuming that a range of global warming-induced decline in productivity has increased by 50%, owing to the adaptation technologies for fruit trees in regions affected by global warming, the positive impact on fruit tree production in Hokkaido and Okinawa will be lower than that in the range of increase in case of the mean value, but the fruit tree production in Tohoku will decrease by 0.52% from +0.08% in the minimum value. While the negative impact on fruit tree production in the west of Kanto will be lower than the range of decline. Consequently, the rate of decline in national fruit tree production improves by 6.70% points from −17.36% in the minimum value. Moreover, a decline in the national equivalent variation will be reduced by 125.47 billion yen to −81.09 billion yen. It falls below 142.69 billion yen when the impact of global warming without adaptation technologies is the minimum value. Given the differences between Hokkaido, which is positively affected by global warming, and Shikoku, which is most negatively affected, the regional gap in the real GRP will slightly reduce from 0.34% to 0.14%. It was also found that the equivalent variation gaps between Hokkaido and Shikoku will reduce from 6476 yen to 2743 yen per person. In terms of farmers' sales, the national mean value with adaptation technologies will increase by 0.13%, a 0.09% decline from the mean value without adaptation technologies, which will increase by 0.22%.

Lastly, we consider the simulation result with the mean value of with adaptation technology and tariff reduction policies. In the cases with only the adaptation technologies mentioned earlier, the supply of fruit trees to the market will decrease by about 51.00 billion yen compared with the base value (2005), as shown in Fig. 15.5. By contrast, the imported amount of fruit trees increases by only about 26.97 billion yen. However, as described earlier, when the simulation is run according to the setting with tariff reduction policy, the decline in the supply of fruit trees to the market will become 35.23 billion yen, and the import amount will increase to 61.07 billion yen but will be less than the increase in case of without adaptation technologies (76.69 billion yen) shown in the right-hand side of Fig. 15.5.[16] As the imported fruit trees are supplied to the market, as described earlier, both fruit tree production in the region and the farmers' sales will change (Table 15.9). Considering the whole country, the domestic fruit tree production as a whole will decrease by 13.10%, a 2.44% point decline from 10.66% decrease without tariff reduction policy. This is somewhat lower than the case of the minimum value without adaptation technology (17.36% decrease). Moreover, farmers' sales decrease by 0.32% as a rise in domestic goods price is suppressed by imported goods. By region, in the west of Kanto, except Okinawa, farmers' sales will reduce by 0.05%–1.19% and will reduce by 0.17%–0.51% in Hokkaido, Tohoku, and Okinawa. However, equivalent variations in all regions are improved, and those in all regions that were negative, except Hokkaido, are reduced. Consequently, the national equivalent variance shows a decrease of 51.57 billion yen from a decrease of 81.09 billion yen, and the per capita value is up to −406 yen from −638 yen. However, the gap between Hokkaido and Shikoku will widen from 2743 to 2875 yen again. Next, considering the changes in the real GRP and the total output, the real GRP and the total output in each region have not remained nearly constant regardless of tariff reduction policy.

On the basis of these results, tariff reduction policy and the development of adaptation technology for global warming are worth considering as measures against global warming for each regional economy, although increasing imports of fruit trees will negatively affect the farmers' income.

---

[16] The reason why the import amount in the case of without the adaptation technology increases by 76.69 billion yen from the base value is that the producer price is relatively higher than the import price of the imported fruit trees because the domestic fruit tree production decreases due to global warming. If a nontariff barrier exists, the import volume does not change significantly from the base value. Therefore, we determined the import tariff rate corresponding to the nontariff barrier by searching the import tariff rate so that the import volume does not increase through some simulations in the CGE model. Moreover, when the estimated import tariff rate is set to zero, a simulation that removes nontariff barriers is possible.

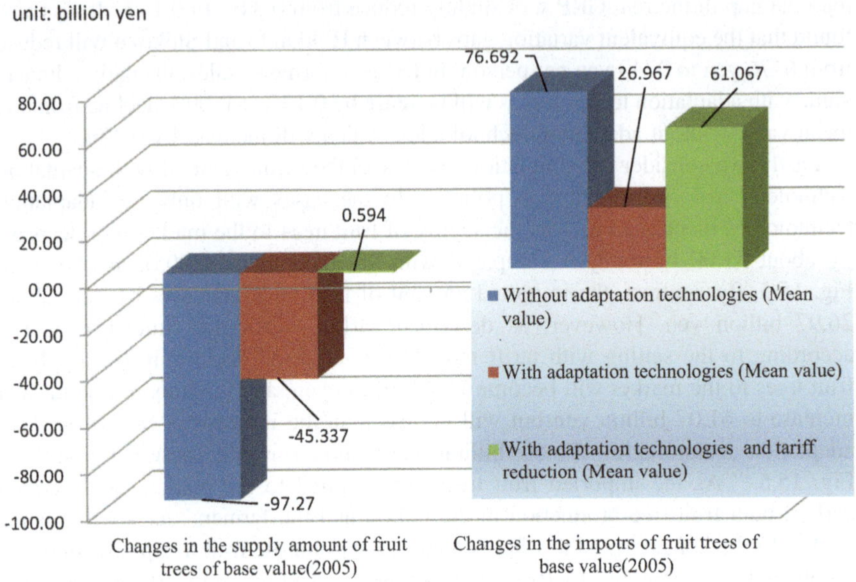

Fig. 15.5 Changes in the supply and in the imports of fruit trees of base value (2005)

15.5 Conclusion and Policy Implications

On the basis of the assumption that only fruit trees are affected by global warming, this study presented the impact of global warming on regional economies through spillover effects from other agricultural products and the industrial sector having an input–output relationship with agriculture. This study found that global warming-induced climate change has different influences on each region and creates regional economic disparities. For example, global warming has a positive impact on regional economies in Hokkaido, Tohoku, and Okinawa, although it is assumed that the impact of global warming on fruit trees is negative in Tohoku and neutral in Okinawa. This is because the outflow (exports) from these three regions to other regions, which is negatively affected by global warming, will increase and the inflow (imports) to these three regions from other regions will decrease because of the decline in fruit tree production of other regions and the differences in costs of fruits trees between these three regions and other regions. Moreover, with these changes in producer prices for fruit trees and other agricultural products alone, farmers' sales will increase with different outcomes among regions. Farmers' sales will increase in Hokkaido, Tohoku, Kanto, Chugoku, except in the case of the maximum value, Kyushu, and Okinawa, and farmers' sales will decrease in Chubu, Kinki, Chugoku, and Shikoku in case of the maximum value. As shown earlier, the impact of global warming on fruit trees has been found to widen the gap in farmers' income among regions. In addition, assuming that adaptation technologies, such as high-temperature-tolerant fruit tree varieties, are developed in each region, the negative impact on fruit tree production in the west of Kanto will be lower than the rate of decline. Consequently, the rate of decline in national fruit tree production improves. Furthermore, a decline in the national equivalent variation will be reduced, and the equivalent variation gaps between Hokkaido and Shikoku will be reduced. When a tariff reduction policy for fruit trees and adaptation technologies is applied, increasing imports of fruit trees will negatively affect farmers' income. Moreover, although equivalent variations in all regions are improved, the equivalent variation gap between Hokkaido and Shikoku will widen again. The study revealed that it is necessary to develop another framework. Therefore, it is essential to draw aggressive policies to further promote a sixth industrialization linking cooperative agriculture, the food processing industry, and the service industry currently undertaken.

References

Ban K (2007) Development of a Multiregional Dynamic Applied General Equilibrium Model for the Japanese Economy; Regional Economic Analysis Based on a Forward-Looking Perspective. RIETI Discussion Paper Series 07-J-043 (in Japanese)

EcoMod Modeling School (2012) Advanced Techniques in CGE Modeling with GAMS. Global Economic Modeling Network, Singapore, January 9–13

Fujimori S, Iizumi T, Hasegawa T, Takakura J, Takahashi K, Hijioka Y (2018) Macroeconomic impacts of climate change driven by changes in crop yields. Sustainability 10:3673

Furuya J, Kobayashi S, Yamamoto Y, Nishimori M (2015) Climate change effects on long-term world-crop production: incorporating a crop model into long-term yield estimates. JARQ 49(2): 187–202

Greene WH (2012) Econometric analysis. Pearson Education, London

Hayashiyama Y, Abe M, Muto S (2011) Evaluation of GHG discharge reduction policy by 47 prefectures multi-regional CGE. J Appl Reg Sci 16:67–91

Hosoe N, Gasawa K, Hashimoto H (2010) Textbook of computable general equilibrium modeling: programming and simulations. Palgrave Macmillan, New York

Japan Meteorological Agency (2017) Global warming projection, vol 9, p 8

Kunimitsu Y (2015) Regional impacts of long-term climate change on rice production and agricultural income: evidence from computable general equilibrium analysis. JARQ 49(2): 173–185

Kunimitsu Y, Iizumi Y, Yokozawa M (2013) Is long-term climate change beneficial or harmful for rice total factor productivity in Japan: evidence from a panel data analysis. Paddy Water Environ 12:213–225. https://doi.org/10.1007/s10333-013-0368-0

Kunimitsu Y, Sakurai G, Iizumi T (2020) Systemic risk in global agricultural markets and trade liberalization under climate change: synchronized crop-yield change and agricultural price volatility. Sustainability 12:10680

Ministry of the Environment (2015) Report on Assessment of Impacts of Climate Change in Japan and Future Challenges (Central Environment Council Comment Submission)

Okiyama M, Tokunaga S (2016) Impact of global warming on a regional economy through fluctuation in agricultural production: utilizing the multi-regional CGE model. J Rural Econ 87(4):341–346. (in Japanese)

Okiyama M, Tokunaga S (2019) Impact of climate change on a regional economy through changes in Japan's crops production: utilizing the 8 interregional CGE model. J Rural Econ 91(2): 293–298. (in Japanese)

Tanaka T, Hosoe N (2009) Productivity Shocks and National Food Security for Japan. RIETI Discussion Paper Series 09-J-009 (in Japanese)

Tokunaga S, Resosudarmo BP, Wuryanto LE, Dung NT (2003) An inter-regional CGE model to assess the impacts of tariff reduction and fiscal decentralization on regional economy: the case of Indonesia. Stud Reg Sci 33(2):1–25

Tokunaga S, Okiyama M, Ikegawa M (2015) Dynamic panel data analysis of the impacts of climate change on agricultural production in Japan. JARQ 49(2):149–157

Tokunaga S, Okiyama M, Ikegawa M (2016) Impacts of climate change on agricultural production: a dynamic panel data analysis. In: Furuya J (ed) Assessing the impacts of climate change on agriculture and countermeasures. Yokendo, pp 61–80

Tokunaga S, Okiyama M, Ikegawa M (2017) Impact of climate change on regional economies through fluctuations in Japan's rice production: using dynamic panel data and spatial CGE models. In: Shibusawa H et al (eds) Socioeconomic environmental policies and evaluations in regional science essays in honor of Yoshiro Higano: new frontiers in regional science: Asian perspectives, vol 24. Springer, Berlin, pp 557–580

Tokunaga S, Okiyama M, Ikegawa M (2020a) Spatial analysis of climate change impacts on regional economies through Japan's rice production changes and innovative food industry cluster: using the nine interregional CGE model. In: Madden J et al (eds) Environmental economics and computable general equilibrium analysis: essays in memory of Yuzuru Miyata: new frontiers in regional science: asian perspectives, vol 41. Springer, Berlin, pp 301–332

Tokunaga S, Okiyama M, Ikegawa M (2020b) Effects of climate change on depopulating regional economies through changes in Japan's rice production and recovery policies. Asia Pac J Reg Sci 4(3):691–712

Yokozawa M, Iizumi T, Okada M (2009) Large scale projection of climate change impacts on variability in rice yield in Japan. Glob Environ Res 14(2):199–206. (in Japanese)

Chapter 16
Economic Value of Coral Reefs in Palau

Yoko Fujita, Kaoruko Miyakuni, and Lincy Lee Marino

Abstract The aim of this research is to estimate how much Palauan people value coral reefs in the Rock Island Southern Lagoon (RISL) in Palau by using the Contingent Valuation Method, which is one of the methods used in Environmental Economics. According to some surveys, Palauan people are comparatively more environmentally conscious than those from other countries. However, in recent years, land development has been rapidly increased, and the number of tourists has been drastically increasing as well. Climate change is a global phenomenon that is affecting the condition of the marine environment. These trends cause serious damages to the natural environment. Since coral reefs provide some of the most important resources to the Palauan people, we conducted this study to understand the value of coral reefs to the people of Palau and as a result develop appropriate and effective conservation policy for Palau's coral reefs. As a result of CVM survey conducted in Koror and Airai states, people's "willingness to pay" and "willingness to work" are estimated at US $8.00 per month with a total annual value that is estimated at US $452,448. These estimated values can be used as critical information for compensation for coral damage, evaluation of economic efficiency of conservation policy, and improving awareness or education for Palauan residents.

Keywords Contingent valuation method · Coral reef · Republic of Palau

Y. Fujita (✉) · K. Miyakuni
University of the Ryukyus, Okinawa, Japan
e-mail: yfujita@eve.u-ryukyu.ac.jp

L. L. Marino
Present affiliation: Palau International Coral Reef Center, Koror, Republic of Palau

M. Kawano et al. (eds.), *Theory and History in Regional Perspective*, New Frontiers in Regional Science: Asian Perspectives 56,
https://doi.org/10.1007/978-981-16-6695-7_16

16.1 Introduction

The Republic of Palau is a small island developing country in the Micronesian Region. According to the Census 2015 of this country, the population is 17,661, and 80.5% of the population is concentrated in Koror State and Airai State.

The target area of this research, The Rock Islands Southern Lagoon (RISL) area is one of the foremost natural sites in Palau and was designated as a UNESCO Mixed Cultural and Natural World Heritage Site in 2012. Coral reefs in this area provide various useful ecosystem services to Palauan residents and their community. Some ecosystem services include the preservation of marine biodiversity, spawning and nurturing space for marine life, purifying water, fishing area and source of food, recreational/tourism sites, beautiful ocean view, effective natural breakwater, and so on. Therefore, The Palau National Government and Koror State Government establish laws and guidelines to maintain good condition of coral reefs including this area. Also, many people in Palau recognize that coral reefs are important for themselves. However, in recent years, people's livelihoods have drastically changed. Construction of road and hotel causes the contamination of seawater and damage coral reefs by sediments. Additionally, the number of tourists has been increasing since 2014, and not every visitor is as environmentally conscious, thus resulting in negative use of the marine resources. Though some would rather conserve and preserve the environment, others are more in favor of economic development. This conflict between preserving the environment and economic development is ongoing, not only in Palau, but also in other small island countries in the world.

Thus, in order to make the proper decisions for sustainable economic development, the country must identify its top priority and its subsequent value to society. It is necessary to draw comparisons between the profits from economic development and the benefits of environmental conservation. In other words, there need to be some discussions regarding environmental conservation and economic development under the same conditions. For this purpose, there are various methods for economic valuation that were developed in the field of Environmental Economics. Thus, with economic valuation, the non-market value of nature can be evaluated in monetary terms.

16.2 Methods

Figure 16.1 shows the categories of the economic valuation method for environment. All methods are divided into preference-independent method and preference-dependent method. Preference-independent methods estimate the value of nature by market price or cost. Preference-dependent method is suitable to estimate non-use values of natural environment (e.g., beautiful views, biodiversity, cultural value, recreational function, etc.). The loss of the natural environment due to economic development was expressed in terms of market value, such as the decrease in

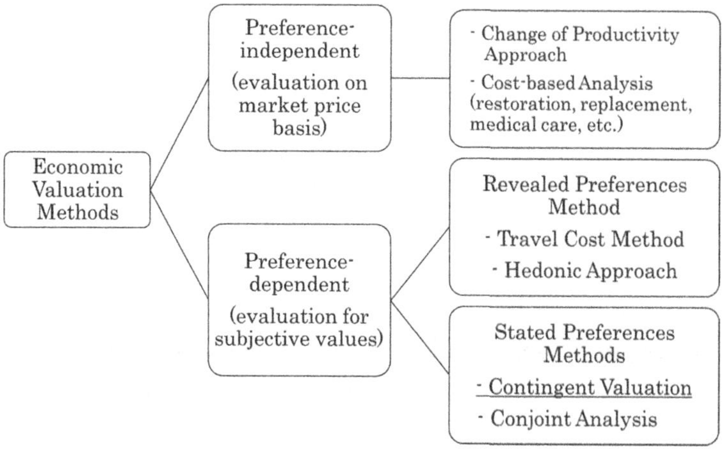

Fig. 16.1 Methods of economic valuation (Source: Turner et al. 1993; Bateman et al. 2002, revised by the author)

production value in related industries, for example, fisheries and tourism, and did not include the decrease in people's utility due to the decline of the nature's quality. As a result, the value of the natural environment was underestimated, and economic development tended to take priority over environmental conservation. However, as awareness of the environment increased not only in developed countries but also in developing countries, the need to express the changes in people's utility caused by environmental changes in monetary term and directly compare them with the benefits of economic development came to be the focus of attention. In the field of environmental economics, the stated-preference method was developed to evaluate the level of people's subjective value that people attach to the natural environment, that is, the non-market value of the natural environment.

The aim of this study is to estimate how much Palauan people value coral reefs and its conservation. Therefore, the Contingent Valuation Method (CVM), which is one of the stated-preference methods, was chosen in order to estimate the subjective values of Palauan people. A famous case back in 1989 was that of the Exxon Valdez oil spill incident which happened off the coast of Alaska. Due to the extent of the damages as a result of the oil spill, Exxon was required to compensate the State for the loss of ecosystem, in addition to recovery cost and fishery product loss (use value). The CVM method was used to estimate the non-use value of the ecosystem for citizens. CVM is a useful method to estimate non-market value of the environment by estimating a person's willingness to pay (WTP) for environmental conservation (Mitchell and Carson 1989). It is important to know resident's WTP because it shows the level of individual preferences for the environment.

This study consisted of a multi-layer approach to obtaining the WTP using the CVM method. First, focus group meetings and interviews were done. Then, a questionnaire was used to ask residents' "WTP" for environmental conservation.

16.3 Focus Group Meetings and Interviews

In order to obtain preliminary information about resident's attitudes and perception towards coral reefs, eight focus group meetings were held, with a total of 81 participants. These participants consisted of community members, non-government organizations staff, tour guides, and government staff. During these focus group meetings, the CVM questionnaire was pretested and finalized.

16.4 Hypothetical Change of Coral Reefs in the Future

With the CVM, the hypothetical scenario of future conditions of coral reefs and conservation measurement needs to be illustrated within the questionnaire. WTP estimated by CVM means the amount that people want to pay for prevention or mitigation of the environmental deterioration in the future. The survey respondents need information about the change of environment to decide their WTP. The hypothesis scenario is helpful for the respondents to image clearly about the nature condition which they evaluate. Additionally, for credibility of survey result, the respondents need to have the same image or their image should be hardly any differences. Therefore, the scenario of hypothetical change of natural condition should be provided in CVM survey. Within the questionnaire, photos are shown, illustrating the hypothetical change of coral reef condition in the RISL area with no conservation efforts for the next 30 years which is based on the scientific information from the expert in coral reefs studies (see the Appendix).

16.5 Hypothetical Measurement

In this hypothetical scenario, NGOs and other environmental organizations conduct regular monitoring of coral reef condition in the area, as well as conduct awareness programs to Palauan residents and tour guides to teach the importance of coral reefs. Normally with the CVM, respondents are only asked for their willingness to pay. However, with this study, through focus group meetings and interviews, it was found that many people hesitate to pay money, but they also would like to do something for environmental conservation. This means they have positive value for coral reefs. Thus, in the questionnaire, a "willingness to work as a volunteer (WTW)" question was added as an additional measurement to people's WTP. A time value was also added in order to convert the time to wage rate, thereby calculating the WTP (see the Appendix).

16.6 How to Estimate the Total Value

WTW was converted into monetary term by minimum wage rate in Palau. By converting the WTW with the wage rate, the WTP was calculated as a result. Then, with these calculations done, the mean and median WTP per household was calculated. To obtain the amount of the total value as a result, multiply the WTP per household multiplied by the total number of households in Koror and Airai States (Fig. 16.2).

16.7 Results

Figure 16.3 is the outline of survey. This research was conducted in Koror State and Airai State where 78% of the Palauan population is concentrated (Office of Planning and Statistics and Bureau of Budget and Planning of Ministry of Finance 2015). The enumerators were hired from each hamlet and worked in their own communities in order to obtain high response rate.

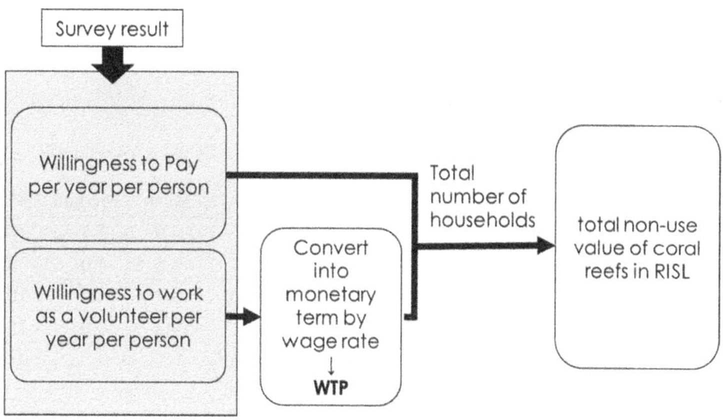

Fig. 16.2 How to estimate the total value

Fig. 16.3 Survey outline

Date: November 2016-December 2016
Target Area: Koror State (3,091 households)
Airai State (624 households)
*78% of total households in Palau
Method: Drop-off and Pick-up
Number of Enumerators: 25
Number of Surveys Given to Enumerators: 1,395
Number of Response: 1,273 (91.3%)
Number of Valid Responses: 1,205 (94.7%)

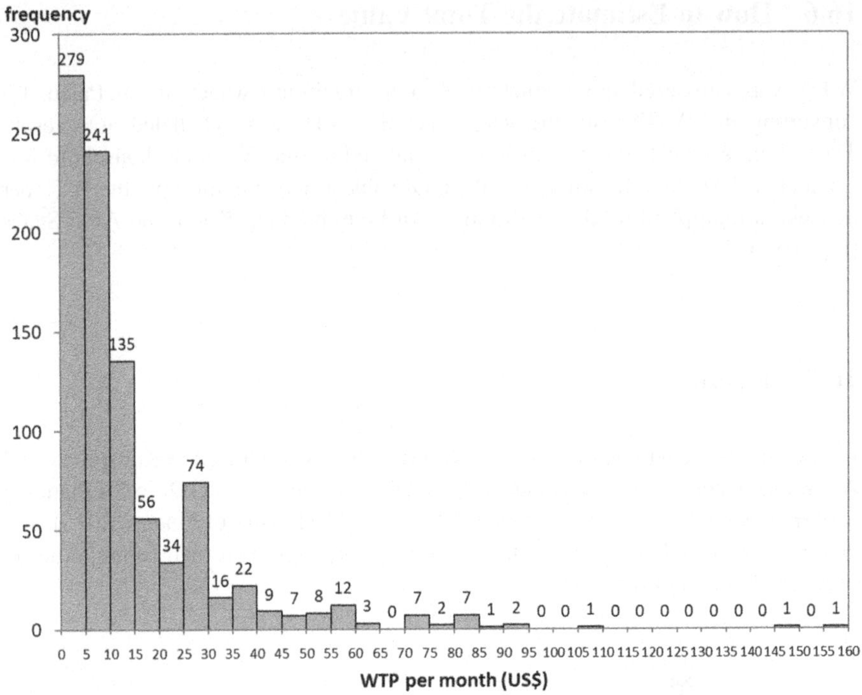

Fig. 16.4 Histogram of WTP per month

Table 16.1 WTP per household per month

	Mean	Median	Maximum
Willingness to pay (per month)	4.9	2.5	50.0
Willingness to work (per month)	5.5	4.0	30.0
Converted WTP from WTW by minimum wage rate (US $3.5/h)	19.3	14.0	105.0
WTP + WTW (per month)	13.2	8.0	155.0

Figure 16.4 illustrates the stated WTP of residents per month. WTPs in this graph are the sum of WTP converted from WTW by minimum wage rate and the WTP for donation. According to the information on the website of Minimum.Wage.org, Palau's minimum wage rate is US $3 per hour (as of 2017). The majority of the respondents stated their WTP was $5–10 per month. Conversely, 279 respondents stated their negative preference to the question.

Table 16.1 shows the estimated economic values. "Willingness to pay (WTP)" in the first row of this table is derived from the answers by the respondents who choose "donation." "Willingness to work (WTW)" in the second row is derived from the answers by the respondents who choose "volunteer work." "WTP+WTW" in the fourth row is the sum of these two values, and these are the results of WTP which can be used to estimate the annual total value. However, average (mean) values are higher than the median, for all the items due to the impact of a few extreme answers. Due to the high likelihood of over-estimation, the median was used in order to provide more reliable results. That is to say, US $8 is to be the base of estimation of the total value. As a result, estimated annual total value of coral reefs in RISL is US $452,448 for the residents in Koror and Airai States. The calculation is as follows: (WTP+WTW) × 12 months × total number of households of Koror and Airai.

Note that the target of this research are the residents in Koror and Airai states. It means that the total values for all the Palauan residents including other states would probably be higher than it.

Due to the scheme of the CVM survey, respondents were asked to provide the reasons as to why they hesitate both to donate and to work as a volunteer. The top two options, "I am not interested in coral reefs" and "It is not important/necessary to protect coral reefs," show their preference that those respondents do not want to preserve coral reefs in RISL positively. This type of answer is called "0-dollar bid." A "0-dollar bid" means they do not appreciate coral reefs and their WTP is at 0 dollar. Those answers should be included in estimation of the total value. Others are called "Protest bid." These respondents are interested in coral reefs, but for some reasons, they do not want to do anything in this scenario. They could possibly change their mind if the hypothetical policies/future condition in the scenario would be different. We have to remove those answers for estimation of total value to prevent from under-estimation. Figure 16.5 shows the distribution of the reasons why they hesitated to do something for coral reefs conservation. Red bars are 0-dollar bids, and blue bars are protest bids. Top answer shows that they do not have extra money and time spending coral reefs conservation. The second one is "Government should do it with the current revenue," and next one is "It should be done with Green Fee." These answers express their incredulity at the government's policy or plans. Others are about the responsibility of payment for conservation effort.

16.8 Discussion and Conclusion

This research shows that Palauan residents value the coral reefs in the RISL, which is their significant resource for food, recreational sites, economy, tourism resources, and so on. How can the estimated value in monetary term be applied to policymaking? First possibility is to calculate amount of compensation to the coral reefs' damage caused by boat stranding, overuse/misuse by tourists, non-sustainable way of fishing (using dynamite, toxic chemicals, etc.). The estimated value will provide useful information for court or negotiation. Second is to evaluate the economic efficiency of conservation measurements by cost–benefit analysis. CVM results can be used as "cost" or "benefit" in cost–benefit analysis, and it is necessary information for the policy assessment. Finally, it will be beneficial to engage with the people in order to raise awareness on the importance of the RISL coral reefs, and how much coral reefs benefit people and human society as non-use values. It will

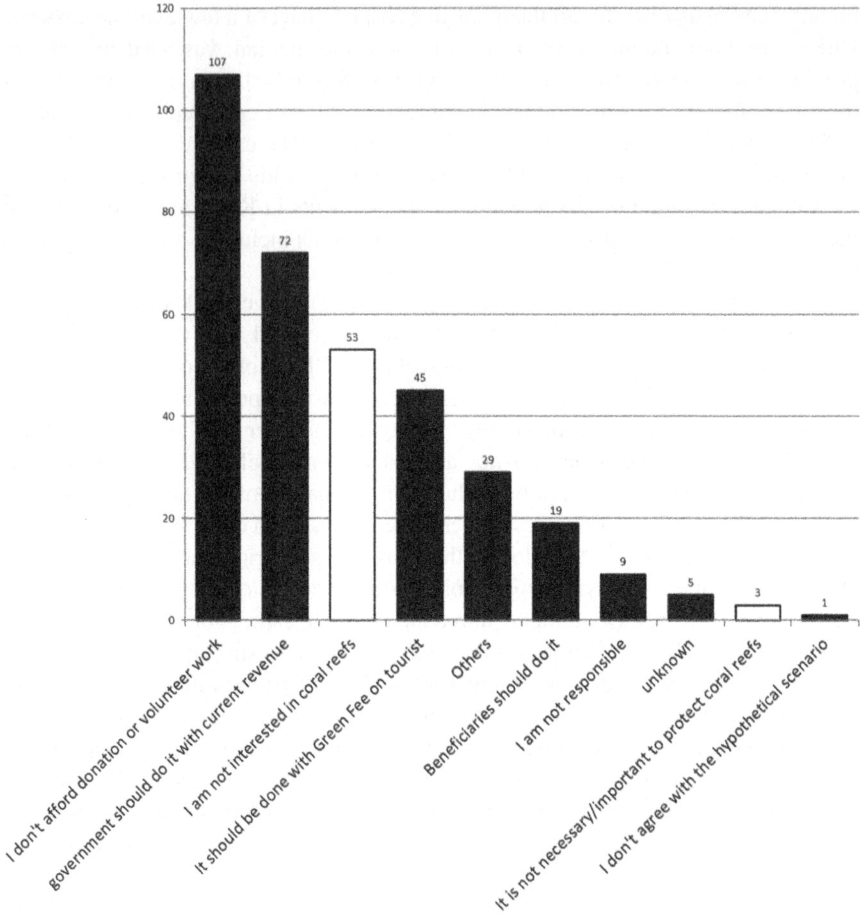

Fig. 16.5 Zero dollar bid (*white*) and protest bid (*black*)

also be beneficial to promote public involvement in conservation activities and promoting community-based management.

At the end of this paper, we propose two policy recommendations as the conclusion to this research (Table 16.2). First recommendation is to conduct an evaluation of conservation policies in terms of economic rationality by cost–benefit analysis regularly and continuously. A monitoring scheme using economic analysis can help improve the conservation policies and be more cost-efficient and effective. Cost–benefit analysis is important for as it can help identify priority among different policies. Second recommendation is to estimate the value of ecosystem services in monetary terms by economic valuation methods for natural environment. Economic valuation research is conducted to obtain parameters for cost–benefit analysis (e.g., benefits from conservation, damage cost caused by natural disruption). In addition, the estimated values in monetary terms can be used as indicators for appropriate

Table 16.2 Policy recommendation

Policy Recommendation
1. To conduct evaluation of conservation policies in terms of economic rationality by cost–benefit analysis 2. To estimate values of ecosystem services in monetary term by economic valuation methods for environment
Aims of Proposal 1
• To improve conservation policy more cost-efficient and effective. • To identify priority among different policies can be identified by B/C – Cost–Benefit Analysis B/C: Benefit from Nature/Cost for Conservation B/C > 1: Economically Rational Policy B/C < 1: Not Economically Rational Policy This policy should be revised; less cost, more benefit
Aims of Proposal 2
• To obtain parameters for cost–benefit analysis (e.g., benefits from conservation, damage cost caused by natural disruption) • To provide objective indicate for appropriate decision-making about environmental policy and economic development • To show how much the nature is important for Palauan people, and to promote environmental awareness/education

decision-making about environmental policy and economic development. Also, it shows how much important the nature is for Palauan people, and it helps to improve environmental awareness/education. For a small island country like Palau, the power and effort of the residents and local communities are extremely critical for conservation and natural resource management. In order to deepen people's understanding in these matters, they should be more involved in such activities or challenges for coral preservation. To encourage people more to join environmental activities, it is necessary to inform how much valuable for them the nature is. Estimated economic values can be effective information to raise people's awareness of importance of natural conservation for themselves. In the end, in order to be more efficient in making policy decisions, economic valuation methods can be utilized to ensure better decision-making for a more sustainable management scheme in Palau.

Acknowledgment This chapter is a revised and reprinted version of the PICRC Technical Report 18-12 "Economic Value of Coral Reefs in Palau"(2018) by courtesy of the Palau International Coral Reef Center (PICRC). This original paper was published as a result of the international collaborative research project "Palau Coral Reef Island Ecosystem (P-CoRIE) Project."

The authors wish to acknowledge Dr. Yimnang Golbuu (CEO, PICRC), Ms. Geraldine Rengiil (Research Director, PICRC), Dr. Seiji Nakaya (former P-CoRIE Project Coordinator), and Ms. Vallin Kloulechad (former P-CoRIE Research Assistant) for all the support and useful suggestions for conducting this research in Palau. Finally, we are grateful to all the residents in Palau who kindly cooperated with our research in these 5 years. P-CoRIE is supported by the project of "Science and Technology Research Partnership for Sustainable Development (SATREPS)" by Japan International Cooperation Agency (JICA) and Japan Science and Technology Agency (JST).

Appendix: CVM Part of the Survey Sheet (English Version)

Description of the Hypothetical Scenario

The pictures on the previous page show *the hypothetical change* of coral reef condition in the RISL area with no conservation efforts for the next 30 years.

In this hypothetical scenario, non-governmental organizations (NGOs) or other organizations for the environment conduct *regular monitoring of coral reef condition in the RISL*, and *awareness programs to Palauan residents (including tour guides) to learn the importance of coral reefs*. Imagine that these monitoring and awareness programs are funded only by donations from contributors like you. Your donation to these NGOs or other environmental organizations will only be used for these activities.

Also, in order to maintain the current condition of coral reefs in the RISL, public involvement is important and dependent on voluntary efforts. In this hypothetical scenario, the activities are "*beach cleanup (e.g., picking up trash and driftage, etc.)*" and "*assisting with conservation efforts that are led by the NGOs/other environmental organizations (e.g., water quality check, checking the condition of coral reefs, assistance in awareness seminars, etc.).*" Imagine you join one or both of these volunteer activities in your leisure time, without compensation.

Q1: Which of the following would YOU be willing to do to prevent degradation of coral reefs in the RISL? Please choose only *ONE of the following options from [A] to [D]*, in the table below.

Options what you want to do	YOUR ANSWER *Check ONE*	Next Question for you
[A] I want to donate to NGO or environmental organization.		➡ If you chose [A], go to Q2.
[B] I want to help NGO or environmental organizations as a volunteer		➡ If you chose [B], go to Q3.
[C] I want to do both [A] and [B].		➡ If you chose [C], go to both Q2 & Q3.
[D] I don't want to do either [A] or [B].		➡ If you chose [D], go to Q4.

Q2: For those who choose [A] or [C]

How much is your household willing to pay per month (for 1 year) for these management strategies? Please note that your donation comes from your household income, which means *you cannot use this amount of money for any other purpose.*

You are willing to pay ... (for 1 year)
Please check *ONE* that applies.

[...] $1.00 per month	[...] $2.50 per month	[...] $5.00 per month
[...] $7.50 per month	[...] $10.00 per month	[...] $12.50 per month
[...] $15.00 per month	[...] $17.50 per month	[...] $20.00 per month
[...] $22.50 per month	[...] $25.00 per month	[...] $27.50 per month
[...] $30.00 per month	[...] $32.50 per month	[...] $35.00 per month
[...] $37.50 per month	[...] $40.00 per month	[...] $42.50 per month
[...] $45.00 per month	[...] $47.50 per month	
[...] $50.00 or more per month		

Q3: for those who choose [B] or [C]

How many hours a month are you willing to spend for these volunteer work (without pay) aside from your regular work? Please note that you have to dedicate this time to the volunteer activities, and *you cannot do anything else during this time.*

You are willing to spend ... (for 1 year)
Please check *ONE* that applies.

[...] 2 h per month	[...] 4 h per month	[...] 6 h per month
[...] 8 h per month	[...] 10 h per month	[...] 12 h per month
[...] 14 h per month	[...] 16 h per month	[...] 18 h per month
[...] 20 h per month	[...] 22 h per month	[...] 24 h per month
[...] 26 h per month	[...] 28 h per month	
[...] 30 or more h per month		

Q4: For those who choose [D]

Why do you hesitate to do both donation and volunteer work?
Please *check ONE* that applies.

[...] I am not interested in coral reef conservation in the RISL.
[...] I don't think coral reef conservation in the RISL is necessary nor important.
[...] These hypothetical conservation plans are useful and necessary, but conservation efforts should be done by government with the current revenue.
[...] These hypothetical conservation plans are useful and necessary, but I am not responsible.
[...] These hypothetical conservation plans are useful and necessary, but I cannot afford the donation and the volunteer work.
[...] Conservation efforts are necessary for coral reefs in the RISL, but I do not agree with the hypothetical scenario (future condition, conservation strategies).

[. . .] The Palau National Government imposes the Green Fee on tourists, so Palauan residents do not have to do anything for the environment of Palau.

[. . .] Only beneficiaries from coral reefs (tourists, tour company, fisherman, etc.) should be responsible for conservation.

[. . .] Others (please specify):

References

Bateman IJ et al (2002) Economic valuation with stated preference techniques: a manual. Edward Elgar, Cheltenham

Minimum-wage.org (n.d.). https://www.minimum-wage.org/international/palau, Retrieved on June 1, 2017

Mitchell RC, Carson RT (1989) Using surveys to value public goods: the contingent valuation method, Resources for the future press. The Johns Hopkins University Press, New York

Office of Planning and Statistics and Bureau of Budget and Planning of Ministry of Finance (2015) Census of population, housing and agriculture for the Republic of Palau, Volume 1, Basic Table.

Turner RK, Pearce D, Bateman I (1993) Environmental economics: an elementary introduction. The Johns Hopkins University Press, Baltimore

Chapter 17
International Trade in Environmental Goods and Environmental Regulation in the Presence of Lobbying

Masakazu Maezuru

Abstract This paper analyzes the relationship between international trade in environmental goods and environmental regulation in the presence of lobbying. We assume an open economy consisting of two countries and two polluting sectors subject to environmental taxation. Thus, we have an environmental goods industry sector supplying pollution abatement goods and services. The pollution abatement goods and services are assumed to be internationally traded, and this is the only industrial interaction between the two countries. Pollution affects consumers in both countries. The impact of lobbying on a politically optimal pollution abatement subsidy is ambiguous and depends on the relative strength of the environmental lobby group.

Keywords Lobbying · Environmental goods · Pollution abatement · Environmental regulation · International trade

17.1 Introduction

This paper analyzes the relationship between international trade in environmental goods and environmental regulation in the presence of lobbying. The incumbent government maximizes its chances of being re-elected. The objective function of the government includes social welfare as well as political contribution.

Our work is based on two strands of the literature. First, we refer to the existing normative studies on the environmental goods industries. These studies explain how the market powers of firms modify the optimal environmental policy chosen by a benevolent regulator. Abatement activities are supplied by the environmental goods industry. The environmental market is composed of two firms, one based in each country and selling indifferently environmental goods and services to firms in both

M. Maezuru (✉)
Osaka University of Economics and Law, Yao, Japan
e-mail: maezuru@keiho-u.ac.jp

M. Kawano et al. (eds.), *Theory and History in Regional Perspective*, New Frontiers in Regional Science: Asian Perspectives 56,
https://doi.org/10.1007/978-981-16-6695-7_17

countries. Imperfect competition between the environmental goods industries tends to push up the optimal second-best pollution abatement subsidy. The interest of the regulator is best served by increasing the subsidy to above the traditional Pigouvian subsidy level and giving enough incentives for abatement activities. The impact of this should be balanced with the negative incentives that the imperfect competition of polluting firms imposes on the optimal pollution abatement subsidy.

Next, we assume an open economy consisting of two countries and two polluting sectors subject to environmental taxation. Thus, we have an environmental goods industry sector supplying pollution abatement goods and services. The abatement goods and services are assumed to be internationally traded, and this is the only industrial interaction between the two countries. Pollution affects the consumers in both countries.

The rest of the paper proceeds as follows: Section 17.2 gives the economic model. Section 17.3 presents the political model. Section 17.4 examines the politically optimal pollution abatement subsidy. Section 17.5 considers the comparative statics and discusses the impact of a change in the number of people in the environmental lobby group. Finally, Section 17.6 summarizes our work.

17.2 The Economic Model

We assume a representative polluting firm with an output $x_i (i = 1, 2)$ and a pollution level $e_i(x_i, a_{\text{di}})$. The net pollution of the firm is positively correlated with its production level and negatively affected by its abatement activities a_{di} purchased from the international environmental goods industry. Polluting firms purchase environmental goods and services because they are subject to environmental taxation.

The environmental market comprises two firms, one in each country, selling different types of environmental goods and services to firms in both countries. We are interested in only the political decisions in country 1, and so for now we assume that the other environmental policies are constant. The profits of polluting firms can be written as

$$\max_{x_i, a_{\text{di}}} \Pi_i = P_i x_i - c_i(x_i) - p a_{\text{di}} - t_i e_i(x_i, a_{\text{di}}), \tag{17.1}$$

where P_i is the price charged by the representative firm; $c_i(x_i)$ the production cost function, twice differentiable, increasing, and convex; p the price of environmental inputs; a_{di} the necessary condition to abate pollution; t_i the level of environmental taxation; $e_i(x_i, a_{\text{di}})$ the emission function; and $t_i e_i$ tax expenditure. We assume that the production cost function is $c_i(x_i) = c x_i$, and that the emission function is continuous and twice differentiable. Partial derivatives have the following signs: $e_{ix_i}(x_i, a_{\text{di}}) > 0$ (more production entails more pollution), $e_{ia_{\text{di}}}(x_i, a_{\text{di}}) < 0$ (more abatement decreases total emissions), $e_{ix_ix_i}(x_i, a_{\text{di}}) < 0$ (emissions from the last unit produced increase with the production level), and $e_{ia_{\text{di}}a_{\text{di}}}(x_i, a_{\text{di}}) > 0$ (abatement is subject to diseconomies of scale). The abatement decisions of a firm are additively separable from its production decisions, and so $e_{ix_i a_{di}}(x_i, a_{di}) = 0$.

We further assume that the emission function is

$$e_i(x_i, a_{di}) = \varepsilon_i(x_i) - w_i(a_{di}), \tag{17.2}$$

where $\varepsilon_i(x_i) = x_i^2/2$ and $w_i(a_{di}) = a_{di} - a_{di}^2/2$.

From the first-order conditions of profit maximization, we obtain the output and inverse demand in environmental goods and services, respectively, as follows:

$$x_i = (P - c)/t_i \tag{17.3}$$

$$a_{di} = (-p + t_i)/t_i. \tag{17.4}$$

The overall demand is

$$A = a_{d1}(p, t_1) + a_{d2}(p, t_2) = [-p(t_1 + t_2) + 2t_1t_2]/t_1t_2 \tag{17.5}$$

The overall inverse demand can then be written as

$$p = [t_1t_2(2 - A)]/(t_1 + t_2) \tag{17.6}$$

The price of environmental inputs decreases in A. An increase in local tax increases both the overall demand and the price of environmental goods and services.

The profit function of the local environmental goods industry is

$$\max_{a_{si}} \Pi_i^{up} = p(A, t_1, t_2)a_{si} - c_{ui}(a_{si}) + \sigma_i a_{si}, \tag{17.7}$$

where A is the world production, a_{si} local production, and $c_{ui}(a_{si})$ the cost function, twice differentiable, increasing, and convex. σ_i is the level of pollution abatement subsidy and $\sigma_i a_{si}$ subsidy revenue. The first-order condition of profit maximization is

$$a_{si} = \left[2t_1t_2 + (t_1 + t_2)(c_{uj} - \sigma_j - 2c_{ui} + 2\sigma_i)\right]/3t_1t_2 \quad (i, j = 1, 2;\ i \neq j) \tag{17.8}$$

All the citizens in country 1 have the same preferences with respect to goods. The utility function of a consumer is

$$u_1 = u_1(x_1) \tag{17.9}$$

From (17.9), we derive the following demand function:

$$u_1'(x_1) = P_1(x_1) \tag{17.10}$$

From (17.9) and (17.10), the consumer surplus is

$$\mathrm{CS}_1 = \int_0^{x_1} P_1 du - P_1 x_1 \tag{17.11}$$

The welfare of this economy is thus

$$W_1 = \mathrm{CS}_1 + t_1 e_1 - \sigma_1 a_{s1} + \Pi_1 + \Pi_1^{\mathrm{up}} - D_1^{\mathrm{E}}, \tag{17.12}$$

where CS_1 is consumer surplus, $t_1 e_1$ tax revenue, $\sigma_1 a_{\mathrm{d}1}$ subsidy expenditure, and $D_1^{\mathrm{E}} = \nu e_1 + \gamma e_2$ damage function in country 1. The government of each country subsidizes firms for pollution abatement activity. The marginal damage of pollution in country 1 is assumed to be equal to ν and strictly positive and constant. γ is the disutility that the environmentalists incur for each unit of pollution abroad. In a traditional normative approach, the government would choose its pollution abatement subsidy rate based on maximizing the abatement function.

A benevolent government would maximize welfare following the condition:

$$\partial W_1 / \partial \sigma_1 = 0. \tag{17.13}$$

From (17.13), we derive the non-cooperative subsidy rate

$$\sigma_1^N = \frac{G - H\nu - I\gamma}{C - D\nu - F\gamma}, \tag{17.14}$$

where

$$C = 2t_1t_2(t_1 + t_2)(5t_1 + 6t_2), \quad D = t_2^2(t_1 + t_2) \quad F = t_1^2(t_1 + t_2)$$

$$G = -2t_1t_2(t_1 + t_2)(4t_1 + 3t_2)c_{u1} + 2t_1t_2(t_1 + t_2)(2t_1 + 3t_2)c_{u2} - 2t_1t_2(t_1 + t_2) \times (2t_1 + 3t_2)\sigma_2 + 11t_1^2t_2^2,$$

$$H = t_2^2\{2t_1t_2 + (t_1 + t_2)(c_{u1} + c_{u2} - \sigma_2)\},$$

$$I = t_1^2\{2t_1t_2 + (t_1 + t_2)(c_{u1} + c_{u2} - \sigma_2)\}.$$

The welfare in country 2 is thus

$$W_2 = \mathrm{CS}_2 + t_2 e_2 - \sigma_2 a_{s2} + \Pi_2 + \Pi_2^{\mathrm{up}} - D_2^{\mathrm{E}}, \tag{17.15}$$

where CS_2 is consumer surplus, $t_2 e_2$ tax revenue, $\sigma_2 a_{\mathrm{d}2}$ subsidy expenditure, and $D_2^{\mathrm{E}} = \nu e_2$ damage function in country 2.

The total welfare of the two countries is

$$W = W_1 + W_2 \tag{17.16}$$

If the government in country 1 were benevolent, it would maximize the total welfare following the condition:

$$\partial W / \partial \sigma_1 = 0. \tag{17.17}$$

We obtain the socially optimal subsidy rate

$$\sigma_1^{\mathrm{SO}} = \frac{L - M\nu - I\gamma}{J - K\nu - F\gamma}, \tag{17.18}$$

where

$$J = 2t_1t_2(t_1 + t_2)(5t_1 + 4t_2), \quad K = \left(t_2^2 - t_1^2\right)(t_1 + t_2),$$

$$L = 4t_1^2t_2^2(5t_1 + 3t_2) - 2t_1t_2(t_1 + t_2)(3t_1 + 5t_2)c_{u1} + t_1t_2(t_1 + t_2)(7t_1 + 5t_2)c_{u2} \\ - 2t_1t_2(t_1 + t_2)(5t_1 + 4t_2)\sigma_2,$$

$$M = \left(t_2^2 - t_1^2\right)\{2t_1t_2 + (t_1 + t_2)(c_{u1} + c_{u2} - \sigma_2)\}.$$

From (17.18), we derive the following condition:

$$\partial W_1 / \partial \sigma_1 \lesseqgtr 0 \quad \text{if and only if} \, \sigma_1 \gtreqless \sigma_1^{\mathrm{SO}}.$$

We obtain the difference between the socially optimal and non-cooperative subsidy rates as follows:

$$\Delta\sigma_1^{\mathrm{SN}} = \sigma_1^{\mathrm{SO}} - \sigma_1^{N} = \frac{(L - M\nu) - I\gamma}{(J - K\nu) - F\gamma} - \frac{(G - H\nu) - I\gamma}{(C - D\nu) - F\gamma} \tag{17.19}$$

The socially optimal subsidy rate in country 1 would be higher than the country's non-cooperative subsidy rate if the subsidy rate in country 2 and the marginal cost of the upstream firm in country 1 are very low and the marginal cost of the upstream firm in country 2 is very high.

17.3 Political Model

Our political model consists of a two-stage game in which the environmental lobby group is the principal and the government the agent. This model has been extensively used in the literature following Grossman and Helpman (1994). The objective of the incumbent government is to be re-elected. Therefore, the government would wish to maximize its weighted function of national welfare and lobby contribution. A solution to this two-stage game has been provided by Bernheim and Whinston (1986) in a discrete case study, and extended by Grossman and Helpman (1994) and Fredriksson (1997), among others, to continuous functions.

In our approach, however, the government will deviate from its policy choice of social welfare maximization if the lobby group offers a positive contribution.

Let $M(\sigma_1)$ be the contribution of the lobby group when the policy chosen is σ_1 in country 1. The payoff function of the government in country 1 will then be

$$v^{g} = \lambda W_1(\sigma_1) + M(\sigma_1), \tag{17.20}$$

where λ is the political weight given to the economy's welfare. We do not consider how the lobby group forms or how it overcomes the free-riding problem [see Olson 1965 for a discussion on the logic of collective action].

We assume that the lobby group is functionally specialized and considers only one particular aspect of the issue, namely pollution.

Some environmentalists might join to create a lobby group. They represent a fraction α_E of the environmentalists in country 1. The menu auctions of environmentalists depend on the impact that a change in subsidy rate causes on pollution, including pollution abroad. Their gross payoff function can be shown as

$$v^{E} = B - \alpha_E D_1^{E} = B - \alpha_E(\nu e_1 + \gamma e_2), \tag{17.21}$$

where B is the budget of an environmental lobby group and $B > D_1^{E} + M^{E}/\alpha_E$.

The net payoff function of the environmental lobby group would then be

$$V^{E} = v^{E} - M \tag{17.22}$$

The first-order condition of the net payoff function of the environmental lobby group is

$$\frac{\partial V^{E}}{\partial \sigma_1} = \frac{\partial v^{E}}{\partial \sigma_1} - \frac{\partial M}{\partial \sigma_1} = -\alpha_E \frac{\partial D_1^{E}}{\partial \sigma_1} - \frac{\partial M}{\partial \sigma_1} = 0 \tag{17.23}$$

17.4 Politically Optimal Pollution Abatement Subsidy

We now present the impact of lobbying on the policy chosen by a regulator. As already mentioned, the incumbent government maximizes its political payoff function (17.20).

The trade-off facing a benevolent regulator dealing with environmental goods industries has already been discussed extensively (David and Sinclair-Desgagné 2010; Canton et al. 2012; Nimubona and Sinclair-Desgagné 2013). Now, the socially optimal policy can be balanced in accordance with the auctions menu proposed by the lobby group. The government would therefore maximize its payoff function as follows:

$$\frac{\partial v^{g}}{\partial \sigma_1} = \lambda \frac{\partial W_1}{\partial \sigma_1} + \frac{\partial M}{\partial \sigma_1} = \lambda \frac{\partial W_1}{\partial \sigma_1} - \alpha_{\mathrm{E}} \frac{\partial D_1^{\mathrm{E}}}{\partial \sigma_1} = 0. \tag{17.24}$$

From (17.24), we derive the politically optimal subsidy rate as follows:

$$\sigma_1^{\mathrm{PO}} = \frac{\lambda G - (\lambda - \alpha_{\mathrm{E}})(H\nu + I\gamma)}{\lambda C - (\lambda - \alpha_{\mathrm{E}})(D\nu + F\gamma)} \tag{17.25}$$

17.5 Comparative Statics

17.5.1 Impact on Politically Optimal Pollution Abatement Subsidy Rate

We now turn to comparative statics. A rise in membership in the environmental lobby group will have the following impact on a politically optimal pollution abatement subsidy rate:

$$\frac{\partial \sigma_1^{\mathrm{PO}}}{\partial \alpha_{\mathrm{E}}} = \frac{(H\nu + I\gamma)\{\lambda C - (\lambda - \alpha_{\mathrm{E}})(D\nu + F\gamma)\} - (D\nu + F\gamma)\{\lambda G - (\lambda - \alpha_{\mathrm{E}})(H\nu + I\gamma)\}}{\{\lambda C - (\lambda - \alpha_{\mathrm{E}})(D\nu + F\gamma)\}^2} \tag{17.26}$$

From (17.26), we derive the following condition:

$$\frac{\partial \sigma_1^{\mathrm{PO}}}{\partial \alpha_{\mathrm{E}}} \underset{<}{\overset{>}{=}} 0 \quad \text{if and only if} \quad \frac{(H\nu + I\gamma)}{(D\nu + F\gamma)} \underset{<}{\overset{>}{=}} \frac{\{\lambda G - (\lambda - \alpha_{\mathrm{E}})(H\nu + I\gamma)\}}{\{\lambda C - (\lambda - \alpha_{\mathrm{E}})(D\nu + F\gamma)\}}.$$

From this condition, we present the following proposition.

Proposition 17.1

1. *A rise in membership of the environmental lobby group will increase the politically optimal subsidy rate if the subsidy rate in country 2 is very high.*
2. *A rise in membership of the environmental lobby group will increase the politically optimal subsidy rate if the marginal cost of the upstream firm in country 1 is very high.*
3. *A rise in membership of the environmental lobby group will decrease the politically optimal subsidy rate if the marginal cost of the upstream firm in country 2 is very high.*

17.5.2 Impact on Difference Between Two Subsidy Rates

The difference between the politically optimal and non-cooperative subsidy rates in country 1 is

$$\Delta\sigma_1^{\mathrm{PN}} = \sigma_1^{\mathrm{PO}} - \sigma_1^{N} = \frac{\alpha_{\mathrm{E}}\{C(H\nu + I\gamma) - G(D\nu + F\gamma)\}}{\{\lambda C - (\lambda - \alpha_{\mathrm{E}})(D\nu + F\gamma)\}\{C - (D\nu + F\gamma)\}}. \quad (17.27)$$

From (17.27), we derive the following condition:

$$\Delta\sigma_1^{\mathrm{PN}} \gtreqless 0 \quad \text{if and only if} \quad \frac{C}{G} \gtrless \frac{D\nu + F\gamma}{H\nu + I\gamma}.$$

From this condition, we present the following proposition.

Proposition 17.2

1. *The politically optimal subsidy rate in country 1 will be higher than its non-cooperative subsidy rate if the subsidy rate in country 2 is very high. Therefore, a rise in membership of the environmental lobby group would increase the difference between the subsidy rates in country 1.*
2. *The politically optimal subsidy rate in country 1 will be higher than its non-cooperative subsidy rate if the marginal cost of the upstream firm in country 1 is very high. Therefore, a rise in membership of the environmental lobby group would increase the difference between the subsidy rates in country 1.*
3. *The non-cooperative subsidy rate in country 1 will be higher than its politically optimal subsidy rate if the marginal cost of the upstream firm in country 2 is very high.*

Therefore, a rise in membership of the environmental lobby group would increase the difference between the subsidy rates in country 1.

The net impact on the subsidy rate would depend on the relative size of the lobby group and relative impact of a change in pollution abatement subsidy rate on the payoff function.

17.5.3 Impact on Global Environmental Pollution Level

The global environmental pollution level is

$$e_{\mathrm{W}} = e_1 + e_2 \tag{17.28}$$

The impact of a rise in pollution abatement subsidy rate in country 1 on the global environmental pollution level is

$$\begin{aligned}\partial e_{\mathrm{W}}/\partial\sigma_1 &= \partial e_1/\partial\sigma_1 + \partial e_2/\partial\sigma_1 \\ &= \frac{t_1^2 + t_2^2}{9t_1^2 t_2^2(t_1 + t_2)}\{2t_1 t_2 + (t_1 + t_2)(c_{u1} + c_{u2} - \sigma_1 - \sigma_2)\}.\end{aligned} \tag{17.29}$$

The impact of a rise in membership of the environmental lobby group in country 1 on the global environmental pollution level is

$$\begin{aligned}\partial e_{\mathrm{W}}/\partial\alpha_{\mathrm{E}} &= (\partial e_1/\partial\sigma_1 + \partial e_2/\partial\sigma_1)(\partial\sigma_1/\partial\alpha_{\mathrm{E}}) \\ &= \frac{t_1^2 + t_2^2}{9t_1^2 t_2^2(t_1 + t_2)}\{2t_1 t_2 + (t_1 + t_2)(c_{u1} + c_{u2} - \sigma_1 - \sigma_2)\} \\ &\quad \times (\partial\sigma_1/\partial\alpha_{\mathrm{E}})\end{aligned} \tag{17.30}$$

We now present the following proposition.

Proposition 17.3

1. *A rise in membership of the environmental lobby group will decrease the global environmental pollution level if the subsidy rate in country 2 is very high.*
2. *A rise in membership of the environmental lobby group will decrease the global environmental pollution level if the marginal cost of the upstream firm in country 1 is very high.*
3. *A rise in membership of the environmental lobby group will increase the global environmental pollution level if the marginal cost of the upstream firm in country 2 is very high.*

17.6 Conclusion

This paper analyzed the relationship between international trade in environmental goods and environmental regulation in the presence of lobbying. We assumed an open economy consisting of two countries and two polluting sectors subject to environmental taxation. Therefore, we have an environmental goods industry sector supplying pollution abatement goods and services. The abatement goods and services are assumed to be internationally traded, and this is the only industrial interaction between the two countries. Pollution affects consumers in both countries.

Our main findings can be summarized as follows: The impact of environmental lobbying on the pollution abatement policy of one country depends on the pollution abatement policy of the other country and the marginal cost of upstream firms in both countries.

We assume that the marginal cost of upstream firms abroad is very high. In such a case, a rise in environmental lobbying in the environmental goods and services industry would decrease politically optimal subsidization and worsen the global environment. Conversely, in case the marginal cost of upstream firms abroad is very low, a rise in environmental lobbying in the environmental goods and services industry would increase politically optimal subsidization and improve the global environment.

This work can be improved in several ways. For example, we can take up the political game and coalition opportunities of the different stakeholders in a future study. We can also make an in-depth study to understand the interactions between the environmental goods industry and polluting goods industry.

References

Bernheim DB, Whinston MD (1986) Menu auctions, resource allocation and economic influence. Q J Econ 101:1–32

Canton J (2008) Redealing the cards: how an environmental goods industry modifies the political economy of environmental taxes. Resour Energy Econ 30:195–215

Canton J (2009) Environmentalists' behavior and environmental policies. In: Fondazione Eni Enrico Mattei Working Papers

Canton J, Soubeyran A, Stahn H (2008) Environmental taxation and vertical cournot oligopolies: how eco-industries matter. Environ Resource Econ 40(3):369–382

Canton J, David M, Sinclair-Desgagné B (2012) Environmental regulation and horizontal mergers in the eco-industry. Strategic Behav Environ 2(2):107–132

Conconi P (2003) Green lobbies and transboundary pollution in large open economy. J Int Econ 59: 399–422

David M, Sinclair-Desgagné B (2005) Environmental regulation and the eco-industry. J Regul Econ 28(2):141–155

David M, Sinclair-Desgagné B (2010) Pollution abatement subsidies and the environmental goods industry. Environ Resource Econ 45(2):271–282

David M, Nimubona A-D, Sinclair-Desgagné B (2008) Environmental taxation and the structure of the eco-industry. In: CIRANO working papers

Fredriksson PG (1997) The political economy of pollution taxes in a small open economy. J Environ Econ Manag 33:44–58

Grossman GM, Helpman E (1994) Protection for sale. Am Econ Rev 84:833–850

Nimubona A-D, Sinclair-Desgagné B (2013) The Pigouvian tax rule in the presence of an eco-industry. Econ Bull 33(1):747–752

Olson M (1965) The logic of collective action: public goods and the theory of groups. Harvard University Press, Cambridge, MA

Part III
Spatial Data Analytics

Chapter 18
A Test for the Herfindahl Index

Gordon F. Mulligan

Abstract Regional scientists have adopted two rather different empirical views of agglomeration. One view, favored by economists, examines the *distribution* of some property across a class of entities (agents, regions). The other view, favored by geographers, examines the spatial correlation of that property based on the *arrangement* of those entities. Adopting the first approach, this paper develops new statistical properties for the Herfindahl–Hirschman concentration index. The methodology is based on the standard occupancy problem in physics, where r particles (points) are distributed across n cells (quadrats). Both $\boldsymbol{r}$ and $\boldsymbol{n}$ are random variables so the Herfindahl index itself is considered a random variable $H(\boldsymbol{r}, \boldsymbol{n})$. Including all the equi-probable states of this random variable, expected values for both the mean and standard deviation are specified. A test compares the Herfindahl score for a specific state (sample) to the score based on all possible states, allowing inferences to be made about whether the observed score conforms to a random process. A few applications follow and then a short discussion concludes the chapter.

Keywords Herfindahl index · Hirschman · Occupancy problem · Observed score for specific state · Expected score for random state · Mean and standard deviation · Test statistic

18.1 Introduction

Regional and social scientists are often interested in understanding why concentration is so pervasive in human activities. This concentration can be considered either aspatial (functional) or spatial (geographic) in nature, but when it does involve some aspect of space the term clustering is often applied. In the first case, analysts are

G. F. Mulligan (✉)
School of Geography, Development and Environment, University of Arizona, Tucson, AZ, USA
e-mail: mulligan@arizona.edu

M. Kawano et al. (eds.), *Theory and History in Regional Perspective*, New Frontiers in Regional Science: Asian Perspectives 56,
https://doi.org/10.1007/978-981-16-6695-7_18

interested in the *non-spatial distribution* of a chosen metric across a class of entities (Carlton and Perloff 1990; Sen 1997; Atkinson 2015; Milanovic 2016; Mulligan and Carruthers 2021). Here much recent interest has turned to the issue of scale, which is important to all forms of life and all types of organizations (Batty 2013; West 2017). But, in the second case, analysts are more interested in the *spatial arrangement* of those metrics, using global statistics, or in identifying their hot spots, using local statistics (Cliff and Ord 1973, 1981; Getis and Ord 1992; Getis 2008). The two approaches are not independent and, when reference is made to agglomerative tendencies in human activities, regional scientists often refer both to concentration in size, as measured by some index of evenness or inequality, and clustering in space, as measured by some index of closeness or contiguity.

In both instances an observed distribution is often compared to an expected distribution where the null hypothesis is that the observed distribution, which is a specific state, has been randomly generated. This hypothesis is violated when the observed distribution is either too concentrated or too even. In the case of functional concentration, the distribution of cities might be dominated by one very large place (indicating primacy) or, instead, the distribution might have places that are all very similar in population size (exhibiting no hierarchy). As either of these two limits is approached, the entire distribution increasingly conforms to a non-random process. Alternatively, in the case of geographic clustering, the distribution of points might either be found too close together (showing positive autocorrelation) or too evenly dispersed (perhaps even showing negative autocorrelation). Again, those specific states that resemble these two extremes suggest that the observed distribution has been non-randomly generated.

In both cases regional scientists typically borrow from statisticians who, instead, prefer to talk about randomly choosing identical balls from a set of urns. But, when spatial statistics are involved, analysts usually invoke geographic *quadrats* and examine the count (integer) data for *points* across those quadrats. So, to be more specific, these quadrats might represent counties or provinces and the analyst might be interested in the degree of evenness in different populations across those spatial units. Surprisingly, however, the most popular aspatial measure for assessing the degree of concentration—the widely known Herfindahl–Hirschman H index—does not appear to have a test for randomization associated with it so, as a result, an observed score for the index cannot be compared to a randomly generated score (Hirschman 1964). In response, this chapter develops such a test procedure, at least one that can address those occupancy problems where r points (particles) are assigned to n quadrats (cells, urns). In doing so, general solutions are given for both the mean and the standard deviation of the Herfindahl (for short) index. Consequently, any specific assignment of r points to n quadrats, where concentration is measured by the Herfindahl index, now leads to testable inferences about the probability of randomness in that assignment.

18.2 The Herfindahl Index

The Herfindahl index H equals the sum of the squared shares (for employment, revenue, etc.) across a group of similar entities (cities, firms, etc.). The index is particularly popular in antitrust legislation, where a market is thought to be uncompetitive if the value of H is too high for firm sales (U.S. Department of Justice 2010). Other applications are often made in the study of employment numbers, where concerns can arise that targeted occupational groups (e.g., STEM) have cross-industry indices that are too high (U.S. Bureau of Labor Statistics 2014). The Herfindahl index can also be applied to domestic or international trade portfolios where nations, or their regions, might want to maintain some diversification in exports to avoid highly excessive vulnerability (Sakai 2018). Unfortunately, though, the index does not reflect any kind of underlying welfare distribution. Moreover, it does not make use of a reference distribution, like an industrial localization or regional specialization coefficient, even though the index for one industry is often compared to the index for a different industry (Isard 1960; Mulligan and Schmidt 2005). Furthermore, the Herfindahl index is sometimes used to discern whether an activity, or industry, is becoming more, or less, concentrated over time (see trade example below).

In the case of r points distributed across quadrats suppose that there are n non-overlapping quadrats where the (integer) count in quadrat k is r_k. Adding numbers across all these n cells the total number r of points is.

$$r = r_1 + r_2 + \ldots + r_k + \ldots + r_n.$$

The computed value of the Herfindahl–Hirschman index is then.

$$H(\boldsymbol{r}, \boldsymbol{n}) = (r_1/r)^2 + (r_2/r)^2 + \ldots + (r_k/r)^2 + \ldots + (r_n/r)^2 \tag{18.1}$$

where the boldface type indicates that $\boldsymbol{r}$, $\boldsymbol{n}$, and the Herfindahl index itself are all viewed as random variables. If $n = 3$, and $r_1 = 2$, $r_2 = 3$, $r_3 = 5$, and $r = 10$, then the score $H(10, 3)$ for this particular state is computed to be 0.04 + 0.09 + 0.25 = 0.38. The other equi-probable states of this distribution can have very different scores and, in establishing the two appropriate statistics for the Herfindahl index, all possible states of $H(10, 3)$ must be considered. The upper limit for this index, computed when all 10 points are found in a single quadrat, is 1; the (theoretical) lower limit, computed when all quadrats share (sometimes approximately) the same number r/n of points, is $1/n$. Sometimes these extreme values are modified (e.g., multiplied by 10,000) or standardized (e.g., adjusted for the minimum observed score) in various ways. For all practical purposes, the scores for the Herfindahl index in this chapter range between 0 and 1. Most known applications of this concentration index in economics involve the study of only a few entities ($n < 10$ cells) but in geography studies often make use of numerous entities ($n > 50$ cells); as a result, the index numbers tend to be much larger in the former studies.

18.2.1 An Example

A straightforward application involves the use of World Bank (1981, 2019) data for the annual value of merchandise trade—as measured in US dollars for the 2 years, 1979 and 2019. A panel data set of the 30 most important trading nations was created, omitting the former Soviet states, a few failed or disrupted states like Iran and Venezuela, and a handful of oil-producing states like Kuwait and Saudi Arabia.

Over the 40-year period, imports and exports in these more developed nations became increasingly similar—earlier, in 1979, the rank (Spearman) coefficient for the two components of trade was $r = 0.911$ while later, in 2019, their rank correlation had grown to $r = 0.976$. This occurred because the relationship between exports ($r = 0.532$) weakened more than the relationship between imports ($r = 0.606$) over the years; in other words, during the four decades the trade pattern for imports proved to be more stable or resilient than the trade pattern for exports. Indeed, once the trade numbers for the various Herfindahl indices were calculated for 1979 and 2019, the results indicated that the concentration index for exports declined appreciably some 7.6% from 0.007978 to 0.006882 but the concentration index for imports declined even more, falling some 8.1% from 0.007902 to 0.007261. These numbers might appear to be small, but only because there were numerous nations being assessed in the panel study.

18.2.2 Some Background

The main intention of the chapter is to provide estimates (or expected values) for the mean and standard deviation of the Herfindahl index, where the solutions conform to the occupancy problem having r indistinguishable particles (points) assigned to n cells (quadrats). As discussed in Feller (1957), Parzen (1960), and elsewhere this problem is commonplace in Bose–Einstein statistics where the number of equi-probable states of the distribution is $m = (n + r - 1)!/r!(n - 1)!$ and there are $m - 1$ degrees of freedom. Of course, when r and n are both large numbers it becomes very convenient to use Stirling's formula for computing factorials (see the Appendix).

To illustrate matters in a little more detail, consider the simple case of $r = 4$ points distributed across $n = 2$ quadrats. Here the $m = 5$ equi-probable states can be represented as (4,0), (3,1), (2,2), (1,3), and (0,4), where the paired integers indicate the number of points in each of the two quadrants, respectively. Each of these states is equally possible so each occurs with probability $1/m = 0.20$. From Eq. (18.1), the score of the Herfindahl index H_m ($m = 1, \ldots, 5$) specific to each of these five states is 1, 0.625, 0.50, 0.625, and 1. This indicates that the most balanced distribution (with low H_m) of points is state three and the least balanced distributions (with high H_m) are states one and five. Computing across all possible states, it follows that the expected values for the mean and the standard deviation of $H(4, 2)$ are $\mu = 0.75$ (3/4) and $\sigma = 0.2338$, respectively. Used together, these two statistics reveal whether the score H_m for each of the five specific states is significantly different from the expected score that would be generated by a random process. For these five samples, the test statistic $V_m = (H_m - \mu)/\sigma$ takes on the values 1.07, −0.53, −1.07, −0.53, and 1.07, respectively. Adopting the *t*-distribution to evaluate the significance of each difference and recognizing $m - 1 = 4$ degrees of freedom in each case, none of the five scores proves to be significantly different from the expected (mean) score of 0.75 according to the tabled *t*-scores of 2.78 (2.13) for the two-tailed test at the 0.05 (0.01) level. But this property will soon disappear for occupancy problems having many particles (points) and many cells (quadrats). However, in these larger occupancy problems the computations can become tedious and time-consuming, so general formulations are needed for computing both the mean and the standard deviation of the Herfindahl index.

18.2.3 Calculating the Mean

The expected value for the number of particles in each of the n cells was not calculated using moment generating functions. A thorny part of the problem with this preferred approach is that the Herfindahl index is computed as a function based on the sums of ratios or quotients, a property that considerably complicates matters. Alternatively, an entirely inductive approach was used to examine a large set of possible situations. In the current exercise all situations having $r = 10$ or fewer particles and $n = 6$ or fewer cells were examined where, in each instance, the equiprobable states were first identified, the various state-specific Herfindahl scores were calculated, and the mean of these various scores was identified. Once the solutions were expressed in fractional as opposed to decimal form a pattern in the mean scores was discernible. As it turns out the expected value E for the random variable $H(\boldsymbol{r}, \boldsymbol{n})$ is.

$$\mu = E\left[H(\boldsymbol{r}, \boldsymbol{n})\right] = (n + 2r - 1)/\left[r(n + 1)\right] \qquad (18.2)$$

This formulation includes those states (as seen in the two-cell example above) where some cells are empty and in this sense Eq. (18.2) represents an unconstrained solution for the expected value. It is straightforward to modify this estimate to include only those states having at least one particle. Some of the scores for the (unconstrained) index are given in Table 18.1, where the values are shown in both fractional and decimal form. As a further test, another five situations were numerically analyzed where both $r > 8$ and $n > 8$ and in each instance the solution for the expected score conformed to that given in Eq. (18.2). Evidently, the mean score shifts lower down each column (where particles change their numbers and cells do not) and lower along each row (where cells change their numbers and particles do not); however, the expected values for $H(\boldsymbol{r}, \boldsymbol{n})$ appear to be more sensitive to the number of cells than to the number of particles.

Table 18.1 Mean μ of Herfindahl index for r particles and n cells

	$n = 2$	$n = 3$	$n = 4$	$n = 5$	$n = 10$	$n = 20$	$n = 30$
$r = 2$	5/6 0.8333	6/8 0.7500	7/10 0.7000	8/12 0.6667	13/22 0.5909	23/42 0.5476	33/62 0.5323
$r = 3$	7/9 0.7778	8/12 0.6667	9/15 0.6000	10/18 0.5556	15/33 0.4545	25/63 0.3968	35/93 0.3763
$r = 4$	9/12 0.7500	10/16 0.6250	11/20 0.5500	12/24 0.5000	17/44 0.3863	27/84 0.3214	37/124 0.2983
$r = 5$	11/15 0.7333	12/20 0.6000	13/25 0.5200	14/30 0.4667	19/55 0.3454	29/105 0.2762	39/155 0.2516
$r = 6$	13/18 0.7222	14/24 0.5833	15/30 0.5000	16/36 0.4444	21/66 0.3182	31/126 0.2460	41/186 0.2204
$r = 7$	15/21 0.7143	16/28 0.5714	17/35 0.4857	18/42 0.4286	23/77 0.2987	33/147 0.2245	43/217 0.1982
$r = 8$	17/24 0.7083	18/32 0.5625	19/40 0.4750	20/48 0.4167	25/88 0.2841	35/168 0.2083	45/248 0.1814
$r = 9$	19/27 0.7037	20/36 0.5555	21/45 0.4667	22/54 0.4074	27/99 0.2727	37/189 0.1957	47/279 0.1684
$r = 10$	21/30 0.7000	22/40 0.5500	23/50 0.4600	24/60 0.4000	29/110 0.2636	39/210 0.1857	49/310 0.1582
$r = 50$	101/150 0.6733	102/200 0.5100	103/250 0.4120	104/300 0.3467	109/550 0.1982	119/1050 0.1133	129/1550 0.0832
$r = 100$	201/300 0.6700	202/400 0.5050	203/500 0.4060	204/600 0.3400	209/1100 0.1900	219/2100 0.1043	229/3100 0.0739

18.2.4 Calculating the Standard Deviation

The next exercise involved solving for the standard deviation (square root of the variance) of the index scores across the various equi-probable states. The same inductive approach was followed and, after some tedious arithmetic involving repeated application of Pascal's triangle, the overall sum ϕ of the deviations for the general situation with r particles and n cells was established as:

$$\phi = [4n(n-1)(n+r+1)!]/\left[r^4(n+1)(n+3)!(r-2)!\right] \qquad (18.3)$$

So, returning to the example above with $r = 4$ particles and $n = 2$ cells, it follows that the overall sum ϕ of the deviates is $(8 \times 1 \times 7!)/(256 \times 3 \times 5! \times 2!) = 336/1536 = 0.2187$. Again, this general solution includes some states that do not have any particles in cells; in fact, for the numerical example above, two of the five states have such an empty cell. As a final step this sum must be standardized by accounting for the appropriate degrees of freedom in the assignment. So, the standard deviation σ is generally solved as follows:

Table 18.2 Standard deviation σ of Herfindahl index for r particles and n cells

	$n = 2$	$n = 3$	$n = 4$	$n = 5$	$n = 10$	$n = 20$	$n = 30$
$r = 2$	0.2886	0.2738	0.2582	0.2439	0.1946	0.1471	0.1228
$r = 3$	0.2566	0.2400	0.2231	0.2087	0.1607	0.1180	0.0974
$r = 4$	0.2338	0.2165	0.1993	0.1843	0.1371	0.0979	0.0798
$r = 5$	0.2186	0.2008	0.1831	0.1678	0.1210	0.0842	0.0678
$r = 6$	0.2078	0.1897	0.1716	0.1561	0.1096	0.0744	0.0594
$r = 7$	0.2000	0.1816	0.1631	0.1474	0.1010	0.0671	0.0530
$r = 8$	0.1939	0.1754	0.1566	0.1407	0.0944	0.0615	0.0481
$r = 9$	0.1891	0.1705	0.1514	0.1353	0.0892	0.0570	0.0442
$r = 10$	0.1852	0.1665	0.1472	0.1310	0.0849	0.0534	0.0309
$r = 50$	0.1564	0.1367	0.1153	0.1072	0.0523	0.0257	0.0170
$r = 100$	0.1520	o.1329	0.1111	0.0936	0.0480	0.0221	0.0139

$$\begin{aligned}\sigma &= [\phi/(m-1)]^{0.5} \\ &= \left\{\left[4n\left(n-1\right)(n+r+1)!\right]/[(m-1)r^4(n+1)(n+3)!(r-2)!]\right\}^{0.5}\end{aligned} \quad (18.4)$$

where m indicates the total degrees of freedom that are available when assigning r points to n quadrats. As already noted, in the numerical example there are only $m - 1 = 4$ degrees of freedom so the standard deviation is calculated to be $\sigma = [(8 \times 1 \times 7!)/(4 \times 256 \times 3 \times 5! \times 2!)]^{0.5} = (336/6144)^{0.5} = 0.2338$.

When large values, certainly exceeding the count of 20, exist for both n and r it is possible to use two different methods to arrive at suitable approximations of the standard deviation. First, Stirling's formula can be used to estimate the appropriate terms and then these can be substituted back into Eq. (18.4); see the Appendix for details. However, an alternative method involves manipulating that equation and simply dropping one degree of freedom so that:

$$\sigma* = \left\{[4(n-1)(n+r+1)(n+r)r(r-1)]/\left[(n+3)(n+2)(n+1)^2r^4\right]\right\}^{0.5}$$

where the asterisk is a reminder that this is an approximation. Moreover, when those values are very large, certainly greater than 100, it is possible to estimate the standard deviation using a very short and simple formula:

$$\sigma** = 2(n+r)/rn^{1.5}$$

Recalling the input data for r and n that were used to estimate the expected values or means in Table 18.1, exact estimates for the matching standard deviations are given in Table 18.2. Once again, the estimates descend in size as larger values are considered for either the number r of particles or the number n of cells.

18.3 Some Applications of the Herfindahl Index

18.3.1 Schools in Toronto

The first example examines data from Boots and Getis (1988) who analyzed the geographic distribution of 119 schools across 72 quadrats in metropolitan Toronto, Canada. Although their main purpose was to test for spatial autocorrelation in the arrangement of these schools, the data also prove useful for current purposes. To begin with, recall that this is only one equi-probable state, or sample, drawn from many billions of possible states. This particular state of $H(119, 72)$ generated a Herfindahl score equal to 0.0259, which was low partly because so many spatial units were used in the study. Boots and Getis also disclosed that the observed distribution had slightly more empty quadrats (17) than would be expected from a Poisson process alone (14.6); see below. In any case, Eqs. (18.1) and (18.2) indicated that the expected value for the mean was 0.0356 and the expected value for the standard deviation was 0.00525. So, the Herfindahl score computed for the specific (observed) state was only about three-quarters the size of what could be expected if the assignment of schools had been entirely random. The test statistic for this specific state, where all 119 schools were assigned across all 72 quadrats, was computed to be $V_m = (0.0259 - 0.0356)/0.00525 = -1.844$, which indicated that the null hypothesis of randomness in school concentration could be rejected at the 0.10 level ($t = 1.65$) but could not be rejected at the 0.05 level ($t = 1.96$) applying the two-tailed test. In other words, there is weak evidence given here that the concentration of schools by quadrats across Toronto was not entirely random, but instead slightly more even or dispersed than a random process would generate. Of course, due to the population density gradient, the prior expectation was not necessarily one of randomness anyways.

One nice feature of these data is that the quadrats could easily be divided into two groups: there were 40 suburban districts located relatively far from Lake Ontario and 32 other urban districts located much closer to the lake. The suburban quadrats contained 53 schools and the urban districts contained the remaining 66 schools. In the suburban areas, the test statistic was computed to be $V_m = (0.0438 - 0.0667)/0.0125 = -1.832$, while in the urban areas the test statistic was computed to be $V_m = (0.0868 - 0.0748)/0.0145 = 0.828$. The signs on the alternative test scores indicate that the concentration in school numbers was somewhat less than expected in the suburban areas but slightly more than expected in the more urban areas. This finding might be related to the variable sizes or ages of the schools, both issues that were not addressed by the authors. Moreover, the two tabled t-scores indicate that the observed school concentration was likely not drawn randomly (but more evenly) in the outer low-density neighborhoods but, in contrast, was drawn randomly in the inner high-density neighborhoods.

18.3.2 Patents in US Metropolitan Areas

The second example uses data on patenting activity that was developed by the author for an earlier paper. As reported in Table 18.1 of Mulligan (2018), America's 380 metropolitan areas were responsible for 43,845 utility patents in 1990 and 134,474 utility patents in 2015, a remarkable increase of some 206%. Moreover, the Herfindahl scores for those patents climbed from 0.0238 in 1990 to 0.0339 in 2015, indicating that an increase of some 42% took place in the concentration of metropolitan patenting activity over those 25 years. In 1990 the expected values for the mean and standard deviation of the Herfindahl index were $\mu = 0.00527$ and $\sigma^{**} = 0.000272$, respectively, while in 2015 the expected values for the concentration index were $\mu = 0.00525$ and $\sigma^{**} = 0.000270$, respectively. The very slight shift seen in these two estimates reflects the convergence that occurs in both the mean and standard deviation when the number r of counts rises but the number n of regions remains constant. Each of the test statistics V_m was computed to be very large, 68.12 in 1990 and 106.11 in 2015, indicating that metropolitan patenting activity was far more concentrated than what would be caused by a purely random process. However, repeating the procedure for metropolitan populations, the corresponding Herfindahl score was computed to be 0.0181 in 1990 and 0.0162 in 2015, indicating that metropolitan populations became less concentrated over time. Although another test statistic was not identified, the patent-to-population ratio of the year-specific Herfindahl scores climbed from 1.322 in 1990 to 2.087 in 2015, or nearly 58%, during the 25-year period. In other words, the assignment of utility patents to different-sized places like New York, San Francisco, Austin (TX), and Boulder (CO) became much more concentrated over time than would be expected by only the differential population changes that took place across metropolitan America.

18.4 Concluding Remarks

This paper has developed new statistical properties for the Herfindahl–Hirschman index, which is widely used to measure size concentration when location is little or no interest. This index, which ranges between 0 and 1, is computed as the sum of the squared shares (percentages) of a chosen metric across a class of entities. The approach taken in the chapter follows the logic of the standard occupancy problem, where r particles (points) are distributed across n cells (quadrats). Both $\boldsymbol{r}$ and $\boldsymbol{n}$ are random variables so the Herfindahl index itself is considered a random variable $H(\boldsymbol{r}, \boldsymbol{n})$. Addressing all the possible states of this random variable, expected values for both the mean and standard deviation were specified. A test was then devised to compare the *observed* score for a specific state, or sample, to an *expected* score reflecting all possible states. This allows inferences to be drawn about whether the observed Herfindahl score conforms to a random process. The discussion ended with two examples showing how test statistics can uncover geographic variation in concentration (suburban versus urban schools in metropolitan Toronto) or longitudinal variation in concentration (1990 versus 2010 patents generated in US metropolitan areas).

As stated at the outset, regional scientists are interested in both non-spatial distributions and spatial arrangements. The former can provide information about the degree of aspatial concentration and the latter information about the degree of spatial concentration, which often seem to be correlated. This suggests the usefulness of developing a 2 by 2 classification matrix, at least for conceptual purposes, where the aspatial and spatial approaches are considered along the two axes. The vertical axis would range between 0 and 1 (for the Herfindahl index) and the horizontal axis would range between -1 and $+1$ (for Moran's coefficient). Those situations devoid of both types of positive concentration would be found somewhere in the bottom, left-hand corner and those situations exhibiting both types of positive concentration would be found somewhere in the top, right-hand corner. Agricultural establishments of approximately the same size might be representative of the former group and manufacturing establishments of different sizes might be representative of the latter group.

That said, it would be very useful in regional science to devise a composite index where both dimensions were addressed together. So, this index would likely have three different components: one coefficient to measure pure (non-spatial) distribution, a second coefficient to measure pure (spatial) arrangement, and a third to account for the interaction between the spatial and non-spatial coefficients. This might sharpen our understanding of how changes in the concentration of some activity take place over time: in some instances, agent locations might remain constant although agent sizes might shift, while, in other instances, agent locations might shift when agent sizes remain constant.

As a final note, the test statistic for *randomness* outlined above could be refined to make it more applicable to various real-word situations. Few cases of interest will exhibit many quadrats with no occupants, but the underlying matrices used to calculate the mean and standard deviation could be truncated and re-examined to identify expected values for those instances having more than a few zeroes across the quadrats. In the same way, these matrices could be truncated to reexamine other cases where all, or nearly all, quadrats have many occupants, as in the merchandise trade example earlier. These operations might lead to test statistics for randomness having a sharper focus on either tail of the overall size distribution and, in other words, examine randomness across designated subpopulations instead of entire populations. Such operations would elevate the Herfindahl–Hirschman index from descriptive to inferential status and give the index wider appeal for understanding any randomness arising only from size differences.

Appendix

The formula for integers developed by James Stirling (1692–1770) has been given much attention by many prominent mathematicians, especially since the advances made in research on complex numbers by Abraham de Moivre (1667–1754). The formula provides an approximate solution for integer factorials where the absolute errors diverge, but the relative or proportional errors converge, as the integers become larger in size. In short, the formula is.

$$n!\tilde{(2\pi)}^{0.5}\, n^{n+0.5} e^{-n}$$

where the sign ~ indicates that the ratio of the formula's two sides approaches unity as the size of the integer n approaches infinity (Feller 1957). Note, when $n = 10$, the LHS of the formula is 3,628,800, while the RHS is 3,598,695.6, and the approximation generates a relative error of less than 1%. In fact, when $n = 8$ the error is 1.03%, when $n = 10$, the error is 0.83%, and when $n = 12$ the error is 0.63%.

As Parzen (1960) points out this factorial approximation for integers is a special case of the gamma function for real numbers, which continues to play an important role in various aspects of probability theory. This function also can be tied to the Riemann Zeta function, which has key applications to the study of prime numbers in mathematics and string theory in physics. It is worth noting that, in general, the gamma function $\Gamma(n + 1) = n!$, where $\Gamma(1) = 1$. When addressing increasingly larger integers, Stirling's formula provides solutions that asymptotically approach the values for the real numbers that are calculated in the various integral solutions of the gamma function.

References

Atkinson A (2015) Inequality. Harvard University Press, Cambridge

Batty M (2013) The new science of cities. MIT Press, Cambridge

Boots B, Getis A (1988) Point pattern analysis. Sage, Beverly Hills

Carlton D, Perloff J (1990) Modern industrial organization. Harper Collins, New York

Cliff A, Ord K (1973) Spatial autocorrelation. Pion, London

Cliff A, Ord K (1981) Spatial processes: models and applications. Pion, London

Feller W (1957) An introduction to probability theory and its applications, vol 1, 2nd edn. Wiley, New York

Getis A (2008) A history of the concept of spatial autocorrelation: a geographer's perspective. Geogr Anal 40:297–309

Getis A, Ord K (1992) The analysis of spatial association by use of distance statistics. Geogr Anal 24:189–206

Hirschman A (1964) The paternity of an index. Am Econ Rev 54:761

Isard W (1960) Methods of regional analysis. MIT Press, Cambridge

Milanovic B (2016) Global inequality. Harvard University Press, Cambridge

Mulligan G (2018) Patent generation in U.S. metropolitan areas. In: Bernhard I (ed) Diversity, innovation, entrepreneurship: regional, urban, national and international perspectives. University West, Trollhättan, pp 299–314

Mulligan G, Carruthers J (2021) City-size distribution: the evolution of theory, evidence, and policy in regional science. In: Fischer M, Nijkamp P (eds) The handbook of regional science, 2nd edn. Springer, Berlin, pp 41–59

Mulligan G, Schmidt C (2005) A note on localization and specialization. Growth Chang 36:565–576

Parzen I (1960) Modern probability theory and its applications. Wiley, New York

Sakai Y (2018) Liverpool merchants versus Ohmi merchants: how and why they dealt with risk and insurance differently. Asia-Pacific J Reg Sci 2:15–33

Sen A (1997) On economic inequality: expanded edition. Clarendon Paperbacks, Oxford

U.S. Bureau of Labor Statistics (2014) Measuring occupational concentration by industry. Beyond the Numbers (Feb issue) 3:1–13. https://www.bls.gov/opub/btn/volume-3/pdf/measuring-occupational-concentration-by-industry.pdf. Last accessed 4/5/20

U.S. Department of Justice (2010) Horizontal merger guidelines. https://www.justice.gov/sites/default/files/atr/legacy/2010/08/19/hmg-2010.pdf. Last accessed 4/5/20

West G (2017) Scale: the universal laws of life, growth, and death in organisms, cities, and companies. Penguin Books, New York

World Bank (1981) World development Bank 1981. International Bank for Reconstruction and Development, Washington, DC

World Bank (2019) World Development Indicators 2019. https://datatopics.worldbank.org/world-development-indicators/themes/economy.html.pdf. Last accessed 1/3/21

Chapter 19
Risk Culture: Comparative Analysis of Risk Management

Yuji Maeda

Abstract Facing the COVID-19 pandemic in 2020, we find quite different people's attitudes among nations toward the same crisis. This is a good timing to analyze why there shows such difference between countries. In this paper, we argue about factors of the culture which determine the characteristics of risk management in the country. Especially referring to insurance industry, we attempt to clarify why, and to what extent, the culture influences risk management in Japan in comparison with Anglo-Saxon and European countries.

Keywords Risk management · Pandemic · Risk culture · Insurance

19.1 Introduction

It is not exaggerated to say that the year of 2020 is a year of COVID-19. People in the world are scared of death from the corona pandemic. This coronavirus, however, has clarified the interesting difference in its response among nations to mitigating the spread of the virus. For example, in Europe, "*test, test and test*" and "*lockdown*" are thought the most important, while Japan fights for it "*case by case*" and "*attacking clusters*" when corona is identified. Then, we come to a question why these responses are so different among nations toward the same virus. We argue that there must be certain reasons for the difference in response or we have distinct characteristics of "risk culture" and the way of the people's thinking or behavior that would make different responses toward risk. Thus, in this study, we discuss the risk management between cultures so that we attempt to clarify this important research question.

Risks have always been a problem but are likely to be ignored since they have been perceived as unavoidable. However, given recent trend of internationalization,

Y. Maeda (✉)
Institute of Business and Accounting, Kwansei Gakuin University, Nishinomiya, Hyogo, Japan
e-mail: ymaeda@kwansei.ac.jp

M. Kawano et al. (eds.), *Theory and History in Regional Perspective*, New Frontiers in Regional Science: Asian Perspectives 56,
https://doi.org/10.1007/978-981-16-6695-7_19

globalization, deregulation, and integration, risks often cause significant impacts to the daily lives of people who can no longer ignore risks.

In the past, there are many arguments in cultural difference in risk management. For example, Mizushima et al. (1995) argued that the risk management of a corporation is very much influenced by its country or corporate culture. According to their argument, the risk management practices of each country should reflect the cultural differences between societies or countries. The argument is supported by Wildavsky and Drake (1990) who demonstrated that the studies of contrasting theories of risk perception consistently find the cultural component to be the most important factor. The authors differentiate the risk perception of "individualistic" cultures. They define the "individualistic" cultures as the cultures where the people value "individual" or the individual identity the most. Those countries are such as the USA and UK. The risk perception of "hierarchies" is different. Here are such "hierarchical" cultures as the culture where the people value the group consensus the most important among others such as Japan and other Asian countries. According to them, Austria, Germany, Italy, and Switzerland among the European countries are the more individualistic, whereas Belgium, France, and Spain take a middle position.

Even though risk management is a strategically important and critical for an organization, until recently in Japan there have been no serious discussions about risks and risk management within companies.

19.2 Risk Perception in Japan

"*Earthquakes, Thunderstorms, Fires and Fathers (Jisin, Kaminari, Kaji, Oyaji)*" is a very famous proverb in Japan. This means that the people fear *earthquakes* the most, then *thunderstorms*, *fires*, and *fathers* (the last). Historically, the Japanese islands are susceptible to earthquakes and/or *tsunami* and typhoons that are natural disasters frequently occurred in Japan. Fires have been scared because most of the residential houses are constructed of woods and have been built very close to each other in scarce flat land. Especially in the *Edo* period (1603–1868), there were fires which destroyed a lot of houses because of fast spread of a fire. Because of this, there is so-called *fire legal* in Japan that makes the person who owns the house of the origin of a fire is free from liability for the spread of fire. Last is "*Fathers.*" It means "*the father is the rule for a family and whom the family members should obey,*" in which it is hierarchy with the father as the head of a family.

It is interesting to note that those risks such as earthquakes, thunderstorms, and fires have two common characteristics, that is, "randomness (or suddenness)" and "ending in a short time period." According to Yamamoto (1971), Japanese people learned that the best risk management for natural disasters is "to tolerate" or "to wait for the bad time gone by." The damage by the disaster then had been burdened for many generations. After the disaster had gone, what the people did was to forget it. None talked about it and none wrote about it. We prayed at shrines and temples for no more disasters. During the certain season every year, we have festivals or *Matsuri (in Japanese)* for praying for no disasters, even now.

Except for those natural disasters, Japan has enjoyed safety all the time. Even now the crime rate in Japan is one of the lowest in the world according to *Crime Rate by Country* 2021. Geographically, Japan is located on islands which are separated from other nations by oceans. Japan is dominantly lived by one race, Japanese, with almost no immigrants. The islands have not invaded by other people in its long history over two thousand years except the occupation of GHQ after World War II.

Yamamoto (1971) said "*in our history of risk, there was no such events as wars, pandemic, genocide, discrimination, or persecution.*" Japan has enjoyed a full of water, plenty of rice harvest, peace, and safety on the tiny islands. One evidence shows that the people did not equip a key to enter their house because of no burglary.

It is indeed true for Japanese people that "safety" is given all the time. They enjoy safety without paying any costs. Contrary to Japan, the nations in Europe have built high rigid walls to protect cities and built water canal bridges to protect the supply of water among others. The people in Europe paid tremendous amount of labor and money for protection for their living, thus for safety.

One evidence is illustrated that the people in Europe and America are willing to pay money for insurance to protect their lives. We have known that insurance started in Europe. Japanese people buy insurance for saving, not for protection. It does not make sense for Japanese people to buy insurance or pay money for "safety." Insurance seller in Japan therefore often promotes insurance as "products" by saying "*This is for your saving, for future!*" They never say that insurance is to protect you from "danger." To illustrate this fact is that Japanese insurance companies are known for offering maturity refund policies that have saving elements built into the insurance (Skipper and Kwon 2007).

19.3 Risk Management Standard in Japan

In the previous section, we demonstrated that the Japanese people attempt to forget such natural disasters as earthquakes, thunderstorms, and fires and do not keep record of what had happened. If they had to face it, they tolerate it and wait for it to go by. Other than those disasters, safety is given to them for free and the people are not willing to pay for the protection from danger because they do not need one in most cases. Under such circumstances, risk management has not been developed as in the western nations or the USA where dangers frequently occur.

Knowledge of risk management was imported into Japan from overseas. Insurance industry had started since the *Meiji* period around 1880 starting with marine insurances by Tokio Marine Insurance Company[1]. Conversely, the standards or rules for controlling and managing risks were imported from *outside*. Those

[1] Tokio Marine Insurance Company started in 1878.

implementation have not been successful in changing the people's attitude. One reason is for the features of the people dealing all the times with "double standards," that is, rules of "*Shakai*" and "*Seken*" separately in the society.

Kohkami (2009) explained their "double standard" by an interesting story of a French man who visited Japan for the first time. The French man said, "*Last week, I forgot my bag in the train. I was very sad for the loss and told this story to a Japanese friend. He said he would call the JR (Japan Rail) immediately. It was foolish! I thought at first. But at JR I found my bag in the same train where I left the bag. I was very surprised.*" He thought it was incredible. "*In France, the bag would be lost for sure. Well, in any European countries, it would be so. If the owner of the bag is not there, someone will steal it. Japanese people are very good in manners. This is miracle!*" Two weeks later, the same French man was at a loss. He said, "*Today, I was in the train when an old lady got on the train. Then, she stood in front of the priority seats but no one sitting in the seats did not offer their seats. They were looking down the smart phones without notice. In France or any European countries, someone would offer her the seats immediately. It is incredible that the old lady with a stick was left standing!*" He continued, "*Yesterday, there was a lady who was carrying a baby in a stroller onto the stair. But no one tried to help the lady mother. She was carrying the baby stroller alone with a lot of efforts! What in the world has happened to this country by not helping her in this situation?*" The French man was stuck by the contradiction of Japanese attitudes.

Kohkami (2009) demonstrates another story for explanation. "*I often come across a group of middle-aged ladies who got on the train. A lady with full of energy jumped in at first and tried to get the seats for everybody of the group and said "I got the seats for you, here here!!*"" The lady who tried to secure the seats did not show a bad manner but instead she must be a very kind person thinking about her group. She must be a generous person who cares for others. Kohkami (2009) explained that she was just separating the world (space) of her interest clearly from the world (space) of her ignorance. We noticed that there is something common among those stories. Japanese people often deal with "*inside*" and "*outside*" with quite different attitudes. *The French person's bag was* "*outside.*" It was separated from the interests of the people and thus ignored.

The world (space) of their interest is called "*Seken (in Japanese)*," while the world of their ignorance is called "Society *(Shakai in Japanese)* (Kohkami 2009)." Unlike Japan, the western nations have one *Society* that an individual belongs to, not two! A notion of *Society* was imported into Japan in the *Meiji* period. In Japan, the people care for others within the same interests, while they are likely to ignore people and/or things outside of their interests. That is the nature of "double standards" in Japan. For example, we treat differently the people from overseas by calling them "*Foreigners (Gaijin).*"

Japan has two different standards or double standards in its daily life. We argue that this double standard of Japanese people makes the effective risk management very difficult to implement. Loftstedt et al. (2000) found similarly that the Japanese traditional consensus-based regulation was based on informal and personal networks among stakeholders where people on the street had to rely on the authorities' decision-making in the dichotomy of "safety" and "danger." In their studies, in Japan the shortage of risk studies on scientific evidence, including epidemiological surveys had forced most Japanese regulatory measures to follow the outside regulations.

Decision-making in risk management is also unique. In every day's life, the word liquidated from *Seken* is "*Kuuki (in Japanese)*" which mind-controls the Japanese people. There are no proper translations in English about *Kuuki*. *Kuuki* means "*read between lines*" in English if we would, "*ruwach*" in Hebraea, or *aer* in Latin (Yamamoto (2018)). *Kuuki in Japanese* means something unwritten, unvoiced, and changing rule depending on a circumstance, that is, a kind of rule that controls the mind of people in a certain group in Japan. It is often "*Kuuki*" which influences the important decision-making for the people. It is said nowadays that he is mocked as "*K.Y. (Kuuki wo Yomenai)*" (who cannot understand *Kuki*) among young people if he did not follow the rule of *Kuuki*. Yamamoto (2018) stated that the foolish strategies were conducted by the Japanese Military during World War II because of the existence of *Kuuki*. Otherwise, no one could explain the reasons for the irrational, and so foolish, strategies at the times of war.

The Japanese people are very sensitive to *Kuuki* and unconsciously comply with *Kuuki*. It is because of *Kuuki* that the leader of Japan made an irrational decision making sometimes, for example, sacrificing many people to death at the time of World War II. We argue that the existence of *Kuuki* leads to unique consequences on the decision-making with respect to risk management. We found an example of creating *Kuuki* successfully in the COVID-19 pandemic recently where almost everyone follows instructions of wearing a mask and staying at home without enforcing lockdowns or penalties. It is therefore critical in Japan to successfully create *Kuuki* in which everyone follows a certain rule so that an effective risk management can be standardized at every level of the people. We doubt about the success because the unwritten and unvoiced nature of *Kuuki* is contradictory to transparent, precise, and rational decision makings for sound risk management. In theory, every person should understand clearly what to do in case of a danger.

19.4 Corporate Risk Management in Japan

A survey conducted by Tokio Marine Nichido Fire Risk Consulting Inc. (from the White Papers/Reports done by Ministry of Economy, Trade and Industry (2006)) showed that about 70% of the surveyed Japanese corporations answered that they have not established risk management practice in place.

Marsh's survey (2012) revealed that earthquake insurances are purchased by 36% of Japanese firms, while 76% of the US firms; business interruption[2] insurances are

---

[2]Business interruption insurance is to indemnify the loss of profits and the continuing fixed expenses during the break of commercial activities due to occurrence of a peril (Rubin 1995).

13% of Japanese firms, while 83% of the US firms. The survey indicated that the perception of insurance is quite different between Japan and the US.

Like insurance, a *pooling* of funds in case of shipwrecks or bankruptcies had been seen among *Ohmi* merchants in the *Edo* period in the 1800s when they started to transport goods by boats from Osaka to *Edo* (current Tokyo) or Hokkaido to *Edo* (Uemura 2005; Sakai 2018). It had been a mutual fund by which losses were paid upon danger.

Insurance started as marine insurance on August 1, 1878 by Tokio Marine Insurance Company, to help develop marine transportation and trading business with overseas. On October 1, 1888, fire insurance started by Tokyo Fire Insurance Company (subsequent *Yasuda Fire* and current *Sompo Japan*).

Japanese firms in the modern times have started since the end of World War II when all the *Zaibatzu* had been broken up by GHQ[3] because the USA considered that *Zaibatsu* conglomerates contributed a lot to providing technologies to the Japanese military force during the war. Japanese firms have then developed the system of *Keiretsu*[4] instead to protect themselves. By holding their shares each other and forming a rigid network of business, *Keiretsu* is in fact to provide a protection from the risk of hostile takeovers by US capitalists.

The modern Japanese management is unique with several distinct characteristics. We can identify quite a few, for example, lifetime employment, seniority-based salary system, enterprise unions, aggregate recruiting, a high level of job security, selection of the company's leader from themselves, among others. In this unique system, the voice of stockholders is comparatively weak. Corporate governance is depending on the *Keiretsu* bank. This bank, called "*Main Bank,*" has been acting strong responsibilities in their corporate governance and financing. The fraternal nature of the firms in *Keiretsu* has created harmony with local communities, between employers and employees, with suppliers, customers, and other stakeholders. Presidents act as coordinators among business units rather than leaders. Enterprise unions have also been strong coordinators between employees and employers. Important information has been shared among the bottom-line workers first and then communicated with the upper management.

Loss information is likely not stored because there is no department in an organization where loss records are filed. Insurance is handled generally by General Affairs[5] departments. Marsh (2012) showed that in the 57% of the surveyed firms "General Affairs Department" oversaw insurance purchase and claims and in the 29% "Accounting and Finance Department." In the USA or European countries,

---

[3]GHQ is General Headquarters, the Supreme Commander for the Allied Powers that were to execute a policy into Japan based on Potsdam Declaration.

[4]Keiretsu is a group of firms connected by holding shares each other. Within Keiretsu, a bank, insurance companies, a trust company act as financing companies for group firms. Keiretsu have firms from different industries. For example, Mitsubishi Keiretsu consists of Mitsubishi Bank, Tokio Fire and Marine Insurance Company, Meiji Life Insurance Company, Kirin Brewery, Asahi Glass, Mitsubishi Electrics among others.

[5]General Affairs Department deals with anything else besides business operations.

there is "Risk Management Department" with a "Risk Manager" in almost every organization. "Risk Manager" is a professional hired from outside and sometimes became a C-level executive[6], overseeing enterprise wide risk management activities and insurance management as well.

Because risk management is not considered as a major function in an organization, expertise of handling risk or losses has not been developed well. College education in Japan does not have a risk management as a "major" course even though many colleges and universities teach "Insurance Theory," to some extent, in commerce or business schools. Conversely, many universities have a faculty of risk management and/or insurance in Europe and the USA but almost none in Japan. Fundamental knowledge and skills of risk management are therefore not shared among people, employees, managers, and leaders. Risk consulting has not become a *money-making* business. We often observe employees and managers did nothing but went into big troubles when they came across emergency events.

Weak leadership is another problem in Japan. Presidents of firms are mostly selected from internal managers within the same organization because they are expected to play good coordinator's role rather than to lead the organization. President of a firm is likely to ignore risk management because it costs money and does not produce profit.

One example is in March 2011 when a large earthquake and the subsequent tsunami caused a devastating damage in the northern part of Japan, known as *Great East Japan Earthquake*. *Fukushima* nuclear power plant melted down as a result. This is a typical example of a poor leadership. The accident was the result of collusion between the government, the regulator, and *TEPCO (Tokyo Electric Power Company)* (Shimizu 2014). Shimizu (2014) pointed out, "*Researchers repeatedly pointed out the high possibility of tsunami levels reaching beyond the assumptions made at the time of construction, as well as the possibility of core damage in the case of such tsunami, TEPCO ignored these warnings. They are aware of the risk of core damage from the tsunami. However, no regulations were created nor did TEPCO take any preventative steps against such an occurrence. This was a disaster "Made in Japan." Its fundamental causes are to be found in the ingrained conventions of Japanese culture. Nobody at TEPCO voiced responsibility. Everybody disguised himself as unrelated to the issue. They made excuses, excuses and excuses . . .*" Later, Prime Minister *Abe* said to the world, "*Fukushima is under control*" when Japan invited Olympic of 2020 to Tokyo, hiding the fact that the situation was still in bad situations.

[6]C-level executives are such as chief finance officers, chief operating officers and chief risk officers.

19.5 Risk Sharing Within a Group or Organization

A feature of risk sharing among the members of a group or an organization is considered as distinct characteristics of Japanese corporate risk management. Wildavsky and Drake (1990) demonstrated that Japan has the "*Hierarchies*" cultures where the people value the group consensus the most among others and its risk perception is built on this group culture. We argue that the group consensus nature also reflects on its corporate risk management. One example is that risk is shared among the member companies of "*Keiretsu*" system.

A characteristic of *Keiretsu* system is its established shareholding ties with one another and the main bank supports their financial ties. Flath (1995) argues that "*Keiretsu*" is a business group that has been an important feature of Japan's industrial organization. "*Keiretsu*" provides not only the financial ties but also business ties between the members of a *Keiretsu* group. This system also provides unconscious trust among members, multilateral relationship (Nishiguchi and Beaudet 1999) for mutual benefits, and more unwritten contracts of agreement for cooperation in case of adverse events. Monthly president's club meetings of the group provide the place where affiliated entities exchange information and built their mutual trust, which is inevitably building multilateral cooperation for business as well. We can demonstrate that the business groups must be purportedly formed to create a rigid and shared system of their risk management in place among the members. Anticipating extreme cases, the members must help a troubled member company if an adverse event had occurred to the troubled member.

Existence of unwritten, but trust-worthy agreement of cooperation from the same business group members in case of an emergency is illustrated by the case of "*Toyota and Aisin Seiki Fire*" in 1997. *Aisin Seiki Company* was a sole supplier of proportioning valves for Toyota and the fire at *Aisin Seiki* suddenly halted the whole process of Toyota's manufacturing to a complete stop mostly because of the famous Toyota's manufacturing system, "*Just-in-Time*[7]."

According to the research of Nishiguchi and Beaudet (1999), the loss of proportional valve supplies because of the fire at *Aisin Seiki* was completely covered by impromptu productions of alternative *P valves* from other 200 suppliers amazingly within a few days after the incident, even though those suppliers had no expertise in producing *P valves*. As a result, the production at Toyota was completely recovered to normal within a week after the loss. The research noted an interestingly story in which there was no written consent for indemnifying extra costs for alternative production, no endangering intellectual property rights, nor forced directions from Toyota. Those suppliers' voluntary cooperation had made a successful and extraordinary speedy recovery.

[7] Just-in-time is a production of Toyota, eliminating all the waste. Warehouse, storage, redundancies among others are considered as waste. They try to produce automobiles, what is needed, when it is needed and the amount needed.

19.6 Anglo-Saxon Countries: USA, UK, Canada, and Australia

Wildavsky and Drake (1990) observe that individualist cultures such as the USA would be expected to support self-regulation, including the freedom to bid and bargain as the means for addressing risk. In the individualistic society, risks are also viewed to offer opportunities and should be accepted in exchange for benefits.

Holstede (1995) introduced the anthropological theory of risk perception that Anglo countries such as Australia, Canada, New Zealand, the USA, and UK tend to be more individualistic, whereas the European countries such as Denmark, Finland, the Netherlands, Norway, and Sweden tend to value solidarity more.

Mizushima et al. (1995) argue that in the USA and UK business models, economically rational decisions are often made in the process of risk management, comparing the cost of protection from risks with the associated benefits. Since corporations behave rationally to maximize their utility and profit, they tend to manage risks that potentially reduce the corporate value. It is more likely that, in the USA businesses react unnecessarily or overreact to risks and try to mitigate them as early as possible. Obviously, their reaction toward risks can be viewed as a reflection of the litigious nature of the USA and, therefore, managing a company in the USA often involves strategic consideration of financial, business, and operational risks, or, insurable and non-insurable risks.

According to the rational behavior of maximizing their utility and profit, their risk management should be determined based on returns relative to risk. Generally speaking, higher risk requires more returns. The Anglo-Saxon firms behave with respect to the tradeoff between risks and return. This behavior is based on the principle of "assumption of risk," on which firms retain risk first before transfer the risk. Reflecting this tendency, the US firms are likely to set high deductibles or high self-insured retention in their insurance contracts. For example, rules of thumb in the US general insurance industry (International Risk Management Institute Inc. 2020) show that rational retention capacity is 2–5% of working capital, 1–5% of total current assets, 1–8% of operating income, 1/2–2% of annual revenue, or 2–5% of cash flows.

With this practice, insurance companies expect firms to control risk by themselves under the set retention level. Firms are also encouraged to manage and control the risks. As a return for this effort, the cost of risk becomes lower. Reduction of risk would lead to a decrease in insurance premiums, in return, creating more efficient market.

19.7 European Countries

In general, European countries tend to value solidarity and are less individualistic than the USA and UK. Risk perception of European countries is positioned somewhere in the middle between the individualistic countries such as the USA and UK and the hierarchical countries such as Japan. Following the discussions of Ren (1992) and Rayer (1992) European countries can be classified into the stratified individuals. The stratified individuals tend to perceive that life is a lottery; risk is out of control; safety is a matter of luck. They also tend to think that risk should be avoided unless it is inevitable to protect the public good. They tend to claim that nature is fragile to justify sharing the earth limited resources. Their peculiar characteristics include the strong cognition of environmental risk management and protection of historical assets from risks.

In this context, Kamei (1998) argues that the risk management in European countries stands its own way, while it has been influenced very much by the US risk management. The research on European risk management started in 1976 by Jacques Charbonnier. Charbonnier identified that the risk management in European countries imported the US style at the beginning but developed one on its own. Thus, in the beginning stage, corporations classified risks as pure risks (insurable risks) and speculative risks (non-insurable risks) and then they concentrated only on the pure risks. The facts indicate that the European corporations follow the US risk management theory. From there, the European corporations have developed uniquely their own way of risk management.

Charbonnier argues that, compared with the US risk management, European risk management has the following four characteristics: first, risks of small to medium size are primary concerns; second, risk management is viewed as equivalent to insurance management; third, risk management is focused on the protection of assets such as human assets, environmental assets, property assets from risks; fourth, environmental and product liability risks are the two of most concern risks for risk managers.

19.8 Comparative Study in Insurance Industries

If the corporate risk management is partially viewed as "*Insurance Management*" as in Anglo-Saxon countries or European countries, it can be explained to a certain extent by analysis on the structure of each insurance industry. Here, we assume that the market reflects the demand of protection from risk, the social and cultural fabric of the people, the political history and philosophy of the country (Skipper and Kwon (2007)).

Table 19.1 provides the scale of premiums in insurance industries among countries. The market in the USA is by far the largest in the world. The US market comprises roughly 30% of the world followed by China (11%) and then Japan

Table 19.1 Life and nonlife premiums by countries in 2018

Top 10 countries by life and non-life insurance (2018)

Unit: US $ million

Total rank	Country	Life premiums ($)	Life rank	Nonlife premiums ($)	Nonlife rank	Total ($)	Percentage of total world premiums
1	The USA	5,93,391	1	8,75,984	1	14,69,375	28.29
2	China	3,13,365	3	2,61,512	2	5,74,877	11.07
3	Japan	3,34,232	2	1,06,405	4	4,40,637	8.49
4	UK	2,35,501	4	1,01,009	5	3,36,510	6.48
5	France	1,65,075	5	92,888	6	2,57,963	4.97
6	Germany	96,439	9	1,45,046	3	2,41,485	4.65
7	South Korea	98,072	8	80,951	7	1,79,023	3.45
8	Italy	1,25,341	6	44,933	9	1,70,274	3.28
9	Canada	54,070	10	73,833	8	1,27,903	2.46
10	Taiwan	1,02,044	7	19,864	10	1,21,908	2.35

Table is created by authors, Data source: Swiss Re, *sigma* (2019)

(8.5%). The ranking can explain as a reflection of the economic power in the world. Interestingly, looking at the size of gross premiums, Anglo-Saxon countries such as the USA and UK come at higher ranks in the table followed by the European countries such as Germany and France.

Though, Japan comes third for the size of "Gross Premiums," it ranks below average among advanced countries, at the 15th in "Insurance Density and Penetration (Swiss Re 2019)." Interestingly, Switzerland is the second following Hong Kong on Insurance Density and penetration. Overall, the data explains that risk is traded intensively in Anglo-Saxon and European countries.

Interestingly, nonlife insurance premiums are larger than life insurance premiums in the USA, while life insurance is larger than nonlife in Japan, China, Korea, and Taiwan. In Asian countries such as China, Korea, and Japan, life insurance industry overwhelms nonlife industry in the market. If we look at the life insurance only, the Japanese market comes second after the US market. The fact illustrated that the high Asian propensity to "save" via life insurance is revealed (Skipper and Kwon (2007)). Skipper and Kwon (2007) explain that the growth of life insurance in those countries is "*driven by increasing life expectancy and governments having to reduce the generosity of the social insurance programs in the face of fiscal imbalances.*"

19.9 Risk Avoidance and Elimination

Techniques of risk management are fundamentally categorized into two: passive and active. The passive approach is avoidance and elimination of risk. This technique includes avoidance of taking risk, contractual transfer or non-insurance transfer of risk, and insurance transfer of risk. Another is an active approach; retaining and controlling risk. The first technique is the one that people would consider in managing risk first of all since it is the best among various risk managements measures. We argue that the tendency of using this first technique, a passive approach, that is risk avoidance or risk elimination, is prevalent in Japan.

Illustrating this evidence, the corporate insurance programs or policies have had low (or none) deductible, or the self-insured retention of risk is set at very low level, which explains that the programs or contracts aim at a total transfer of risk to insurance companies. Elements of risk sharing between insurance carriers and purchasers of insurance are negligible.

In such total transfer of risk to insurance companies, the cost of purchasing insurance tends to be high because insurance companies charge their own profits, administrative costs, and the cost of moral hazard added to losses. Contrary to this is the USA where the transfer of risk is negotiated, as a rational economic behavior, between purchasers of insurance and insurance carriers as to how much, and to what extent, risk is transferred for how much money. The US firms normally agree with higher self-insured retention and thus can minimize the cost of insurance, leading to efficient risk transfer. Rather they consider that they can save the cost saved from self-insurance at *low-loss* levels to spend for more coverage at *high-loss* levels so that the firm can sustain from bankruptcy from a large loss ignoring the costs of paying for small losses. Contrary, Japanese firms do not have such a rational idea for efficient purchase of insurance. They consider that they must purchase insurance from zero dollar because "*it is necessary!*"

Figure 19.1 which shows comparative costs of nonlife insurance between Japan and the USA, supports this argument. In Fig. 19.1, for example, in 2019 the 138% in the US versus 148% in Japan means that US firms pay $1.38 for the loss of $1.00, while Japanese firms pay $1.48 for $1.00 of loss. This indicated the cost of insurance is around 10% higher in Japan than in the USA. We consider that the Japanese firms could have purchased insurance much cheaper.

Manufacturers in Japan have expertise in elimination of risk over time by their renowned practice of "*Kaizen*" or continuous improvement. According to Imai (1986), "*Kaizen*" is the gradual, unending improvement, doing "little things" better; setting and achieving even higher standards in the manufacturing process. This management practice, as many researchers agree, is unique for Japanese production reflecting Japanese culture of group orientation and continuous efforts. The Imai's analysis supports that Japanese companies are likely to take gradual but rigid approach to progress and the process has successfully led to the world premier quality assurance and in such a way eliminating risks of producing defective products and therefore creating safer products over the long-run. We argue that

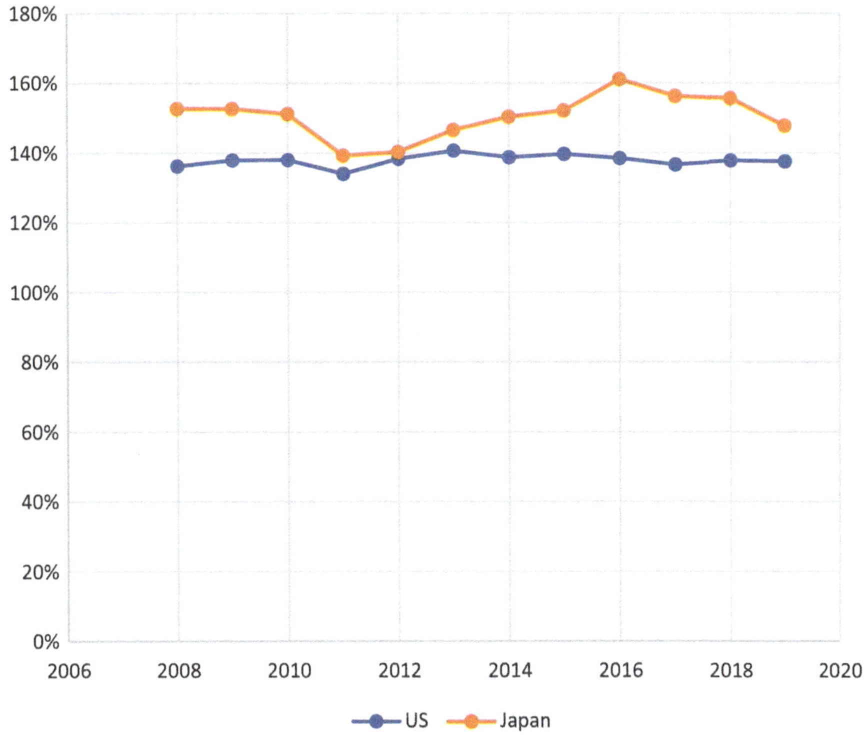

Fig. 19.1 Cost of Insurance between Japan and the USA in Nonlife Insurance Industry (How much do you need to pay for insurance if you have a loss value of 100%? The values in Fig. 19.1 are calculated by the authors based on the data. Source: Insurance Research Institute of Japan "*The Statistics of Japanese Non-life Insurance Business* 2009–2019" and the US NAIC (National Association of Insurance Commissions 2019) "*U.S. Property and Casualty Insurance Industry, 2019 Full Year Results*")

this practice represents the risk elimination, a distinctive nature of the Japanese risk management process.

These empirical findings are consistent with the argument that Japanese companies tend to rely on risk avoidance or risk elimination as a primary risk management strategy.

19.10 Reserving Monetary Fund for Risk

Japan is more serious in the aging problem than any other country. Especially worried about anticipated shrinking consumer demand because of a lower birthrate (1.36 in 2019 per Ministry of Health Labor and Welfare), insecurity of job market (the unemployment rate is 2.4% in 2020 as compared to 2.0% in 1980), longer after-retirement life (the life expectancy is an age of 81.41 in 2020 for men and 87.45 for women in 2020 as compared with an age of 78 and 85, respectively, in 2002 per Ministry of Health Labor and Welfare), and endangered government pension plans, people would have a strong tendency to save for anxious future. Reflecting this, in 2018, Japan owned net global assets of 328 trillion yen, the world largest. Germany was the second largest global creditor, owning 262 trillion yen, followed by China in the third place, owning 205 trillion yen according to Japan Times (2018). The saving rate in Japan has gradually declined to 2.7%, however, from the level as high as 20% in the 1970s. Even though the saving rate is lower than some European countries such as France and Germany presently, but it has never been below those of Anglo-Saxon countries such as Australia, Canada, and the USA (Horikawa (2004)).

On May 29, 2020 *Nikkei Asia's* article indicated that Minister of State for Economic and Fiscal Policy Yasutoshi Nishimura joined a chorus of self-congratulation for cash-hoarding by Japanese corporations as a "clairvoyant" defense against the rainy days brought on by COVID-19. "*Large Japanese corporations have internal cash reserves of up to 100 trillion yen ($930 billion)," he said, "that have been built up precisely for times like these and should now be used*" *to weather the storm* (Nikkei Asia (2020)). This article illustrated strong tendency to "*save*" *for risk* which can be seen in recent years at Japanese corporations whose retained earnings from profits have been accumulated to a historically highest level.

The high level of cash balance is a noticeable tendency of Japanese corporations in preparing for adverse events. The recent statistics of Ministry of Finance also stated that about 50–60% of the total capital account for the accumulated retained earnings. This is contrary to the Anglo-Saxon capitalism in which the modern corporate finance teaches that cash does not create enough returns for the risk their shareholders bear and thus is inefficient use of their invested capitals. The phenomenon in Japan dictates that Japanese firms consider cash is not "waste" but the best to prepare for risk.

Even if we look closely at the purchase of insurance, the Japanese people prefer an element of cash reserving in insurance rather than one solely for indemnity. Responding to such requests, Japanese insurance companies are offering maturity refund policies that have a savings element built into the products. This is the policy that an owner of the policy gets some refund at the time of policy expiration. In addition, dividends may be paid based on the actual yield on the premiums paid. Skipper and Kwon (2007) indicated that those policies carry higher premiums than policies without a refund from an actuarial viewpoint. The fact that the product has been very popular among Japanese people explains that people unconsciously want that policies for risk management.

Figure 19.2 shows the balance of maturity refund payment in comparison with written premiums in nonlife insurance industry. The figure shows, however, the decreasing amount of maturity refund payment. This trend is explained by the recent very low interest rates on savings. Even though issues of such policies are getting less and less in recent years, we would like to express that the existence of maturity refund policies is a distinctive feature of Japanese general insurance industry as it is

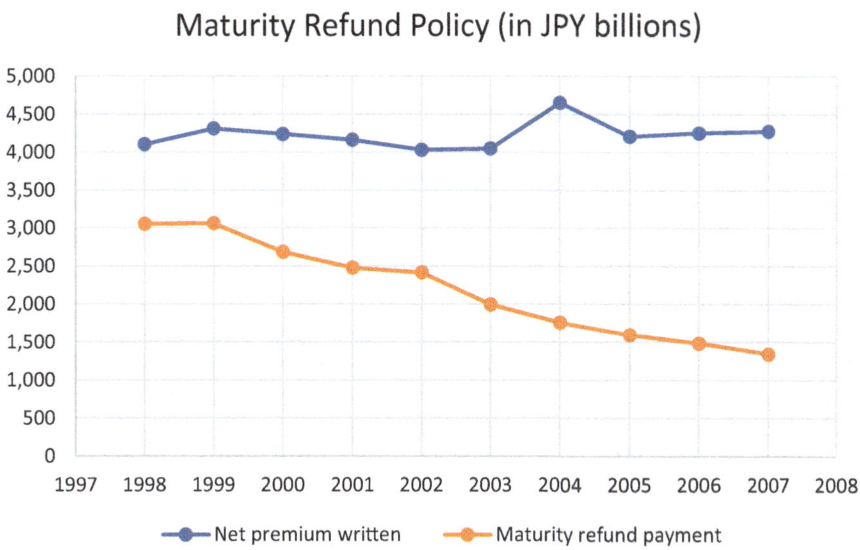

Fig. 19.2 Trend of maturity refund payment versus net written premium (Nonlife Insurance Fact Book 2007)

very rare in other countries. Again the existence of maturity refund policy explains Japanese risk management characteristics to a certain extent.

19.11 Conclusion

This paper has discussed that the Japanese risk management has three characteristics: first, risk avoidance; second, reserving monetary fund for risk; the third, risk sharing among the group members. All of them are of "proactive" approaches to risk rather than "reactive" approaches. We argue that Japan must have imbedded the "proactive" approaches into its system over its long history, though most of the people have not recognized their original functions as risk management. These imbedded risk management have become effective only within the Japanese culture; however, the people are likely to rely too much on them and thus are often puzzled at what to do when they found the system was not functioning well upon the event. The system made the people poor in "*management*" and "*Leadership*" upon disaster and thus they were not able to respond quickly. Obviously, lack of strong leadership and poor management attribute to the weakness of the system.

Conversely, the Anglo-Saxon style of risk management is very dynamic. It continues to identify an origin of failure (loss exposure), implement a solution, monitor and control losses. The leader is not afraid of making changes if the current management is found ineffective.

In Japan, further the responsibility of losses or adverse accidents is not clearly sought or identified within an organization. The organizational culture in Japan would rather not prefer to make a clear cut-off between "right" and "wrong." We argue that this ambiguous nature of not making clear cut-off is much due to the cultural faucets of "*saving face.*" The group-focused culture does not want to have an individual stand with public embarrassment, and thus they prefer "*saving face*" in the Japanese culture. Especially if the individual can be identified easily as a source of the failure. Skipper (1998) identified this characteristic as they stated that the individuals and businesses in societies that place a greater emphasis on solidarity are less likely to seek legal redress for perceived wrongs.

This faucet of "*saving face*" worked favorably in such instance as "*Toyota and Aisin Seiki Fire.*" *Aisin* was not accused for the failure nor sought for monetary compensations from others at that time. Further, Toyota group members helped *Aisin* without expecting any compensations. Had other group members insisted on getting compensation from *Aisin* for monetary loss, such early recovery would not have happened. In other words, this "*saving face*" discipline worked excellently in this case. This is a virtue of Japanese risk culture. In a western company, this individual company would be punished as a source of failure to show a sample of bad performance. Even the failed company would be left bankruptcy. The western risk management starts from eliminating a failed part.

In the contrary, this Japan system invites easily negligence of the management because people are satisfied solely with the system, while they are not willing to change once it has been placed. Continuous improvement of the system is not likely to occur.

Current COVID-19 pandemic fortunately, or unfortunately, made it apparent which risk management is effective or not. We observe puzzled attitudes of Japan's leader, Prime Minister Suga, in coping with the current pandemic. The pandemic has revealed poor management controls in Japan. This is a good timing, however, for the people in Japan to re-construct the risk management to be more "reactive" with a strong leadership.

References

Flath D (1995) The Japanese economy, 2nd edn. Oxford University Press, New York

Holstede G (1995) Insurance as a product of national values. Geneva Paper of Risk and Insurance 20(77):423–429

Horikawa Y (2004) Dankai Sedai no Taishoku to Nihon no Kakei Chochikuritu (in Japanese)

Imai M (1986) Kaizen: the key to Japan's competitive success. Random House Business Division, New York

Inurance Research (2007) The statistics of Japanese non-life insurance business. Hoken Kenkyujo Ltd.

Insurance Research Institute (2009–2019) Insurance: the statistics of Japanese non-life insurance business

International Risk Management Institute Inc. (2020) Risk financing: insurance cash flow and alternative funding. vol. I. Retention capacity

Japan Times (2018) Japan, savings superpower of the world. https://www.japantimes.co.jp/opinion/2018/09/02/commentary/japan-commentary/japan-savings-superpower-world/ Date of access: Jan 25, 2021
Kamei K (1998) Managing strategies and risk management in French enterprise (in Japanese). Horitsu Bunkasha, Kyoto
Kohkami S (2009) Kuuki and Seken (in Japanese). Kohdansha Gendai Shinsho 2006
Loftstedt ER, Ikeda S, Thompson MK (2000) Risk management across the globe: insights from a comparative look at Sweden, Japan and the United States. Risk Anal 20(2):157–161
Marsh (2012) Risk finance survey analysis report (in Japanese). Marsh Japan.
Ministry of Economy, Trade and Industry (2006) White Papers/Reports. Report of the Risk Finance Study Group. http://www.meti.go.jp/ Date of access: March 10, 2006
Mizushima K et al (1995) Insurance culture—risk and Japanese people (in Japanese). Chikura, Tokyo
NAIC (2019) U.S. property and casualty insurance industry, 2019 full year results
Nikkei Asia (2020) Japanese companies must stop gloating about cash-hoarding. https://asia.nikkei.com/Opinion/Japanese-companies-must-stop-gloating-about-cash-hoarding Date of access: Jan 25, 2021
Nishiguchi T, Beaudet A (1999) Self organization in chaos: Toyota Group and Aisin Seiki Fire (in Japanese). J Org Sci 32(4):58–72
Rayer S (1992) Cultural theory and risk analysis. In: Krimsky S, Golding D (eds) Social theories of risk. Praeger, Westport
Ren O (1992) Concepts of risk: a classification. In: Krimsky S, Golding D (eds) Social theories of risk. Praeger, Westport
Rubin HW (1995) Dictionary of insurance terms, 3rd edn. Barron, New York
Sakai Y (2018) Liverpool merchants versus Ohmi merchants: how and why they dealt with risk and insurance differently. Asia-Pacific J Reg Sci 2(1):15–33
Shimizu S (2014) Japanese-style management. LID, London
Skipper HD Jr (1998) International risk and insurance—an environmental-managerial approach. Irwin/McGraw Hill, Boston
Skipper HD Jr, Kwon W J (2007) Risk management and insurance: perspectives in a global economy. Blackwell, Malden
Swiss Re Institute (2019) World Insurance. sigma No. 3/2019 https://www.swissre.com/dam/jcr:b8010432-3697-4a97-ad8b6cb6c0aece33/sigma3_2019_en.pdf. Date of access: Jan 27, 2021
Uemura M (2005) Ohmi merchants' management and diffusion of risk (in Japanese). Economic Theory 325:71–86
Wildavsky A, Drake K (1990) Theories of risk perception: who fears what and why? Daidalus 229(4):41–60
World Population Review (2021) Crime rate by country 2021. https://worldpopulationreview.com/country-rankings/crime-rate-by-country. Date of access: Jan 16, 2021
Yamamoto H (1971) Japanese and Jews (Nihonjin to Yudayajin in Japanese). Kadokawa, Tokyo
Yamamoto H (2018) Research on Kuuki (Kuuki no Kenkyu in Japanese). Bunshun, Tokyo

Chapter 20
What Is Our Study of Risk for? The Case of the Japanese "Go To Campaign"

Kami SEO

Abstract As a research field, risk analysis does not have a long history. However, its theoretical advances have been remarkable, and many lessons have been learned. It has made great contributions to such fields as chemical regulation and food safety. Although it is only at the beginning of addressing complex, uncertain systemic risks, risk analysis can provide some tools for those difficult risks including transparency in decision making and risk communication. In Japan, however, these tools and knowledge are not fully utilized. Japanese risk scientists are needed to think more actively about "implementation science." This paper presents lessons learned from "lessons not learned" by the Japanese government, using a case of the travel subsidy program aimed at boosting the economy amid the COVID-19 pandemic.

Keywords Tourism subsidy · Low-probability-high-consequence risk · Systemic risk · COVID-19 pandemic · Implementation science

20.1 Introduction

The COVID-19 pandemic, which began in 2019, has quickly spread around the world, and as of January 2021 at the time of writing, the number of infected people worldwide has exceeded 100 million. Governments are facing at least two different problems: the spread of the infectious disease and economic stagnation. The risk of COVID-19 is an example of a global-scale multi-risk, which is sometimes called a "systemic risk" (Renn et al. 2020). Over the past half-century, risk research has made significant contributions to conventional risk management. However, assessment and management of large-scale risks with low probability are still challenging, because people often ignore the risk of small probabilities (Sakai 2006). In fact, a

K. SEO (✉)
School of Politics, Economics and Communication, Aoyama Gakuin University, Shibuya, Tokyo, Japan
e-mail: t31313@cc.aoyama.ac.jp

M. Kawano et al. (eds.), *Theory and History in Regional Perspective*, New Frontiers in Regional Science: Asian Perspectives 56,
https://doi.org/10.1007/978-981-16-6695-7_20

pandemic is not a totally new risk; on the contrary, infectious diseases have been "the biggest killers" worldwide (OECD 2003, p. 102). Yet, with the increasing inter-connection of regions, even traditional hazards become more complex. Consequently, conventional risk management policies are "likely to be increasingly faced with 'surprise'" (OECD 2003, p. 31).

The conventional definition of "risk" is the multiplication of the magnitude of hazard and its probability. This is a tool for decision-making based on long-term and scientific perspectives, not short-term interests or mass media-influenced public opinion. However, it has become inappropriate to compare low-probability, high-consequence (LPHC) risk with high-probability, low-consequence risk by using the same index. Risks of the former are complex and contain uncertainty, while those of the latter are relatively simple and processable with the law of large numbers.

Risk analysis gives us the flexibility to set endpoints. This flexibility is both an attraction and a source of controversy. Large events usually result in many different types of effects. These effects should be evaluated with a single parameter for comparison. However, it is not easy to weigh different types of effects: for instance, how can we compare the small probability of human death and quality of life? This is the matter of a value system, not science (Renn 1992).

Risk analysis still can play a role even in systemic risks that are complex, non-linear, uncertain, and value-dependent. It makes the decision-making process transparent by setting scientific evaluation axes and by distinguishing between physical and metaphysical issues. This helps the public to see at which point and how policymakers made a mistake. When times and/or other social and environmental changes require changes in decision-making, it is easier to know where and how these changes should be made. Risk analysis clarifies why the policy required changing: whether it is a result of a misunderstanding, a lack of data, and/or a change of a value system. Consequently, it presents what kind of research and communication is needed. As risk analysis has been developed without fixed endpoints, it can be a tool to assist two-way communication and democracy.

Early risk studies suffered from the difference between the "scientific" decision of experts and the opinion of the lay public. Then, the experts tried to "persuade" the public in various ways. Showing the comparison between the risk of nuclear power plants and that of aflatoxin in peanuts is an example. Today's risk science does not conclude that public perceptions are unscientific, although they are not always consistent with the magnitude of actual risk. Often there is some rationality, not just cognitive distortion, in that people perceive some risks as greater than the actual level of risk, and some others as smaller than they really are. Experts realized that the lay public is not a target of education about risk but a partner to improve decision-making together. At this point, risk analysis has deepened from a persuasion tool to a communication tool. Risk communication and public involvement can help mutual understanding. Meanwhile, are the risk ideas and knowledge, which have evolved over half a century, used for actual policymaking? Unlike the study of, say, the Big Bang, which is interesting itself, risk analysis is a tool to be used.

This paper discusses actual policy and the policymaking process in response to the COVID-19 pandemic in Japan. Our case is the so-called Go To campaign. This campaign is a subsidy for tourism involving a government expenditure of 2.7 trillion yen (26 billion USD), which is about 4.3% of the national tax income. The campaign gives people an incentive to travel by offering a 35% discount plus a 15% free coupon on their travel costs. Conversely, Japanese hospitals today are struggling to raise funds for additional equipment to accommodate the increasing number of COVID-19 patients, and staff salaries are being cut despite wartime-like overwork. Some local governments are underfunded and raising funds through the cloud-funding systems. The problem is not just the inappropriate resource allocation, but the very policy of promoting travel at a time when infectious disease is spreading. Prime Minister Suga stated that there is no evidence of a relationship between Go To and the spread of infection. But, in general, is travel with lodging unrelated in the spread of infection?

By epidemiological analysis, Anzai and Nishiura (2021) estimated the effects of the Go To campaign and concluded that the travel-associated incidence of COVID-19 cases during the campaign was about 1.5–3 times greater than in the pre-campaign period. This is an important warning, but it may have underestimated the total effects of the spread of infection because while this study has been carefully tracking the tourists, the tourists could be the spreaders of the disease to non-travelers, and these non-travelers have not been counted. In fact, it is natural that travel-associated cases increase as the number of travelers increases. In addition, it may not be appropriate to compare different periods, because the variables are not only the number of travelers but other factors, including weather conditions, other policies, or number of holidays on the calendar. In any case, policymakers should not ignore these warnings.

In the next section, we try to determine the relationship between travel and the spread of the infectious disease with a simple statistical model. We believe it is not difficult to determine the approximate effects—at least if the effect of the campaign is positive, negative, or zero with open datasets.

20.2 Analysis

20.2.1 Method

We performed multiple regression assuming a linear model.

$$y = a + bx_1 + cx_2 + dx_3 + e \tag{20.1}$$

The dependent variable y is the number of cumulative infections from October 8th to November 23rd per capita by prefecture*. The target is the period that the Go To campaign was fully implemented. The campaign started in all prefectures in July apart from Tokyo, where it started on October 1st. We allowed a week for the incubation period.

Explanatory variable x_i is

x_1: number of total guests from October to November 2020 by prefecture**
x_2: population density of each prefecture***
x_3: a dummy for prefectures in commuting distance from major cities: Saitama, Kanagawa, Chiba, and Nara.

The number of data $n = 47$, which is the number of prefectures in Japan.

Data source
*Ministry of Health, Labor and Welfare (Japan)
**Japan Tourism Agency
***Statistics Bureau of Japan

20.2.2 Results

Regression results are shown in Tables 20.1–20.3.

The model explains approximately 65% of each prefecture's infection during the target period. From the t-state and p-value, the contribution of the number of tourists is significant, while that of population density is almost none. In other words, tourists are much more likely to spread epidemic disease than residents. The analysis without considering travelers may show correlation between the number of infected and population density. However, this is only because population density is a rough proxy variable of travelers; facilities such as international airports and long-distance

Table 20.1 Regression statistics

R	0.811359
R^2	0.658303
Adjusted R^2	0.634434
Standard error	14.26441
Observations	47

Table 20.2 Dispersion analysis table

	df	SS	MS	F	Significance F
Regression	3	16856.26	5618.752	27.6142	4.11E-10
Residual	43	8749.36	203.474		
Total	46	25605.62			

Table 20.3 Regression analysis output: coefficients

	Coefficients	Standard error	t-state	P-value
Intercept	1.608299	3.022002	0.532197	0.597329
x_1	1.45E-06	2.48E-07	5.851703	6.01E-07
x_2	−0.00337	0.003175	−1.0613	0.294479
x_3	0.49399	0.218081	2.265173	0.028597

Regression statistics (May 2020)

R	0.693655
R^2	0.481157
Adjusted R^2	0.444959
Standard error	1.107979
Observations	47

Table 20.5 Dispersion analysis table (May 2020)

	df	SS	MS	F	Significance F
Regression	3	48.95333	16.31778	13.29223	2.82E-06
Residual	43	52.78755	1.227618		
Total	46	101.7409			

Table 20.6 Regression analysis output: coefficients (May 2020)

	Coefficients	Standard error	t-state	P-value
Intercept	−0.09687	0.249037	−0.38897	0.699216
x_1	4.25E-06	1.66E-06	2.558501	0.014117
x_2	0.00034	0.000221	1.542683	0.130236
x_3	0.066965	0.298101	0.224639	0.823324

train stations are often located in large cities with high population density. In essence, migration is a better indicator of the spread of infection than the density or attributes of the people living there. Now we have returned to the old golden rule: "When people move, viruses move."

For reference, we implemented the same analysis in the period before the Go To campaign started in May 2020. The results are shown in Tables 20.4–20.6.

This time, only x_1 is significant, but with a lesser contribution, and the model is less significant. In other words, before the Go To campaign started, travel was only a moderate factor among many, but the subsidies have accelerated the effects. The number of infected per million people on May 1st, before the campaign started, was 0.185, but it increased more than a hundred times by December 1st.

If travel itself is simply correlated with the number of infected people, then the same model should work for all time periods. One possible reason for the weak correlation before the Go To campaign is that the campaign promoted tourism travel, whereas before the campaign, a higher percentage of travel was business travel, because business travel is less price elastic than tourism travel. If the effect of tourism is greater than that of business travel, then the difference between the two periods can be explained.

20.3 Discussion

We have shown the high possibility that travel accelerates the spread of infectious disease. This possibility could also be true in the next epidemic. However, we are not trying to insist that these quantities are exact. In fact, analyzing the quantitative effect of one of the many causes of systemic risk is very difficult, if not impossible, partly because of complexity and time lag. Our point is that if one understands the characteristics of systemic risk—including exponential change, complexity, and uncertainty—s/he can have discussions with open-access data and insight. For example, the OECD (2003) warned that the risk of infectious disease would increase with the growing number of travelers. This happens as a matter of course because a virus needs carrier to spread.

The Japanese government has provided incentives to travel in order to stimulate the economy. Indeed, travel expenditure is highly price elastic, and thus the response to the incentives is expected to be good. The actual discount rates from the Go To campaign were great and motivated many people to travel. Conversely, against the world's movement, the government has been limiting the number of tests; the number of PCR tests per capita for Japan is 149th in the world (world coronavirus cases data site). Recently in Japan, more than a few people have died at home while waiting for the test. A limited number of tests means that nobody knows which of these travelers are asymptomatically infected. Why are they trying to accelerate travel at taxpayers' expense and at the same time trying to save the cost of tests? Many Japanese people are starting to question whether it is possible to stimulate the economy while tolerating the spread of infection.

The most serious problem of the Japanese government is not that it has made many mistakes, but that it has ignored all warnings and questions from many people and has rejected communications. As mentioned, Prime Minister Suga stated that there is no evidence of a relationship between Go To and the spread of infection; however, evidence can be found only when one looks for it. And many researchers and experts in different fields have some pieces.

What is our risk study for? Risk research is developing, but knowledge has not been utilized to any great extent, at least in Japan. What Japanese risk scientists should do now is not only accumulate further knowledge, but to think about how to achieve its implementation.

References

Anzai A, Nishiura H (2021) "Go To Travel" campaign and travel-associated coronavirus disease 2019 cases: A descriptive analysis, July–August 2020. J Clin Med 10(3). https://doi.org/10.3390/jcm10030398

Japan Tourism Agency n.d.. https://www.mlit.go.jp/kankocho/siryou/toukei/shukuhakutoukei.html#cp1. Accessed 30 Dec 2020

Ministry of Health, Labor and Welfare (n.d.). https://www.mhlw.go.jp/index.html. Accessed 30 Dec 2020

OECD (2003) Emerging risks in the 21st century—an agenda for action. OECD, Paris

Renn O (1992) The social arena concept of risk debates. In: Krimsky S, Golding D (eds) Social theories of risk. Praeger, Westport, pp 179–196

Renn O, Laubichler M, Lucas K, Kröger W, Schanze J, Scholz RW, Schweizer PJ (2020) Systemic risks from different perspectives. Risk Anal. https://doi.org/10.1111/risa.13657

Sakai Y (2006) Risk shakai wo miru me [Eyes on risky societies]. Iwanami-Shoten, Tokyo. (in Japanese)

Statistics Bureau of Japan (n.d.). http://www.stat.go.jp/english/index.html. Accessed 30 Dec 2020

worldometer (n.d.) Coronavirus cases. https://www.worldometers.info/coronavirus/. Accessed 30 Jan 2021

Chapter 21
The Sales Channel of Life Insurance and Relationship Marketing

Nobuko Aoba

Abstract In Japan, sales agents stimulate the demand for insurance by building a relationship of trust with customers. In recent years, the growth of new life insurance policies has become sluggish owing to the low birthrate and an aging population. Therefore, the need to build good relationships further increases to maintain the existing insurance contracts. Studies have examined the factors that lead consumers to buy life insurance through sales agents, but rarely have any explored how sales agents' activities affect the contract amount. We explain relationship marketing in the Japanese life insurance market using the accumulation of human capital theory as well as estimate its effect on the insurance contract amount. The study therefore contributes to the literature in determining whether relationship marketing helps in increasing the contract amount. This study used panel data analysis and insurance data were obtained from the annual reports of individual insurance companies. The empirical results reveal that as the number of sales agents increases, a decrease is seen in the total amount of individual insurance in force in traditional and Japan Post insurers. This implies that sales agents fail to build good relationship marketing. The employee turnover rate is high because anonymity of labor does not dissipate. Japanese life insurers need to evaluate the proficiency of labor and improve skills to decrease employee turnover.

Keywords Sales channel · Relationship marketing · Japanese life insurance market · Dissipation of anonymity

---

Thank you for providing the opportunity to submit this paper to Professor Yasuhiro Sakai commemorative theses.

N. Aoba (✉)
Naruto University of Education, Naruto, Japan
e-mail: aoba@naruto-u.ac.jp

M. Kawano et al. (eds.), *Theory and History in Regional Perspective*, New Frontiers in Regional Science: Asian Perspectives 56,
https://doi.org/10.1007/978-981-16-6695-7_21

21.1 Introduction

In 1980, there were only 24 life insurers in Japan. When the Insurance Business Act was radically reformed in 1996 to promote deregulation and a liberalized life insurance market, it aimed to (1) promote competition, (2) secure soundness in management, and (3) enhance transparency. By 1996, life insurance had become the biggest industry. In August of the same year, 11 non-life insurance companies had entered the life insurance market. However, a policy of very low interest rates caused negative spread in Japan, and the Nissan Life Insurance Company went bankrupt in April 1997. Toho Mutual Life Insurance, Daihyaku Mutual Life Insurance, Taisho Life Insurance, and Chiyoda Mutual Life Insurance also successively went bankrupt, and five of these (except for Taisho and Tokyo) were placed under the umbrella of foreign-affiliated capital. Thereafter, Nihon-dantai Life Insurance, Heiwa Life Insurance, Nicos Life Insurance, and Orico Life Insurance were acquired by foreign-affiliated life insurance companies.

In 2000, the number of life insurers in Japan grew to 49. The Japan Post was privatized in 2007, and the SBI Axa Insurance Company, the first life insurance company specializing in the Internet, opened for business in April 2008. In 1996, the life insurance industry was worth 1496 trillion yen, but this number fell to 848 trillion yen in 2019. The number of life insurance decreased due to industry reorganization and continues to do so amid Japan's declining birth rate and aging society. Depopulation decreases the total amount of life insurance and increases the amount of medical insurance—the third sector of insurance ("Trend of Life Insurance 2020"). Medical insurance is mainly sold by non-life insurance companies, foreign-affiliated life insurance companies, and companies specializing in the Internet. It is simple, and customers need not provide detailed explanations. However, the number of registered sales agents has been increasing in recent years.

Before the deregulation of diversified sales channels, life insurance was sold mainly by sales agents and non-life insurance companies and through insurance agents by foreign-affiliated life insurance companies. The General Survey on Life Insurance (2018) showed that approximately 70% of new insurance contracts were bought through sales agents (53.7% were sales agents at life insurance companies, and 17.8% were sales agents at life insurance agencies).

In Japan, sales agents play an important role in life insurance. The Japanese are poor in stochastic thinking, and therefore, lack sufficient understanding of the price and details of life insurance (Mizushima 2006; Tamura 2006; Sakai 2008). It is difficult to recognize the demand for life insurance because of its long coverage, and the insured is different from the beneficiary. By building relationships of trust and providing information catered to each individual, sales agents stimulate demand for insurance.

Few studies have examined the role of sales agents in the Japanese life insurance industry. In this study, we considered their role in the sales of life insurance and estimated how much their sales activities have increased insurance demand. The sales method through which sales agents build a relationship of trust and stimulate demand is known as "relationship marketing." This study examines the role of sales agents using research findings on relationship marketing.

The remainder of this paper is organized as follows: Sect. 21.2 presents a brief literature review; Sect. 21.3 presents the state of the Japanese life insurance market; Sect. 21.4 uses the human capital model of Otaki (2012, 2013) and explains the role of life insurance sales agents in Japan; Section 21.5 presents the data sources, variable definitions, and panel data analysis; Sect. 21.6 presents our empirical results; and finally, conclusions are outlined in Sect. 21.7.

21.2 Literature Review

The explanation given by sales agents increases the demand for insurance because consumers cannot attach a specific value to it. In the first study that analyzed sales efforts in individual life insurance markets, Mathewson (1982) argued that the purchase of insurance does not maximize social welfare when sales agents persuade consumers to purchase unnecessary insurance. Aoba (1995) place transportation cost into the Mathewson model and concluded that educating sales agents is important. The author showed that an increase in insurance demand increases social welfare if sales agents are able to give clients a proper explanation. Tanaka (2009) also reviewed details on sales agents in the life insurance market, but did not analyze it theoretically.

Under price regulation, the Japanese life insurance industry conspired to create a substantial price cartel, which provided large-scale insurers with excess profits relative to price and made small-scale insurers avoid competition. The restriction of competition owing to price regulation led to the strong promotion and considerable turnover of agents. Japanese life insurance companies had employed many sales agents before the bubble, but their managers unintentionally fired them thereafter. Although there was potential demand for sales agents, employing too many of them wreaked havoc on the management of insurers. In a study that estimated the profitability of sales agents in traditional life insurance companies, Maebayashi (2005) proved that reducing the new hiring of sales agents decreases profitability and educates sales agents, while decreasing their retirement increases profitability.

After the deregulation in 1996, newcomers, non-life insurance companies, and foreign-affiliated life insurance companies sold the third sector of insurance (e.g., medical insurance) without a detailed explanation because of its simplicity. Meanwhile, traditional life insurance companies sold individual insurance and annuity. If consumers buy this type of insurance, and sales agents build good relationships with them, insurance companies can receive premiums covering long periods. Moreover, traditional insurance companies could offer various riders on the existing coverage. In 2005, a non-payment of insurance claims occurred. In 2008, the Financial Services Agency investigated the administrative actions of ten traditional life insurance companies that paid the main insurance claims, but not the added riders. Subsequently, life insurance companies were thoroughly audited.

Consumers must be connected to sales agents to obtain information about life insurance. One way life insurance companies inform potential customers that sales agents can provide custom-made insurance is through television commercials. In this regard, Aoba (2006) investigated the advertisements of domestic life insurance companies, foreign-affiliated companies, and non-life insurance companies from 1996 to 2001 and proved that domestic and foreign insurers use television and newspaper advertisements. Non-life insurers also used these types of advertisements, the cost of which was a quarter of that of domestic or foreign insurers. Domestic insurers inform potential customers that sales agents are always kind and attentive. Foreign insurers are not well known; thus, broadcasting for an unspecified large number of people is desirable for them. In contrast, targeting advertisements is desirable for non-life insurance companies because they sell insurance at independent agencies.

Sales agents can survive if they build a good relationship with customers and provide them with custom-made insurance. In one study, Washio (2016) used relationship marketing to analyze the sales channels of life insurance. He concluded that insurance companies centrally manage customer information to respond to customers' needs according to their future life stages. In this process, a one-to-one relationship is less important; however, there is a risk of one's personal information being retained by private companies. In another study, Koyama (2016) conducted a questionnaire survey of 1035 people who bought life insurance within 3 years. His results proved that "death protection," "nursing care protection," "old age income protection," and "benefit for surviving family" were affected by sales channels.

21.3 State of the Japanese Life Insurance Market

The scale of individual life insurance and the labor force participation rate are positively correlated. The scale of the Japanese individual life insurance market shrunk after it grew to its largest in 1996. The rate of labor force participation also shrunk after it peaked in 1997 (Uchino 2017). In this section, insurance data were obtained from the annual reports of individual insurance companies in Japan. Japanese life insurers are described in the Table 21.1. The number of registered sales agents, however, has continued to increase in recent years (Fig. 21.1).

There are 21 life insurance companies that use sales agents.[1] While the relationship between the total number of registered sales agents and the total amount of life insurance was negative during 2014–2019 (Fig. 21.2), this relationship was positively correlated in 21 companies in 2019 (Fig. 21.3). That is, an increase in sales

[1] There are ten life insurance companies with sales agents: all traditional life insurance companies, Japan Post Insurance, and five third sector life insurance companies (Metlife Life, Tokyo Marine Nichido Anshin Life, Axa Life, MS Aioi Life, Sompo Himawari Life), and six others insurers (Gibralta Life, Sony Life, MS Primary Life, Prudential Life, Manulife Life, Midori Life).

Table 21.1 Japanese life insurance companies

Traditional life insurance companies	Nippon Life, Meiji-Yasuda Life, Dai-ichi Life, Taiyo Life, Daido Life, Fukoku Life, Sumitomo Life, Asahi Life, Taiju Life
Japan Post Insurance life insurance companies	
Insurance companies selling the third sector of insurance	Axa Life, MS Aioi Life, Sompo Himawari Life, Tokyo Marine Nichido Anshin Life, Metlife Life, Medicare Life, Aflac Life, Zurich Life, Orix Life, AIG Fuji Life
Insurance companies specializing in Internet sales and other insurance companies	The Prudential Gibraltar Financial Life (PGF), Gibraltar Life, Dai-ichi Frontier Life, NN Life, MS Primary Life, Nissei Wealth Life, Sony Life, Manulife Life, Fukoku Shinrai Life, Sony Life With Life, T&D Life, Credit Agricole Life, Ion Allianz Life, SBI Life, Cardif Life, Rakuten Life, Midori Life, Hanasaku Life, Lifenet Life, Axa Direct Life, Neo First Life, Prudential Life

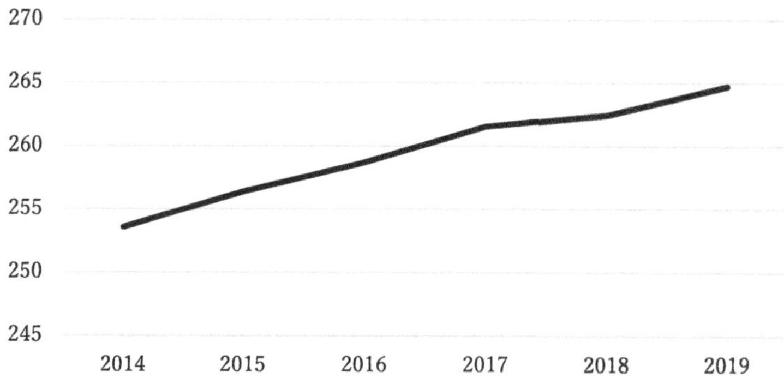

Fig. 21.1 Number of registered sales agents (thousands)

agents decreased the amount of life insurance in the case of total value, but the more sales agents the life insurer had, the greater the amount of life insurance in 2019. For this reason, life insurance companies increased the number of their sales agents.

Figure 21.4 shows the relationship between the total amount of life insurance of 41 life insurance companies and their total operating expenses from 2014 to 2019.[2] Increases in operating expenses did not raise the total amount of life insurance; however, the two had a positive correlation in 2019 (Fig. 21.5). The operating cost

[2]Operational expenses are divided into three types: marketing operation expenses, marketing administration expenses, and general and administrative expenses. Marketing operation expenses primarily include those related to the solicitation and assessment of new policies; marketing administration expenses primarily include those related to advertising and the sales force; and general and administrative expenses include expenditures for maintaining contracts and other costs of managing assets (Nippon Life Insurance 2020, p. 156).

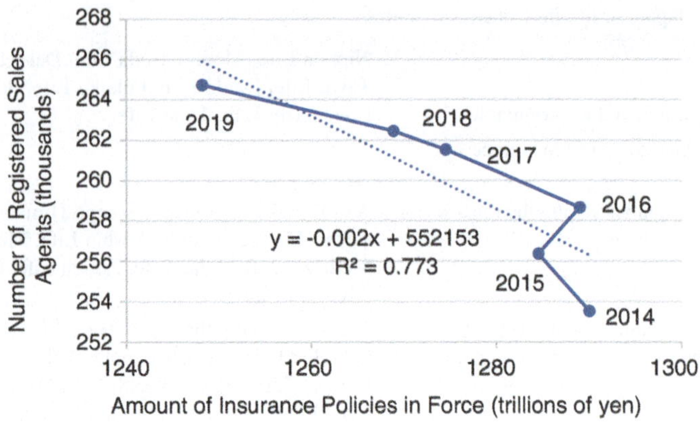

Fig. 21.2 Relationship between the number of registered sales agents and the amount of insurance policies in force (2014–2019)

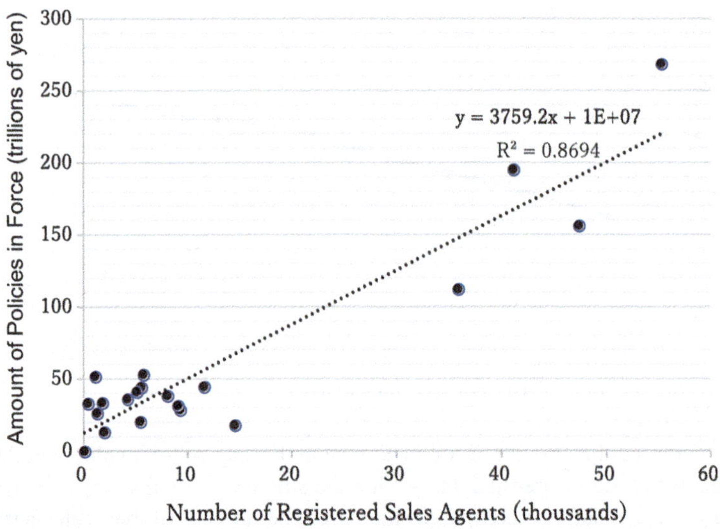

Fig. 21.3 Relationship between the number of registered sales agents and amount of policies in force (2019)

and amount of insurance of the third sector of insurance are lower than that of life insurance. Therefore, many insurers have low operating costs and amounts of insurance. However, some insurers may pay more in operating expenses, but have

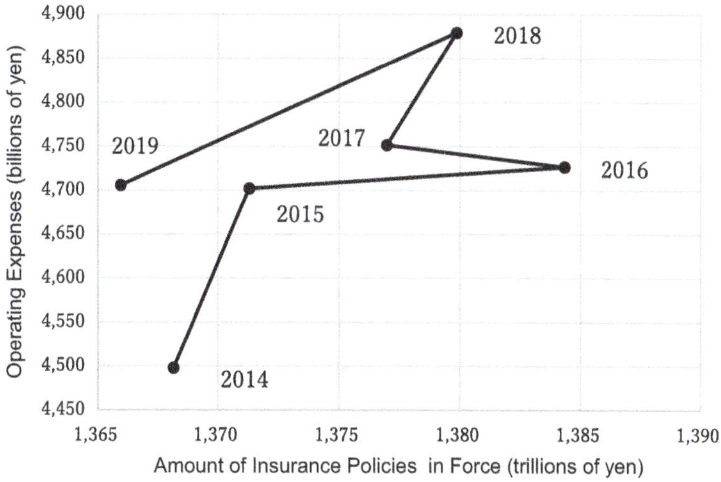

Fig. 21.4 Relationship between the amount of operating expenses and insurance policies in force (2014–2019)

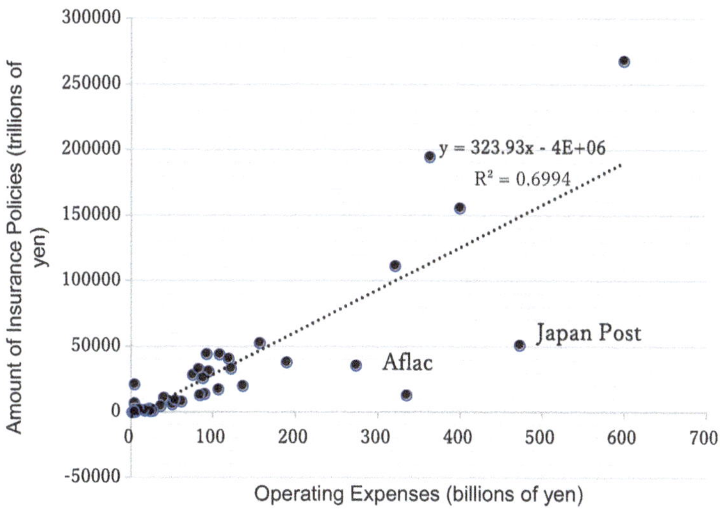

Fig. 21.5 Relationship between the amount of operating expenses and insurance policies in force (2019)

a small amount of insurance. The operating cost of Japan Post Life is 70% of commission fees from the Japan Post.[3] Aflac pays for general and administrative expenses, which include expenditures for maintaining contracts.

[3] http://pdf.irpocket.com/C7181/BXIb/fM0I/v7Qn.pdf (Interim Settlement in 2019 [Japan Post]).

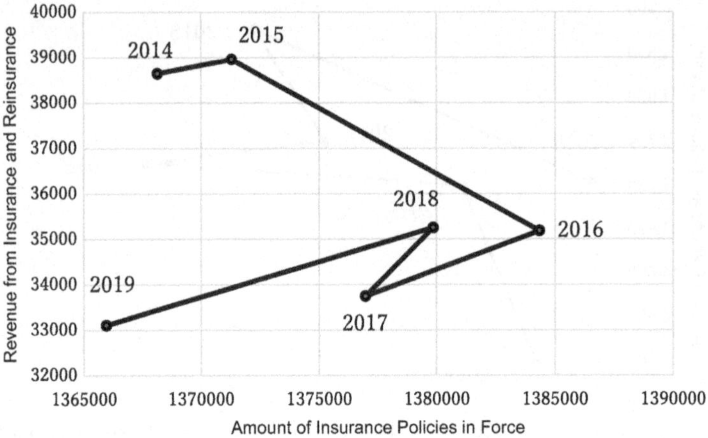

Fig. 21.6 Relationship between the revenue from insurance and reinsurance and amount of insurance policies in force (2014–2019)

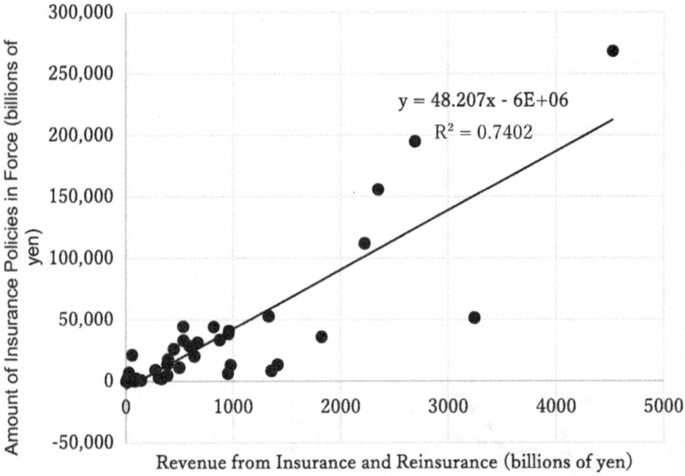

Fig. 21.7 Relationship between the revenue from insurance and reinsurance, and the amount of insurance policies in force (2019)

Figure 21.6 shows the relationship between the total amount of insurance and revenue from insurance and reinsurance from 2014 to 2019. While both the total amount of insurance and revenue from insurance and reinsurance decreased, the relationship between the two was positively correlated in 2019. That is, life insurers that have huge revenue from insurance and reinsurance also have a huge amount of insurance (Fig. 21.7).

21.4 Dissipation of Anonymity of Labor and Relationship Marketing

21.4.1 Dissipation of Anonymity

It is difficult to identify the demand for life insurance. Consumers purchase insurance recommended by reliable sales agents who build relationships based on trust and continuously provide information individually. If proficient life insurance sales agents build good relationships with their client and maintain contracts for a long time, the degree of proficiency and productivity is closely related. Therefore, a client cannot change sales agents because the employer can evaluate the proficiency and anonymity of labor. Conversely, the effect of proficiency is not accurately evaluated when labor is normalized, and when employers are indifferent to the characteristics of labor. That is, the employer cannot evaluate proficiency when labor is anonymous. In the following section, we explain the relationship marketing of life insurance based on Otaki (2012, 2013), which utilized the Horndar effect.[4]

21.4.2 Horndar Effect

If the employer ensures an environment in which sales agents can develop their skills and accurately evaluate proficiency, then the firm becomes more productive.

$$K = \Psi(L, k)$$

$$\frac{\partial \Psi}{\partial L} > 0, \quad \frac{\partial \Psi}{\partial k} > 0$$

where K denotes capital input, L denotes the employment of proficient labor, and k denotes real capital. Then, the capital input is described as a function $\Psi(L, k)$ of L and k. It is assumed that Ψ is a first-order homogeneous function. $(\partial\Psi/\partial L) > 0$ means that an increase in proficiency raises productivity, even if capital endowment is constant (Horndar effect).

The production function y was assumed as the first-order homogeneous function:

$$y = F(K, L) = F(\Psi(L, k), L)$$

Proficiency is not evaluated exactly when labor is anonymous.

[4]This is a typical example of the learning effect. In 1835, the proficiency of labor increases average 2% product per person and hour a year at Horndar ironworks in Sweden. The economic effect of proficiency is called the Horndar effect.

Proposition 21.1 *Life insurance companies consider decreasing returns to scale when labor is anonymous. Therefore, the long-term growth rate is 0.*

Proof When labor is anonymous, proficient labor is evaluated exactly.

$$\frac{\partial F}{\partial K}\frac{\partial \Psi}{\partial k} = 1, \quad \frac{\partial F}{\partial L} = w^R \tag{21.1}$$

Then, optimal (k, L) is independent of time, and firms do not grow without changes in external conditions. Based on the assumption of the first-order homogeneous production function and Euler's theorem:

$$y = \frac{\partial F}{\partial K}\frac{\partial \Psi}{\partial k}k + \left[\frac{\partial F}{\partial K}\frac{\partial \Psi}{\partial L} + \frac{\partial F}{\partial L}\right]L = \left[k + w^R L\right] + \frac{\partial F}{\partial K}\frac{\partial \Psi}{\partial L}L \tag{21.2}$$

When the production function is decreasing returns to scale:

$$\lambda^a y = G(\lambda k, \lambda L), 0 < a < 1 \Leftrightarrow ay = k + w^R L \Leftrightarrow y > k + w^R L$$

Therefore, firms recognize the production function as decreasing returns to scale when they do not evaluate the proficiency of labor exactly. Then, the third term on the right-hand side of Eq. (21.2) should be expanded for labor. However, the employer receives it as good will.

Proposition 21.2 *A firm recognizes that its production function becomes a first-order homogeneous by labor proficiency when the anonymity of labor dissipates. It evaluates the proficiency of labor exactly and achieves a positive steady-state growth rate.*

Proof When the proficiency of labor is evaluated exactly, the net cash flow for each period is as follows:

$$F(\Psi(L,k),L) - k - w^R L - \varphi(g)L, g \equiv \frac{\dot{L}}{L}$$

Here, $\varphi(g)L$ is the training cost for new employees.[5] Based on the assumption of the first-order homogeneous function, we can reformulate it as:

$$[F(\Psi(\kappa,1),1) - \kappa]L - w^R L - \varphi(g)L, \kappa \equiv \frac{k}{L}$$

From Uzawa (1969), the steady state of growth rate is

[5]Otaki (2012, 2013) assumes that new employees are acquire skills through training and become proficient labor.

$$\varphi'(g^*)* = \frac{[F - \kappa] - w^R - \varphi(g^*)}{\rho - g^*} \tag{21.3}$$

where ρ is the discount rate.

From Eq. (21.2), we obtain the following:

$$[F(\Psi(\kappa, 1), 1) - \kappa] - w^R = \left[F(\Psi(k, L), L) - \left[k + w^R L\right]\right] \frac{1}{L} = \frac{\partial F}{\partial K} \frac{\partial \Psi}{\partial L} \tag{21.4}$$

After substituting Eq. (21.4) into Eq. (21.3) we get

$$\varphi'(g^*) = \frac{\frac{\partial F}{\partial K} \frac{\partial \Psi}{\partial L} - \varphi(g^*)}{\rho - g^*} \tag{21.5}$$

Equation (21.5) means that the improvement of labor skills increases the efficiency of capital equipment ($\partial \Psi / \partial L$) and the productivity of capital as a result. This is the management resource of Uzawa-Penrose.

21.4.3 Economic Effect of Relationship Marketing

The process of learning by doing is mastered as tacit knowledge, which is not limited to the world of artisans. This process is generally related to human behavior.[6] Learning by doing in the Japanese life insurance market is useful for building good relationships between sales agents and customers and maintaining contracts. Life insurance companies recognize that their production function is first-order homogeneous if they can evaluate the proficiency of sales agents. Therefore, we assume that an increase in the employment of sales agents raises the amount of insurance. We examine this using a panel data analysis.

21.5 Methodology

21.5.1 Estimation of the Effect of Sales Activities

We estimated the effect of the sales activities of Japanese life insurance firms. Customers of sales agents maintain insurance for a long period if sales agents succeed in building good relationships with them; therefore, we considered insurance as an effect of sales activities and the individual as the target of relationship marketing. We set the total amount of individual insurance and individual annuity,

[6] Otaki (2013), p. 135.

revenue from insurance and reinsurance, and net surplus as the dependent variables. The explanatory variables were the number of sales agents, number of employees (non-sales agents and sales agents), and operational expenses. Total assets were used as proxy variables for the scale.

21.5.2 Data Sources

This study employed panel data gathered from 42 firms operating in the Japanese life insurance market from 2014 to 2019. Insurance data were obtained from the annual reports of individual insurance companies, which were divided into three groups.

The first group is composed of traditional life insurance companies and the Japan Post Insurance life insurance companies, which were established before the deregulation. While Japan Post Insurance life insurance companies have supplied region-based relationship services, the second group of companies has the advantage of selling the third sector of insurance. Life insurance companies specializing in Internet sales and the remaining companies make up the third group (Table 21.1).

21.5.3 Variable Definition

Products

In Japan, about 70% of new insurance contracts were bought through sales agents. The degree of proficiency and productivity is closely related if proficient sales agents build good relationships or trust and maintain contracts for a long time in the sales of life insurance. Now, we define products of life insurers as amounts of policies in force.

Capital Input

By applying the law of large numbers, small premium assures large insurance. In other words, as population gets larger, the difference between frequency of accidents and probability of accidents decreases. Therefore, larger-scale insurers get smaller difference between premium and insurance. This difference reduces to insurance premium. In addition, all insured do not meet with accidents at once. Since insurers keep many premiums, they employ part of premium and get interests. A part of interests reduces to insurance premium, too. Now, we define capital input as total assets.

Labor

Employees in life insurance companies are divided into non-sales personnel and sales representatives. Some of the insurers have no sales representatives. Therefore, we estimate the production function in the case of total employees at the first step and estimate it in the case of non-sales personnel and sales representatives at the second step.

Operating Expenses

Change of sales channel decreases employees. Some insurers have no sales representatives. Therefore, we substitute operating expenses for employees.

Let insurance contracts be y_{it}, let number of employees be L_{it}, and let total assets be K_{it}. Increase of employees increases insurance contracts. Increase of total assets decreases insurance premium and increases insurance contracts. Therefore, we estimate as follows:

$$y_{it} = \alpha_i + \beta_1 L_{it} + \beta_2 K_{it} + u_{it} \quad (i = 1, \ldots, N; t = 1, \ldots, T) \tag{21.6}$$

where u_{it} is residuals and we suppose that the u_{it} are independent with zero mean, and their variance is σ^2. As described above, relationship marketing increases demand of insurance and we expect $\beta_1 > 0$. The marginal products of sales agents increase if they build relationship of trust.

21.5.4 Panel Data Analysis

As the number of insurers are small, we used a panel data analysis. With panel data analysis there are fixed effects model and random effects model.

Fixed Effects Model

Adding firm-specific constants μ_i to Eq. (21.6), the model may be estimated by OLS as a "fixed effects" model.

$$y_{it} = \alpha_i + \beta_1 L_{it} + \beta_2 K_{it} + \mu_i + u_{it} \quad (i = 1, \ldots, N; t = 1, \ldots, T) \tag{21.7}$$

Here μ_i reflects company-specific inefficiency.

Random Effects Model

Transforming firm-specific constants into random variables, we can obtain the random effect model. Random effects model is assumed to have no correlation among μ_i and the other explanatory variables. By Hausman test, we use fixed effects model if we reject the hypotheses that firm-specific terms μ_i do not correlate with L_{it} and K_{it}. By F test, we use pooled OLS model if we do not reject the hypotheses that firm-specific terms μ_i are the same value. By Breusch and Pagan test, we use random effects model if we reject the hypotheses that the u_{it} are independent with zero mean.[7]

The descriptive statistics are presented in Tables 21.2 and 21.3. Descriptive statistics shows that traditional life insurance companies and Japan Post Insurance have 18 times as many sales agents as third sector life insurance companies (Internet selling life insurance companies and others). Traditional insurers sell life insurance mainly sales agents. However, third sector insurers and others sell simple insurance and it needs explanation by sales agents. Therefore, we compare the effects of sales agents on individual insurance among four groups and we expect these effects are large in traditional insurers. The regression results are presented in Tables 21.4, 21.5, 21.6, 21.7, 21.8, 21.9, 21.10, 21.11, and 21.12. From Tables 21.4, 21.5, 21.6, and 21.7 we show the effects of sales activities on individual insurance and annuity purchases. From Tables 21.8, 21.9, and 21.10 we show the effects of the number of sales agents on individual insurance and annuity purchases. Table 21.11 shows the effects of sales agents and non-sale employees on insurance premium. Table 21.12 shows the effects of sales agents and non-sale employees on net surplus.

21.6 Empirical Results

21.6.1 Individual Insurance and Sales Activities

First, we estimated the relationship between individual insurance and total operating expenses (Table 21.4). Next, we divided the operational expenses into three types: marketing operation expenses, marketing administration expenses, and general and administrative expenses (Table 21.5).

The coefficients of total assets are negative in the case of traditional life and Japan Post Insurance insurers (significant at 1% level). The coefficients are positive in the case of insurers who mainly sell the third sector of insurance and other insurance companies. Life insurance companies play an important role in financial and loan markets, both as institutional investors and providers of loans to various industries. They also hold the stocks of many companies. In addition, traditional life insurance

[7]Matsuura (2010).

Table 21.2 Descriptive statistics (1)

Total (millions of yen)					Traditional life insurance companies and Japan post insurance (millions of yen)			
Average	Standard deviation	Max.	Min.		Average	Standard deviation	Max.	Min.
21,300,382	30,095,827	146,649,364	0	Individual insurance	54,734,320	40,657,776	146,649,364	14,223,825
2,610,801	4,744,945	24,812,800	0	Individual annuities	7,827,543	7,126,516	24,812,800	1,167,574
895,297	1,190,618	6,080,915	84	Revenue from insurance and reinsurance	2,088,370	1,709,984	6,080,915	383,776
36,729	67,303	303,758	−165,454	Net surplus	97,456	85,854	303,758	724
9,517,443	17,111,390	84,911,946	5571	Total assets	28,404,110	25,682,926	84,911,946	5,356,358
117,726	144,812	611,973	929	Operating expenses	266,698	188,939	611,973	75,077
47,225	55,449	262,362	7	Marketing operation expenses	97,252	75,915	262,362	21,200
14,018	20,400	85,035	0	Marketing administration expenses	35,433	26,430	85,035	5967
56,460	76,419	346,095	881	General and administrative expenses	133,921	98,701	346,095	43,255
8536	15,778	74,557	29	Labor	27,419	22,191	74,557	6846
2047	3329	19,747	29	Not-sale	4969	5294	19,747	1076
6489	13,053	55,132	0	Sales total	22,450	18,138	55,132	1075
240				Sample no	60			

Table 21.3 Descriptive statistics (2)

Advantage of the third sector life insurance companies (million yen)					Internet selling life insurance companies and others (million yen)			
Average	Standard deviation	Max.	Min.		Average	Standard deviation	Max.	Min.
14,732,802	10,102,900	31,906,435	105,994	Individual insurance	8,767,203	13,476,519	48,778,991	0
869,088	899,246	3,564,819	0	Individual annuities	873,288	1,158,301	4,995,231	0
629,538	596,654	2,285,779	13,359	Revenue from insurance and reinsurance	431,640	500,726	1,899,783	84
30,278	67,261	294,293	−165,454	Net surplus	9590	24,015	136,685	−100,072
4,590,489	4,154,885	12,379,316	22,637	Total assets	2,537,586	3,353,636	11,662,953	5571
117,126	99,946	341,090	8164	Operating expenses	43,540	52,214	191,160	929
46,458	39,506	167,323	2959	Marketing operation expenses	22,595	25,884	89,059	7
12,285	14,554	52,442	1016	Marketing administration expenses	4176	7351	26,478	0
58,380	58,938	217,909	3339	General and administrative expenses	16,768	23,679	110,667	881
3233	2901	9270	173	Labor	1745	3344	13,612	29
1882	1574	5134	173	Not-sale	668	948	4062	29
1352	1927	9270	173	Sales total	1077	2436	9695	0
60				Sample no	120			

Table 21.4 Individual insurance and operating expenses

	Total	Traditional + JP	Third sector	Others
Stock	−1.345552***	−2.069091***	1.126214***	1.528861***
totalexp	74.63798***	135.1018**	49.70114**	42.07974***
Const.	2.59e+7**	7.75e+7***	3,741,657	2,315,748***
R2(within)	0.2156	0.4072	0.3581	0.6040
F-value	161.43***	24.02***	241.26***	477.89***
Breusch and Pagan Lagrangian multiplier test			133.06***	
Hausman test	86.18***	181.45***	1.28(0.5263)	17.25***
	Fixed effect	Fixed effect	Random effect	Fixed effect
No of Obs.	235(40)	60(10)	60(10)	115(20)

F-value; ***Rejection of the null hypothesis at the 1% confidence level (fixed effect model)
Hausman test; ***Rejection of the null hypothesis at the 1% confidence level (fixed effect model)
Breusch and Pagan Lagrangian multiplier test; ***Rejection of the null hypothesis at the 1% confidence level (random effect model)

Table 21.5 Individual insurance and marketing operation expenses, marketing administrative expenses, and general and administrative expenses

II	Total	Traditional + JP	Third sector	Others
Stock	−0.4290521**	−2.323164***	0.3551203	0.7508275***
MOE	54.21032*	207.1092***	−6.771336	9.418344
MAE	546.0788***	−1142.634**	−102.4408**	216.2232***
GAE	243.0986***	21.29429	288.7202***	235.8535***
Cons.	1,503,779	1.38e+8***	−2,179,835	1,087,621**
R2(within)	0.7273	0.4770	0.7701	0.7703
F-value	66.64***	23.83***	241.74***	362.35***
Breusch and Pagan Lagrangian multiplier test	319.89***		63.33***	192.33***
Hausman test	−93.34	26.53***	171.68***	11.25(0.0239)**
	Random effect	Fixed effect	Fixed effect	Fixed effect
No. of obs.	228(39)		60(10)	108(19)

F-value; ***Rejection of the null hypothesis at the 1% confidence level (fixed effect model)
Hausman test; ***Rejection of the null hypothesis at the 1% confidence level (fixed effect model)
Breusch and Pagan Lagrangian multiplier test; ***Rejection of the null hypothesis at the 1% confidence level (random effect model)

companies decreased individual insurance, but increased individual annuities and total assets.

The coefficient of operating expenses is positive and significant at the 1% or 5% level; thus, increasing sales activities will raise the amount of individual insurance, which also increases as new policy solicitation increases. The coefficient of marketing administration expenses in traditional and Japan Post Insurance insurers is positive and significant at the 10% level; thus, expenses of the sales force increased the amount of individual insurance in force. The coefficient of marketing administration expenses of traditional and Japan Post Insurance insurers is negative and significant at the 5% level.

Third sector insurance is simple and can be purchased at an independent agency or from the Internet. Hence, a decrease in marketing expenses increases the amount of individual insurance in force. The negative coefficient in traditional and Japan Post Insurance insurers reflects inefficient management, that is, there is a possibility that they do not make use of labor's ability. The coefficients of general and administrative expenses, which include expenditures for maintaining contracts, are not significant in the case of traditional insurers. In the case of long-period insurance, relationship marketing was effective in maintaining contracts. There is a possibility that sales agents building good relationships with customers do not increase maintaining contracts and the amount of individual insurance in force in traditional and Japan Post Insurance insurers.

21.6.2 Individual Annuities and Operating Expenses

First, we estimated the relationship between individual annuities and the total operating expenses (Table 21.6). Next, we divided operational expenses into three types (Table 21.7). The coefficients of total assets are positive, but third sector insurance is significant at the 1% or 5% level. Increasing individual annuities raises total assets.

Table 21.6 Individual annuities and operating expenses

	Total	Traditional + JP	Third sector	Others
Stock	0.686027***	0.1054124**	0.0379056	0.2900763***
totalexp	238.1497***	13.18523*	2.1091	5.692098
Const.	−78,150.22	1,316,922	502,113.8*	−119,598.5
R2(within)	0.8857	0.4171	0.3563	0.2964
F-value	396.77	247.10***	21.97***	51.15***
Breusch and Pagan Lagrangian multiplier test	506.80***	107.70***	16.10***	174,051***
Hausman test	2.41(0.3003)	−4.46	−263.67	7.00(0.0302) **
	Random effect	Random effect	Random effect	Fixed effect
No. of obs.	210(35)	60(10)	54(9)	96(16)

F-value; ***Rejection of the null hypothesis at the 1% confidence level (fixed effect model)
Hausman test; ***Rejection of the null hypothesis at the 1% confidence level (fixed effect model)
Breusch and Pagan Lagrangian multiplier test; ***Rejection of the null hypothesis at the 1% confidence level (random effect model)

Table 21.7 Individual annuities and marketing operation expenses, marketing administrative expenses, and general and administrative expenses

IA	Total	Traditional + JP	Third sector	Others
Stock	0.1430831***	0.1075778**	0.0919571	0.2964714***
MOE	4.425766	15.91103*	0.0637972	5.870799
MAE	58.98945***	−14.98287	62.17202***	11.80252
GAE	−9.907046	−7.478035	−15.82495***	2.690904
Cons.	906,283.2	4,756,879	679,659**	−121,144.3
R2(within)	0.2538	0.3434	0.3588	0.2970
F-value	110.11***	96.17***	22.65***	14.53***
Breusch and Pagan Lagrangian multiplier test	422.23***	76.30***	21.54***	95.02***
Hausman test	184.29***	10.91**	−82.48	11.66(0.0201) **
	Fixed effect	Fixed effect	Random effect	Fixed effect
No. of obs.	207(35)	60(10)	54(9)	93(16)

F-value; ***Rejection of the null hypothesis at the 1% confidence level (fixed effect model)
Hausman test; ***Rejection of the null hypothesis at the 1% confidence level (fixed effect model)
Breusch and Pagan Lagrangian multiplier test; ***Rejection of the null hypothesis at the 1% confidence level (random effect model)

The coefficient of total operation expenses is positive and significant at the 1% and 5% levels in traditional, Japan Post Insurance, and total insurers. Traditional and Japan Post Insurance insurers focus on selling death benefit insurance and individual annuities at higher amounts.

The coefficients of marketing operation expenses are positive in the case of traditional and Japan Post Insurance insurers and are significant at the 10% level, which is a reflection of their sales activities.

The coefficient of marketing administration expenses—including advertising and sales forces—of total insurers and third sector insurers is positive and significant at the 1% level. Third sector insurers sell simple insurance, so a decrease in sales force increases individual annuities.

The coefficient of general and administrative expenses, including expenditures on maintaining contracts and advertising, is negative and significant at the 1% level in third sector insurers. Third sector insurers are not famous because of their short history, so advertising costs are high. Traditional and Japan Post Insurance insurers can increase individual annuities the more they train sales agents to maintain contracts.

21.6.3 Individual Insurance, Individual Annuities, and Labor

Table 21.8 shows that the coefficients of labor are negative and significant at the 1% level in traditional, Japan Post Insurance, and total insurers. The coefficient of labor is positive and significant at the 1% level. This means that traditional, Japan Post,

Table 21.8 Individual insurance and labor

II	Total	Traditional + JP	Third sector	Others
Stock	−0.8544917***	−1.2354***	1.532601***	1.128686***
Labor	−1780.883***	−2978.922***	846.3383	1,629.228***
Const.	4.56e+7***	1.72e+8***	4,960,862	22,970,970***
R2(within)	0.2128	0.4627	0.4572	0.5871
F-value	58.48***	38.07***	224.72***	380.54***
Breusch and Pagan Lagrangian multiplier test			141.28***	
Hausman test	132.11***	90.73***	0.55(0.76)	4.76*
	Fixed effect	Fixed effect	Random effect	Fixed effect
No. of obs.	235(40)	60(10)	60(10)	115(20)

F-value; ***Rejection of the null hypothesis at the 1% confidence level (fixed effect model)
Hausman test; ***Rejection of the null hypothesis at the 1% confidence level (fixed effect model)
Breusch and Pagan Lagrangian multiplier test; ***Rejection of the null hypothesis at the 1% confidence level (random effect model)

Table 21.9 Individual annuities and labor

IA	Total	Traditional + JP	Third sector	Others
Stock	0.1093094***	0.0794535***	−0.2620828***	0.2390854***
Labor	311.1917***	268.2025***	406.6807**	201.3133
Const.	−1,230,965*	−1,783,047	848,386.4	−94,511.91
R2(within)	0.2816	0.3766	0.3259	0.2961
F-value	109.46***	116.79***	43.46***	32.20***
Breusch and Pagan Lagrangian multiplier test		132.67***		153.13***
Hausman test	9.41(0.0090) ***	3.56(0.1690)	54.1***	10.46(0.0053) ***
	Fixed effect	Random effect	Fixed effect	Fixed effect
No. of obs.	210(35)	60(10)	54(9)	96(16)

F-value; ***Rejection of the null hypothesis at the 1% confidence level (fixed effect model)
Hausman test; ***Rejection of the null hypothesis at the 1% confidence level (fixed effect model)
Breusch and Pagan Lagrangian multiplier test; ***Rejection of the null hypothesis at the 1% confidence level (random effect model)

and other insurance companies sell simple insurance, so they do not need many employees. They manage to be more efficient than traditional insurers.

Table 21.9 shows the relationship between individual annuities and labor. The coefficients of the number of employees are positive and significant at the 1% and 5% levels in the case of traditional, Japan Post Insurance, third sector, and total insurers; thus, labor increases individual annuities for these groups. Traditional insurers sell custom-made insurance. While the insurance is suited to each customer, it needs to be explained by sales agents. However, other insurers sell simple insurance that customers can understand it without explanations from sales agents.

21.6.4 Sales Agents and Non-sales Agents, Individual Insurance, and Individual Annuities

There are 21 life insurance companies that use sales agents.[8] Since data could not be obtained from Midori Life for the past 6 years, it was omitted from the analysis. As seen in Tables 21.10 and 21.11, an increase in sales agents decreases individual insurance, but increases individual annuities. This is the reason insurance shifted from the death benefit to the living benefit, and depopulation reduces the total amount of life insurance. Therefore, traditional insurers sell custom-made insurance, which is suitable for customers. Individual annuities need to be explained by sales agents, so that the coefficient of sales agents will be positive in third sector and other insurance companies. Traditional life insurers sell individual annuities that support their lives in various stages. Sales agents combine various protections and build custom-made annuities. In contrast, life insurance companies that have the advantage of selling third sector insurance sell individual annuities as an over-the-counter savings-type insurance. Third sector insurers do not need sales agents when they want to sell their individual annuities.

Table 21.10 Individual insurance and sales agents and non-sale agents

II	Total	Traditional + JP	Third sector and others
Stock	−0.8945054***	−1.211217***	1.973429***
Salestotal	−2019.763***	−2941.077***	−44.08918
Non-sale	−84.45544	−2437.367	2522.423**
Const.	8.21e+7***	1.67e+8	7,759,694*
R2(within)	0.2964	0.4645	0.4246
F-value	45.05***	31.64***	409.99***
Breusch and Pagan Lagrangian multiplier test			134.50***
Hausman test	96.05***	42.27***	1.53(0.6746)
	Fixed effect	Fixed effect	Random effect
No. of obs.	119(20)	60(10)	59(10)

F-value; ***Rejection of the null hypothesis at the 1% confidence level (fixed effect model)
Hausman test; ***Rejection of the null hypothesis at the 1% confidence level (fixed effect model)
Breusch and Pagan Lagrangian multiplier test; ***Rejection of the null hypothesis at the 1% confidence level (random effect model)

[8]There are ten life insurance companies with sales agents: traditional life insurance companies, the Japan Post Insurance, five third sector life insurance companies (Metlife Life, Tokyo Marine Nichido Anshin Life, Axa Life, MS Aioi Life, Sompo Himawari Life), and six other insurers (Gibralta Life, Sony Life, MS Primary Life, Prudential Life, Manulife Life, Midori Life).

Table 21.11 Individual annuities and sales agents and non-sale agents

IA	Total	Traditional + JP	Third sector and others
Stock	0.1215399***	0.1494018***	−0.2075877**
Salestotal	357.033***	343.2162***	314.4597*
Non-sale	900.6699***	906.323***	1829.934***
Const.	−5,592,874***	−8,624,866***	−2,539,459***
R2(within)	0.4624	0.5710	0.4107
F-value	116.11	167.49	29.71***
Breusch and Pagan Lagrangian multiplier test	246.74***		58.36***
Hausman test	29.12***	18.56***	7.75*(0.0514)
	Fixed effect	Fixed effect	Fixed effect
No. of obs.	114(19)	60(10)	54(9)

F-value; ***Rejection of the null hypothesis at the 1% confidence level (fixed effect model)
Hausman test; ***Rejection of the null hypothesis at the 1% confidence level (fixed effect model)
Breusch and Pagan Lagrangian multiplier test; ***Rejection of the null hypothesis at the 1% confidence level (random effect model)

21.6.5 Sales Agents and Non-sale Agents and Revenues from Insurance

In Table 21.12, an increase in sales agents will decrease revenue from insurance and reinsurance and net surplus in traditional and Japan Post Insurance insurers. This means that traditional insurers and the Japan Post do not make use of sales agents. As

Table 21.12 Revenue from insurance and reinsurance and sales agents and non-sale agents

Premium	Total	Traditional + JP	Third sector and others
Stock	0.111826***	0.1215769***	0.0440878*
Salestotal	−296.6399***	−389.9978***	32.99557
Non-sale	−239.1297***	−378.2557***	145.6698*
Const.	4,261,378***	9,269,996***	161,466.3
R2(within)	0.3492	0.4616	0.6375
F-value	8.87***	5.79***	40.79
Breusch and Pagan Lagrangian multiplier test	38.07***	0.03(0.4335)	106.45***
Hausman test		34.56***	2.26(0.5209)
	Fixed effect	Fixed effect	Random effect
No. of obs.	119(20)	60(10)	59(10)

F-value; ***Rejection of the null hypothesis at the 1% confidence level (fixed effect model)
Hausman test; ***Rejection of the null hypothesis at the 1% confidence level (fixed effect model)
Breusch and Pagan Lagrangian multiplier test; ***Rejection of the null hypothesis at the 1% confidence level (random effect model)

mentioned in Sect. 21.4, companies that evaluate the proficiency of labor grow in the long run.

21.7 Conclusion

In Japan, sales agents play an important role in life insurance. The Japanese are poor in stochastic thinking, and therefore, lack sufficient understanding of the price and details of life insurance (Mizushima 2006; Tamura 2006). It is difficult to recognize the demand for life insurance because the period of life insurance is very long, and the insured is different from the beneficiary. As sales agents build a relationship of trust and continue to provide information individually, these sales activities stimulate demand for insurance. In this study, we examined the role of sales agents in the sales of life insurance using research findings on relationship marketing and estimated how their sales activities increase insurance demand. In this chapter, we showed the dissipation of anonymity of labor yields in sales activities in the Japanese life insurance market using Otaki (2012, 2013).

The empirical results show that an increase in the number of employees will decrease the individual insurance in force in traditional and Japan Post Insurance insurers. In the case of long-period insurance, relationship marketing is effective in maintaining contracts. The empirical results also show that sales agents do not build good relationships with customers, and the anonymity of labor does not dissipate, causing a high employee turnover rate. Japanese life insurers need to evaluate the proficiency of labor and develop skills to reduce the rate of employee turnover.

While we estimated the effect of sales agents' sales activities on the Japanese life insurance industry, we did not examine the trust relationship between customers and sales agents. In the future, we hope to prove that this trust relationship exists through a questionnaire research.

References

Aoba N (1995) Visiting-sales and advertising. Tsukuba Econ Stud 14:1–8

Aoba N (2006) Life insurance and advertisement. J Jpn Inst Life Insur 154:77–92

Koyama K (2016) Marketing channels' influence affecting life insurance's purchase. J Insur Sci 635:141–161

Life Insurance Association of Japan (2018) The general survey on life insurance. https://www.jili.or.jp/files/research/zenkokujittai/pdf/30/2018honshi_all.pdf

Life Insurance Association of Japan (2020) Life insurance fact book. https://www.seiho.or.jp/english/statistics/trend/pdf/2020.pdf

Maebayashi Y (2005) A study of profit verification of sales staff channel. Proc Inst Actuaries Jpn 58:75–93

Mathewson GF (1982) Sales efforts in individual life insurance markets. In: Information, entry, and regulation in markets for life insurance. Ontario Economic Council, Ontario, pp 70–80

Matsuura T (2010) Stata niyoru deta-bunseki nyuumon (Introduction of data analysis by Stata). Tokyo Publisher, Tokyo

Mizushima K (2006) Hoken no keizaigaku (Economics of insurance). Chikura Publisher, Chuo

Otaki M (2012) Growth of firms and accumulation of human capital: management right and conflict of firms' growth. DBJ discussion paper series, no 1208, pp 1–19

Otaki M (2013) Shihon chikuseki sairon (Revisitation of accumulation of human capital). Kokusai Kinyu and Keizai Seicyo riron no kiso (Fundamentals of the theory of International Economics and Economic Growth)

Sakai Y (2008) Risk to hoken bunka (Risk and insurance culture). In: Tamura Y, Takao A, Okada T (eds) Hoken-sisutemu no shin-tyoryu (The new trend of insurance system). Chikura Publisher, Chuo

Tamura Y (2006) Kake-zute kirai no hoken-sisou: Hoken to bunka (Insurance thought such that "Kake-zute" is disliked: insurance and culture). Chikura Publisher, Chuo

Tanaka T (2009) A study on sales agents in the life insurance sales. J Jpn Inst Life Insur 169:1–28

Uchino H (2017) Nijunengo no seimeihoken gyokai no yukue (The trend of 20-year life insurance industry). Daiwa institute of research financial analysis. https://www.dir.co.jp/report/research/capital-mkt/it/20171013_012369.pdf

Uzawa H (1969) Time preference and the penrose effect in a two-class model of economic growth. J Polit Econ 77:628–652

Washio K (2016) Personal finance service sectors and creation of marketing strategy model (4). Takachiho Ronso 49(1):311–350

Chapter 22
Differences in State Level Impacts of COVID-19 Policies

Kingsley E. Haynes, Rajendra Kulkarni, Meng-Hao Li, and Abu Bakkar Siddique

Abstract This paper compares COVID-19 infections between selected pairs of neighboring states where the policies of the non-pharmaceutical interventions (NPI) such as lockdown/stay-at-home differ. This analysis uses a difference-in-differences (Diff-in-Diff) model to test the effectiveness of NPI in mitigating COVID-19 infections at the state level. The states are Iowa and Illinois, the Dakotas (North and South) and Minnesota, and Arkansas and Mississippi. In each case the policies for each pair of states differ. Based on the difference-in-difference model output, state policies appear to make a significant difference in infection rates but these differences vary. This is for the first phase (wave) of the pandemic (April–June 2020). State level results are mixed reflecting spatial heterogeneity and interaction across the inter-state system. However, there appears to be a significant positive lag effect following the lifting of these mitigation/lockdown policies.

Keywords COVID-19 · US Infection rates · Difference-in-difference model · Mitigation policies · Comparative analysis

JEL Z18 · R00 · R10 · B00 · B49

This research in one of a series drawn from the COVID Research Grant funded by the Schar Foundation Initiative examining the first wave of the COVID disease diffusion in the USA (May–Sept/2020)—Kingsley E. Haynes, Principal Investigator.

K. E. Haynes (✉) · R. Kulkarni · M.-H. Li · A. B. Siddique
Schar School of Policy and Government at George Mason University, Arlington, VA, USA
e-mail: khaynes@gmu.edu

M. Kawano et al. (eds.), *Theory and History in Regional Perspective*, New Frontiers in Regional Science: Asian Perspectives 56,
https://doi.org/10.1007/978-981-16-6695-7_22

22.1 Introduction

Studies on COVID-19 are rising exponentially. By early August (2020), among the non-epidemiological and non-medical science publications, the National Bureau of Economic Research (NBER) has released over 220 working papers that are related to the pandemic. Similarly, about 130 discussion papers on the pandemic were released by the IZA Institute of Labor Economics during the same period[1]. Many other health and medical science-related research platforms are also releasing articles that are partially or fully focused on socio-economic components of the COVID-19 pandemic.

The majority of this literature covers the characteristics and consequences of the pandemic[2]. Broadly, they can be grouped as follows: (a) the measurement of the spread of COVID-19 and the role of mitigation such as masks, crowding limitation, and social distancing, (b) the degrees of disease transmission, plus the effectiveness and compliance with social distancing, (c) the economic impacts of COVID-19 such as the impact on employment, (d) the socio-economic consequences of extreme measures such as shelter-in-place or lockdowns, and (e) the governmental response to the pandemic (Brodeur et al. 2020).

Some literature attempts to relate COVID-19 to key socio-economic variables as causes for the different impacts. Most of these have yet to be peer-reviewed (Chin et al. 2020; Li et al. 2020). Other studies focus on spatial analysis (Sun et al. 2020), ethnic disparities (Li et al. 2020), development of online dashboards for tracking COVID-19 (Wissel et al. 2020), use of vulnerability indices (Mukherjee 2020), and issues in equitable COVID-19 response (Chin et al. 2020). None of these studies examined differences in mitigation consequences.

22.1.1 Background

Unlike much of the world where a central governing body has the authority to respond to health emergencies, the USA, with its federal governing structure, became a 50 state patchwork of responses to fighting the disease. Each state's governor issued that state's emergency response (State Orders 2020) through a series of state level executive orders. These orders spelled out a variety of action plans that her/his government had the constitutional authority to execute so that the state would be able to manage the growing threat of COVID-19. The main goals of this multitude of mainly non-pharmaceutical intervention/mitigation plans were focused on slowing the epidemic, reducing the impact on the health care system, and reducing health care emergencies.

[1]NBER website: https://www.nber.org/wp_covid19.html and IZA: https://covid-19.iza.org/publications/

[2]See Brodeur et al. (2020) for a review of these literature.

With respect to implementation details (US state 2020) the 50 states fall into two broad categories: states where governments issued "lockdown" or "stay-at-home" orders and the states that did not. Early in the pandemic, there were just five states that did not require its residents to "stay-at-home," namely Arkansas, Iowa, South Dakota, North Dakota, and Nebraska. We look at states that are neighbors but had different mitigation policies this is in contrast to other studies which have examined this issue on a within state basis such as Friedson et al. (2020) in California or cross sectionally (Dave et al. 2020) or even more generally across public and private sector responses (Courtemanche et al. 2020; Gupta et al. 2020)

The following phrases refer to the stay-at-home states as "stay@home" states and include "lockdown," "shelter-in-place" or "shutdown" because these are the dominant control elements but they also often included other components such as mask wearing, distancing between individuals, closing of some "nonessential" business, limits on crowding and group activities.

This situation presents a unique opportunity to test the outcomes of these mitigation policies. As a policy intervention measure, did stay-at-home make an effective difference? Do the results provide empirical evidence of the slowing of the disease computed in concrete terms? Is there a reduction in the rate of infections as well as a reduction in the total (or cumulative) infections at the end of this policy intervention stay-at-home period?

The next section presents the methodology and results of the comparative analysis across each pair of neighboring states. The following pairs of neighboring states are used.

1. Stay@home Illinois (IL) and Non-Stay@home Iowa (IA)
2. Stay@home Minnesota and Non-Stay@home North and South Dakota
3. Stay@home Mississippi (MS) and Non-Stay@home Arkansas

Next, for each of the above pairings of states, we analyze how policy intervention at the state level is reflected in the number of COVID-19 infections per 10,000 population.

To determine the effect of the policy intervention measure on the number of infections in the states study during the policy intervention period we used a difference-in-differences assessment model specified below in (22.1) and (22.2).

The basic underlying perspective is that a neighboring state pair has specific trends in rates of infection relative to each other before a policy change in one of these states occurs. In other words, we would not expect to see any change unless one of the states adopts a policy change, while the other does not. In such a scenario, the null hypothesis is to assume that policy intervention would have no effect on the outcome of state rates. However, if the state with policy intervention does show statistically significant change then we reject the null hypothesis. This approach is sometimes referred to in the public health literature as a natural experiment (Craig et al. 2017). We look at the state scale in our analyses since policy decision on health is a state responsibility in the US Federal system. However, states are heterogeneous with differences in densities, metropolitan areas, economic structures, and employment patterns but neighboring states should be more similar than states at greater distances from each other. Further by using a difference-in-difference analysis we control for many of these local effects as they impact the rate changes over time (see Lechner 2011; Conley and Taber 2005).

22.1.2 Difference-In-Difference Model

The specification below applies to each neighboring pairs of states sharing a common boundary. For convenience the explanation below is described in terms of two neighboring states A and B with a common border and we build our model from the county level data aggregated to the state to make sure we are building from the smallest spatial data units that are available. Since the state data is aggregated from the county level, the model is specified as:

$$n = C_{\mathrm{a}} + C_{\mathrm{b}} \tag{22.1}$$

where C_{a} and C_{b} are counties in state A and state B, respectively.

Both states have COVID-19 infections. State B decides to implement "stay-at-home" policy intervention to control infections for a duration T.

Let InfP10K(t,i) represent number of infections per 10K population in county i at time t.

Infections per 10K population at time t in a spatial unit i can be expressed as a summation of an intercept, a spatial term, a temporal term, and an interaction term between the spatial and temporal terms.

The spatial term refers to a dummy variable $C(i)$ that represents whether a county i is in a stay@home state, such that $C(i) = 1$ when county i is in stay@home; otherwise, it is 0.

The temporal term is a dummy variable $D(t)$ that refers to whether the time variable is in the interval (duration T) or outside of it. Thus $D(t) = 1$ when the intervention policy is in effect and zero outside the interval.

The interaction term is a multiplication between the two dummy variables $D(t)$ and $C(i)$.

After running the DiD regression model, the value of the coefficient of the interaction term will represent the number of infections per 10K population per day in the stay@home state where the "stay-at-home" NPI is used as a mitigation policy to reduce the number of COVID-19 infections.

The difference-in-difference (DiD) regression model is represented as:

$$Inf\mathrm{P10k}(t, i) = \beta_0 + \beta_1\, D(t) + \beta_2\, C(i) + \beta_3\, D(t) \times C(i) + \in \tag{22.2}$$

where β_0 is an intercept and $\in$ is the error term and β_3 is the coefficient of interest and it represents the impact of the interaction term $D(t) \times C(i)$. The interaction term equals to 1 when a county has an NPI policy in place otherwise zero.

A DiD model does not require two entities to have a geographic border (be neighbors). However, for our current experiment, we are restricting the DiD model comparison to neighboring spatial units (states) that share a geographic border. As noted above, states are the decision-making units in terms of public health.

The DiD model was run on the repeated cross-sectional data of daily COVID-19 infections per 10K population at the state level where two states share a common border. The model is run from the time (in days) from when the first case appeared in the state through the start of the stay-at-home order to the end of the stay-at-home order in that study area or region. Below is a brief description of the data and the model output for each of these state level comparisons.

22.1.3 Discussion and Results

In this section, we briefly outline information related to the neighboring state comparisons[3].

Johns Hopkins University (JHU) "time series confirmed COVID-19_US" data is used for the analyses (JHU 2020). The cumulative confirmed COVID-19 infections cover the time interval (first wave) from Jan 22, 2020 to Aug 31, 2020 for neighboring states.

The raw cumulative confirmed COVID-19 infections data were processed to create a non-decreasing cumulative COVID-19 infections time series data.[4] This data was normalized with the 2019 population estimates from the Census (County 2010–2019) to generate a decreasing time series of cumulative level of COVID-19 infections per 10,000 population. The data was further processed to compute daily COVID-19 infections per 10,000 population by county and aggregated to the state level. A subset from the output was generated for the following states: Arkansas, Illinois, Iowa, North Dakota, South Dakota, Minnesota, and Mississippi.

These daily infections per 10K population (also referred to as cross-sectional PInf10K) were used as input for the DiD analysis for neighboring pair(s) of states. The pairs of neighboring states are referred to as A and B where states B followed a "stay-at-home" NPI/mitigation policies for time duration T, while states A did not follow this NPI.

The time series data for each study area covering duration *T* was serialized by date and further processed by adding a time, location dummy variables, and the interaction variable. The time dummy variable signifies the time period of the stay-at-home

[3]JHU's time series cumulative confirmed COVID-19 cases data were downloaded. The DiD analyses for neighboring states have COVID-19 data up to Aug 31, 2020.

[4]A time series with daily cumulative counts is expected to be a non-decreasing by date, i.e., the values either stay the same or increase with time as fresh counts are added. However, in the JHU time series data, the confirmed COVID-19 cases may show an aperiodic drop in the cumulative counts. This is due to noise in the data, as it is compiled continuously from various sources.

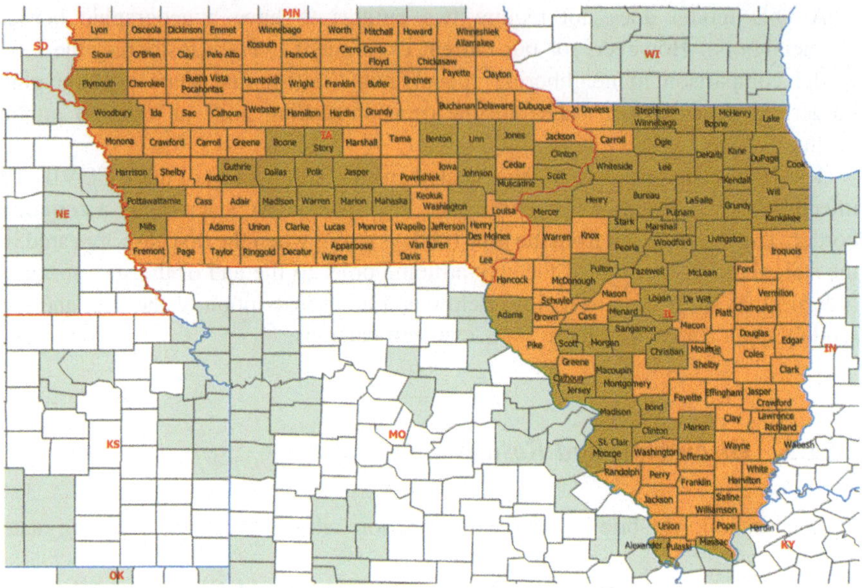

Map 22.1 Iowa (Not-stay@home_state) and Illinois (Stay@home_state)

or shutdown, while the location dummy variable is set to 1 for states with the lockdown policy and zero otherwise.

The results obtained with DiD models are for each state are specified for 10-day intervals as well as for the entire duration that spanned each states' "stay-at-home" policy. Discussion related to the neighboring border states and based on the DiD results is in the following section.

22.2 Neighbor State Comparisons

For each of the following pairs of neighboring states, one of the states followed a "stay-at-home" equivalent NPI/mitigation policy for a limited duration compared to its neighbor(s) which did not enforce such a policy.

22.2.1 Stay@home Illinois (IL) and Not Stay@home Iowa (IA)

There are a total of 201 counties in this two states, of which 102 counties are in Illinois and Iowa has 99 (Map 22.1). The Illinois Governor issued a "stay-at-home" order (Illinois 2020a) that took effect on Mar 22, 2020 and was lifted (Illinois 2020b)

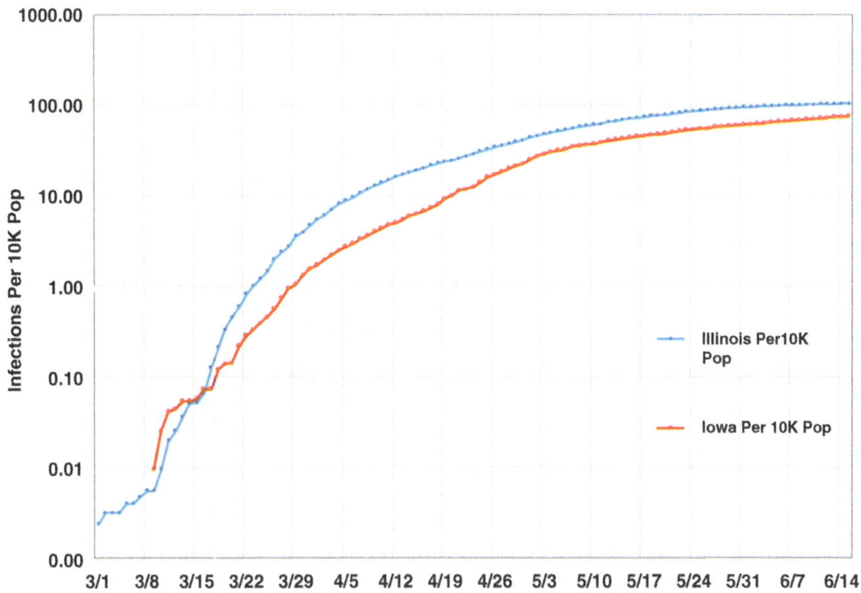

Fig. 22.1 Statewide infections per 10K population in all of Illinois and Iowa during Illinois' shelter-in-place of 71 days duration

Table 22.1 COVID-19 cumulative total and per 10K population Infections in Iowa and Illinois

	Iowa	Illinois
Pop 2019	31,55,070	1,26,71,821
Total cases May 30	19,244	1,18,917
Cases per 10K pop May 30	60.99	93.84
Total cases Aug 31	65,139	2,36,724
Cases per 10K pop Aug 31	206.46	186.81

on May 30, 2020, for a total duration of 71 days, while Iowa did not. Iowa recorded its first infections in Johnson county on Mar 9, 2020, while Cook county, IL recorded its first infection on Jan 24, 2020. For the DiD analyses, only those infections that occurred between Mar 1 to Jun 20, 2020 are included. Throughout this early time period, Illinois continued to have higher numbers of infections per 10K population compared to Iowa (Fig. 22.1).

For the entire shutdown interval (Mar 21–May 30, 2020), the total number of confirmed cases in Iowa grew from 69 to 19,244, while the confirmed cases in Illinois counties grew from 753[5] to 118,927. The corresponding data normalized by the population for each side are 60.99 per 10K population for IA and 93.84 per 10K population for Illinois (Table 22.1). However for the following period (to August 31) these numbers grew quickly for Iowa and by the end of August, Iowa had more

[5]Majority of infections (548) are from Cook County in Illinois

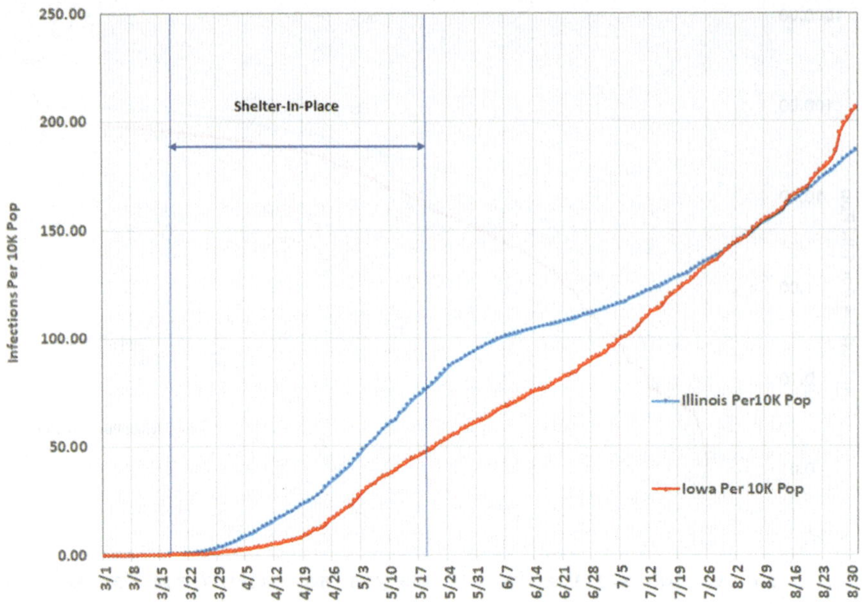

Fig. 22.2 Statewide infections per 10K population in Iowa and Illinois: before, during, and after Illinois' 71-day shutdown

Table 22.2 DiD Estimates for coefficient of infections per day per 10K population for Illinois at 10-day interval and the entire shutdown duration

Time interval	Coeff per 10K pop	Std Err	t	$P > \|t\|$	95% Conf interval		# Observations
Mar 22–31	−0.0381	0.0084	−4.54	0.000	−0.0545	−0.0216	6293
Apr 1–10	−0.0096	0.0233	−0.41	0.68	−0.0552	0.0360	6293
Apr 11–20	−0.2285	0.0618	−3.7	0.000	−0.3497	−0.1073	6293
Apr 21–30	−0.1651	0.0491	−3.36	0.001	−0.2613	−0.0689	6293
May 1–10	−0.3222	0.0501	−6.43	0.000	−0.4204	−0.2240	6293
May 11–20	−0.3427	0.0635	−5.4	0.000	−0.4671	−0.2183	6293
May 21–30	−0.8083	0.1611	−5.02	0.000	−1.1242	−0.4924	6293
Mar 22–May 30	−0.2735	0.0754	−3.63	0.000	−0.4212	−0.1258	18,473[a]

[a]Total number of observations for the entire span of stay-at-home

confirmed cases per 10K population (206) compared to 187 per 10K population in Illinois (Fig. 22.2). It would appear there was a significant and positive lag effect from Illinois closure policy.

Table 22.2 shows the output of the DiD model at 10-day intervals as well for the entire shutdown duration of 71 days. Except for the second 10-day interval (Apr 1–10, 2020), the negative valued coefficient of Illinois infections (decrease) is statistically highly significant indicating the stay-at-home policy intervention is associated with keeping the infections down on the Illinois side of the border. The policy intervention for the entire shutdown period (from March 22, 2020 to May 30, 2020) resulted in Illinois having 0.27 cases less per day per 10K population than might have been expected. Illinois' 71-day shutdown helped reduce infections by 24,260 for the state's population of nearly 12.7 million. These findings parallel those of Lyu and Wehby (2020) and Gostin and Wiley (2020). Also, there appears to be a continuing (positive lag) effect of the lockdown after it is lifted.

22.2.2 Stay@home Minnesota (MN) and Not Stay@home North and South Dakota

There are a total of 206 counties in this study area, of which 87 counties are in Minnesota; 66 in North Dakota and 53 in South Dakota, for a combined total of 119 counties between the North and South Dakotas (Map 22.2). On the map North and South Dakota are on the west and Minnesota is on the east.

Minnesota observed "stay-at-home" policy (Minnesota 2020a) from Mar 25, 2020 to May 18, 2020 (10), for a total duration of 53 days, while there was no "shutdown" in either of the neighboring states of North Dakota and South Dakota. Minnesota recorded its first infection in Ramsey county on Mar 6, 2020, while a number of counties in South Dakota (Beadle, Bonne Homme. Charles, Davidson, Minnehaha, etc.) recorded their first cases on Mar 11, 2020 (Minnesota 2020b). For the DiD analyses, only those infections that occurred between Mar 1 and Jun 20, 2020 are used. Throughout this time period, Minnesota continued to have fewer numbers of infections per 10K population compared to either North Dakota or South Dakota or the combination thereof (Fig. 22.3).

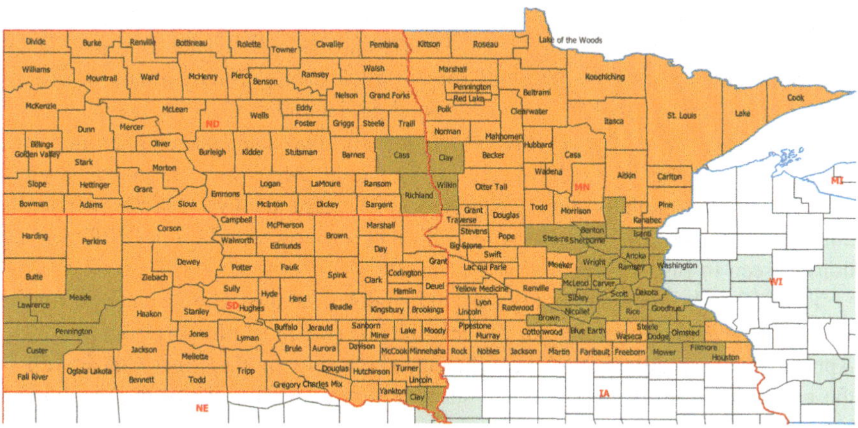

Map 22.2 Minnesota (a Stay@home_state), North and South Dakota (Not_stay@home_states)

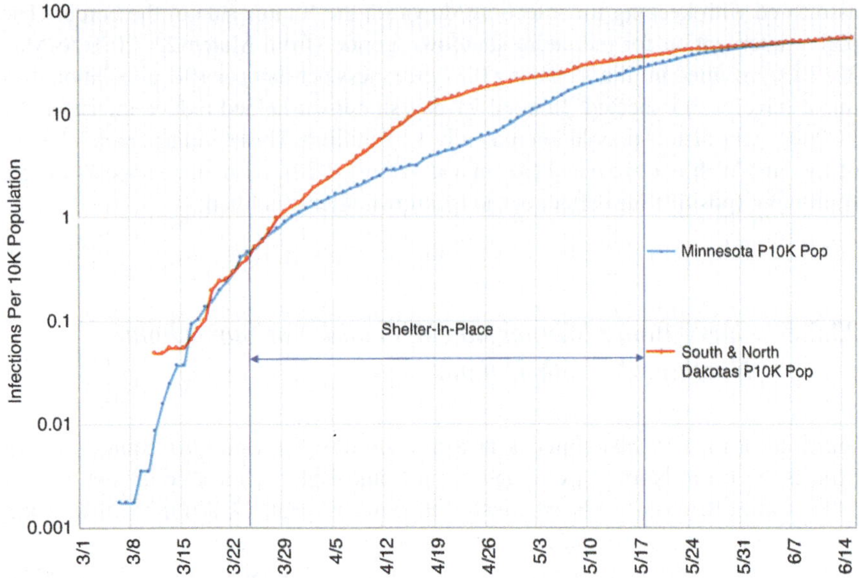

Fig. 22.3 Statewide infections per 10K population in South and North Dakotas and Minnesota during Minnesota's 53-day shelter-in-place shutdown duration

Table 22.3 Statewide COVID-19 cumulative total and per 10K population infections

	South and North Dakotas	Minnesota
Pop 2019	16,46,721	56,39,632
Total cases May 18	5958	16,372
Total cases Aug 31	25,325	75,864
Cases per 10K pop May 18	36.2	29.0
Cases per 10K pop Aug 31	153.8	134.5

For the entire shutdown interval (Mar 27–May 18, 2020), the total number of confirmed cases in the two Dakotas rose to 5968 cases, while Minnesota saw its cases nearly triple to 16,322. The corresponding data normalized by the population for each state are 36.2 per 10K population for two Dakotas and 29 per 10K population for Minnesota (Table 22.3). The total infections continued to grow over the next two months and, by end of Aug 31, 2020, the two Dakotas had nearly 20 more cases per 10K population (153.8) than Minnesota (134.5 per 10K population) as seen in Fig. 22.4.

Table 22.4 shows the output of the DiD model at 10-day intervals as well for the entire shutdown duration of 53 days. Only the first two-time intervals from Mar 27 to Apr 16, have a slightly negative coefficient. The following three intervals as well as the entire duration of the shutdown show a highly significant positive coefficient

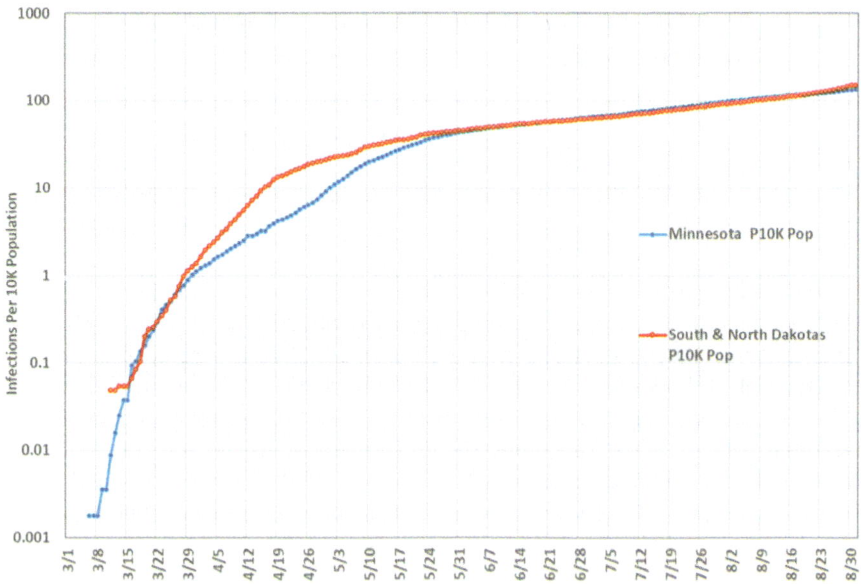

Fig. 22.4 Statewide infections per 10K population in all of South and North Dakotas and Minnesota: before, during, and after Minnesota's 53-day shutdown

Table 22.4 DiD estimates for coefficient of infections per day per 10K population for Minnesota at 10-day intervals and the entire shutdown duration

Time interval	Coeff per 10K pop	StdErr	t	$P > \|t\|$	95% conf interval		# Observations
Mar 27–Apr 6	−0.0477	0.0182	−2.62	0.009	−0.083	−0.012	7733[a]
Apr 7–16	−0.0831	0.0201	−4.14	0.000	−0.122	−0.044	7524
Apr 17–26	0.1836	0.0401	4.58	0.000	0.105	0.262	7524
Apr 27–May 6	0.6484	0.0779	8.32	0.000	0.496	0.801	7524
May 7–18	0.4744	0.0373	12.7	0.000	0.401	0.548	7492[b]
Mar 27–18	0.2453	0.0433	5.67	0.000	0.161	0.330	16,511[c]

[a]This interval is 11 days instead of 10
[b]This interval is 12 days
[c]Total number of observations for the entire span of stay-at-home

which means the during the period of the shutdown the number of infections for Minnesota's 5.6 million people were not reduced. However over the longer period (to Aug. 30) the rate of infections in Minnesota fell. This appears to indicate a positive lag effect from the shutdown.

22.2.3 Stay@home Mississippi (MS) and Not-stay@home Arkansas (AR)

There are a total of 157 counties in this two-state study area, of which 82 counties are in Mississippi and 75 in Arkansas (Map 22.3). Mississippi had "stay-at-home" policy (Mississippi 2020a) from Apr 3, 2020 and through an extension (Mississippi 2020b) to May 25, 2020 for a total duration of 53 days (Mississippi 2020c), while there was no "shutdown" in Arkansas.

Mississippi recorded its first infection in Forrest county on Mar 12, 2020, while Arkansas recorded its first case in Washington county on Mar 18, 2020. Only those infections that occurred between Mar 1 and Jun 20, 2020 are included in the DiD analyses. It is important to note that throughout this time period, Mississippi continued to have higher numbers of infections per 10K population compared to Arkansas (Fig. 22.5). For the entire shutdown interval (Apr 3–May 25, 2020), the total number of confirmed cases in Arkansas rose to 18,000, while in Mississippi the numbers rise to 24,100. The corresponding data normalized by population for each side are 60 per 10K population for Arkansas and 89 per 10K population for Mississippi (Table 22.5). The total infections continued to grow over the next two months and by Aug 31, 2020, Arkansas had 73 per 10K more infections (279 per 10K population) than Mississippi (206 per 10K population) but the gap was closing (see Fig. 22.6). This suggests a positive lag effect following the shutdown period.

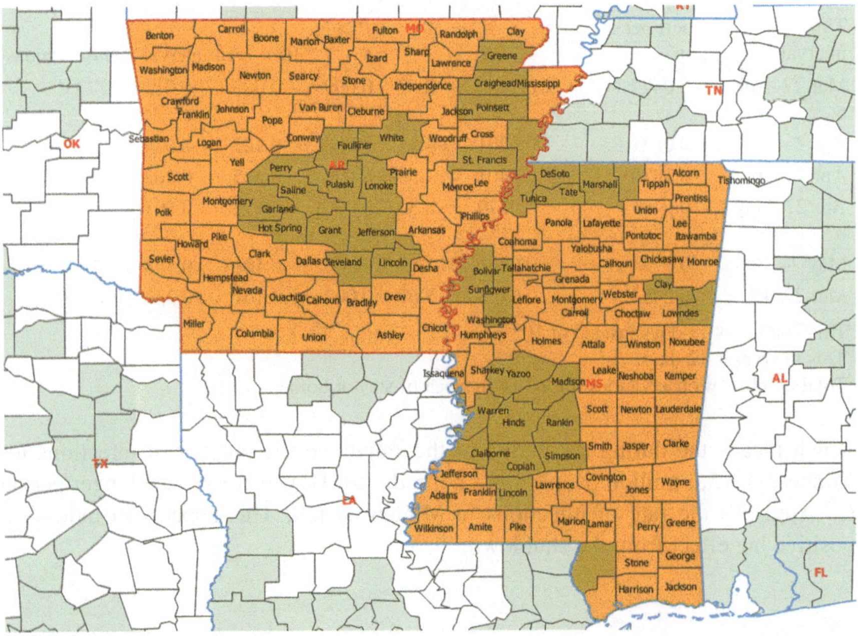

Map 22.3 Counties in Mississippi (a Stay@home_state) and Arkansas (a Not_stay@home_state)

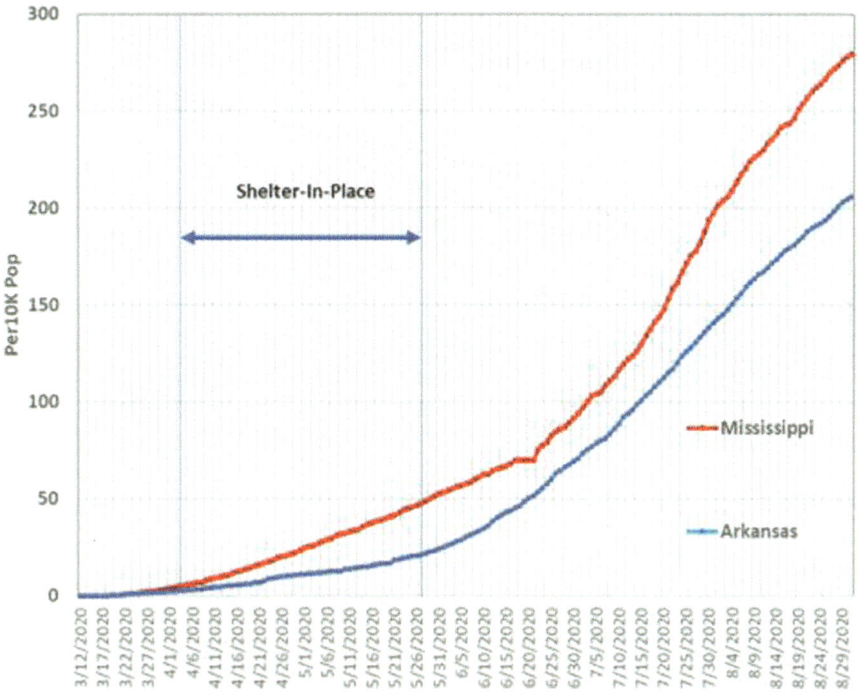

Fig. 22.5 Statewide infections per 10K population in all of Mississippi and Arkansas counties during Mississippi shutdown

Table 22.5 Statewide COVID-19 infections: cumulative total and per 10K population

	Arkansas	Mississippi
Pop 2019	29,76,149	30,17,804
Total cases May 25	18,067	24,610
Cases per 10K pop May 25	59.87	82.69
Total cases Aug 31	62,156	83,046
Cases per 10K pop Aug 31	205.96	279.04

Table 22.6 shows output of the DiD model at 10-day intervals as well for the entire shutdown duration of 53 days. Each of the 10-day intervals shows a highly significant positive coefficient for infections in Mississippi. The shutdown failed to reduce the infections in Mississippi relative to Arkansas.

22.3 Conclusions and Future Research

This analysis is for the first wave of COVID-19 infections in the USA in the spring and summer of 2020. The USA did not pursue a nationwide mitigation policy to fight the COVID-19 pandemic. Instead there appeared to be different attempts/strategies

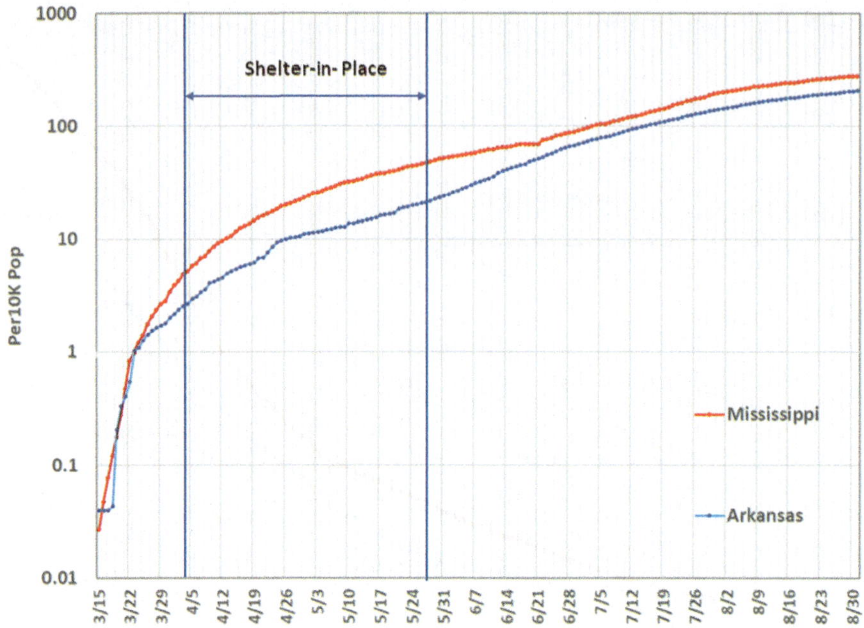

Fig. 22.6 Statewide infections per 10K in Mississippi and Arkansas before during and after shutdown in Mississippi through Aug 31

Table 22.6 DiD by 10-day infection intervals for Mississippi and Arkansas

Time interval	Coeff per 10K pop	Std Err	t	$P > \|t\|$	95% conf interval		# Observations
Apr 3–12	0.2679	0.0352	7.61	0	0.1989	0.337	5244
Apr 13–22	0.3121	0.135	2.31	0.021	0.0475	0.5767	5244
Apr 23–May 2	0.6134	0.1287	4.77	0	0.3611	0.8657	5244
May 3–12	0.6390	0.0904	7.07	0	0.4618	0.8162	5244
May 13–25	0.5000	0.0921	5.43	0	0.3195	0.6806	5244
Apr 3–May 25	0.2919	0.0764	3.82	0	0.1421	0.4417	11,734

across the fifty states to control the spread of the disease and reduce the burden on state health care systems. The mitigation strategies ranged from strict stay-at-home orders to issuing loose guidelines and advisories to state residents. 45 states that issued a limited duration stay-at-home executive orders under emergency powers, and five states that did not. These two approaches created an opportunity for an analytical comparison for applying the DiD model to pair(s) of neighboring states. We applied the DiD model to three pairs of neighboring states.

At the state level both for Iowa and Illinois, the 71-day "stay-at-home" mitigation strategy appears to have helped Illinois reduce the potential increase in COVID-19 infections by over 24,000 cases. In the case of Minnesota and the combined states of North and South Dakota, the diff-in-diff results indicate that the 50-day plus shutdown did not help in the reduction of statewide cases for Minnesota during the shutdown period. For the DiD model applied to Arkansas and Mississippi, the 50-day plus Mississippi shutdown continued to see statistically significant increases in statewide COVID-19 cases in Mississippi during the shutdown period. However, in all cases stay-at-home states appeared to do better in the long run (through Aug 31) with strong positive lag effects slowing infections after the lockdowns ended.

The shelter policy immediate effects (effects limited to the shutdown period) work sometimes in some places but the results are not consistent across the board at least in these examples in the USA. This may be due to high variability in implementation, density, and urban variability and to high cross region mobility patterns. However we did see consistent positive lag effects from shelter-in-place policies over the longer run. In the absence of a national policy and instead of each state on its own fighting the disease, a national, regional, or a least multi-jurisdictional cooperation strategy with uniform regional policies may help in fighting infectious diseases such as COVID-19. In our future research, we plan to study issues of county level infections and metropolitanization, residential density and population interaction as elements in regional mitigation policies (Goolsbee et al. 2020). These we hypothesize might hold potential solutions to developing better mitigation responses to COVID-19 like pandemics in the decentralized US/federal policy context.

References

Brodeur A, Grey DMJ, Islam A Bhuiyan S (2020) A literature review of the economics of COVID-19k. Global Labor Organization. https://www.ecostareu/bitstream/10419/222316/1/GLO-DP-0601.pdf

Chin T, Kahn R, Li R, Chen JT, Krieger N, Buckee CO, Balsari S, Kiang MV (2020) U.S. county-level characteristics to inform equitable COVID-19 response. medRxiv: the preprint server for health sciences, 2020.04.08.20058248. https://doi.org/10.1101/2020.04.08.20058248

Conley T, Taber C (2005) Inference with "difference in differences" with a small number of policy changes. Technical Working Paper 312. https://www.nber.org/papers

County (2010–2019) Population totals. https://www.census.gov/data/datasets/time-series/demo/popest/2010s-counties-total.html

Courtemanche C, Garuccio J, Le A, Pinkston J, Yelowitz A. (2020) Strong social distancing measures in the United States reduced the COVID-19 growth rate. Health Aff (Millwood). 39 (7):1237-1246 doi:https://doi.org/10.1377/hlthaff.00608

Craig P, Katikireddi SV, Leyland A, Popham F (2017) Natural experiments an overview of methods, approaches, and contributions to public health intervention research. Annu Rev Publ Health 38:39–56. https://www.annualreviews.org/doi/full/10.1146/annurev-publhealth-031816-044327

Dave DM, Friedson AI, Matsuzawa K, Sabia JJ (2020) When do shelter-in-place orders fight COVID-19 best? In: Policy heterogeneity across states and adoption time, IZA Discussion Papers 13190. Institute of Labor Economics (ZA), Bonn

Friedson AI, McNichols D, Sabia JJ, Dave D (2020) Did California's shelter-in-place order work? Early Coronavirus-related public health effects. NBER Working Papers 26992. National Bureau of Economic Research, Cambridge

Goolsbee A, Luo NB, Nesbitt R, Syverson C (2020) COVID-19 lockdown policies at the state and local level. Working Paper No. 2020-116, Sept 1. Becker Friedman Institute for Economics, University of Chicago, Chicago. https://papers.ssrn.com/sol3/papers.cfm?abstract_id=3682144

Gostin LO, Wiley LF. (2020) Governmental public health powers during the COVID-19 pandemic: stay-at-home orders, business closures, and travel restrictions JAMA 323(21):2137-2138. doi: https://doi.org/10.1001/jama.2020.5460

Gupta S, Nguyen TD, Rojas FL, Raman S, Lee B, Bento A, Simon KI, Wing C (2020) Tracking public and private responses to the COVID-19 epidemic: evidence from state and local government actions. NBER Working Papers 27027. National Bureau of Economic Research, Cambridge

Illinois (2020a) Govenor's Office. https://www2.illinois.gov/sites/gov/Documents/APPROVED%20-%20Coronavirus%20Disaster%20Proc%20WORD.pdf

Illinois (2020b) Governor's Office. Gubernatorial disaster proclamation. https://www2.illinois.gov/sites/gov/Documents/CoronavirusDisasterProc-5-29-2020.pdf

JHU (2020) Time series confirmed COVID-19 US. county data. https://github.com/CSSEGISandData/COVID-19/tree/master/csse_covid_19_data/csse_covid_19_time_series

Lechner M (2011) The estimation of causal effects by difference-in-difference methods. Found Trends Econom 4(3):165–224

Li AY, Hannah TC, Durbin JR, Dreher N, McAuley FM, Marayati NF, Spiera Z, Ali M, Gometz A, Kostman JT, Choudhri TF (2020) Multivariate analysis of factors affecting COVID-19 case and death rate in U.S. counties: the significant effects of Black race and temperature. medRxiv. https://doi.org/10.1101/2020.04.17.20069708

Lyu W, Wehby GL (2020) Comparison of estimated rates of coronavirus disease 2019 (COVID-19) in border counties in Iowa without a stay-at-home order and border counties in Illinois with a stay-at-home order. AMA Netw Open 3(5):e2011102. https://doi.org/10.1001/jamanetworkopen.2020.11102. https://jamanetwork.com/journals/jamanetworkopen/fullarticle/2766229

Minnesota (2020a) Emergency Executive Order 20-20 directing Minnesotans to stay at home. Governor's Office. https://mn.gov/governor/assets/3a.%20EO%2020-20%20FINAL%20SIGNED%20Filed_tcm1055-425020.pdf

Minnesota (2020b) Emergency Executive Order 20-56. Safely reopening Minnesota's economy and ensuring safe non-work activities during the COVID-19 peacetime emergency. Governor's Office. https://mn.gov/governor/assets/EO%2020-56%20Final_tcm1055-433768.pdf

Mississippi (2020a) Office of Governor. Executive Order No 1466. https://www.sos.ms.gov/content/executiveorders/ExecutiveOrders/1466.pdf

Mississippi (2020b) Office of Governor. Executive Order No 1477. https://mcusercontent.com/08cb3e52aa1308600f84d49ea/files/e24a9045-8ab7-4aa0-bb23-bb49d342c816/Executive_Order_1477_Safer_at_Home.pdf

Mississippi (2020c). https://www.sos.ms.gov/content/executiveorders/ExecutiveOrders/1480.pdf

Mukherjee (2020). https://www.medrxiv.org/content/10.1101/2021.05.19.21257455v1.full

Smittenaar P, Stewart N, Sutermaster S, Coome L, Dibner-Dunlap A, Jain M, Caplan Y, Campigotto C, Sgaier SK (2021) A COVID-19 community vulnerability index to drive precision policy in the US (unpublished). https://doi.org/10.1101/2021.05.19.21257455

State Orders (2020) "Shelter-in-place" and "stay-at-home". https://www.finra.org/rules-guidance/key-topics/covid-19/shelter-in-place

Sun F, Matthews SA, Yang T-C, Hu M-H (2020) A spatial analysis of the COVID-19 period prevalence in U.S. counties through June 28, 2020: where geography matters? Ann Epidemiol 52:54–59.e1, ISSN 1047-2797. https://doi.org/10.1016/j.annepidem.2020.07.014. https://www.sciencedirect.com/science/article/pii/S104727972030274X

U.S. State (2020) State and local government responses to the COVID-19 pandemic. https://en.wikipedia.org/wiki/U.S._state_and_local_government_responses_to_the_COVID-19_pandemic#cite_note-Coronavirus_Oklahoma-74

Wissel BD, Van Camp PJ, Kouril M, Weis C, Glauser TA, White PS, Kohane IS, Dexheimer JW (2020) An interactive online dashboard for tracking COVID-19 in U.S. counties, cities, and states in real time. J Am Med Inform Assoc: JAMIA 27(7):1121–1125. https://doi.org/10.1093/jamia/ocaa071

Chapter 23
Integrating the Internal and External Structure of Metropolitan Economies: Some Initial Explorations

Lei Wang and Geoffrey J. D. Hewings

Abstract While there has been a great deal of attention directed to the structure and structural changes in world trade, there is a growing interest in exploring the integration of international and interregional trade. The paper focuses on the Beijing–Tianjin–Hebei mega-metropolitan region (hereafter JingJinJi) through the development of a five-region model (Beijing, Tianjin, Hebei, rest of China, and rest of world) by merging the China Multi-Regional Input–Output Table and World Input–Output Table. The initial explorations explore the internal and external structure of the multi-region economies to understanding the nature and strength of internal interdependence, using measure of feedback effects, fields of influence and hypothetical extraction, and average propagation lengths. The second section of the paper examines the nature and strength on interregional income formation employing the Miyazawa framework. We conclude that the flow of goods and labor inside JingJinJi is stronger than that in the outside area. And there is a close interdependence between Beijing and Tianjin within the JingJinJi metropolitan area.

Keywords JingJinJi Mega-region · Interregional interdependence · Miyazawa interrelational income matrix · Economic structure

L. Wang
School of Economics & Management, China Three Gorges University, Yichang, China

Regional Economics Applications Laboratory, University of Illinois, Urbana, IL, USA

G. J. D. Hewings (✉)
Regional Economics Applications Laboratory, University of Illinois, Urbana, IL, USA
e-mail: hewings@illinois.edu

M. Kawano et al. (eds.), *Theory and History in Regional Perspective*, New Frontiers in Regional Science: Asian Perspectives 56,
https://doi.org/10.1007/978-981-16-6695-7_23

23.1 Introduction

The JingJinJi mega-metropolitan region is an almost circle of areas centered around the capital city of China. As shown in Fig. 23.1, the JingJinJi mega-metropolitan region covers Beijing, Tianjin, and 11 prefectural cities of the neighboring Hebei province. This metropolitan area contains 8.5% of China's GDP and 8.1% of population and is the most dynamic region in northern China. The functions of the three regions in the JingJinJi mega-metropolitan region are as follows: Beijing has four major centers of politics, culture, international communications, and science and technology; Tianjin is a national advanced manufacturing R&D base, an international shipping core area, a financial innovation demonstration area, and a pioneering area for reform and opening up, while Hebei is an important base for

Fig. 23.1 The JingJinJi Mega-Metropolitan Region. Note: Jing indicates Beijing; Jin stands for Tianjin; and Ji means Hebei

modern commercial logistics in China, a national pilot zone for industrial transformation and upgrading, a national demonstration zone for new-type urbanization and urban-rural co-ordination, and a support zone for the ecological environment of JingJinJi (LGFEA 2017).

The arrangement of the regional functions in JingJinJi complements the non-capital core functions in the short term; however, the deteriorating ecological environment in Beijing and the uncoordinated relationship between population and resources made Hebei and Tianjin natural choices for non-capital core functions. The specific goal of JingJinJi's development is to control Beijing's permanent population to approximately 23 million by 2020 while establishing a regional transportation network to facilitate intra-regional interaction, with the ultimate goal of improving the quality of the ecological environment without compromising the strength and growth of the economic base. It is expected that by 2030, the JingJinJi integration pattern will be basically formed, and Beijing, Tianjin, and Hebei have become important regions with strong international competitiveness and influence, supporting and enhancing national economic and social development goals.

To become important regions with strong international competitiveness and influence, it will be important to explore the integration of *international* and *interregional trade*. The prior literature has focused on the interaction within the JingJinJi metropolitan areas, with attention to regional development issues (Liu et al. 2013; Li et al. 2017), energy flows (Zhang et al. 2016; Wang and Chen 2016), and urbanization (Li 2011; Tang et al. 2017) in the JingJinJi metropolitan regions. A missing perspective is the link between internal and external dependencies and to explore the strength of different types of dependencies; in this paper, the focus will be on trade in goods and services and trade in income. To accomplish these tasks, this paper develops a five-region model (Beijing, Tianjin, Hebei, rest of China, and rest of world) by merging a China Multi-Regional Input–Output Table with a World Input–Output Table. Some appropriate analytical techniques are employed to uncover the structure of these dependencies.

The remainder of this paper is organized as follows: Sect. 23.2 provides some background about the JingJinJi region. In Sect. 23.3 we introduce the method of merging the two input–output systems; thereafter, the nature and strength of internal and external interdependence in goods and services are examined. In addition, income flows are also traced, using the methodological contributions pioneered by Miyazawa (1976). Section 23.4 reports the estimation results of internal and external interdependencies, while Sect. 23.5 provides the details for the direction and strength of trade flows of labor, that is, journey-to-work with income data. Finally, Sect. 23.6 summarizes the main results of this paper and provides some concluding remarks.

23.2 The JingJinJi Region: An Introduction

Coordinated development of the JingJinJi region was launched in 2014. The JingJinJi region covers 216,000 square kilometers with a total population that exceeds 110 million allocated across the three subregions as shown in Fig. 23.2. Hebei accounts for 75 million, followed by Beijing and Tianjin, with nearly 21 million and 15 million, respectively. Although Hebei province has the largest population, there are fewer high-income jobs located there; Fig. 23.3 presents the number of employees in the top three sectors, ICT, financial, and R&D, with the highest wages in the JingJinJi region. As can be seen, 70% high-income jobs in the region are concentrated in Beijing, while less than 20% of these jobs are found in Hebei. While the population of Hebei is 3.4 times that of Beijing, Beijing's GDP exceeds that of Hebei in 2019 as shown in Table 23.1. The concentration of higher-paying jobs in Beijing and Tianjin is reflected in the per capita GDP; this ratio for Hebei province in 2019 is 46.24 thousand Chinese Yuan which is 1/3 of Beijing's per capita GDP and 1/2 of Tianjin's per capita GDP. Hence, the significant income gap has created a

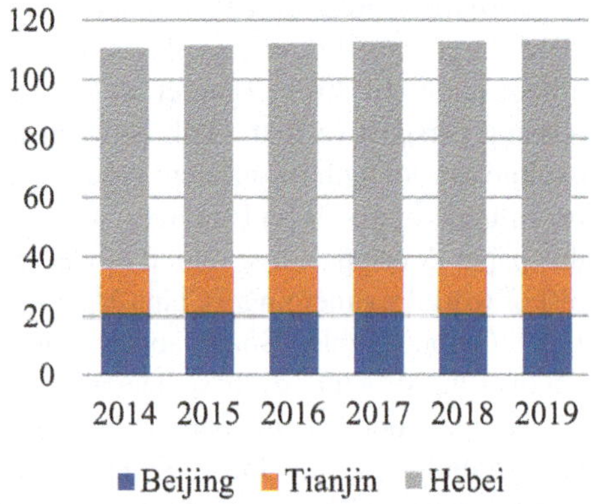

Fig. 23.2 The allocations of JingJinJi population. (Data Sources: China Statistical Yearbook)

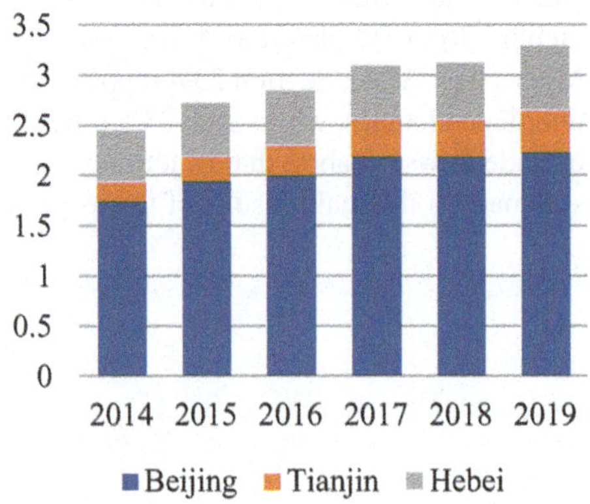

Fig. 23.3 JingJinJi high-income employment (million). (Data Sources: China Statistical Yearbook)

Table 23.1 The internal GDP and industrial structure of the JingJinJi Region

	GDP (billion)	Per capita GDP (thousand)	Primary industry as percentage to GDP (%)	Secondary industry as percentage to GDP (%)	Tertiary industry as percentage to GDP (%)
Beijing	3537.13	164.21	0.32	16.16	83.52
Tianjin	1410.43	90.30	1.31	35.23	63.45
Hebei	3510.45	46.24	10.02	38.73	51.24
China	99,086.51	70.89	7.11	38.97	53.92

Data Sources: China Statistical Yearbook

Table 23.2 The internal harmful emissions of the JingJinJi Region

	Sulfur dioxide (thousand ton)	Nitrogen oxides (thousand ton)	Particulates (thousand ton)	Emission density per unit value added
Beijing	4.7	112.4	32.4	0.04
Tianjin	23.7	141.0	37.5	0.14
Hebei	402.2	1523.0	666.1	0.74

Data Sources: China Statistical Yearbook

situation that while more people live in Hebei, many commute to work in Beijing and Tianjin for higher wages and, for non-workers, access to better education.

If we compare the economic activities in the JingJinJi region with that of China as a whole, some additional perspectives on the internal uneven distribution of high-income, high tech jobs in the region will become clearer. In 2019, China's per capita GDP is 70.89 thousand Chinese Yuan, which is less than that of Beijing and Tianjin, while more than that of Hebei. Further, the industrial structure of the whole of China is similar to Hebei that still retains a considerable share of agriculture and manufacturing industry. However, the proportion of agriculture and manufacturing in Beijing and Tianjin is less than 20% and 40%, respectively. It indicates that the creative, productive, and green sectors of the JingJinJi region are concentrated in Beijing and Tianjin, but the high pollution or lower value-added industries are concentrated in Hebei which has become the main source for the internal supply chain as shown in Tables 23.1 and 23.2. Hence, Beijing and Tianjin are the developed regions of JingJinJi, while Hebei can be characterized as more of a developing region of JingJinJi, with a much higher concentration of polluting activities. The huge factor endowment gap generates a high, frequent volume of internal flows of labor and goods. To speed up the internal flows of the JingJinJi region, 9 high-speed rail projects have been constructed in the region by 2017, with a total mileage of about 1100 km, and an investment of about 247 billion Chinese Yuan. This includes 4 north-south, 4 east-west, and 1 circular rail lines; as a result of this investment, the commuting time has been reduced by one-third from 2015 to 2020 as shown in Table 23.3. If we take Beijing as the center, it would be easy to reach the other major internal cities of the JingJinJi region within one hour. In

Table 23.3 The internal commuting time in the JingJinJi Region (minutes)

	Beijing	Tianjin	Hebei
Beijing		30	90 To 57
Tianjin	30		91 To 63
Hebei	90 To 57	91 To 63	

The range shows the reduction in average commuting time between 2015 and 2020

addition, the new Beijing Daxing international airport was opened in 2019; it is located at the junction of Beijing and Hebei Province. The new airport implements a policy of 144-h transit visa exemption for foreigners and 24-h transit exemption from border inspection procedures. It will greatly enhance the flows between JingJinJi, the rest of China, and the rest of the world.

23.3 Methodology

To integrate the internal and external structure of metropolitan economies, this section first presents the method for merging Multi-Regional Input–Output Table (MRIOT) in 30 provinces and cities in China with a World Input–Output Table (WIOT). Then, based on the newly merged input–output Table (MR-WIOT), this section uses measures of feedback effects, fields of influence, hypothetical extraction, and average propagation lengths to explore the nature and strength of internal and external interdependence. Finally, this section transfers the interdependence indicators to income information with the Miyazawa (1976) framework.

23.3.1 Merging the Multi-regional Input–Output Table and World Input–Output Table

There are two primary methods for constructing a link between MR-WIOT. The first one is mainly based on WIOT, using the total data of WIOT's total output, final product output, and value-added as exogenous variables. At the same time, based on the MRIOT and the Chinese Customs Database, the input–output structure of intermediate products and final products between Chinese provinces and cities and between China and other countries in the world is obtained. Finally, the data of China in WIOT is gradually disaggregated into provincial and municipal data. Meng (2013), Pei (2015), and other studies adopted this method. The second approach is mainly based on MRIOT and retains the input–output data of intermediate products among the provinces. Then, the MRIOT's import and export values, total output, and value-added data are used as exogenous variables. These data are supplemented and the MRIOT is expanded with the input and output coefficients of WIOT China and other countries in the world to obtain a more detailed and complete MR-WIOT. Dietzenbacher et al. (2013) used this method to merge Brazilian regional input–output tables and WIOT. Since the research focus of this paper is to reveal the structure and strength of internal and external connections of the JingJinJi Metropolitan, this paper follows the merger method of Dietzenbacher (2013), focusing on the MRIOT, and incorporating relevant information in WIOT.

The direct consumption coefficient matrix of WIOT is shown in the left half of Eq. (23.1). A_{12} is an $(n \times n)$ matrix and its typical element a_{12} denotes the intermediate inputs per unit total input from country 1 to country 2. The direct consumption coefficient matrix of WIOT would be converted to the right half of Eq. (23.1) when we merge the WIOT and MRIOT. The subscript R, S, or T represents a region of country 1. Hence, the typical element a_{R2} of A_{R2} reveals the intermediate inputs per unit total input from country 1's region R to country 2.

$$\begin{bmatrix} A_{11} & A_{12} & A_{13} \\ A_{21} & A_{22} & A_{23} \\ A_{31} & A_{32} & A_{33} \end{bmatrix} \rightarrow \begin{bmatrix} A_{RR} & A_{RS} & A_{RT} & A_{R2} & A_{R3} \\ A_{SR} & A_{SS} & A_{ST} & A_{S2} & A_{S3} \\ A_{TR} & A_{TS} & A_{TT} & A_{T2} & A_{T3} \\ A_{2R} & A_{2S} & A_{2T} & A_{22} & A_{23} \\ A_{3R} & A_{3S} & A_{ST} & A_{32} & A_{33} \end{bmatrix} \tag{23.1}$$

MRIOT already provides the information of interregional direct consumption coefficient, such as A_{RR}, A_{RS}, and A_{SR}. WIOT provides data for international trade flows like A_{22}, A_{23}, and A_{32}; to construct the MR-WIOT, we need to add input and output information between regions and countries, such as A_{R2} and A_{2R}. If the intermediate inputs from country 1 to country 2 can be decomposed to E^i_{R2}, E^i_{S2}, and E^i_{T2}, as shown in Eq. (23.2), we can estimate the export share of region, R σ^i_{R2}. E^i_{R2} that indicates the intermediate inputs from country 1's region R to country 2.

$$\sigma^i_{R2} = E^i_{R2} / \left[E^i_{R2} + E^i_{S2} + E^i_{T2} \right] \tag{23.2}$$

$$\sigma^i_{R2} + \sigma^i_{S2} + \sigma^i_{T2} = 1 \tag{23.3}$$

However, the MRIOT lacks detailed export data between Chinese regions and other countries. China Customs Database provides import and export data from Chinese provinces and cities to various countries. This paper employs the China Customs Database to obtain the intermediate input information between regions and countries. Combining the information of export shares σ^i_{R2} and direct consumption coefficient matrix A^i_{12} at the country level, the direct consumption coefficient matrix from region R to country 2 for product i, A^i_{R2} can be obtained as shown in Eq. (23.4).

$$\sigma^i_{R2} A^i_{12} = A^i_{R2} \tag{23.4}$$

Given the import information between Chinese regions and various countries ($E^i_{2R}, E^i_{2S}, E^i_{2T}$) listed in China Customs Database, the import shares from country 2 to region R for product i, λ^i_{2R}, are presented in Eq. (23.5).

$$\lambda^i_{2R} = E^i_{2R} / \left[E^i_{2R} + E^i_{2S} + E^i_{2T}\right] \tag{23.5}$$

$$\lambda^i_{2R} + \lambda^i_{2S} + \lambda^i_{2T} = 1 \tag{23.6}$$

The same applies to the imports by region R. We combine the import shares λ^i_{2R} and the typical element of direct consumption matrix a^i_{21} . Equation (23.7) is transformed to the ratio of intermediate input from country 2 to region R, z^{ij}_{2R}, and total input of country 1 for product j, x^j_1. There is still one more step needed to compute the direct consumption coefficient from country 2 to region R. Equation (23.8) provides the method of decomposing the total input x^j_1 by using the regional total input information of MRIOT (x^j_R, x^j_S, and x^j_T). Hence, we will compute the direct consumption coefficient from country 2 to region R, a^{ij}_{2R}, as shown in Eq. (23.9) with the help of total input shares μ^i_R.

$$\lambda^i_{2R} a^{ij}_{21} = \lambda^i_{2R} \left[\frac{z^{ij}_{21}}{x^j_1}\right] = \frac{z^{ij}_{2R}}{x^j_1} \tag{23.7}$$

$$\mu^i_R = x^j_R / \left[x^j_R + x^j_S + x^j_T\right] \tag{23.8}$$

$$\lambda^i_{2R} a^{ij}_{21} \left(\mu^i_R\right)^{-1} = \left[\frac{z^{ij}_{2R}}{x^j_1}\right] \left[\frac{x^j_R + x^j_S + x^j_T}{x^j_R}\right] = \left[\frac{z^{ij}_{2R}}{x^j_R}\right] = a^{ij}_{2R} \tag{23.9}$$

$$\lambda^i_{2R} A^i_{21} \left(\mu^i_R\right)^{-1} = A^i_{2R} \tag{23.10}$$

Through this round-by-round approach, this paper realizes the conversion of WIOT matrix to MR-WIOT matrix in Eq. (23.1).

23.3.2 *The Indicators for Measuring the Nature and Strength of Internal and External Interdependence of Metropolitan Economies*

A selection of many available techniques will be used to explore the internal and external interdependence of the metropolitan economies within JingJinJi. A brief description of these techniques will be presented in this subsection, while the method for uncovering the income-related flows will form the following sub-section. The results can be found in Sect. 23.4.

Feedback Effects

With the preparation of the MR-WIOT data complete, the nature and strength of feedback effects (see Guccione et al. 1988) will be explored to measure internal and external interdependence. An increase in demand by region R will stimulate new output in region S or country 2, referred to as interregional spillovers. To meet these demands, output in region S or country 2 will have to expand and, in the process, inputs sourced in region R may be purchased generating a multiplier effect in region R. Then, all of the direct and indirect inputs generated in region R by the initial change in region R from demands originating in region S or country 2 that were required are referred to as interregional feedback effects.

To capture the feedback effects in the MR-WIOT, we assume that there is an increased demand for the final products of region R, ΔY_R. The change of gross output in region R is indicated as ΔX_R. As shown in Eqs. (23.11) and (23.12), the well-known Leontief matrix reveals the relationship of ΔY_R and ΔX_R.

$$\begin{bmatrix} I-A_{RR} & -A_{RS} & -A_{RT} & -A_{R2} & -A_{R3} \\ -A_{SR} & I-A_{SS} & -A_{ST} & -A_{S2} & -A_{S3} \\ -A_{TR} & -A_{TS} & I-A_{TT} & -A_{T2} & -A_{T3} \\ -A_{2R} & -A_{2S} & -A_{2T} & I-A_{22} & -A_{23} \\ -A_{3R} & -A_{3S} & -A_{ST} & -A_{32} & I-A_{33} \end{bmatrix} \begin{bmatrix} X_R \\ X_S \\ X_T \\ X_2 \\ X_3 \end{bmatrix} = \begin{bmatrix} Y_R \\ Y_S \\ Y_T \\ Y_2 \\ Y_3 \end{bmatrix} \tag{23.11}$$

$$\Delta Y_R = (I - A_{RR})\Delta X_R - A_{RS}\Delta X_S - A_{RT}\Delta X_T - A_{R2}\Delta X_2 - A_{R3}\Delta X_3 \tag{23.12}$$

$$\Delta Y_S = (I - A_{SS})\Delta X_S - A_{SR}\Delta X_R - A_{ST}\Delta X_T - A_{S2}\Delta X_2 - A_{S3}\Delta X_3 \tag{23.13}$$

Since we are assessing the impacts in five regions of a change in final demands in region R only, this paper assumes that $\Delta Y_S = \Delta Y_T = \Delta Y_2 = \Delta Y_3 = 0$. Under these conditions, solving the equation in Eq. (23.13) for ΔX_S yields.

$$\begin{aligned} \text{If } \Delta Y_S = 0, \quad \text{then } \Delta X_S \\ = (I - A_{SS})^{-1}(A_{SR}\Delta X_R + A_{ST}\Delta X_T + A_{S2}\Delta X_2 + A_{S3}\Delta X_3) \end{aligned} \tag{23.14}$$

Inserting Eq. (23.14) into Eq. (23.12), the loop connecting R output to itself, via region S's output, is presented in Eqs. (23.15) and (23.16). $A_{SR}\Delta X_R$ captures the spillover effect on S due to the increased output of R. $(I - A_{SS})^{-1}A_{SR}\Delta X_R$ translates this stimulation into the direct and indirect needs in S to satisfy the demand from R. S needs inputs from multiple locations, including R, shown as $A_{RS}(I - A_{SS})^{-1}A_{SR}\Delta X_R$.

$$\Delta Y_R = (I - A_{RR})\Delta X_R - A_{RS}(I - A_{SS})^{-1}(A_{SR}\Delta X_R + A_{ST}\Delta X_T + A_{S2}\Delta X_2 + A_{S3}\Delta X_3) - A_{RT}\Delta X_T - A_{R2}\Delta X_2 - A_{R3}\Delta X_3 \tag{23.15}$$

$$FB_{RSR} = A_{RS}(I - A_{SS})^{-1}A_{SR}\Delta X_R \tag{23.16}$$

Fields of Influence

To complement the analyses of the feedback effects, attention will then be directed to the identification of which transactions are the most important from the perspective that if they change, they would generate the most important system-wide effects. Hence, the analysis will reveal the most important linkages of economic and trade flows inside and outside of metropolitan economies.

Sonis and Hewings (1989, 1992) developed and applied the concept of a "field of influence" associated with the effects of coefficient change. This indicator explores the impact of changes in unit trade flow between regions. Sonis and Hewings define the first-order field of the incremental change as $F[i,j]$. Let the column sum i and row sum j of the Leontief inverse matrix, B, be denoted as $B_{\bullet i}$ and $B_{j\bullet}$, respectively, as shown in Eq. (23.17). Thus, the matrix $F[i,j]$ shows the change in each element of B caused by direct input changes can be presented in Eq. (23.18).

$$B_{\bullet i} = \begin{bmatrix} l_{1i} \\ \vdots \\ l_{ni} \end{bmatrix}; \quad B_{j\bullet} = \begin{bmatrix} l_{j1} & \cdots & l_{jn} \end{bmatrix}; \quad B = \begin{bmatrix} I - A_{11} & -A_{12} & -A_{13} \\ -A_{21} & I - A_{22} & -A_{12} \\ -A_{31} & -A_{32} & I - A_{33} \end{bmatrix}^{-1} \tag{23.17}$$

$$F[i,j] = B_{\bullet i}B_{j\bullet} = \begin{bmatrix} l_{1i}l_{ji} & \cdots & l_{1i}l_{jn} \\ \vdots & \vdots & \vdots \\ l_{ni}l_{ji} & \cdots & l_{ni}l_{jn} \end{bmatrix} \tag{23.18}$$

Then, we can identify the inverse-important coefficients by comparing their fields of influence. This paper chooses the largest fields of influence and terms them as *inverse-important coefficients* (see Sonis and Hewings 1992).

$$\|F\| = \max\left|f_{ij}\right| \tag{23.19}$$

Hypothetical Extraction

To complement the previous analyses of analytically important transactions, the attention will now be directed to an examination of the impacts of the loss of complete sectors. The hypothetical extraction was introduced by Dietzenbacher et al. (1993) and more recently used by Los and Timmer (2018) to highlight trade linkages.

Define V as a vector of factor payments (salary, rent, tax) per unit of output; the vector and thus V_1 provides the share of domestic factor payments in total output of region 1; B is the well-known Leontief inverse matrix; Y is the final demand vector; and Y_1 stands for the total final production of region 1. The amount of region 1's value-added generated from the international trade can be obtained from Eq. (23.20):

$$\mathrm{VBY} = \begin{bmatrix} V_1B_{11}Y_1 & V_1B_{12}Y_2 & V_1B_{13}Y_3 \\ V_2B_{21}Y_1 & V_2B_{22}Y_2 & V_2B_{23}Y_3 \\ V_3B_{31}Y_1 & V_3B_{32}Y_2 & V_3B_{33}Y_3 \end{bmatrix} \tag{23.20}$$

Region 1's GDP can be computed by aggregating region 1's value-added or factor payments as in Eq. (23.21).

$$\mathrm{GDP}_1 = V_1B_{11}Y_1 + V_1B_{12}Y_2 + V_1B_{13}Y_3 \tag{23.21}$$

In Eq. (23.22), Y_{12} is the export of final products from region 1 to region 2 and B' denotes the Leontief inverse matrix without the intermediate inputs from region 1 to 2 in the direct consumption coefficient matrix A (hence A_{12}=0). Since the model presented in Eq. (23.22) omits the value-added embedded in intermediate export and final export in the calculation of the hypothetical GDP (noted GDP′), Dietzenbacher et al. (2019) refer to this as the hypothetical extraction method.

$$\begin{aligned} Y_1 = Y_{11} + Y_{12} + Y_{13} \quad \mathrm{GDP}_1' \\ = \left[V_1B_{11}'(Y_1 - Y_2) + V_1B_{12}'Y_2 + V_1B_{13}'Y_3\right]; \end{aligned} \tag{23.22}$$

$$\text{where } A = \begin{bmatrix} A_{11} & 0 & A_{13} \\ A_{21} & A_{22} & A_{23} \\ A_{31} & A_{32} & A_{33} \end{bmatrix}; \quad B' = \begin{bmatrix} I - A_{11} & 0 & -A_{13} \\ -A_{21} & I - A_{22} & -A_{23} \\ -A_{31} & -A_{32} & I - A_{33} \end{bmatrix}$$

$$\mathrm{VAXD}_{12} = \mathrm{GDP}_1 - \mathrm{GDP}_1' \tag{23.23}$$

Equation (23.23) represents the value-added that region 1 absorbs from the direct export to region 2. Since the trade flows for VAXD_{12} between countries 1 and 2 belong to direct exports, this formulation only accounts for direct cross-border transactions between 1 and 2. The indirect export from 1 to 3 and 3 to 2 is not included. In other words, the value VAXD_{12} corresponds to the GDP in region

1 (GDP_1) minus the hypothetical GDP without direct export from region 1 to region 2 (GDP'_1).

Average Propagation Lengths

Not only is the size of interregional sector linkage relevant to interdependence but also the *economic distance* between sectors. To compute economic distance, Dietzenbacher et al. (2005) introduced the notion of the average propagation length as the average number of steps it takes an exogenous change in one sector to affect the value of production in another sector. The measure provides a way of measuring the degree of intermediation (intermediate flows between sectors) characterizing an economy; the higher the connectivity between sectors, the smaller the average propagation length. More recently, Romero et al. (2009) have elaborated the idea by linking it with the role of fragmentation and complexity in characterizing the structure of an economy.

In this paper, the output coefficients are defined as m_{ij}. This coefficient shows the proportion of the output of industry i that is employed by industry j as shown in Eq. (23.24).

$$m_{ij} = x_{ij}/x_i \tag{23.24}$$

Therefore, the well-known Ghosh's input–output model can be written as Eq. (23.25). M is the output coefficients matrix, V is the value-added vector as before. This supply driven model can be rewritten as Eq. (23.26), where G denotes the Ghosh inverse. It has been widely used to calculate the changes in output ($\Delta X'$) due to a change in value-added (ΔV).

$$X' = X'M + V \tag{23.25}$$

$$X' = V(I - M)^{-1} = VG \tag{23.26}$$

Since the cost-push in industry i raises the output value in industry j by g_{ij}, the average propagation length is defined by Eq. (23.27). δ_{ij} is the Kronecker delta, i.e. $\delta_{ij} = 1$ if $i = j$, and 0 otherwise, which help us neglecting the initial effects with $g_{ij} - \delta_{ij}$. $[M^k]_{ij}$ denotes the element of output coefficient matrix M. The numerator of the right side of Eq. (23.27) tells us the sum of output coefficients weighted by distance. After this numerator is divided by complete output coefficients ($g_{ij} - \delta_{ij}$), we would know the average propagation length coefficients, p_{ij} as follows:

$$p_{ij} = \left[1m_{ij} + 2\left(M^2\right)_{ij} + 3\left(M^3\right)_{ij} + \ldots\right] / \left(g_{ij} - \delta_{ij}\right) \tag{23.27}$$

where $\delta_{ij} = \begin{cases} 1 & \text{if } i = j \\ 0 & \text{if } i \neq j \end{cases}$

Equations (23.28) and (23.29) give the method to compute the sum of output coefficients matrix weighted by distance H. Hence, the average propagation length coefficients can be denoted as Eq. (23.30).

$$H = M(M - I) \tag{23.28}$$

$$H = M + 2M^2 + 3M^3 + \ldots = (I - M)^{-1}(G - I) = G(G - I) \tag{23.29}$$

$$p_{ij} = \begin{cases} h_{ij}/\left(g_{ij} - \delta_{ij}\right) & \text{if } g_{ij} - \delta_{ij} > 0 \\ 0 & \text{if } g_{ij} - \delta_{ij} = 0 \end{cases} \tag{23.30}$$

23.3.3 Estimating Income Flows in the Metropolitan Economies Using Miyazawa's Formulation

In addition to the flow of goods and services between regions, there is also the movement of labor, that is, commuting and the associated income flows. Since 300 million migrant workers in China work in cities and sent their income back to their rural hometowns, journey-to-work and income flows are common phenomenon. To find the source of income for the regions within the metropolitan area, this paper employs the Miyazawa's (1976) framework to measure the income flows. A similar analysis for the metropolitan region of Chicago revealed that the flows of income from work–home interactions (and subsequent journey-to-shop flows) generated the most significant part of the inter-economy interdependence (Hewings and Parr, 2007).

The Miyazawa's (1976) input–output model in a five-partition hierarchical model can be presented as follows:

$$Z = \begin{bmatrix} A_{RR} & A_{RS} & A_{RR} & A_{RR} & A_{RR} & C_1 \\ A_{SR} & A_{SS} & A_{ST} & A_{S2} & A_{S3} & C_2 \\ A_{TR} & A_{TS} & A_{TT} & A_{T2} & A_{T3} & C_3 \\ A_{2R} & A_{2S} & A_{2T} & A_{22} & A_{23} & C_4 \\ A_{3R} & A_{3S} & A_{3T} & A_{32} & A_{33} & C_5 \\ V_1 & V_2 & V_3 & V_4 & V_5 & 0 \end{bmatrix} = \begin{bmatrix} \widehat{A} & \widehat{C} \\ \widehat{V} & 0 \end{bmatrix} \tag{23.31}$$

The vector $\widehat{V}$ denotes the value-added ratio for employee's wage income. And the vector $\widehat{C}$ represents the compensation coefficients in the metropolitan economies. Combined with other data in the IO table, Miyazawa considered the system shown in Eq. (23.32). X and W are the vectors of the total output and income. f denotes the vector of final demand without household consumption. T is exogenous income like transfer payment from outside the metropolitan area.

$$\left[\frac{X}{W}\right] = \begin{bmatrix} \widehat{A} & \widehat{C} \\ \widehat{V} & 0 \end{bmatrix} \left[\frac{X}{W}\right] + \left[\frac{f}{T}\right] \tag{23.32}$$

With matrix manipulation, Eq. (23.32) can be rewritten as:

$$\left[\frac{X}{W}\right] = \begin{bmatrix} B(I + \mathrm{CKVB}) & \mathrm{BCK} \\ \mathrm{KVB} & K \end{bmatrix} \left[\frac{f}{T}\right] \tag{23.33}$$

where $K = (I - L)^{-1}$; $L = \mathrm{VBC}$ where L is the direct and indirect value-added income from the household consumption. K denotes the Miyazawa interrelational income multiplier matrix, which shows how the increase in income in one region can generate income in the remaining regions. In essence, the Miyazawa framework closes the model with respect to income receipts and expenditures.

23.4 Estimation Results

In this section, we will report the empirical analysis results of feedback effects, fields of influence, hypothetical extraction, and average propagation lengths for the JingJinJi metropolitan areas, ROC (rest of China), and ROW (rest of world). By comparing the results using these indicators, additional insights will be revealed documenting the nature and degree of interdependence of the JingJinJi metropolitan areas with internal (to China) and external economies. The concluding part of this section will examine the results that focus on income flows.

23.4.1 The Strength of Internal and External Interdependence for the JingJinJi Metropolitan Area

The hypothetical extraction method can help us trace the source of value-added by measuring the difference of real GDP and hypothetical GDP without the contribution of targeted region. If Beijing would lose the value-added absorbed from Tianjin, the figure of Beijing's GDP would decrease by \$16.04 billion. It accounts for 5.41% of Beijing's GDP, which indicates the importance and contribution of Tianjin market to Beijing's regional economy.

The information in Table 23.4 shows the allocation of the percentage dependence of each region at the left on the other regions (including itself). For example, its own market provides 40.26% of Beijing's total GDP, followed by 32.92% from the ROC and 17.25% GDP from the products sold in the rest of the world. Compared to ROC and foreign countries, which include 27 provinces or hundreds of countries, the other 2 JingJinJi metropolitan areas contribute 9.57% of Beijing's GDP. In total, the three

Table 23.4 The source of value-added in the five regions in 2012 (Unit: $USD billion)

	Beijing	Tianjin	Hebei	ROC	ROW	Total
Beijing	40.26%	5.41%	4.16%	32.92%	17.25%	**100%**
	119.26	16.04	12.33	97.53	51.10	**296.26**
Tianjin	6.08%	41.32%	3.05%	30.32%	19.22%	**100%**
	12.69	86.21	6.36	63.26	40.10	**208.62**
Hebei	3.07%	1.92%	48.96%	34.26%	11.79%	**100%**
	13.54	8.47	215.83	151.01	51.95	**440.80**
ROC	0.86%	0.88%	1.62%	78.25%	18.38%	**100%**
	73.90	75.17	138.80	6685.74	1570.55	**8544.16**
ROW	0.16%	0.09%	0.04%	2.36%	97.34%	**100%**
	104.17	59.52	24.80	1498.03	61,770.19	**63,456.71**

Data Sources: Authors calculations based on the IO tables of WIOD and Mi et al. (2017)

JingJinJi areas contribute just under 50% to Beijing's GDP. The structure of Tianjin's GDP presents a similar distribution, while Hebei is more dependent on its own market than the other two regions; it is also less dependent on external to China markets.

Unlike Beijing and Tianjin, which are the two developed regions in the JingJinJi metropolitan regions, Hebei is the least developed of the three JingJinJi regions with lower wages and less skilled labor. Hebei absorbs more value-added from the domestic market (48.96%), while less value-added from the JingJinJi metropolitan regions (4.99% in total with 3.07% from Beijing and 1.92% from Tianjin) and foreign countries (11.79%). Essentially, Hebei is a provider of lower value-added intermediate products for the JingJinJi metropolitan regions. Analyses of regional development challenges (Liu et al. 2013; Li et al. 2017), energy flows (Zhang et al. 2016; Wang and Chen 2016), and urbanization (Li 2011; Tang et al. 2017) in the JingJinJi metropolitan region also highlight similar findings. The development in the JingJinJi metropolitan regions suggest that activities in the Beijing and Tianjin regions focus more on products and services that are much more upstream in terms of value chains than is the case for Hebei. In addition, the pull effects of both Beijing and Tianjin on the more peripheral areas of Hebei are comparatively weak.

Focusing on the contribution of JingJinJi metropolitan regions to the external areas, ROC and ROW, due to the magnitude of these two areas, JingJinJi's contribution to these regions' GDP appears to be very small, with only 3.36% and 0.29%. However, in value terms, ROC and ROW's GDP from some regions of JingJinJi has exceeded their own contribution to the GDP of these regions. For instance, ROW obtains $104.17 billion from Beijing, while Beijing only absorbs $51.10 billion from ROW. This means although China's overall import and export trade shows a surplus in value-added terms, the imports from ROW that come from Beijing and Tianjin exceed the exports by these two regions from ROW. The trade deficit of Beijing and Tianjin also confirms that Hebei cannot meet Beijing and Tianjin's demand for high-quality products; it may be specializing in products and services not provided

Table 23.5 The feedback effects in the five regions in 2012 (Unit: $USD billion)

	Beijing	Tianjin	Hebei	ROC	ROW	Total
Beijing	0	0.26%	0.10%	0.27%	0.19%	0.82%
	0	2.06	0.76	2.09	1.44	6.35
Tianjin	0.19%	0	0.01%	0.06%	0.11%	0.37%
	1.14	0	0.06	0.38	0.65	2.23
Hebei	0.02%	0.01%	0	0.10%	0.05%	0.18%
	0.24	0.08	0	1.14	0.62	2.08
ROC	0.10%	0.04%	0.11%	0	0.18%	0.43%
	22.76	8.78	26.10	0	42.13	99.76
ROW	0.004%	0.004%	0.003%	0.15%	0	0.16%
	5.12	4.91	3.23	182.76	0	196.01

Data Sources: As for Table 23.1

competitively from other parts of China or ROW. According to these data in Table 23.4, we can understand the strength of external interdependence for the JingJinJi metropolitan areas. The economic and trade exchanges between Hebei and external regions are mainly concentrated in ROC, while Beijing and Tianjin are more interdependent with ROW.

The economic development of a region can spill over to other regions, contributing to the GDP growth of other regions as can be seen from Table 23.4. Further, these spillover effects can also feedback to the domestic region through the interdependence of upstream and downstream industries between regions. For example, an increase in demand in Beijing will stimulate new output in Tianjin, an interregional spillover. The direct and indirect inputs needed to supply this new output in Tianjin might also include components made in Beijing, generating an interregional feedback.

First, we will analyze the strength of internal interdependence for the JingJinJi metropolitan areas. The results in Table 23.5 reveal that the interregional feedback from Tianjin to Beijing is $2.06 billion, accounting for 0.26% of the gross output in Beijing in 2012. The proportion of interregional feedback from Hebei to Beijing is 0.10%. The strength of economic interdependence between Beijing and Tianjin is greater than that of Beijing and Hebei. The contributions of feedback effects from JingJinJi metropolitan areas to Tianjin reflect the fact that these two regions have a similar structure, generating more intraindustry trade that enhances the strength of the economic interdependence between Tianjin and Beijing in contrast to that say between of Hebei and Tianjin. The percentage of interregional feedback from Hebei to Tianjin accounts for 0.19% of Tianjin's gross output, while the feedback from Hebei to Tianjin only accounts for 0.1% of Tianjin's output. This is further confirmed by the feedback from Beijing and Tianjin on the output share returned to Hebei, with 0.02% and 0.01%, respectively.

Next, the focus will be on a comparison of the strength of the internal and external interdependence of the JingJinJi metropolitan areas. The figure of output value returned to Beijing from ROC is $2.09 Billion, a value very similar to the $2.06

Billion from Tianjin. The value of output returned to Beijing from ROC is less than that from Tianjin. Given that the interregional feedback between Beijing and Tianjin is similar to the sum of 27 other regions in China, and stronger than the sum of ROW, we believe that Beijing and Tianjin have a stronger internal interdependence than with the external regions of the JingJinJi metropolitan areas. There is no evidence that the interdependence between Hebei and internal regions is stronger than that of the external regions, since the interregional feedback between Hebei and the internal regions (\$0.24 Billion and \$0.08 Billion) is weaker than that of the external regions of JingJinJi metropolitan areas (\$1.14 Billion and \$0.62 Billion).

23.4.2 The Nature of Internal and External Interdependence for the JingJinJi Metropolitan Areas

The indicators of hypothetical extraction and feedback effects help us to understand which regions are highly interdependent within JingJinJi metropolitan areas and whether the interdependence within JingJinJi's internal areas is stronger than their interdependence with external areas. However, the strength of interdependence does not reflect the nature of economic and trade exchanges between regions. To highlight the industries that drive the internal and external interaction for the JingJinJi metropolitan areas, this section will report the results using the field of influence and average propagation length methodologies.

Figure 23.2 shows a complete surface graph for 2012 of the fields of influence coefficients in five regions. Table 23.3 summarizes industries with the largest and second largest coefficient, which are the most important linkages of economic and trade flows inside and outside of metropolitan economies. Beijing mainly builds the linkages to the other regions and industries with electricity and hot water production and supply (14). Within the JingJinJi metropolitan regions, Tianjin's petroleum refining, coking (9), and metallurgy (7) show strong linkage with the electricity and hot water production and supply of Beijing. This is because the raw material industries such as metallurgy and coal mining have been relocated from Beijing 30 years ago. Tianjin has a long history for the development of coal mining. Further, more than 30% of the iron products in China are made in Hebei. Therefore, Hebei and Tianjin mainly provide the metal products and energy products that provide the most important inputs for the downstream industries in Beijing.

The chemical industry (9) and textile, clothing, leather, fur, etc. (4) of ROC are the critical industries connected with the internal JingJinJi metropolitan regions. The information in Fig. 23.4 and Table 23.6 reveal that the interdependence within the JingJinJi metropolitan region focuses on the exchange of raw materials and energy, while the interactions between ROC and JingJinJi metropolitan region are centered around the transfer of raw materials and manufacturing products.

The coefficients of fields of influence present the industries with the most important influence on the metropolitan economies. To fully understand the nature

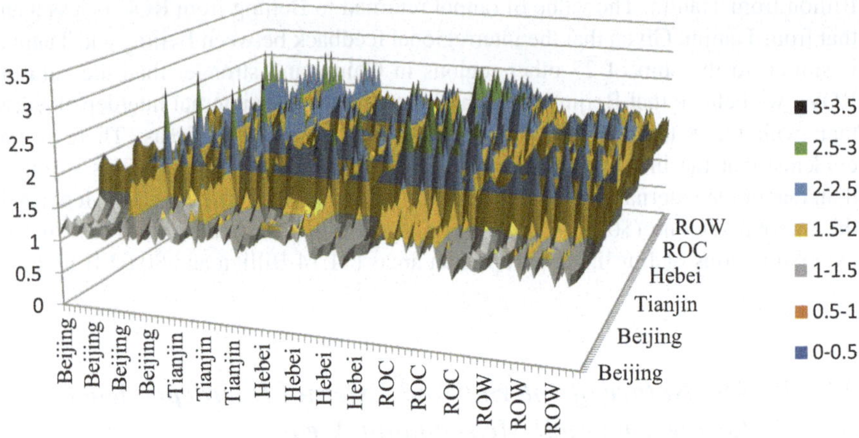

Fig. 23.4 The fields of influence for the five regions. (Data Sources: Author calculations from the IO tables of WIOD and Mi et al. (2017))

Table 23.6 Fields of influence, JingJinJi Metropolitan Areas

	Industry with the largest coefficient		Industry with the second largest coefficient	
Beijing	14	3.23	17	2.31
Tianjin	9	3.28	7	2.61
Hebei	9	2.84	7	2.52
ROC	4	3.16	7	3.12
ROW	9	2.67	14	2.57

Data Sources: As for Table 23.1

Notes: Industry 4 representatives textile, clothing, leather, fur, etc.; industry 7 representatives petroleum refining, coking, chemical industry; industry 9 representatives metallurgy, metal products; industry 14 representatives electricity and hot water production and supply, gas and water production and supply; industry 17 representatives other services

of internal and external interdependence for the JingJinJi metropolitan areas, we should also explore where these industries are located in the production chains. We will derive a general idea of the role of a certain sector using average propagation length coefficients. In Fig. 23.5, the figure of average propagation lengths in mining industry is 5.05, meaning that it takes almost 5 steps from the mining industry to the final demand of this industry. Further, the mining industry can be viewed as being situated at the beginning of the regional production chain with the largest coefficients, followed by electricity and hot water production and supply, gas, and water production and supply (industry 14). Table 23.6 reveals that the industry 14 is a strong driving force in JingJinJi, while Fig. 23.3 shows that industry 14 is located in the upstream of the JingJinJi's production chain. Compared to the industry 14 of external production chain in Fig. 23.6, which is in a relatively downstream position with a lower average propagation lengths coefficient, industry 14 of JingJinJi's production chain has more related industries and extends further. Another interesting

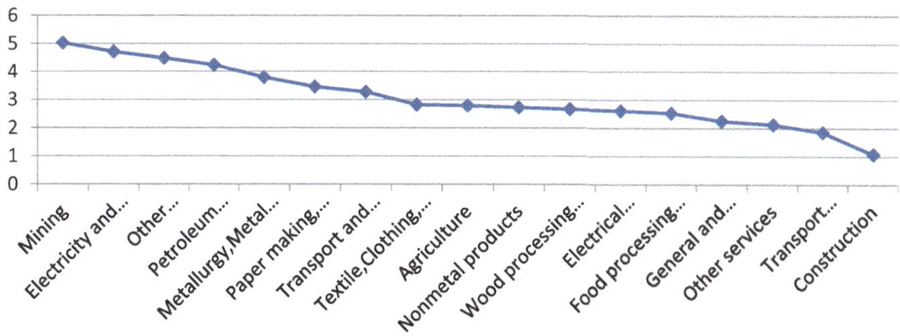

Fig. 23.5 The average propagation lengths of 17 industries within JingJinJi Metropolitan Areas. (Data Sources: As for Table 23.1)

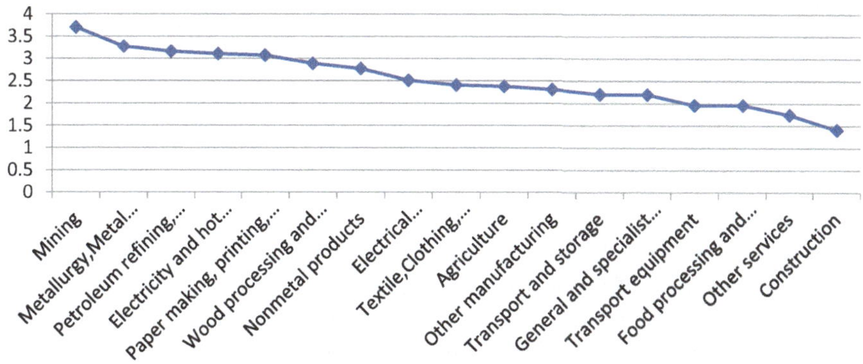

Fig. 23.6 The average propagation lengths of 17 industries outside JingJinJi Metropolitan Areas. (Data Sources: As for Table 23.1)

phenomenon is that some service industries, like transport and storage industry, traditionally located in the downstream of production chain also have higher coefficients in the JingJinJi's production chain. This shows that the flow of goods and labor inside JingJinJi is stronger than that in the outside area. Finally, the overall average propagation length coefficients of JingJinJi's production chain are larger than that of the external production chain ($3.10 > 2.54$). This reflects the greater industrial connectivity within the JingJinJi metropolitan areas.

23.5 Income Formation in JingJinJi

Labor is another form of trade flow, which appears to have a significant impact in generating interdependence between regions. The flows of labor, that is, journey-to-work, provide significant linkages between regions in two important ways. First, income associated with labor flows moves from one region to another in response to

Table 23.7 Miyazawa's interregional income multiplier

	Beijing	Tianjin	Hebei	ROC	ROW	Total
Beijing	1.208	0.021	0.021	0.007	0.001	**1.258**
Tianjin	0.025	1.243	0.010	0.004	0.001	**1.283**
Hebei	0.069	0.063	1.554	0.023	0.002	**1.711**
ROC	0.348	0.302	0.329	1.699	0.039	**2.717**
ROW	0.403	0.374	0.207	0.299	2.116	**3.399**
Total	**2.053**	**2.003**	**2.121**	**2.032**	**2.159**	

Data Sources: As for Table 23.1

Table 23.8 Percentage allocation of interregional income impacts

	Beijing (%)	Tianjin (%)	Hebei (%)	ROC (%)	ROW (%)
Beijing	19.75	2.09	1.87	0.68	0.09
Tianjin	2.37	24.23	0.89	0.39	0.09
Hebei	6.55	6.28	49.42	2.23	0.17
ROC	33.05	30.11	29.35	67.73	3.36
ROW	38.27	37.29	18.47	28.97	96.29
Total	100.00	100.00	100.00	100.00	100.00

Data Sources: As for Table 23.1

home–work separation. Second, households receiving this income will choose to spend it on a variety of goods and services, and again, there may be considerable variations in the propensities to consume within the region of residence. Using data from the merged input–output Table (MR-WIOT), it has been possible to generate a matrix of Miyazawa's interrelational multipliers.

Table 23.7 shows Miyazawa's interrelational multipliers, the expression K, from Eq. (23.33). Here the ripple effects indicate the direct and indirect income generate by a unit change in income in the zone at the top of the columns. The rows reveal how this income change reverberates throughout the JingJinJi metropolitan area, generating direct and indirect income changes in other regions that finally sum to the entries shown in this table. Their interpretation may be illustrated by reference to Beijing. For each $1 of income increase in Beijing, a further $0.208 of income is generated in Beijing itself, $0.025 in Tianjin, $0.069 in Hebei, $0.348 in ROC, $0.403 in ROW, and $2.053 in the Whole world. Among this five-zone system, there is a modest variation in the overall income-generating effects (from 2.003 in Tianjin, 2.032 in ROC, 2.053 in Beijing, 2.121 in Hebei to 2.159 in ROW). Even though Tianjin and Beijing generate a smaller total impact than Hebei and ROW, the interregional effect is larger in Tianjin and Beijing. Beijing generates $0.094 for the internal regions and $0.751 for the external regions of JingJinJi. Tianjin's coefficients are similar to Beijing ($0.084 and $0.676). By contrast, Hebei's income growth mainly drives local consumption and further drives local income growth but only provides $0.031 for other 2 regions of JingJinJi. Table 23.8 recomputes the percentage distribution of the indirect flows of income effects. Between 6.55% and

6.28% of the indirect income generated in Beijing and Tianjin ends up in Hebei, while Hebei only provides 1.87% and 0.89% of indirect income for Beijing and Tianjin.

A feature that stands out from this information, perhaps more than any other, is that the income flows associated with the journey-to-work and consumption-expenditure patterns involve interactions among regions that are largely absent from the dominant production and trade relationships among regions. For instance, there are a large number of labors flow from the less developed region Hebei and ROC to the developed region Beijing and Tianjin. The workers from Hebei receive their wages in Beijing and Tianjin, and then a major share of this income is consumed in Hebei during the Spring Festival. What's more, many people who work in Beijing cannot afford Beijing's housing price or rent and choose to live in Hebei. The average commute time from Yanjiao in Hebei to Beijing is 75 min. For every minute of commuting time, house prices will fall by $6500 in 2017. Hence, a significant share of the income earned in Beijing and Tianjin is spent in Hebei. This scale is a fundamental determinant of the nature and extent of spatial interaction, an issue which may not have received the attention that it deserves.

23.6 Conclusions

To better understand the nature and strength of internal and external interdependence of JingJinJi metropolitan areas, this paper merges the China Multi-Regional Input–Output Table (Mi et al. 2017) and World Input–Output Table (Timmer et al. 2015) into a five-zone system. By measuring the feedback effects, fields of influence, hypothetical extraction, average propagation lengths, and Miyazawa income multipliers, the following results were obtained.

1. **Beijing and Tianjin's ability to obtain GDP across JingJinJi metropolitan regions is stronger than that of Hebei.** The JingJinJi metropolitan areas contribute 9.57% for Beijing's GDP and 9.13% for Tianjin's GDP with interregional trade. However, this figure is only 4.99% when it comes to Hebei since Hebei lacks the qualified products to satisfy the demands of Beijing and Tianjin with the latter two regions meeting their demands by importing from the external regions of the ROC and ROW. For example, the imports from ROW to Beijing and Tianjin exceeded the exports.
2. **There is a close interdependence between Beijing and Tianjin within the JingJinJi metropolitan area.** The interregional feedback from Tianjin to Beijing accounts for 0.26% of the gross output in Beijing. This interregional feedback proportion is similar to that from the sum of 27 other regions in China to Beijing (0.27%) and stronger than that from the sum of ROW to Beijing (0.19%). There is no evidence that the interdependence between Hebei and internal regions is stronger than that of the external regions.

3. **Interdependence within the JingJinJi metropolitan region focuses on the exchange of raw materials and energy.** Beijing's electricity and hot water production and supply, Tianjin and Hebei's petroleum refining, coking, chemical industry and metallurgy, metal products industry are the main industries with the largest field of influence coefficients, which builds the linkages to the other regions and industries.
4. **The overall JingJinJi's production chain is longer than that of the external production chain.** Compared to the industry 14 of external production chain, which is in a relatively downstream position with a lower average propagation lengths coefficient, the industry 14 of JingJinJi's production chain has more related industries and extends further. Transport and storage industry, traditionally located in the downstream of production chain also have higher coefficients in the JingJinJi's production chain. The flow of goods and labor inside JingJinJi is stronger than that in the outside area.
5. **Many workers from Hebei received their wages in Beijing and Tianjin and then consumed the income derived in Hebei.** Beijing and Tianjin generate more Miyazawa income for the internal regions of JingJinJi and the external regions of JingJinJi. By contrast, Hebei's income growth mainly drives local consumption and further drives local income growth.

In 2013, The United Nations Development Programme and the Chinese Academy of Social Science reports that China's urbanization level will reach 70% in 2030, which means that China's urban population will reach 1 billion. This reflects the perspective that a policy commitment to enhance domestic demand will need to be centered on strong, vibrant cities and city-regions. JingJinJi is one of those (multi) city-regions and one of the challenges over the coming decades will be addressing environmental quality heterogeneity within the region and the concomitant differences in levels of income. In addition, the policy decisions to limit the size of large cities such as Shanghai and Beijing will generate important new dynamics on the internal distribution of population within the mega-metropolitan regions in which they are located. An additional dynamic that will need to be addressed is the problem of an aging population and a concomitant decline in the size of the active labor force. Future research will need to address household heterogeneity since with an aging population (forecasts indicate 25% will be >60 years old by 2030), sources of income will shift from wage and salaries to government transfers, pensions, and dividends. Similar explorations in Chicago by (Kim et al. 2015; Kim and Hewings 2019) revealed significant differences in the structure of the Miyazawa interrelational income matrix over time with increasing concentrations of the indirect effects of income changes in the older households and a decline in the share accruing to younger households. Since households of different ages have different consumption patterns, the impact on different sectors of the economy is likely to be profound.

One limitation of this paper is that the spatial distribution of consumer expenditures and transfers of income from temporary migrants are not measured. This is because the IO table does not divide the final product consumption into the consumption of the permanent population and the consumption of temporary migrants;

without this information, it is not possible to reveal the places of work and consumption of the temporary migrants. In addition, it was difficult to provide a formal link between place of work, place of residence, and place(s) of consumption since journey-to-shop data were not available. An additional avenue of exploration would be a comparison of the degree to integration that occurs within JingJinJi in contrast to that recorded in western cities such as Chicago (Hewings and Parr 2007). In the latter case, the journey-to-work and journey-to-shop flows generated a far greater degree of interdependence than that associated with the flows of goods and services.

References

Dietzenbacher E, van der Linden JA, Steenge AE (1993) The regional extraction method: applications to the European Community. Econ Syst Res 5:185–206

Dietzenbacher E, Luna IR, Bosma NS (2005) Using average propagation lengths to identify production chains in the Andalusian economy. Estudios de Economía Aplicada 23(2):405–422

Dietzenbacher E, Guilhoto J, Imori D (2013) The role of Brazilian regions in the global value chain. Working papers 2013_15, Department of Economics, University of São Paulo (FEA-USP), Brazil

Dietzenbacher E, van Burken B, Kondo Y (2019) Hypothetical extractions from a global perspective. Econ Syst Res 31:505–519

Guccione A, Gillen WJ, Blair PD, Miller RE (1988) Interregional feedbacks in input-output models: the least upper bound. J Reg Sci 28(3):397–404

Hewings GJD, Parr JB (2007) Spatial interdependence in a metropolitan setting. Spat Econ Anal 2: 7–22

Kim K, Hewings GJD (2019) Bayesian estimation of labor demand by age: theoretical consistency and an application to an input-output model. Econ Syst Res 31:44–69

Kim K, Kratena K, Hewings GJD (2015) The extended econometric input-output model with heterogeneous household demand system. Econ Syst Res 27:257–285

LGFEA (2017) The outline of collaborative development of Beijing, Tianjin and Hebei Province. http://www.en.cnki.com.cn/Article_en/CJFDTotal-LLYX201601011.htm. Accessed 1 2016

Li Y (2011) Urban-rural linkages and spatial-temporal land use change in Beijing-Tianjin-Hebei metropolitan region: a new perspective. J Sustain Dev 4(4):61–72

Li M, Wang T, Xie M, Zhuang B, Li S, Han Y, Cheng N (2017) Modeling of urban heat island and its impacts on thermal circulations in the Beijing–Tianjin–Hebei region, China. Theor Appl Climatol 128(3–4):999–1013

Liu Y, Xu Y, Guo T, Wang Z (2013) Visual simulation of regional development differentiation in Beijing-Tianjin-Hebei Metropolitan Region. J Geogr Sci 23(3):549–566

Los B, Timmer MP (2018) Measuring bilateral exports of value added: a unified framework. Working paper no. 24896. National Bureau of Economic Research, Cambridge

Meng B, Zhang Y, Inomata S (2013) Compilation and applications of IDE-JETRO's international input–output table. Econ Syst Res 25(1):122–142

Mi Z, Meng J, Guan D, Shan Y, Song M, Wei Y-m, Hubacek K (2017) Chinese CO2 emission flows have reversed since the global financial crisis. Nat Commun 8(1):1–10

Miyazawa K (1976) Input-output analysis and the structure of income distribution. Springer, Berlin

Pei J, Meng B, Wang F, Xue J (2015) Production sharing, demand spillovers and CO2 emissions: the case of Chinese regions in GVCs. IDE discussion papers 493. Tokyo, Institute of Developing Economies, Japan External Trade Organization (JETRO)

Romero I, Dietzenbacher E, Hewings GJD (2009) Fragmentation and complexity: analyzing structural change in the Chicago regional economy. Revista de Economía Mundial 23:263–282

Sonis M, Hewings GJD (1989) Error and sensitivity input-output analysis: a new approach. In: Miller RE, Polenske KR, Rose A (eds) Frontiers of input-output analysis. Oxford University Press, New York, pp 232–244

Sonis M, Hewings GJD (1992) Coefficient change in input–output models: theory and applications. Econ Syst Res 4(2):143–158

Tang Y, Zhao W, Gu C (2017) Urbanization and rural development in the Beijing–Tianjin–Hebei metropolitan region: coupling-degree model. J Urban Plan Dev 143(1):04016028

Timmer MP, Dietzenbacher E, Los B, Stehrer R, de Vries GJ (2015) An illustrated user guide to the world input–output database: the case of global automotive production. Rev Int Econ 23 (3):575–605

Wang S, Chen B (2016) Energy–water nexus of urban agglomeration based on multiregional input–output tables and ecological network analysis: a case study of the Beijing–Tianjin–Hebei region. Appl Energy 178:773–783

Zhang Y, Zheng H, Yang Z, Li Y, Liu G, Su M, Yin X (2016) Urban energy flow processes in the Beijing–Tianjin–Hebei (Jing-Jin-Ji) urban agglomeration: combining multi-regional input–output tables with ecological network analysis. J Clean Prod 114:243–256

Chapter 24
Negative Exponential Land Price Function and Impacts of Sale and Deemed Tax on the City Development: Analysis with an Alternative to Alonso–Muth Model in the Dynamic Content

Yoshiro Higano

Abstract This aimed to derive an exponential land price function based on explicit analytical assumptions on the spatial and dynamic urban model which is an alternative to conventional Alonso–Muth type model in a dynamic context. With homogeneous space conventionally adopted, it was assumed that landowners are differentiated with the distance to the CBD boundary so that landowners having land located at outer location ring cannot sell their land with higher land price than landowners having land at inner location ring. It was shown that dynamic land price function becomes negative exponential function in the distance to the city center and its growth rate becomes discounting rate in case land demand function is negative exponential function in land traded which is faced by differentiated landowners. Tax on sales of tracts of land and deemed tax on reserved land for speculation were introduced into the model and their impact on the urban sprawl was analyzed. It was shown that both deemed tax on reserved land and revenue tax on utilization of land enhance city development although urban sprawl is inevitable elsewhere and increase in tax rates will shorten the period when urban sprawl is observed in the city. Conversely, sale tax itself is of course neutral to the speculation but its effects become unclear if it is charged together with deemed tax. The differentiation of landowners was extended to incorporate other location attributes than the distance to the city center and meaning of non-geographical space was analyzed on which human activities are developed. A possible experimental analysis was suggested which utilizes estimated hedonic land price function.

This is an extended version of Higano (1985).

Y. Higano (✉)
University of Tsukuba, Tsukuba, Ibaraki, Japan
e-mail: higano@jsrsai.jp

M. Kawano et al. (eds.), *Theory and History in Regional Perspective*, New Frontiers in Regional Science: Asian Perspectives 56,
https://doi.org/10.1007/978-981-16-6695-7_24

Keywords Monopolistic land markets · Sale tax · Deemed tax · Urban sprawl · Non-geographical space · Exponential land price function

24.1 Introduction

In the conventional location theory, the geographical space is taken as *homogeneous* and *continuous space* and, therefore, it can be mapped into the geometric space. Perception and therefore analytical treatment of location, namely where housing should be located, where goods should be produced, etc., in the homogeneous space is made with choosing *distance*, e.g., distance from the city center in the traditional monocentric city model that is mapped into one-dimensional coordinate, distances from city centers in the multi-centric city model that are mapped into multi-dimensional coordinates, etc. In the continuous coordinate space, tract of land where, e.g., house is to be located is analytically described as infinitesimal ring, lot, etc.

Typically, in the traditional Von Thünen–Alonso–Muth model (Alonso 1964; Muth 1969; Mills 1972), land price (rent) is determined by the household (firm) which makes highest bid price through utility (profit) maximization subject to budget constraint (production function). The utility (profit) is dependent on consumption (intermediate input) of goods and housing space (land area or office space) subject to income (price of products at the city center with CIF term of trade) that is exogenously given. Disposable income (net profit) of household (firm) is dependent on the location ring, that is perceived as distance from the city center, since household (firm) must pay for transportation cost to the city center. The bid price is endogenously determined dependent on the exogenously given utility (profit) level which is to be attained by all households (firms) in the city with the closed model. City outer boundary and the number of households (firms) dwelling (existing) in the city are both determined endogenously dependent on agricultural land rent exogenously given. In the conventional analysis, it is implicitly assumed that the tracts of land are monopolized at each location ring, which means households (firms) face (virtual) monopolistic landowners who occupy all the tracts of land at each location ring. Using intuitive and somewhat petitio principii diagrammatical method, it is shown that price of land is decreasing with the distance from location ring to the city center (although it is not necessarily decreasing with distance monotonically according to empirical analyses).

A typical experimental research of urban land price is analysis of land price gradients in cities (e.g., Atack and Margo 1998; Colwell and Munneke 2009; Rehák and Káčer 2019, etc.). It is often shown that urban land price is exponentially and negatively dependent on the distance to the city center and other location factors such as social infrastructures, environmental condition, land and architectural regulation, etc. (e.g., Ueno 2021), using hedonic price approach. However, those empirical results eventually mean that land price is (exponentially) decreasing with distance to the city center or to a certain specific location based on extrapolation analysis with estimated land price function under assumption that all the other location factors were same in the city, namely the city is geographically homogeneous space except for the distance to the city center.

It is strange that no mathematical analysis with the monocentric city model is made to conclude that land price is decreasing (exponentially) in distance to the city center somehow. As far as the author knows, none has tried to give answer to the question (Question A), e.g., what functional form of utility function derives what functional form of land price in distance to the city center. Conversely, it is empirically true, ceteris paribus, that urban land price is decreasing function in distance to the city center or to any specific location such as NIMBY (not in my yard) facility as land price gradient analysis has shown. However, it does not necessarily mean that the conventional Alonso–Muth type of determinant mechanism is working behind the observed phenomenon.

A kind of arbitrage condition, namely attained maximized utility (profit) must be same through the city, is the only mechanism through which bid land price is determined to be decreasing in distance as household (firm) must pay for transportation cost of commuting (products) to the city center, which means bid land price has to be decreasing due to the commuting (transportation) cost that increases in distance in order to attain the same level of utility (profit) irrespective of housing (firm) location.

Moreover, in Japan, basically all the commuting cost is paid by the company irrespective of commuting distance. This means that urban land which is decreasing in distance in Alonso–Muth model is only due to time cost of commuting. It is easy to raise a counterexample against it. A kind of official (residential) land price that is assessed by a qualified real estate appraiser, near (800 m away from) Yoyogi-Uehara Station of Odakyu Railway is around 1,350,000 JPY/m^2 in 2020. Yoyogi-Uehara has an image of nice residential area and many embassies are located there. Residential land price near (800 m away from) Machida Station along the same railway line is around 320,000 JPY/m^2. Machida used to be a typical bed-town in the suburbs of Tokyo. Average land area of house which is now on sale in Yoyogi-Uehara and Machida may be assumed to be 60 and 130 m^2, respectively. Difference in commuting hours from Machida and Yoyogi-Uehara to Tokyo (Otemachi) is around 27 min (0.45 h). Assuming the number of working days per month is 20, the time value is estimated between 6080 JPY/h and 9537 h/JPY.

$$\frac{1,350,000 \times 60 - 320,000 \times 130}{0.45 \times 2 \times 20 \times 12 \times 30} = 6080$$

$$\frac{1,350,000 \times 60 - 320,000 \times 60}{0.45 \times 2 \times 20 \times 12 \times 30} = 9537$$

Average working hours in Tokyo in October 2020 is 155.5. The average annual income in 2020 in Tokyo is 6,203,944 JPY. So, calculated average time value is 3324 JPY/h.

$$\frac{6,203,944}{155.5 \times 12} = 3324$$

This means that time value derived on the hypothesis of Alonso–Muth model that land price is only dependent on the distance to the city center is too high compared to estimated figures on actual data in Tokyo (MILT 2020; TMG 2018). Considering intolerable time during commuting on the train (and it is not necessarily for all people), this is still too high, which means that household lay more weight on the distance to the city center that is perceived as commuting costs including patience to the city center.

Original idea of the paper can be back to Higano (1985). In the 1980s, the Japanese economy was just in the midst of the so-called bubble economy. Demand was decisively huge compared to supply in the land market and land price was skyrocketing. It was argued reservation demand for land price speculation was one cause for skyrocketing land price. Another cause was the excessive credit easing. In the media and on the Congress, it was argued that reserved vacant land should be taxed in order to control rapid increase in land price. Also, it was argued that lending rate should be raised. However, arguments were different among expertise with question (Question B) whether those policies are effective to induce an increase in supply of land in the city as designed.

In this paper, we present a different urban land price model that could be considered as an alternative to Alonso–Muth model. Geographical space itself is not directly specified or mapped into geometrical coordinate(s) but it is implicitly or indirectly specified and analyzed through ordering tracts of land following their preferability that is dependent on location attributes. The model will give us more fruitful answers to the above two questions. In Sect. 24.2, assumptions and terminologies are explained (Sect. 24.2.1), simple land reservation model of discrete time and continuous time is specified in order to show the essence of urban sprawl (Sects. 24.2.2 and 24.2.3), and the results in Sect. 24.2.3 (continuous time) are extended to the case of two landowners (Sect. 24.2.4), which gives an idea how to expand the model into a continuous spatial and continuous dynamic model in Sect. 24.4. In Sect. 24.3, the model in Sect. 24.2.4 is expanded to a multiple landowner case and impacts of deemed tax and sale tax are analyzed by showing that substance of the impacts is proved with the timing with which landowners sell up the total amount of land they each have reserved so far for speculation (Question B is solved). In Sect. 24.4, the model in Sect. 24.3, which is formulated with the case of multiple landowners, applied to the monocentric city, in which CBD is a disk and road network is ubiquitous but it connects the CBD and the suburb only a la spoke, and Manhattan city where CBD is a square and road network is ubiquitous but only of the grid pattern (Question B is solved). In Sect. 24.5, a short discussion is made related to the two questions. Section 24.6 suggests possibility of how to expand the model in an experimental and positive content in which a monocentric city cannot be assumed. Section 24.7 summarizes results of this chapter and points out shortage of the model which shall be fixed in future.

24.2 Model

24.2.1 Assumptions and Definitions

We assume each landowner in the objective space (city or region) has a certain fixed amount of land. Landowners intend to dispose of all tracts of land by sale and maximize the discounted sum of sales over time. For a while, it is assumed that land which is reserved for future sale is left vacant, namely no economic activities which earn income/profits, and no tax is charged on land kept vacant, and so on. Tracts of land can be differentiated by location (e.g., latitude and longitude) as well as other location attributes in any sense. Landowners can be differentiated by location attributes of the ordered tracts of land they own. For simplicity and without loss of generality, it is assumed that all tracts of land which have same location attributes of a certain level or on which consumers have same preference ordering are owned by one landowner. This means there exists one-to-one correspondence between the landowner and a certain level of location attributes or preference ordering of consumers. So, landowners can be ordered according to the superiority of location attributes or preference ordering as well. The order may be ordinary one. Based on the ordering, landowners are indexed with i $(i = 1, 2, \ldots N_{\mathrm{L}})$, where N_{L} is the number of landowners assuming tracts of land are discretely countable.

We assume the land market in the objective space in which all providers (landowners) and all consumers (households, firms, etc.) sell and purchase tracts of land.

For a while, we assume that land demand price function of households is exogenously given over time and will focus on the behavior of landowners.

Dominance Relation Among Landowners in the Land Market

Landowner i is dominant over landowner j in the land market in that landowner j cannot sell any tract of land with higher price than price with which landowner i sells tract of land at the same period $(i \leq j \leq N_{\mathrm{L}})$.

Dominance relation means each landowner i has its own monopolized (divided) land market in which landowner j cannot enter $(i < j)$.

Discriminating Monopolist

For simplicity, it is assumed that landowners are discriminating monopolists of the first degree in each divided land market in Pigou's sense (1932).

As it is usual case that same location attributes are owned by multiple landowners, a question which must be cleared is whether one of the landowners who own land that has same location attributes tries to sell tract of land with lower price than the other landowners having land of same location attributes. It is easy to prove that it never happens since arbitrage, e.g., by other landowners works since there exist consumers (households) who are willing to buy the land with a slightly higher price and land prices with which tracts of land having same attributes will increase and land is traded with same discriminated price following the land demand price function exogenously given. Therefore, it is safe to assume that land having same location attributes is owned by one landowner for simplicity of analysis.

No conflict exists between dominance relation and discriminating monopolist of first degree in Pigou's sense. At all, whether the assumption of monopolistic land market is plausible or not although it is assumed in Alonso–Muth model? First of all, land is not producible and supply of land having same location attributes is limited. So, the assumption of monopolistic land market becomes clear and robust due to introduction of dominance relation. It does not matter the economy is glowing or not as far as demand against land exists and land market is monopolized to whatever degree.

24.2.2 Simple Reservation Demand Model of Two Periods

For a while, neglecting *space* in any sense, we assume that a landowner owns tracts of land and the total area is A ($A > 0$) in order to see why and how land is reserved (demanded) by landowner over time for speculation. We assume that the landowner faces land demand price function at each period:

$$p = a - bx \tag{24.1}$$

in which a (>0) is the intercept of the demand price function with the vertical axis of land price, b (>0) is the slope of the demand function, and x is the quantity of land traded that is put on the horizontal axis. This presumes the number of households who are willing to buy tracts of land is stable over time due to some growth factor of the economy (city) because households once purchased land quit the land market. For simplicity of analysis, it is also assumed that the landowner intends to dispose of his/her land over two periods. For further simplicity, it is assumed that reserved land produces no revenue and there exists no expectation for, e.g., increase in land price at period 2 due to increases in demand pressure against land. Main concern of the landowner should be how much land he/she should sell at period 1 to reserve the remaining for sale at period 2 in order to maximize his/her revenues in terms of present value considering time preference.[1] There can be two extreme strategies for

[1]Typical pedagogical explanation of *time preference* is that nobody knows what will happen in future and usual people discount what will be obtained in future in order to compare it with what is certain now. Or, everybody has opportunity to invest what is obtained now in order to obtain more in future, which is of course risky, and an easy way is to deposit it in a bank with interest rate of i. So, one Japanese yen certain now becomes $(1 + i)$ JPY at one period later, which means one JPY at period 2 is equivalent to $1/(1 + i)$ JPY that is certain now. Considering the risk related to the opportunities with which revenues certain now are invested, with a rate of $\rho > i$, it should be

the landowner. Strategy 1: the landowner sells all the tracts of land at period 1 (presuming he/she can sell up all the tracts of land at one period) and Strategy 2: the landowner sells all the tract of land at period 2. Apparently, Strategy 2 is not wise because Strategy 2 is inferior to Strategy 1 in the sense that the total revenue obtained by Strategy 1 is preferred to the total revenues obtained by Strategy 2 due to time preference, namely the expected revenues in future must be discounted when it is compared to the current revenue. Strategy 1 itself is not wise, too, because the landowner must sell land at the cheaper price as he/she sells the more due to down-sloping land demand price function he/she faces. This means that an optimal strategy must be between Strategies 1 and 2 in terms of the amount of land sold at period 1 (2).[2] Therefore, his/her optimization problem is defined as follows:

$$\max_{\{x_1,x_2\}} V = \int_0^{x_1} (a - bx)\mathrm{d}x + \frac{1}{1+\rho}\int_0^{x_2} (a - bx)\mathrm{d}x, \tag{24.2}$$

$$\text{s.t.} \quad x_1 + x_2 \leq A, \tag{24.3}$$

$$x_1, x_2 \geq 0. \tag{24.4}$$

Trivial and non-interesting case is $2a \leq bA$, which means the landowner cannot sell all the tracts of land he/she owns within two periods and the best strategy is that he/she sells land as far as he/she can sell land with positive land price, and solutions are $x_1^* = x_2^* = \frac{a}{b}$. In this case, dead stock of land is $A - \frac{2a}{b}$.

Non-trivial and interesting case is $2a > bA$ and the first-order necessary conditions are given as follows:

$$a - bx_1 - \lambda = 0 \tag{24.5}$$

$$\frac{1}{1+\rho}(a - bx_2) - \lambda = 0 \tag{24.6}$$

$$x_1 + x_2 = \mathrm{A}, \tag{24.7}$$

in which λ is the Lagrangian multiplier associated with the constraint of Eq. (24.7).

Solutions are derived as follows:

---

equivalent to $1/(1 + \rho)$ JPY certain now. $1/(1 + \rho)$ is called a discounting factor that discounts nominal monetary value at period 2 to at (the initial of) period 1 (if the nominal value at period t is discounted, the discounting factor becomes $1/(1 + \rho)^t$) and ρ is a discounting rate in order to compare nominal monetary values at different periods. In Sect. 24.2.3, a continuous time model is shown and discounting factors become $e^{-\rho t}$. Further explanation is skipped as it is a well-known formula.

[2] It is apparent that Strategy 1 is best if the land market were perfect, which means the amount of land owned by landowners is negligibly small and he/she can sell land at constant land price.

$$x_1^* = \frac{a\rho + bA}{2b + b\rho} \tag{24.8}$$

$$x_2^* = \frac{bA + b\rho A - a\rho}{2b + b\rho}. \tag{24.9}$$

Reservation demand by the landowner himself/herself at the first period is

$$\mathrm{A} - x_1^* = \frac{bA + b\rho A - a\rho}{2b + b\rho}. \tag{24.10}$$

Average land price at the first (second) period is.

$$\bar{p}_1^* = \frac{1}{x_1^*}\int_0^{x_1^*}(a - bx)\mathrm{d}x = \frac{4a + a\rho - bA}{4 + 2\rho} \tag{24.11}$$

$$\bar{p}_2^* = \frac{1}{x_2^*}\int_0^{x_2^*}(a - bx)\mathrm{d}x = \frac{4a + 3a\rho - bA - b\rho A}{4 + 2\rho} \tag{24.12}$$

$$\bar{p}_2^* - \bar{p}_1^* = \frac{\rho(2a - bA)}{4 + 2\rho} \tag{24.13}$$

As far as $2a > bA$ holds, the average land price at the second period is greater than the average land price at the first period. This is due to discounting (preference) over time.

$$\frac{\partial \bar{p}_1^*}{\partial \rho} = \frac{2(bA - 2a)}{(4 + 2\rho)^2} < 0 \leftrightarrow bA - 2a < 0 \tag{24.14}$$

$$\frac{\partial \bar{p}_2^*}{\partial \rho} = \frac{2(2a - bA)}{(4 + 2\rho)^2} > 0 \leftrightarrow bA - 2a < 0. \tag{24.15}$$

When discount rate increases, the average land price at the first (second) period decreases (increases) as the amount of land sold at the first (second) period increases (decreases), respectively.

24.2.3 Simple Reservation Demand Model of Continuous Time

Assuming continuous time, the reservation demand model of landowner (called landowner A) having tracts of land of area A (>0) is given as follows:

$$\max_{\{x_A(t),N_A\}} \int_0^{N_A} e^{-\rho t} \int_0^{x_A(t)} f(s)\mathrm{d}s\mathrm{d}t, \tag{24.16}$$

$$\text{s.t.} \quad \dot{y}_A(t) \equiv \frac{\mathrm{d}y_A}{\mathrm{d}t} = -x_A(t), \tag{24.17}$$

$$y_A(0) = A, \tag{24.18}$$

$$y_A(N_A) = 0, \tag{24.19}$$

in which: $e^{-\rho t}$ is the discounting factor in order to add (integrate) over time streams of revenues of land sales at different periods into the present value at period $t = 0$; $y_A(t)$ is reservation demand by landowner A himself/herself at time t; $x_A(t)$ is the amount of land sold at time t; $f(\cdot)$ is the land demand price function which landowner A faces. For simplicity, we may assume it is stable over time especially with the growing economy. It is further assumed that the land demand price function is exponential function in quantity traded in the market:[3]

$$p = f(x) \equiv e^{-bx} \quad (b > 0). \tag{24.20}$$

Solution to the above model is obtained by applying the dynamic optimization method (Hestens 1966).

Hamiltonian Function

$$H = e^{-\rho t} \int_0^{x_A(t)} e^{-bs}\,\mathrm{d}s - \psi_A(t)x_A(t). \tag{24.21}$$

Euler–Lagrange–Hamiltonian Equations

$$\dot{\psi}_A(t) = -\frac{\partial H}{\partial y_A(t)} = 0 \tag{24.22}$$

[3] Adjusting land unit, we may assume intercept with the vertical axis is one (1).

$$\frac{\partial H}{\partial x_A(t)} = \mathrm{e}^{-\rho t}\mathrm{e}^{-bx_A(t)} - \psi_A(t) = 0, \quad \text{Equations (24.17), (24.18), and (24.19)} \tag{24.23}$$

Transversality Condition[4]

$$H(N_A) = \mathrm{e}^{-\rho N_A}\int_0^{x_A(N_A)} \mathrm{e}^{-bs}\mathrm{d}s - \overline{\psi}x_A(N_A) = 0. \tag{24.24}$$

Equation (24.22) gives

$$\psi_A(t) = \overline{\psi}. \tag{24.25}$$

Equations (24.23) and (24.25) give

$$x_A(t) = -\frac{1}{b}(\rho t + \log\overline{\psi}) \quad (0 \leq t \leq N_A). \tag{24.26}$$

It is obvious that $x_A(t) = 0$ for all t such that $N_A \leq t$.
Equation (24.17) gives

$$y_A(t) = -\int_0^t x_A(s)\mathrm{d}s + C. \tag{24.27}$$

Equations (24.27) and (24.18) give

$$C = A. \tag{24.28}$$

Equations (24.19), (24.26), and (24.28) give

$$-\frac{1}{b}\left(\frac{1}{2}\rho N_A^2 + N_A\log\overline{\psi}\right) = A. \tag{24.29}$$

It is obvious:

[4] N_A is the timing at which landowner A finishes sale of land (stops reservation of land, namely no further land reserved for sale of the next instance). It is a control variable and of course endogenous, which needs to satisfy the transversality condition.

$$x_A(N_A) = 0 \tag{24.30}$$

since exponential land demand price function is assumed. This means transversality condition (24.24) holds with N_A which satisfies Eq. (24.29). Eqs. (24.26) and (24.30) give

$$\overline{\psi} = \mathrm{e}^{-\rho N_A}. \tag{24.31}$$

Equations (24.29) and (24.31) give

$$N_A = \sqrt{2bA/\rho}\,. \tag{24.32}$$

Equations (24.31) and (24.32) give

$$\overline{\psi} = \mathrm{e}^{-\sqrt{2b\rho A}}. \tag{24.33}$$

Equations (24.26) and (24.33) give

$$x_A(t) = \frac{1}{b}\left(\sqrt{2b\rho A} - \rho t\right). \tag{24.34}$$

Equation (24.34) shows that all the tracts of land A may be sold at once in case A is very small, b is very small (though A may increase if only unit of land area does matter) and further ρ is large, which means that issue of reserved land for speculation will not originally arise in case landowners have small tracts of land. Of course, this is uninteresting case and we will not consider it.

As $t \le N_A = \sqrt{2bA/\rho}$, Eq. (24.34) gives $x_A(t) \ge 0$ for all t such that $0 \le t \le N_A$. For other range of t, $x_A(t) = 0$. By definition, we obtain

$$y_A(t) = A - \frac{1}{b}\left(\sqrt{2b\rho A}\, t - \frac{1}{2}\rho t^2\right) \quad (0 \le t \le N_A). \tag{24.35}$$

It is obvious that $y_A(t) = 0$ for all t such that $N_A < t$.

24.2.4 *Land Reservation Model of Landowner* B

We assume landowner B who is dominated by landowner A in the land market and having tracts of land of area B. Analogically, being given $x_A^*(t)$ that is the optimal sale of land by landowner A, the land reservation model of landowner B can be formulated as follows:

$$\max_{\{x_B(t), N_B\}} \int_0^{N_B} \mathrm{e}^{-\rho t} \int_{x_A^*(t)}^{x_A^*(t)+x_B(t)} \mathrm{e}^{-bs} \mathrm{d}s\mathrm{d}t, \tag{24.36}$$

$$\text{s.t.} \quad \dot{y}_B(t) \equiv \frac{\mathrm{d}y_B(t)}{\mathrm{d}t} = -x_B(t), \tag{24.37}$$

$$y_B(0) = B, \tag{24.38}$$

$$y_B(N_B) = 0\,. \tag{24.39}$$

Comparing Eqs. (24.16)–(24.19) and Eqs. (24.36)–(24.39), we can construct the following slightly modified dynamic optimization problem, with which we can derive solutions for the land reservation strategy by landowner B:

$$\max_{\{x_{A+B}\ (t), N_{A+B}\ \}} \int_0^{N_{A+B}} \mathrm{e}^{-\rho t} \int_0^{x_{A+B}\ (t)} \mathrm{e}^{-bs} \mathrm{d}s\mathrm{d}t, \tag{24.40}$$

$$\text{s.t.} \quad \dot{y}_{A+B}(t) \equiv \frac{\mathrm{d}y_{A+B}(t)}{\mathrm{d}t} = -x_{A+B}(t), \tag{24.41}$$

$$y_B(0) = A + B, \tag{24.42}$$

$$y_B(N_{A+B}) = 0. \tag{24.43}$$

The above problem is just the land reservation strategy for a virtual landowner who had tracts of land of area $A + B$. Replacing A with $A + B$, we will analogically obtain solutions for the above problem as follows:

$$\overline{\Psi}_{A+B} = \mathrm{e}^{-\rho N_{A+B}} \tag{24.44}$$

$$N_{A+B} = \sqrt{2b(A+B)/\rho} \tag{24.45}$$

$$\overline{\Psi}_{A+B} = \mathrm{e}^{-\sqrt{2b\rho(A+B)}} \tag{24.46}$$

$$x_{A+B}(t) = \frac{1}{b}\left(\sqrt{2b\rho(A+B)} - \rho t\right) \tag{24.47}$$

$$y_{A+B}(t) = A + B - \frac{1}{b}\left(\sqrt{2b\rho(A+B)}\, t - \frac{1}{2}\rho t^2\right) \quad (0 \le t \le N_{A+B}). \tag{24.48}$$

Equation (24.45) shows $N_A < N_{A+B}$ and Eq. (24.47) shows $x_A(t) < x_{A+B}(t)$ as far as A and B are positive, which have critical and essential meaning for the recursive algorithm applied for Eqs. (24.16)–(24.19) and Eqs. (24.40)–(24.43) in order to obtain solutions for the land reservation strategy of landowner B.

As landowner A is dominant over landowner B and therefore the optimality for the land reservation model of Eqs. (24.16)–(24.19) is inclusive in the model of Eqs. (24.40)–(24.43) (this is also meaning given to the model by the first degree of discrimination in Pigou's sense), we obtain solutions for the land reservation strategy of landowner B as follows:

$$\overline{\Psi}_{A+B} = \mathrm{e}^{-\rho N_{A+B}} \tag{24.49}$$

$$N_B = \sqrt{2b(A+B)/\rho} \tag{24.50}$$

$$\overline{\Psi}_{A+B} = \mathrm{e}^{-\sqrt{2b\rho(A+B)}} \tag{24.51}$$

$$x_{B(t)=}x_{A+B}(t) - x_A(t). \tag{24.52}$$

As for t such that $0 \leq t \leq N_A$,

$$x_{B(t)=} \frac{1}{b}\left(\sqrt{2b\rho(A+B)} - \sqrt{2b\rho A}\right). \tag{24.53}$$

As for t such that $N_A \leq t \leq N_B$, since the partial forward optimality must hold at any point of time with the overall dynamic optimal path,

$$x_{B(t)} = \frac{1}{b}\left(\sqrt{2b\rho(A+B)} - \rho t\right). \tag{24.54}$$

As for t such that $N_B \leq t$,

$$x_{B(t)} = 0. \tag{24.55}$$

As for t such that $0 \leq t \leq N_A$,

$$y_B(t) = B - \frac{1}{b}\left(\sqrt{2b\rho(A+B)} - \sqrt{2b\rho A}\right)t. \tag{24.56}$$

As for t such that $N_A \leq t \leq N_B$,

$$y_B(t) = A + B - \frac{1}{b}\left(\sqrt{2b\rho(A+B)}\, t - \frac{1}{2}\,\rho t^2\right). \tag{24.57}$$

As for t such that $N_B \leq t$,

$$y_B(t) = 0. \tag{24.58}$$

As $t \leq N_B = \sqrt{2b(A+B)/\rho}$, Eq. (24.54) gives $x_B(t) \geq 0$ for all t such that $0 \leq t \leq N_B$. For other range of t, $x_B(t) = 0$.

It is interesting that landowner B sells same amount of land, while landowner A sells tracts of land even at around $t = 0$. This result (the sale is constant over time till $t = N_A$) is not changed by discounting ratio ρ, gradient of land demand price function (demand pressure), and initial total land A and B owned by landowners A and B although the constant amount itself of course dependent on b and ρ. Intercept of the land demand price function does not matter because it can be always one (1) by adjusting unit of land area.

24.3 Inclusion of Policies Which Is Designed to Enhance Sale of Land Earlier

During the 1970s in Japan when the Japanese economy had experienced rapid economic growth, it was so often argued that landowners had reserved land in order to gain more by speculation and it causes shortage in supply in land market, which had caused skyrocketing land price. The phenomenon is further enhanced by immigrants into Tokyo and other large cities in Japan for pursuing jobs of high income.

One policy argued to be introduced was increase in rate of transfer tax on sale of land which had been already introduced. The other is *deemed taxation*, which means tax is charged on normal revenue that should have been obtained even if land is reserved vacant (a kind of opportunity cost by keeping land just vacant). Property tax has aspect of deemed tax and increase in property tax has same impacts if any. In case land is actually utilized and revenue is obtained, "deemed tax" becomes income tax. In this section, impact and effectiveness of such policies are discussed using the landowner reservation model in order to show effectiveness of the model as a framework for such policy agendas (Question B).

24.3.1 *The Model with Taxes*

We assume multiple landowners index by j ($j = 1, 2, \ldots, n$). Each has tracts of land of total area A_j ($A_j > 0$, $i = 1, 2, \ldots, n$). We define $L_j = \sum_{k=1}^{j} A_k$. Dominance relation defined in Sect. 24.2 is assumed such that landowner j dominates k in the land market as far as $j < k$ ($1 \leq j < k \leq n$). In order to apply the recursive land reservation model in Sect. 24.2 to the policy issues, we specify the following land reservation model:

$$\max_{\{x_j(t),\ N_j\}} V_j = \int_0^{N_j} \left\{ e^{-\rho t} \alpha \int_0^{x_j(t)} e^{-b\xi} d\xi + \beta y_j(t) \right\} dt, \tag{24.59}$$

$$\text{s.t.} \cdot \ \dot{y}_j(t) \equiv \frac{dy_j(t)}{dt} = -x_j(t), \tag{24.60}$$

Equations (24.65), and (24.66).

In which $\alpha = 1 - \tau > 0$; τ is rate of transfer tax; $\beta = (\delta - \Pi)R$; δ is equal to 1 in case reserved land is utilized for economic activities like agriculture, parking, etc. which actually produce revenue (income R per unit tract of land per unit period) or is equal to 0 in case it is left vacant and deemed tax is charged on vacant land reservation, and Π is rate of income tax. Solutions for the above problem are obtained as follows:

Hamiltonian Function

$$H_j(t) = \mathrm{e}^{-\rho t}\left\{\alpha\int_0^{x_j(t)} \mathrm{e}^{-b\xi}\mathrm{d}\xi + \beta y_j(t)\right\} - \psi_j(t)x_j(t). \tag{24.61}$$

Euler–Lagrange–Hamiltonian Equations

$$\dot{y}_j(t) \equiv \frac{\partial H_j(t)}{\partial \psi_j} = -x_j(t) \tag{24.62}$$

$$\dot{\psi}_j(t) = -\frac{\partial H_j}{\partial y_j(t)} = -\beta e^{-\rho t} \tag{24.63}$$

$$\frac{\partial H_j}{\partial x_j} = \mathrm{e}^{-\rho t}\alpha e^{-bx_j(t)} - \psi_j(t) = 0, \tag{24.64}$$

$$y_j(0) = L_j, \tag{24.65}$$

$$y_{Bj}(N_j) = 0. \tag{24.66}$$

Transversality Condition

$$H_j(N_j) = \mathrm{e}^{-\rho N_j}\left\{\alpha\int_0^{x_j(N_j)} \mathrm{e}^{-b\xi}\,\mathrm{d}\xi + \beta y_j(N_j)\right\} - \psi_j(N_j)x_j(N_j) = 0. \tag{24.67}$$

Equation (24.63) gives

$$\psi_j(t) = \frac{\beta}{\rho}\,\mathrm{e}^{-\rho t} + C_{j.} \tag{24.68}$$

As $x_j(N_j) = 0$, Eq. (24.64) gives

$$\alpha e^{-\rho N_j} - \psi_j(N_j) = 0. \tag{24.69}$$

Equations (24.68) and (24.69) give

$$C_j = \left(\alpha - \frac{\beta}{\rho}\right) \mathrm{e}^{-\rho N_j}, \text{ and} \tag{24.70}$$

$$\psi_j(t) = \frac{\beta}{\rho} \mathrm{e}^{-\rho t} + \left(\alpha - \frac{\beta}{\rho}\right) \mathrm{e}^{-\rho N_j}. \tag{24.71}$$

Equation (24.64) gives

$$-\rho t + \log \alpha - bx_{j(t)} = \log \psi_j(t) \text{ , and} \tag{24.72}$$

$$x_j(t) = \frac{1}{b}\left\{ \log \alpha - \log \psi_j(t) - \rho t \right\}. \tag{24.73}$$

$x_j(t)$ satisfies the following condition:

$$\int_0^{N_j} x_j(t) \mathrm{d}t = L_j. \tag{24.74}$$

N_j satisfies the following condition:

$$N_j \log \alpha - \int_0^{N_j} \log \psi_j(t) \mathrm{d}t - \frac{1}{2} \rho N_j^2 = bL_j. \tag{24.75}$$

By totally differentiating both sides of Eq. (24.75) with respect to L_j, we obtain as follows ($\dot{N}_{JL} \equiv \frac{\mathrm{d}N_j}{\mathrm{d}L_j}$):

$$\dot{N}_{jL} \log \alpha - \log \psi_j(N_{jL}) \dot{N}_{jL} - \int_0^{N_j} \frac{\mathrm{d} \log \psi_j(t)}{\mathrm{d}L_j} \mathrm{d}t - \rho N_j \dot{N}_{jL} = b \tag{24.76}$$

$$\frac{\mathrm{d} \log \psi_j(t)}{\mathrm{d}L_j} = -\frac{1}{\psi_j(t)} (\rho\alpha - \beta)\, \mathrm{e}^{-\rho N_j} \dot{N}_{jL}. \tag{24.77}$$

As $x_j(N_j) = 0$ and N_j does not dependent on t, Eqs. (24.76) and (24.77) give

$$\int_0^{N_j} \frac{1}{\psi_j(t)} (\rho\alpha - \beta)\, \mathrm{e}^{-\rho N_j} \mathrm{d}t \dot{N}_{jL} = b > 0. \tag{24.78}$$

Necessary condition for landowners to start sale of tracts of land, which is only interesting case, is

$$\left(\alpha - \frac{\beta}{\rho}\right) > 0, \tag{24.79}$$

which means that the net value obtained by sale of land at the highest price (=1) is greater than the discounted value of net revenue obtained by utilizing land. It is a kind of opportunity criteria for selling land. As far as Eq. (24.79) holds, we obtain the following relation between timing when reserved land for speculation by landowners becomes zero since Eqs. (24.78) and (24.79) mean $\dot{N}_{jL} > 0$:

$$N_1 < N_2 < \cdots N_{j-1} < N_j \cdots. \tag{24.80}$$

Landowner j reserves land longer than the landowners k ($k < j$) who dominate over landowner j in the land market. Of course, the timing when landowner j ($k < j$) starts to sell land cannot be earlier than landowner k ($k < j$) since landowner j cannot sell land at higher price than landowner k.

24.3.2 Comparative Analysis of N_j with Policy Variables

Total differentiation analogical to Eqs. (24.76)–(24.78) gives the followings:

$$\int_0^{N_j} \frac{1}{\psi_j(t)} e^{-\rho N_j} dt - \int_0^{N_j} \frac{1}{\psi_j(t)} (\rho\alpha - \beta)\, e^{-\rho N_j} dt \dot{N}_{j\alpha} = \frac{N_j}{\alpha} > 0, \tag{24.81}$$

$$\int_0^{N_j} \frac{1}{\psi_j(t)} \frac{1}{\rho} \left(e^{-\rho t} - e^{-\rho N_j}\right) dt - \int_0^{N_j} (\rho\alpha - \beta)\, e^{-\rho N_j} dt \dot{N}_{j\beta} = 0, \tag{24.82}$$

in which: $\dot{N}_{j\alpha} \equiv \frac{dN_j}{d\alpha}$ and $\dot{N}_{j\beta} \equiv \frac{dN_j}{d\beta}$.

Equation (24.81) implies sign of $\dot{N}_{j\alpha}$ is indeterminate. Conversely, Eq. (24.82) implies sign of $\dot{N}_{j\beta}$ is positive.

Assuming monocentric city and the dominance relation in the land market in the city is determined by distance to the city center, we obtain the following proposition:

Proposition 24.1

1. *Increase in deemed tax rate Π $\left(= \delta - \frac{\beta}{R}\right)$ results in decrease in N_j, which means the city experiences relatively speedy (and compact)*[5] *development although still*

[5] This term is nothing related to a so-called compact city. It simply means that, e.g., more housing are built inner suburb at earlier timing as N_i decreases and such utilization of land can be said relatively compact development compared to the case in which no deemed tax is charged or it is charged with a less rate, especially at an earlier timing. Eventually, it may happen a compact city will appear in a long run as the land price is higher with the less tax rate and it induces, e.g., a small lot size housing development.

some of the land in the city is kept for reservation demand for a while till all tracts of land are sold following the dominance order in the land market.

2. *In case $\beta \neq 0$, impact of tax on sale of land (a kind of transfer tax) is indeterminate. In case $\beta = 0$, namely in case deemed tax is not charged on opportunity cost of vacant land reservation, apparently impact of transfer tax is neutral.*
3. *In case deemed tax is firstly charged on vacant land reservation, of course N_j decreases as $\beta = -\Pi R$ and $\frac{d\beta}{dR} < 0$ with any deemed tax rate $\Pi > 0$.*

These results confirm the arguments that property tax discourages reservation of land for speculation and enhances development in the city (e.g., Benetick 1979; *Beneticks* 1980) *with a different context.*

The above proposition mean that transfer tax is only effective in case deemed tax is charged on vacant land reservation or revenue (profit) tax is charged on gains from utilization of reserved land although the impact of tax on sale of land is indeterminate.

24.4 Continuous Space Model

24.4.1 Case of Multiple Landowners

In case $\beta = 0$, where reserved land is left vacant and no tax is charged, applying analogically results obtained in Sect. 24.2, we obtain the following land reservation demand strategy of the virtual landowner who owns the total tract of land having area of L in the city:

Land Reservation Strategy of the Virtual Landowner

$$x_L(t) = \frac{1}{b}\left(\sqrt{2\rho bL} - \rho t\right) \tag{24.83}$$

$$y_L(t) = L - \frac{1}{b}\left(\sqrt{2\rho bL}\, t - \frac{1}{2}\rho t^2\right) \tag{24.84}$$

$$\psi_L(\mathrm{t}) = \alpha \exp\left(-\sqrt{2\rho bL}\right) \tag{24.85}$$

$$N_L = \sqrt{\frac{2bL}{\rho}}. \tag{24.86}$$

Conversely, we obtain the following land reservation strategy for each land owner j, who owns tracts of land of area A_j in discrete space, is dominated by other landowners k such that $k < j$, and dominates other landowners k such that $j < k$:

Land Reservation Strategy of Landowner j ($j = 1, 2, \ldots$)

$$X_j(t) = x_j(t) - x_{j-1}(t) \text{ for } t \text{ such as } t \le N_j, \tag{24.87}$$

$$X_j(\mathrm{t}) = 0 \text{ for } t \text{ such as } N_j < t, \tag{24.88}$$

$$Y_j(t) = A_j - \frac{1}{b}\left(\sqrt{2\rho b L_j} - \sqrt{2\rho b L_{j-1}}\right)t \quad \text{for } t \text{ such as } t \le N_{j-1}, \tag{24.89}$$

$$Y_j(t) = L_j - \frac{1}{b}\left(\sqrt{2\rho b L_j}\, t - \frac{1}{2}\rho t^2\right) \text{ for } t \text{ such as } N_{j-1} \le t \le N_j, \tag{24.90}$$

$$N_j = \sqrt{\frac{2bL_j}{\rho}}, \tag{24.91}$$

in which:

$X_j(t)$ (upper case letter X) is sale of tracts of land by landowner j at t;
$Y_j(t)$ (upper case letter Y) is reservation of land by landowner j at time t;
$x_k(t)$ (lower case letter x) is sale of tracts of land by the virtual landowner who owns all tracts of land of area $L_k\left(= \sum_{s=1}^{k} A_s\right)$ in the city, which is given by Eq. (24.83) and $x_0(t) = 0$ for all t;
N_j is the time at which all tracts of land owned by landowner j are sold up and no land is reserved by landowner j. As apparently $N_{j-1} < N_j$, Eqs. (24.83) and (24.87) give the following:

$$X_j(t) = \frac{1}{b}\left(\sqrt{2b\rho L_j} - \sqrt{2b\rho L_{j-1}}\right)\text{for } t \text{ such as } t \le N_{j-1}, \text{ and} \tag{24.92}$$

$$X_j(t) = \frac{1}{b}\left(\sqrt{2b\rho L_j} - \rho t\right)\text{for } t \text{ such as } N_{j-1} < t \le N_j. \tag{24.93}$$

It can be considered that parameter b is demand pressure in the land market and it is represented by b, namely b increases as it increases. Equations (24.91), (24.92), and (24.93) imply that speculation of landowner will heat up, namely N_j increases and $X_j(t)$ decreases with all landowners, as demand pressure increases in the land market.

24.4.2 The Model with Dominance Relation by the Accessibility to the City Center in Continuous Space

In Case of the Circular City of Alonso–Muth Type

We assume a city having compact CBD surrounded by small suburb and it is surrounded by spacious almost arid land. It is growing economically and population in the city is increasing due to migration. Market starts to exist with arid land surrounding the city. Landowners of arid land try to sell tracts of land by speculation. The dominance relation in the land market is determined by linear accessibility to the city edge. In case land having same level of dominance relation is owned by multiple landowners, still the model developed can be applied to it by assuming that landowners belong to same level of dominance are *competitive* with each other due to arbitrage. So, we can take it as if tracts of land having same level of dominance relation belong to one landowner.

We may assume location attribute is only distance to the city edge and the edge of existing city is located at an infinitesimally small location ring having distance ε to the CBD center. Area of tracts of land owned by at ring r of which distance to the city edge is between r and $r + dr$ is given as $2\pi(r + \epsilon)dr$. So, the total arid land between the city edge and ring r is

$$A(r) = \int_0^r 2\pi(\xi + \epsilon)\mathrm{d}\xi = \pi\left(r^2 + 2\epsilon r\right), \tag{24.94}$$

in which π is the circular constant.

Equations (24.83)–(24.86) can be rewritten as follows by replacing L with $A(r)$:

$$x(t,r) = \frac{1}{b}\left(\sqrt{2\rho bA(r)} - \rho t\right) \tag{24.95}$$

$$y(t,r) = A(r) - \frac{1}{b}\left(\sqrt{2\rho bA(r)}\, t - \frac{1}{2}\rho t^2\right) \tag{24.96}$$

$$\psi_L(t,r) = \alpha \exp\left(-\sqrt{2\rho bA(r)}\right) \tag{24.97}$$

$$N(r) = \sqrt{\frac{2bA(r)}{\rho}}. \tag{24.98}$$

Or, they are given

$$x(t,r) = \frac{\rho}{b}(N(r) - t) \tag{24.99}$$

$$y(t,r) = \frac{\rho}{2b}\,(N(r) - t)^2 \tag{24.100}$$

$$\psi(t,r) = \alpha\,\exp\left(-\sqrt{2\rho b\pi(r^2 + 2\epsilon r)}\right) \tag{24.101}$$

$$N(r) = \sqrt{\frac{2b\pi(r^2 + 2\epsilon r)}{\rho}}. \tag{24.102}$$

Using an analogy to Eq. (24.87), sale of land by landowner at ring r is given as follows:

$$\begin{aligned} X(t,r) &= \lim_{\delta \to 0} \frac{x(t, r+\delta) - x(t,r)}{\delta} = \frac{\partial x(t,r)}{\partial r} = \frac{\rho}{b}\frac{\mathrm{d}N(r)}{\mathrm{d}r} \\ &= \sqrt{\frac{2\rho\pi}{b}}(r^2 + 2\epsilon r)^{-\frac{1}{2}}(r+\epsilon) \end{aligned}$$

$$\text{for } r \text{ and } t \text{ such that } \omega_0(t) \le r \le \omega_1(t) \text{ and } 0 \le \mathrm{t} \ \le N(r), \tag{24.103}$$

in which: $\omega_0(t)$ is inner boundary of urbanization area, where land are traded and some of land are reserved, at t and $\omega_1(t)$ is outer boundary at t. As expected, $X(t, r)$ is constant over t. All the landowners start to sell tracts of land at $t = 0$ as no opportunity cost for reserved land and no deemed tax is charged on reserved land. So, $\omega_0(t)$ is solution ω_0 to $N(\omega_0) = t$ with r and $\omega_1(t)$ is infinity or ω_1 which is solution to $R_A = \mathrm{e}^{-b\omega_1}$, in which R_A is revenue for rural use of land (apparently $R_A < 1$ as the highest selling land price is one (1)). More specifically, $\omega_0(t) = -\epsilon + \sqrt{\epsilon^2 + \frac{\rho}{2b\pi}t^2}$ and $\omega_1 = -\frac{1}{b}\log R_A$.

We should note that the amount of sale is constant over time but variant at location. We can confirm that the integral of $X(t,r)$ from 0 to $N(r)$ is the amount of land owned by landowner located at an infinitesimal location ring at r, namely $2\pi(r+\epsilon)$.

Since the total amount of land sold at the land market by the virtual landowner who owns (reserves) all tracts of (vacant) land at location s ($\epsilon \le s \le r$) is $x(t,r)$ and landowners at infinitesimal location ring s ($\epsilon \le s \le r$) are discriminating monopolists of the first degree in Pigou's sense in the market, who follow the dominance relation among them, the selling land price at location r and time t is the lowest price among differentiated prices with which land are sold by the virtual landowner who owns (reserves) land at all infinitesimal location rings s ($\epsilon \le s \le r$). Therefore, it is given by replacing x in Eq. (24.20) by $x(t,r)$:

$$\begin{aligned} &\Gamma(t,r) = \exp\{-bx(t,r)\} = \exp\{-\sqrt{2\rho b\pi(r^2 + 2\epsilon r)} + \rho t\} \\ &\text{for } r \text{ and } t \text{ such that } \omega_0(t) \le r \le \omega_1(t) \text{ and } 0 \le \mathrm{t} \ \le N(r). \end{aligned} \tag{24.104}$$

Equation (24.104) implies that market price of land at time t, with which land is traded in the (discriminated) market at r, is a negative exponential function with $\sqrt{(r^2 + 2\epsilon r)}$ for r and t such that $\omega_0(t) \le r \le \omega_1(t)$ and $0 \le t \le N(r)$. As the inner edge of urbanization area, $\omega_0(t)$, expands to outward as time elapses and landowners located around (farther from but close) the existing city edge ϵ have sold up all tracts of land which they owned (reserved), only land is traded at location rings far farther from the existing city edge and selling land price increases especially near the inner urbanization edge that moves outward as time elapses. Using a two-dimensional graph of horizontal axis of location r and vertical axis of land price Γ, traded land price function Γ in r is drawn as a negatively sloped curve. Infinitesimal location rings where no trades of land are made eventually appear close to the existing city edge ϵ and the area of no trade of land and, therefore, no records of traded land prices expand as time elapses. In other words, the land price with which landowners still having (reserving) land to sell increases along the land demand price function as they become able to obtain higher discriminating prices. As a result, traded land price increases at each location where land is still traded as time elapses. Graph of the traded land price function shifts toward right horizontally, which means that as time elapses, traded land price increases at all location rings where land are still traded and the rate of increase in traded land price per (infinitesimal) time (growth rate with infinitesimal time) is ρ irrespective of location r. It is plausible because an opportunity cost of future sales of land through reservation of land is a loss due to discounting and gain by reservation of land is an expected increase in selling land price in future which is realized through horizontal shift of traded land price function toward right. For small ϵ, the traded land price function is approximated by a negative exponential function in r for r and t such that $\omega_0(t)\leq r \leq\omega_1(t)$ and $0\leq t \leq N(r)$. This is an answer to Question A.

If the land demand price function is shifted upward by growth factor e^{gt} (g is growth rate of land demand price and, of course, interesting case is $\rho > g$), namely Eq. (24.20) is replaced by $p = f(x) \equiv e^{-bx + gt}$, then price of land traded in the market at r, $\Gamma(t,r)$, will increase with growth rate of $\rho - g$ for r and t such that $\omega_0(t)\leq r \leq\omega_1(t)$ and $0\leq t \leq N(r)$, which is directly obtained by replacing ρ in the formular of Eq. (24.40) by $\rho - g$, namely the growth rate of land price decreases when it is expected that future land demand price increases. It is also plausible because substantial discounting rate becomes $\rho - g$. However, as the positive growth factor, g, of the land demand price function induces more land reservation for speculation and in that case, of course, speculation causes longer period of urban sprawl observed elsewhere in the city since $N(r)$ will increase as real discount rate decreases. As the growth factor, g, the more increases, the more decreases the amount of land sold in a period of time (an infinitesimal time), becomes the more gentle the slope of curve of the traded land price function in r within the range of urbanization area, which is the more slowly shifting outward as time elapses, the more increases at any time an average traded land price over the urbanization area, and eventually the more decreases at a certain time t_0 the growth rate of the traded land price at all location r where land are traded till time t_0.

In Case Accessibility Is Ordered in Manhattan Distance

In case accessibility is measured in the Manhattan distance, similar development and discussion can be applied to the above formulation analogically and we obtain:

$$A_M(r) = 2(u_0 + v_0)r + 2r^2, \tag{24.105}$$

$$N_M(r) = 2\sqrt{b\{(u_0 + v_0)r + r^2\}/\rho}, \tag{24.106}$$

$$\Gamma(t, r) = \exp\{-2\sqrt{\rho b\{(u_0 + v_0)r + r^2\}} + \rho t\}, \tag{24.107}$$

in which: it is assumed that road is ubiquitously facilitated with grid patterns parallel to a rectangle CBD; u_0 and v_0 are length of boundaries of CBD (or existing city). Equation (24.107) also implies land price is a negative exponential function in r for small u_0 and v_0. It is also considered that Eq. (24.107) gives a solution to Question A.

We have shown analytically schemes of city model in which traded land price gradients are exponentially decreasing function in distance to the city center, which have been so often adopted hypotheses with experimental analysis of urban land price.

24.5 Discussion

Equation (24.100) clearly shows reserved land (for speculation) is positive till $t = N(r)$ that is the timing for landowners located at location ring at r to sell up his/her reserved land and given by Eq. (24.102). This proves necessity of a leap-frog type of urban development (an urban sprawl) from the rationality of landowners who occupies all the land in the city (e.g., Bahl 1968; Markusen 1978; Mills 1981). Namely, at a location r_1 and a timing of $t_1(<N(r_1))$, reserved land by landowner at location r_1 is $y(t_1, r_1) = \frac{\rho}{2b}\,(N(r_1) - t_1)^2 > 0$ since $t_1 < N(r_1)$ and at location r_2 $(>r_1)$ and a timing t_1, sales of land by landowner at location r_2 is $x(t_1, r_2) = \frac{\rho}{b}\,(N(r_2) - t_1) > \frac{\rho}{b}\,(N(r_1) - t_1) > 0$ since $t_1 < N(r_1) < N(r_2)$ (Eq. 24.102). This implies while land is reserved inner location ring r_1, land at outer location ring r_2 is sold (and developed). As we see in Sect. 24.4.2, if landowners speculate increase in land price with which he/she can sell land, urban sprawl exists longer period because it can be taken that growth factor with the land demand price function represents landowners' speculation of selling land price in future.

With introduction of deemed tax, the formular of land price function becomes complicated and even it cannot be shown in an explicit form. However, whether land price increases or not due to increase in deemed tax rate can be predicted based on Proposition 1 by knowing if $x(t, r)$ increases or not because $x(t, r)$ is basically dependent on $N(r)$ as it can be seen by Eq. (24.73). For example, decrease in $N(r)$ means increase in $x(t, r)$ since a same amount of the total land must be sold up in a shorter period and this implies a decrease in land price with which land is traded.

Introduction of the deemed tax rates differentiated location by location, i.e., increase in deemed tax rate in inner suburb (urbanization area) more discourage speculation closer the city center and it may increase lot size due to decrease in net land price, an increase in deemed tax rate may make the suburb compact as it enhances inner city development more speedy, etc. (cf. Ermini and Santolini 2017). However, the model developed here cannot say precisely about whether deemed tax enhances realization of a *compact city* or not because density is dependent on the ratio of land that are not developed and the lot size of housing on developed area that is dependent on the price with which land is traded (cf. Banzhaf and Lavery 2010).

Equation (24.73) shows that amount of developed land is very small in case b is large (which means urban sprawl must continue for a long period since a larger sale of land would face a larger decrease in land price with which land would be traded) and effects of deemed tax may be inefficient even if it enhances development (Owen 1974). Land value taxation is favored by economist as it is neutral with resource allocation. However, it has been pointed out that it distorts the city development (e.g., Wyatt 1994). The model developed in this chapter is incomplete to analyze the impacts of land value tax because it has no mechanism which determines land price where trade of land is not made. In order to make the analysis, the model of markets of housing, office, factories, etc. must be constructed.

When sale tax is only charged (namely $\alpha > 0$ and $\beta = 0$), it is neutral as seen by Eq. (24.59). However, when it is charged together with deemed tax ($\alpha, \beta > 0$), the impacts of sale tax is indeterminate and possibility cannot be excluded that increase in sale tax rate may rather enhance urban sprawl. Using numerical simulation, complicated impacts of uniform deemed and sale taxes as well as those taxes differentiated location by location may be identified with the circular city of Alonso–Muth type, e.g. deemed tax enhances inner city development or, on the contrary, outer city development, i.e., urban sprawl, etc. This should be a good exercise in order to confirm general applicability of the model discussed in the next section.

24.6 Implication and Applicability of the Model

The model developed here reminds us what is space in which we are interested. It is the space where people perceive in order to behave and do actions. It is not necessarily geographical space. It can be seen that the functional form $A(\cdot)$ is critically important and essential in the above analysis. It is true with any geographical space. The point is that variable r is not necessarily distance. It can be a variable (index) that specifies the dominance relation between monopolistic landowners.

For example, we may use a hedonic land price function that is estimated using data of location attribute $R = (r_1, r_2, ..., r_m)$ of traded land and land price p with which land having location attribute R is traded in the land market in the suburb of a city at a certain specific period.[6] We define an estimated hedonic land price function as follows:

$$\overline{p} = h(r_1, r_2, \ldots, r_m) = h(R). \tag{24.108}$$

Contrary, as $\overline{p}$ can be taken as land price with which tracts of land having attribute $\overline{R}(\overline{p}) = h^{-}(\overline{p})$ were to be traded. The point is $h^{-}(\cdot)$ is a correspondence and there are many tracts of land which have different location attributes and give same (estimated) land price $\overline{p}$. Namely $\overline{R} = \{R | \overline{p} = h(R)\}$.

Using all the reserved tracts of land in the suburb and their location attribute data, we may construct $A(\cdot)$ as follows:

$$A(\widetilde{p}_i) = \sum_{k=1}^{i} | a(\widetilde{p}_k) | \qquad (i = 1, 2, \ldots, \widetilde{I}_L), \tag{24.109}$$

in which:

$a(\widetilde{p}_k)$ is a set of tracts of reserved land of which attributes give estimated hedonic price of $\widetilde{p}_k$;[7]

$|a(\widetilde{p}_k)|$ is the total area of tract of land which belongs to $a(\widetilde{p}_k)$; and

$\widetilde{p}_1$ and $\widetilde{p}_{\widetilde{I}_L}$ are the highest and lowest estimated hedonic prices among tracts of reserved land.

Conversely, the land demand function in the suburb may be estimated using questionnaire data, e.g., survey data of households, who are tenants of house or living in apartments, about willingness to have an owned house in 10 years, etc. Using functions of Eq. (24.109) and estimated land demand price function which landowners will face, the analysis can be developed in the same way in the above. Experimentally, useful is reformulating the mode into a model of discrete space and time. Point is that elements (tracts of land) in the set of $a(\widetilde{p}_k)$ have names with which tracts of land are associated with location in the geographical space of the suburb. However, there may still exist critical indeterminateness as $a(\widetilde{p}_k)$ may include tracts of land which are scattered in the geographical space. In that case, it is one possible way to nullify continuity of preference ordering and adopt lexicographic ordering though hedonic hypothesis is adopted.

The model presented in this chapter has a defect. It assumes a kind of dichotomy. Originally, the land demand price function in a year is depending on growth of the city as well as trade of land and housing (and office, etc.) services in previous year.

---

[6] Precisely speaking, land price data must be adjusted depending on the size of traded land as land having the bigger lot size is traded at the more discounted land price.

[7] Identification whether land is reserved or not is practically difficult under complicated laws and regulations.

Assumption of stability of stably growing land demand price function may relieve the dichotomy assumption and it is not usual case. Inter-related feedback loops must be built in between the model which derives land demand price function and the monopolistic land market model developed in this chapter. It requires a more comprehensive and unified model approach at a higher level. We leave it as a subject in future. The author just makes comments that a meaningful approach should be empirical-oriented. Recent rapid developments in the informatic science and devices and software of big-data mining make it possible to get a grid of reality of such approach.

24.7 Conclusion

The land reservation model has been proposed related with old and still new topic of land speculation and urban sprawl. It treats *geographical space* in a dynamic content in different ways than conventional static (continuous) space model like Alonso–Muth type. Real meaning of space is perceived as barrier (friction) to various human activities, which are closely related with each other and, therefore, have advantage if they are located closely. In this sense, distance itself is sometimes important in the spatial analysis of human activities. Space must be formulated with which distance can be explicitly defined. Conversely, distance in the real world and space is very complicated geographically as well as economically as it is perceived as, e.g., time cost resulting by real settings like social infrastructures. This is one reason why analytical results obtained by conventional continuous spatial model have been seldom applied to a real setting or no linkage has been observed between the theoretical and empirical analysis.

It may cause misunderstanding to say that explicit incorporation of geographical space into analytical framework itself is not substantial. Analysis of human activities ruled by what should be defined as *space* is important. In this sense, more substantial perception of space should be more important than physical and geographical one.

The proposed model treats substance of space with location attributes and distance defined over geographical space is one of them. It is the hypothesis empirically adopted without clear analytical evidence that land price (rent) in the city exponentially decreases with distance to the city center. The model developed in this chapter has shown one possible evidence. The model also gives a clear conclusion to the argument on the effectiveness of sale tax and deemed tax on reserved land demand in the spatial and dynamic context. Deemed revenue tax on reserved idling land is effective in that it enhances and hastens development in the suburb near city center by giving negative incentive to the landowners to speculate higher selling land price in future as well as is effective tax on revenues earned by utilizing reserved land for rural or other purposes. However, sale tax itself is of course neutral to the speculation but its effects are unclear if it is charged together with deemed tax.

It is a defect of the model that it assumes a kind of dichotomy. However, it can be applied to any locational and spatial topic by using big data set and advanced technology of informatic sciences. Thus, it is highly expected that dichotomy issues are eventually solved.

References

Alonso W (1964) Location and land use. Harvard University Press, Cambridge
Atack J, Margo RA (1998) "Location, location, location!" The price gradient for vacant urban land: New York, 1835 to 1900. J Real Estate Financ Econ 16:151–172. https://doi.org/10.1023/A:1007703701062
Bahl RW (1968) A land speculation model: the role of the property tax as a constraint to urban sprawl. J Reg Sci 8:199–208. https://doi.org/10.1111/j.1467-9787.1968.tb01324.x
Banzhaf HS, Lavery (2010) Can the land tax help curb urban sprawl? Evidence from growth patterns in Pennsylvania. J Urban Econ 67:169–179. https://doi.org/10.1016/j.jue.2009.08.005
Benetick BL (1979) The capitalization of the property tax and idle land: comment. Land Econ 55: 545–552. https://doi.org/10.2307/3145777
Beneticks BL (1980) Capitalized property taxes and the viability of rural enterprise subject to urban pressure. Land Econ 56:451–456. https://doi.org/10.2307/3146221
Colwell PF, Munneke HJ (2009) Directional land value gradients. J Real Estate Financ Econ 39:1–23. https://doi.org/10.1007/s11146-007-9104-0
Ermini B, Santolini R (2017) Urban sprawl and property tax of a city's core and suburbs: evidence from Italy. Reg Stud 51:1374–1386. https://doi.org/10.1080/00343404.2016.1190448
Hestens MR (1966) Calculus of variations and optimal control theory. John Wiley & Sons, Inc., New York
Higano Y (1985) Monopolistic land market model in the metropolitan area. Stud Reg Sci 16:103–114. https://doi.org/10.2457/srs.16.103
Markusen JR (1978) Ownership concentration and market power in urban land. Rev Econ Stud 45: 519–526. https://doi.org/10.2307/2297253
Mills ES (1972) Studies in the structure of the urban economy. The John Hopkins Press, Baltimore
Mills DE (1981) Growth, speculation and sprawl in a monocentric city. J Urban Econ 10:210–216. https://doi.org/10.1016/0094-1190(81)90015-2
Ministry of Land, Infrastructure and Transport (MILT) (2020) 2020 official land price. https://www.mlit.go.jp/common/001333710.pdf. Accessed 4 Mar 2021
Muth RF (1969) Cities and housing. The University of Chicago Press, Chicago
Owen MS (1974) Land taxes and idle land: a case study of Houston. Land Econ 50:251–260. https://doi.org/10.2307/3145035
Pigou AC (1932) The economics of welfare, 4th edn. Macmillan, London
Rehák Š, Káčer M (2019) Estimating price gradient in Bratislava with different distance measurements. J Eur Real Estate Res 12:190–206. https://doi.org/10.1108/JERER-10-2018-0045
Tokyo Metropolitan Government, Bureau of General Affairs, Statistics Division (TMG) (2018) Monthly labor statistics, Table 1 and Table 6. http://www.toukei.metro.tokyo.jp/homepage/ENGLISH.htm. Accessed 4 Mar 2021
Ueno K (2021) A study on the relation between residential land value and the distance to the center of Tokyo Metropolitan Area (1970-2016). In: Asami Y, Higano Y, Fukui H (eds) Frontiers of Real Estate Science in Japan (New frontiers in regional science: Asian perspectives 29). Springer Nature, Singapore
Wyatt MD (1994) A critical view of land value taxation as a progressive strategy for urban revitalization, rational land use, and tax relief. Rev Radical Polit Econ 26:1–25. https://doi.org/10.1177/048661349402600101

